STUDY GUIDE FOR WASHINGTON REAL ESTATE

FUNDAMENTALS

JOHN JEDDELOH

VOLUME I
STUDY TEXT

Published in the United States of America by
Real Estate Publishers, Inc.
8316 N. Lombard #329
Portland, Oregon 97203-3727

WWW.REALESTATEPUBLISHERS.COM
E-mail: INFO@REALESTATEPUBLISHERS.COM

Library of Congress Catalog Card Number 99-66090
ISBN 1-87857-204-0

First printing, July, 2004

REALTOR® Affiliate member, Washington Association of REALTORS®.

Member, Real Estate Educators Association.

Contents

Introduction

The *Study Guide for Washington Real Estate Fundamentals, Study Text* offers a thorough introduction to Washington real estate. It is especially structured to meet the curriculum required by the Department of Licensing for the Washington Real Estate Fundamentals course that salesperson applicants must take. This text is divided into 25 chapters that not only meet the curriculum requirements, but also provide special emphasis on those subjects that are problem areas on the examinations.

The text is designed to accompany *Study Guide for Washington Real Estate Fundamentals, Practice Questions*, a text comprised of practice questions to prepare applicants for the examinations. Each section in the practice questions text corresponds to chapters in this text, so students can easily use the practice questions to review and gain a better understanding of the text material.

The author, John Jeddeloh, began his real estate career in 1971 and since then has worked in brokerage, property management, appraisal and investment real estate. He began teaching real estate in 1976 and since then has successfully prepared thousands of students for their exams. He also holds a degree in education and did graduate work in business, law and finance. In addition he is a member of the Real Estate Educators Association, a national organization of professionals dedicated to the furtherance of real estate education. Little wonder that he is considered to be one of today's leading experts on real estate and on licensing exams!

His unequaled ability to explain complex subjects clearly and understandably stems from his years in the classroom. Any text will give you facts to memorize. But if you want to *understand* real estate, this is the text you need!

Getting a real estate license

Real estate brokerage is a relatively young profession compared to other professional fields such as medicine and law. Real estate agents were almost completely unregulated until the National Association of Real Estate Boards was formed (currently the National Association of Realtors®). In fact, the chief purpose for which the National Association of Real Estate Boards was formed was to create a code of ethics and encourage government licensing of real estate brokers.

Even then, membership and adherence to the code of ethics was voluntary. Over the ensuing decades state after state adopted licensing laws. Today real estate agents must be licensed in all states and territories of the United States, all Canadian provinces, and many other countries as well. In Washington agents are licensed by the Washington Department of Licensing.

In order to engage in real estate practice in Washington you must hold one of several different licenses. Most persons new to the real estate profession obtain a salesperson license as their first license. A salesperson may conduct any kind of real estate activity (except appraisal), but must do so only under a broker or designated broker. A salesperson cannot operate independently. To be independent you must have a broker's license, which requires additional experience and education. A broker can be the supervising broker for a company, in which case the broker is referred to as a designated broker. The licensing requirements for brokers and designated brokers are the same, however.

In addition, a broker can be licensed as an associate broker. An associate broker is simply a person who has met all the requirements to become a broker or designated broker, but chooses to work under another broker or designated broker instead of running his or her own company. In essence, an associate broker steps into the shoes of a salesperson. The only distinction is that an associate broker may be a branch manager, which is not permitted for a salesperson licensee. And, of course, an associate broker can become a broker or designated broker at any time just by having the Department of Licensing reissue the license, since the associate broker has already met all the education and examination requirements.

Appraisal deserves a special mention. Appraisers must be licensed or certified in Washington, but appraisal is considered a separate field. A licensed or certified appraiser cannot engage in sales or property management activity, and a broker or salesperson cannot perform most appraisals. Of course, you could hold a license or certificate as an appraiser and a broker's or salesperson's license at the same time, but this is unusual. However, while salespersons and brokers are not allowed to appraise, they are required to know the basics of appraisal so they can understand and interpret appraisal reports and to help them advise sellers and buyers about listing and offering prices.

Salesperson license requirements

To obtain a salesperson's license in Washington there are three requirements. You must –
- Be eighteen years of age or older,
- Complete an approved 60 clock-hour course in Washington Real Estate Fundamentals, and
- Successfully complete the national and state salesperson exams with a score of 70% or better on each.

The above are the requirements to be eligible for the license. In addition, since salespersons are not permitted to be independent, you must be licensed under a broker. Your broker must sign when you go to activate the license, although you can take the courses and the national and state exams without first having a broker. The license fee is $146.25 for two years and for each renewal thereafter. For each renewal a salesperson must have completed 30 clock hours of continuing education. In addition, for the first renewal salespersons must complete an additional 30 clock-hour course in Real Estate Practices (total 60 hours of education for the first renewal).

The Department of Licensing has procedures for substitution of other courses in lieu of the Fundamentals course. Typically, the alternative courses will be from degree-granting institutions and consist of equivalent educational experience. To secure approval for substitute courses that you have already taken you must submit transcripts and other information to the Department of Licensing (see *Contact information* at the end of this section).

Many states today contract with an outside testing service to conduct the national and state examinations. In Washington the testing agency is Promissor, Inc. (Promissor is the successor to Assessment Systems, Inc., which provided the examinations previously.) Promissor administers both examinations at the same time. Test questions for the national portion (80 questions) are written by Promissor. Questions for the state portion (30 questions) are written by Department of Licensing staff. Naturally, test questions are not disclosed to the public, but applicants can obtain sample test questions and other information about the exams in the Real Estate Candidate Handbook from Promissor. Promissor also has practice exams which applicants can purchase. These materials are made available because the philosophy of Promissor and the Department of Licensing is to minimize exam phobia as much as possible, while maintaining security over the testing process to ensure fairness and accuracy. You can be assured that examination questions are carefully reviewed for correctness and relevance by persons in the field. In addition, Promissor uses sophisticated statistical analysis on test questions to maintain a consistent overall difficulty level for each examination.

The state portion of the exam covers only Washington real estate licensing law and administrative rules (RCW 18.85, 18.86, 18.235 and WAC 308-124). All other real estate issues will be on the national exam. However, there is a problem the student should be aware of. The Promissor national exam is general in nature and covers laws from all states. There is no simple way for the exam to exclude laws that do not apply in Washington. For example, nine states (including Washington) follow community property laws. Most of the rest follow dower and curtesy law instead, or follow neither. Therefore, the national exam may have questions on both community property as well as dower and curtesy. In other words, you will have to learn about dower and curtesy, even though it is not used in Washington. While this may seem a bit unfair, there is an advantage. Practically all states today break their exams down into a national and a state portion. Since the Promissor national exam covers material in all states, if you ever wish to obtain a license in another state they will probably waive the national exam and require only that you take their state exam.

To take the examinations you must first receive a Candidate Examination Document from the school where you took the Fundamentals course, certifying that you have completed the course and the final examination. Once you have this in hand you can call Promissor to make an exam reservation, or you can make the reservation on Promissor's website or by fax. You must make the reservation at least three business days before the exam date (four days for online or fax reservations). On the day of the examination you must present the Candidate Examination Document and pay the exam fee of $138.25 to Promissor staff. The fee can be paid by credit card if paid in advance, but if the candidate wishes it can be paid by cashier's check, certified check or money order at the exam site. Personal checks and cash are never accepted.

Promissor has test centers in Everett, Kennewick, Lacy, Seattle/Tukwila, Spokane, Vancouver, Wenatchee and Yakima. Seattle/Tukwila is the largest facility and will schedule exams any day of the week Monday through Saturday. Other centers may offer fewer days per week, and centers in outlying areas may offer only one day a week. You may schedule your examination at whichever center you wish without regard to where you live. To make an exam reservation or order practice exams, see the *Contact information* at the end of this section.

The examinations will be administered on an electronic examination terminal called EXPro. EXPro presents the test question and response options on a touch-sensitive screen. The system is operated by an internal computer, but there is no keyboard, mouse, or other input systems like most computers today. Instead, you select the answer by just touching the screen. Candidates need absolutely no computer experience to operate the system. Promissor staff will instruct candidates in operation of the device, but it is so simple that it takes them just a couple minutes to explain how it works. The system holds a memory card that works like a floppy disk, that is, it records your responses. You can change your answers, skip over questions and come back to them later, and mark questions for review. As soon as you are finished your examination is scored on the spot and you leave the test center with your score report in your hand.

Passing scores are good for one year. If you do not become licensed within one year of passing the exams you will have to retake the exams. If you

passed one section of the exam but not the other, you only need to retake the portion you failed, provided you pass within six months. Passing score reports just say that you passed. If you failed an exam your score report will give a numeric score and a diagnostic analysis to help you determine weak areas.

Once you have the passing score report you are ready to become licensed. To do so you must send an application for the license, signed by you and your broker, together with the license fee to the Department of Licensing. You will be given the application for the license at the test center along with your passing score report. However, it will take some time before the license can be processed and mailed out. In the meantime, it would be illegal to practice real estate. To eliminate this problem the score report will have a second portion that is an interim license good for 45 days after the postmark when you mailed the application and license fee to the Department of Licensing.

In a few cases the interim license is not valid because of Personal Data Information the applicant was required to submit at the time of the examination. The Personal Data Information includes questions such as whether you have ever been convicted of a crime, and so on. In many cases the applicant merely needs to submit further information to allow the Commission to issue the license. Occasionally, however, the Commission denies the license based on the results of their investigation.

Broker license requirements

To obtain a broker's license in Washington there are five requirements. You must –
• Be eighteen years of age or older,
• Be a high school graduate or the equivalent (GED certificate),
• Have at least two years verified experience as a licensed salesperson within the past five years,
• Complete 120 clock hours consisting of 30 hours each in Real Estate Law, Brokerage Management, Business Management, and one elective course. If any of the above courses were used for continuing education as a salesperson, then additional real estate courses must be taken to make up the total of 120 clock hours, and
• Successfully complete the national and state exams for brokers with a score of 75% or better on each.

The license fee is $210.00 for two years and for each renewal thereafter. For each renewal a broker must have completed 30 clock hours of continuing education.

The Department of Licensing has procedures for substitution of other courses in lieu of the above listed courses. Typically, the alternative courses will be from degree-granting institutions and consist of equivalent educational experience. To secure approval for substitute courses that you have already taken you must submit transcripts and other information to the Department of Licensing.

Examination procedures are the same as for the salesperson's license, with a couple of differences. The state portion has 40 questions instead of 30. Not only are there more questions and a higher score is required, but the questions on both broker examinations tend to be somewhat more difficult. Also, the focus of the questions is more toward the type of activity a broker would be involved with – e.g., more emphasis on supervising, office management, closing procedures, etc.

To take the examinations you must first receive a Candidate Examination Document from the Department of Licensing, certifying that you have completed the courses, have the high school degree or equivalent, and have the required experience. The Department will have to verify the experience and education, which can take some time, especially if they are from out of state.

Once you have passed the examination you will be given a license application form at the test center together with your score report. To become licensed as a broker you must send in the application with the required license fee, plus your old license (released by previous broker). If you wish to become the designated broker for an organization, you must also submit the required documentation for the organization. Unlike salespersons, there is no automatic 45-day interim license.

Exam reservation and other procedures are the same as for salesperson applicants, except for the differences in the exams noted above.

Contact information

Real Estate Commission –
    Department of Licensing
    Real Estate Licensing
    Post Office Box 9015
    Olympia, WA 98507-9015
Street address:
    2004 – 4th Avenue West, Olympia
Salesperson applicant phone number: 360-664-6488
Broker applicant phone number: 360-664-6500
Fax: 360-586-0998
Web: http://www.wa.gov/dol/bpd/refront.htm
E-mail: realestate@dol.wa.gov
Promissor –
    CAT*ASI
    Washington Real Estate
    Post Office Box 8588
    Philadelphia, PA 19101-8588
Exam reservation phone: 800-274-5985
Exam reservation fax: 888-204-6291
Information faxback system: 888-204-6246
To order salesperson or broker practice
    exams: 800-618-2565
Web: http://www.asisvcs.com

Study hints

Successful students know that if you master the terminology of a subject you will have mastered that subject. This is particularly true of real estate because you will encounter an overwhelming number of new terms. Don't let a new term get by you without learning its meaning and how it is used. About half the items you will find on the exams are really just vocabulary questions – testing your knowledge of real estate terminology. So if you have a thorough grasp of the language of real estate, you will have matters well in hand at exam time.

To assist you in mastering real estate terminology, you will find a *Key terms* section at the end of each chapter. Each of the key terms listed is in bold and italics where it first appears in the text, so you can easily check its meaning and usage. You can use the Key Terms section to review a chapter just by scanning down the list to make sure you remember the meaning of each term.

The most efficient way to study is to be sure you understand one lesson before proceeding to the next. Some of the chapters build on knowledge from previous material. To make your study work well, proceed through the chapters in an orderly fashion, or follow the course outline from your instructor.

A good study trick is to look for common elements and ways to tie information together. Learning facts in isolation makes it harder to retain them. Once you get an overall picture your mind will create a framework in which to store the data. Understanding how parts fit together is the most powerful aid to memory.

Exam questions also make great use of lists of items, e.g., "Which of the following is required for … ," followed by several choices, only one of which is required. Successful test takes know they must pay attention any time they encounter a list of items in their textbook.

However, memorizing lists of items is hard for many people. Yet teachers know there are tricks to make it easier. One technique is to write down the list in addition to reading it in the text. The act of writing down each item is much more memorable than just reading it. To help you with this, every time there is a list of items that is a popular source of test questions, we have included a blank checklist box next to the text where a list of items appears. Filling out the box will help cement the items in your memory.

Item list box
❶
❷ *Write the list in this box*
❸

Right from the beginning you should start a routine of systematic review. The mind retains facts initially only for a brief time. But each time you re-learn the fact you retain it longer before forgetting it. For example, think about learning a phone number. The first time you dial the number you will probably have completely forgotten it within half an hour. But if you have to call that person again, the next time you dial the number you will probably remember it for several hours before forgetting it. Each time you have to look the number up again you remember it for a longer time, until eventually you have it memorized. This is because the mind retains facts by a process of learning – forgetting – re-learning – forgetting – re-learning, and so on. Each time you learn – forget – re-learn you just about double the time before you will forget the material.

Beginning students are sometimes dismayed at their retention. It is not uncommon to retain only a third to a half of the information after the first reading, and even then for only a short time. Systematic review is the solution. Plus, after you have a fair mastery of the material in a chapter, going through the practice questions in *STUDY GUIDE FOR WASHINGTON REAL ESTATE FUNDAMENTALS, PRACTICE QUESTIONS*, the companion to this text, will give you another exposure to the same material and further cement it in your mind. If you continue reviewing you will eventually get to the level where *nothing can stand in the way of your success!*

Chapter 1

The real estate profession

PEOPLE JUST BEGINNING their study of real estate are usually surprised when they discover the variety within the field. The average consumer thinks of a real estate agent as someone who drives people around showing them houses until they find one they like and buy it. Of course, residential sales and showing property are certainly very important functions in the real estate profession, but there are many other roles that real estate agents take as well. Real estate is a huge business encompassing many specialties, not to mention allied fields such as title insurance, mortgage lending, and others.

Each year trillions of dollars worth of real estate changes hands in the form of millions of individual transactions, the vast majority of which are generated by real estate agents. The fees charged in connection with these transactions, not just for the services of the agents, but also for title insurance, escrow, mortgage lending, and dozens of others, contribute hundreds of billions of dollars to the economy. In addition, additional billions of dollars are generated in residential and commercial property management, as well as development, construction, and other aspects of the real estate field. Real estate is directly or indirectly responsible for millions of jobs. Adding up everything that real estate agents do, real estate is a major factor in the economy. Real estate is such an enormous economic force that it is a favorite component used by the government to control the economy. In fact, it is often said that the stock market may take us into a recession, but real estate always leads us out of it.

Specialists and their professional organizations

Real estate is such an enormous field that no one person can do everything. While many real estate agents are involved in more than one aspect of real estate, there are still specific ways we categorize real estate activity. These include –

Brokerage – Real estate *brokerage* means bringing a buyer and a seller together. We call it brokerage, even though probably the majority of the sales are generated by salespersons working for brokerage firms. Successful brokerage requires great negotiating skill. Just because a seller wants to sell and a buyer wants to buy, doesn't automatically create a sale. Bringing about a meeting of the minds sometimes requires the wisdom of Solomon and the patience of Job. And even after the contract is signed, there are still many hurdles the broker must surmount to bring the transaction to a successful closing.

Real estate brokerage is also subcategorized by type of property (see *Categories of real estate* later in this chapter). For example, the most common type of brokerage activity is residential brokerage. But there are also investment brokerage, farm and land brokerage, and many other kinds of brokerage.

In the past brokers almost always represented the seller, and represented the buyer rarely, if ever. Today the world of real estate has changed. Washington law, for example, creates a presumption that an agent who shows property to a buyer is usually a ***buyer's agent***. The agent can also act as a ***dual agent***, representing both parties, and even as a ***facilitator***, in which case the agent represents neither party. Modern licensing laws create specific duties for the agent depending on what type of agency or facilitator arrangement the agent accepts.

The majority of real estate brokers and salespersons are members of the National Association of REALTORS® (NAR), founded in 1908 and now the largest trade association in the country. The NAR has created an extensive code of ethics which its members must adhere to. Early in its history the NAR registered the term ***REALTOR***® as a service mark, so its members can be referred to as REALTORS® to distinguish themselves from non-members. Non-members can call themselves agents, brokers, salespersons or anything else they wish, but cannot use the term REALTOR®. The headquarters of the NAR is in Chicago, although they also maintain a large office in Washington, D.C. which is involved in lobbying efforts on behalf of their membership. Each state has a state association which, in turn, grants charters to local associations and boards.

The logo of the National Association of REALTORs®

In Washington, the state association is the Washington Association of REALTORs®. Local associations and boards are formed along the boundaries of a market area rather than on a county by county basis, so many of them cover more than one county. In Washington there are 29 local associations and boards, plus the Washington State Commercial Association of REALTORs®, which is an overlay association throughout the state. Local associations also operate the real estate multiple listing service in most market areas.

The NAR also has subsidiary organizations which their members can join for greater assistance in specialty areas, such as the Real Estate Buyer's Agent Council (REBAC) and the Council of Residential Specialists. Buyers agents can also join the National Association of Exclusive Buyers Agents (NAEBA), which is not affiliated with the NAR. A difference between REBAC and the NAEBA is that NAEBA members work only with buyers and their membership rules do not allow them to take listings. REALTORs® involved in commercial properties may wish to join the Certified Commercial and Investment Member Institute or perhaps the Society of Industrial and Office REALTORs®. Similarly agricultural property agents would benefit from membership in the REALTORs® Land Institute. And REALTORs® managing real estate companies would probably find membership in the Council of Real Estate Brokerage Managers useful. The Women's Council of REALTORs® was originally created just for women members, but today focuses on leadership training for all REALTORs®.

Property management – The majority of property owned by investors is managed by professional property managers. As with brokerage, ***property management*** is subcategorized by type of property – residential, office space, retail property, and so on. But regardless of what kind of property it is, the job of the property manager is not easy. On the one hand, the investor wants the maximum return on the investment, which usually means the highest rent income and the lowest expenses possible. At the same time, tenants want low rents and the property maintained in perfect condition. Keeping both satisfied is a juggling act every bit as difficult as the job of a broker in bringing about a sale. In the vast majority of cases property managers represent the owners, but in a few cases they might represent a tenant.

Professional property managers are likely to be members of the Institute of Real Estate Managers or, if managing commercial property, the Society of Industrial and Office REALTORs®, both subsidiaries of the NAR. Commercial and investment property managers will probably also choose to be members of the Building Owners and Managers Association (BOMA), an organization representing a membership which owns or manages over 80% of the country's prime office space. One of the most important services BOMA provides to its members is a statistical index on building costs. Many commercial leases provide for rent increases tied to the BOMA index.

Appraisal – Almost all *appraisal* work today is ordered by lenders when making loans. Occasionally an appraiser is hired by a seller or a buyer, but that is unusual. Appraisers are also sometimes called on to appraise a property for legal purposes; a divorce settlement, for example. And property tax appeals also often require the services of an appraiser.

Federal law requires all appraisers to be state licensed or certified in order to perform appraisals for loans involving any federal agency, which includes practically all new loans today. The type of license or certificate the appraiser holds determines what kind of appraisals the appraiser is permitted to perform. For example, a licensed appraiser might be limited to residential properties up to $250,000 in value and non-complex income properties up to $1 million in value. More expensive residential property must be done by a certified residential appraiser, and commercial property probably requires a certified general appraiser. Each state defines what the different licenses and certificates permit the holder to do.

Many appraisers join any of several appraisal organizations for professional association and advancement. The largest of these is the Appraisal Institute, but many prefer the American Society of Appraisers or the National Association of Independent Fee Appraisers. None of these are affiliated with the NAR, as appraisers generally feel it is a conflict of interest for an appraiser to be associated with anyone in real estate brokerage.

Real estate brokers and salespersons are not allowed to appraise without obtaining an appraiser's license or certificate. However, salespersons and brokers are permitted to give estimates of value to buyers and sellers in the course of negotiating a transaction. This includes a *competitive market analysis*, which is similar to an appraisal, but less formal. Even if salespersons and brokers are not permitted to appraise, they must still be conversant with the study of appraisal because they must be able to read and interpret appraisal reports prepared by licensed and certified appraisers.

Real estate development – Real estate *development* includes subdividing raw land and constructing improvements, and has long been an integral part of the real estate field. In fact, until the 1900s this was the main function of a real estate broker. Of course, back then there was great demand for new subdivisions to house the population that was growing quickly due to immigration. Development is no longer the most important part of the real estate field, but it still plays a significant role. And today it is generally done by licensed contractors, although many are also licensed real estate brokers.

Mortgage lending – Most real estate sales require new financing, so there are almost as many people in *mortgage lending* as there are in real estate brokerage. In the past a borrower would obtain a mortgage loan by talking to a mortgage loan officer at a local bank, savings and loan, or mortgage banking firm. Today, these institutions still make the majority of the residential loans, but the borrower usually deals with them through a *mortgage broker*. This extends the geographic reach of the lending institution, allowing them to make loans anywhere in the country. It also increases competition among lenders, reducing costs for borrowers.

The role of the mortgage broker is very similar to that of the real estate broker. The real estate broker brings a buyer and a seller together, and the mortgage broker brings a lender and a borrower together. In fact, it is not unusual today to find large residential real estate brokerage firms with their own in-house mortgage brokerage company. However, the position of the mortgage broker in the transaction has become so important that many states now require them to be licensed. In Washington mortgage brokers must be licensed by the Consumer Services Division of the Department of Financial Institutions.

Real estate counseling – Real estate *counseling* involves advising property owners and prospective buyers and tenants about real estate decisions they need to make. This can involve everything from land development alternatives to financing questions and everything in between. Most real estate counselors are people who have been in the business a long time because offering advice requires a vast knowledge of real estate. Unlike most specialties in real estate, real estate counselors usually charge on an hourly basis. Professional counselors may belong to the Counselors of Real Estate, which is affiliated with the NAR.

Home inspection – Modern housing can have many hidden defects that not even the seller may be aware of. Because of this, and because of increased awareness of consumer protection issues, it has become the custom in residential transactions for the buyer to ask for a professional inspection. A residential inspector may spend a long time at the property, inspecting areas that the buyer and the seller never look at. In most states today residential inspectors must be licensed, usually by the same agency that licenses contractors. In addition, professional inspectors can belong to the American Society of Home Inspectors which has a code of ethics and standards of practice that members must adhere to.

It should be noted that the organizations mentioned above all offer courses and educational materials for their members. Most of them also offer professional designations, some of which are very prestigious. Some of the more commonly encountered and the organizations which grant them are –

GRI	Graduate of the REALTOR® Institute (NAR)
CRS	Certified Residential Specialist (NAR –Council of Residential Specialists)
CRB	Certified Real Estate Brokerage Manager (NAR – Council of Real Estate Brokerage Managers)
CCIM	Certified Commercial and Investment Member (NAR – Certified Commercial and Investment Member Institute)
ARM	Accredited Residential Manager (NAR – Institute of Real Estate Managers)
CPM	Certified Property Manager (NAR – Institute of Real Estate Managers)
ABR	Accredited Buyer Representative (NAR – Real Estate Buyer's Agent Council)
CEBA	Certified Exclusive Buyer's Agent (National Association of Exclusive Buyers Agents)
SIOR	Specialist, Industrial and Office Real Estate (NAR – Society of Industrial and Office REALTORS®)
LTG	Leadership Training Graduate (NAR – Women's Council of REALTORS®)
EBA	Exclusive Buyer's Agent (National Association of Exclusive Buyers Agents
MAI	Member of the Appraisal Institute (Appraisal Institute)
SRA	Senior Real Estate Appraiser (Appraisal Institute)
IFA	Independent Fee Appraiser (National Association of Independent Fee Appraisers)
AM	Accredited Member (American Society of Appraisers)

Many of the above designations require substantial experience in the field as well as numerous courses. Some even require college degrees to qualify.

A list of real estate organizations would not be complete without mentioning the Association of Real Estate License Law Officials (ARELLO). While membership is not open to licensees, its impact on licensing laws and regulations is significant. ARELLO assists state real estate licensing officials by sharing problems and solutions discovered by other members, ultimately benefiting licensees as well as the public. After all, real estate licensing requirements were first proposed by brokers as a tool to maintain a clean industry. When the public has faith and confidence in real estate agents, both sides benefit.

While the above discusses some of the main types of real estate activity and professional associations, there are other specializations that are not so commonly encountered. For example, government agencies and large corporations frequently employ in-house real estate staff who become expert in their employers' real estate needs. Every human activity requires a location, and that means real estate will be involved. Real estate is fundamental to everything we do.

Categories of real estate

In real estate we not only categorize by real estate specializations, but also by type of property. The principal categories are –

Residential – If people live there, it's *residential real estate*. Residential varies from a single-family house in the country to apartments in an urban high-rise. It can be on a lot in a subdivision or it can be a condominium. It can be owned by the occupant, or possession can be through a rental agreement or lease. Most of it is owner-occupied, but nearly a third of it is owned by investors. All of these are classed as residential real estate.

Commercial – *Commercial real estate* is the broadest of all the categories. It includes all kinds of property used in business, including retail property, office space, entertainment property, and even a parking lot. Of course, the different kinds of commercial property present special issues to an agent. When we talk about retail property we think in terms of foot traffic, attracting buyers, and similar issues. When we think about office space we may be concerned with how easily it can be partitioned for specific users. Because of the differences among the various kinds of commercial property, real estate agents tend to specialize within the category.

Industrial – As with commercial property, *industrial real estate* is comprised of different subcategories. It includes factories as well as warehouses and every other kind of real estate needed by industries which produce goods.

Agricultural – Farms and ranches are clearly *agricultural real estate*, as are orchards and truck farms. In Washington timberland is also considered agricultural property, since it is clearly a crop.

Special use – *Special use real estate* (also sometimes called special purpose property) includes everything that doesn't fit in the other categories. For example, a church is not residential, not commercial, not industrial and not agricultural. Similarly, a school would also be considered a special use property. And some property owned by the government would be special use property, for example, the state capitol building. However, if the government owns an office building, it is still considered commercial, since the government could always rent it to others. The usual idea of special use property is that it was built for a specific purpose and cannot easily be converted to some other use.

As with specializations, these categories are sometimes not exact. For example, a high-rise building may have retail space on the ground floor, office space for the next several floors, and condominiums or apartments above. Should we categorize this property as residential or commercial? Or we might have a warehouse in an industrial area that is being used as a retail bargain liquidation business. Is it industrial or commercial? In the real world things are not always as cut and dried as textbooks might have you believe.

Furthermore, bear in mind that an agent might become involved with a property in any of the above categories either in a sales transaction or in a rental or leasing transaction. Again, agents tend to specialize. Some might deal in commercial property, for example, but only to represent the owner's interests to a tenant. Others might deal only in the sale of the same kind of property. And yet other agents might do either.

Real estate regulatory bodies

When Washington agents think of how their activities are regulated their thoughts immediately turn to the Department of Licensing. Anyone who practices real estate is required to be licensed by the Department of Licensing and to abide by the license law. The license law is contained in Revised Code of Washington (RCW) 18.85, 18.86 and 18.235. While the legislature is the only body which can make changes to RCW, the Director has the authority to create regulations to implement the purposes of the license law and specify the details. The regulations are considered administrative law and licensees are required to obey them the same as the laws created by the legislature. Regulations of the Director are contained in Washington Administrative Code (WAC) Chapter 308-124.

The Director is appointed by the governor, who also appoints six commissioners. The commissioners, plus the Director, are referred to as the Real Estate Commission. The commissioners are charged with the duty to advise the Director on matters affecting the real estate industry, to provide educational programs for the benefit of licensees, and to conduct license examinations.

The Department of Licensing issues real estate licenses

The license law and administrative rules are extensive and detailed. It is so important for licensees to know them thoroughly that the entire state portion of the licensing exam is devoted to them. The license law and administrative rules are covered in depth in Chapter 19.

Licensees are also regulated by **anti-trust laws**, such as the federal Sherman Act and the Clayton Act, among others. These laws are enforced by the Federal Trade Commission. The Washington legislature has adopted similar laws as well. The most common anti-trust violations by real estate agents are **price-fixing** (e.g., brokerage firms agreeing on minimum commission rates), **group boycotting** (e.g., real estate companies refusing as a group to do business with another company because they charge lower commissions), or **allocation of customers** (e.g., real estate companies agreeing to divide up a market area into protected territories. Anti-trust laws are covered in more detail in Chapter 18.

There are also numerous **discrimination laws** that licensees must be aware of, both federal and state. The chief federal law is the Fair Housing Act, which is enforced by the Department of Housing and Urban Development. Federal laws also include the Americans with Disabilities Act, enforced by the Department of Justice. And, although the Equal Credit Opportunity Act applies mostly to lenders, there are possibilities for violations by real estate agents as well. Portions applying to real estate agents are generally enforced by the Federal Trade Commission.

Washington also has discrimination laws, more or less echoing federal laws. Real estate transactions are covered primarily in RCW 49.60.222 – 49.60.225. The Washington State Human Rights Commission has investigatory authority, and enforcement is by a Washington administrative law judge. Federal and state discrimination laws are covered in detail in Chapter 22.

The Truth in Lending Act and Federal Reserve Regulation Z are also laws which apply mostly to lenders, but which also impact real estate agents. In the case of real estate agents the main area of concern is in making disclosure of loan terms when advertising credit in connection with advertising a property for sale. Enforcement of the Truth in Lending Act and Regulation Z is by the Federal Trade Commission. Detailed coverage of these laws is contained in Chapter 14.

The Real Estate Settlement Procedures Act applies to lenders, closing agents and real estate agents. Its purpose is to make full disclosure of closing costs and to encourage home buyers to shop for the services they need. It is enforced by the Department of Housing and Urban Development and is covered in detail in Chapter 14.

Environmental issues have become a significant issue in today's world of real estate, requiring considerable attention to disclosure requirements by real estate agents, and occasionally even cleanup requirements. The federal Environmental Protection Agency (EPA) is the organization that regulates and enforces most of these requirements. In addition, Washington requires a seller to complete an extensive **property transfer disclosure** form for the buyer of a residential property, although there is no specific agency regulating its use. Nevertheless, real estate licensees must be familiar with the requirement in order to ensure that the seller complies with the law.

From looking at the above it is apparent that real estate agents are highly regulated by a great variety of federal and state agencies. And the above list includes just the high points – there are many more agencies with regulatory authority over things a licensee does in the course of a real estate practice. The world of real estate today is a complex place requiring a great deal of knowledge of regulatory law to protect the licensee and his or her clients and customers.

A career in real estate

Every year hundreds of thousands of people enter the real estate field. A little more than half will start in residential sales, and the rest will go directly into some of the other fields mentioned earlier. However, real estate people tend to change specializations over time. A residential agent may discover a preference for property management, for example. The nice thing about real estate is the variety within the field. Once you are in real estate your options are extensive. Also, unlike a complete career change, you can change specializations slowly. A residential agent who discovers a liking for property management doesn't have to stop selling abruptly in order to start doing property management. It's easy to try out new directions and move into a different specialization without suddenly cutting off what you were doing before.

Regardless of what specialty you prefer, real estate is a career that can provide above average income for a lifetime, and a comfortable retirement as well. Successful real estate agents invest in real estate over the years and eventually become financially independent. However, beginners should be aware that their income potential is exactly proportional to how good they are. Almost all real estate agents work on a commission basis. If you produce nothing, your income will be nothing. No one in real estate gets a paycheck just for showing up at work. An old adage among agents is that real estate is the best paid hard work and the poorest paid easy work there is. If you work hard your income will be well above average. If you think real estate is an easy way to get rich, you are surely heading for a disappointment.

Everyone in real estate will agree that the attrition rate among new agents is worse than most fields. There are a number of reasons for this –

Unrealistic income expectations – The general public looks at the total commission paid on a typical sale and gets the impression that real estate agents must have a very high income. But the public doesn't realize that in most sales that commission is split between the listing company and the selling company, and the listing and selling agents each get only a portion of what their company receives. It's a lot less after it gets split four ways. Furthermore, an agent has some pretty heavy expenses – multiple listing service dues, errors and omissions insurance, auto expenses, and many more.

There is also a psychological effect when a prospective new agent looks at the income potential of a real estate career. Real estate is a second career for over 90% of new agents. Since most new agents are accustomed to a paycheck from their previous employment, they tend to think of their income from commissions as being something they will have on top of a paycheck. Every prospective new agent knows that this is not so, but there is a strong tendency to think of the commission as a bonus to their income. A few months after going into sales they get hit with reality as they struggle to pay their bills.

This is not made easier by the fact that it can be hard to get established in sales. A new agent's income is likely to be small at first, and slow to come in. Plus, commission income is far from regular. Even established agents frequently go for more than a month without a check. Because of these factors brokers recommend that most new agents have enough cash ahead to hold themselves for six months.

Another problem encountered by many new agents is replacing the benefits they had at their previous employment. In real estate you will have no retirement plan or other benefits. Most firms offer a group health insurance plan, but the agent will probably be expected to pay the full premium. There will also probably be no withholding for income tax and social security. The agent has to set enough money aside to cover these expenses. Some new agents have a hard time adjusting to the lack of benefits and financial hand-holding.

Working hours – Agents in commercial and industrial real estate enjoy the luxury of being able to work regular business hours. Everyone else is on call 24 hours a day and seven days a week. When a seller calls to come and list a house, you have to respond right away. When the buyers say they want to make an offer, you have to be available. Evenings and weekends are seldom your own.

In most cases the new agent can handle the hours, but the agent's family cannot, or at least doesn't understand. All the family sees is dwindling income and 80-hour work weeks. The family doesn't always realize that this will change. After a few years in the business the income usually becomes more than what the agent was previously earning, and the agent also develops the resources to handle the variability of the income. The hours are still long, but the agent and family adjust and learn how to manage.

Dealing with people – It is often said that real estate is a people business. That's just another way of saying that it's a service industry. When you provide a service you must deal with the public, and the public can frequently be unreasonable and demanding. Yet the job of the agent is always to solve someone's problem. Until you solve a client's problem, there will be no paycheck. Some people are not cut out for dealing with the public in this way. It requires patience, perseverance, and sometimes a thick skin.

Handling rejection – Even the most skillful agent gets told "no" far more often than "yes." Some people find this is hard to take. Successful agents just shrug off rejection and move on to the next prospect. They know that the rejections are irrelevant. Unsuccessful agents are sometimes unable to grasp that a "no" is only a "no" to their services; not a personal rejection; leading to depression and an early departure from the field.

Time management – Almost all real estate agents are independent contractors. This means that you will be responsible for your own time. If you wish to take the afternoon off, that's your decision. But it doesn't take a genius to realize that you can't do this all the time and still maintain your income. Some new agents have never worked at a job where they had to decide these things for themselves. To be successful in real estate you have to learn how to handle this for yourself.

Who is likely to be successful in real estate? Many studies have been made in an attempt to create a psychological profile of a successful agent. However, human psychology is far from an exact science and it's difficult to make hard and fast statements. Nevertheless, there are a few factors that everyone agrees on.

For example, agents who derive a sense of satisfaction from a successful transaction do better than those whose primary motivation is money. Some psychologists call it ego drive; that is, your ego is bolstered by accomplishing the sale, and this keeps you coming back for more. The money is nice too, but a secondary consideration. You'd sell real estate even if you didn't get paid, just because you get a thrill out of making the sale.

Successful agents are also self-starters and self-directed. You don't need anyone to tell you to get out of bed and go to work. Every job, including real estate, has some things you don't enjoy doing. Maybe you don't like calling people on the phone, or maybe you can't stand driving in traffic. Whatever it is, successful agents have the self-discipline to do it anyway.

Getting started

Selecting a broker – If you don't already have a broker to go to work for after passing the exam, then you need to find one. Luckily, this is not as difficult as most beginners think it is. Brokers are always happy to hire new agents. Remember, if you produce nothing, your paycheck is nothing, so it costs a broker very little to give you a chance. Of course, an unsuccessful agent does the broker no good, so most brokers who take on new agents offer considerable support to help them become successful.

One of the most important things to look for when selecting a broker to work for is what kind of sales training the company offers. This ranges from "follow me around and do what I do," to formal classes given by industry leaders. Each has its advantages. And every new agent comes to the field with different backgrounds, skills and abilities, so there is no one training plan that is perfect for everyone.

Of course, new agents need to start by selecting brokers who work on the kind of property they want to sell and in the area they wish to cover. If you want to sell commercial real estate, then a residential company would be a silly choice. However, there are probably numerous companies that meet your initial criteria, so you need to consider other issues as well. For example, if you can, find out what the average agent in the office earns. This can be a very revealing statistic. Also, ask the broker whether the broker or office manager is a competing broker. In the industry, a **competing broker** is one who takes listings and makes sales along with the salespersons. While there is nothing wrong with this, a non-competing broker may be better. A non-competing broker is one whose sole function is to be in the office to support the sales staff.

New agents frequently consider the idea of starting out on a part-time basis. Most brokers won't take part-timers, and those who do usually discourage it. The problem is that it's harder to be successful as a part-timer. It's difficult to keep up with new listings, new financing being offered, and all the rest of the things an agent must keep abreast of. The public doesn't trust a part-timer and neither do other agents.

However, there is another way to get started in real estate that might allow part-time work without the usual problems associated with it. Many successful agents find that they have too much business to take care of themselves and are looking for a personal assistant to take some of the workload. This can be an excellent entry into the field.

When selecting a broker many new agents run frantically from one company to the next checking out what their commission splits are. This is almost always pointless. Real estate companies depend on keeping good agents. If their competition offered commission splits that were even a little bit better, they would lose their agents to other companies, and soon be out of business. The result is that real estate companies offer commission splits that are different, but on average are very competitive with each other. Worry about whether the company will help you get started and not about commission splits. After all, even if a company gave you all of the commission, if you make no sales, then 100% of no commission at all is zero.

Your future in real estate

The preceding may have left the impression that it is hard to be successful in real estate. In some respects, that is true. But real estate offers an excellent future to anyone able to make it past the first year or two. Every sale you make and every new contact leaves you with so many referrals that eventually you can stop beating the pavement for new business. There are many agents who arrive at this point after as little as a couple years in the business. It is faster to develop a viable clientele in real estate than any other field.

Factors that influence home purchase decisions

Everyone has to live somewhere. In the U.S. we are lucky because we have the highest percentage of home ownership of any country in the world. Over two-thirds of all U.S. households are owner-occupied. Of course, many of the remaining households would not buy a home simply because they don't want the commitment and responsibility. Nevertheless, many would if they could. Factors that prospective home buyers need to consider include –

- The amount and stability of their income
- Current mortgage interest rates and loan terms
- Current cost of housing
- How permanent their employment is and the possibility of having to move
- Tax benefits of home ownership in relation to their income
- Potential for appreciation or depreciation in the future

Housing affordability index – The first three of the above factors are summarized in the ***housing affordability index***. For many years the National Association of REALTORS® has maintained this index to measure whether the income of a typical family is enough to buy a home at the current average national sales price and at current average interest rates, assuming an 80% loan. If the typical family income is exactly enough, then the index is at 100. If the typical family income is greater than what they need, then the index will be above 100, and vice-versa. For example, if the index is at 107, then the typical family has 107% of what they need to buy the average home with an 80% loan at current interest rates. Naturally, the higher the index, the more robust the residential real estate market.

In addition to the housing affordability index, real estate agents sometimes use computer programs to assist prospective buyers in making the rent vs. buy decision. These programs present the actual cost of home ownership as opposed to renting after taking into account income tax savings and potential for appreciation.

NOTES

Regardless of what area of real estate you go into, real estate is a huge and exciting marketplace. If you study and work hard you will enjoy an above average income and a solid career. What you can accomplish in is completely up to you and how hard you work. There is no upper limit to your potential in real estate.

KEY TERMS

The key to understanding any new field is the vocabulary used in that field. To maximize your comprehension of the material presented in this chapter, be sure you know the meaning and significance of the following terms. Remember that the majority of test questions primarily test knowledge of vocabulary.

Agricultural real estate

Allocation of customers

Antitrust laws

Appraisal

Brokerage

Buyer's agent

Commercial real estate

Competing broker

Competitive market analysis

Counseling

Development

Discrimination laws

Dual agent

Facilitator

Group boycotting

Housing affordability index

Industrial real estate

Mortgage broker

Mortgage lending

Price fixing

Property management

Property transfer disclosure

REALTOR®

Residential real estate

Special use real estate

Chapter

Starting out in real estate law

SINCE THE VERY BEGINNING of history man has found the need to create rules to live by. In our modern society, the rules have become codified into a complex legal system. A basic understanding of how that system works is essential for persons engaging in business endeavors, especially if the business is real estate.

Sources of law

Most laws relating to real estate are the result of court decisions. This is sometimes referred to as ***common law***, or ***case law***. Whenever two individuals have a dispute and that dispute is brought to court, the judge will render a decision. Now, the interesting thing is that whenever a decision is made which involves a new problem which the court has never addressed before, the case usually creates a ***precedent***. When a precedent has been established, all subsequent cases involving essentially the same problem must be decided the same way. The decision which creates this precedent is called a ***landmark decision***, or ***landmark case***. Today landmark cases are normally decided by a court of appeals (appellate court) or by the Washington or U.S. Supreme Court, depending on jurisdiction. Since the early colonists brought English common law with them, judges in this country frequently rely on decisions made centuries ago in England. However, most decisions today are based on the great body of American case law, which by now has become substantial.

The common law of the land is, unfortunately, not uniform throughout the United States. Since each state has its own court system, the precedents established in one state tend to vary slightly from those established in another state. In spite of this, a decision rendered in one state usually commands attention in other states, even though a judge in another state is not bound to follow it. Washington has a relatively small population and not as many years of history as most states, and therefore has a shortage of case law of its own. As a result, Washington courts tend sometimes to look strongly at decisions from other states.

A second source of law is that law which is created by elected officials. In the United States the basis of this law is the U.S. Constitution, upon which all legal authority in this country ultimately rests. The Constitution authorizes Congress to create law by the democratic vote of duly elected senators and representatives. Each state also has a constitution and a legislature, patterned after the federal model. Even at the local level (city or county), there are elected officials who are given the power to create laws. Law created by these elected officials is called ***statutory law***. Individual state laws are called ***statutes***, while local laws are generally referred to as ***ordinances***. In Washington statutory law created by the state legislature is referred to as the Revised Code of Washington, or RCW, and applies throughout the state.

What happens when there is a conflict between the common law and a statute? The major purpose of a statute is to modify the common law, so statutes take precedence over the common law. But there is always an interesting interplay between the common law and statutory law. While the statutes modify the existing law, the courts have the power to declare a statute or ordinance unconstitutional, and the courts also have the power to interpret statutes. However, if the courts interpret a statute in a manner which the elected officials did not intend, the elected body can simply rewrite the statute or ordinance, and if necessary can even ask the people to amend the constitution. Ultimately the people, through their elected officials, can force the courts to change the law.

Sometimes a statute is created which gives some appointed or elected officials the authority to create additional rules or regulations in order to implement the purposes of the statute. For example, many times the purpose for which the statute was created requires the creation of detailed rules which are too involved for the legislature itself to take the time to consider. Or sometimes it is desirable to allow other appointed or elected officials to make rules or regulations so the law can easily be kept up to date. Statutes which create this authority are called **enabling statutes**. The rules created under the authority of an enabling statute are called **administrative law**, or **administrative rules and regulations**. In your real estate studies you will come across many enabling statutes. The most important enabling statute you will encounter is the Real Estate License Law, which empowers the Director of the Department of Licensing to create administrative rules which real estate licensees must adhere to, just as if the rules were part of the statute itself. In Washington administrative law is referred to as the Washington Administrative Code (WAC), and the portions that apply to real estate licensees are in Chapter 308-124.

Real property and personal property

Basic to an understanding of real estate law is a clear definition of what **real estate** is. Many times you will hear people refer to real estate as **real property** or as **realty**, or even as **land**. While there are technical distinctions in the meanings of these terms, for our purposes we will use them interchangeably. Likewise, **personal property** (things which are not real property) are often referred to as **personalty** or as **chattels**.

The entire universe is divided legally into real property and personal property. The definition of personal property is "that which is not real property." Now, if you think about it for a minute, you will realize that this is a very neat definition because it leaves out nothing – everything must fit into one category or the other. But at the same time, it places a great burden on the definition of real property. In other words, if we define personal property as "that which is not real," then we have to know exactly what is real in order to know what is personal.

Most people would agree that a parcel of bare land is real property. But what about the improvements on the land? And how deep does your ownership extend? How high? These are some of the questions we will explore next.

Real property consists of the land and everything that is **appurtenant** to the land. When we say that something is appurtenant to the land we mean that the item is part of the land and is conveyed automatically to the buyer when the land is sold, even if it is not mentioned in the deed or sales agreement. In other words, if you own a lot which has a house on it, the house is considered an **appurtenance** to the land. If you sell the lot to your neighbor, the neighbor is automatically presumed to be entitled to the house as well as the lot. Of course, if you specifically exclude the structure, it is possible to sell the house and the lot separately. Remember though, that the legal presumption is that the house is part of the real estate, so if you wish to keep it you must say so in the sales (earnest money) agreement. Things which are appurtenant to the land are said to "run with the land."

Most appurtenances are obvious and present no problems. A house, or other major physical improvement is clearly part of the real estate. However, some appurtenances are more subtle. Many times an appurtenance will not be a physical improvement, but rather a right which runs with the land, such as an easement over adjacent land. Appurtenances which have no physical existence are said to be **incorporeal** – that is, they are intangible, cannot be touched. Physical improvements, on the other hand, are said to be **corporeal** – they are tangible and have physical existence. Typical incorporeal appurtenances include not only easements, but water and mineral rights, the right to lateral support from adjacent land, and many others.

Fixtures – Many times you will be faced with a questionable item. For example, suppose you are selling a house and there is a swag lamp in the living room. It is hanging from a hook which is securely fastened to the ceiling. Is the lamp part of the real estate? Or is just the hook part of the real estate? Or are both the lamp and the hook personal property? Consider also a television antenna on a roof, a drop-in range, unattached carpeting cut to fit a room, or any of numerous other items which leave you wondering. You can imagine countless such problems which a real estate agent would be likely to encounter in the daily practice of selling real estate. Knowing when these items are real and when they are personal is crucial to anyone involved with real estate.

These items are referred to as *fixtures* and a complex set of legal rules exist to determine if they should be part of the real estate or not. If it is determined that an item is a fixture, then it is real. If it is not a fixture, then it is personal.

Usually a fixture started out as personal property and became a fixture because someone decided to make it part of the real estate. For example, consider a deposit of clay lying beneath the ground. While it is in the ground, it is clearly real. If the owner of the land removes the clay and turns it into bricks, then the bricks are personal property, so the owner has converted real property into personalty. Now suppose a homeowner comes along, buys the bricks and uses them to construct a brick barbecue. The bricks have now become real estate again. As you can see, a fixture usually started out as personal property and became real property later because of someone's actions. However, even a fixture can be turned back into personal property.

Note, however, that we are usually only concerned about the item at the point of a sale or lease. If you own a house with a brick barbecue, you probably don't really care if the barbecue is real or personal – either way you may use and enjoy the barbecue. But if you sell or lease the property to someone, it suddenly becomes important to know if you must leave the barbecue, or if you may dismantle and remove it when you leave.

There are various rules involved in determining if an item is a fixture. These rules are commonly referred to as the *tests of a fixture*. The tests of a fixture were designed to be applied by a judge in making a decision.

The most basic test is the test of *annexation*. Annexation refers to how firmly the item is physically attached to the real estate. We refer to the party who installed or involved the item with the real estate as the *annexor*.

Make careful note that Washington courts normally recognize the modern concept that the item need not always be physically attached to the real estate to be a fixture. For example, equipment which is designed to be used with the land and is not readily usable elsewhere would probably be held to be a fixture, even though the equipment was not in the least attached. An everyday example might include the separate remote control unit for an automatic garage door opener. The idea is that if the garage door and the opener motor are part of the real estate, and if the control unit is essential to their operation, then the control unit must be considered part of the real estate as well.

On the other hand, it is possible that an item which is firmly attached may be construed to be personal property. This could occur because the intent of the annexor was that the item remain personal or because there was an agreement relative to the item (see later). The point you must grasp here is that if it is not attached it still may be a fixture, and if even if it is attached, it may sometimes remain personal. You cannot assume that if it is attached it is always real estate, and if it is not attached it is always personal property.

The second test is the adaptability of the item (*adaptation*). Stated simply, if an item has been customized or is vital to the use of the real estate, then it will likely be considered a fixture. For example, think of a gas range in a house. While it may be connected to the real estate via the gas pipe, it is not considered a fixture because it has not been customized, it is not vital to the use of the property, and it is easily replaced with a substitute range which would serve as well. But now consider draperies which were custom made to fit a window of an unusual shape. Since the draperies cannot readily be used elsewhere, they would normally be considered part of the real estate. Note that the draperies are also an example of fixtures which are not physically attached.

The third, and most powerful, test of a fixture is **intention**. Intention refers to the intent of the annexor in installing or involving the item with the real estate. Intention is so powerful an argument that in some cases annexation and adaptation are really just evidence of the intention of the annexor. For example, if the annexor installs an item so firmly that it cannot be removed without irreparable harm to the premises, is this not evidence that the annexor intended for the item to remain permanent? And if the annexor has an item custom made for the property, should this not be considered as evidence that the annexor intended to leave the item with the real estate?

Tests of a fixture
❶
❷
❸

The relationship between the parties is another important factor in determining the intent of the annexor. If an owner installs an item on his or her real estate, there is normally a presumption that the owner did so in order to improve the value of the property, and therefore intended for the item to become a fixture.

But if the item is installed by a tenant, then we must conclude that the tenant probably intended to remove the item at the end of the tenancy. Of course, if the tenant has a long term lease, and installs an item which would normally be worn out by the end of the lease, we might draw a different conclusion. When such items are installed on commercial premises they are referred to as **trade fixtures**. You may also occasionally hear the terms **domestic fixture** and **agricultural fixture** to refer to items installed by a tenant on residential or agricultural premises respectively. Of course, as would seem logical, if the tenant is to be allowed to remove the items, then it is only fair that the tenant restore the premises and repair any damage caused by the removal.

Another important consideration in determining the intent of the annexor is the existence of an agreement. In other words, if a buyer and a seller (or lessor and lessee) enter into an agreement that an item will or will not be considered a fixture, the courts will generally hold them to their bargain. In fact, the courts will not only enforce the agreement, but will usually even ignore other evidence such as provided by the tests of annexation and adaptation. In other words, if you have an agreement, you can normally assume that it will render other factors irrelevant.

The fact that an agreement relative to an item is generally enforceable is crucial to real estate agents. Questions about fixtures are constantly arising in real estate practice. As a result, standard form contracts for the sale and leasing of real estate contain places for the parties to list which items are included with the real estate (called **inclusions** by real estate agents), and which items are not included (commonly referred to as **exclusions**).

While the law of fixtures is vital for real estate agents to know, there are practical considerations as well. For example, what should you do if the seller, when listing a property for sale, wants to exclude the chandelier in the dining room? It is common for sellers to want to remove certain prized possessions, including even shrubs and trees. A good practice is to have the seller remove the items before the first potential buyers ever see the premises. In the case of shrubs and trees, it is common to have the seller mark them with tags so buyers can see which shrubs and trees will be removed.

Surface, subsurface and air rights

Ownership of real estate is really the ownership of a volume of space. This space extends from the surface boundaries down to the center of the earth. Originally, the common law concept of ownership extended to "the heavens above forever and ever." However, if we still followed this concept, air travel would be impossible because anyone flying over your land would be guilty of trespass. Therefore, your ownership interest today extends above the surface only to a height necessary for the ordinary and reasonable use and enjoyment of the property.

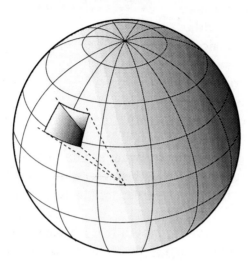

One of the attributes of real estate is that it is a volume of space. Your ownership of real estate extends to the center of the earth and to a height above the land necessary for the ordinary and reasonable use and enjoyment of the property.

Because the owner of land really owns a volume of space, we say that real estate is *indestructible* and *immobile*. After all, no one can destroy space, nor can you move a piece of real estate to another location. In contrast, personal property is easily destroyed or moved.

What about the material which happens to be located within the volume of space? The soil, improvements and other features of an owner's real estate clearly affect the nature, character and value of the property, but they do not change how much property is owned. The concept that real estate is a volume of space and therefore immovable and indestructible is sometimes referred to as *the legal definition of real estate*

An interesting concept is that an owner can sell any part of the property separately from the rest. Thus, an owner could sell the *mineral rights* or the *air rights* while retaining ownership of the rest of the land. In urban areas the sale of air rights is common. For example, a railroad might need the surface only to a height necessary for their trains to clear. The space above could be sold for development as offices, commercial retail space, or even residential purposes. Or rail lines could be elevated above the surface, as in urban areas where elevated mass transit lines run above the surface streets.

Another feature of real property is that it is always unique. No two pieces of real property are ever exactly the same. Even if the value, size and appearance are identical, at least the location is always different. This is not necessarily true of personal property. It is possible for two chattels to be identical in every significant respect. Personal property that is of a sort which consists of identical units is said to be *fungible*.

Sometimes we have personal property which is closely related to real property. For example, a lease is really nothing more than a piece of paper. But since it involves an interest in real property, we refer to it as a *chattel real*. Other examples of chattels real include deeds, mortgages, easements, and the like.

Mineral rights – Rules regarding mineral rights depend on whether the minerals are solid or not. In the case of solid minerals, an owner can sell them easily simply by designating the space below the surface where they lie. Oil and gas rights, on the other hand, are considerably more difficult.

Oil and gas are usually under great pressure, so when a well is drilled into the land, the oil or gas tends to migrate toward the point at the bottom of the well. This makes it difficult for the owner to take just the oil and gas which lies beneath his or her own land. As a result, oil and gas are usually governed by the ***rule of capture***. The rule of capture means that you own all the oil and gas that you can produce from wells on the surface of your own land, even including oil and gas which comes from under your neighbor's land. Once you have removed the oil or gas it becomes your personal property. Naturally, this rule forces your neighbors to drill their own wells quickly, in order to get their fair share.

Crop rights – Growing plants are legally categorized as those which are naturally occurring (called ***fructus naturales***), and those which are planted or cultivated (called ***fructus industriales***). Both naturally occurring plants and perennial cultivated crops are considered real property until ***severance***. Severance means the physical severing of the crop from the land, and in this case normally refers to the harvest. Once you have severed the plants from the land they are still yours, but now they are personal property. Annual crops, however, are considered personal property, even while still in the ground.

On the other hand, what if you planted a crop on land you were renting or leasing? In this case, we must address what happens if the lease or rental arrangement should be terminated prior to the time when the crops are ready to harvest. It would not be fair for the landlord to deprive a tenant of the fruits of the tenant's labors by terminating possession just before the crops were ready to harvest. Therefore, the law grants the tenant the ***right of emblement***, that is, the right to return to cultivate and harvest the crops even after the tenancy is terminated. Of course, the tenant only has this right if the tenancy did not have a fixed term or if the tenancy was terminated through an act of God or other problem not caused by the tenant. A lease, for example, is a tenancy for a fixed term. If the tenant plants a crop that would take longer to harvest than the remaining term on the lease, then the tenant knew this before planting the crop, and therefore has no right of emblement.

Crop liens are a potential real estate problem. It is common for farmers to borrow money in the spring to purchase seed and fertilizer and hire labor to cultivate the crops. The loans are then paid off from the proceeds of the sale of the crop. Most such loans are secured by the future crop, giving the lender a lien on the crop. The problem occurs when the property is sold before the loan is paid off. If the seller defaults on the loan, the buyer may find that the lender has the right to enter the premises and harvest the crop even after the sale has closed.

Agricultural property is frequently rented on a year-to-year basis or leased for several years at a time. This can create a problem when the owner goes to sell the land. As will be discussed in more detail later, when you sell a leased or rented property, the buyer takes title subject to the rights of the tenant. To avoid problems, real estate agents who sell agricultural property should inquire when taking a listing if the property is subject to any leases, rental agreements, potential rights of emblement or crop liens.

Lateral and subjacent support – When you own real estate one of the rights you enjoy is the right to ***lateral support***, that is, the right to insist that adjacent owners do nothing to cause your land to collapse. For example, if your neighbor excavates a hole and, as a result, your land collapses into the hole, it is your neighbor's responsibility to shore up the side to prevent the collapse of your land.

However, the absolute right to lateral support only exists when your land remains in its natural condition. If you place improvements on your land and the weight of the improvements causes your land to subside into your neighbor's excavation, then your neighbor is liable to you only if the neighbor failed to give you reasonable advance notice before excavating. Similarly, even if you place no structures on your land, but you alter the grade or contour of the land, as with landscaping, the result is the same – your neighbor only need give you proper advance notice of the excavation. The responsibility to shore up the land to prevent a loss is then yours.

A parallel problem is the matter of **subjacent support**. Subjacent support refers to the support of the land from underneath, as where a mine has been excavated beneath the surface. Washington is not a state in which a great deal of underground mining activity occurs, so there is little case law on the subject of subjacent support. However, most authorities agree that the principles are generally the same as for lateral support. An owner has the right to expect support from beneath the land, but the right is only absolute if the land remains in its natural conditions. If there are improvements whose weight increases the possibility of collapse, then the person creating the mine is only obligated to give reasonable advance notice.

Water rights

The use of water is an important public concern which the law has addressed since the earliest recorded history. Until recently water laws have involved merely the quantity of water and how it should be distributed. Modern legislation, however, is now beginning to address the issue of water quality as well. We will focus here on water rights as they constitute appurtenances to real property in Washington and other water issues that real estate agents need to be aware of.

Since the beginning of our legal heritage the law has recognized the distinction between **surface water** and **ground water**. The meanings are fairly obvious – surface water is that water which naturally occurs on the surface of the land, including lakes and streams. Ground water is generally all water located beneath the surface. However, in Washington water beneath the surface may have flowed from a surface water source, in which case it is still treated as surface water due to the principle of **hydraulic continuity**. Ground water is also occasionally referred to as **percolating water** or **subterranean water**. The distinction between ground water and surface water is important because in Washington a landowner's rights to ground water and surface water are sometimes very different.

In most states east of the Mississippi rights to surface water, as in a stream, are based on a law known as the **Doctrine of Riparian Right** (sometimes just called "riparian water law" or other similar terms). Under the Doctrine of Riparian Right a property owner has the right to use and appropriate water from a stream only if the owner's property abuts the stream or if the stream flows through the property. Such properties are said to be **riparian** properties and their owners are described as riparian owners. The word "riparian" is derived from the Latin word *ripa*, meaning "the bank of a stream." In similar fashion, properties which lie along a lake are called **littoral** properties and rights to the lake water enjoyed by their owners are called littoral rights.

How the water rights of a riparian owner are reconciled with the rights of upstream and downstream owners is the subject of laws which differ substantially from state to state.

The most significant problem with the Doctrine of Riparian Right is the plight of a non-riparian owner. In most riparian right states, only riparian owners are allowed to appropriate and use water from the stream. Non-riparian owners can use stream water in some states, but even then, not in all cases. However, ground water is generally available for appropriation, so a non-riparian owner can simply drill a well to obtain water.

The Doctrine of Riparian Right predominates in eastern states where there is moderate to heavy precipitation which is relatively evenly spread throughout the year. In these states, if an owner does not have riparian rights, the water table is usually high enough that it is easy to obtain ground water from a well. In the western states, however, the climate tends to be arid, so ground water is not always available. In many instances, the land would simply be unusable unless the owner could divert water from a stream and transport it across the riparian land to use on a non-riparian property.

The ***Doctrine of Prior Appropriation***. (also known as "appropriation water law," etc.) was created to resolve the problems of non-riparian owners. Under the Doctrine of Prior Appropriation water is not apportioned to an owner merely because the owner's land happens to be riparian. Instead, water rights are granted according to the date of the first use. In other words, water rights are on a first-come, first-served basis. The first property owner to use water from a stream establishes the oldest priority date for that stream. In times of inadequate supply the holder of the oldest water right will be the last to be shut off.

Of course, if an owner has a right to appropriate water from a stream, but his or her property is not riparian, then a ditch or pipeline must be created across the land in between. The owner of the riparian property cannot refuse an easement for the ditch or pipeline. However, the riparian owner can demand just compensation for the loss of market value as a result of having the easement across his or her land.

A major advantage of this system is not only that it allows use of stream water on non-riparian land, but that it encourages development. Property owners realize that the older the water right, the more valuable it is. A water right, once established, is appurtenant to the property, which makes the property worth more.

In most prior appropriation states another benefit of the Doctrine of Prior Appropriation is that, by statute, the right to create water rights is vested in the state. This allows the state to create a system of permits and certificates in order to keep clear records of water rights. The state can also maintain minimum stream and ground water levels.

Washington is among only a handful of states that recognize both the Doctrine of Riparian Right and the Doctrine of Prior Appropriation. In Washington some early water rights were created by the Doctrine of Riparian Right and were grandfathered into current water rights law, which requires water rights to be established under the Doctrine of Prior Appropriation.

Water Rights Acts – The first significant legislation affecting water rights in Washington came with the passage of the ***Water Code of 1917***. The Water Code of 1917 established Washington as a prior appropriation state for the creation of future water rights and further established the Water Resources Department, which later became part of the Department of Ecology. It also specified that all water lying within the boundaries of the state is owned by the state, thus clarifying the right of the state to regulate and grant rights for the appropriation of water. Property owners must now obtain a water right by making application to the Department of Ecology. However, the Water Code of 1917 addressed only surface water rights. Nevertheless, appropriating ground water now requires the same basic procedures as for surface water. This requirement was added in 1945 with the passage of the ***Ground Water Code***.

Obtaining a water right – All waters within the state may be appropriated except those which have been closed to appropriation to preserve minimum stream flows and ground water levels. A property owner should check with the Department of Ecology before submitting an application. Real estate agents should never represent to a potential buyer that a water right can be obtained without first verifying with the Department that the area has not been closed.

Uses of ground water, however, are exempt if they do not exceed a total of 5,000 gallons per day and they are for –

- Stock watering,
- A lawn or non-commercial garden up to one-half acre,
- Single or group domestic use, or
- Industrial use.

Uses of ground water for the above purposes are exempt, but a water right is required if the property owner needs to exceed 5,000 gallons per day or use the water for a purpose not listed.

If a water right is needed the first step is to apply to the Department of Ecology for a **water right permit** and publish a public notice written by the Department. The Department reviews the application and applies four tests –

- The proposed use must be a beneficial use,
- There must be water available,
- There must be no impairment to existing rights, and
- The proposed use must not be detrimental to the public interest.

If the review is affirmative the Department issues the water right permit. If the permit is denied the applicant can appeal the decision.

The sprinklers in this farmer's field are probably using water from a stream or a well. The amount used is undoubtedly over 5,000 gallons per day, so the farmer certainly has a water right to make use of the water. The water right may have been created by common law before the Water Code of 1917 or afterwards by filing for a permit with the Department of Ecology. Regardless of how it was created, it is an appurtenance to the title, so it runs with the land unless it is lost by non-use. An agent taking a listing on this farm can verify the water right with the Department of Ecology.

A water right permit is not initially a title right and does not run with the land. No water rights can be granted unless the landowner actually makes a beneficial use of the water, so the purpose of a water right permit is to allow an owner to make a legal use of water to the extent necessary to prove that there is water to be taken, and the owner did, indeed, make a beneficial use of the water.

After making a beneficial use of the water, the owner can ask the Department of Ecology to issue a and record a **water right certificate**, which is the evidence of the existence of the water right as an appurtenance to the title. As a technicality, the water right exists as an appurtenance as soon as the beneficial use is made, but the certificate makes it a matter of public record and eliminates any question as to its existence. If a property is sold after the application process is started but before the certificate is issued and recorded, the application can be assigned to the buyer, who can then complete the process.

The water right certificate will stipulate the amount of water allowed both as an instantaneous rate (rate of flow) and, if used for irrigation, as an annual maximum amount. The instantaneous rate is usually expressed as a number of cubic feet per second of flow. The annual maximum is expressed in acre-feet. One **acre-foot** is the amount of water necessary to cover one acre to a depth of one foot.

As noted previously, many of the surface water rights established before the Water Code of 1917 are still valid. In order to determine the existence of these water rights, an **adjudication** process was required, i.e., the matter had to be submitted to a court hearing. This process resulted in many water rights being established. Most of these water rights have been recorded by the Department of Ecology where they can be verified.

Once a water right is created it becomes an appurtenance to the title and runs with the land forever. However, a water right can be lost in Washington either through common-law abandonment or statutory relinquishment. **Common law abandonment** occurs if the owner stops using the water and there is evidence of an intent to abandon it; e.g., failing to maintain the ditch or pipeline necessary for its use. In 1967 the Legislature passed a statute providing for **statutory relinquishment** if the owner fails to use the water for five years without good cause.

Water rights are usually appurtenant only to the property for which established. For example, if you own a section of land (640 acres), but have a water right for only 40 acres, then the water right can only be used on the 40 acres, not the other 600. The legal description of the property to which the water right is appurtenant must be included in the application for the permit and will appear on the final water right certificate. However, some of the very early water rights were less specific about the portion of the property on which the water could be used.

While a water right is established for a specific property, a water right can be transferred. To transfer a water right to another property, or even to change a point of diversion or the nature of the use, requires filing an application with the Department of Ecology. Assuming that the transfer or other change will not injure other water right holders or the public interest, the Department will issue a new water right certificate.

You can check on whether a water right exists for a property by contacting the Department of Ecology where all water rights are kept on record, with the exception of a few very old water rights which may be found only in the county records. Eventually the Department plans to make this information available on their website.

Wells – Washington law requires all wells to be constructed by a well contractor licensed by the Department of Ecology. The well contractor must also be registered as a general contractor. At least 72 hours before commencement of the well construction the property owner must file a notification form to the Department of Ecology along with a fee. Upon completion of the well a well log must be filed with the regional office of the Department of Ecology, and a well tag issued by the Department must be affixed to the well.

If the well will be used for exempted purposes (see above) then no water right will be needed. While the vast majority of wells in Washington have been constructed for exempted purposes, if the owner will be exceeding the 5,000 gallon per day limit, or using the water for a purpose other than the exempted uses, then a water right permit will be required before construction of the well. If the well will serve more than one dwelling there are additional requirements for health and safety issues.

The important issue about water rights for real estate agents is that an agent should never represent that a property has a water right without first verifying the accuracy of the statement. Nor should an agent let a potential buyer believe that obtaining a water right is a simple or automatic process, or unnecessary. Buyers might even assume that they have the right to drill a well themselves and not understand the legal need to maintain well logs and other requirements. Agents must understand these issues in order to ensure that the parties to a transaction are not disappointed because of misapprehensions about water rights.

KEY TERMS

The key to understanding any new field is the vocabulary used in that field. To maximize your comprehension of the material presented in this chapter, be sure you know the meaning and significance of the following terms. Remember that the majority of test questions primarily test knowledge of vocabulary.

Acre-foot	Intention
Adaptation	Land
Adjudication	Landmark case
Administrative law	Landmark decision
Agricultural fixture	Lateral support
Air rights	Littoral
Annexation	Mineral rights
Appurtenance	Ordinance
Appurtenant	Percolating water
Case law	Personal property
Chattel real	Personalty
Chattels	Precedent
Common law	Real estate
Common-law abandonment	Real property
Corporeal	Realty
Doctrine of Prior Appropriation	Right of emblement
Doctrine of Riparian Right	Riparian
Domestic fixture	Rule of capture
Enabling statute	Severance
Exclusion	Statute
Fixture	Statutory law
Fructus industriales	Statutory relinquishment
Fructus naturales	Subjacent support
Fungible	Subterranean water
Ground water	Surface water
Ground Water Code	Tests of a fixture
Hydraulic continuity	Trade fixture
Immobile	Unauthorized practice of law
Inclusion	Water Code of 1917
Incorporeal	Water right certificate
Indestructible	Water right permit

Chapter

3

Ways to own real estate

NOTES

MANY DIFFERENT KINDS of interests can exist in real estate at the same time. For example, an owner may have leased the property to a tenant, so both the owner and the tenant have interests in the property simultaneously. Or perhaps the owner has mortgaged the property to a bank. Then the bank clearly has an interest in the property also. The word *interest* is a broad term that encompasses any kind of right in the real property.

There are many kinds of interests that can exist in the same property simultaneously. In addition to leasing or mortgaging your property, you can give your neighbor an easement across it, you can give a buyer an option to buy it, and you can even list it for sale with a real estate broker, among many other possibilities.

Most of these interests will be discussed in more detail in later chapters, but one particular kind of interest that we will explore in detail in this chapter is an *estate*. An estate is a possessory interest in real estate. In other words, if you have a right of possession, your interest is properly referred to as an estate. A possessory interest could arise through ownership of the property or by being a renter or lessee.

Estates are further classified as *present estates* and *future estates*, that is, the right to current possession, or the right to possession at some time in the future. For example, if you own a property but lease it to a tenant, the tenant has the present estate, and you have the future estate – the right to possession after the lease is over. There are many ways to create a future estate, as we shall see later.

Modern Washington real estate law is based on English common and statutory legal principles. Early England was a class society with serfs at the bottom of the social scale and various levels of lords rising up to the king or queen at the top. In the beginning, serfs were not permitted to own real estate – only the lords were allowed that privilege. Later, a third class arose, called "freemen." A freeman was not a lord, but did have the right to own real property. With the signing of the Magna Charta in 1215, all Englishmen who were not lords became freemen – the serf class was abolished. From that point on, any Englishman could own real property. For the most part, women were accorded the same rights in real property as men.

What does all this have to do with modern real estate? Today we still use the terms and concepts developed during this early period of history. One important concept is *ownership*. In early England, ownership was a right which could only be held by a freeman or better, so ownership interests today are still called *freeholds* or *freehold estates*. Possessory interests which are not ownerships are called *less than freehold estates* or more commonly today, *leaseholds*.

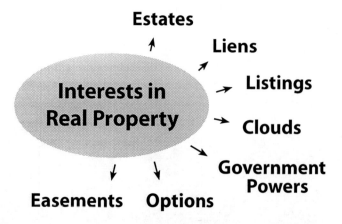

There can be an unlimited number of interests in a given piece of real estate, most of which can exist at the same time. For example, you can own the property (an estate), but have a mortgage to the bank (a lien), lease it to a tenant, grant your neighbor an easement across it, give your brother an option to buy it, and list it with a real estate broker.

There are so many possible interests that we categorize them. There are many different kinds of estates, for example, so many that we will devote this entire chapter to them. The diagram shows only some of the major groups of interests.

Feudal versus allodial system of land tenure

In feudal English society, an owner held the land only at the pleasure of the sovereign. This is referred to as the **feudal system of land tenure**. The word **tenure** means "holding," so this really implies that the king or the queen was the ultimate owner of all the land. Freeholders did not even have the right to sell or will their property without the permission of the lord from whom they held the land until the year 1290. Of course, this means that, since the land already belonged to the sovereign, if the king or queen wished to place a road across your land, there was no legal need to pay you any compensation.

By the time of the American revolution, totally new social and legal concepts had become popular. In fact, these concepts were, in large part, the cause of the American revolution. The thrust of these new ideas was a lessening of the powers of the sovereign and the democratization of society – placing more power in the hands of the people. As this developed, a new concept of land tenure came into being, called the **allodial system of land tenure**. The allodial system of land tenure is just the opposite of the feudal system. That is, the owner is a true owner and not just a holder of the land at the pleasure of the government. While the government does retain certain incidents of sovereignty, true ownership is vested in the citizen who holds title to the land.

Some of the rights the government has retained include the right to take property for the public good (**eminent domain** or **condemnation**). But eminent domain can be exercised today only by paying the owner just compensation. The government also has the right to regulate an owner's use of the land in order to maintain public order (an example of a regulation would be a **zoning ordinance**). One of the government's major rights is the right to tax privately owned land. And the government has the right to acquire all property for which no owner can be found (**escheat**). While these powers are not technically encumbrances, they nevertheless restrict an owner's use of the property, so we will discuss them in more detail in Chapter 4 on encumbrances.

Estates of inheritance

As we have seen, estates in real property are divided into freeholds and less than freeholds (leaseholds). Let us begin our discussion of these interests with the freehold estates. Freeholds are further classed as **estates of inheritance** (usually called **fees**) and **estates not of inheritance** (more commonly referred to as **life estates**).

A fee estate (or estate in fee) is said to be an estate of inheritance because the owner can leave it to his or her heirs. A life estate, on the other hand, is said to be an estate not of inheritance because the estate terminates upon the death of the owner. That is, if you have a life estate, you own the property, but only for your lifetime. Your ownership ends upon your death. And if your ownership ends upon your death, then there is nothing for you to leave to your heirs. Of course, ownership must continue to be vested in someone even after your death. Who the property would go to after your death (the future possessory estate) is determined by rules which we will discuss later.

Fees are further divided into **fees tail** and **fees simple**. A fee tail (also sometimes called an **estate in fee tail** or an **entailed estate**) is an estate which is granted to the holder and to a certain class of the holder's heirs, normally the children or other family members. The idea is to keep the property in the family. Therefore, if a holder of a fee tail were to attempt to deed the property outside of the class of heirs, the deed would be void. Fees tail are not recognized in Washington. If you wish to keep property within the family, then the modern approach is to set up a family trust. The advantage of a trust is that the trust is a separate legal entity which can also own stocks, bonds and other personal property as well.

The word "simple" in the expression "fee simple" really just means "not tail." In other words, if you have a fee simple, you can leave the estate to whomever you wish and you can also sell or give away the property during your lifetime. Because the fee tail is not recognized in Washington, the only kind of fee that still exists is the fee simple. As a result, many knowledgeable persons leave the word "simple" out. In Washington today, a "fee title" is a "fee simple title."

Fees simple are further divided into those fees which are ***absolute*** and those which are ***defeasible*** (also called ***qualified fees*** or fees which are ***subject to divestiture***). The words "absolute" and "defeasible" refer to how the owner's title is vested. The ***vesting*** of title means delivery of the ownership rights and is normally accomplished by a deed. The opposite of vesting is ***divestiture*** (or ***divestment***). In other words, when you buy a property you are vested in title, and when you no longer own it, we say that you are divested.

If your title is vested absolutely, this means that the only way you can be divested is your voluntary act (you deed or will it to someone else), or involuntarily through an operation of law (condemnation, foreclosure, etc.). But if your title is defeasible, then the person you acquired title from has created some ***condition*** and if you violate the condition, you can be divested. Therefore, a defeasible title can be divested voluntarily or involuntarily the same as a title which is vested absolutely, and in addition can be divested if the owner violates the condition. Fortunately, defeasible fees are very rare so real estate agents are unlikely to run into them in a normal real estate practice.

Of course, if a title is defeasible, then there is a question as to who will gain ownership if the present owner violates the condition and is divested. Normally, the title will revert to the person who set up the condition in the first place. For example, suppose someone deeds property to you and adds to the deed a clause which says that the conveyance is "only so long as the premises shall be used for residential purposes, and if they should cease to be used for residential purposes, then the estate herein granted shall automatically revert to the grantor or the grantor's heirs." Now, if you violate the condition, the title will automatically go back (revert) to the person you got it from. The right to take the title back is called a ***right of reverter, estate in reversion, reversionary interest (estate)*** or just simply a ***reverter.***

In some cases, the grantor does not wish to get the property back, but rather wishes it to go to a third party. But if the property goes to a third party we can't call the future estate a right of reverter, since the word "revert" implies that it returns to the grantor. Instead, if the property is to go to a third party we say that the third party has an ***executory interest***.

As a practical matter, Washington law recognizes three types of defeasible fees. A ***fee simple determinable*** or ***determinable fee simple***, which is also sometimes called a ***fee simple upon special limitation*** is created by using words such as "for so long as," "while," "during" and the like, together with a statement of the grantor's automatic right of reverter. For example, the language "only so long as the premises shall be used for residential purposes, and if they should cease to be used for residential purposes, then the estate herein granted shall *automatically* revert to the grantor or the grantor's heirs" is an example of a determinable fee. Note that the fee reverts to the grantor automatically upon the violation of the condition.

A ***fee simple on a condition subsequent*** is similar, except that the right of reverter is actually is a ***right of (re)entry***, sometimes also called a ***power of termination*** or ***possibility of reverter.*** The grantor has the right to get the property back, but the right is not automatic. Upon violation of the condition, the grantor must re-enter the premises and take action to recover the estate. Language used to create this interest typically includes phrases such as "on condition that," "provided" and the like. The same residential-only restriction as in the fee simple determinable above could be recast as a fee simple on a condition subsequent by changing it to read "on condition that the premises are used for residential purposes, and if they should not be used for residential purposes, then the grantor or the grantor's heirs may re-enter and terminate the estate herein created."

When it is desired to have the property go to a third party in the event the condition is breached, then the grantor can create a *fee simple subject to an executory interest*. This estate is frequently used when the grantor wishes to make the conveyance force someone to act in a certain way, e.g., "I hereby convey this property to Susan, provided that she marry within the next ten years, and if she should fail to do so, then the fee shall vest absolutely in her brother, Joe." In this case Joe has an executory interest and Susan has a fee simple subject to her brother's executory interest.

From the preceding discussion, you can see that a fee simple title which is vested absolutely is the highest ownership interest in real property that is possible. You will commonly hear people refer to this interest as a "fee simple absolute" as a short way of describing it. In fact, since the word "simple" is unnecessary in Washington, you could really shorten this to just "fee absolute." And since defeasible fees are rare, if you say just "fee" or "fee title," everyone normally assumes that you mean a fee simple title absolutely vested.

Estates not of inheritance

A fee title is called an estate of inheritance because the owner can leave it to his or her heirs. A life estate, on the other hand, is said to be an estate not of inheritance because the estate terminates upon the death of the owner. Nevertheless, always remember that life estates are ownership interests in real property (freeholds). The difference is that the duration of a fee title is potentially perpetual, where life estates have a duration measured by someone's life. The life which measures the ownership period is called the *governing life*. This can be the life of the donor, of the recipient, or it can be the life of an unrelated third party. It can even be for the life of the survivor of a stipulated group of persons.

The governing life is normally simply the life of the holder of the life estate – called the *life tenant*. In fact, unless there is some language stating otherwise, the legal presumption is that the governing life is that of the life tenant. If the life estate is for another person's life, then it is called a life estate *pur autre vie*. The term pur autre vie is Old French which, literally translated, means "for another life." A life estate pur autre vie can be created directly by the grantor – e.g., "I hereby convey this property to you for the life of your brother." But a life tenant can sell the life estate, and if a life tenant were to do so, a life estate pur autre vie would also be created.

For example, suppose you convey a life estate to your sister. Since you specify no other governing life, we presume the governing life is the life of the life tenant; in this case, your sister. Now suppose your sister deeds the property to your brother. An ordinary deed, without any special language, is presumed to convey all of the grantor's right, title and interest in the property. Therefore, your brother has now received exactly the interest your sister had, no more and no less. Since your sister held an ownership interest for her life, that is exactly what your brother now holds – an ownership interest for your sister's life. In other words, your brother now has a life estate pur autre vie.

Your brother in the preceding example may also be motivated to see that your sister lives a long and healthy life since, upon her death, fee title reverts to you. Life estates always terminate upon the death of the governing life and thereafter fee title must vest in someone. The presumption is (unless there is language to the contrary), that the life estate reverts to the grantor. Note then, that the life estate is normally followed by a right of reverter (also called an estate in reversion or reversionary interest). Of course, these are the same familiar terms we used previously to describe the right of the grantor to get the property back when the estate was a defeasible fee.

When the life estate is to go to a third party rather than back to the grantor, then the future interest is called a ***remainder***. Notice here that the concept of the remainder and the concept of the executory interest we discussed earlier are the same. Nevertheless, when the future estate follows a life estate it is called a remainder and when it follows a fee estate it is normally an executory interest.

Life estates are sometimes created when an owner in fee title conveys a remainder to someone but retains a life estate in the property. Parents frequently convey a remainder in their property to their children, reserving a life estate. This reduces the dollar value of their estate and thereby lowers future estate taxes. At the same time that they are lowering future estate taxes, the parents can take advantage of the gift exclusions which allow them to give substantial sums to any individual without any tax liability. A tax benefit also accrues when you donate property to a qualified charitable or religious organization. Older people frequently donate property to such organizations, but reserve a life estate in the property. The donation gives them a tax break while they are alive and can still enjoy the tax savings.

You can also create a life estate that is defeasible. For example, suppose you want to grant a life estate to someone, but you also want to receive monthly income from the life tenant, and you want the life estate to terminate if the rent is not paid. Then you might grant a life estate "for so long as the sum of X dollars is paid monthly, and if not so paid, then the estate herein created shall automatically terminate and revert and revest in the grantor." This would create a determinable life estate. Note that you now have two rights of reverter – you have the right to get the property back when the life tenant dies, and you also have the right to get the property back if the life tenant violates the condition by not paying the monthly rent.

Since a life estate is an ownership interest, the life tenant is free to use the property in any way, including selling it. The only restriction is that the life tenant cannot do anything which would be injurious to the interests of the holder of the future estate. And, of course, the life tenant has no power or authority to bind the holder of the future estate to any agreements with others.

Even though the rights of the life tenant are subsidiary to the rights of the holder of the future estate, the life tenant can mortgage or lease the life estate or create other interests within it. But what would happen if a life tenant mortgaged the property on a 30-year mortgage, and then died before the mortgage was paid off? In this case, the lender's mortgage would be extinguished. The holder of the future interest would become vested in fee simple absolute, unencumbered by the mortgage. The logic is that the lender took a mortgage on a life estate, so the lender should have known that the life estate could terminate at any time. If the mortgage is an interest which depends on the life estate, then it is extinguished if the life estate is extinguished. The same results would occur if the life tenant were to lease the life estate. If the life tenant dies, the lessee may be forced to move even if the lease is not yet over. Lenders and lessees in these situations commonly protect themselves by obtaining the signature of the holder of the future interest on the mortgage or lease. Then the future interest is also mortgaged or leased – so if the property reverts, the mortgage or lease remains intact.

Legal life estate – In some states a life estate can be created by the automatic operation of a law, as opposed to being created deliberately by the owner. Such a life estate is sometimes called a *legal life estate*. Legal life estates are usually created by dower and curtesy laws, which are not recognized in Washington. (See *Dower and curtesy*, later in this chapter.)

Anyone who holds a future interest in real estate has a right to expect that the holder of the present interest will maintain the premises in reasonable condition and not allow *waste*. Waste occurs when a holder of a present possessory estate acts (or fails to act) in such a fashion as to cause a lowering of the value of the interest of those who have a future estate in the property. So while a life tenant can do anything with the property, this right does not extend to waste.

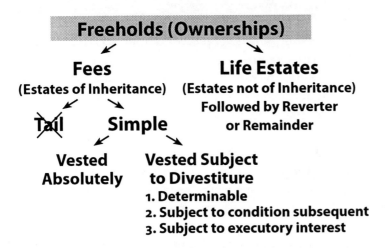

Estates are categorized as freeholds and less than freeholds. Here we see a diagram showing how the freeholds are further categorized as fees and life estates. Fees were originally either tail or simple, but the fee tail is not recognized in Washington, leaving us with only the fee simple. Ordinarily a fee simple is vested absolutely, but if the grantor wishes it can be vested with a condition. Violating the condition makes the grantee lose the title, so if there is a condition we say the vesting is subject to divestiture, or defeasible. There are three ways to vest the title subject to divestiture.

The bundle of rights

All freeholders (owners) are said to be vested with *seizin* (also frequently spelled "seisin") to the property they own. A legal expression commonly used is to say that the owner is "seized of the estate."

Seizin makes the person vested with it responsible for the property. Chief among these responsibilities is the duty to pay the taxes. The owner's responsibilities also include liability for certain damages that might be caused by the land. For example, if a handrail is loose and, as a result, the local letter carrier falls and is injured, the owner is liable. Even if the letter carrier was delivering mail to a renter in the property, the owner is still liable. The owner also has the responsibility to obey the law and to abate any nuisances caused by the land.

On a more pleasant note, the party vested with seizin also has rights. These rights are referred to as the *bundle of rights*. The bundle of rights is like a bundle of sticks, each of which represents one of the rights of ownership. These sticks include the right to do anything the owner wishes with the property. The owner may use and enjoy it, rent or lease it, mortgage it, sell it, or give it away. Every conceivable thing that could be done with the property is another stick in the bundle of rights. The bundle of rights even includes the right of the owner to do nothing at all.

The owner may exercise any of these rights with the entire property or just part of it. And the owner may simultaneously exercise one or more rights on part of the land while exercising other rights on another part of the land. The owner may exercise some or all the rights for a period of time and then change the use in the future. All or part of the rights may be granted to another for a period of time, for life, or forever. Or the owner may divide the rights and grant them to different individuals, again, for a period of time, for life or forever. The possibilities are endless.

When we refer to an owner granting one of these rights we say that the owner has given one of the "sticks from the bundle of rights." The idea that an owner can give or keep any stick is a concept that is used throughout the study of real estate. For example, when an owner gives a real estate broker a listing, the owner has given the broker one of the sticks from the bundle of rights – the right to sell the property. Always remember that any single stick or combination of sticks can be granted to anyone for any period of time the owner desires. At the same time, if the owner has not given a stick to another, then the owner must still have the stick.

Less than freehold estates

Leaseholds are created by a **lease** or **rental agreement**. The act of leasing or renting the property is legally referred to as a **demise**. When the leasehold terminates, the owner retakes possession of the property. The right of the owner to retake possession is called a right of reverter (or estate in reversion, reversionary interest or estate, etc.) – the same term we encountered earlier for the future interest after a defeasible fee or a life estate.

A leasehold estate is frequently referred to as a **tenancy**. This term describes the act of possessing the property by the **tenant**. A tenant is the party in possession. Legally, we use the word tenant to describe even an owner when the owner is in possession. Note that an "estate" is the possessory interest or right, and the "tenancy" is the act of possessing. While these concepts are slightly different, from a practical standpoint, when describing different interests in property, most people use the terms interchangeably.

In the rest of this section we will discuss the various leasehold tenancies and the rights and duties of landlords and tenants generally. However, there is a special statute in Washington called the "Washington Residential Landlord-Tenant Act" which governs the relationships between landlords and tenants in residential tenancies. This is covered in detail in Chapter 24.

Creating a less than freehold – To create a less than freehold estate generally requires only the signature of the owner. The tenant signifies acceptance of the terms by taking possession and paying rent. The common practice today, however, is to have the tenant sign the lease or rental agreement as well. If the tenant did not sign the lease or rental agreement, the tenant always has the potential claim that certain provisions of the contract were unknown, and therefore should not be binding.

Responsibilities of the parties – A common question is the issue of maintenance. The original English common-law rule provided that the landlord had no responsibility for maintenance of the premises. Today, modern courts give the landlord the responsibility to provide at least some maintenance, particularly of items which involve health or safety hazards. The Washington Residential Landlord-Tenant Act places extensive maintenance requirements on the landlord. However, in a non-residential setting, the landlord is usually only obligated to maintain the premises if there is an agreement to that effect, although the landlord may be liable for defects unknown to the tenant and for maintenance of common areas under the control of the landlord.

By the same token, the tenant is only obligated to maintain the premises as necessary to prevent waste. The tenant is not obligated to make extensive additions or improvements. Again, the Washington Residential Landlord-Tenant Act, which only applies to residential rentals, relieves the tenant of most of the burden to maintain the premises and places it on the shoulders of the landlord.

What would happen if someone were injured on the premises during the tenancy? The general rule is that the landlord is liable unless the injury was caused by something under the tenant's control or by some improvement made by the tenant. For example, if you rent a property to a tenant and there is a loose step which causes a visitor to be injured, you are normally liable. If the rental agreement contains language which requires the tenant to perform all maintenance, then the tenant and you would most likely both be liable. On the other hand, if the stair was in good condition at the start of the tenancy, but the tenant damages it beyond ordinary wear and tear, then any resulting injury could conceivably be just the responsibility of the tenant. The issue of responsibility for injuries to each other and to third parties is an area of law where it is difficult to escape liability. The best course for both landlord and tenant is to assume that they will always be liable and plan accordingly.

The law recognizes an implied **covenant of quiet enjoyment** on which the tenant may rely. The covenant of quiet enjoyment means that the landlord is obligated to defend the landlord's title against any claims which would interfere with the tenant's right to uninterrupted possession of the premises. If the landlord cannot meet this requirement, then the tenant is relieved of the responsibility to pay rent. For example, suppose you have leased space from the owner of a shopping center in which you operate a business. An owner whose property is adjacent to the shopping center claims an easement through the shopping center, and in fact, right through your space. If the owner of the shopping center is not successful in warding off the claim, and as a result you are forced to leave your space, then your lease is terminated and you have no further obligations to the lessor.

Types of less than freehold estates – There are four types of less than freeholds – a **tenancy at sufferance** (without the owner's permission), and a **tenancy at will** (with permission), plus a **tenancy for years** (for a fixed term, i.e., a lease) and a **tenancy from period to period** (also known as a **periodic tenancy**), which has a period that continuously renews until one party gives notice to the other, i.e., a month-to-month rental.

Tenancy for years – The tenancy which gives the most rights to the tenant is the **tenancy for years**. Do not be confused by the word "years" – a tenancy for years is a tenancy for any fixed term, whether the term is a day, a month, a year, or longer. The tenancy for years is what most people think of when they think of a **lease**. As everyone knows, a lease has a definite term with a beginning and an ending date. How often the rent is paid, or even whether there is rent, is irrelevant; it is the fixed term which makes the agreement a lease.

Leases also occasionally call for a fixed dollar amount during the term. As a result, lay people commonly presume that there is some legal requirement that this be so. The truth is that leases commonly contain cost-of-living clauses, or tie the rent to some index, or provide that the rent will be a percentage of the tenant's gross sales, among other possibilities. It is unusual to find a lease with a fixed amount of rent.

Although most less than freeholds require the parties to give proper notice to each other in order to terminate the agreement, this is not the case with a tenancy for years. No notice is required to terminate a tenancy for years because it has a definite expiration date and the parties obviously knew when it would be over at the time they entered into the lease. Of course, if either party wishes to terminate the lease sooner, then notice may be required. Note that a party wishing to terminate a lease before its expiration has to have a valid reason, such as a breach by the other party.

When the tenant holds a tenancy for years, the owner's title is encumbered by the leasehold. Therefore, if the owner subsequently sells the property, the buyer will take title subject to the lease. Of course, it is possible to place a special termination clause in a lease which allows the lessor to cancel the lease upon a sale. It is also common to find leases where the tenant also has a right to cancel the lease upon the happening of some event such as the death or incapacity of the lessee, for example.

Unless a lease contains language prohibiting it, a lessee may **assign** his or her interest to another. An **assignment** occurs when you transfer rights under a contract to another. In the case of a lease, this means that you would transfer all of your rights for the entire premises and for the entire remaining term to a new tenant. Many times a lease will contain a clause requiring the lessor's approval for an assignment. The lessor, in this case, cannot unreasonably withhold consent without the risk of becoming liable to the tenant for damages the tenant might suffer as a result.

What if you transfer your rights to just a portion of the premises, or for only a part of the remaining term of the lease? Then this is called a **sublease** and, as with the assignment, the lessee may sublease unless the lease specifically prohibits it. Make note that a prohibition on assignment does not create a prohibition on subleasing, and vice-versa. And as with the assignment, if the lease requires the lessor's approval for a sublease, the approval cannot be unreasonably withheld. When a sublease has been created there will be two leases in existence. The lessee of the original lease will have become the lessor to the new tenant. In this situation we say the original lessee holds a **sandwich lease**.

When the tenant assigns or subleases to another, this does not normally relieve the original tenant from the obligation to pay the rent. If the new tenant fails to pay, the landlord has the right to look to the original tenant for payment. However, it is possible for the lessor to accept the new tenant and release the original tenant from liability. This is called a **novation**. A novation occurs when an original contract is extinguished and replaced with a new contract.

When a lessee abandons the premises the lessor is nevertheless entitled to demand that the rent continue uninterrupted. The common-law rule is that the lessor can hold the tenant to the tenant's promise to pay the rent, regardless of whether the tenant has possession, because moving out was the tenant's own choice. However, in Washington a landlord has a duty to **mitigate**. To mitigate means to lessen a loss. Therefore, if the tenant moves out, the lessor must make a good faith attempt to locate a new tenant. When an acceptable tenant is found, the lessor must offset the obligations of the old tenant with whatever the new tenant pays. Of course, the old tenant remains liable for the period when the premises were vacant, and for the expenses the lessor incurred in obtaining the new tenant.

Another factor which may hinder the landlord's right to collect rent from the tenant is the possibility of a **surrender**. A surrender occurs any time a holder of a present possessory interest relinquishes the premises and allows the holder of the future estate to take over immediately. A surrender of a lease would occur when the lessee moves out and gives possession of the premises back to the lessor prior to the termination of the lease. Of course the lessor need not accept the surrender. However, if the lessor does accept the surrender, the lessee is relieved of any further obligation under the lease.

Tenancy from period to period – A more common tenancy (particularly in residential property) is the **tenancy from period to period**, or **periodic tenancy**. This type of tenancy is characterized by a rental period, rather than a fixed term as in the tenancy for years. The period may be any period desired by the parties, such as month to month, week to week and the like. Agricultural properties are frequently rented on a year to year basis. Washington code abolishes the tenancy from year to year unless the parties specifically agree to it in writing.

Sometimes we refer to a periodic tenancy by the period involved. For example, a **month-to-month tenancy** is a type of periodic tenancy where the period is monthly, and so on. Usually the parties in a periodic tenancy are referred to as **landlord** and **tenant** rather than as lessor and lessee, although the distinction is not carefully observed today.

A tenancy from period to period continues for an indefinite time, but can be terminated by either party upon giving proper notice to the other. At common law, the amount of the notice required is the amount of the period, so for a month-to-month tenancy the notice required would be one month. However, there are special statutes in Washington which modify the common law rule. Non-residential tenancies require a 30-day notice and the Washington Residential Landlord-Tenant Act provides for 20 days notice.

Since proper notice is required to terminate a periodic tenancy, it is also required if there is to be a substantial modification of the tenancy. This would include matters such as rent increases. Washington law requires a 30-day notice for rent increases or other modifications to the agreement.

Tenancies from period to period are encumbrances on the owner's title, the same as tenancies for years, so if the owner sells the property, the buyer must respect the rights of the tenant. Of course, the new owner can terminate a periodic tenancy with a relatively short notice, so the matter is not as significant as where a long term lease is involved.

Also, as with leases, a periodic tenancy can be assigned or subleased, assuming there is no provision in the rental agreement which prohibits assignment or subleasing. Again, if the landlord declines to allow an assignment or sublease, the matter is not significant because the tenant can just give notice and terminate the tenancy.

Tenancy at will – A **tenancy at will** is created when an owner gives someone permission to occupy the premises. A tenancy at will does not stipulate how long the permission is good for, because if it did, it would really be a lease (tenancy for years). A tenancy at will usually exists only for a brief period, such as after the termination of a lease where the tenant remains in possession with the landlord's permission while they are negotiating a new lease. However, it could be for a very long time. For example, an owner might let a friend stay in a house for years without rent or formal rental agreement.

Tenancies at will can be terminated by the owner only by giving proper notice. After all, the owner did give permission for the tenant's occupancy, so it is only fair that the owner give the tenant reasonable notice to vacate the premises.

A tenancy at will cannot be assigned or subleased. Also, tenancies at will are not considered encumbrances on the owner's title, so a sale of the property extinguishes the tenant's rights and converts the tenancy into a tenancy at sufferance (see below).

Tenancy at sufferance – When a right of possession is terminated, but the tenant does not leave, this is normally called a **tenancy at sufferance**, although Washington code refers to it as a "tenancy by sufferance." Regardless of its name, it does not constitute a true interest in the property since the tenant has no legal grounds upon which to base a right of possession. Therefore, the owner can terminate a tenancy at sufferance without notice.

In order to create a tenancy at sufferance, the tenant must have originally entered into possession lawfully through some prior right which is now ended. For example, if you own the house you live in, sell the house to another, but then not leave after your sales contract requires you to deliver possession to the buyer, you are a tenant at sufferance. Or you might remain in possession wrongfully after the termination of a lease. The term **holdover tenant** is sometimes applied to a tenant at sufferance.

When a tenant never had a legal right, but instead just takes possession of the property, it is called a **trespass**. A trespasser, the same as a tenant at sufferance, has no legal right to possession, so the owner can terminate the possession without notice. A tenancy at sufferance and a trespass are both civil wrongs, so the owner can sue the tenant at sufferance or trespasser for possession or damages. But, unlike a tenancy at sufferance, a trespass is also a criminal act.

An owner faced with a tenant at sufferance or trespasser should be careful. What if the tenant at sufferance or trespasser offers money to the owner? Accepting money from a tenant at sufferance or trespasser may be held to constitute granting permission. Permission means the tenancy is at will (or better), so the owner must now give the tenant proper notice to terminate the tenancy.

Eviction – An *eviction* occurs when an owner forces a tenant to leave the premises. This can be an *actual eviction* (filing a suit) or a *constructive eviction* (forcing the tenant out). Actual evictions occur when the owner files a suit commonly called a *forcible entry and detainer*, (frequently abbreviated "F.E.D."). Sometimes you encounter the term with a extra word, such as *forcible entry and wrongful detainer* or *forcible entry and unlawful detainer*. While these are the terms commonly used in other states, Washington law makes further distinctions between a detainer (being in possession wrongfully) which was forcible (e.g., by breaking and entering) or merely unlawful (not moving out when the tenancy has terminated). Landlords rarely have to deal with persons breaking and entering, so the usual legal action in Washington is a suit for unlawful detainer.

Assuming that the owner files a suit for unlawful detainer and wins the suit, the judge will grant the owner a *writ of restitution*. This means that the tenant is required to restore possession to the owner. If the tenant still refuses to comply, then the owner can ask the court to order the sheriff to remove the tenant and the tenant's possessions, by force if necessary.

When the owner takes matters into his or her own hands and forces the tenant out, this is called a constructive eviction. For example, if the owner cuts off essential services or locks the tenant out, these actions would constitute constructive eviction. Constructive eviction of a residential tenant would give the tenant various remedies, including damages, so the use of constructive eviction is generally limited to non-residential tenancies. However, merely cutting off a service or taking other action detrimental to the tenant's interests is not constructive eviction until the tenant actually moves out. The tenant cannot claim constructive eviction and still retain possession.

Where the rental agreement or lease requires the owner to maintain the premises, and the owner fails to do so to the point where the premises become unusable or uninhabitable, this also constitutes constructive eviction. Because the Residential Landlord-Tenant Act places extensive maintenance requirements on the landlord, a claim that the owner has constructively evicted the tenant by failure to maintain the premises is a common complaint by a residential tenant.

Another remedy is a *landlord's lien* on chattels owned by the tenant and brought upon the premises. By statute, the lien attaches to the chattels when the rent becomes due and remains unpaid, although the amount cannot exceed two months rent (four months rent for a mobile home space). If necessary, the landlord may have the chattels sold to satisfy the tenant's obligations.

Whenever a party holds the personal property of another in order to force the payment of money, it is called *distraint*. In this case, enforcement of the landlord's lien is really *distraint for rent*. However, Washington code refers to it as "distress for rent." Distress for rent is not permitted if the rental is residential.

Lease-options – In an *option to buy* the seller grants the buyer the right to buy the property at a certain price and terms for a period of time. For an option to be enforceable, the buyer must give something of value to the seller as consideration. Note that an option does not have to be an option to buy; it can be an option to sell, option to lease, or option to do anything else the parties desire. For example, suppose a buyer gives you a written document stating that the buyer will buy your property for $500,000 any time you are ready to sell it provided that you agree to sell it within the next 90 days and provided that you give the buyer $10. Upon receipt of the offer, you tender the $10 to the buyer. You now hold an option to sell.

Options to buy are frequently coupled with a lease. This is commonly called a **lease-option**. In a lease-option, the optionee (holder of the option right) also has possession of the property through a lease. Always remember that a lease-option is really two separate documents – a lease, and an option. Either the lease or the option can stand on its own. This can create a problem if the tenant breaches the lease. Since the option is a separate agreement, the tenant could still exercise the option. To avoid this, lease-option agreements almost always provide that a breach of the lease extinguishes the option.

Lease-options are popular with some buyers and sellers. Buyers see the lease-option as a way to buy a property when they don't have sufficient cash for a down payment. And even those who have the funds to buy might be unsure if their employer might require them to move to another region. A lease-option gives the tenants the option to buy, but does not obligate them to do so, leaving them free to move if they wish.

However, many buyers misunderstand what financial arrangements are typical of lease-options. It is not unusual to find buyers who think that they will receive credit for their entire lease payment toward the down payment. Of course, an owner and a lease-optionee can agree to anything they wish, but it would be unusual to find an owner who would agree to give credit for the entire lease payment.

More commonly, lease-options provide a base sales price, to which is to be added all the owner's expenses of operating the property, including taxes, insurance, maintenance, and so on. The owner also expects a rate of return on the investment, usually stated as an "interest rate" as though the entire purchase price were cash deposited in a bank account. After adding all these things to the sales price, then the full lease payments are deducted to find the final option price.

Because this may not ultimately give the lease-optionee much credit toward the nominal sales price stated in the lease-option, it is customary for the parties to structure the agreement with rent payments higher than market. If the lease-optionee is going to obtain outside financing in order to exercise the option, then it is also important to be sure the agreement makes it clear that the price is the market value and the credit being given to the lease-optionee is toward that value. Otherwise a bank may not consider the credit to be the equivalent of down payment.

In addition to the above it is important to understand that an option to buy must contain all the details necessary to close an ordinary real estate sale. This includes matters such as prorating of expenses, condition of the title, if and how the property will be financed, and everything else that is contained in a normal earnest money agreement. Therefore, a lcase-option must include the same things. This even includes any disclosures required by law, such as environmental issues and the property transfer report required for residential properties (see Chapter 9).

Concurrent tenancies versus severalty estates

In the previous section we defined the word "tenancy" as the "holding" of the real estate. We discussed it in terms of the extent and duration of a tenant's right of possession (estate). Now we will use the word "tenancy" in terms of how many persons own the property at any given time, and their relationships with each other.

Real estate can be owned by one person at a time, or by more than one. When title is vested in more than one person (or legal entity), this is called a **concurrent tenancy** or sometimes **co-tenancy** or **co-ownership**. The parties are referred to as **co-tenants** or **concurrent tenants**.

When one person owns the property alone we call it a **tenancy** (or **estate**) **in severalty**. Do not let the term "severalty" here confuse you – it sounds as though it should mean "more than one" because of its similarity to the word "several." In reality, it is closely related to the word "sever." In other words, the legal concept of a severalty estate is that the owner's property is severed from all other adjacent property, so the ownership is individual.

In contrast, concurrent tenants enjoy an **undivided right of possession**, also called a **unity of possession**. The unity of possession means that all co-tenants have an undivided right to possession of the entire property simultaneously and no individual owner can be restricted from possession of any portion of the property. Therefore, no co-tenant can be charged rent for his or her possession of the property. If any co-tenant is excluded from any portion of the property, then that portion of the property has been severed and the common ownership ends with respect to it. The unity of possession is fundamental to the creation of all concurrent tenancies. Without it, the tenancy reverts to separate severalty estates.

In some concurrent tenancies there must also exist certain other unities. A **unity of title** means that they acquired their interests through the same deed. A **unity of interest** means that their interests are equal. And a **unity of time** means that the co-tenants acquired their interest at the same time.

Right of survivorship

Of course, ownership of property by one person or entity (severalty) does not produce many legal problems to resolve. Concurrent tenancies, on the other hand, involve complex rules of law. Of these, none is more important than the **right of survivorship**, or lack of it. Whether or not there is a right of survivorship determines the disposition of the interest of a co-tenant in the event of the co-tenant's death.

For example, suppose you and your brother own property together as co-tenants. If your brother dies and you survive him, do you receive his half interest in the property automatically, or does it go to the persons named in his will, or to his natural heirs if he dies without a will? In some concurrent tenancies his interest would automatically vest in you upon his death. If this is the case we would say that you and he owned it with right of survivorship. But if his interest goes to his heirs (even if you happen to be one of his heirs), then the co-tenancy was without a right of survivorship. The existence of a right of survivorship means that the surviving co-tenant(s) automatically take the interest of the deceased co-tenant, share and share alike.

As noted above, some concurrent tenancies have a right of survivorship, while others do not. For example, if you specify that you and a friend wish to hold title as "joint tenants without right of survivorship," you will likely end up with a right of survivorship anyway. A right of survivorship is a feature of the joint tenancy (defined in detail later), and you and your friend cannot enter into a contract to change that fact. If you did not wish a right of survivorship, you should have chosen a type of concurrent tenancy which did not have a right of survivorship. Notice that kinship and other relationships are generally irrelevant. The fact that the co-tenants are related does not, in and of itself, create a right of survivorship, nor would it bar them from having as right of survivorship if they should so choose.

Of course, in the example above, if your friend's interest in the property is without right of survivorship, you could still wind up owning it if the friend makes out a will and leaves it to you. However, owning the property with a right of survivorship is better than mutually leaving your interests to each other in your wills. For one thing, a will can be changed unilaterally, whereas removing the right of survivorship can be changed only by mutual agreement in writing. In addition, by making wills leaving your respective interests in the property to each other, you would eventually gain title to your friend's interest if you should be the survivor, but you would gain title to them friend's half interest only after probate of the will. Probate proceedings can take considerable time and expense. If you had owned the property with right of survivorship, you would be legally vested in title to the friend's half interest automatically and immediately upon the friend's death.

Types of concurrent tenancies

Tenancy in common – Of the different types of concurrent tenancies, one of the most popular is the *tenancy in common*. Practically everywhere the English brought their legal system, you will find the tenancy in common. Although the rules for a tenancy in common vary slightly from one jurisdiction to the next, in most states it is virtually the same.

There is no right of survivorship in a tenancy in common. This makes it a favorite vehicle for ownership of small investment properties. Two or more people can get together and create a simple investment just by taking title as tenants in common. Upon the death of a co-tenant, the interest of the deceased co-tenant will simply be part of the deceased co-tenant's estate and ultimately go to his or her heirs.

A tenancy in common can have any number of co-tenants and they can be natural persons or other entities such as corporations, government agencies, and so on. They can be husband and wife, or unmarried. There is no restriction on what kind of kinship can exist between or among the co-tenants, nor need there be any kinship at all. A natural person can hold property as a tenant in common with any other entity, including corporations. In other words, any kind of legal entity, natural or otherwise, can be a tenant in common with any other. In addition, the percentage of interest held by each co-tenant can be equal or unequal in whatever percentages the parties desire. The only requirement is that there be a unity of possession – each co-tenant must have an undivided right of possession of the entire property.

In a tenancy in common each co-tenant's interest is freely transferable without the permission of any other co-tenant, another feature which makes the tenancy in common popular for an investment. Normally, however, no co-tenant has the right to act with respect to the interests of another co-tenant. In other words, co-tenants do not have an automatic right to sign for each other.

Not only is each co-tenant's interest freely transferable without the permission of the other co-tenants, but each interest can also be independently liened as well. In other words, if you own an interest as a tenant in common, you may mortgage it to the bank without affecting the interests of your co-tenants. Similarly, a judgment, income tax levy, or other personal obligation of a co-tenant can only affect the interest of the debtor co-tenant, not the interests of the other co-tenants.

In a tenancy in common, each co-tenant is entitled to share pro-rata according to percentage of ownership in all the rents and profits from the property. If one co-tenant is managing the property for the others, then the others are entitled to an accounting of all income and benefits received from the property. In the event one of the co-tenants is in possession, and while in possession permits waste or removes produce, shrubs or trees, or improvements on the property, he or she may be liable to the other co-tenants for damages.

By the same token, while each co-tenant is entitled to share in the profits from the property, each co-tenant is also responsible for his or her share of the expenses and liabilities of the property. If one co-tenant pays insurance premiums, property taxes, mortgage payments, and similar expenses which benefit all co-tenants, then he or she is entitled to reimbursement from the other co-tenants for their share of the expense.

An important note should be made of the issue of personal liability. While each co-tenant is only responsible for his or her share of the expenses of the property, there is nevertheless potentially unlimited personal liability for the property. If a visitor, for example, is injured on the premises and it is adjudged to be the fault of the owners, then the visitor can probably obtain judgment against each owner "jointly and severally." This means that the visitor can reach any assets of any co-tenant for an amount up to the total of the judgment. The visitor has no obligation to make any attempt to collect the judgment equally from the co-tenants. If a co-tenant ends up paying more than his or her share, he or she has a right to demand offsetting contributions from the other co-tenants. However, if they have no resources, the one whose assets were taken is out of luck, from a practical perspective.

An interesting feature of the tenancy in common is the right of each co-tenant to a ***suit for partition*** (partition action). A suit for partition can be brought by any co-tenant who wishes to terminate the co-tenancy. When a suit for partition has been brought by a co-tenant, the judge must either order the property physically surveyed and parceled out pro-rata to the co-tenants, or the judge must order the property sold and divide the resulting cash sales proceeds. Since dividing the property is not usually practical, and in fact, would probably be a violation of land use and subdivision laws, the normal procedure is to order the property sold and divide the proceeds.

Joint tenancy – Practically all states recognize a survivorship estate in real property known as a ***joint tenancy***. Because it has a right of survivorship, all four unities must be present for it to be created. That is, in addition to undivided rights of possession, it must be created at the same time and through the same document (deed or will), and the interests must be equal. However, Washington law provides a minor exception to the normal rules. If an owner of a property in severalty deeds the property to himself or herself and another person as a co-tenant, and stipulates that the purpose is to vest title as joint tenants, this is held to be adequate to create the joint tenancy. In reality, since the grantor owned the entire property the deed conveys only a half interest to the other person. Thus the grantor received his or her interest in the original deed, and the new co-tenant received his or her interest in the later deed. Nevertheless, Washington law allows this as an exception to the unities of time and title.

Note that the interests must always be equal, without exception. If you think about it, equality of interest is only fair when there is a right of survivorship. Remember, in a right of survivorship the surviving co-tenant will end up owning the property in severalty. Who will die last is a gamble, and in gambling everyone is expected to place the same amount on the table.

Also because of the right of survivorship, the co-tenants must be natural persons. A corporation can be a tenant in common, but it cannot be a joint tenant. The reason is that corporations can have a perpetual life. Thus, if a corporation were one of the joint tenants it could ultimately outlive all the others. However, as long as the co-tenants are natural persons, the law makes no distinction as to their anticipated lifespan. Also, the co-tenants may be related, but they do not have to be related.

In a joint tenancy, the same as in a tenancy in common, each interest can be independently liened. In other words, if you own an interest as a joint tenant, you may mortgage it to the bank without affecting the interests of your co-tenants. Similarly, a judgment, income tax levy, or other personal obligation of a co-tenant can only affect the interest of the debtor co-tenant, not the interests of the other co-tenants. However, there is a catch. The right of survivorship is primary and takes precedence over encumbrances. For example, suppose one co-tenant mortgages his or her interest, and then dies. The death of the co-tenant extinguishes his or her interest as it merges into the interest(s) of the surviving co-tenants. If the deceased co-tenant's interest is extinguished, then the mortgage on it ceases to exist as well.

Because of this feature, lenders do not lend on individual interests in a joint tenancy. Instead, they demand the signatures of all the joint tenants. Thus, if one dies, the mortgage still reaches the entire property.

Personal liability of joint tenants is the same as for tenants in common – joint and several. As in a tenancy in common, the co-tenants should make sure they have adequate insurance or other resources to handle unforeseen legal liabilities.

A joint tenancy can be terminated in various ways. As noted above, to create a joint tenancy there must be the four unities of possession, time, title and interest. Not only must they be present to create the joint tenancy, but they must remain present. If any ceases to exist, the joint tenancy is terminated. When a joint tenancy is terminated, it is converted to a tenancy in common.

For example, suppose A and B buy a property together as joint tenants. Later, A deeds his interest in the property to a friend. The friend and B now own the property as tenants in common and the joint tenancy is terminated.

A joint tenancy may also be terminated by the bankruptcy of any of the co-tenants, although not in all cases. For example, if the bankrupt co-tenant owned the property with another as a personal residence, the exemption in the bankruptcy laws for a personal residence may be adequate for the co-tenant to be allowed to keep the property.

A joint tenancy may also be terminated by a suit for partition, the same as a tenancy in common.

The usual reason people choose joint tenancy is the feeling that it will give the survivor relief from the delay and expense of probate. In fact, this is true, as the survivorship vests instantly upon the death of the co-tenant, and probate fees are based on the value of the estate being probated. The survivorship interest passes directly to the survivor without going through the probate proceedings, so it does not add to the estate value.

An additional advantage is that any debts of the deceased co-tenant that might have attached to the property are extinguished. For example, suppose you and a friend own a property as joint tenants. Your friend is involved in an auto accident and ends up with a judgment for damages. The judgment reaches your friend's interest in the property, but if the creditors have not done anything to initiate a foreclosure action on his or her interest before your friend dies, you receive the friend's interest free of the judgment.

However, there are some disadvantages to a joint tenancy. For one thing, the co-tenants are no longer able to leave their interest to heirs by will, as the survivorship supersedes the provisions of a will. But the most important disadvantage is in the area of estate taxes. While the value of the deceased co-tenant's interest in the property is not included when calculating probate fees, it is included for purposes of estate taxes. In fact, if the survivor cannot prove the amount that the survivor contributed to the initial acquisition, the entire value of the property is included in the estate when calculating estate taxes. There are substantial exemptions in the estate tax laws, however, so there may be no estate taxes anyway. Yet, at the same time, joint tenancies may create liability for gift tax and/or income tax for the survivor. This is an area where the real estate agent should refer the clients to appropriate estate planning counsel, as the issues involved can be extremely complex.

In the graphic below assume that four persons, A, B, C and D purchase a property together. On the left side they purchase as joint tenants. On the right side they purchase as tenants in common –

Joint Tenants	**Tenants in Common**

The four owners have an undivided right of possession, and also a right of survivorship. Each has a one-fourth ownership interest.

The four owners have an undivided right of possession, and each has a one-fourth interest, but they have no right of survivorship.

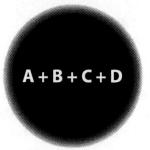

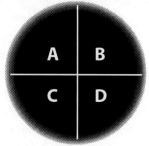

Now, suppose B sells to Z –

Now, suppose B sells to Z –

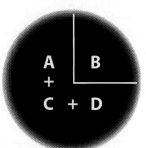

The result is that Z becomes a tenant in common with the others, who remain joint as to each other.

Now, suppose C dies and his son is his only heir. The son will take nothing, as the right of survivorship takes precedence over inheritance. A and D will own three-quarters jointly with right of survivorship and B will still own one quarter –

The result is that Z takes the position of B, so the tenancy in common remain unchanged except that there is a new owner.

Now, suppose C dies and his son is his only heir. The son will take the interest of C, as there is no right of survivorship, so the son inherits and becomes a new owner with the others –

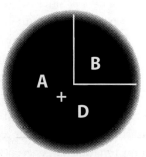

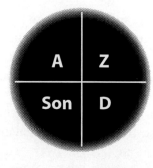

Tenancy by the entirety – While a joint tenancy as to real property is common in Washington, a **tenancy by the entirety** (also sometimes called **tenancy by the en-tireties**) is not used. The tenancy by the entirety is also a common-law tenancy, and it is used in the majority of states, but not all. To be tenants by the entirety, the co-tenants must have been legally married to each other at the time they took title.

In a tenancy by the entirety each co-tenant is considered the owner of the entire property, not the owner of just a half-interest. However, each person's ownership of the entire property is subject to the spouse's right of survivorship, which cannot be broken as long as the tenancy remains by the entirety. Therefore, when one spouse dies, the survivor does not "inherit" anything; rather, the interest of the deceased spouse is simply extinguished, leaving the surviving spouse vested in severalty.

While death of either spouse turns a tenancy by the entirety into a severalty estate vested in the survivor, a tenancy by the entirety could also be converted into a tenancy in common. This could occur through the voluntary act of the parties, but occurs more commonly as the result of a divorce. When parties who held property as tenants by the entirety become divorced, but continue to own the property after the divorce, the presumption is that their tenancy by the entirety is converted to a tenancy in common. Once it is a tenancy in common, the right of survivorship is, of course, extinguished.

In most states that recognize tenancy by the entirety, either co-tenant may uni-laterally encumber or convey the entire property, but only subject to the other's right of survivorship. This can create an interesting situation. Suppose you and your spouse own a property free and clear together as tenants by the entirety. You deed all your right, title and interest in the property to your brother. Your brother now owns a 100% interest in the property, but subject to your spouse's right of survivorship. The right of survivorship is governed by the lives of the married parties, (you and your spouse), not your brother. In other words, if your brother dies, his heirs simply inherit his position. If, on the other hand, you die first, your spouse takes the entire property back from your brother because your spouse still has a right of survivorship. On the other hand, if your spouse is the first one to die, then your spouse's interest is extinguished and your brother's ownership is no longer subject to your spouse's right of survivorship.

While tenancy by the entirety is not used in Washington, both of its neighboring states do. Therefore, Washington real estate agents selling property to married couples moving from those states should be aware of what they mean when they say they want tenancy by the entirety. Because of the survivorship issue, they would probably want a joint tenancy in Washington, but making the decision for them would be dangerous. A better practice would be to refer them to estate planning counsel.

Tenancy in partnership – Washington has adopted the Uniform Partnership Act, which makes tenancy in partnership possible. In a **tenancy in partnership** the partnership acquires the property, and the individual partners are not in title. The usual way for the partnership to acquire title is for it to be named as the grantee in the deed. However, if a seller deeds property to an individual partner with an indication that it is for the partnership, this is also deemed to vest title in the partnership.

Instead of an interest as a tenant in common or joint tenant in the real estate, each partner has a share in the partnership, which is deemed to be personal property. Upon the death of a partner his or her heirs take the interest of the deceased partner as they would any other assets of the deceased. (See *Partnerships*, later in this chapter.)

Creating concurrent tenancies – The type of co-tenancy is established by the words in the deed. In other words, when you buy property in a concurrent tenancy you must instruct the seller how to deed it to you. Normally the seller does not care how you take title, since the seller gets the same price for the property regardless. The decision is usually made at the time the buyers sign the earnest money agreement, although it is also common to leave the issue until it is time for the transaction to close and the deed is being prepared.

Fortunately, real estate agents do not normally have to draft a deed. Nevertheless, real estate agents should be familiar with the language used on deeds so they can tell who the owners are when it comes time to take a listing.

In Washington, if a deed conveys property to two or more persons, the presumption is that they take title as tenants in common, unless special language is used to create a different concurrent tenancy. Similarly, if the tenancy is in common, the presumption is that the interests are equal unless otherwise stated. Of course, in a joint tenancy the interests are always equal.

Thus, a deed conveying title "to Bill and Sam" creates a tenancy in common and each has a half interest. If Bill and Sam wish to be joint tenants, the deed should convey title "to Bill and Sam as joint tenants." These are examples of the minimum required by the law. In actual practice, if Bill and Sam wish to be tenants in common the standard procedure would be for the deed to say "to Bill and Sam, each to an undivided one-half interest as tenants in common," just to make matters crystal clear. And if they are to be joint tenants the deed would probably say "to Bill and Sam as joint tenants with right of survivorship." The latter is especially common because, in a few states, joint tenancy does not automatically create a right of survivorship unless it is specified. While this is not the case in Washington, nevertheless, it gives rise to the common practice of adding "with right of survivorship."

In addition, because of community property laws (see below), it is common to state the marital status of the buyer(s). In this respect, "single" means "never married," and "unmarried" means "previously married, but not married at the time of the conveyance." Washington law also presumes that when a husband and wife take title as concurrent tenants (whether in common or as joint tenants), the property is deemed to be community property (see below).

Community property versus dower and curtesy

Dower and curtesy – Although the rule has been abolished in Washington, many states still follow the English rule of *dower and curtesy*. Dower and curtesy refer to the right of a surviving spouse to a life estate in real property owned by the deceased spouse (sometimes called a *legal life estate*). The wife's right is called her *dower right* and the husband's interest is called his *curtesy right*. The idea was to ensure that you could not completely disinherit your spouse, while at the same time permitting you to leave the remainder interest to others. You might, for example, have a family inheritance which you wished to leave to your family, rather than have it descend in the future down your spouse's lineage.

The significance of dower and curtesy is that if you own property in a dower and curtesy state, and you are married, your spouse automatically has the right to the life estate if your spouse survives you, even if you alone are in title to the property (own it in severalty). If you sell the property, your signature on the deed will convey all rights in the property, except your spouse's dower or curtesy right. Therefore, your buyer may own the property, but is always at risk that your spouse may survive you and return to claim the life estate. As a result, in dower and curtesy states, as a practical matter, no one will accept a married person's deed to a property, even if held in severalty, without the spouse's signature to convey the potential dower or curtesy right as well.

Community property – In a minority of states (but including Washington), community property laws are followed. *Community property* is a concept from Spanish common law. Under community property laws, each spouse brings certain assets to the marriage, called **separate property**. Separate property also includes property acquired by either spouse after marriage if it was acquired by gift or inheritance, plus all the profits from separate property. All other property (i.e., property acquired during the marriage) is community property. However, under Washington law, if a husband and wife are legally separated and living apart, the income of each during the separation is their separate property. Otherwise all income from either spouse during the marriage is also considered community property.

Upon the death of either spouse, the surviving spouse has an automatic right to one-half the community property, although the deceased spouse may will his or her separate property to others. The right of survivorship, as such, does not automatically exist between a husband and wife in community property states.

The difficulty with community property laws is that, as a general rule, separate property can become community property by a simple agreement to that effect by the spouse who owns it. Even if no formal agreement is made, if community assets are used to make improvements to the separate property of one spouse, the value of the improvements will be considered community property. Of course, a buyer of the property has no way of knowing if the property is still separate property or has become community property. The result is that, in community property states, no one is likely to accept a deed signed by a married person without the signature of the spouse to convey the spouse's possible community property interest, even if only one spouse is in title.

In an attempt to clarify this problem, Washington law provides that a buyer is presumed to have good title to property if the deed is signed by a married person who is alone in title, unless the other spouse recorded a document claiming a community property interest in the property. Still, there are too many possible problems, so title insurance companies almost always require that both spouses sign a deed, even if only one is in title. A deed signed by both spouses would convey the property and all possible community property interests, thus eliminating any question.

Types of business organizations and how they hold title

Real estate agents frequently encounter business organizations which need to buy or sell real property. Understanding the basics about these entities and how they take title to real estate is essential.

Of all the ways in which a business can be organized, the simplest is the **sole proprietorship**. A sole proprietorship is an individual operating on his or her own in business. The business is the person and the person is the business – they are legally indistinguishable. Needless to say, the sole proprietor has complete liability for the activity of the business, because the actions of the business are the actions of the individual. In spite of this drawback, the sole proprietorship is a very popular form of organization because it is easy to form – you just put your name on a sign and you are in business. Many large corporations started as sole proprietorships.

Suppose you wanted to form a real estate brokerage firm as a sole proprietorship, and suppose further that you wanted to call it "Aardvark Realty." Unless your name happens to be Aardvark, this is called an **assumed business name**. The term "assumed business name" is usually abbreviated "ABN." You also frequently hear people refer to it as a "DBA." which stands for "doing business as." And Washington code refers to it as a **trade name**, so that is probably the most common term that Washington licensees will encounter.

When you use an assumed business name (trade name) Washington law requires that you register it with the Department of Licensing. If you fail to register you lose your right to sue others. However, registering a name does not guarantee that someone else is not already using the name. The right to a trade name in Washington is determined by who used the name first, not who registered it first.

Since a sole proprietorship is the same as the individual, when a sole proprietor owns real estate, the title is usually just vested in the personal name of the proprietor. However, it is also possible to vest title in the assumed business name, if the owner desires.

Partnerships – A *partnership* form of organization comes about when there are two or more persons (or other legal entities) who desire to engage in business together. Partnerships are categorized as *general partnerships*, *limited liability partnerships*, and *limited partnerships*.

At common law, general partners of a partnership are all agents of each other and can bind the partnership to contracts with third parties with their signature alone. Of course, when they do, they have a fiduciary obligation of good faith and loyalty to their partners. Also, in a general partnership, all the general partners have the same liability as if they were sole proprietors. For example, if a customer suffers a personal injury and sues, the customer can reach not only the partnership's assets, but all the personal assets of each general partner as well.

A limited partnership offers a way around the liability problem. In a limited partnership, most of the partners are usually *limited partners*, that is, their liability is limited to the amount they have invested, the same as stockholders in a corporation. Creditors of a limited partnership cannot generally reach the personal assets of the limited partners. However, a limited partnership must have at least one *general partner*. The general partner can be held personally liable. The general partner is also responsible for management of partnership affairs.

Of course there is a trade-off. In order to have the benefits of limited liability, the limited partners must give up the right to manage the affairs of the partnership. If a limited partner steps in and starts running things, the limited partner might be deemed to have become a general partner, and therefore personally liable.

Washington law also provides for the creation of a limited liability partnership. A *limited liability partnership* is a partnership that provides professional services for which a license is required. Because the partners are regulated by a licensing agency the requirements to form a limited liability partnership are simpler than for a regular limited partnership. Professionals find the limited liability partnership an attractive alternative to other forms of organization because it shields the partners from vicarious liability, is easier to operate and more flexible than a corporation, and is taxed the same as a partnership.

General partnerships can be created just by agreement of the partners, but limited partnerships and limited liability partnerships can be created only by registering with the Washington Secretary of State. As with a corporation (see below), a limited partnership must have a registered agent whose name and physical address are on file with the Secretary of State. The function of the agent is to receive service legal process on the partnership.

Whether the partnership is general or limited, real property can be held in the name of the partnership or it can also be held in the name of one or more of the general partners. If it is held in the name of the partnership, then the signature of any one general partner is sufficient to convey it. If it is vested in the personal names of the partners, then the entire interest in the property cannot be conveyed without the signatures of all the partners in whose name the title is vested.

Corporations – Corporations are the subject of a great body of law. A corporation is said to be a "creature of the state," that is, it is created by the Washington Secretary of State when a citizen files **articles of incorporation**. Upon receipt of proper articles of incorporation and the required fee, a **certificate of incorporation** is issued and the corporation has been created. The articles and certificate of incorporation are sometimes referred to as the corporate **charter**.

Once created, the corporation may conduct any business the charter allows – and corporate charters typically contain a clause authorizing "any lawful activity." Corporations filed in Washington are called **domestic corporations** and are authorized to conduct business only in Washington. If a Washington corporation wishes to conduct business by maintaining a physical presence in another state (i.e., a corporate office), then it must first become registered as a **foreign corporation** in that state and receive a **certificate of authority** or **certificate of qualification** from the appropriate officials in that state.

The interesting thing about corporations and limited partnerships is that they are legal entities. General partnerships and sole proprietorships are not legal entities, so any act of the business is an act of the individuals. When it comes to ownership of real estate, unlike partnerships, a corporation may hold title only in the name of the corporation.

A corporation or a limited partnership may sue or be sued in its own name the same as a natural person. And since corporations are legal entities, they must also designate a natural person as the **registered agent** upon whom demands and legal papers can be served, the same as a limited partnership. The registered agent does not have any legal liability with respect to such demands or service, except the obligation to forward them to the appropriate corporate officials or general partners.

Corporations are run by a **board of directors** who are elected by the stockholders. The board of directors also creates **bylaws** for the corporation. The bylaws set forth the duties and powers of the officers, when directors and stockholder's meetings will be held, how votes will be cast, and so forth. The stockholders must elect the board of directors and approve the bylaws.

A corporation cannot act except through authority of the board of directors – that is, during its meetings the board must authorize everything the corporation does. And, since a corporation does not have a physical existence, it can only act through agents. That is, eventually, all contracts the corporation enters into have to be signed by a natural person and this person must be authorized as an agent of the corporation by the board of directors.

Of course, in the bylaws various officers will be granted authority to sign documents for day-to-day functions. However, special authority is frequently required in order to buy or sell real estate. When conducting business with a corporation, it is common practice to ask for a special **resolution** to be made by the board. The resolution is an excerpt from the minutes of a board meeting during which the board authorized someone to sign a document on behalf of the corporation. Typically, the resolution must be signed by the president and the secretary.

If someone signs a contract on behalf of a corporation, but was not authorized, the corporation cannot generally be held to the contract. However, the person who signed the contract as agent of the corporation did so wrongfully, and is therefore generally liable personally for any damages suffered by the other party to the contract. To avoid such a legal tangle, real estate agents should always insist on a corporate resolution signed by the president and secretary and authorizing the signer to sign the specific contract on behalf of the corporation.

Warning: Many persons believe that if you incorporate you will shield yourself from legal liability. While generally true, this may not always be so. The trend in the law is to make it easier for a plaintiff to pierce the corporate veil and find the officers personally liable for corporate obligations. Anyone running a business as a corporation should seek appropriate legal counsel to conduct the affairs of the corporation in a manner to minimize legal exposure of the officers.

Corporations are sometimes organized as ***non-profit corporations***. Such corporations follow the same general rules as ordinary for-profit corporations, except that there are no stockholders. The purpose of having stockholders is to divide up the profits pro-rata according to the number of shares of stock held by each stockholder. If there is to be no profit, then there will be no need for stockholders. There are also other special rules for non-profit corporations, but the rules for ownership of real estate and entering into contracts remain the same – all authority must come from the board of directors and the usual procedure is to obtain a resolution authorizing someone to sign the agreement on behalf of the corporation.

Another special kind of corporation is the ***Subchapter S corporation***. A Subchapter S corporation can be created in order to avoid taxation of corporate profits. Ordinary for-profit corporations must file income tax returns and pay tax on their profits. Subchapter S corporations file "informational returns" only – telling the Internal Revenue Service how much was paid to each stockholder during the year. Each stockholder is responsible for his or her own taxes on the corporate income that was distributed during the year. Subchapter S corporations are subject to a number of other regulations, including a limitation on the number of stockholders.

Note that a Subchapter S corporation takes on many of the aspects of a limited partnership. Assuming that investors wish to limit their liability to the amount of their investment, this can be accomplished with either a limited partnership or a corporation. But the ordinary corporation suffers the disadvantage of double taxation – corporate profits are subject to corporation income taxes, and then when the after-tax profits are distributed to the stockholders as dividends, they become taxable again as income to the stockholders. Limited partnerships are not subject to income taxes, so double taxation is avoided. But if the investors really want the corporate form of ownership, they can have the best of both worlds by creating a Subchapter S corporation. Another advantage of the Subchapter S corporation over the limited partnership is that the Subchapter S corporation can have a perpetual life, where the limited partnership must be created with a finite life.

Washington law also permits the creation of professional service corporations for persons engaging in an activity for which a license or other authorization is required. In a professional services corporation all stockholders must be licensed or authorized. The advantage of a professional services corporation is that the income tax laws allow the corporation to deduct all of the expense of health and accident insurance coverage for the licensed employees. In other forms of organization the business can deduct only a portion of this expense. There are other tax advantages as well, which make professional corporations popular among real estate brokers and other professionals.

Limited liability companies – In the early 1990s various states began to enact legislation to create a new type of business entity, the ***limited liability company***. Limited liability companies combine the benefits of the limited partnership with the flexibility of the corporation. As in a partnership, the limited liability company pays no taxes itself. Tax liabilities and benefits are passed directly through to the owners of interests. But like the corporation, the limited liability company can have any number of owners of interests (usually called members), all of whom are shielded from liability. There does not need to be a general partner to take liability.

Limited liability companies are formed by filing a certificate of formation with the Washington Secretary of State. The process is similar to a corporation, including the appointment of a registered agent. Although the limited liability company appears to be a special type of corporation, it is unrelated to the corporation form of business. Limited liability companies should be considered a completely separate type of business entity.

In forming a limited liability company the organizers must create a limited liability company agreement setting forth how the company is to be run and what its business will be. In many respects this is analogous to the bylaws of a corporation. One difference, however, is that the members of a limited liability company are deemed to be agents of each other in running the company, the same as partners in a general partnership, unless the limited liability company agreement specifically gives that authority to a manager.

In the few years since limited liability companies have become available, they have become very popular as the vehicle for ownership of investment real estate. However, there are a few drawbacks to limited liability companies. For one, not all states have enacted legislation to recognize limited liability companies. If a Washington limited liability company were to attempt to conduct business in such a state, there would be a question whether the company's actions would be legal. Another problem is that, even in Washington, there may be legal questions about limited liability companies which cannot be answered due to lack of precedent.

Business trusts – Although not commonly encountered, the **business trust** has special significance in the field of real estate. A business trust (frequently referred to in Washington as a **Massachusetts trust**) has many of the same characteristics as a corporation, yet it is legally constituted in a completely different way. All trusts involve three parties, a **trustor**, a **trustee**, and a **beneficiary**. The trustor entrusts some asset to a trustee, who holds it for the benefit of the beneficiary. It is possible for the trustor and beneficiary to be the same person – that is, you could give your own assets to a trustee to manage them for yourself, thus making you both the trustor and the beneficiary. This is precisely what happens in a business trust. The investors (trustors) turn over their assets (e.g., cash) to a trustee, who manages the asset for the benefit of the investors (beneficiaries of the trust).

In a business trust the trustee is normally composed of a **board of trustees** who are usually elected by the investors. The investors are said to hold **shares of beneficial interest**, and are therefore commonly called beneficiaries or shareholders (but not stockholders, since that term applies only to corporations). Business trusts are usually taxed the same way as corporations. Business trusts also conduct business the same way as corporations – by granting authority to agents to act for the trust through resolutions issued by the board of trustees. However, when business trusts take title to real estate, the title may be vested in the name of the trust, or may be vested in the names of the trustees as joint tenants with right of survivorship.

Because there is little advantage to a business trust over a corporation the corporation is more popular. Corporations are better understood by the public, so it is easier to raise capital for a corporation than for a business trust. However, there is one kind of organization which uses the business trust exclusively – the **Real Estate Investment Trust** (REIT). Real Estate Investment Trusts were authorized by revisions made in 1960 to the Internal Revenue Code. The essential advantage of a REIT is that it can avoid paying income tax on its income provided that it is created as a business trust and not as a corporation, that it pays substantially all its income to its beneficiaries, and that certain other investment criteria are met. In effect, REITs function the same as mutual funds, except that where mutual funds invest in stocks and other securities, REITs invest in mortgages and real estate equities.

Joint ventures and syndicates – Any time two or more persons or other legal entities get together in a business enterprise, this can be called a **joint venture**. Joint ventures are frequently formed for just one single purpose. For example, suppose you own some land whose highest and best use is for development as a subdivision. Although you own the land, perhaps you know little about how to go about subdividing it. A developer makes an arrangement with you to use the developer's knowledge and experience to develop your land to its maximum potential as a subdivision, in exchange for a portion of the profits. This is a classic example of a joint venture.

Notice that a joint venture could be formed by two investors simply to acquire real estate as an investment. The term "joint venture" is a loose term used to describe many kinds of enterprises. Joint ventures can be complex, or can be nothing more complicated than a couple of investors buying property as tenants in common.

When a business venture takes on the aspect of an ongoing enterprise, we usually refer to it as a ***syndicate***. The word "syndicate" just means a group of persons or entities who have pooled their resources in a common enterprise. Investing in real estate is a popular purpose for a syndication. Note that a syndicate could take any form of business organization. Syndicates are commonly created to invest in large properties. Real estate agents frequently find that it is easier to find several small investors for such properties than to look for one investor who could swing the deal alone.

A principal benefit of investing in real estate is the potential for tax shelter. Because of this, the corporate or business trust form of organization is rarely used, since the tax benefits cannot usually be passed through to the investors. General partnerships involve too much personal liability, so the favored form of organization is the limited partnership or the limited liability company. For small investment properties, a simple tenancy in common is also frequently encountered.

Caution: If you should be involved in a transaction where the promoter of the investment (possibly yourself) will control and direct the investment of another (such as where you agree to manage the real estate for the investors after they buy it), you may be involved with a ***security***. Although there are exemptions, securities must usually be registered with the Securities Division of the Washington Department of Financial Institutions, or the federal Securities and Exchange Commission (SEC).

⚷ *KEY TERMS*

The key to understanding any new field is the vocabulary used in that field. To maximize your comprehension of the material presented in this chapter, be sure you know the meaning and significance of the following terms. Remember that the majority of test questions primarily test knowledge of vocabulary.

Absolute	*Board of directors*
Actual eviction	*Board of trustees*
Allodial system of land tenure	*Bundle of rights*
Articles of incorporation	*Business trust*
Assignment	*Bylaws*
Assumed business name	*Certificate of authority*
Beneficiary	*Certificate of incorporation*

Certificate of qualification

Charter

Community property

Concurrent tenancy

Concurrent tenant

Condemnation

Condition

Constructive eviction

Co-ownership

Co-tenancy

Co-tenant

Covenant of quiet enjoyment

Curtesy right

Defeasible

Demise

Determinable fee

Distraint (distress) for rent

Divestiture (Divestment)

Domestic corporation

Dower and curtesy

Dower right

Eminent domain

Entailed estate

Escheat

Estate

Estate in fee tail

Estate in reversion

Estate in severalty

Estate not of inheritance

Estate of inheritance

Eviction

Executory interest

Fee

Fee simple

Fee simple determinable

Fee simple on a condition subsequent

Fee simple subject to an executory interest

Fee simple upon special limitation

Fee tail

Feudal system of land tenure

Forcible entry and (unlawful) detainer

Foreign corporation

Freehold

Freehold estate

Future possessory estate

General partner

General partnership

Governing life

Holdover tenant

Interest

Joint tenancy

Joint venture

Landlord

Landlord's lien

Lease

Lease-option

Leasehold

Legal life estate

Less than freehold estate

Life estate

Life tenant

Limited liability company

Limited liability partnership

Limited partnership

Massachusetts trust

Mitigate

Month-to-month tenancy

Non-profit corporation

Novation

Option

Ownership

Partnership

Periodic tenancy

Possibility of reverter

Power of termination

Present possessory estate

Pur autre vie

Qualified fee

Real Estate Investment Trust

Registered agent

Remainder

Rental agreement

Resolution

Reversionary interest

Reverter

Right of (re-)entry

Right of reverter

Right of survivorship

Sandwich lease

Security

Seizin

Separate property

Shares of beneficial interest

Sole proprietorship

Statute of Frauds

Subchapter S corporation

Subject to divestiture

Sublease

Suit for partition

Surrender

Syndicate

Tenancy

Tenancy at sufferance

Tenancy at will

Tenancy by the entirety (entireties)

Tenancy for years

Tenancy from period to period

Tenancy in common

Tenancy in partnership

Tenancy in severalty

Tenure

Trade name

Trespass

Trustee

Trustor

Undivided right of possession

Unity of interest

Unity of possession

Unity of time

Unity of title

Unlawful detainer

Vesting

Waste

Writ of restitution

Zoning ordinance

Chapter 4

Encumbrances

A MAJOR AREA of concern to real estate agents is the condition of the title to the property being sold. When we talk of the condition of the title, we are generally referring to whether or not there are any *encumbrances* on the title. Encumbrances are things which burden the title. There are countless ways in which real estate can be encumbered. In this chapter we will explore some of the more common encumbrances.

An important consideration about encumbrances is that if the property is encumbered, then the owner cannot convey the title to another unless it is conveyed subject to the encumbrance. In other words, selling the property does not extinguish the encumbrance – the new owner must take the title subject to all the encumbrances which existed at the time of the conveyance. Therefore, part of the definition of an encumbrance is that it survives a sale of the property. If an interest would be extinguished by a sale of the property, then the interest was not an encumbrance.

There are so many kinds of encumbrances that it is difficult to discuss them without some kind of categorization. Most beginning real estate texts start out by categorizing encumbrances as *financial encumbrances* and *non-financial encumbrances*. Financial encumbrances (technically referred to as *liens*) include interests such as mortgages, judgments, property taxes, and other matters which make the real property collateral for a debt. Non-financial encumbrances include easements, leases, and private land use restrictions, among other possibilities.

Encumbrances are interests held by others which burden the title. The definition of an encumbrance is that it survives a sale of the property. It an interest would be extinguished by a sale, then it is not an encumbrance. We categorize encumbrances as financial and non-financial. Clouds are defined as possible interests, and can ripen into either a financial or a non-financial encumbrance.

Encumbrances

Financial (Liens)	Non-Financial
Mortgages	Easements
Property Taxes	Profits
Special Assessments	Covenants
Income Tax Levies	Tenancies for Years
Judgments	Periodic Tenancies
Attachments	Clouds
Notices of Lis Pendens	
Construction Liens	
Clouds	

Priority of encumbrances

Another important issue which real estate agents must understand about encumbrances is the matter of *priority*. Priority affects all kinds of encumbrances, both financial and non-financial, although it is usually of greater importance when dealing with financial matters. The issue of priority relates to the order in which rights fall in the event there should be a forced sale of the property, i.e., a foreclosure sale.

The issue of priority is very complex and there are many exceptions. The general rule, however, is that rights are apportioned in date order. The date is generally the date when documents were recorded in the public records. In other words, a "first mortgage" means that it was recorded before the "second mortgage," and so forth. Notice that the date the parties signed the mortgage is irrelevant as to the issue of priority – only the date it was recorded matters. Similarly, it doesn't matter what is written in the document – it may say "first mortgage" at the top of the page, but if another mortgage was recorded first, it is a second mortgage.

The issue of priority has two important impacts in real estate. First, the holder of a prior lien has first claim on the proceeds of the sale, and holders of subsequent liens have subsequent claims, in order of their priority. So if the property is sold at a forced sale, the holder of the first mortgage gets paid first, if there is anything left from the sales proceeds, the holder of the second mortgage gets paid next, and so on until the funds are exhausted.

The second impact is that whenever a lienholder forces the sale of the property by foreclosure, subsequent encumbrances are extinguished, although sometimes the lienholders have a right of redemption. (Redemption rights are explained in Chapter 11.) This is true, not just of liens, but of non-financial encumbrances as well. For example, suppose you mortgage your property to the bank, and then lease it to a tenant. If the bank forecloses its mortgage, the foreclosure will extinguish the lease. But if the order were reversed and you leased it first and then mortgaged it, the bank will have to take the title subject to the lease, since the lease enjoyed priority.

There are numerous exceptions to the "date rule" above, some of which are significant to real estate agents. The first exception is property taxes and special assessments. As a rule, unpaid property taxes and special assessments are a prior lien ahead of all others, regardless of when the other liens were recorded or the year(s) for which the taxes are due. This is the reason most lenders insist that the borrower establish a reserve account so the taxes will be collected along with the monthly principal and interest payment. This allows the bank to ensure that the taxes were paid so their mortgage lien will not be in second position.

Another exception is the possibility of a voluntary **subordination**. This is a simple agreement where one lienholder, who currently enjoys priority, agrees to step down in favor of another lienholder.

Real estate agents should also be aware of the special priority of **mechanics' liens** and **materialmen's liens**, sometimes referred to collectively as construction liens. Construction liens can enjoy a priority which is ahead of other recorded liens. Construction liens will be discussed in more detail later in this chapter.

Easements appurtenant and in gross

If your neighbor needed to use your property on a continual basis for some purpose, he or she would normally need an **easement**. When we think of easements the purpose that comes most quickly to mind is a driveway – legally referred to as an **easement for ingress and egress**. While this is certainly a very ordinary kind of easement, easements are also commonly created for virtually every conceivable use that someone might make of another's land. For example, easements can be created for utility lines (electric, water, sewer, gas, etc.), for public roads, for use of air space, and even to keep a neighbor from blocking sunlight (solar easement) or a view (scenic easement). Sometimes an easement is even created to prohibit a certain use (negative easement). Easements are also sometimes created in favor of the government as a means to preserve open space or create other land use controls.

An important concept to remember about an easement is that it is a **right of use**, not a right of possession. A right of possession is an estate, not an easement.

Before we can go any deeper into the subject of easements, we need to define some terms. In the drawing on the next page, the property over which the easement runs is called the **servient tenement** or **servient estate**. The land which has the right to use the easement is called the **dominant tenement** or **dominant estate**. The owners are referred to as the **servient tenant** and **dominant tenant**, respectively.

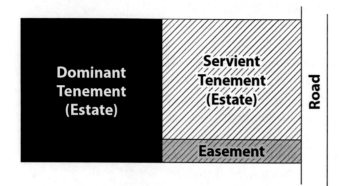

Easements are a common way of granting access to land which would otherwise have no access. An easement appurtenant is a title right which runs with the dominant tenement and is an encumbrance on the servient tenement. A buyer of the dominant tenement automatically receives an existing easement whether it is mentioned in the deed or not. Similarly, a buyer of the servient tenement takes title subject to the easement

Appurtenant and indestructible – An easement is normally an appurtenance to the dominant tenement and simultaneously an encumbrance on the servient tenement. Therefore, when the dominant tenement is sold, the buyer will gain title to the easement as well – even if it is not mentioned in the deed. Similarly, when the servient tenement is sold, the buyer will take title subject to the easement.

An easement appurtenant to one property can be appurtenant to others as well, such as where one driveway serves two or more properties. In this situation, it is not uncommon for the easement to be appurtenant to properties to which it is not physically adjacent. This might occur if, for example, the dominant tenement is divided after the easement was created.

Easements are normally perpetual and indestructible unless terminated voluntarily or involuntarily (see *Termination of easements* later in this chapter). Although easements are normally indestructible, it is possible to create a defeasible easement which can be terminated if the dominant tenant violates a condition imposed when the easement was created. (Creating conditions and defeasible interests is discussed in Chapter 3.) Easements are also sometimes created with a time limit.

Occasionally an easement is created which is an encumbrance on the servient tenement, but is not simultaneously an appurtenance to another property. Such easements are called **easements in gross**. For example, suppose you grant to a friend an easement for ingress and egress across your land. But suppose your friend does not own any real estate. Obviously, the easement cannot be appurtenant, since there is no land to which it can be appurtenant. Therefore, we call this an easement in gross instead of an easement appurtenant.

Even if the easement holder does own real estate, an easement in gross can be created just by granting the easement to the individual, rather than specifying the property to which it is appurtenant. Easements in favor of utility companies are almost always easements in gross. Utility easements are also sometimes referred to as **commercial easements**.

Maintenance – Whenever an easement exists, a question arises as to who is responsible for the maintenance of the easement. The general rule is that the person receiving the benefit of the easement has the right and the responsibility to maintain the easement. The servient tenant cannot normally interfere with this right. However, easements can be contractual, so if the document creating the easement stipulates a different arrangement, the courts will generally hold the parties to their bargain. When the easement benefits more than one property, the maintenance expenses are normally shared equally among the dominant tenants.

Exclusivity – Whether or not the servient tenant can use the easement as well is a question which commonly arises. The general rule is that, unless there is a specific agreement to the contrary, the easement is non-exclusive and the servient tenant may use the easement as well. Of course, the rights of the dominant tenant are paramount, so use of the easement by the servient tenant must be in a manner which does not interfere with the rights of the dominant tenant.

Community drives – In urban areas it is not uncommon to encounter *community drives*. A community drive is created where each lot has an easement along the adjacent lot for one-half the width of the driveway which runs between the lots.

Creation of easements – There are many ways that easements can come about, but the most common is where an owner simply grants the easement to another, either as an easement appurtenant or as an easement in gross. Washington law requires that the grant be in writing. And since the easement is a right of use, the use(s) for which the easement is granted should be specified. If the easement is less than perpetual, then its duration, as well as any other provisions and conditions should be listed. Such an easement is said to have been created by *express grant*.

Easements are also commonly created when an owner sells off the frontage, but retains an easement over it in order not to become landlocked. This is commonly referred to as an *easement by reservation*. Again, the reservation should stipulate the uses to which the easement can be put and any other desired provisions.

Note that an easement usually needs to have a location. This should be done with the same precision and care that one would describe the boundaries of land being sold. One of the most common legal problems faced by attorneys is the *floating easement*, that is, an easement where the person granting the easement failed to specify its location. For example, an owner sells off the frontage and reserves an "easement for a driveway." Where is the driveway to be located? How wide is it to be? These and other issues should be covered in the document creating the easement.

Easements created by express grants or by reservation are considered to have been created by agreement of the parties. But easements can also be created involuntarily by a process called *prescription*. An *easement by prescription* (*prescriptive easement*) can be created when someone uses another's land for ten uninterrupted years. The use must be with the knowledge but without the permission of the owner. It is important to note that the use must be without permission. If the servient tenant can demonstrate that permission was granted, then the claim for a prescriptive easement will be denied. In addition, an easement by prescription can be claimed only on privately owned land; it cannot be created on lands owned by the government.

Note that the unauthorized use of the property is only a claim, not an easement, until the ten years have elapsed and the claim has been perfected. The claim is a *cloud on the title* (see *Clouds* later in this chapter), and must be perfected by court action.

The law implies the creation of an easement under certain other special circumstances. Such easements are called *easement by implication of law*. Easements by implication of law occur because fairness and justice demand that someone have an easement.

One such circumstance might occur when a parcel of land is severed into two parcels. For example, suppose you purchase the frontage to a parcel of land and the seller retains the back portion. At the time of your purchase, the seller had already been driving across the frontage and a driveway was clearly evident and visible, yet your deed made no mention that the seller reserved an easement. Will you be able to deny the existence of an easement for the seller? Probably not, although the case could go either way depending on the specific testimony and evidence in the case. If allowed, such an easement would be called an *easement by prior use*.

Another case where implication of law would create an easement is an *easement by way of necessity*. At common law, an owner of a landlocked parcel can demand an easement for ingress and egress over adjacent land. To be fair, the landlocked owner would have to pay the servient tenant just compensation for loss of market value, to be determined by an appraiser if necessary. The principle of law is that, while it is unfair to the servient tenant to have to allow an easement, the alternative is even more unfair – the landlocked owner would have to forfeit all use of the landlocked parcel.

An easement by way of necessity cannot be granted if the landlocked owner had any other legal remedy or if the property is landlocked as a result of the actions of the landlocked owner. In order to perfect the easement the landlocked owner would have to file suit and obtain a judicial decree. The location of the right of way would be determined according to what portion would cause the least harm to the servient tenement.

Washington code also recognizes that an easement in the public was created in the past when a developer created a plat map of a subdivision and then sold the lots, where the plat map showed roads, streets and other public areas. The legal concept is that the plat map itself expressed the intent to grant an easement to the public in the common areas. There are now strict requirements that common areas be formally conveyed to the city or county when a plat is created. This subject is covered in more detail in Chapter 10.

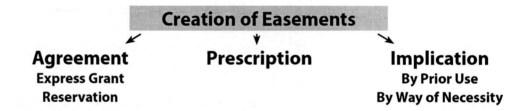

Creation of Easements

Agreement	Prescription	Implication
Express Grant		By Prior Use
Reservation		By Way of Necessity

Termination of easements – Probably the simplest way to terminate an easement is for the holder of the easement to relinquish it to the owner of the servient tenement. This is normally accomplished by a quitclaim deed (deeds are discussed in Chapter 5).

There are a few other simple ways to terminate easements. For example, easements sometimes have expiration dates, in which case they are obviously terminated when the expiration date arrives. Easements created by way of necessity are generally terminated if the need for the easement ceases to exist. Even if the easement was an express grant, it may be terminated by lack of further need, depending on the exact language used in the grant.

One of the more interesting ways an easement can be terminated is by *merger*. This is best explained by an example. Suppose you own a parcel of real estate and you enjoy access to the road via an easement across another parcel which lies between your property and the road. Now suppose further that you purchase the property through which your easement runs, so now you own both properties. By the principle of merger, you now own all the rights to both properties, but the rights have merged into *one* set of rights. In other words, the easement rights were merged into the entire estate, and therefore *the easement no longer exists*. Now suppose you decide to sell the frontage parcel to another. If you don't reserve an easement to yourself, you will leave yourself landlocked.

Easements can also be terminated by *abandonment*. As a general rule, abandonment can only occur if there was a clear intent by the dominant tenant to abandon the easement. Mere non-use alone is not ordinarily evidence of an intent to abandon, although the circumstances surrounding the non-use can lead a court to conclude that there was an intent to abandon.

As previously noted, an easement can be created by *prescription*, but it can also be terminated by prescription. As you recall, an easement is created by prescription when someone uses another's land for ten years, adverse to their interests, with their knowledge and without their permission. Then, if you held a valid easement across your neighbor's land, yet your neighbor blocked your use of it continuously for ten years, with your knowledge and without your permission, the easement would be extinguished by prescription.

Termination of Easements
▼
Agreement (Quitclaim)
Expiration
Lack of Further Need
Merger
Abandonment
Prescription

Licenses and profits

A **profit** (more formally called a **profit à prendre**) is the right to severance of a benefit from another's land. The profit usually involves crops, timber or minerals. The existence of the profit is an encumbrance on the land and the owner cannot convey the land except subject to the profit.

A **license** is created when someone grants to another a personal privilege or right to use land. Unlike easements, however, licenses are revocable. The hallmark of the license is "revocable permission" – in fact **permit** is frequently used as a synonym for license. Of course, since a license can be terminated at will, it is not considered an encumbrance on the title – a sale of the land extinguishes the license.

Sometimes people will attempt to create an "irrevocable license." In fact, the licensee may expend substantial money and effort in the belief that his or her license was irrevocable. Depending on the circumstances, a court may agree that the license is not revocable. Technically, this is a contradiction in terms so, depending on the circumstances, a court would likely interpret it as an easement. Many times owners grant "permits" – "hunting permits," "grazing permits," "wood permits" and the like. Such permits may be interpreted as easements or even profits, depending on the exact language used.

Deed covenants

There are countless ways in which an owner's use of the property can be restricted. Chief among these, of course, are zoning ordinances, building codes, and other **public restrictions**. However, it is also possible to create **private restrictions** as well. Private restrictions are commonly created in the deed, so they are sometimes also called **deed restrictions**. You frequently hear people refer to "covenants, conditions and restrictions," or "CC & Rs" as a catch-phrase to summarize these private restrictions.

The term "restriction" is a generic term which applies to anything which lessens the owner's unfettered right to use the property, including both public and private controls. Private restrictions are further categorized as **conditions**, **covenants** and **equitable servitudes**.

A condition is a serious matter which occurs only rarely. A condition creates a defeasible fee title – e.g., "I, the grantor, hereby convey this property provided you never build over thirty feet high at any point on the premises, and if you should ever do so, the fee shall automatically revert and revest in me." As discussed in Chapter 3, this is a determinable fee title. The penalty for violation is loss of title. Since the penalty is so severe, they are not commonly created.

Covenants and equitable servitudes, however, are very common. Both are mere restrictions on the use of a fee title which is vested absolutely – in other words, the title is not defeasible. The distinction between a covenant and an equitable servitude is technical and beyond what ordinary real estate agents need to understand. They go by numerous terms – ***covenants running with the land***, ***covenants for the benefit of adjacent land***, ***negative easements***, ***real covenants***, ***general plan restrictions***, ***subdivision covenants***, and so on. Usually the reason for the different terms is that there is a slight difference in the desired effect.

Unlike conditions, covenants and servitudes cannot be enforced by taking back the fee title. Instead, covenants and servitudes are enforced by a suit for damages, a suit to enjoin the offending action, or occasionally a suit for specific performance. A suit for damages seeks a monetary award, a suit to enjoin is a suit which seeks an injunction, and a suit for specific performance is a suit which asks the court to compel the other party to comply with an agreement.

When we discuss covenants and servitudes, we must remember that there is a distinction between the burden on one party and the benefit to the other. Covenants and servitudes can be created so the burden is personal, or they can be created so the burden is an encumbrance and runs with the land. Similarly, the benefit to the other party can be personal, or it can be created as an appurtenance which runs with the land. Notice that these concepts are similar to the differences among an easement appurtenant, an easement in gross, and a license.

Frequently a subdivider will wish to create a set of covenants for a subdivision. The concepts are still the same, the only difference is that the subdivider will want to create dozens of restrictions instead of just one. In other words, instead of a "covenant for the benefit of adjacent land" we have a "declaration of subdivision covenants," or other similar term.

Because a declaration of subdivision covenants could run to many pages, it would be inconvenient to reproduce them inside the deeds to the individual lots. To keep the deeds simple, it is common practice to record the subdivision covenants. Recording a document means that it has been placed in the public records and therefore everyone is deemed to be given notice of it. When a document is recorded, it is given an index number by which it can be referenced in the future. Therefore, when the subdivider sells a lot, the deed can be made subject to the recorded covenants just by referring to the index number where they were recorded. Such deeds are commonly called **covenant deeds**.

This leads to an interesting dilemma. Most land is subject to government zoning and planning regulations. Therefore, if a subdivider creates a set of subdivision covenants, there is the possibility of a conflict between the covenants and the zoning. The resolution is simple. Clearly, the owner must follow both the private covenants and the zoning ordinances. Violation of the covenants will invite legal action by a private party, and violation of zoning ordinances will result in local government action. Logically, if the owner were to follow the more restrictive of the two, this would normally ensure compliance with both the zoning and the covenants.

Less than freehold estates as encumbrances

Less than freehold estates are covered in Chapter 3, however, it should be noted here that a tenancy for years (lease) and a periodic tenancy are encumbrances. Therefore, if an owner leases the property to a tenant, and then sells the property, the buyer will take title subject to the lease. Similarly, a periodic rental of the property creates an encumbrance which the buyer must take the title subject to. However, tenancy at will and tenancy at sufferance are not encumbrances.

Encroachments and other clouds

A title problem which (fortunately) occurs only occasionally is the existence of a *cloud*. Clouds are defined as "possible interests" in the property. In other words, if someone has a cloud on your title, it means that the person has a claim which is uncertain, as yet unproved. Eventually, the cloud could ripen into title, or into a lien – or it could simply be extinguished. Until its status becomes certain, it remains an encumbrance on the title.

Clouds can arise through a variety of circumstances. They are typically caused by errors, defects in legal documents, and even as a result of fraud and misrepresentation. For example, suppose your neighbor builds a fence which is placed one foot over the lot line onto your land. This is called an *encroachment*. After a period of time your neighbor may actually gain title to the extra one-foot wide strip of land. In the meantime, however, the existence of the encroaching fence is a cloud. (The exact rules of law for turning this encroachment into ownership of the strip of land are covered in detail in Chapter 5.)

An owner's normal protection against a cloud is the title insurance policy. But what could be done if a cloud does show up? The normal remedy is to obtain a *quitclaim deed* from the party claiming the interest. On the other hand, if the claimant will not voluntarily relinquish the claim, you can force the issue by filing a *suit to quiet title (quiet title action)* or a *suit for slander of title*. The suit for slander of title would normally be used if you wished to assert that the claimant deliberately and maliciously clouded your title. Note that a *quiet title* is a title which is free of clouds.

Financial encumbrances (liens)

While real property can be subject to many kinds of non-financial encumbrances, it is the financial encumbrances which can be more problematical in a real estate transaction. Financial encumbrances include liens such as mortgages and trust deeds, property tax liens and special assessments, income tax levies, judgments, construction liens, and many more.

It is important to understand the difference between a *lien* and an obligation to pay (debt). A lien makes the real property collateral for a debt, but a debt can exist unsecured. In other words, you can borrow money as a personal obligation without giving the lender any collateral. Or you could borrow money and give the lender collateral. When you use your real property as collateral, you have allowed it to be liened. And since liens are encumbrances on the real estate, if you sell the real estate, your buyer will take the title subject to the lien. If the debt was personal (without collateral), then it could not affect your real estate, so you can sell the real estate any time without having to pay off the personal obligation. When property has been pledged as collateral, we say it has been *hypothecated*.

Categories of liens

Liens are categorized as *voluntary liens* and *involuntary liens*. A voluntary lien is a lien which the debtor agreed to, such as a mortgage, trust deed, and the like. An involuntary lien occurred without the debtor's agreement, such as an Internal Revenue Service lien, property taxes, special assessments, judgments and construction liens.

Liens are also categorized as **general liens** and **specific liens**. A general lien reaches everything the debtor owns. Judgments and income tax levies are examples of general liens. A specific lien reaches only the property specified in the document. Examples of specific liens include mortgages and trust deeds, construction liens, and property tax liens.

Mortgages, trust deeds and land sales contracts are the three documents used when financing real estate. Each has its differences and each is governed by an extensive body of law. Financing is involved in practically every transaction, so real estate agents need to have a thorough understanding of these encumbrances. Because of their importance, all of Chapter 11 is devoted to them.

Judgments

Whenever you are owed money and the other party fails to pay, you are entitled to file a suit to compel them to pay. There are innumerable ways in which an obligation to pay can arise – services rendered, goods purchased, money borrowed, damages for wrongful acts – the list is endless. In this section we will not dwell on the means by which the obligation to pay is created. However, since a judgment is a lien against the debtor's real property, real estate agents should know the procedures by which a forced sale can occur and the effects of a judgment on a sale of the property.

The first step the creditor takes is to file a suit against the debtor. Assuming the creditor wins, this will result in a judgment in favor of the creditor and against the debtor. From this point on, we refer to the parties as the **judgment creditor** and the **judgment debtor**. The judgment will be entered on the court records (court docket).

Judgments properly docketed become liens against all real and personal property owned by the judgment debtor in the county where docketed. Each county has its own courts, so if you obtain a judgment in one county, but the judgment debtor owns property in another county, you must have your judgment copied into the court records for the county where the property is located before it will be a lien against that property.

With a few exceptions a judgment is good for ten years, and upon motion to the court, can be renewed for ten additional years. Therefore, one approach to collection of the debt is just to wait. Once your judgment has become a lien on the debtor's property, the debtor will probably have to deal with you in order to sell the property. A judgment debtor may always sell the property, but once the judgment has reached the property, the property can only be sold subject to the judgment. Most buyers will have nothing to do with this, so it forces the judgment debtor to pay off the judgment in order to give clear title to the buyer.

Of course, a judgment creditor is frequently at the mercy of senior lienholders. For example, suppose you obtain a judgment against someone who owns property, but at the time your judgment is docketed there is already a first mortgage and several other judgment creditors ahead of you. Foreclosure by any of the senior lienholders will extinguish your judgment as to the property in question, so a judgment creditor has to be careful of his or her position in the property.

An alternative approach to collection is to force the sale of the property. The judgment creditor is free to proceed against any or all property of the judgment debtor. The process starts by filing a **writ of execution** with the court. When signed by the judge, the writ becomes a court order directed to the sheriff to sell the property described in the writ at public auction. Such a sale is commonly referred to as an **execution sale** or *sheriff's sale*. If there is more than one property listed, the sheriff will sell them in order until the judgment is satisfied or the properties exhausted.

In order to sell the property the sheriff must advertise the sale. The judgment creditor must advance the funds to pay all costs, but the costs are then added to the total judgment. At the auction sale anyone may bid, including the judgment creditor, the judgment debtor, and any member of the public, but not the sheriff holding the sale. All bids must be all cash, except that the judgment creditor can bid up to the amount of the judgment without paying anything at all, since that amount is already owed.

If the property sells for more than the amount of the judgment, the surplus is turned over to the judgment debtor. The judgment, of course, is then satisfied in full. If the property does not sell for enough, then there will be a **partial satisfaction** of the judgment.

Regardless of who is the high bidder at the sheriff's sale, upon proper payment, the sheriff will issue to the high bidder a **sheriff's certificate**, or **certificate of sale**. The certificate of sale entitles the holder to a **sheriff's deed** unless the judgment debtor or a junior lienholder redeems within the statutory period. The judgment debtor has a **statutory right of redemption** for eight months or one year, depending on various factors. Junior lienholders have 60 days in which to redeem (unless the junior lienholder is the federal government, in which case the right of redemption is 120 days). Any person redeeming must do so by paying back the successful bidder whatever the successful bidder paid for the property, plus anything the successful bidder paid on unpaid property taxes or on prior liens, plus 8% interest. During the redemption period, the successful bidder is entitled to possession of the property unless the property is agricultural. However, any benefits of ownership, such as rents received, are credited to the debtor if the debtor redeems.

Homestead exemption

Washington law provides certain protections for homeowners when a judgment has been entered against the homeowner. One of these protections is the **homestead exemption**. A **homestead** is simply defined as your place of personal residence. The homestead exemption provides that the homeowner is entitled to save a certain amount of the equity in a homestead from an execution sale arising out of a judgment. The homestead exemption is generally only applicable to judgments and specifically does not apply to mortgages, trust deeds, construction liens or government liens.

The judgment debtor may claim any personal residence as a homestead, including manufactured housing (mobile homes). The maximum amount of the exemption is normally $40,000 or, if the homestead is a manufactured dwelling not located on land owned by the judgment debtor, $15,000. There is no limitation on the amount of land included with the homestead. The owner must record a declaration of homestead in order to claim the property as a homestead and can have only one homestead.

If the judgment creditor cannot prove that the market value of the homestead is over the amount of the exemption, the court will refuse to allow the creditor to force the sale of the homestead. However, if it is in excess of the exemption, then the court will order an execution sale of the property, with special instructions to the sheriff holding the sale not to accept bids under the amount of the exemption.

When the execution sale takes place the sheriff must place the homestead claim ($40,000 or $15,000, as the case may be) immediately prior to the claim of the judgment creditor. In other words, just before the judgment creditor gets any of the sales proceeds, the sheriff must hold out the homestead claim. The funds will be turned over to the judgment debtor and remain protected from claims of the judgment creditor so the judgment debtor will have them available to purchase a new homestead.

Notices of lis pendens and attachments

When a suit is filed the plaintiff does not have judgment against the defendant until the case is decided. Meanwhile, the defendant's assets are free of the plaintiff's claims. To prevent a debtor from liquidating and wasting his or her assets, the law provides two potential remedies for the plaintiff.

Sometimes the suit involves real property, such as a divorce case where one party is requesting that the decree grant him or her exclusive ownership of certain real property. In this case, to prevent the other party from selling the property prior to finalization of the case, the party claiming the property can file a **notice of lis pendens**. ("Lis pendens" is a Latin phrase that means "litigation pending.") When the notice of lis pendens has been properly filed, it constitutes a cloud on the title. Any buyer of the property will take title subject to the claims of the party who filed the notice.

In other cases, the plaintiff wants to have a lien against the defendant's property and ask the court to order the sheriff to seize the property and hold it. In this case, the plaintiff can apply to the court for permission to file an **attachment** against the defendant's assets. The effect is the same as a notice of lis pendens, that is, any buyer of the property will take title subject to the claims of the party who filed the attachment.

It is important to note that if the plaintiff files an attachment or a notice of lis pendens and later loses the suit, the defendant may have cause of action against the plaintiff for damages due to the wrongful attachment or notice of lis pendens. An attachment of notice of lis pendens can be a dangerous tactic for the plaintiff.

Mechanics' and materialmen's liens

Real estate agents who deal with new construction, or even property which has recently been remodeled, frequently find that the property is subject to a **construction lien**. The laws relating to construction liens are complex, but real estate agents should have a basic understanding of the subject.

Construction liens (also referred to in Washington code as **mechanics' liens** and **materialmen's liens**) are special liens which can be claimed by certain individuals who supply labor or materials for improvements on another person's real estate. The usual purpose is to block a sale of the property until the claimant gets paid.

Construction liens can be claimed by anyone who supplies labor or materials for improvements. While this obviously includes carpenters, bricklayers, roofers, and the like, the statute includes architects, engineers, surveyors and landscapers.

To claim a construction lien, the claimant merely records a claim of lien. Although some claimants may be required to file a claim even earlier, no claims are valid unless recorded within 90 days of substantial completion of the construction project. The claimant must also deliver a notice to the property owner prior to recording the claim of lien. The claim of lien is normally valid for eight months. If the claimant wishes to continue the claim after that time, a suit to foreclose must be filed within the eight months.

The priority of a construction lien is prior in right to all other liens that were recorded after construction was begun or materials supplied. This could create a problem for a lender. Suppose a bank lends funds to the property owner and the documents were recorded on April 1. However, unknown to the lender, the owner hired a contractor to perform work which was begun on March 15. If the contractor is not paid and files suit to enforce a construction lien, the contractor's lien will be ahead of the bank's mortgage. To protect against this possibility, lenders almost always require a type of title insurance policy which covers against construction liens.

Many times an owner wishes to dispute a construction lien. In order to gain clear title immediately, the owner can record a surety bond for 200% of the claim, but not less than $5,000 or, if the claim is over $10,000, 150% of the amount of the claim.

Powers of the government

Although not technically encumbrances, certain rights in real property are reserved to the government. The exercise of these powers by the government must be within constitutional limits. These rights include police power, eminent domain, taxation and escheat.

Police power –One of the most commonly exercised of these powers is **police power**. Police power is the right of the government to maintain public order and to protect the public health, safety, morals and general welfare. While police power obviously includes everything from police forces to traffic control, its particular impact on real estate is the area of zoning and land use laws. These laws include comprehensive planning, building codes, subdivision control laws, condominium regulations and environmental restrictions, to specify just a few. Note that it is constitutional for a government to exercise police power without paying any compensation to the owner.

Mention should also be made that police power does not create just land use laws. For example, real estate licensing laws are an exercise of the police power of the state. Every government regulation is an exercise of police power.

Eminent domain – When the government takes privately owned property it is exercising **eminent domain**. The process is called **condemnation**. In order to exercise eminent domain, the government must be able to demonstrate that the use they will make of the property is a public purpose and that they are paying the owner just compensation. Note that even utility companies and quasi-utilities such as railroads can exercise eminent domain. Even a private citizen has a limited right of eminent domain, such as where a landlocked owner can demand an easement of necessity across adjacent land.

Many times the government wants only a portion of the owner's property. If the taking of the portion results in a loss in value to the remainder of the property, the owner may be entitled to **severance damages**.

Sometimes the actions of the government will cause loss to an owner, even without taking any part of the owner's land. An example might be the construction of a freeway which causes noise and air pollution on nearby properties. In this case, the owners of the affected properties may be entitled to **consequential damages**.

If the government zones an owner's land with such severe restrictions that they leave the owner with little or no economic benefit to be made of the land the owner could claim damages by filing a suit for **inverse condemnation**.

Escheat –When a property owner dies without natural heirs capable of inheriting and without a will, we say that the property **escheats** to the state. In Washington it will be managed by the Department of Natural Resources.

⚷ KEY TERMS

The key to understanding any new field is the vocabulary used in that field. To maximize your comprehension of the material presented in this chapter, be sure you know the meaning and significance of the following terms. Remember that the majority of test questions primarily test knowledge of vocabulary.

Abandonment	Hypothecate
Attachment	Inverse condemnation
Certificate of sale	Involuntary lien
Cloud on the title	Judgment creditor
Commercial easement	Judgment debtor
Community drive	License
Condemnation	Lien
Condition	Materialman's lien
Consequential damages	Mechanic's lien
Construction lien	Merger
Covenant	Negative easement
Covenant deed	Non-financial encumbrance
Covenant for the benefit of adjacent land	Notice of lis pendens
Covenant running with the land	Partial satisfaction
Deed restriction	Permit
Dominant tenant	Police power
Dominant tenement	Prescription
Easement by implication of law	Prescriptive easement
Easement by prescription	Priority
Easement by prior use	Private restriction
Easement by reservation	Profit à prendre
Easement by way of necessity	Public restriction
Easement for ingress and egress	Quiet title
Easement in gross	Quiet title action
Eminent domain	Quitclaim deed
Encroachment	Real covenant
Equitable servitude	Right of use
Escheat	Servient tenant
Execution sale	Servient tenement
Express grant	Severance damages
Financial encumbrance	Sheriff's certificate
Floating easement	Sheriff's deed
Forfeiture	Sheriff's sale
General lien	Specific lien
General plan restriction	Statutory right of redemption
Homestead	Subdivision covenant
Homestead exemption	Subordination

Suit for slander of title   Way of necessity

Suit to quiet title   Writ of execution

Voluntary lien

Chapter

5

Conveying and insuring title

ALTHOUGH WASHINGTON real estate agents do not draft deeds, a basic understanding of them is nevertheless essential background. Real estate agents frequently encounter deeds in their daily practice and they must be able to read and understand them. And real estate agents must be able to converse with escrow agents and others who do draft deeds.

A transfer of real estate is called a **conveyance** or **alienation**. Conveyances are categorized as **voluntary conveyances** and **involuntary conveyances**. For example, selling your property is a voluntary conveyance, but losing it to the bank in a foreclosure is involuntary. When the conveyance is voluntary you sometimes hear people call it a **grant**. The party giving up the property is called the **grantor**, and the party receiving it is the **grantee**.

Involuntary conveyances

Let us turn our attention first to involuntary conveyances. As noted above, a foreclosure is an involuntary conveyance. Involuntary conveyances also result from a many other situations – divorce decrees, bankruptcy, condemnation, suits for partition, even conceivably the forfeiture of a defeasible title – all are examples of involuntary conveyances. In most of these cases (although not all) the actual conveyance is a deed which the grantor is forced to sign under court order. Most of these involuntary conveyances have been, or will be, covered elsewhere in this text. However, two possible involuntary conveyances require a special note.

Riparian right of accession – When property along a stream is increased in size as a result of the addition of soil deposited by the stream, the owner is said to have a right of **accession** to the additional land area. Accession is the legal right of an owner to that which is incidental to the item owned.

The process of building up soil along a riparian property is called **accretion**, that is, the silt and other solids "accrete" to the riparian property. The soil itself is called **alluvium**, or occasionally **alluvion**.

However, the accretion will result in gaining title to new land only if it is a gradual addition. If the accretion is the result of a sudden flood, then no title changes. A sudden or violent tearing away is called **avulsion**.

Adverse possession – Gaining title to property by **adverse possession** occurs when someone possesses another's property without permission for at least the statutory time period. In this respect it is essentially the same process as obtaining an easement by prescription (discussed in Chapter 4). The main difference is that in obtaining an easement by prescription the claimant *used* the property, but in gaining title by adverse possession, the claimant *possessed* the property. Note the distinction between a right of possession (estate), and a right of use (easement).

Various common-law and statutory rules govern a successful claim of adverse possession. The obvious first rule is that the claimant must have been in possession of the property. Under Washington law, the possession must have been for at least ten years and, in rare cases, even longer is required. Being in possession does not necessarily mean the claimant never left the premises. Being in possession merely means that the claimant possessed the property in the normal way as any owner of the property would.

Adverse possession cannot result in gaining title if the possession was secret. The possession must have been **open and notorious**. The test of whether or not the possession was sufficiently open and notorious is fairly rigorous. The possession must have been of such character that it would leave no doubt in the true owner's mind that the party in possession intended to claim the property.

Another rule is that the adverse possession must have been **hostile**. Hostility means that the claimant possessed the property with the intent to claim it or with **color of title**. Color of title means that the claim arises from a written conveyance which purports to convey title to the claimant, but was somehow defective and failed to convey the title.

A fundamental element of hostility is that it cannot co-exist with permission. That is, if the true owner gives the adverse possessor permission to occupy the property, then the hostility is extinguished. Without hostility, the claimant cannot prevail. Therefore, a defense commonly asserted by an owner whose land is adversely claimed, is that the claimant had permission.

The adverse claimant must also demonstrate that the possession was **exclusive**. This does not mean that the adverse claimant may not allow others on the land. It does mean that the claimant must exclude other potential adverse claimants. Invitees and guests are not potential adverse claimants, so an adverse possessor does not diminish his or her claim by allowing ordinary visitors on the property.

The adverse possession must be **continuous** for the statutory time period. The statutory time period in Washington is normally ten years. This means that you cannot adversely claim the property for a couple of years, move away, then return and possess it again for another eight years, and still maintain your claim of title. The ten year requirement must be met by continuous possession. Note, however, that the continuity can be met by more than one claimant through a process known as **tacking**. For example, you could adversely claim the property for a couple of years, and then deed your interest to another. Your grantee could continue the possession for another eight years, and then successfully claim the title adversely.

Washington law provides exceptions to the ten-year rule. If the adverse possessor was in possession under color of title and paid the taxes for at least seven years, this is sufficient to gain title by adverse possession. However, if the defendant (true owner) was mentally incompetent, then the time period is unlimited provided the true owner sues to recover the land within three years after recovering competence.

Another requirement is that the property must have been privately owned. Although the government, acting on behalf of the public, can gain title to privately owned property by adverse possession, a claim of title by adverse possession cannot normally be asserted by private parties against property owned by the government.

For real estate agents, claims of adverse possession are unusual events. After all, owners of land usually notice someone in possession of their land and take measures to prevent the adverse possession from ripening into a legally enforceable claim. When a claim of adverse possession does occur, the most common case involves a fence or other encroachment. Even then, the owner can usually assert the defense of permission.

Creation of and requirements for deeds

The document used in almost all voluntary conveyances is a **deed**. The parties are called the **grantor** (seller) and the **grantee** (buyer). There are numerous kind of deeds, each with its own special legal effects, which we will discuss later.

Many legal terms end in –or and –ee. The rule is that the –or is the giver of the thing, and the –ee is the receiver. Thus, in the case of a deed, the thing is the grant, the grantor is the giver (seller) and the grantee is the receiver (buyer). If you remember this rule it will help when you encounter other –or and –ee terms in your study of real estate.

There are various legal requirements for the creation of a valid and enforceable deed. Primary of these is that the deed must be *in writing*.

In addition to being in writing, a deed must be ***signed by the grantor(s)***. All parties who are in title to the property must sign it. If a party with an ownership interest fails to sign the deed, then his or her interest is not conveyed. In the event one or more of the parties cannot sign the deed it is common practice for the deed to be signed by an authorized representative, such as an attorney in fact (acting under recorded power of attorney), a conservator or a legal guardian. Washington law also requires an ***acknowledgment*** of the signature of the grantor(s), although this is not required in most states. Acknowledgment means that someone has witnessed the grantor's signature. It is normally done by a notary public. (Acknowledgment is covered in detail later in this chapter.) The grantor or the grantor's authorized representative must also be legally ***competent*** at the time of the conveyance.

Note that it is not usually required for the grantee to sign the deed. It logically follows then that the grantee need not necessarily be competent. Therefore, it is possible to deed property to minors and others without legal competence. Of course, such persons are limited in their ability to deal with the real estate, since they must convey it through the signature of a conservator or guardian.

Normally the grantee merely accepts the title, but there are occasions where the grantee specifically agrees to something. In such occasions the grantee should sign the deed as well. An example might be a deed where the grantee agrees to a restrictive covenant.

Although the grantee need not ordinarily be competent, the deed must at least state an ***identifiable grantee***. Technically, this does not have to be by name, but if the name is not used, later title problems may result. For example, it may create a legal conveyance to deed property to someone's "first-born daughter," but when that first-born daughter goes to sell the property, she will have to prove that she was indeed the individual named as grantee. It is also not required to spell the name of either the grantor or the grantee correctly. The law follows the principle of ***idem sonans***, that is, that if it sounds the same then it is the same, regardless of the spelling.

A related problem occurs when the grantee's name changes. For example, suppose Mary Smith takes title to property while a single woman. Later she gets married to Bob Jones and decides to call herself Mary Jones from then on. When she sells the property, how should she sign the deed? That answer is that it doesn't matter as long as it is clear that the person signing the deed is the same person who was listed as grantee in the previous deed. As a courtesy to title examiners it is customary for her to sign her name "Mary Jones, who took title as Mary Smith." This makes it clear to all that she is the same person.

There must also be ***acceptance*** of the conveyance by the grantee. The evidence of the grantee's acceptance normally occurs when the grantee pays money for the property. Even if the grantee paid nothing for the property, the grantee's acceptance is evidenced by moving into the property or accepting the benefits of ownership, such as rental income. Note that the acceptance is the last requirement to be met.

Deeds must also contain an ***adequate description of the premises*** being conveyed, sufficient to permit the location of the property to be determined with certainty. The description of the real estate is normally a formal description, although an informal description is adequate as long as it is sufficient to leave no doubt as to the boundaries.

A deed must contain ***words of conveyance***, also sometimes referred to as a ***granting clause.*** In many states there is a specific word or phrase which is required. In

Washington, however, there is no particular wording required unless the deed is a statutory form deed (see *Types of deeds* later in this chapter).

Washington law does not specifically require a recital of the actual **consideration** for normal deeds. However, if a grantor deeds property without stating the actual consideration, and a creditor feels that the purpose of the deed was to hide the asset from the creditor, the creditor may be able to have the deed set aside. The customary practice today is, therefore, to state the actual consideration. However, many deeds are still written today stating a nominal consideration, such as "for $10 and other good and valuable consideration."

Many states have enacted statutes requiring the actual consideration be stated so that appraisers and tax assessors have a means to determine market values. Washington has no such requirement, although Washington does require that an excise tax be paid based on the actual consideration. Therefore, anyone can calculate the sales price from the amount of excise tax paid.

One of the more interesting requirements is **delivery**. Although volumes have been written about the issue of delivery, it can be summarized succinctly as "the intent of the grantor to convey." It is conceivable that the grantor could physically hand the deed to the grantee intending some purpose other than to convey the title, in which case there would be no conveyance. Of course, proving that the grantor did not intend delivery would be difficult. To avoid disputes over delivery, in modern real estate practice it is customary for the grantor to hand the deed to a neutral escrow agent with instructions to record it when the buyer has complied with the terms of the sale. Once handed to the escrow, the grantor cannot ordinarily withdraw the deed unless the buyer breaches the terms of the escrow.

A fundamental principal of delivery is that it must generally occur within the lifetime of the grantor. After all, consider the impossibility of a dead person forming the intent to convey title. A technical exception occurs if the deed is delivered to a neutral escrow agent with irrevocable instructions to deliver it to the buyer upon the grantor's death. Since the instructions are irrevocable, it is generally held that the grantor has relinquished dominion and control over the title, therefore there is a valid conveyance at the time of handing the deed to the escrow. The grantee's right of possession is just deferred until the death of the grantor.

There are certain matters which are not required. For example, a deed does not require a date to be enforceable. Although the date is evidence of the time when the seller's warranties take effect there is no legal requirement to place a date on a deed. And deeds from corporations do not require a seal in Washington, although a corporate seal is required in some states.

Essential elements for deeds
❶
❷
❸
❹
❺
❻
❼

The preceding has been a discussion of what is required to make the deed valid and enforceable as a conveyance of the property. However, deeds should also be recorded for the protection of the buyer. Recording is discussed in detail later in this chapter.

Persons reading textbooks published in other states may find reference to a **habendum clause**. The habendum clause starts with the words "to have and to hold" and proceeds to describe the quantity or extent of the estate being granted. It is commonly required in some states, but although it can be used, the habendum clause is not required for a valid conveyance in Washington and its use is increasingly rare.

It must always be remembered that a deed lasts for a brief instant at the moment of conveyance, and then has no further effect. Its only function is to convey the title and (possibly) create warranties. Therefore, the grantee cannot further convey the title by endorsing the deed or by delivering it to another person. A new deed must be used each time the property is conveyed, even if the conveyance is back to the original grantor.

Types of deeds, their warranties, and typical uses for them

There are many, many types of deeds – sheriff's deeds, trust deeds, conservators deeds, deeds in lieu of foreclosure, gift deeds – the list is long. Each of these deeds is a deed which has been specially printed for certain uses. For example, a sheriff's deed is designed to be used by a sheriff when deeding property which has been sold at a foreclosure sale. However, all Washington deeds fall into one of three categories based on the warranties they contain. These three categories will be discussed in detail below.

(There are samples of commonly used deed forms on the following pages.)

Deeds are very important documents, but at the same time, an ordinary deed is a very simple document. Nevertheless, over the centuries numerous extra phrases were added to deeds (such as the habendum clause mentioned previously). Preprinted deed forms eventually came to the point where no one but attorneys could understand their language.

To simplify and clarify deed forms, the Washington Legislature enacted statutes creating **statutory form deeds**. The statutory deeds are created by copying the statutory language exactly (RCW 64.04.030 to 64.04.050). The statutes then prescribe the precise legal effect of each form. Since there was already a great body of law regarding the three categories of deeds, the Legislature created a statutory form for each.

Because the legal effect of the simple statutory form deeds is adequate for practically all transactions, they have become virtually the only deeds used today. Therefore, we will confine our discussion of the various deed formats to their statutory forms.

Warranty deed – The deed which gives the buyer the best protection is the **warranty deed**, also sometimes referred to as a **full warranty deed** or **general warranty deed**. As the name would imply, it contains warranties for the grantee's protection.

The statutory warranty deed contains three warranties, frequently referred to as **covenants**. Covenants can be used in the deed to restrict the grantee's use of the property. In that sense, they are encumbrances. Now we find the term used in a somewhat opposite sense. The covenants of a warranty deed are promises that the grantor makes to the grantee regarding the condition of the title, as warranties instead of encumbrances. The three covenants are –

Covenant (warranty) of seizin – By the **covenant** or **warranty of seizin** the grantor warrants that he or she actually has the estate which the deed purports to convey and the right to convey it.

Covenant (warranty) against encumbrances – As the term would imply, the **covenant** or **warranty against encumbrances** is the seller's promise that the property is free and clear. Many times the property is to be conveyed subject to an encumbrance, such as where the buyer is buying the property subject to the seller's old loan. In this case, standard preprinted forms provide a place for the seller to exclude such encumbrances from the warranty.

Covenant (warranty) of quiet enjoyment – The **covenant** or **warranty of quiet enjoyment** guarantees the buyer the right to peaceable possession of the property and obligates the seller to defend against any claims existing as of the moment of the conveyance that interfere with the buyer's right of possession.

Sometimes deeds are created with additional warranties not specified in the statutory forms, especially in other states. Some of these warranties include –

Covenant (warranty) of title – The *covenant* or *warranty of title* requires the grantor to pay the grantee's expense of defending the title against claims of third parties.

Covenant (warranty) of further assurance – When there is a *covenant* or *warranty of further assurance* the buyer can force the seller to sign whatever additional documents may become necessary in the future to perfect the buyer's title. For example, if an error in the description is discovered in the original deed, the buyer can force the seller to sign and deliver a correction deed (see later).

Bargain and sale deed – The statutory *bargain and sale deed* specifies that the grantor gives none of the above three covenants. The seller is under no obligation to defend the title. Bargain and sale deeds are commonly used in fulfillment of land sales contracts. Sheriff's deeds and deeds from other government agencies are also normally bargain and sale deeds in format.

Quitclaim deed – Using either the warranty deed or the bargain and sale deed creates two presumptions – that the grantor had a fee title absolutely vested (unless the deed states a lesser interest), and that the deed not only conveys all the grantor's present interest, but any interest the grantor might acquire in the future. The fact that the above deeds contain these presumptions creates the need for the *quitclaim deed*. A statutory quitclaim deed not only contains none of the above warranties of title, but also creates no presumption that the grantor had any interest at all. Furthermore, using a quitclaim deed conveys only the interest the grantor had at the time of the conveyance. Any interest acquired by the grantor in the future (*after-acquired title*) is not conveyed.

This makes the quitclaim deed the ideal deed when the grantor wishes to release a possible interest (cloud), without promising that the interest being conveyed is genuine. Remember that using even a bargain and sale deed creates the presumption that the grantor had the interest stated in the deed. If the grantee can later demonstrate that the grantor had no interest at all, the grantor could conceivably be found guilty of fraud. By using the quitclaim deed, the grantor conveys all his or her present interest in the property, but does not promise that anything at all was conveyed.

Note that it does not matter what kind of deed was used; the grantee gets all the grantor's right, title and interest in the property unless, of course, the grantor stipulates a lesser estate. The differences among the three Washington deed forms is not the quantity of interest conveyed, but rather the extent to which the grantor will stand behind the conveyance and defend the title in the future.

Special warranty deed – In some states there is a *special warranty deed*, which is similar to the warranty deed. The covenants are identical except that the grantor limits the covenant against encumbrances in that the grantor warrants only that the title is free of encumbrances created or suffered by the grantor. Like the bargain and sale deed, a common use of the special warranty deed is in fulfillment of a land sales contract where the seller has not been in possession of the property for years and does not wish to warrant any actions but his or her own.

In today's world of real estate, it is an unusual transaction where the buyer does not obtain title insurance. As a result, buyers today are less concerned about the kind of deed they receive, as long as the title insurance policy reflects that the buyer is getting the interest bargained for. Note however, that title insurance policies are limited in the scope of their coverage. The covenants of a warranty deed are broader than the coverage of typical title insurance policies. Nevertheless, the chances of recovering from a financially secure title insurance company are probably greater than from the seller.

Reservations and exceptions – It is not unusual in a real estate transaction for the seller to retain some rights in the property being conveyed. For example, the seller may wish to retain an easement. Retaining rights in the property being conveyed is

AFTER RECORDING MAIL TO:

Name

Address

City, State, Zip

Filed for Record at Request of:

_____

STATUTORY WARRANTY DEED

THE GRANTOR(S)

for and in consideration of   Dollars ($),

in hand paid, conveys, and warrants to

the following described real estate, situated in the County of   , state of Washington:

Assessor's Property Tax Parcel/Account Number:

Dated:

STATE OF   )
)-ss
COUNTY OF   )

I certify that I know or have satisfactory evidence that
(is/are) the person(s) who appeared before me, and said person(s) acknowledged that (he/she/they) signed
this instrument and acknowledged it to be (his/her/their) free and voluntary act for the uses and purposes
mentioned in this instrument.

Dated:
                    Notary Public in and for the state of
                    My appointment expires:

                                                                              LPB-10(i) 7/97

*Limited Practice Board statutory warranty deed. The Limited Practice Board has created standard real es-
tate documents that qualified closing agents can use.*

AFTER RECORDING MAIL TO:

Name

Address

City, State, Zip

Filed for Record at Request of:

_____

BARGAIN AND SALE DEED

THE GRANTOR(S)

for and in consideration of   Dollars ($),

in hand paid, bargains, sells and conveys to

the following described real estate, situated in the County of   , state of Washington:

Assessor's Property Tax Parcel/Account Number:

The Grantor(s) for himself/herself/themselves and for his/her/their successors in interest do(es) by these presents expressly limit the covenants of the deed to those herein expressed, and exclude all covenants arising or to arise by statutory or other implication, and do(es) hereby covenant that against all persons whomsoever lawfully claiming or to claim by, through, or under said Grantor(s) and not otherwise, he/she/they will forever warrant and defend the said described real estate.

Dated:

STATE OF   )
)-ss
COUNTY OF   )

I certify that I know or have satisfactory evidence that
(is/are) the person(s) who appeared before me, and said person(s) acknowledged that (he/she/they) signed this instrument and acknowledged it to be (his/her/their) free and voluntary act for the uses and purposes mentioned in this instrument.

Dated:

          Notary Public in and for the state of
          My appointment expires:

                                                                 LPB-15(i) 7/97

Limited Practice Board bargain and sale deed. The Limited Practice Board has created standard real estate documents that qualified closing agents can use.

AFTER RECORDING MAIL TO:

Name

Address

City, State, Zip

Filed for Record at Request of:

_____

QUITCLAIM DEED

THE GRANTOR(S)

for and in consideration of   Dollars ($),

conveys and quitclaims to

the following described real estate, situated in the County of   , state of Washington:

Assessor's Property Tax Parcel/Account Number:

together with all after acquired title of the grantor(s) therein:

Dated:

STATE OF   )
)-ss
COUNTY OF   )

I certify that I know or have satisfactory evidence that
(is/are) the person(s) who appeared before me, and said person(s) acknowledged that (he/she/they) signed this instrument and acknowledged it to be (his/her/their) free and voluntary act for the uses and purposes mentioned in this instrument.

Dated:

            Notary Public in and for the state of
            My appointment expires:

                                                                    LPB-12(i) 7/97

Limited Practice Board quitclaim deed. The Limited Practice Board has created standard real estate documents that qualified closing agents can use.

called a *reservation*. Other times the seller may wish to retain complete ownership of a portion of the property. This is commonly referred to as an *exception*.

Reformation (correction) deed – Real estate agents occasionally run into a *reformation deed*, also sometimes called a *correction deed*. A reformation deed is used to correct an error in an already executed deed. For example, the original deed may have mis-stated the legal description. The usual practice is to obtain the original incorrect deed, type the correction on it, have the grantor sign it a second time with a note that it is being signed again to correct the error, and then re-record the deed.

Excise tax on conveyances

Washington law requires an *excise tax* on transfers of real estate. The tax is collected by the county treasurer and remitted to the Department of Revenue. Deeds and contracts cannot be accepted for recording until the treasurer has certified that the tax has been paid or that the transaction is exempt (See *Notice and recording*, later in this chapter.) The tax is calculated on the gross selling price, including the amounts of loans. Normally it is the seller's obligation to pay the tax. However, the tax is a lien on the property until paid, so if the seller doesn't pay it the buyer will become obligated to do so.

The amount of the tax varies according to the city and county in which the property is located. The basic rate is 1.28%, which is the state rate. In addition, cities and counties can add 0.25% for capital improvement projects. Cities and counties can also add an additional 0.25% for capital improvements specified in a comprehensive plan. Counties are also authorized to add 1.0% for acquisition and maintenance of conservation areas. In a couple dozen areas in the state the minimum of 1.28% applies. The most common rate is 1.53%. The maximum rate that could be charged is 3.28%.

For more detail on the real estate excise tax, see Chapter 8.

Patents

Title to all real estate in Washington which is currently in private ownership was originally conveyed by the federal government to a private individual at some time. The instrument used was called a *federal patent*, or just *patent*. Patents are seldom used in Washington today, except when the federal government grants just the mineral rights. Note that the patent is the original conveyance of the land. Subsequent conveyances, even when the grantor is the federal government, are by deed.

Starting in the 1850s, federal patents were granted to settlers in what was then the Oregon Territory (what is now Oregon and Washington). The grants were made under the provisions of the federal Donation Land Law of 1850. Settlers would first file a *Donation Land Claim*. After living on the land and making improvements, they would be granted a federal patent to their claims. Many modern surveys continue to refer to the corners of these donation land claims as starting points for property boundaries. Many times these patents reserved the mineral rights to the federal government. You will frequently find reference to this in documents like purchase and sale agreements or title insurance policies, where the document says the title is to be "free and clear of encumbrances except reservations in the federal patent."

Dedications

A *dedication* is a grant of land to the public. Most commonly, it occurs when a developer conveys property to a city or a county for the roads and streets in a new subdivision. Occasionally other common areas, such as parks, school sites, and so on are included. The instrument is normally a deed, although the conveyance can also be made by recording a plat map showing the areas to be dedicated and containing formal language conveying them to the city or county.

Sometimes a dedication is created between an owner and the public by a formal deed and acceptance by the government. In many cases in the past the conveyance was not by a formal deed but, rather, because the owner failed to stop the public from using the land. Either way, it is considered a **common-law dedication**. Today, it is illegal to divide land without recording a plat map and placing on the map the words creating a formal conveyance to the city or county of any roads or streets shown on the map. Since such dedications today are required by land use statutes, they are called **statutory dedications**.

Transfer of title to personal property

Where deeds are the normal instrument used to convey real property, we transfer personal property by a **bill of sale**. A bill of sale is to personal property what a deed is to real property. Many real estate transactions involve personal property as well as the real estate – e.g., a range and a refrigerator included in the sale price. Therefore it is not uncommon to find a bill of sale in a real estate transaction, as well as a deed.

Basics of wills, inheritance and estate law

At one time or another most real estate agents become involved in the sale of property in an estate. Inheritance laws are complex, but a knowledge of at least the terminology can be useful in these situations. A gift of real property by will is called a **devise** and the recipient (heir) is the **devisee**. A gift of personal property in a will is called a **bequest** or a **legacy** and the recipient is called the **legatee**. The deceased person is called the **decedent**. When the decedent leaves a will, we say that he or she died **testate**. A decedent who died without leaving a valid will is said to have died **intestate**. A **codicil** is an amendment to a will.

Ordinarily, the only wills recognized in Washington are formal, written, witnessed wills. Some states also recognize a **holographic will**, which is a will written entirely in the decedent's own handwriting, but not witnessed. Washington recognizes a holographic will if it was made in a state which allows it and the person later moved to Washington and never made a new will. A **nuncupative will** is an oral will made to at least two witness on the decedent's deathbed. Washington recognizes a nuncupative will, but only for personal property not over $1,000 in value and only if the decedent was in the armed forces or merchant marine at the time. If the person recovers it is no longer valid.

When the decedent dies intestate there is a question of the disposition of the estate. Of course, if there are no heirs, the estate will escheat to the state (see Chapter 4). If there is a spouse, and no other heirs or children, the spouse will take all. If there is a spouse and children, the spouse will take all the community property and one-half of the separate property, and the children will share the other half of the separate property. There are also provisions for further distribution in the event there is no spouse, which are too involved for our discussion here. The important point to bear in mind that a surviving spouse will take half the deceased spouse's separate property unless the deceased spouse made a will. Thus, if a married person wants separate property to pass to others, it is important to make a will.

Although there are ways to avoid it, the estate of a decedent must usually go through **probate**. Probate is the process of submitting the estate to the scrutiny of the probate court for final distribution of the decedent's assets. There are ways to avoid probate, but whether this is wise is a complicated issue. Real estate agents should always advise and encourage clients to seek estate planning counsel. Failing to do so can cost heirs many thousands of dollars in taxes and costs which could have been avoided by proper planning.

A decedent who died testate may have named a **personal representative** in his or her will. If not, or if the decedent died intestate, the probate court will appoint a personal representative. Personal representative is the modern term for "executor" ("executrix" if female) and "administrator" ("administratrix" if female). The personal representative has broad powers in Washington, including the right to list property for sale, accept offers, sign deeds, contracts, leases, etc. – as long as the action is consistent with the provisions of the will and the orders of the probate court.

Washington law provides that heirs receive title to real property instantly on the death of the decedent. However, until the provisions of the will or intestate succession have been approved by the probate court, there is no way to be positive that an heir has really inherited the property. Therefore, the heirs usually have to wait until probate is finalized before doing anything with the property.

Acknowledgments

There are many times in the course of business transactions when it is desirable to have a signature on a legal document verified by another person. This is usually done by an **acknowledgment**. It is called an acknowledgment because the party signing the document acknowledges before an official that it was a voluntary act. The party who witnesses or verifies the signature is said to "take an acknowledgment."

We have signatures acknowledged for a variety of reasons, but the most important is that a document ordinarily cannot be recorded in Washington unless it has been acknowledged. Acknowledgment also creates prima facie evidence that the signature on the instrument was a voluntary act (not under duress). And it is also prima facie evidence that the official taking the acknowledgment either knew the individual personally or verified the identity of the signer, so we know the signature was not a forgery.

An acknowledgment is most commonly taken by a **notary public**. You can usually find notaries in banks, escrow offices, title insurance companies and attorneys' offices, since such people constantly deal with instruments which must be acknowledged and recorded. The maximum fee for a notarization is a nominal amount and many notaries

---

State of Washington
County of _____
I certify that I know or have satisfactory evidence that _____ is the person
who appeared before me, and said person acknowledged that (he/she) signed this instrument and acknowledged it to be
(his/her) free and voluntary act for the uses and purposes mentioned in the instrument.

Dated: _____

_____ (Signature)   (Seal or stamp)

Title _____

My appointment expires _____

A short form acknowledgment suitable for an individual signing for himself or herself. If the individual is signing for a corporation or other entity, then the language is changed to reflect the capacity of the signer.

perform the service at no charge. Many real estate agents find it is convenient to become notaries. Washington judges and their clerks can also take acknowledgments, as can certain officers of the armed forces. Washington law also recognizes acknowledgments taken by notaries and authorized officials of other states.

Notice and recording

At its simplest, **notice** is the concept that people should not be held responsible for things that were unknown to them or, to put it in legal terms, of which they had no notice. While this may seem fair and just, it raises a problem. You could easily escape legal responsibility just by saying "I didn't know." To prevent this, there are various situations where the law provides that you are deemed to have been given notice, whether you actually knew it or not.

One such case is that everyone is deemed to have notice of the law, therefore ignorance of the law is no excuse. While a court might be sympathetic to a lay person who was unaware of the law, everyone has access to attorneys, so everyone will be held responsible for their actions, whether they knew the law or not.

In other circumstances, it is often necessary to be able to prove that you gave someone notice. For example, if you sue someone, you cannot prevail in court unless the defendant was properly served with the complaint. The service puts the defendant on notice of the pending suit and the process server files papers with the court attesting to the service. And in civil contracts it is also often necessary for one party to give notice to the other. Certified mail is a common device to demonstrate proof that notice was given.

When it comes to real estate transactions, the issue of notice becomes crucial because of the doctrine of the **bonafide purchaser** (also sometimes called an **innocent purchaser**). When a bonafide purchaser buys property **in good faith**, **for value**, and **without notice of defect**, the bonafide purchaser will be held safe from any claims against the title. For example, if you buy a parcel of real estate without any notice that there is a mortgage on the title, the lender may find that your purchase caused their mortgage to be extinguished. Any person who holds an interest in another's real estate has a duty to give notice to the world of the interest, lest it be extinguished when the property is sold.

Of course, this is impossible. There is no way a lender or other party with an interest in another's real estate can actually notify the entire world. Therefore, in matters involving title to real estate, the law imposes a duty on anyone dealing in the real estate to make certain inquiries, and the party is deemed to have been given notice of anything which would be revealed thereby, whether the person actually inquired or not.

One matter which the buyer is required to investigate is the rights of any parties in possession. A party in possession of real estate is deemed to have given the entire world notice of his or her rights by the mere act of being in possession.

Another matter which must be investigated is the **public record**. The public record consists of all documents which have been recorded and which affect the property (see *Recording* later). In other words, if a lessee is in possession, the buyer takes title subject to the lease, whether the buyer knew of it or not, because being in possession gave the buyer notice. Or the lessee could simply record the lease, in which case the buyer would also be given notice of it. Either notice is sufficient to protect the lessee from having his or her lease extinguished by a sale of the property.

Notice given by being possession or notice given by recording is called **constructive notice**. Notice can also be given by personally informing someone of a fact, verbally, in writing or by actions. This is called **actual notice**. Again, it makes no difference if the notice was constructive or actual – the interest is protected as long as the buyer was given notice.

Notice can also arise when a buyer had a duty to inquire about a suspicious situation. Suppose, for example, that a seller sold a property to a buyer, but the buyer did not record the deed. Subsequently, the seller sold the property to you. If you record your deed, then normally you would be held to be the "innocent purchaser in good faith for value without notice of the defect," so your title would be good. But suppose the first buyer ordered improvements to be made. When you inspect the premises, you notice the improvements being made and there is further evidence that the improvements were not being made by the seller. Nevertheless, you do nothing. Because the situation was suspicious, you had an obligation to investigate. Such investigation would have revealed the truth, so your title is not good. The duty to investigate suspicious situations is called *inquiry notice*.

The doctrine of the bonafide purchaser also extends to encumbrances, particularly as to priority. If a lender takes a mortgage on property, but does not record it, is not in possession, and gives no actual notice, then a subsequent lender who does record is deemed to have the first mortgage. The subsequent lender who recorded is an innocent party in good faith for value without notice of the defect. An unrecorded encumbrance is always last in priority.

Recording – It is important to understand that neither recording nor acknowledgment make a document legally enforceable. Acknowledgment merely creates evidence that the signatures were legitimate and voluntary. Recording gives constructive notice. But a neither a notary nor a recording officer has the authority to pass judgment as to the legal enforceability or effect of a contract.

In early England the concept did not exist that a bonafide purchaser in good faith for value should be held safe from claims of which he or she had no notice. The idea did not become law until 1640 in the Massachusetts Bay Colony. But from that beginning, modern recording statutes have spread throughout the United States, and in much the same format.

In the early days of recording, an exact copy of the document to be recorded would literally be bound in a book. As it was bound into the book it was given a page number. Thus, it became possible to refer to the document by the "book and page number" where it was recorded.

Today, each county has its own system for recording documents. However, a common thread runs throughout, so most things are very similar, if not identical, from one county to the next. In some counties, for example, deeds are recorded in one set of books, while mortgages and other liens are recorded in another set of books. In other counties, there is just one set of books for all real estate records. In some counties they use the Latin terms for book and page, "liber and folio." In other counties they have adopted the nomenclature of modern microphotography, so documents are referred to by the "reel and instrument number" where they can be found on the microfilm. It is also common to encounter counties where each document is just given a sequential "file" or "document" number. As long as the document can be found in readable format in the location where it belongs, proper notice is given.

Of course, in order to find anything in the public records, there must be an index. In Washington the records will be indexed by last name of the grantor (the direct index) and grantee (the inverted index). Mortgagors are considered "grantors" and mortgagees are considered "grantees."

In Washington the official usually responsible for recording is the county auditor. Fortunately, Washington real estate agents rarely find it necessary to deal with the auditor's office. The majority of transactions today are handled by escrow agents (or the escrow department of a title insurance company). These professionals close hundreds of real estate transactions every day and are experts at recording requirements. Most will record any document as a courtesy if you just reimburse them the recording fee.

Nevertheless, real estate agents should be familiar with some of the requirements for recording documents. Of course, we have already noted that most documents must be acknowledged to be recorded. And there are statutory as well as local ordinances which set the fees charged for the service. The fees vary according to the type of document and the number of pages.

In addition, certain documents create additional requirements. For example, deeds and land sales contracts must bear the stamp of the county treasurer stating that the excise tax on real estate transfers has been paid, or that the transaction is exempt.

As we have seen, a buyer would be foolish not to record his or her deed or land sales contract. However, there are times when the parties wish to keep their transaction from the public. There are other times when the document (especially a land sales contract) may be many pages in length and the recording charges could be avoided by not recording. For these situations, the law permits the recording of a ***memorandum*** of the document. The memorandum must meet the same requirements as the original – that is, it must have the signature(s) of the parties, which must be acknowledged, and it must bear the stamp of the county treasurer that the excise tax has been paid, or that the transaction is exempt. Once recorded, it gives the same notice as recording the entire original would.

Evidence of title

As we have seen, there are many complicated laws which buyers must deal with in a real estate transaction. Yet buyers are typically ill-prepared to ensure that the interest they bargained for is, in fact, the interest the seller is delivering. At the same time, they have to be sure. An error could cost them their ownership in the property.

To assist buyers (as well as lenders, lessees and others) in determining the condition of the seller's title, an entire title insurance industry has arisen. In this chapter we will explore the origins of this industry and the types of title insurance policies which are commonly available today.

Abstracts and the chain of title

In the early days the seller would provide a buyer with an ***abstract of title***. The abstract would be prepared by an abstract company (commonly called title companies or title and trust companies). The abstract was a bulky document, sometimes containing of hundreds of pages, bound together in date order. Each page in the abstract would be a summary of some recorded document which affected the title to the property. Normally, the very first page in an abstract would be a summary of the original federal patent to the first homestead claimant. Subsequent pages would describe everything that followed, right up to the date the abstract was prepared.

Each recorded document is referred to as a ***link*** in the ***chain of title***. Researching the public records relative to a property to determine the current status of the title is called ***chaining the title*** or conducting a ***title search***.

Abstract companies were able to prepare an abstract easily because they had developed their own files of recorded documents. Over the years, the abstract companies would take down a summary of each document recorded at the recorder's office every day, and re-file these summaries in their own company records. These records are referred to as a ***title plant***.

An interesting feature of the title plant is that it was arranged in a ***tract index*** – property by property, rather than by grantor-grantee. Keeping all the records relating to a given property in a single file greatly simplified the creation of the abstract. Even today, modern title insurance company records are kept much the same way.

The job of the abstract company was only to provide information about documents in the public records, not to pass judgment on their legal effect or the quality of the title. Therefore, buyers would receive the abstract of title, and would also obtain the opinion of a title attorney as to the condition of the seller's title. For this reason, we usually refer to this system as ***abstract and opinion***.

Torrens title registration

Although abstract and opinion was better than no evidence of the condition of the seller's title, it was expensive and it afforded relatively limited protection. In most parts of the country the abstract and opinion system has been replaced.

One of the earliest alternative methods was the Torrens system. The Torrens system was created in the mid 1800s by Sir Robert Torrens, a businessman who was experienced in registering ship titles.

Under the Torrens system, an owner would apply to register the title to his or her property with a county registrar of titles. In order to ensure that the title was correctly registered in the beginning, a suit to quiet title would be filed. Once the court decreed the condition of the title, the initial registration was made. In the future, any encumbrances, conveyances, or other matters would be filed with the registrar of titles. Each filing with the registrar would require a fee, and a portion of each fee would be set aside as a recovery fund for losses caused by registration errors.

The Torrens system can be an effective and inexpensive way to assure buyers of the condition of the title. Its major drawback is the time and expense involved in the initial registration. Although it is still used in several other countries and in 19 states, today its use in the United States is limited mostly to certain counties in Hawaii, Massachusetts, Minnesota and Illinois, and even within those counties not all properties are in the Torrens system. In Washington the legislature created a Torrens Act in 1907 (RCW 65.12), which is still part of state law. Its use today is very limited, although approximately 3,500 properties in King County are still in Torrens registration.

Title certificates

In a few parts of the United States a system of ***title certificates*** is used. The title certificates are issued by an attorney who researches the condition of the seller's title. Generally speaking, the certificate is really nothing more than the attorney's opinion as to the condition of the title. Not only is the system expensive, but in the event of an error, the buyer has little recourse other than the attorney's malpractice insurance.

Title insurance policies, coverages and exclusions

In the western United States today the most common way for the buyer to get evidence of the condition of the seller's title is title insurance. Although the concept of title insurance began much earlier, it was not until the 1920s that it first appeared as a serious alternative to the abstract and opinion or Torrens registration.

An interesting footnote in the development of the title insurance industry is that it was the abstract companies who formed the original title insurance companies. After all, you cannot issue a title insurance policy without first investigating the title, which requires a title plant, and the abstract companies had the only title plants. So when people started asking for title insurance instead of abstracts, the abstract companies simply became licensed as insurance companies and began issuing title insurance.

Title insurance has a number of advantages over earlier systems. For one thing, a title insurance policy is only a few pages and is reissued anew each time the property is sold. With abstracts, the buyer always had to hold onto the abstract so it could be updated and turned over to the next buyer. But the biggest advantage is that it is *insurance* – if the buyer suffers a loss covered by the policy, the buyer can simply present a claim. In addition, title insurance companies are regulated by the Washington Insurance Commissioner, so consumers can be assured that each company will maintain adequate resources to protect their policyholders.

Policy types – Today there are numerous different title insurance policies available, each specifically tailored to a certain situation. For example, you would no doubt be embarrassed if you built a building on a long-term leasehold, only to discover that the lessor's title was in question and you were about to be dispossessed by someone else claiming ownership. A wise move would have been to obtain a **leasehold policy** to protect your lessee's interest.

In addition to leasehold policies, title insurance companies issue various other policies, but none is more common than the **owner's policy**. The owner's policy, obviously, insures the interest of an owner. But many times a seller will carry a land sales contract from the buyer. In this case, the seller retains legal title, so the buyer does not become the owner. Yet the buyer needs coverage, so the buyer obtains a **purchaser's policy**. Except that it is issued to a contract buyer rather than a buyer who receives a deed at closing, the purchaser's policy is essentially the same as the owner's policy.

When property is financed through an outside lender (such as a bank), the lender will normally insist on a **mortgagee's policy**. The mortgagee's policy insures that the lender has a good lien and is issued in the amount of the loan balance, rather than the purchase price. The coverage declines as the loan balance is paid off and ceases upon full satisfaction.

Although real estate agents seldom have use for them, title insurance companies also issue **foreclosure guaranties**, **trustee's sale guaranties** and **litigation guaranties**. When a lienholder forecloses, or when other litigation is commenced, all other parties with an interest in the property must be served with notice of the suit. Therefore, the purpose of these policies is so the plaintiff will know all the parties claiming an interest in the property.

Coverages – Different title insurance policies offer different coverages, but all insure that the insured's title is a **marketable title**. (In contracts, marketable title is sometimes referred to as **insurable title**). Marketable title does not mean that the property is completely free of encumbrances. Rather, marketable title means that the title is free of financial encumbrances but not other encumbrances which are normal in the area. For example, utility easements are encumbrances, but when they benefit all the properties in the area, the buyer is ordinarily expected to accept the title subject to them.

A common point of confusion for beginners is that, unlike other types of insurance, title insurance only insures the condition of the title at one specific moment in time. Title defects which are created in the future are not covered. Note the difference between a title defect which *occurs* in the future (not covered) and a title defect which *is discovered* in the future, but which existed at the time the policy was issued (covered defect).

While coverage is as of a given point in time, the term of a policy is unlimited. You would be covered even after selling the property, if called upon by your buyer to honor a warranty in the your deed to the buyer, for example.

The coverage afforded under the policy depends on the form on which it was issued. Today there are several title insurance forms in general use in Washington. The most common of these is the **standard form** policy – normally the American Land Title Association (ALTA) standard form policy. The American Land Title Association has also created an **extended form** policy. There is an example of the ALTA standard form policy on the following pages.

An owner's, purchaser's or mortgagee's policy could be issued on any one of the forms. However, usually the owner's or purchaser's policy to be issued on an ALTA standard form, while the mortgagee's policy is usually an ALTA extended coverage policy. Nevertheless, buyers of new construction frequently ask for the ALTA extended coverage policy, since it covers construction liens which the standard form does not. And there are few lenders who are satisfied with a standard form mortgagee's policy, so a mortgagee's policy is almost always an ALTA extended coverage policy. There are also endorsements available for these policies.

The ALTA standard form policy insures
- That the title is vested as stated in the policy
- That there are no defects in, or liens on, the title
- Against lack of a right of access
- Against the title not being marketable

However, there are numerous exclusions from coverage. These include –
- Government exercise of police power or eminent domain, including environmental protection laws
- Defects of which the insured had actual notice
- Taxes or special assessments not already shown as liens by the taxing authority, i.e., future property taxes
- Interests of others which could be ascertained from an inspection of the premises
- Unrecorded easements
- Unpatented mining claims, reservations in federal patents (mineral rights)
- Water rights
- Construction liens
- Encroachments, discrepancies or shortages which would be disclosed by a survey

In addition, the title search frequently reveals encumbrances such as mortgages, property taxes and other liens which the buyer is assuming, easements appurtenant to adjacent land, and others. Such defects do not necessarily mean the transaction will fail, if the buyer already knew of them and has agreed to buy the property subject to them. However, they will be excluded from the coverage under an additional schedule appended to the policy.

The American Land Title Association extended coverage form was originally created in response to the needs of the secondary mortgage market. A "secondary lender" is a lender who purchases loans, usually in large "pools" from a "primary" or originating lender. When a primary lender sells a loan to a secondary lender the mortgagee's title insurance policy is assigned to the secondary lender. In the early days of title insurance, policies were not uniform throughout

Standard form exclusions

❶

❷

❸

❹

❺

❻

❼

❽

❾

AMERICAN LAND TITLE ASSOCIATION
OWNER'S POLICY
(10-17-92)

CHICAGO TITLE INSURANCE COMPANY

SUBJECT TO THE EXCLUSIONS FROM COVERAGE, THE EXCEPTIONS FROM COVERAGE CONTAINED IN SCHEDULE B AND THE CONDITIONS AND STIPULATIONS, CHICAGO TITLE INSURANCE COMPANY, a Missouri corporation, herein called the Company, insures as of Date of Policy shown in Schedule A, against loss or damage, not exceeding the Amount of Insurance stated in Schedule A, sustained or incurred by the insured by reason of:

1. Title to the estate or interest described in Schedule A being vested other than as stated therein;
2. Any defect in or lien or encumbrance on the title;
3. Unmarketability of the title;
4. Lack of a right of access to and from the land.

The company will also pay the costs, attorney's fees and expenses incurred in defense of the title, as insured, but only to the extent provided in the Conditions and Stipulations.

In witness whereof, CHICAGO TITLE INSURANCE COMPANY has caused this policy to be signed and sealed as of Date of Policy shown in Schedule A, the policy to become valid when countersigned by an authorized signatory.

Issued by: CHICAGO TITLE INSURANCE COMPANY
CHICAGO TITLE INSURANCE COMPANY   By:
1111 MAIN STREET
SUITE 200
VANCOUVER, WA 98660
360-696-0551   President

                                                  By:

*An **ALTA** standard form owner's title insurance policy. Reproduced with the kind permission of the Chicago Title Insurance Company.*

ALTA Owner's Policy (10/17/92)

SCHEDULE A

Date of Policy: October 10, 2004
Policy No.:   564321w
Order No.:   564321w
Amount of Insurance: $260,000.00
Premium: $905.00

1. **Name of Insured:**
   Donald Duck and Daisy Duck

2. **The estate or interest in the land which is covered by this policy is:**
   an estate in fee simple

3. **Title to the estate or interest in land is vested in:**
   Donald Duck and Daisy Duck, husband and wife, as joint tenants

4. **The land referred to in this policy is situated in the State of Washington, County of** King **and is described as follows:**

   Lot 17, Block 4, FRED & ETHEL'S PLACE, in the City of Seattle, County of King and State of Washington.

SCHEDULE B
EXCEPTIONS FROM COVERAGE

This policy does not insure against loss or damage (and the Company will not pay costs, attorneys' fees or expenses) which arise by reason of:

1. Taxes or assessments which are not shown as existing liens by the records of any taxing authority that levies taxes or assessments on real property or by the public records; proceedings by a public agency which may result in taxes or assessments, or notice of such proceedings, whether or not shown by the records of such agency or by the public records.
2. Any facts, rights, interests or claims which are not shown by the public records but which could be ascertained by an inspection of said land or by making inquiry of persons in possession thereof.
3. Easements, claims of easements or encumbrances, not shown by the public records reservations or exceptions in patents or in acts authorizing the issuance thereof; water rights, or claims or title to water.
4. Any lien, or right to a lien, for unemployment taxes, workman's compensation, services, labor, equipment rental or material, heretofore or hereafter furnished, imposed by law and not shown by the public records.
5. Discrepancies, conflicts ion boundary lines, shortage in area, encroachments, or any other facts which a correct survey would disclose.
6. An easement created by instrument, including the terms and provisions thereof, Recorded July 1, 1956, Book 352, Page 20
7. Trust deed, including the terms and provisions thereof,
   Recorded : October 9, 2002 in Book 1105, Page 243
   Grantors : Donald Duck and Daisy Duck, husband and wife
   Trustee   : Chicago Title Insurance Company
   Beneficiary : Perpetual Loan Company, a Washington Corporation
   Amount   : $220,000.00

EXCLUSIONS FROM COVERAGE

The following matters are expressly excluded from the coverage of this policy and the Company will not pay loss or damage, costs, attorneys' fees or expenses which arise by reason of:

1. (a) Any law, ordinance or governmental regulation (including but not limited to building and zoning laws, ordinances, or regulations) restricting, regulating, prohibiting or relating to (i) the occupancy, use, or enjoyment of the land; (ii) the character, dimensions or location of any improvement now or hereafter erected on the land; (iii) a separation in ownership or a change in the dimensions or area of the land or any parcel of which the land is or was a part; or (iv) environmental protection, or the effect of any violation of these laws, ordinances or governmental regulations, except to the extent that a notice of the enforcement thereof or a notice of a defect, lien or encumbrance resulting from a violation or alleged violation affecting the land has been recorded in the public records at Date of Policy.

(b) Any governmental police power not excluded by (a) above, except to the extent that a notice of the exercise thereof or a notice of a defect, lien or encumbrance resulting from a violation or alleged violation affecting the land has been recorded in the public records at Date of Policy.

2. Rights of eminent domain unless notice of the exercise thereof has been recorded in the public records at Date of Policy, but not excluding from coverage any taking which has occurred prior to Date of Policy which would be binding on the rights of a purchaser for value without knowledge.

3. Defects, liens, encumbrances, adverse claims or other matters:
(a) created, suffered, assumed or agreed to by the insured claimant;
(b) not known to the Company, not recorded in the public records at Date of Policy, but known to the insured claimant and not disclosed in writing to the Company by the insured claimant prior to the date the insured claimant became an insured under this policy;
(c) resulting in no loss or damage to the insured claimant;
(d) attaching or created subsequent to Date of Policy; or
(e) resulting in loss or damage which would not have been sustained if the insured claimant had paid value for the estate or interest insured by this policy.

4. Any claim, which arises out of the transaction vesting in the Insured the estate or interest insured by this policy, by reason of the operation of federal bankruptcy, state insolvency, or similar creditors' rights laws, that is based on:
(a) the transaction creating the estate or interest insured by this policy being deemed a fraudulent conveyance or fraudulent transfer; or
(b) the transaction creating the estate or interest insured by this policy being deemed a preferential transfer except where the preferential transfer results from the failure:
(i) to timely record the instrument of transfer; or
(ii) of such recordation to impart notice to a purchaser for value or a judgment or lien creditor.

CONDITIONS AND STIPULATIONS

1. DEFINITION OF TERMS.
The following terms when used in this policy mean:
(a) "insured": the insured named in Schedule A, and, subject to any rights or defenses the Company would have had against the named insured, those who succeed to the interest of the named insured by operation of law as distinguished from purchase including, but not limited to, heirs, distributees, devisees, survivors, personal representatives, next of kin, or corporate or fiduciary successors.
(b) "insured claimant": an insured claiming loss or damage.
(c) "knowledge" or "known": actual knowledge, not constructive knowledge or notice which may be imputed to an insured by reason of the public records as defined in this policy or any other records which impart constructive notice of matters affecting the land.
(d) "land": the land described or referred to in Schedule [A][C], and improvements affixed thereto which by law constitute real property. The term "land" does not include any property beyond the lines of the area described or referred to in Schedule [A][C], nor any right, title, interest, estate or easement in abutting streets, roads, avenues, alleys, lanes, ways or waterways, but nothing herein shall modify or limit the extent to which a right of access to and from the land is insured by this policy.
(e) "mortgage": mortgage, deed of trust, trust deed, or other security instrument.
(f) "public records": records established under state statutes at Date of Policy for the purpose of imparting constructive notice of matters relating to real property to purchasers for value and without knowledge. With respect to Section 1(a)(iv) of the Exclusions From Coverage, "public records" shall also include environmental protection liens filed in the records of the clerk of the United States district court for the district in which the land is located.
(g) "unmarketability of the title": an alleged or apparent matter affecting the title to the land, not excluded or excepted from coverage, which would entitle a purchaser of the estate or interest described in Schedule A to be released from the obligation to purchase by virtue of a contractual condition requiring the delivery of marketable title.

2. CONTINUATION OF INSURANCE AFTER CONVEYANCE OF TITLE.
The coverage of this policy shall continue in force as of Date of Policy in favor of an insured only so long as the insured retains an estate or interest in the land, or holds an indebtedness secured by a purchase money mortgage given by a purchaser from the insured, or only so long as the insured shall have liability by reason of covenants of warranty made by the insured in any transfer or conveyance of the estate or interest. This policy shall not continue in force in favor of any purchaser from the insured of either (i) an estate or interest in the land, or (ii) an indebtedness secured by a purchase money mortgage given to the insured.

3. NOTICE OF CLAIM TO BE GIVEN BY INSURED CLAIMANT.
The insured shall notify the Company promptly in writing (i) in case of any litigation as set forth in Section 4(a) below, (ii) in case knowledge shall come to an insured hereunder of any claim of title or interest which is adverse to the title to the estate or interest, as insured, and which might cause loss or damage for which the Company may be liable by virtue of this policy, or (iii) if title to the estate or interest, as insured, is rejected as unmarketable. If prompt notice shall not be given to the Company, then as to the insured all liability of the Company shall terminate with regard to the matter or matters for which prompt notice is required; provided, however, that failure to notify the Company shall in no case prejudice the rights of any insured under this policy unless the Company shall be prejudiced by the failure and then only to the extent of the prejudice.

4. DEFENSE AND PROSECUTION OF ACTIONS; DUTY OF INSURED CLAIMANT TO COOPERATE.
(a) Upon written request by the insured and subject to the options contained in Section 6 of these Conditions and Stipulations, the Company, at its own cost and without unreasonable delay, shall provide for the defense of an insured in litigation in which any third party asserts a claim adverse to the title or interest as insured, but only as to those stated causes of action alleging a defect, lien or encumbrance or other matter insured against by this policy. The Company shall have the right to select counsel of its choice (subject to the right of the insured to object for reasonable cause) to represent the insured as to those stated causes of action and shall not be liable for and will not pay the fees of any other counsel. The Company will not pay any fees, costs or expenses incurred by the insured in the defense of those causes of action which allege matters not insured against by this policy.
(b) The Company shall have the right, at its own cost, to institute and prosecute any action or proceeding or to do any other act which in its opinion may be necessary or desirable to establish the title to the estate or interest, as insured, or to prevent or reduce loss or damage to the insured. The Company may take any appropriate action under the terms of this policy, whether or not it shall be liable hereunder, and shall not thereby concede liability or waive any provision of this policy. If the Company shall exercise its rights under this paragraph, it shall do so diligently.
(c) Whenever the Company shall have brought an action or interposed a defense as required or permitted by the provisions of this policy, the Company may pursue any litigation to final determination by a court of competent jurisdiction and expressly reserves the right, in its sole discretion, to appeal from any adverse judgment or order.
(d) In all cases where this policy permits or requires the Company to prosecute or provide for the defense of any action or proceeding, the insured shall secure to the Company the right to so prosecute or provide defense in the action or proceeding, and all appeals therein, and permit the Company to use, at its option, the name of the insured for this purpose. Whenever requested by the Company, the insured, at the Company's expense, shall give the Company all reasonable aid (i) in any action or proceeding, securing evidence, obtaining witnesses, prosecuting or defending the action or proceeding, or effecting settlement, and (ii) in any other lawful act which in the opinion of the Company may be necessary or desirable to establish the title to the estate or interest as insured. If the Company is prejudiced by the failure of the insured to furnish the required cooperation, the Company's obligations to the insured under the policy shall terminate, including any liability or obligation to defend, prosecute, or continue any litigation, with regard to the matter or matters requiring such cooperation.

5. PROOF OF LOSS OR DAMAGE.
In addition to and after the notices required under Section 3 of these Conditions and Stipulations have been provided the Company, a proof of loss or damage signed and sworn to by the insured claimant shall be furnished to the Company within 90 days after the insured claimant shall ascertain the facts giving rise to the loss or damage. The proof of loss or damage shall describe the defect in, or lien or encumbrance on the title, or other matter insured against by this policy which constitutes the basis of loss or damage and shall state, to the extent possible, the basis of calculating the amount of the loss or damage. If the Company is prejudiced by the failure of the insured claimant to provide the required proof of loss or damage, the Company's obligations to the insured under the policy shall terminate, including any liability or obligation to defend, prosecute, or continue any litigation, with regard to the matter or matters requiring such proof of loss or damage.
In addition, the insured claimant may reasonably be required to submit to examination under oath by any authorized representative of the Company and shall produce for examination, inspection and copying, at such reasonable times and places as may be designated by any authorized representative of the Company, all records, books, ledgers, checks, correspondence and memoranda, whether bearing a date before or after Date of Policy, which reasonably pertain to the loss or damage. Further, if requested by any authorized representative of the Company, the insured claimant shall grant its permission, in writing, for any authorized representative of the Company to examine, inspect and copy all records, books, ledgers, checks, correspondence and memoranda in the custody or control of a third party, which reasonably pertain to the loss or damage. All information designated as confidential by the insured claimant provided to the Company pursuant to this Section shall not be disclosed to others unless, in the reasonable judgment of the Company, it is necessary in the administration of the claim. Failure of the insured claimant to submit for examination under oath, produce other reasonably requested information or grant permission to secure reasonably necessary information from third parties as

required in this paragraph shall terminate any liability of the Company under this policy as to that claim.

6. OPTIONS TO PAY OR OTHERWISE SETTLE CLAIMS; TERMINATION OF LIABILITY.
In case of a claim under this policy, the Company shall have the following additional options:

(a) To Pay or Tender Payment of the Amount of Insurance.
(i) To pay or tender payment of the amount of insurance under this policy together with any costs, attorneys' fees and expenses incurred by the insured claimant, which were authorized by the Company, up to the time of payment or tender of payment and which the Company is obligated to pay.
(ii) Upon the exercise by the Company of this option, all liability and obligations to the insured under this policy, other than to make the payment required, shall terminate, including any liability or obligation to defend, prosecute, or continue any litigation.

(b) To Pay or Otherwise Settle With Parties Other than the Insured or With the Insured Claimant.
(i) to pay or otherwise settle with other parties for or in the name of an insured claimant any claim insured against under this policy, together with any costs, attorneys' fees and expenses incurred by the insured claimant which were authorized by the Company up to the time of payment and which the Company is obligated to pay; or
(ii) to pay or otherwise settle with the insured claimant the loss or damage provided for under this policy, together with any costs, attorneys' fees and expenses incurred by the insured claimant which were authorized by the Company up to the time of payment and which the Company is obligated to pay.
Upon the exercise by the Company of either of the options provided for in paragraphs (b)(i) or (ii), the Company's obligations to the insured under this policy for the claimed loss or damage, other than the payments required to be made, shall terminate, including any liability or obligation to defend, prosecute or continue any litigation.

7. DETERMINATION, EXTENT OF LIABILITY AND COINSURANCE.
This policy is a contract of indemnity against actual monetary loss or damage sustained or incurred by the insured claimant who has suffered loss or damage by reason of matters insured against by this policy and only to the extent herein described.
(a) The liability of the Company under this policy shall not exceed the least of:
(i) the Amount of Insurance stated in Schedule A; or,
(ii) the difference between the value of the insured estate or interest as insured and the value of the insured estate or interest subject to the defect, lien or encumbrance insured against by this policy.
(b) In the event the Amount of Insurance stated in Schedule A at the Date of Policy is less than 80 percent of the value of the insured estate or interest or the full consideration paid for the land, whichever is less, or if subsequent to the Date of Policy an improvement is erected on the land which increases the value of the insured estate or interest by at least 20 percent over the Amount of Insurance stated in Schedule A, then this Policy is subject to the following:
(i) where no subsequent improvement has been made, as to any partial loss, the Company shall only pay the loss pro rata in the proportion that the amount of insurance at Date of Policy bears to the total value of the insured estate or interest at Date of Policy; or
(ii) where a subsequent improvement has been made, as to any partial loss, the Company shall only pay the loss pro rata in the proportion that 120 percent of the Amount of Insurance stated in Schedule A bears to the sum of the Amount of Insurance stated in Schedule A and the amount expended for the improvement.
The provisions of this paragraph shall not apply to costs, attorneys' fees and expenses for which the Company is liable under this policy, and shall only apply to that portion of any loss which exceeds, in the aggregate, 10 percent of the Amount of Insurance stated in Schedule A.
(c) The Company will pay only those costs, attorneys' fees and expenses incurred in accordance with Section 4 of these Conditions and Stipulations.

8. APPORTIONMENT.
If the land described in Schedule [A][C] consists of two or more parcels which are not used as a single site, and a loss is established affecting one or more of the parcels but not all, the loss shall be computed and settled on a pro rata basis as if the amount of insurance under this policy was divided pro rata as to the value on Date of Policy of each separate parcel to the whole, exclusive of any improvements made subsequent to Date of Policy, unless a liability or value has otherwise been agreed upon as to each parcel by the Company and the insured at the time of the issuance of this policy and shown by an express statement or by an endorsement attached to this policy.

9. LIMITATION OF LIABILITY.
(a) If the Company establishes the title, or removes the alleged defect, lien or encumbrance, or cures the lack of a right of access to or from the land, or cures the claim of unmarketability of title, all as insured, in a reasonably diligent manner by any method, including litigation and the completion of any appeals therefrom, it shall have fully performed its obligations with respect to that matter and shall not be liable for any loss or damage caused thereby.
(b) In the event of any litigation, including litigation by the Company or with the Company's consent, the Company shall have no liability for loss or damage until there has been a final determination by a court of competent jurisdiction, and disposition of all appeals therefrom, adverse to the title as insured.
(c) The Company shall not be liable for loss or damage to any insured for liability voluntarily assumed by the insured in settling any claim or suit without the prior written consent of the Company.

10. REDUCTION OF INSURANCE; REDUCTION OR TERMINATION OF LIABILITY.
All payments under this policy, except payments made for costs, attorneys' fees and expenses, shall reduce the amount of the insurance pro tanto.

11. LIABILITY NON-CUMULATIVE.
It is expressly understood that the amount of insurance under this policy shall be reduced by any amount the Company may pay under any policy insuring a mortgage to which exception is taken in Schedule B or to which the insured has agreed, assumed, or taken subject, or which is hereafter executed by an insured and which is a charge or lien on the estate or interest described or referred to in Schedule A, and the amount so paid shall be deemed a payment under this policy to the insured owner.

12. PAYMENT OF LOSS.
(a) No payment shall be made without producing this policy for endorsement of the payment unless the policy has been lost or destroyed, in which case proof of loss or destruction shall be furnished to the satisfaction of the Company.
(b) When liability and the extent of loss or damage has been definitely fixed in accordance with these Conditions and Stipulations, the loss or damage shall be payable within 30 days thereafter.

13. SUBROGATION UPON PAYMENT OR SETTLEMENT.
(a) The Company's Right of Subrogation.
Whenever the Company shall have settled and paid a claim under this policy, all right of subrogation shall vest in the Company unaffected by any act of the insured claimant. The Company shall be subrogated to and be entitled to all rights and remedies which the insured claimant would have had against any person or property in respect to the claim had this policy not been issued. If requested by the Company, the insured claimant shall transfer to the Company all rights and remedies against any person or property necessary in order to perfect this right of subrogation. The insured claimant shall permit the Company to sue, compromise or settle in the name of the insured claimant and to use the name of the insured claimant in any transaction or litigation involving these rights or remedies.
If a payment on account of a claim does not fully cover the loss of the insured claimant, the Company shall be subrogated to these rights and remedies in the proportion which the Company's payment bears to the whole amount of the loss.
If loss should result from any act of the insured claimant, as stated above, that act shall not void this policy, but the Company, in that event, shall be required to pay only that part of any losses insured against by this policy which shall exceed the amount, if any, lost to the Company by reason of the impairment by the insured claimant of the Company's right of subrogation.
(b) The Company's Rights Against Non-insured Obligors.
The Company's right of subrogation against non-insured obligors shall exist and shall include, without limitation, the rights of the insured to indemnities, guaranties, other policies of insurance or bonds, notwithstanding any terms or conditions contained in those instruments which provide for subrogation rights by reason of this policy.

14. ARBITRATION.
Unless prohibited by applicable law, either the Company or the insured may demand arbitration pursuant to the Title Insurance Arbitration Rules of the American Arbitration Association. Arbitrable matters may include, but are not limited to, any controversy or claim between the Company and the insured arising out of or relating to this policy, any service of the Company in connection with its issuance or the breach of a policy provision or other obligation. All arbitrable matters when the Amount of Insurance is $1,000,000 or less shall be arbitrated at the option of either the Company or the insured. All arbitrable matters when the Amount of Insurance is in excess of $1,000,000 shall be arbitrated only when agreed to by both the Company and the insured. Arbitration pursuant to this policy and under the Rules in effect on the date the demand for arbitration is made or, at the option of the insured, the Rules in effect at Date of Policy shall be binding upon the parties. The award may include attorneys' fees only if the laws of the state in which the land is located permit a court to award attorneys' fees to a prevailing party. Judgment upon the award rendered by the Arbitrator(s) may be entered in any court having jurisdiction thereof.
The law of the situs of the land shall apply to an arbitration under the Title Insurance Arbitration Rules.
A copy of the Rules may be obtained from the Company upon request.

15. LIABILITY LIMITED TO THIS POLICY; POLICY ENTIRE CONTRACT.
(a) This policy together with all endorsements, if any, attached hereto by the Company is the entire policy and contract between the insured and the Company. In interpreting any provision of this policy, this policy shall be construed as a whole.
(b) Any claim of loss or damage, whether or not based on negligence, and which arises out of the status of the title to the estate or interest covered hereby or by any action asserting such claim, shall be restricted to this policy.
(c) No amendment of or endorsement to this policy can be made except by a writing endorsed hereon or attached hereto signed by either the President, a Vice President, the Secretary, an Assistant Secretary, or validating officer or authorized signatory of the Company.

16. SEVERABILITY.
In the event any provision of the policy is held invalid or unenforceable under applicable law, the policy shall be deemed not to include that provision and all other provisions shall remain in full force and effect.

17. NOTICES, WHERE SENT.
All notices required to be given the Company and any statement in writing required to be furnished the Company shall include the number of this policy and shall be addressed to the Company at the issuing office or to:
Chicago title Insurance Company
Claims Department
171 North Clark Street
Chicago, Illinois 60601-3294

the United States and the coverage was sometimes poor. As a result, secondary lenders developed, jointly with the American Land Title Association, a uniform mortgagee's policy with extended coverage. Originally it was available only for lenders, but today a modified extended coverage policy can also be issued in owner's, purchaser's and lessee's forms.

The ALTA extended coverage mortgagee's policy insures
- That the title is vested as stated in the policy
- That there are no defects in, or liens on, the title
- Against lack of a right of access
- Against the title not being marketable
- Against the unenforceability of the mortgage, including the unenforceability of any assignment of it, listed in the policy, unless unenforceable due to violation of usury or consumer protection or disclosure law
- Against any other encumbrance having priority
- Against construction liens

Exclusions from coverage include
- Government exercise of police power or eminent domain, including environmental protection laws
- Defects of which the insured had actual notice

Note that the number of issues covered is considerably greater under the ALTA extended coverage policy than under either standard form policy. At the same time, the exclusions are far fewer. Additional endorsements are also available for a small additional charge.

In addition to the standard and extended coverage ALTA policies, title insurance companies issue various endorsements upon request. One commonly encountered in Washington is the **homeowner's endorsement**, which gives coverage for existing violation of restrictive covenants, damages caused by encroachments, and a few other matters. Sometimes a policy with this endorsement is referred to as a **homeowner's policy**, although it is really just an endorsement on a standard form policy.

Real estate agents sometimes refer to the ALTA mortgagee's extended coverage policy as an "ALTA" policy, without stipulating "mortgagee's extended coverage." The buyer may be receiving an ALTA standard form owner's policy in the same transaction, which is commonly just referred to as the "standard form" policy. In other words, when real estate agents speak of an "ALTA" policy they mean "ALTA mortgagee's extended coverage" and when they say "standard form" they mean either the ALTA owner's or ALTA purchaser's standard form policy.

While it is customary for the seller to pay the premium for the owner's or purchaser's policy, there is no law requiring the premium to be paid by the seller. Similarly, the borrower is the party who is normally responsible for the mortgagee's policy, but the parties can negotiate otherwise if they desire. Washington real estate agents should be aware that these customs also prevail in most of the rest of the western United States, but not everywhere. In some areas it is customary for the buyer to pay for the owner's policy, and in other areas the normal practice is for the buyer and the seller to split the cost. Clients moving to this area may be surprised by our customs.

Preliminary title reports

A problem occurs in the closing of real estate transactions. The buyer does not want the cash to be released to the seller without first receiving the title insurance policy. The seller, on the other hand, does not want the deed recorded without getting the cash. The title insurance policy insures that the buyer has good title, so it cannot be issued until the seller's deed to the buyer has been recorded. This creates an impasse with no apparent solution.

The remedy lies in the **preliminary title report**, or **preliminary title commitment** sometimes just called a **title report**, or in common jargon, a "PTR" or "prelim." The preliminary title report is issued prior to closing and is a summary of what the title insurance company found when searching the seller's title. It will show the seller in title, and will report all encumbrances, even those which the seller plans to pay off on closing. The preliminary title report is not insurance and does not create any liability on the part of the company.

When the buyer and the seller sign an earnest money (purchase and sale) agreement, there is typically a clause where the buyer agrees to accept the preliminary title report as conclusive evidence of the seller's title and to close the transaction if the preliminary title report shows the seller's title to be as the seller represented it. This allows the transaction to close, the seller can receive the cash and the seller's deed can be recorded, all without the actual policy being issued. A short time after closing the title insurance company will issue the owner's or purchaser's policy.

Drafting documents and unauthorized practice of law

Real estate agents should take special note of the role of the attorney in drafting documents used in a real estate transaction. Obviously, real estate agents should be sure their clients see their attorneys when a legal question comes up. Trying to give legal advice yourself might result in being guilty of **unauthorized practice of law**, not to mention the legal liability if you are wrong. It is unauthorized practice of law whether you charge a fee for the advice or not. Even selecting which form the client should use is giving legal advice. In Washington, unauthorized practice of law is a misdemeanor as well.

Nevertheless, you should remember that it is never unauthorized practice of law to draft documents to which you are a party personally. Of course, be sure the old adage does not apply – "when you represent yourself you have a fool for a client."

It is also not considered unauthorized practice of law for agents to fill in the blanks on attorney-prepared standard form earnest money agreements, provided no special fee is charged. And whenever you draft an earnest money agreement for your clients, the courts have made it clear that you will be held to the same standard of care as an attorney.

When it comes to land sales contracts, deeds, and other forms commonly used in real estate transaction, a real estate licensee cannot prepare them, but Washington law does allow them to be filled out by a **certified closing officer** of a title insurance company or escrow agency under the Limited Practice Rule of the Washington State Bar. The closing officer must pass an examination given by the Bar and can use only specific real estate forms prepared by the Bar. In addition, the certified closing officer cannot give legal advice about the forms and must make certain disclosures to the buyer and seller. Because of the Limited Practice Rule most ordinary transactions in Washington can be closed without an attorney.

KEY TERMS

The key to understanding any new field is the vocabulary used in that field. To maximize your comprehension of the material presented in this chapter, be sure you know the meaning and significance of the following terms. Remember that the majority of test questions primarily test knowledge of vocabulary.

Abstract and opinion

Abstract of title

Acceptance

Accession

Accretion

Acknowledgment

Actual notice

Adequate description of the premises

Adverse possession

After-acquired title

Alienation

Alluvium (or alluvion)

American Land Title Association

Avulsion

Bargain and sale deed

Bequest

Bill of sale

Bonafide purchaser

Certified closing officer

Chain of title

Chaining the title

Codicil

Color of title

Common-law dedication

Competent grantor

Consideration

Constructive notice

Continuous possession

Conveyance

Correction deed

Covenant

Covenant against encumbrances

Covenant of further assurance

Covenant of quiet enjoyment

Covenant of seizin

Covenant of title

Decedent

Dedication

Deed

Delivery

Devise

Devisee

Donation Land Claim

Exception

Exclusive possession

Extended form

Federal patent

For value

Foreclosure guaranty

Full warranty deed

General warranty deed

Grant

Grantee

Granting clause

Grantor

Habendum clause

Holographic will

Homeowner's endorsement

Homeowner's policy

Hostile

Idem sonans

Identifiable grantee

In good faith

In writing

Innocent purchaser

Inquiry notice

Insurable title

Intestate

Involuntary conveyances

Leasehold policy

Legacy

Legatee

Limited practice license

Link

Litigation guaranty

Marketable title

Memorandum

Mortgagee's policy

Notary public

Notice

Nuncupative will

Open and notorious

Owner's policy

Patent

Personal representative

Preliminary title report (commitment)

Probate

Public record

Purchaser's policy

Quitclaim deed

Reformation deed

Reservation

Signature of the grantor(s)

Special warranty deed

Standard form policy

Statutory dedications

Statutory form deeds

Tacking

Testate

Title certificate

Title plant

Title report

Title search

Tract index

Trustee's sale guaranty

Unauthorized practice of law

Voluntary conveyances

Warranty deed

Without notice of defect

Words of conveyance

Chapter

6

Legal descriptions

A**N ESSENTIAL ELEMENT** of any contract is a clear meeting of the minds of the contracting parties. If the parties to a transaction have differing ideas as to the boundaries and location of a property, then the contract could well be unenforceable. And if the failure to agree was caused by the negligence of the agent, then the agent could be held liable for damages as well. Fortunately, getting an accurate, enforceable legal description of the property is usually a simple matter. If the owner does not have an accurate description of the property, you can generally get one free from the customer service department of any title insurance company.

To be adequate, a description of the property must describe the property sufficiently that a disinterested third party could locate the property, find the boundaries of the property, and clearly segregate it from all other property. As a general rule, there is no requirement that any particular system for creating legal descriptions be used in an ordinary contract, although documents to be recorded in Washington must meet somewhat more stringent requirements as part of the recording statutes.

There are numerous ways to describe property adequately. Three of these are called **legal descriptions** because their methodology is considered to be part of the law. These include the **government** or **rectangular survey**, **metes and bounds**, and **lot and block** descriptions.

In addition, Washington has a **grid coordinate system**. The grid coordinate system is used by government agencies to describe very large tracts of land using computer programs. Since real estate agents rarely encounter it, its inclusion here is unnecessary. It is also not acceptable for use in documents to be recorded, so you are not likely to encounter it in real estate practice.

Real estate agents sometimes use other methods, such as giving constructive notice by referring to the description in a recorded deed. These methods may be adequate to meet the requirements of contract law, but are not considered legal descriptions. Real estate agents should also be aware that the law holds different standards for different types of contracts. An accurate, but informal, description may be acceptable in a listing agreement or month-to-month rental agreement, but might fail if used in a deed.

The Federal System of Rectangular Surveys

Although the oldest method of creating legal descriptions is by metes and bounds, all property in Washington (and most of the rest of the western United States) was originally surveyed by the government. These government surveys form the base from which all subsequent private surveys are made. Therefore, we must understand the government survey system before turning to other methods.

Prior to independence, the English colonies in America were surveyed by metes and bounds in much the same way that England had been surveyed. Metes and bounds is simply a description of the monuments and boundary lines for a property. But after the new United States government was formed, Congress looked westward. Lands lying west of the original thirteen colonies were called the "Wilderness." That these lands should be settled was inevitable, and to facilitate settlement, surveys were essential.

In 1785 Congress passed the first law for surveying this new territory. The initial part of the Wilderness to be surveyed was the eastern portion of what is now Ohio. Each time new areas were surveyed, the law was amended, with the result that the government surveys of Ohio were not done with exactly the same system as was used in the rest of the country. The final format was adopted in 1796, essentially the same format which would be used eventually in the Oregon Territory, part of which later became the State of Washington.

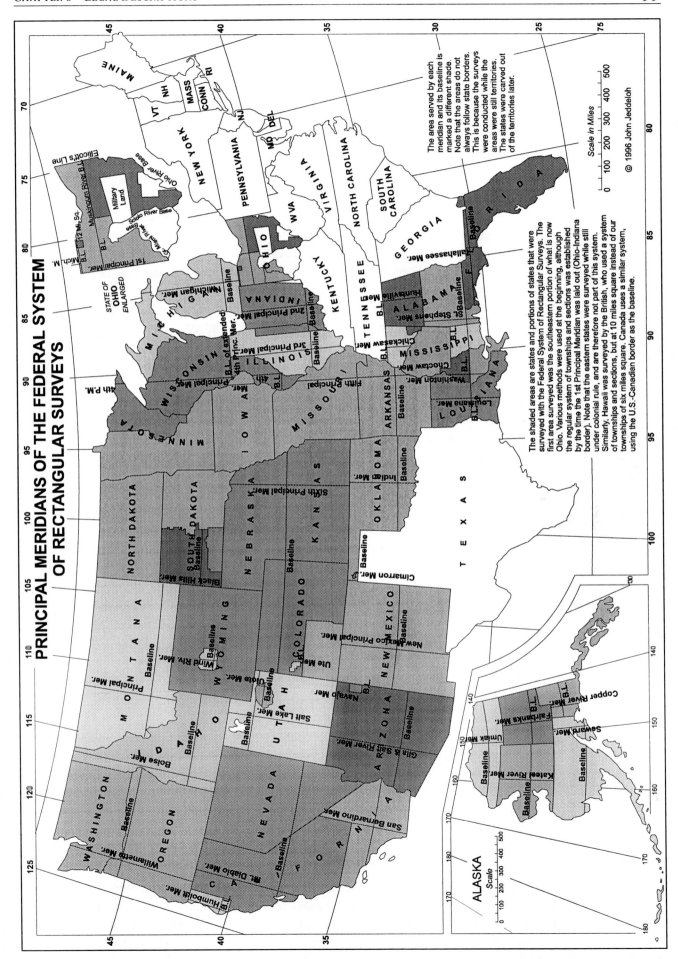

PRINCIPAL MERIDIANS OF THE FEDERAL SYSTEM OF RECTANGULAR SURVEYS

The area served by each meridian and its baseline is marked a different shade. Note that the areas do not always follow state borders. This is because the surveys were conducted while the areas were still territories. The states were carved out of the territories later.

Scale in Miles
0 100 200 300 400 500

© 1996 John Jeddeloh

The shaded areas are states and portions of states that were surveyed with the Federal System of Rectangular Surveys. The first area surveyed was the southeastern portion of what is now Ohio. Various methods were used at the beginning, although the regular system of townships and sections was established by the time the 1st Principal Meridian was laid out (Ohio-Indiana border). Note that the eastern states were surveyed while still under colonial rule, and are therefore not part of this system. Similarly, Hawaii was surveyed by the British, who used a system of townships and sections, but at 10 miles square instead of our townships of six miles square. Canada uses a similar system, using the U.S.-Canadian border as the baseline.

ALASKA
Scale
0 100 200 300 400 500

The official name of this system is the ***Federal System of Rectangular Surveys***. As you can see from the map of the United States on the preceding page, it covers several states east of the Mississippi and all western states (except Texas and Hawaii).

At the middle of the 1850s Washington and Oregon comprised the Oregon Territory. (Oregon split off in 1859 and became a separate state, at which time the remainder was renamed the Washington Territory, which was admitted to statehood in 1889.) The largest town in the early days of the Oregon Territory was Portland, itself not much more than a small settlement. However, exploration parties had traveled over the majority of the Oregon Territory, so the early surveyors were aware of the basic geography of the region. Of course, at that time no one had any idea that the Oregon Territory was to become two separate states, so the survey lines were established to cover the entire Oregon Territory. Because Portland was the largest settlement at the time the surveys were begun, it was decided to start surveying near Portland, moving out to the rest of the territory as settlers arrived and other areas became populated.

To start the surveys the government surveyors did the same as they had done for other new territories; that is, they began by establishing a starting point. For the Oregon Territory they wanted a point near Portland, and which would run through the thin shelf of land between Mt. Hood and the Columbia River in the east-west plane, and which would go through the central valleys in the north-south plane. They named this point the ***Willamette Stone***. It is located just outside what is now Portland city limits in the northwest corner of the city. After the beginning point was selected, a ***principal meridian*** (sometimes called a ***prime meridian***) was surveyed straight north and south through the beginning point. There are 31 such principal meridians throughout the United States, each with a unique name. Ours is called the ***Willamette Meridian***, and runs from the Willamette Stone north to Canada and south to the California border.

An east-west line, called the ***baseline*** was also surveyed for each territory surveyed. Our baseline runs from the Willamette Stone west to the ocean and east to the Idaho border. Thus the Willamette Meridian and its baseline formed the north-south and east-west coordinates from which all further surveys in Oregon and Washington would be made.

As you can see by looking at the map on the preceding page, all of Oregon and Washington (and only the states of Oregon and Washington) were surveyed from the Willamette Stone and its baseline. It is also interesting to note that all property in Washington, is north of the baseline.

Following the establishment of the Willamette Stone, the surveyors moved out to survey the rest of the Oregon Territory, using the same grid system which had been used previously in other territories. The drawing on the next page shows the Willamette Meridian and its baseline, and the Willamette Stone.

Referring to the drawing, notice that at a distance of 24 miles east and west the baseline is intersected by a major north-south line called a ***guide meridian***. The guide meridians are numbered consecutively, so the first ones shown in the drawing are the "First Guide Meridian East" and the "First Guide Meridian West." Guide meridians were laid out to make sure that the curvature of the earth was properly adjusted for.

Between each guide meridian you will find three additional north-south lines called ***rangelines***. The rangelines are six miles apart, except at the top where they converge due to the curvature of the earth.

In similar fashion, there are ***standard parallels***, also called ***correction lines***, laid out at distances of 24 miles north and south along the Willamette Meridian. The same as the guide meridians, their purpose was to ensure that the curvature of the earth was properly adjusted for. They are also numbered, the same as the guide meridians. The

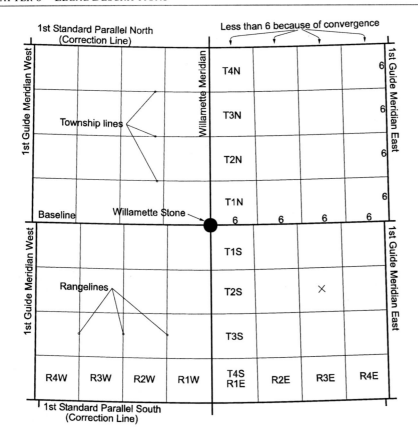

The Willamette Stone forms the point through which the baseline and Willamette Meridian were surveyed (the black dot in the center of the drawing). The baseline and parallels are continuous arcs, following the curvature of the earth. Guide meridians and rangelines were surveyed toward true north.

drawing shows the First Standard Parallel South and the First Standard Parallel North.

Just as there are three rangelines between each guide meridian, so there are three **township lines** between each standard parallel. Notice that this system creates a regular grid of large, more or less square blocks which are 24 miles on a side, each of which is further divided into 16 smaller squares. Each of the smaller squares is approximately six miles by six miles, and is called a **township**.

Townships are referred to by their distance north or south of the baseline and their distance east or west of the Willamette Meridian. In the drawing you will notice the first range of townships east of the Willamette Meridian has been labeled. The numbering to the north starts at T1N (read as "township one north"), and continues until you reach the Canadian border. To the south the number starts with T1S (read as "township one south") and continues until the California border. Each township line or standard parallel creates a **tier of townships**. In similar fashion the rangelines form **ranges** which are numbered consecutively east and west of the Willamette Meridian. In the drawing the first four to the east and west have been labeled.

By numbering the tiers of townships and the ranges we can identify any given township very easily. For example, locate the small × in the township which is the second township south of the baseline and third east of the Willamette Meridian. Since it is the second south and the third east, it would be referred to as "T2S, R3E, W.M." (read as "township two south, range three east of the Willamette Meridian"). It is customary to state the "township" first and the "range" second, followed by reference to the principal meridian. Notice also that "Willamette Meridian" is usually abbreviated "W.M."

Townships, in turn, are divided into smaller pieces called **sections**. (See the drawing on the next page.) Each township is more or less six miles on each side, so each township contains approximately 36 square miles (6 miles × 6 miles = 36 square miles). Therefore, we simply divide each township into 36 regular sections, each of which is approximately one square mile.

North boundary of a section is a township line, a standard parallel, or the baseline.

6	5	4	3	2	1
7	8	9	10	11	12
18	17	16	15	14	13
19	20	21	22	23	24
30	29	28	27	26	25
31	32	33	34	35	36

West boundary of a section is a rangeline, a guide meridian, or the principal meridian.

East boundary of a section is a rangeline, a guide meridian, or the principal meridian.

1 mile (each side)

1 mile   1 mile   1 mile   1 mile   1 mile   1 mile

South boundary of a section is a township line, a standard parallel, or the baseline.

Representation of a typical township, divided into 36 sections of more or less one square mile. Adjustment for the curvature of the earth and for accumulated errors were thrown into the northernmost and westernmost sections of each township, leaving as many full sections as possible.

So that we can identify any given section easily, sections are numbered consecutively 1 through 36. The numbering starts in the northeast corner and zigzags back and forth until the last section is found in the southeast corner of the township. Much has been written about the reason for this numbering system, all of which is speculation since the records of its creation have been lost. The section numbering system in the early Ohio surveys was different and this arrangement did not appear until 1796, although it has been used consistently ever since.

In order to describe a given square mile, it is only necessary to state the section number, followed by the township in which it is located and a reference to the principal meridian. For example, suppose the above drawing represents Township 2 South, Range 3 East of the Willamette Meridian (the township with the × in it on the previous drawing). Now suppose that Section 15 is for sale and you want to take the listing on it. You could describe it simply as "Section 15, T2S, R3E, W.M." Note that it is customary to state the section first, followed by the township, range, and principal meridian. (A good rule to remember is that you always state the smallest piece first, followed by successively larger pieces.)

At one square mile, a section is a lot of area, so sections are divided into even smaller pieces. See the drawing on the next page –

There are an unlimited number of ways this can be done, but there are certain rules which must be followed –

- The only fractions that you can use are quarters and halves. If you want to make one sixteenth, you have to say it as "a quarter of a quarter." If you want to make one-eighth, you have to say "a half of a quarter," and so on.
- You can have halves of halves or halves of quarters, but you cannot have quarters of halves. If there are any "one-half's" in the description, they have to come first.
- If you are describing a half of something, then the word "half" must be preceded by only one compass direction, e.g., "the S ½," "the W ½," and so on. You cannot use two compass directions with the fraction ½. Similarly, quarters must be preceded by two compass directions, e.g., "the SW ¼," "the NE ¼," and so on. You can never say "the SW ½" or "the S ¼."
- Commas are read "of the," or just "of." Semicolons are read "and the." If you mistake a semicolon for a comma or vice-versa, it could make a drastic difference in the amount of property being described.

A normal section is one mile on each side (5,280 feet)

2640'	1320'	1320'
NW ¼ 160 acres	W ½, NE ¼ 80 acres	E ½, NE ¼ 80 acres

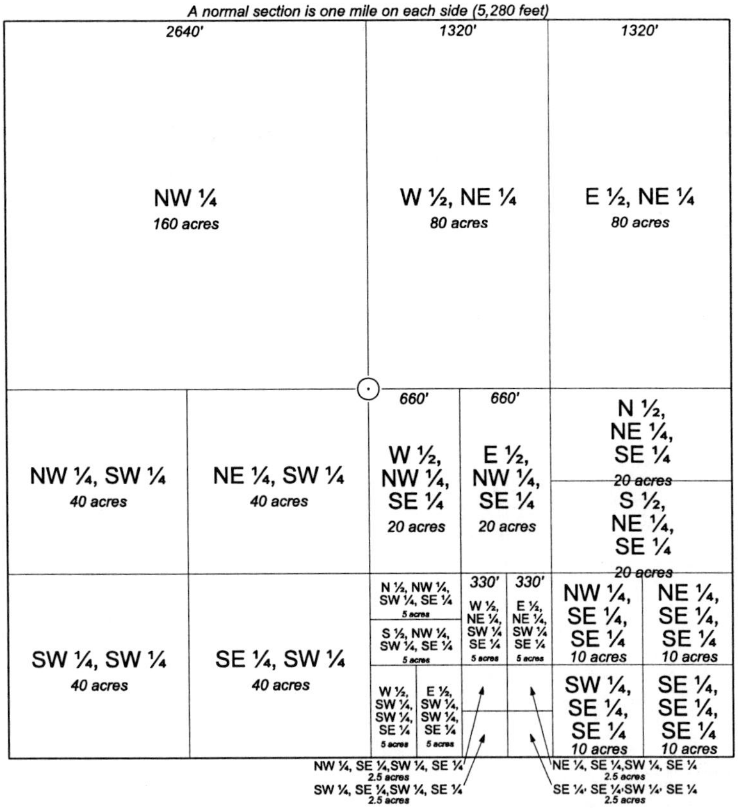

Drawing of a regular section containing 640 acres. A normal 40-acre parcel (quarter of a quarter section) is called a "lot." Most of Washington has been surveyed by the government surveyors down to the quarter section corners.

		660'	660'	N ½, NE ¼, SE ¼ — 20 acres
NW ¼, SW ¼ 40 acres	NE ¼, SW ¼ 40 acres	W ½, NW ¼, SE ¼ 20 acres	E ½, NW ¼, SE ¼ 20 acres	S ½, NE ¼, SE ¼ — 20 acres

		N ½, NW ¼, SW ¼, SE ¼ 5 acres	330' W ½, NE ¼, SW ¼, SE ¼ 5 acres	330' E ½, NE ¼, SW ¼, SE ¼ 5 acres	NW ¼, SE ¼, SE ¼ 10 acres	NE ¼, SE ¼, SE ¼ 10 acres
SW ¼, SW ¼ 40 acres	SE ¼, SW ¼ 40 acres	S ½, NW ¼, SW ¼, SE ¼ 5 acres				
		W ½, SW ¼, SW ¼, SE ¼ 5 acres	E ½, SW ¼, SW ¼, SE ¼ 5 acres		SW ¼, SE ¼, SE ¼ 10 acres	SE ¼, SE ¼, SE ¼ 10 acres

NW ¼, SE ¼,SW ¼, SE ¼ 2.5 acres
SW ¼, SE ¼,SW ¼, SE ¼ 2.5 acres
NE ¼, SE ¼,SW ¼, SE ¼ 2.5 acres
SE ¼, SE ¼,SW ¼, SE ¼ 2.5 acres

As a further tip, if you are having difficulty interpreting a complex government survey legal description, try working the description backwards from the word "Section" toward the front. Written descriptions always place the smallest piece at the beginning, but in locating a property it is sometimes easier to work from the largest piece down to the smallest. For example, consider the description "the S ½, NE ¼, SW ¼, NW ¼, Section 27, T21N, R3E, W.M." The first piece immediately before the word "Section" is the NW ¼, so put your finger on the NW ¼ of a section. The next piece is the SW ¼, so find the SW ¼ of the piece your finger is on. Repeat the process until you get it down to the smallest piece in the description.

Notice the dimensions on the drawing on the preceding page. A normal section is exactly one mile square (5,280 feet on a side). Therefore, a regular quarter section will be one-half mile (2,640 feet) on a side, a quarter of a quarter section will be one-quarter mile (1,320 feet), and so on.

A regular section is 640 acres. Real estate agents find it useful to remember the areas of certain configurations. For example, a quarter section is 160 acres, a quarter of a quarter is 40 acres, and so on. By knowing the dimensions of standard parcels you can save yourself a lot of time in making calculations.

In the original surveys the survey lines would run into lakes, rivers and the ocean. In addition, some sections were less than full size because of the curvature of the earth. The parcels left over are commonly called *fractional sections*. In fractional sections the odd portion would be taken up in the "quarter-quarters" (40 acre parcels) along the north and west of the section. A quarter of a quarter is commonly referred to as a "lot" in early surveys. It was not uncommon for title to these odd parcels to be vested in the state or federal government, so these odd quarter-quarters are also sometimes called *government lots*.

You may also find references to a *school section*. In most of the midwest the federal government would reserve section 16 of each township and convey it to a local school district once the area was settled and a local government was formed. The local school district would typically locate the schoolhouse in a corner of this section, since it is centrally located in the township, and sell or rent out the rest of the section as a source of operating funds.

Metes and bounds surveys

Metes and bounds is the oldest and most direct method for describing land. To survey by metes and bounds a surveyor just describes the boundaries of the property by stating the distance and direction from one corner to the next. The drawing below is an example of a typical simple metes and bounds description.

Example of a metes and bounds description for a property which lies slightly askew of true compass directions. It is customary, although not required, to survey the distances counterclockwise around the parcel. For practice, read the written description in the lower left corner and trace the boundaries in the drawing as you do so. Real estate agents frequently have to trace the boundaries to make sure the written description matches the map of the property.

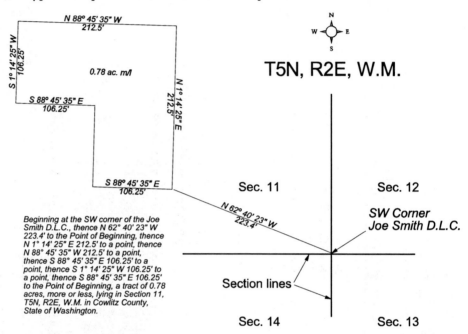

Beginning at the SW corner of the Joe Smith D.L.C., thence N 62° 40' 23" W 223.4' to the Point of Beginning, thence N 1° 14' 25" E 212.5' to a point, thence N 88° 45' 35" W 212.5' to a point, thence S 88° 45' 35" E 106.25' to a point, thence S 1° 14' 25" W 106.25' to a point, thence S 88° 45' 35" E 106.25' to the Point of Beginning, a tract of 0.78 acres, more or less, lying in Section 11, T5N, R2E, W.M. in Cowlitz County, State of Washington.

Notice that the description of the property above actually starts in the corner of the section. In the description above it is referred to as the "SW Corner of the Joe Smith D.L.C." The Donation Land Law of 1850 allowed each married settler to claim 640 acres (one section), or a half-section if single. The claims were called **donation land claims**. Therefore a section corner is probably also the corner of some early settler's donation land claim. Since these land claims were recorded, it is common practice to refer to the section corner by reference to the corner of the donation land claim, although reference to the section corner is also commonly encountered. The term "donation land claim" is usually abbreviated "D.L.C."

In describing a property by metes and bounds, a surveyor frequently starts the survey at some point other than the boundary of the property. The drawing of a metes and bounds description above is a typical example of this. The description of the property itself starts at a point called the **point of beginning**, frequently abbreviated just "POB." Whenever you read the phrase "point of beginning" in a metes and bounds description, it means that you are now reading the description of the actual property boundaries. Everything before the words "point of beginning" was just a reference to where the land lies on the earth. However, occasionally a survey will use the term "point of beginning" for a starting point outside the property, and then **true point of beginning** for the point where the property actually starts.

Direction is given in **quadrant bearings**. The drawing on the next page shows a circle divided into four quadrants of 90° each. To describe any direction, start in the center of the circle and draw an imaginary line through the edge of the circle in the direction of travel. For example, direction *A* in the drawing below runs from the center of the circle through the edge of the circle at exactly 73°, so it is written "N 73° W" (read as "north 73 degrees west"). Similarly, direction *B* is "N 45° E" because it is north, deflected 45 degrees toward the east. Direction *C* travels south from the center, deflected 24° toward the east, so it is "S 24° E."

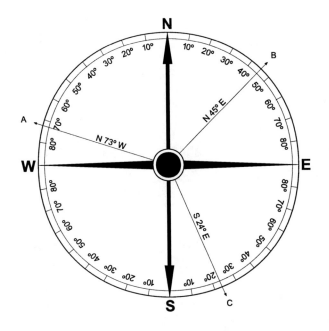

Circle showing the four quadrants of 90 degrees each. Each degree is divided into 60' (minutes) and each minute is divided into 60" (seconds). By using degrees, minutes and seconds surveyors can pinpoint direction very accurately.

All bearings start with either north or south, followed by the number of degrees of deflection toward the east or west. When the direction is absolutely north, south, east or west, we just say the direction without any number of degrees of deflection. That is, "North" is the same as saying "North 00° East (or West), so we just say "North."

In the real world, surveyors divide each degree into 60 minutes and each minute into 60 seconds. Thus, a direction stated as "N 23° 29' 15" W" would be about midway between 23° and 24°. Using degrees, minutes and seconds allows surveyors to state a direction with great precision. Notice that there can never be a quadrant bearing greater than 89° 59' 59". One more second of arc would be just "East" or "West."

Real estate agents find it is useful to understand quadrant bearings because it helps them locate property. For example, if you were reading a legal description which contained the direction "S 88° 45' 22" E," it would be helpful to know that this describes a direction which is almost due east. (Use the drawing of quadrant bearings above to prove that to yourself.) Thus, if you were out showing a property and one of the compass directions in the description said "S 88° 45' 22" E," you should be looking for a boundary fence that is running more or less east–west, not north–south.

In the past, surveyors would sometimes describe a compass direction by *azimuth bearing*. Azimuth bearings are the same as quadrant bearings except that the circle is not divided into quadrants. Instead, north is 0°, east is 90°, south is 180° and west is 270°. The circle is just continuously numbered with degrees starting with north (0°) through 359° 59' 59". A quadrant bearing of S 1° W would be stated as Azimuth Bearing 181°.

Descriptions by recorded plat

When a subdivision is created, Washington law requires the developer to record a ***plat map*** showing how the land has been divided. The plat map must be drawn by a surveyor and must meet statutory drafting standards. An example of an actual plat map is reproduced on the following pages (Tiffany Park – 3).

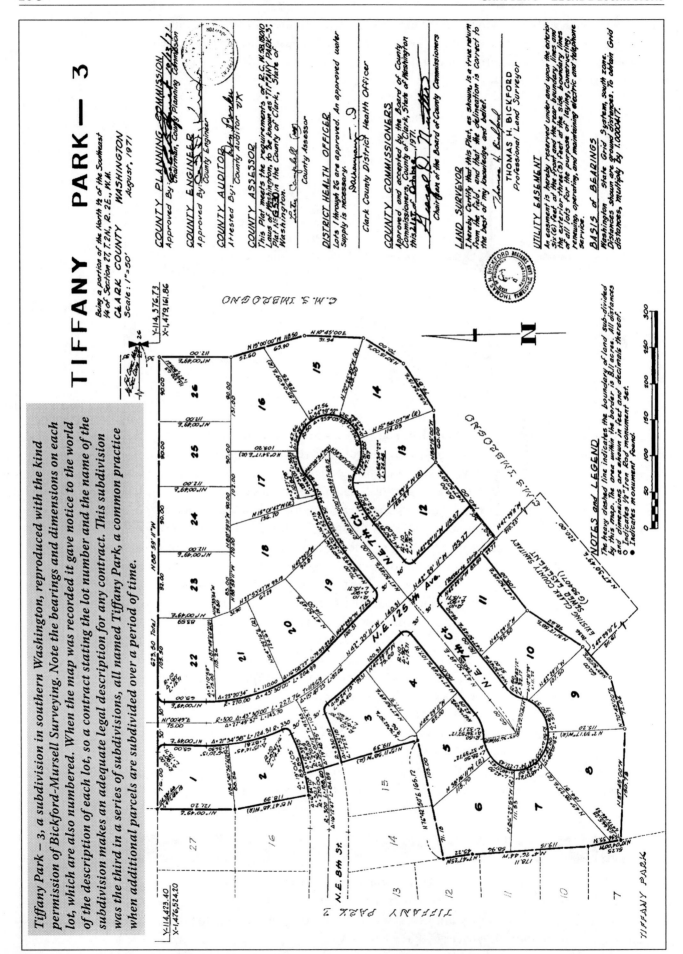

Tiffany Park – 3, a subdivision in southern Washington, reproduced with the kind permission of Bickford-Mursell Surveying. Note the bearings and dimensions on each lot, which are also numbered. When the map was recorded it gave notice to the world of the description of each lot, so a contract stating the lot number and the name of the subdivision makes an adequate legal description for any contract. This subdivision was the third in a series of subdivisions, all named Tiffany Park, a common practice when additional parcels are subdivided over a period of time.

To record a subdivision plat map, the subdivision must be given a unique name, not used on any other subdivision in the county. Each lot must be numbered or otherwise given a unique designation. Of course, since the plat map was drawn by metes and bounds, all the distances and bearings of each lot will be shown. In fact, anyone who was looking at the map would know the dimensions of each lot. And since the map is recorded, the result is that we can now legally refer to any given lot by the designation on the map. In other words, if you wanted to sell the lot on the northernmost corner of N.E. 7th Court and N.E. 125th Avenue, you could describe it in your documents as "Lot 19, Tiffany Park – 3, Clark County, Washington." This description will be legally enforceable because the world was given constructive notice of the dimensions and location of the lot when the plat map was recorded (for further discussion of notice and recording see Chapter 5).

We call such a description a **lot and block** legal description, or sometimes a description by **recorded plat**. Notice that the lots in Tiffany Park – 3 are numbered 1 to 26. Most subdivisions are considerably larger, so it is customary to divide the subdivision into blocks, and then divide the blocks into lots (hence "lot and block" legal description). But there is no legal requirement to create blocks and divide the blocks into lots. And it is also possible to use other nomenclature, such as "tracts," "divisions," "parcels" and the like. The following examples will give you a feel for how lot and block descriptions are used.

"Lot 8, Block 12, Gray's Addition to the City of Klickitat, Idaho County, Washington"

"Tract 2, Division 3, The King Ranch, Evergreen County, Washington"

"Parcel 3, Olympic Heights Addition to the City of Polk, Everett County, Washington"

As you can see, lot and block legal descriptions are simple and easy to use. Typically, you will find that large tracts of land, such as ranches, timberland, and the like, will be described with government survey descriptions. Suburban land which was not part of a formal subdivision is more commonly described by metes and bounds. And the more populated the area, the more likely the land will be described by lot and block.

Other ways to describe real estate

Assessor's property tax numbers – Metes and bounds descriptions, as we have seen, tend to be lengthy and difficult to copy accurately. This is a problem not only for real estate agents, but also for the property tax assessor. To avoid having to include lengthy legal descriptions on tax bills, the tax assessor in some counties creates large maps of the county which are recorded. The assessor assigns a property tax number (or other description) to a parcel that has a long legal description and marks it on the map. Along with the map the assessor records a list of the original legal descriptions and the descriptions assigned on the map. The maps and the lists are part of the public records, so everyone has constructive notice of the dimensions and location of the properties on them. It has become common practice to use the assessor's description for parcels in private contracts.

Reference legal descriptions –Real estate agents occasionally make use of a previously recorded document as a reference for a legal description. For example, if you take a listing, the seller's deed is recorded, and you know the deed is an excellent source of an accurate description of the property. Every recorded document gives constructive notice of its contents, so you could create an enforceable description of the property in your listing or earnest money agreement just by making reference to the seller's recorded deed and where it is recorded. Reference descriptions in this fashion are not acceptable for the final closing documents which are going to be recorded, such as deeds and mortgages, but they are adequate to meet the test of contract law for listing and earnest money agreements.

Street addresses – Street addresses should be used only when no alternative is available. There is no way to tell the dimensions of the land or its location on the surface of the earth from a street address. Nevertheless, real estate agents sometimes use addresses when there is no other choice. If you use a street address you should consider that the contract is not legally enforceable until you have the parties sign an addendum clarifying the legal description. An exception might be an informal contract such as a month-to-month rental agreement. Remember, if you create a document that is not legally enforceable, and as a result a client is damaged, you could be held liable for the client's loss.

Air rights – When air rights are created it becomes necessary to describe a volume of space in three dimensions, using not just the surface boundaries, but elevation as well. Just as land surveys require an anchor point, elevations also need a reference. The base reference point for elevations is called a *datum*. In Washington it is generally mean sea level. Based on the datum in use in the area additional bench marks are created. A *bench mark* is typically a round brass marker set into a sidewalk or other permanent public fixture. Each bench mark indicates its elevation based on the datum, so surveyors can use it as a point of reference.

Personal property – Personal property is quite commonly included with the sale of real estate. Describing the personal property properly is frequently overlooked, even by experienced agents. To make sure that you will not have to spend your commission buying a new range or refrigerator for the buyer, be sure to identify all personal property sufficiently so the seller cannot switch one item for another of lesser quality or remove the item altogether.

Handy equivalents to remember

One section	=	One mile square*
	=	One square mile*
	=	640 acres
One acre	=	43,560 square feet
	=	208.71 feet square
One mile	=	5,280 feet
One township	=	36 sections
	=	6 miles square*
One hectare	=	10,000 square meters
	=	2.47 acres

*Note that "miles square" means "miles on a side," so "two miles square" is a square whose sides are two miles long and which contains four square miles. The expression "two square miles" describes a property (of any shape) which contains two square miles, and is not at all the same thing as "two miles square."

One chain contains 100 links, or four rods, and is equal to 66 feet. A rod is 16½ feet. Real estate agents today rarely encounter rods, chains and links.

🔑 KEY TERMS

The key to understanding any new field is the vocabulary used in that field. To maximize your comprehension of the material presented in this chapter, be sure you know the meaning and significance of the following terms. Remember that the majority of test questions primarily test knowledge of vocabulary.

Azimuth bearing

Baseline

Bench mark

Correction line

Datum

Donation land claim

Federal System of Rectangular Surveys

Fractional section

Government survey

Government lot

Grid coordinate system

Guide meridian

Legal description

Lot and block

Metes and bounds

Plat map

Point of beginning

Prime meridian

Principal meridian

Quadrant bearing

Range

Rangeline

Recorded plat

Rectangular survey

School section

Section

Standard parallel

Tax lot number

Tier of townships

Township

Township line

True point of beginning

Willamette Meridian

Willamette Stone

Chapter

7

Condominiums and cooperatives

IN WESTERN CIVILIZATION, the condominium form of ownership is known to have been used at least as far back as ancient Rome. Of course, today's condominium and cooperative developments are governed by laws and regulations which are vastly more sophisticated than early Roman law. Nevertheless, the basic concept remains the same – ownership of your own unit, while sharing the use and expense of the common areas.

The underlying legal concept of a **condominium** today is relatively simple. Each owner owns his or her own unit, and owns the surrounding common areas as a tenant in common with the other unit owners. The percentage of interest in the common areas is usually apportioned according to the value of each unit, so the owners of larger units have a larger share than the owners of smaller units, and vice-versa.

Note that the tenancy in common gives each owner the same undivided right of possession to the common areas, regardless of the percentage interest. Therefore, the amount of interest in the common elements would seem to be unimportant. However, it is normal to apportion common expenses, profits and occasionally voting privileges according to the percentage of interest in the common elements.

Each condominium development must have a **unit owners' association**. In the case of a residential condominium development, the association is commonly referred to as a **homeowners' association**. Of course, condominiums can be created for any type of property – including offices, industrial parks, recreation property, mobile home parks – the list of possibilities is endless. The association is run by board members who are elected by the unit owners. The main function of the association is to manage and maintain the common areas, although it may have other duties as well. To cover the cost of maintenance and other expenses, the association has the right to levy assessments against each unit.

Many times condominiums are built on leased land. Since most buyers need financing, a buyer will have to give the lender a mortgage on the leasehold. While leasehold mortgages are common, a problem will arise if the lessor should evict the unit owner. Eviction extinguishes the leasehold, and thereby the leasehold mortgage as well. This would leave the lender without collateral for the debt.

Lenders have several ways to protect themselves from this situation. The most common solution is to insist that the lessor subordinate the lease to the mortgage. This will allow the mortgage to be senior to the lease, even though recorded later. Then, if the lessor evicts a tenant, the lessor must take the unit back subject to the mortgage. It is common to find such a subordination clause in the master lease.

The Washington Condominium Act

The **Washington Condominium Act** (RCW Chapter 64.34) has been created to answer the many questions involved in the creation and operation of condominiums. The Act also contains regulations to protect the public from fraud, deceit and misrepresentation in the sale of condominiums. The Washington Condominium Act was enacted in 1989 as a replacement for the original condominium law, the **Horizontal Property Regimes Act** (RCW Chapter 64.32). The Condominium Act applies to all condominiums created after July 1, 1990, and substantial portions of it apply to previously created condominiums as well.

The creation of a condominium starts when the developer records a **declaration**. The developer is called the **declarant**, because the developer is declaring that the property described in the declaration is now under the provisions of the Washington Condominium Act. The declaration must include numerous matters. While not a complete list, the following are the most important –

- A legal description of the entire property
- A list of the units and the designation by which each shall be known, to be shown on the survey and plans for the structure(s)
- The name by which the development will be known, which must be a unique name not used for any other condominium in the county
- The percentage interest in the common elements which appertain to each unit
- Limited common elements (see below) and the unit(s) to which they appertain

As noted previously, when a condominium is created, each unit owner also owns an undivided interest as a tenant in common to the **common elements**. The common elements can be thought of as "the entire development, less the units themselves." The majority of the common elements are classed as ordinary common elements. However, the common elements may also include **limited common elements**. Remember that in a tenancy in common each co-tenant has an undivided right of possession of the entire property. Thus, in a condominium, no unit owner could ever be legally excluded from any portion of the common elements. This would make it impossible to have parking spaces or other portions of the common elements reserved for specific units. The Condominium Act fixes this problem by creating the possibility of limited common elements. Limited common elements are portions of the common areas which are reserved for the exclusive use of a particular unit owner.

Once a condominium has been created, the Condominium Act provides that the interest in the common elements, both ordinary and limited as set forth in the declaration, becomes an inseparable appurtenance to the unit. This means that a deed conveying the unit will also automatically convey the interest in the common elements. Such deeds are sometimes called **unit deeds**. Were it not for this provision in the Condominium Act owners would be constantly deeding their unit to a buyer and forgetting to include their interest in the common elements, leaving the buyer owning a landlocked property. To create a unit deed the Condominium Act requires the name of the condominium, the recording number for the declaration, the county where the condominium is located, and the identifying number of the unit (RCW 64.34.212).

At common law, any tenant in common always has the right to partition of the tenancy. This can't be allowed for the common elements in a condominium, so another provision of the Condominium Act is that, once a development has been declared to be a condominium, there can be no suit for partition of the common elements.

An important part of the process of creating a condominium is the recording of a survey map and the **plans** of the structure(s). The plans must be created by a surveyor, who must certify that they accurately depict the building(s) and the boundaries of the units. Note that the plans will be in three dimensions, since each condominium is a volume of space. The unit number as listed in the declaration must be shown on the plans.

The purpose of recording the plans is to create a public record which will give constructive notice of the dimensions of each unit. Once this has been accomplished, the legal description of any given unit can simply be the unit designation. Note that this process is conceptually identical to the creation of a lot and block legal description.

The developer normally creates the initial **bylaws** which will govern the operation of the association of unit owners. Of course, once the units have been sold, each owner has the right to vote to amend the bylaws. The bylaws contain matters such as the officers of the association and their duties and powers, calling special meetings, quorums, election of board members, procedures for amending the bylaws, and the like. Operational matters are also included, such as collection of assessments, maintenance of the units, insurance coverage, financial statements, hiring personnel, and so forth.

Under the Condominium Act a developer may create a condominium on which the development is to take place all at once, or where a developer reserves the right to build additional units later. If the developer has reserved the right to build additional units this fact must be contained in the declaration.

The association of unit owners may levy on each unit an assessment for common expenses. The levy is considered a lien on the unit, which can be foreclosed, if necessary. In some cases the levy can be prior to a mortgage or other loan, so lenders typically require that the assessment be paid along with the monthly payment. This way the lender can pay the assessment using the borrower's funds, thus ensuring that the assessments are paid.

Conversion – Existing structures can be turned into a ***conversion condominium*** with little problem in Washington. However, if the structure is residential, the owner must give 90 days advance notice to each tenant. The notice may be waived if 100% of the tenants agree to do so. The notice does not constitute a notice to terminate the existing tenancy, although an owner can give such notice separately if the tenant breaches the lease or rental agreement.

The owner must offer to sell each unit to the tenant in the unit. The offer must be left open for 60 days. This means that the developer may not be free to sell the units to the public for 60 days after recording the declaration and other documents. Following the offer period, the owner cannot offer the unit to the public on terms more favorable than the terms on which it was offered to the tenant for 180 days, unless the owner gives the same offer to the tenant and leaves it open for ten days.

These provisions were made a part of the Condominium Act to protect tenants from having their apartments sold out from under them and to ensure that such units would be offered to the tenants at reasonable prices. However, in reality, when apartments are converted to condominiums, the owner usually offers more favorable terms to the tenants since a sale to a tenant can be faster and cheaper.

Amendments to the declaration – Supplemental declarations or amendments to the declaration must be approved by the unit owners. The Condominium Act requires the vote in favor to be as required in the original declaration. However, if the condominium is residential the vote must be at least 67% of the unit owners.

Removal from condominium status – The unit owners (with the permission of lienholders) may remove a property from the provisions of the Condominium Act and convert it to a tenancy in common by recording an agreement to that effect.

Structural warranty – As an additional consumer protection, a declarant of a condominium must give buyers an ***implied warranty*** on the improvements, including the common elements. Actions under the warranty must be commenced "within four years after the cause of action accrues" (RCW 64.34.452). The declarant may limit the warranty by excluding certain matters provided the buyer agrees in writing. However, if the unit is residential general disclaimers such as "as is," "with all faults," and so forth will not be effective. For residential units the only limitation allowed is an exclusion for a specific defect.

Sales regulations – In the event the condominium development is residential the declarant must comply with certain sales regulations. The most significant part of these regulations deals with the creation of a ***public offering statement***, a copy of which must be given to each buyer. The developer must create the disclosure statement according to extensive statutory requirements The statement must include a copy of the declaration, survey map and plans, the articles of incorporation of the association, bylaws and regulations, the current or proposed budget for the association, and the balance sheet of the association if assessments have been collected for 90 days or more.

If the transaction is a resale, then the seller must give the buyer a **resale certificate**. A resale certificate must be signed by an officer of the association. The resale certificate must include a long list of items such as the amount of the assessment and if any assessments are in arrears, the previous year's annual financial statement of the association, information that would be required by a lender, and so on. It must also include a copy of the declaration, bylaws, and the rules and regulations. Upon request by a unit owner the association must provide the resale certificate within ten days. The association may charge up to $150 for the certificate, but the Condominium Act does not specify whether the fee must be paid by the buyer or the seller. Any sale agreement the buyer has entered into is voidable by the buyer until five days after the certificate has been furnished, or until the buyer accepts the seller's deed, whichever occurs first.

Cooperatives

A **cooperative** is another form of common ownership. In some day-to-day aspects, cooperatives appear very similar to condominiums, but the underlying legal principles are very different. A cooperative is created by forming a corporation (or occasionally a limited partnership or trust), which then sells shares to the unit owners. The organization uses the funds acquired from sales of shares to purchase a property. Ownership of shares entitles the shareholder to occupy a particular unit.

Note, however, that each owner holds shares – personal property – not title to real property. Title to the real property is vested in the organization. Nevertheless, income tax laws generally treat ownership of cooperative apartments the same ownership of condominiums and ordinary homes.

As in any organization, each shareholder is entitled to vote his or her shares in the election of board members. The board, in turn, takes care of the operation of the property. The organization assesses each shareholder for his or her share of the common expenses, such as taxes, insurance, maintenance, and so on.

From a practical standpoint, creating a cooperative would appear to accomplish the same ends as a condominium. But a difficulty arises when the cooperative organization borrows in order to acquire the property. For example, if the organization finances the property, then each owner only needs enough cash to pay his or her share of the down payment. This makes the acquisition easier, but it also means that each owner must be assessed his or her share of the mortgage principal and interest, in addition to the amount needed to cover the taxes, insurance, maintenance and other operating expenses. And if an owner defaults on paying the assessment, then the other owners will have to be assessed additional amounts until the default can be cured.

Cooperatives are common in some areas, particularly the cities of New England. In Washington, however, cooperatives are unusual. By far the preferred form of common ownership here is the condominium.

Planned communities

A **planned unit development** (PUD) (sometimes called a **planned community**) is in some respects a hybrid between a condominium and a subdivision. As in a subdivision, each owner owns an individual lot, separately platted. But, as in the condominium, each owner is a member of a homeowners' association. As in the condominium, the association takes care of matters such as exterior maintenance and the like. In many planned communities, there are also common areas (e.g., a golf course, recreation buildings, and so on) which the owners hold as tenants in common. Instead of tenancy in common, title is sometimes vested in the association. In either case, the association will also manage and maintain the common areas. And, as in a condominium, the association levies assessments against each owner's property to cover the costs of operation.

Planned communities also frequently contain commercial enterprises for the convenience of the lot owners, such as convenience stores and other local service businesses.

In creating a planned community it is common to find the concept of **cluster zoning**. Cluster zoning stipulates a total density for the area, but allows the developer to place all the units compactly in one area and leave other areas as open space. Planned unit developments and cluster zoning offer the developer a higher density and lower cost per dwelling unit, while providing more open space for the enjoyment of the residents.

Timeshares and the Washington Timeshare Act

A **timeshare** (sometimes referred to as **interval ownership**) is a relatively new concept in the real estate marketplace. Any interest in property, whether fee title, leasehold, condominium, cooperative, or otherwise can be marketed as a timeshare. Since the bundle of rights to any property can be divided in any manner, to create a timeshare, a seller simply sells the right of occupancy for a specific time, recurring each year.

Timeshares have been an especially attractive way to market vacation property, where the buyer really only intends to occupy the property for a week or two each year. Timeshare developments usually have a management team to maintain the property. In most cases, the management can also rent the property to others for those times when the owner is unable to use the occupancy period. In some timeshares the owner has the option to trade their time for time in another timeshare.

Timeshare regulation – Timeshares in Washington are regulated by RCW Chapter 64.36. A timeshares is defined as "a right to occupy a unit or any of several units during three or more separate time periods over a period of at least three years" [RCW 64.36.010 (11)]. It should be noted that a timeshare is frequently an interest in a condominium unit, but it could also be a regular house in an ordinary subdivision or planned community, or even a parcel of vacant land. Also, a timeshare can be created out of a leasehold as well as a fee. The timeshare can be deeded or it can be a recurring leasehold, or even a license to occupy a fee or a leasehold.

A timeshare must be registered with the Director of the Department of Licensing before any advertising or offering of a timeshare can be made. The registration must be renewed annually. Note that, if the property is a condominium, the condominium must first be created in the usual manner, and then the timeshare can be registered. The code list specific facts which the registration must contain, including matters involving the business background of the registrant, the registrant's financial statements and so forth. The registration must be signed individually with personal liability of the promoter, and if the registrant is a corporation, by each person with ten percent or greater ownership interest. The corporate shield does not apply to these individuals.

Timeshares can be sold only by persons registered as timeshare salespersons with the Department of Licensing. However, anyone licensed as a real estate salesperson or broker is exempt from registration as a timeshare salespersons.

Sales regulation – A person selling a timeshare must give each buyer a **timeshare disclosure document**. The disclosure document must include a series of disclosures required by RCW 64.36.140. For seven days after receiving the disclosure document the purchaser may rescind the purchase agreement. The disclosure document must contain a notice of the buyer's right to rescind.

When a promoter offers free gifts to the public as an inducement to attend a sales presentation the promoter must first file with the Department of Licensing a security bond to ensure that the gift will be produced. If a potential buyer does not receive a promised free gift the buyer can sue the promoter and obtain judgment for up to three times the value of the gift.

In addition, all advertising of the timeshare must be submitted to the Director of the Department of Licensing at least seven days before the advertising appears.

⚷ KEY TERMS

The key to understanding any new field is the vocabulary used in that field. To maximize your comprehension of the material presented in this chapter, be sure you know the meaning and significance of the following terms. Remember that the majority of test questions primarily test knowledge of vocabulary.

Bylaws	*Interval ownership*
Cluster zoning	*Limited common elements*
Common elements	*Planned community*
Condominium	*Planned unit development (PUD)*
Condominium public offering statement	*Plans*
Conversion condominium	*Resale certificate*
Cooperative	*Timeshare*
Declarant	*Timeshare disclosure document*
Declaration	*Unit deed*
Homeowners' association	*Unit owners' association*
Horizontal Property Regimes Act	*Washington Condominium Act*
Implied warranty	

Chapter

8

Property taxes

R EAL PROPERTY is permanent, indestructible and immovable. Because of this we say that real estate has fixity. And because of its fixity, governments have always enjoyed certainty that they would be able to collect taxes levied on real property. After all, the owner can't just pick it up and leave town.

We have had real property taxes since feudal times, although in early England taxes were levied in very different ways. Lands held by tenant farmers were taxed a portion of the production of the land. Property owned by knights was taxed in the form of a certain number of days of military service, and so forth. Today we have reduced this system to just a monetary tax, yet the operation of today's property tax system is far more complex than the feudal system from which it is derived.

The property tax was the first tax ever levied in Washington, created even before statehood in 1889. Although the majority of tax revenue in Washington today is derived from sales and other taxes, property taxes still account for roughly 30% of state and local taxes. Property taxation today is a function mostly of county government and other local taxing districts. In addition, the state of Washington levies property taxes to help pay for schools. There are no federal property taxes.

Within each county there are many small and some large political units which depend primarily on property taxes for their source of revenue. School districts come foremost to mind as examples of such districts, since school districts are typically the largest property tax district on the tax bill. Other examples include city governments, port authorities, public library districts, community college districts, and even the county itself. Regardless of its size or purpose, each local government unit which levies property taxes is called a ***tax levy district***.

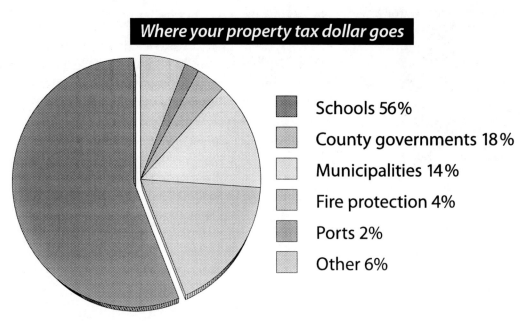

Where your property tax dollar goes

- Schools 56%
- County governments 18%
- Municipalities 14%
- Fire protection 4%
- Ports 2%
- Other 6%

Every year each tax levy district creates a budget for its operations during the coming year. This process results in a property tax ***levy***. On January 1 the levy becomes a lien on all taxable property in the district. Each owner will pay his or her share of the levy ***ad valorem***, that is, according to the value the property.

Because the tax is levied ad valorem, someone must determine the values of all the properties in each tax levy district, and this person is the ***tax assessor***. The process of appraising all taxable properties each year is called ***assessment***. The tax assessor's job is endless. No sooner than one year's valuations are finished and it's time to start on the next year. The important thing to remember about assessment is that its sole function is

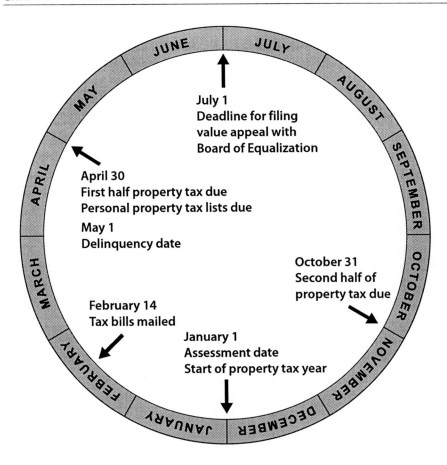

July 1
Deadline for filing
value appeal with
Board of Equalization

April 30
First half property tax due
Personal property tax lists due

May 1
Delinquency date

October 31
Second half of
property tax due

February 14
Tax bills mailed

January 1
Assessment date
Start of property tax year

The Washington real property tax year. Each property is valued for its real market value as of January 1. The tax levy becomes a lien on all taxable property within each tax levy district on January 1. The first one-half of the property tax bill is due on April 30. The second half is due October 31. Payment in full pays the taxes for the period from the preceding January 1 through the coming December 31. This fact is very important when prorating the tax liability between a buyer and a seller. If any portion of the tax or interest remains unpaid on November 1 it is delinquent.

to apportion the tax burden fairly according to value among all property within each tax levy district.

Each year the tax rate for each tax levy district is calculated. The tax rate is computed from the amount of each district's levy and the total value of all property from which the levy must be raised. Once the levies have been approved and the valuations have been determined, the collection process begins. This job falls to the county ***treasurer***.

Tax bills are sent in February. Property owners can pay their bills one-half at a time, or all at once. At least the first half is due on April 30. If the taxes are not paid, ultimately the treasurer will foreclose on the property.

The foregoing has been a brief overview of real property taxation in Washington. You should note that there are three separate entities which are responsible for our property tax bills. The tax levy districts determine how much they are going to spend. This, more than any other single factor, determines how much our property tax bills will be. Next comes the tax assessor. The job of the tax assessor is to value every taxable property so that each owner can be billed for his or her share of the total levy according to the value of the property. And finally comes the county treasurer, who functions as the tax collector.

Many people blame the county treasurer or the tax assessor when they feel their bills are too high. This is usually incorrect. The county treasurer's function in this process is merely to collect the taxes. The amount of an owner's tax bill is determined by the amount of the levy and the amount of the owner's assessment. If the assessment is too high, then the owner is paying more than his or her share of the total tax burden. But if the property is valued at its market value, then the owner's real complaint is that the tax levy districts are spending too much.

In the following pages we will discuss the details of the levy process, tax assessment, and collection procedures. We will also discuss exemptions and deferrals, among other matters affecting real property taxation in Washington.

The levy process

Creating a tax levy is a complicated affair, not made easier by the fact that it is a purely political process. Each duly constituted tax levy district is run by a group of elected officials. For example, school districts are run by a school board, county commissioners run the county government, cities are run by council members, and so forth. These are all elected positions, so each member is sensitive to the fact that voters wish the budgets to be kept low. Nevertheless, voters also want more and better services, so the job of the politician is always a balancing act.

While the majority of a property owner's bill funds the functions of local government, the state also imposes a levy on all taxable property. The revenue from the state levy is used primarily for support of schools. The amount is generally set at $3.60 per thousand dollars of assessed valuation. However, because assessments are not generally at the ideal rate of 100% of true and fair value, and because accuracy of actual assessments vary from one county to the next, the Department of Revenue applies an adjustment factor to the $3.60 rate to equalize the amounts every property owner will pay statewide. Thus, the actual rate on a given tax bill may be a bit higher or lower than the $3.60 amount.

Limitations on levy amounts – Starting in the 1980s voters nationwide have become angry about ever-escalating property tax bills. In states like Washington which allow voters to amend the state constitution by direct vote, there have been numerous measures passed which limit property taxes in one way or another.

The Washington constitution limits the total regular tax levy to not more than 1% of the market value of the property. This is sometimes referred to as the ***one-percent constitutional limit***. The "regular" levy means the amount levied by all local tax districts as part of their regular budget and does not include what are sometimes called "voted" levies. A "voted" levy means a special levy for a temporary increase to meet unusual needs. For example, an area experiencing heavy growth may discover that they need to make substantial alterations to the local sewer and water facilities. To meet the expense the districts involved with water and sewer may ask the voters for a temporary special levy.

In addition Washington voters approved a limitation on the amount that levies can increase each year. The law (commonly called the ***levy limit***) prohibits taxing districts from increasing their levies by more than 1% over the highest amount that could have been levied since 1985. Like the one percent constitutional limit, the levy limit applies only to non-voted levies. It also does not apply to new construction or annexed areas, so the actual increase in a levy may be greater than the 1% limit.

The assessment process

As noted previously, property taxes are levied according to value (ad valorem). Therefore, accurate valuation of each property is important if the total tax burden is to be distributed fairly among all property owners.

We must distinguish between the market value and the ***assessed value***. Taxes are levied on the assessed value, which is a percentage of the market value. The percentage is called the ***assessment ratio***. By basing the tax on the assessed value, we can shift the tax burden from one class of property onto another class, if we wish. For example, if we make a law which assesses personal residences at half their market value (an assessment ratio of 50% for owner-occupied residences), this would significantly lower the tax bills for personal residences, but at the same time shift a higher portion of the overall burden to other classes of property (e.g., business, agricultural and industrial property). In the past this has been done and is still being done in many states. Of course, lowering taxes on homes at the expense of business and industrial property is popular, but in reality may be a bad idea. Businesses must cover their costs, which means charging more for their products. But if their competition is located in a region with lower costs, local businesses will have no choice but to move or go out of business. Having a lower property tax bill may be desirable for a homeowner, but not if the homeowner becomes unemployed as a result. With some minor exceptions, all Washington property today must be assessed at 100% of its *true and fair value in money*.

The tax assessor is required by law to establish the values of all taxable property as of January 1, which is called the *assessment date*.

Some counties have as many as hundreds of thousands of property tax accounts. To appraise each of these properties every year would cost an enormous amount. To maintain accurate values, yet keep the costs down, some counties uses a process called *trending*. Washington law requires each county assessor to reappraise each property at least once every four years, or in some cases every six years. Thus, the assessor can divide the county *tax maintenance districts*. Appraisers from the assessor's office reappraise each property in one district every year, on a rotating basis ensuring that each property will be reappraised within the requirements of the code.

Because six years is a long time to go between appraisals, if a county wishes to reappraise only every six years a computer generated adjustment must be made every year for the five intervening years. The tax assessor simply programs the computer to change the values of all properties in each of the districts not reappraised by a certain percentage. The percentages are different for each district, and are determined primarily from the values of recent sales. Some counties that are on a four-year cycle also use computer adjustments for the intervening years.

Although the majority of Washington's 39 counties are on a four-year cycle, the code merely allows a four-year cycle; it does not require it. Many counties, therefore, reappraise every year, and a few do so on a two-year or three-year cycle. Washington code provides that the Washington Department of Revenue has jurisdiction over all county property tax activity. Because counties use different methods for maintaining valuations current, the law requires each county to submit its valuation plan to the Department for approval.

The tax assessor must send a *change of value notice* to the property owner whenever the valuation is changed. If the owner feels the new valuation is incorrect the first step should be to contact the assessor's office. Many times the assessor's office will assign an appraiser to reevaluate the valuation. Frequently this is all that is necessary to gain relief.

If the owner wishes to appeal, he or she may file a petition with the *Board of Equalization*. The deadline is July 1, or within 30 days of the mailing of a change of value notice, whichever is later. Most petitioners receive at least some of the relief they ask for.

In all property valuation appeals the property owner must prove by preponderance of the evidence that the assessor's valuation of the property was too high. There are various types of evidence which an owner can use toward this end. An independent appraisal is certainly admissible as evidence, but may not be cost-effective. Comparable sales are considered valid evidence, whether contained in an appraisal report or not. A recent purchase of the property at a price under the assessed value is also excellent evidence. After all, a sale of the property itself is the very best comparable sale, provided, of course, that it was an open market, arms-length transaction. The best argument occurs when the property has been listed for sale in the open market for a reasonable period of time and has not sold. In hearings before the Board of Equalization the burden of proof is on the taxpayer.

Many times property owners will attempt to argue that the assessor has valued their property higher than other similar property, and therefore their valuation should be lowered. This argument will usually fail, since it only demonstrates that the valuations are unequal. It does not prove the value of the owner's property is less than what the assessor says it is.

If the owner is dissatisfied with the results of the petition to the Board of Equalization, a further appeal can be taken to the **State Board of Property Tax Appeals**. As an alternative, the owner can pay the tax under protest and then file a suit for a refund in Superior Court.

Tax collection

When the levies for each district and the total amount of the assessed values for all property in each district has been determined, the **tax rate** for each district can be calculated. The tax rate in Washington is expressed in dollars of tax per thousand dollars of assessed valuation. In the past, the tax rate was computed using **mills**. A mill is one-thousandth of a dollar (one-tenth of a cent). For example, a typical overall tax rate in Washington today would be about $15.00 per thousand. A $200,000 house taxed at this rate would have a tax bill of $3,000 each year (200 × $15 = $3,000). The same rate expressed in mills would be "15 mills," or 15 thousandths of a dollar per one dollar of value. Because people have difficulty with the mathematics of mills, we now state the tax rate in terms of dollars of tax per thousand dollars of value rather than mills of tax per one dollar of value. Still, it is not uncommon to hear the term **millage rate**.

Calculating a tax rate is very simple, but is easier to see if we use an example. Let us assume that the county treasurer is determining the tax rate for a very small fire protection district. The district has a levy of $150,000 to fund operations in the coming year. The total assessed values of all property lying within the boundaries of the district is $500 million. The calculation is to divide the total assessed values into the amount of the levy –

$$150,000 \div 500,000 = .0003$$

Therefore, the tax rate is $0.0003 per dollar. Multiplying by 1,000, we get the tax rate expressed in dollars per thousand dollars of valuation, or –

$$\$0.00030 \times 1,000 = \$0.30$$

In other words, the tax rate for this district will be 0.30 dollars, or 30¢, per thousand dollars of property value. Translated into real world terms, the tax bill for a $200,000 house will include $60 per year for fire protection (200 × $0.30 = $60.00).

Now the treasurer can calculate the rates for all the other districts in the county in the same way. After calculation these rates are entered into the computer. The computer was programmed earlier with all the assessed values. And years earlier each property was coded in the computer for the property tax levy districts within whose boundaries it lies. Thus it is a simple matter to turn on the computer and start producing tax bills. The computer will automatically charge each owner for the districts in which the property is located.

Tax bills are mailed on February 14 of each year. The bill is sent to the owner of record. It is important for real estate agents to realize that the bill does not arrive until February, but there has been a lien against the property since January 1. The Washington tax year runs from January 1 through the following December 31, so if the owner pays the bill in full on the due date (April 30), the taxes will be paid for the period from the preceding January 1 through the coming December 31. The fact that the due dates do not coincide with the tax year is important when prorating property taxes between a buyer and a seller.

Property taxes in Washington can be paid one-half at a time. The first half is due on or before April 30. Unless already paid, the second one half becomes due on October 31. Unpaid taxes are subject to an interest penalty of 1% per month. In addition, if the first half are not paid by June 1 there is an added penalty of 3%. And if any part of the year's taxes remain unpaid after December 1 an additional 8% penalty is added.

If at least half the tax bill is not paid by April 30 they are considered **delinquent** as of May 1. Becoming delinquent means that the clock starts running for foreclosure. By law, the county cannot foreclose on your property until the tax has been delinquent for three full years. Thus, in late May, three years after delinquency, the county treasurer will file in superior court for an order for the sale of the property at public auction. The minimum bid is always the amount of all taxes, interest and penalties owing. The sale is normally absolute to the high bidder. If no one bids, the county will receive title to the property.

Property taxes are prior to all other liens, regardless of when the other liens were recorded. This means that a property tax foreclosure will extinguish any mortgage, trust deed, land sales contract, or other financial encumbrance on the property. Because of this, mortgage lenders take great care to be sure that the borrower pays the property taxes. A common mechanism to ensure this is to require the borrower to pay one-twelfth the projected annual property taxes along with the principal and interest each month. The lender accumulates these funds in a **reserve account** and uses the funds to pay the taxes for the borrower on the due dates.

Deferrals and exemptions

Homeowner additions – Homeowners who make improvements in the form of an addition to their single-family residences may qualify for a three-year exemption on the value of the improvements. Normal maintenance costs do not qualify for the exemption. The homeowner must apply through the local assessor's office prior to the project.

Senior citizens deferral – Washington law provides for the **deferral** of taxes on a homestead owned by certain senior citizens and disabled persons. The taxes are deferred, not forgiven. The taxes must be paid eventually. In reality, it is not the county which defers payment of the tax and interest. Rather, when a qualified homeowner elects to defer payment of property taxes the Department of Revenue, using state funds, lends the funds to the owner by paying the owner's taxes to the county. When the deferred taxes and accrued interest are repaid, the repayment is to the Department of Revenue.

To qualify, the owner must be 60 years of age by December 31 or be a surviving spouse 57 years of age, or the owner must be unable to work because of disability. The property must be the personal residence of the owner, and the owner must have a fee title or be buying on a land sales contract; a life estate does not qualify. The applicant's total household income (both taxable and non-taxable) cannot exceed $34,000. Household income includes income of spouses and all persons residing in the property who have an ownership interest.

The deferral is lost if the owner dies, sells the property, changes ownership or ceases to live permanently on the property. All deferred taxes and accrued interest must be paid when the deferral is terminated.

The program can be used even if the property is mortgaged or if the owners are buying on a land sales contract. However, this could create a problem, since property taxes are a prior lien. To protect the interests of lenders, the homeowner must secure the approval of the lender. In addition, the homeowner must add the state of Washington to the fire insurance policy as a loss payee, the same as when there is a mortgage loan on the property.

Senior citizens exemption – In addition to the deferral, certain seniors and disabled persons may be eligible for an *exemption*. The program freezes the assessed valuation of their homestead, exempts all non-voted levies and, depending on income, may exempt part of regular levies as well.

To qualify the homeowner must be 61 years of age or a surviving spouse 57 years of age, or a person who is unable to work because of disability. In addition, the owner's household income cannot exceed $30,000. The amount of the exemption varies according to the household income.

Open space – Property must normally be appraised according to its highest and best use. When applied to bare land that means what the land would be worth if developed for the most profitable use. Owners of such land frequently feel pressure to sell the land for development, partly due to constantly increasing tax bills. In an effort to use taxation as a tool to encourage open space, Washington created the *Open Space Tax Act* in 1970.

Under the Act the owner of certain open space, agricultural or timber lands can apply to the local assessor to have the land assessed at its current undeveloped use. Normally this is a much lower valuation than its highest and best use. The owner can remove the land from the open space classification, but doing so will result in seven years back taxes on the difference between the open space valuation and the normal valuation suddenly becoming due. However, the back taxes can be avoided if the property is transferred as a result of the death of the owner or certain other reasons.

Historic properties – Owners of certain qualified historic properties in Washington may apply for a limitation on increases in assessed values due to rehabilitation. The limitation is valid for ten years. If the limitation is lost the owner must pay back the tax not assessed, plus interest and penalties.

Special assessments

Public capital improvements typically must be paid for at once. Raising the funds with annual property taxes would take too long. Local governments solve this problem with a *bond issue*. The local government issues bonds to raise the capital to pay for the project. The bonds are bought by investors, who are repaid from future taxes – in fact, sometimes by property taxes. Sometimes the bonds are to be paid off from the income produced by the improvement. For example, the local government may decide that a bridge is needed. By making it a toll bridge, the income generated from the tollgate can be used to pay off the bonds which were sold to finance its construction. Bonds which are to be paid off from the profits generated by the improvement are called *revenue bonds*.

When local improvements are desired which will serve only certain properties, a *special assessment* is used. Special assessments are used to fund improvements such as street paving, curbs, gutters and sidewalks, sewer systems, street lighting, and so on. Special assessments are apportioned to the owners in various ways. For example, the total cost of a street improvement project may be allocated to adjacent property owners on a front-foot basis. The cost of a sewer system may be based on the number of bedrooms per house, etc. Special assessments are a lien against the property, the same as property taxes and can usually be assumed by a buyer.

Personal property taxation

Many people are not aware that personal property is sometimes also subject to property tax. Like most states today, personal property used in business is taxable in Washington. Washington law exempts intangible items – securities and debt obligations, copyrights, patents and trademarks, service contracts such as listing agreements, certificates of deposit, franchise agreements, and the like. Inventories held for resale or for use in manufacturing are also exempt. And motor vehicles are usually exempt, since they are subject to an excise tax upon registration. However, tangible items used in business such as office equipment, computers, desks, signs and so forth are all taxable. Leasehold improvements made by a tenant are considered personal property if the tenant has the right to remove them at the termination of the tenancy, and as such are also subject to personal property taxation.

Washington law provides an exemption if the total value of the personal property is $500 or less. And if the owner of the personal property is a head of household, the exemption is $3,000. Most real estate salespersons and associate brokers will be exempt under one or the other of these provisions. However, brokers running a brokerage firm will probably have enough personal property in the office that they will have to pay tax on it.

Anyone who has non-exempt personal property must complete a personal property tax listing form and submit it to the county assessor no later than April 30 each year. The form must list all taxable personal located in the county as of January 1. Failing to file in timely fashion subjects the owner to a penalty of 5% of the tax due up to a maximum of 25%.

Collection procedures are considerably more strict than for real property taxes. If at least the first half of the taxes are not paid by April 30 the bill becomes delinquent on May 1, which subjects the bill to interest charges of 1% per month until paid, plus 3% penalty for the first month and an additional penalty of 8% if not paid by December 1. In addition, the treasurer may place a lien on any real property of the owner. The treasurer may also seize and retain the personal property until the tax is paid. And if the treasurer has reason to believe that the personal property is about to be removed from the county, the treasurer may demand that the owner pay all current taxes plus an advance amount to ensure that the taxes are paid before removal.

The assessment and taxation of mobile homes follows the same procedures as for the assessment of real property when it is classified as real property. However, floating homes are always taxed as personal property, as are mobile homes in some cases. If the owner of the mobile home also owns the land on which the manufactured dwelling is situated and the mobile home has substantially lots its character as a mobile home by being place on posts or a foundation, then the dwelling and the land are both taxed as real property. If the owner is renting or leasing the land on which the mobile home is situated (i.e., it is in a park) it is taxed as personal property. The reason for taxing mobile homes as personal property when the owner does not own the land on which it is situated is simply because it has no fixity. If the owner of a mobile home owns land as well, the taxes can always be collected from the land, so we can give the owner the more liberal collection procedures of real property taxation.

Real estate excise tax

For many years Washington law has required the seller to pay an ***excise tax*** to the county on the sale of property. The purpose of the tax is to provide funding for schools. The tax is levied on all sales of real estate, including used mobile homes and floating homes, except –

- Fulfillment deed at the end of a land sales contract where the contract was already recorded earlier and the excise tax paid at that time
- Deed of trust (a deed of trust is really a financing document)
- Correction or reformation deeds
- Conveyances between husband and wife or parent and child
- Sheriff's deeds (used at the end of a foreclosure), or any other conveyance caused by a foreclosure or forfeiture proceeding
- Conveyances resulting from gifts, probate of an estate, divorce proceeding, or a partition action among co-tenants
- Assignment of a land sales contract by the seller in order to sell the contract
- Conveyances as a result of condemnation actions
- A transfer where the purpose is merely a change of ownership name, e.g., a deed to a corporation where the corporation is wholly owned by the grantor
- The sale of a cemetery lot
- Any sale by a government entity

A sale includes sales on land sales contracts or by deed of the property or any interest in the property. For example, the sale of timber or mineral rights would require payment of the tax. It does not apply to a rental or lease, but it does apply to a lease-option.

A credit is available if a single-family residence is transferred to a real estate broker and the broker resells the property within nine months. The credit is in the amount of the tax paid for the transfer to the broker and is applied to the tax due on the resale. Many real estate brokers take properties "in trade" like this for buyers and this provision keeps the costs down.

The amount of the tax varies statewide from 1.28% to a maximum of 3.28%, although the most common rate is 1.53%. Of the total, 1.28% goes to the state, of which 92.3% goes to the counties for the common school fund and 7.7% goes to the state general fund. Anything the county levies above this rate is for other county purposes. The county treasurer acts as collection agent for the state's share. It is calculated on the total selling price, including any encumbrances assumed by the buyer. It is easy for the county to enforce collection because deeds and contracts cannot be accepted for recording without an affidavit stamped by the county treasurer that the tax was paid or that the sale was exempt. (For more detail on recording, see Chapter 5.) Until paid, the tax constitutes a lien against the property. For late payment there are substantial penalties, plus interest,

⚿ KEY TERMS

The key to understanding any new field is the vocabulary used in that field. To maximize your comprehension of the material presented in this chapter, be sure you know the meaning and significance of the following terms. Remember that the majority of test questions primarily test knowledge of vocabulary.

Ad valorem

Assessed value

Assessment

Assessment date

Assessment ratio

Board of Equalization

Bond issue

Change of value notice

Deferral

Delinquent

Excise tax

Exemption

Levy

Levy limit

Mill

Millage rate

One percent constitutional limit

Reserve account

Revenue bond

Special assessment

State Board of Property Tax Appeals

Tax assessor

Tax levy district

Tax maintenance district

Tax rate

Treasurer

Trending

True and fair value in money

Chapter 9

Essentials of real estate contract law

ONTRACT LAW is the basis of all commerce, and a firm understanding of it is the foundation upon which any business career must be based, including a career in real estate. In fact, understanding contract law is essential for all citizens. Every time you make a purchase, however trivial and routine, you are entering into a contract. As you go about your daily business you are performing numerous contracts that you entered into previously. For most of us, hardly a day goes by without entering into several contracts. It seems that our lives are an endless series of contracts.

In this chapter we will explore the fundamentals of contract law. Unfortunately, we cannot discuss here more than basic principles, although we will pay extra attention to those special problems which present themselves in real estate contracts. In the world of contracts there are innumerable ramifications, exceptions and special circumstances which may apply in a specific situation. Since we do not have the time and space for an exhaustive study of contracts, persons entering into real estate contracts are well advised to seek competent counsel when faced with an individual case.

Before getting into specifics of contract law it is important to understand where laws relating to contracts come from. Laws in the United States are derived originally from English common law; that is, the law of England at the time of the colonies. With independence and the formation of the United States came the adoption of the U.S. Constitution. The Constitution gives each state the right to create its own laws, within the constraints of the U.S. Constitution, as each state sees fit.

As time went on contract laws in each state drifted slightly from the original. Eventually it got to the point where commerce between people in different states was becoming difficult. Each party had to hire an attorney in the other state to sort out which state would have jurisdiction and what the laws in that state said.

To simplify this the American Law Institute created a uniform model for contract law called the **Uniform Commercial Code** (UCC). Over time each state adopted this by statute for contracts in their state. Today all states have adopted the UCC (except Louisiana, which ratified about half of it). This means that the basic provisions of contract law are now usually the same from one state to the next, simplifying commerce and making it easier for people to understand the provisions of their contracts. Except for certain special requirements of Washington law, everything in this text is based on the UCC.

Classification of contracts

A **contract** is a legally enforceable promise made by at least one party to another. Although a unilateral promise does constitute one sort of contract, most contracts involve mutual promises, where both parties agree to give something or do something for the other. When only one party has made a promise, the contract is said to be **unilateral**. Where both parties have made promises to each other, the contract is **bilateral**. For example, suppose you agree to sell your house to Joe Jones for $300,000 and he agrees to buy it from you for that price. Both parties have made promises to each other, so the contract is bilateral. An important feature of bilateral contracts is that either party can enforce the contract on the other.

Not so the unilateral contract. Suppose Joe Jones wishes to buy your house, but you are not yet ready to sell. He prevails upon you to grant him a **right of refusal**, that is, whenever you decide to sell it you must offer it to him first. Note that Joe is under no obligation to exercise his right of refusal. Thus the unilateral contract is really little more than a standing offer – a promise which becomes binding on both only upon performance by the other party. In addition to rights of refusal, common unilateral contracts in real estate include options and certain agency contracts (e.g., an open listing agreement).

Contracts are frequently created by implication rather than a formal, expressed agreement. These are called *implied contracts*. Since implied contracts are not created by an oral or written agreement, they must be deduced from the actions of the parties. Many unimportant and informal contracts are created and performed this way every day. Of course, the more important the contract, the more likely we are to state the contract, at least orally, and preferably in writing. Such contracts are called *expressed contracts*.

In fact, the law recognizes that some contracts are so important that statutes have been written which require these contracts to be in writing to be enforceable. These laws are called the *Statutes of Frauds*, and they vary from state to state. They are called Statutes of Frauds because they were enacted to prevent frauds upon the courts by requiring that certain contracts be in writing. The following excerpts from Washington Statutes of Frauds apply to contracts which involve real property –

RCW 19.36.010 Contracts, etc., void unless in writing.

In the following cases, specified in this section, any agreement, contract and promise shall be void, unless such agreement, contract or promise, or some note or memorandum thereof, be in writing, and signed by the party to be charged therewith, or by some person thereunto by him lawfully authorized, that is to say: (1) Every agreement that by its terms is not to be performed in one year from the making thereof; (2) every special promise to answer for the debt, default, or misdoings of another person; ... (5) an agreement authorizing or employing an agent or broker to sell or purchase real estate for compensation or a commission.

Thus it would appear that practically any real estate contract, including a deed, listing, lease, and so on, must be in writing lest it be void.

Many times we enter into contracts which exist for a brief instant of time, such as a contract of sale. Other times the contract lasts over a long term. A contract which, by its nature, is to be performed over a period of time is called an *executory contract*. A land sales contract, to be paid off over many years, is an example of an executory contract. The term is also used to describe the current status of a contract. For example, a land sales contract which has not yet been paid off is said to be executory. In this sense, an executory contract is contrasted with an *executed contract*. Strictly speaking, an executed contract is one which was executory, but has now been fully performed. In common usage, however, people often refer to the execution of a contract as the signing or act of entering into the contract.

Void, voidable and unenforceable contracts

A *void contract* is a contract which never existed, a nullity. To say that a contract is void is, technically speaking, improper usage, for if it is void, it is no contract. A *voidable contract*, on the other hand, does have some existence, but because of certain circumstances (which we will discuss later), one of the parties has the right to avoid performance. When a contract is voidable, the party who has the right to avoid performance must *ratify* (affirm) or *rescind* (disaffirm) the contract within a reasonable period of time.

Ratification (affirmation) makes the contract fully enforceable. Its opposite (called *rescission*) has an important legal effect. Upon rescission of the contract, all parties must be placed in the same position they were in before they entered into the contract, as far as practical. For example, suppose you agree to buy a parcel of land, but the owner fails to tell you that the land is unbuildable due to lack of sewers in the area. Assuming the owner knew the truth, this may constitute fraud, which gives you the right to rescind. In this case, you could rescind the contract even after the transaction is closed and the deed recorded. If you do so the seller must return your money and you must deed the property back to the seller. Note that sometimes a rescission becomes very difficult, especially with executory contracts which have already been performed over a period of time. In these cases, the courts do the best they can to put the parties in the same position they were in before they entered into the contract.

A ***cancellation*** of a contract is different from a rescission. Cancellation occurs when a contract is being performed over a period of time, the contract is subsequently terminated, but the parties do not necessarily return the goods or benefits already received.

Contracts are said to be ***unenforceable*** if a court would refuse enforcement. A void contract is clearly unenforceable by either party, and a voidable contract is unenforceable by one of the parties. A contract may also be unenforceable even though neither void nor voidable. For example, you cannot enforce a contract after an unreasonable period of time has elapsed, even though the contract appears to be otherwise acceptable. There are numerous matters (which we will discuss later) which render contracts unenforceable besides being void or voidable.

If a contract is not unenforceable, it is said to be ***valid*** or ***valid and enforceable***. A basic premise of contract law is that any contract is valid and enforceable, unless there is some defect or circumstance which renders it unenforceable. In other words, the purpose of the contract is irrelevant to its enforceability. You can enter into a valid contract for any legal purpose whatsoever, regardless of how bizarre the subject of the contract, and the courts will enforce the contract. The courts leave it up to the parties to decide if the contract made sense.

The preceding definitions have been fairly technical. In the real world it is more common to find contract terms being used loosely. It is not unusual to hear even attorneys and judges stating that a contract is "void" when they mean voidable or unenforceable. It is also typical for people to refer to a contract as "legal" or "illegal" when they simply mean that it is enforceable or unenforceable. And people frequently say they wish to "void" a contract, when they mean they wish to cancel or rescind it. We will use the terms here in their correct technical meaning so as to avoid confusion and because that is the way the terms will be used on exams.

Creation of a contract

Although, as we have seen, there may be many factors which would render a contract unenforceable, a contract is not even formed unless certain essential elements are present. These always include –
- Mutual agreement
- A legal object

And in many types of contracts, also include
- Consideration
- Identified and competent parties
- A sufficient writing
- An adequate description of the property

Since a contract is not formed unless these essential elements are present, we would say that when one of them is required, but nevertheless lacking, the contract is void.

Agreement

Of all the elements required to form a contract, the very heart of the matter is the existence of **mutual agreement**. Many people refer to this as **mutual assent** or **meeting of the minds**, among other terms. It is typically brought about by one party making an offer to the other and the other's acceptance of the offer, so it is also sometimes called the **offer and acceptance**.

Although an agreement can come into existence without a formal offer and acceptance, the offer and acceptance is the normal manner in which contracts are formed in real estate transactions, so we will limit our discussion to the offer and acceptance.

In every offer and acceptance there is an **offeror** (party making the offer) and an **offeree** (party to whom the offer is made). In the creation of sales contracts it is certainly possible for the seller to offer to sell to the buyer, but more commonly, a buyer offers to buy from the seller. In real estate transactions people frequently become confused because the seller has listed the property for sale with a real estate broker. It appears that by listing the property with the broker, the seller is offering it for sale. But in reality, the listing is only an employment contract between the seller and the broker, not an offer to sell. The buyer is not affected by it because the buyer is not a party to the listing. When someone is not a party to a contract we say the party does not have **privity of contract**.

Advertisements are another source of confusion. People sometimes take an advertisement as an offer to sell, which can be accepted by the first person on the scene with the cash. This is not generally true. In most cases, advertising is merely an announcement of the availability of the item, not an offer to sell. For example, an ad that says "House for sale, $350,000" is merely an announcement. But an ad that says "Lot 12, Block 2, Jones Addition to Seattle, first $350,000 takes it" might be construed by a court as an offer to sell. In that case someone showing up with $350,000 might be considered as having created an enforceable contract of sale, even if the seller does not sign anything.

For an offer to exist it must be definite and certain and made with the intention of entering into a contract. As a simple rule of thumb, for an offer to be valid it must be sufficiently complete that, if the offeree accepted it, a binding contract would result. For example, the Statute of Frauds requires contracts involving real property to be in writing to be enforceable. Therefore a verbal offer to buy real property is no offer, because if the seller accepted a verbal offer, no contract would result.

Nevertheless, an offer is still a valid offer even though some matters may not have been specifically stated. A common example is a contract to buy property "for its appraised value." The contract is considered sufficiently definite and certain because the appraised value can be determined by independent appraisal. It is not at all uncommon to enter into contracts where not every detail was thought of at the time the contract was entered into. As long as the essential elements were stated the contract is deemed to exist.

Once made, the offer continues to exist and a contract can be formed by the offeree's acceptance at any time prior to the termination of the offer. Offers can be terminated by –

- Expiration of a time limit (or a reasonable time if no limit is specified in the offer)
- Revocation by the offeror
- Rejection by the offeree
- Death or future incompetence of either offeror or offeree
- Destruction of the subject matter of the contract
- The purpose of the contract becomes illegal

Expiration of a time limit – Although it is customary to make an offer with a time limit, it is not necessary to do so. If the offeror does not specify a time limit, then the offer expires after a reasonable period of time has elapsed. How long would be reasonable would depend on the circumstances and the nature of the contract.

Revocation by the offeror – Offers may generally be revoked at any time prior to acceptance, even though a stated time limit has not yet expired. An exception occurs in commercial transactions where a firm offer is made and the offeree is granted a time period in which to accept. In cases where the offeree must expend considerable money and effort to determine whether or not to accept the offer, the offeror may be required to leave the offer open for the stated time period.

Another exception occurs where the offeror accepts consideration in exchange for leaving the offer open. This could be viewed as a "contract within a contract" – that is, the offeror has entered into a contract with the offeree, supported by consideration, to leave an offer open. If you think this situation through, you will realize that this is precisely what happens when an option is created.

The offeror may revoke the offer, sometimes even after acceptance. The rule is that the offer can be revoked at any time prior to the offeree's acceptance and ***communication*** of the acceptance back to the offeror. As a rule, communication is effective when the acceptance leaves the hands of the offeree, even though not yet received by the offeror. This is especially true when the offeror mailed the offer to the offeree. Thus, if the offer is mailed to the offeree, the acceptance is good immediately when it has been deposited in the mails properly addressed to the offeror, provided the offer was not otherwise already terminated.

Complex problems can easily arise in the matter of the communication of the acceptance. As a preventive measure, the Administrative Rules state "a copy of the agreement to purchase bearing the signature of the seller(s) shall be delivered to the purchaser as proof that the purchaser's offer was accepted" [WAC 308-124D-020 (3)].

Rejection by the offeree – If the offeree rejects the offer, it is extinguished. As a rule, once the offer has been rejected, the offeree cannot later have a change of heart and accept it, for it no longer exists. To be effective, the rejection must be communicated to the offeror. Unlike an acceptance, the rejection must be received by the offeror before the offer is extinguished.

The fact that rejection of an offer extinguishes the offer is an important point that real estate agents must communicate to the offeree when presenting an offer. For example, suppose you have written an offer to buy and are presenting it to the sellers. The sellers may wish to reject the offer but may not be aware that doing so is final. The sellers may think they can change their mind later as long as the buyers haven't bought another property.

Many times an offeree will make a ***counteroffer***. In fact, real estate agents deal with offers and counteroffers on a daily basis as they try to bring about a meeting of the minds. It is important to understand that a counteroffer is usually really two things – it is a rejection of the offer, coupled with a new offer back to the offeror. The offeror and offeree have traded positions. If the original offer was made by a buyer, now the buyer is the offeree, and can accept, reject or otherwise deal with the seller's counteroffer the same as the seller could with the buyer's original offer.

Nevertheless, it is possible to make a counteroffer without extinguishing the original offer. Suppose, for example, you offer to buy your brother's property for $300,000 and agree to leave the offer open for two weeks. Your brother responds that he is considering your offer, but that he is ready to sell right now for $325,000. In this situation, the offeree (your brother) did not reject the original offer, in fact he definitely stated that he may yet accept it. Your brother has merely made you an offer to consider, an offer whose only relationship to the original offer is that it deals with the same property. Thus, there are two offers on the table – your offer to buy for $300,000 and your brother's offer to sell for $325,000. Either of you can create a contract by accepting the other's offer.

Death or incompetence – Death or incompetence of either the offeror or the offeree terminates most offers if the death or incompetence occurs before the offer is accepted and communicated back to the offeror. Death or incompetence does not terminate ordinary contracts for the sale of property if the contract was already entered into (offer made, accepted and communicated) prior to the death or incompetence of the party.

Destruction of the subject matter of the contract – When the subject of the contract no longer exists, a contract relative to it can no longer be created. If you offer to buy a house, but before the seller accepts and communicates the acceptance back to you, the house burns to the ground, your offer immediately ceases to exist at the time of the fire. Destruction doesn't have to be total. The reason it extinguishes the offer is that there is no longer a meeting of the minds. If a buyer offers to buy a house, then the house as it stood at the time of the offer is what the buyer thought he or she was buying. If the house is altered significantly, then a court would say there was no longer an agreement regarding the subject of the contract, so there is no contract.

The purpose of the contract becomes illegal – A change in the law which makes the purpose of the contract illegal terminates the offer. After all, a contract for an illegal purpose is void, so even an offer to enter into an illegal contract is terminated at the moment it becomes illegal. For example, you might offer to buy a building lot which is zoned commercial, intending to build a retail structure on it. Before the seller accepts your offer the zoning is changed to residential only. Then, at the moment the zoning was changed, your offer was extinguished. Note that if the seller accepted your offer and communicated the acceptance back to you before the zone change, then the contract was already entered into and you are stuck and you must complete the transaction. To avoid these problems we commonly use contingency clauses in real estate contracts (which we will discuss later).

Acceptance – The offer starts the parties on the road to agreement, and the *acceptance* brings them to their destination. Acceptance is said to terminate the offer because it turns it into a contract. We have already observed several points about the acceptance, but there are other issues we must discuss.

For there to be a valid acceptance, the acceptance must be unqualified. The offeree cannot add to, subtract from, or in any way alter the offer. If the offeree makes a change in the original offer, then the offer was not accepted, so no contract was formed. The slightest change means that there is no acceptance. However, when the offeree makes a change in the offer and communicates back to the offeror a willingness to enter into a contract on the new terms, this actually constitutes a counteroffer. If the original offeror (now the offeree) accepts the counteroffer, then a contract will be formed on the new terms.

The acceptance must be made in the manner called for in the offer. Normal offers merely expect the offeree to sign the offer indicating acceptance and return the papers to the offeror. But if the offeror were to state in the offer "if you agree to these terms, then you must accept by telegram to my attorney at the following address _____ ," then the acceptance must be made in this manner or there is no acceptance. Similarly, the acceptance must clearly express acceptance and agreement. For example, this statement by the offeree "yours is the high bid, stop by my office tomorrow" does not constitute an acceptance of the bid, since it did not specifically state that the offeree did, in fact, accept the high bid.

Normally, the offeree must take some action to express the acceptance. Silence or inaction do not generally create an acceptance. For example, suppose an offer is made which states "I will sell you my house for $300,000 and I will assume you accept unless I hear from you by the close of business on Friday." If the offeree remains silent or takes no action, the silence or inaction does not normally create an acceptance. An exception is if the parties have established this as a common custom between them.

Real estate contract essentials

❶

❷

❸

❹

❺

❻

❼

Actions can also create an acceptance, sometimes even when the offeror specifically requires another form of acceptance. For example, suppose that you offer to sell your house to your friend, Mary, and you further state that if she accepts she must do so by returning a signed copy of the earnest money agreement to you. Instead, she calls you and orally states her acceptance. Ordinarily, no contract would occur at this point. But then she arranges a mortgage loan as the buyer of the property. When the loan is approved, she calls you to announce the fact. At this point you open an escrow and order title insurance, naming her as the buyer. A contract has been formed because your actions now indicate your willingness to perform the contract.

Reality of consent

So far, in discussing the formation of a contract, we have limited ourselves to the manner in which the parties manifest their promises. Now we must consider the possibility that the contract may appear to have been agreed to, but one or more of the parties entered into the contract under undue pressure or without complete knowledge of the facts.

These problems normally fall into the categories of undue influence, duress, incompetence, mistake, misrepresentation or fraud. Such contracts are generally voidable, not void. For example, a seller misrepresents the property to the buyer and the buyer buys in reliance on the seller's misrepresentation. The contract is therefore voidable at the option of the buyer. However, if the buyer ratifies the contract, the buyer can then compel performance by the seller. In other words, voidable contracts cannot be enforced on the party who was wronged, but the party who was wronged does have the option of enforcing the contract on the party who committed the wrong.

Undue influence – *Undue influence* occurs when one party takes unfair advantage of the other because there is a position of trust between the parties. Examples of such relationships include parent and child, conservator and ward, pastor and parishioner, attorney and client, principal and agent, among many others. A child, for example, trusts his or her parent, so if the parent proposes a contract with the child, the child may have grounds to assume that it is a fair contract.

It is the principal and agent relationship that is of greatest importance to real estate agents, for this is the relationship that determines the duties and responsibilities of real estate agents to sellers and buyers. When you take a listing on a property you become the seller's agent and you place yourself in a position of utmost trust and loyalty. Now if you wish to enter into a contract with the seller to buy the property yourself, the seller may be entitled to assume that the price and terms you offer are fair market terms. To minimize their legal exposure, agents entering into contracts with their clients typically make clear disclosures that they are acting only on their own behalf and in expectation of profit.

Many people misunderstand the requirements for undue influence. Merely buying a property below market value does not mean there was undue influence. Nor was it undue influence if the seller was foolish or uninformed as to the value. Talking someone into a contract also does not create undue influence as long as there was no position of trust. For it to be undue influence there had to be a position of trust which the wronged party relied upon and, therefore, did not bother to check market value first.

For example, a parent says to a child "buy this property from me for $300,000, which is a fair price." The child assumes the parent would be fair, so the child enters into the contract without verifying the value. Thus there was undue influence. Even then, if the child checks the value and realizes the price is too high, and nevertheless agrees to the price, it is not undue influence.

Duress – Reduced to its simplest form, *duress* occurs when one party forces another to enter into a contract unwillingly. A pointed gun is an obvious example. But other types of threats are not so obvious. A threat of turning someone in to the authorities because of a criminal act the other committed is generally held to be duress, on the grounds that such a threat takes on the aspects of blackmail. But a threat to bring a civil suit against another to recover money or property is not duress because there is nothing wrong in threatening to exercise your rights. It is also not duress if someone buys your property cheaply because you are financially distressed and need to raise cash.

Incompetence – An *incompetent* is incapable of entering into a binding contract because the incompetent does not have the mental faculties to comprehend the impact or consequences of the act. Incompetence can be temporary, as when a party is under stress to the point of insanity, or under the influence of drugs or intoxicants. Or it can be permanent, as in the case of persons who are judged by a court to be mentally incapable of entering into contracts. Such persons are sometimes called ***adjudicated incompetents***. In the case of an adjudicated incompetent, the court will appoint a conservator for the incompetent. The conservator has the power to enter into contracts on behalf of the incompetent, but contracts entered into by the incompetent are void. In contrast, contracts entered into by those who are temporarily incompetent are voidable, and the incompetent must ratify or rescind the contract within a reasonable time after regaining competence.

How incompetent must a party be before the contract is considered voidable? If a real estate agent buys a drink for a buyer and then the buyer makes an offer on a property, was the buyer incompetent? Clearly not, but knowing where the line is could be important. The law says that a party is incompetent if the party was unaware they were entering into a contract or, even if they knew it was a contract, they did not know all of its terms and implications.

Most contracts entered into by minors are also voidable. Persons under 18 years of age in Washington are considered minors, unless emancipated or married to a person of legal age. It is important to note that if a minor enters into a contract, the contract cannot be enforced on the minor, but can be enforced by the minor on the other party. Although minors cannot generally be held to contracts, they are nevertheless responsible for acts constituting libel, fraud or negligence. Minors can also be held to contracts where the minor misrepresented his or her age and the other person relied on the misrepresentation in good faith (RCW 26.28.010 to 26.28.050).

In the case of minors the law creates an exception in the case of a necessary. A ***necessary*** is something the minor needs in order to live, or for the minor's education, or to preserve the minor's station in life. Thus, if a minor absolutely has no way to get to school without a car, then a contract for the purchase of a car can be enforced on the minor.

A question similar to competence also arises when a corporation enters into a contract. A contract entered into by a corporation must be signed by some person who is authorized as the agent of the corporation, otherwise the corporation cannot be held to the contract. Real estate agents should always remember that the fact that a person is an officer of a corporation is no guarantee that the person was authorized.

Corporations usually give certain officers authority to sign contracts on behalf of the corporation in the corporate bylaws. However, the bylaws usually run to many pages, so getting a copy of the bylaws is usually impractical. A simpler course is to obtain a corporate **resolution**, signed by the president and secretary, which authorizes someone named in the resolution to sign a contract on behalf of the corporation. A corporate resolution need only be a couple sentences long.

Even if a contract with a corporation was signed by someone who did not have authority, the other party to the contract may have some recourse. When someone signs for a corporation without authority it is called an **ultra vires** act. The corporation cannot be held to the contract, but the other party to the contract has cause of action against the individual for damages.

Mistake – Mistakes take two forms – **mistake of fact** and **mistake of law**. A mistake of fact may render a contract voidable, but a mistake of law generally has no effect on the enforceability of the contract. Suppose you agree to sell your car to another, but unknown to both of you, the model year is other than what you both believed. This is a mutual mistake of fact and renders the contract voidable by the party who got the bad end of the deal. On the other hand, suppose you enter into a contract believing the terms of the contract to have a particular legal meaning, when in fact, the legal meaning is otherwise. This is a mistake of law and you cannot avoid the contract because everyone is responsible for knowing the law.

To render a contract voidable, a mistake of fact must generally be mutual. That is, both parties must have made the same error. By example, suppose you agree to sell your Ford, but in fact intended to sell your Chevrolet. If the buyer accepts your offer to sell the Ford, then you have sold the Ford. Your error was a unilateral error, not mutual, and the courts consider it a good lesson so you will be more careful in the future. But if the buyer also intended to buy the Chevrolet, then there was a mutual mistake of fact and the contract is voidable.

Nevertheless, it is not considered a mutual mistake, even if both parties are ignorant, as long as both parties know they are ignorant. For example, suppose you sell a gemstone for $10 and neither you nor the buyer know its value, and you both know that neither knows its value. Regardless of its true value, the contract stands because both were aware they were taking a risk.

Misrepresentation and fraud – Contracts entered into in reliance upon a **misrepresentation** or a **fraud** are voidable at the option of the party to whom the misrepresentation or fraud was made. A **fraud in the inducement** occurs when a false statement is made (or material facts are concealed), and the party making the false statement (or concealing the facts) knew the truth. In contrast, a misrepresentation occurs when the party making the false statement (or failing to disclose) did not know the truth. Fraud and misrepresentation are both civil wrongs, that is, the party who was harmed can sue the other. Fraud, however, is also a criminal matter which can land the perpetrator in prison.

Misrepresentation is further categorized as **negligent misrepresentation** and **innocent misrepresentation**. Negligent misrepresentation occurs when the party making the misstatement, or failure to disclose, should have investigated, but failed to do so. Innocent misrepresentation occurs when the party making the misstatement, or failure to disclose, did check the facts from reliable sources, but the information obtained was incorrect. Note that the contract is still voidable by the party who was harmed by the misrepresentation, whether it was negligent or innocent.

To summarize, there are three levels of false statements –

Fraud – False statement deliberately made or deliberate concealment of material facts known to the perpetrator. Fraud is both a civil wrong and a criminal act.

Negligent misrepresentation – False statement made or concealment of material facts where the perpetrator did not know the truth, but should have investigated. A civil wrong only.

Innocent misrepresentation – False statement made or concealment of material facts where the perpetrator did not know the truth and is relying on information deemed to be reliable. A civil wrong only.

Either fraud or misrepresentation can be actual or constructive. ***Actual fraud*** and ***actual misrepresentation*** occur when an actual untrue statement is made orally or in writing. ***Constructive fraud*** and ***constructive misrepresentation*** occur where a party has a duty to disclose a material fact, yet remains silent. In other words, making a statement is actual, keeping quiet is constructive. Again, it does not matter if the fraud or misrepresentation is actual or constructive, in either case the result is a voidable contract.

As we have noted, fraud or misrepresentation can occur either through a false statement (actual), or by failing to disclose (constructive). Failure to disclose creates the majority of problems, so we need to understand what must be disclosed and when. In general, a seller's silence does not constitute fraud or misrepresentation unless the failure to disclose involves a ***latent defect***. A latent defect is any defect which would not be observed during an ordinary examination. Unfortunately, real property has a high potential for latent defects – leaking roofs, bad wiring, poor soil conditions, and the like – all of which could easily be hidden from view.

Even where a latent defect does not amount to fraud or misrepresentation, the injured party may have the right to damages for breach of warranty. And even where no formal warranty exists, the courts will impose an implied warranty of fitness for use.

However, a buyer would have no cause to take legal action against a seller for fraud or misrepresentation unless the matter also involved a ***material fact***. Reduced to its simplest, a material fact is something which is significant. The test is whether a buyer would have offered less, offered different terms, or not have bought at all, if the buyer had known the truth.

In addition, incorrect statements are not misrepresentations or frauds unless the party had a ***right to rely*** on the representation. That is to say, the fraud or misrepresentation must have been committed by someone who would be considered a reliable source of information. As a general rule, the buyer has the right to rely on anything the seller says, or fails to say. This right can sometimes extend to the right to rely on anything the seller's real estate agent says or fails to say.

Many people still believe in the old common-law concept of ***caveat emptor*** (let the buyer beware). While this concept may have been true at one time, courts today tend to disregard it. The modern view is that the doctrine of caveat emptor exalts deceit and dishonesty, and therefore has no place in our system of jurisprudence. Of course, the issue of disclosure and liability for failure to disclose is an evolving area of law with great lack of clarity. Nevertheless, some issues are clear. It is established that if a buyer makes specific inquiry, the seller and the seller's agent are obligated to respond truthfully.

It is also clear that the circumstances of the sale have a great bearing on whether or not a specific fact is material. For example, suppose you sold a wheat farm to another farmer, knowing that the buyer intended to grow grapes on the land. If you know the land is unsuitable for grapes, and you know the buyer is unaware of this fact, then disclosure must be made to the buyer. On the other hand, if the buyer is purchasing the property for a residential subdivision, then the condition of the soil probably becomes irrelevant.

In a 1984 California case, the seller's agent was found equally as liable as the seller for failure to disclose that the soil on the property was subject to landslides (*Easton v Strassburger,* 152 Ca 3rd 90). The California Supreme Court stated "if a broker were required to disclose only known defects, but not also those that are reasonably discoverable, he would be shielded by his ignorance of that which he holds himself out to know … ." Subsequent statutes were enacted in California which hold the broker liable only for those defects which can be ascertained from a visual inspection of the property. This case is not law in Washington, but the trend is clearly toward requiring greater disclosure and toward making the seller's agent liable as well as the seller.

As a result, following the lead of California and other states, the Washington legislature added provisions to Revised Code of Washington specifying the obligations of a real estate agent with respect to property condition disclosures –

RCW 18.86.030 Duties of licensee.

(1) Regardless of whether the licensee is an agent, a licensee owes to all parties to whom the licensee renders real estate brokerage services the following duties, which may not be waived:

(a) To exercise reasonable skill and care;

(b) To deal honestly and in good faith;

...

(d) To disclose all existing material facts known by the licensee and not apparent or readily ascertainable to a party; provided that this subsection shall not be construed to imply any duty to investigate matters that the licensee has not agreed to investigate;

...

(2) Unless otherwise agreed, a licensee owes no duty to conduct an independent inspection of the property or to conduct an independent investigation of either party's financial condition, and owes no duty to independently verify the accuracy or completeness of any statement made by either party or by any source reasonably believed by the licensee to be reliable.

From the preceding it is clear that regardless of which party an agent represents in a sale transaction the agent ordinarily has no duty to investigate matters not apparent upon a visual inspection. However, the agent may still have the duty to disclose matters such as violations of land use laws and housing codes and other things which a court might feel are within the scope of the agent's expertise.

At the same time there are certain statements which are clearly not fraud or misrepresentation, regardless of whether made by the seller or an agent. An **opinion**, clearly stated as such, is not a statement of fact, and therefore not fraud or misrepresentation. Real estate agents should be leery of stating opinions, as they have a tendency to be viewed by the other party as statements of fact. **Puffing** (sometimes called **puffery**) is also not fraud or misrepresentation. Puffing consists of statements made by a agent which are clearly sales talk and not meant to be taken literally. Statements such as "this is the best buy for the money" are considered puffing.

Disclaimers – Many people believe that a disclaimer will protect them from liability. This is frequently inaccurate. In general, the courts will not permit a person to insulate himself or herself from liability for a misrepresentation or fraud merely by refusing to guarantee the statement. However, in cases of innocent misrepresentation a disclaimer can be effective, at least to the extent that it allows the agent to shift the burden to someone else.

Legal object

As we have seen above, forming the agreement between the parties is by far the most complex part in the creation of a contract. But the other essential elements are no less important. The second requirement is that a contract must have a **legal object** (lawful purpose). This simply means that a contract which is in violation of the law is altogether void.

Sometimes, however, the subject of a contract is only partially illegal. For example, in decades past it was not unusual for a developer to place racial and ethnic restrictions in a declaration of subdivision covenants. Today, of course, such restrictions are illegal. But if the declaration also contains restrictions as to the height of fences, setback requirements, and the like, these requirements are still valid and enforceable. In other words, if a portion of a contract is illegal, it does not necessarily render the entire contract void.

Consideration

Most contracts must be supported by **consideration** or they will be void. There are not many exceptions, although real estate agents should be aware that common agency contracts (listings, property management agreements, and so forth) are generally enforceable even without a consideration. For example, if a real estate agent gives free advice, an agency contract may have been created with the other party. Therefore, the agent could be found liable if the advice was faulty.

At its most basic, consideration is whatever is given in exchange for something else. Consideration can be mutual promises (a promise for a promise), it can be a promise for an act, or it can even be a promise in exchange for a forbearance to act. For example, "I give you my car and you give me $10,000" expresses a promise for a promise. Or "I will give you $2,500 and you will paint my house" is a promise for an act. A promise for a forbearance to act could be "I will give you $10,000 and you will take no further legal action against me." Consideration can also be a change of position – taking a different posture in exchange for some benefit. Consideration can even be love and affection. The main idea is that the parties have bargained with each other at arms length; both have given and both have received.

Legal sufficiency – The fact that there is consideration may not be enough for the contract to be enforceable. To be legally sufficient, the consideration must be *either* a legal detriment to the donor, *or* a legal benefit to the recipient. It is not required that both elements be present. A **legal benefit** is something the recipient was not previously entitled to and a **legal detriment** is something a party will do which the party was previously under no compulsion to do. Consider the following agreement "I, Jane Doe, will pay all your tuition and fees if you will attend and graduate from Washington State University." If you do, indeed, perform your part of the bargain, Jane obtains no actual benefit, yet she obtains a legal benefit because she receives something to which she was not previously entitled. The fact that your having attended college is useless to her, is irrelevant. You, of course, receive both an actual benefit and a legal benefit. This can create some interesting effects. Consider the following cases –

1. Jones owes $1,000 to Markel. Markel and Jones later agree that Jones will tender and Markel will accept $500 as payment in full. Jones tenders the $500 to Markel. Markel then successfully sues for the remaining $500. The legal principle is that in tendering $500 to Markel, Jones (donor) suffers no legal detriment, because he was already obligated to pay at least that much to Markel. Markel gains no legal benefit, because he already has the right to expect payment of $1,000, a greater sum than *the sum tendered. Hence, the contract to tender $500 as payment in full fails for lack of consideration.*

2. Smith owes $5,000 to Gatsby due on December 31. Smith tenders $2,500 to Gatsby on December 15, and in so doing, marks the check "payment in full." Gatsby sees what Smith wrote on the check, endorses it, and deposits it to his account. Gatsby then tries to collect the remaining $2,500 and is unsuccessful. The legal principle is that tendering payment prior to its due date is a legal detriment to the donor (Smith) and also a legal benefit to the recipient (Gatsby). While it is true that receipt of the $2,500 prior to its due date may be of no actual benefit, it is neverthe-less a legal benefit, since Gatsby did not have the right to demand payment before December 31. And even if it were not a legal detriment to Gatsby, it is still a legal detriment to Smith, which fact alone would be sufficient for the $2,500 to qualify as consideration.

Adequacy of consideration – In general, the courts will refuse to be the arbiters of the bargain. If you make a bad deal, you must live with it. There are exceptions, how-ever, particularly when the contract was entered into as a result of duress or undue influ-ence. In these cases, the courts will refuse to enforce the contract for lack of adequate consideration if the court feels the contract was not at arms length. Contracts where the consideration is grossly inadequate and undue influence is present are called **unconscio-nable contracts**. The test is that the contract must "shock the conscience of the court."

Cases of no consideration – In some cases, the courts may find there to be no consideration, even though at first blush it may appear to exist. For example, past consid-eration is no consideration. That is, a promise made on account of something the other party has already done or given, is not consideration.

There is also deemed to be no consideration when the consideration is stated to be "all of a certain commodity the buyer may want or desire." This type of expression is considered too vague and uncertain. The buyer may buy none of the commodity, and in buying none would exactly fulfill the contract. Hence, the promise is illusory – it appears to be consideration, but in fact, is no promise at all.

Good vs. valuable consideration – Consideration is **valuable consideration** if it derives from a moral duty or from love. It is **good consideration** if it is of a nature that anyone would accept. For example, if you deed your property to your child for the child's love and affection, this is valuable consideration. But it is not good consideration because your child's love and affection for you is probably of no value to anyone else. Money, in contrast, is always good consideration because anyone will accept money. Similarly, a parcel of real estate in an exchange transaction is good consideration to the party receiv-ing it, as would anything else that has a market value.

Identified and competent parties

As noted previously, a contract entered into by one who is incompetent is either void or voidable. As a rule, if the incompetence is permanent, as where the individual has been adjudicated incompetent by a court, then the contract is void. On the other hand contracts entered into by those who are temporarily incompetent, including minors, are voidable at the option of the incompetent.

An important question arises when a party to a contract was competent at the time of entering into the contract, but becomes incompetent in the future. In these cas-es, normally the contract stands unaffected by the future incompetence. It is generally only in the creation of the contract that the parties must have been competent.

However, a future incompetence does render certain contracts unenforceable. Most notably, these include *personal service contracts*. Personal service contracts cover all kinds of employment arrangements, including a real estate agent's listing contract, buyer service agreement, or property management agreement. Thus, if a broker has a listing on a property, the listing is terminated if either the broker or the seller become incompetent.

In most cases, a contract will be void if it fails to identify the parties with certainty. The exact name is not required, nor must the name be spelled accurately. The legal test is whether or not the parties can be ascertained. Therefore, if a contract identifies one of the parties as "my brother's wife by his first marriage," the person is identified adequately, since this identifies only one person in the world. As to misspelled names, the law goes by the rule of *idem sonans* – that is, if it sounds the same when pronounced, it is the same in the eyes of the law, regardless of how badly it is misspelled.

A sufficient writing

We discussed previously that contracts which involve real property must generally be in writing to be enforceable. Note that the statutes declare that such contracts are void, not voidable, if they are not in writing.

While a contract involving real estate must normally be in writing, the law does not imply any firm rule for the nature of the writing. The statute merely requires a "note or memorandum" of the contract. The sufficiency of the writing is a matter for a court to decide on a case-by-case basis.

An adequate description of the property

The last of the essential elements for the formation of a contract is that there be an adequate description of the property. The description is required only for contracts involving property, of course. Note that this does include contracts involving personal property, as well as real property.

Washington courts do not generally require any particular format for the description. The test is whether a disinterested party could segregate the property from surrounding property with certainty. The standard generally required is that it must be accurate to within two inches per hundred feet. Thus a statement that the property boundaries are certain natural objects on the land (a large rock, a tree, etc.) is adequate as long as the objects are described with sufficient certainty and accuracy that anyone can locate and identify them.

Luckily real estate agents rarely have a problem getting an adequate description of the property. The description is on all important documents, so it is readily available. For example, when taking a listing the agent can just ask the seller for their latest tax statement, a copy of their loan papers, or some other document involving the property. All will have a description that will probably be adequate.

However, there are certain exceptions that agents should be wary of. One is using an assessor's *tax parcel number*, also sometimes called a *tax lot number*. Tax parcel numbers are assigned by the county tax assessor. The tax assessor is constantly changing the official tax parcel numbers for properties, which causes a great deal of confusion and potential error. Tax parcel numbers should be used with caution.

Agents should also avoid using a street address. Except for rental agreements and leases, a street address is legally insufficient. Still, there may be cases where you have no choice. Suppose, for example, you are taking a listing from the sellers over lunch in a restaurant. They probably wouldn't have any documentation with them from which to get an accurate legal description. If they are ready to list it would be poor sales practice to delay. So you take the listing with the street address, knowing the listing is not enforceable. As soon as you are back in your office you can prepare some communication with the sellers to clarify the legal description, which will then become an addendum to the listing.

In many cases the legal description is very long, which becomes very cumbersome to work with. In these cases you can adequately describe the property by reference to a document that is recorded and which contains the full description (e.g., the sellers' deed). When a document has been recorded it creates what the law calls constructive notice. **Constructive notice** means that everyone is legally deemed to know it, whether they actually did or not. Thus you could describe the property in your listing or earnest money agreement as "as described in owners' deed recorded under auditor's recording number _____ ."

Real estate contracts generally need the adequate description only once. Subsequent references to the property in the contract can use an abbreviated description. For example, most earnest money forms say "the property being sold is described as [legal description], also known as [street address]." Now you have tied the street address to the legal description, so from now on the contract can just use the street address, including addendums, exhibits, counteroffers, and other subsequent documents.

Unenforceable contracts (discharge)

As we have seen, there are countless obstacles to the creation of a contract. Nevertheless, people regularly enter into binding and enforceable contracts and somehow manage to meet the requirements of the law in the process. But now we must consider the possibility that a valid contract, duly entered into with the required formalities, might still be rendered unenforceable by other factors. Legally speaking, we would say that the duties of the parties under the contract have been discharged.

Some of the ways in which a duty to perform can be discharged are simple. For example, no obligation is intended to survive forever, so a contract which has been fully performed (executed) is no longer enforceable. Also, when a contract contains an expiration date and the date has come and gone, the contract is no longer enforceable. Such matters are obvious.

Conditions – Not so obvious is the possibility of a condition. A condition is any event, the happening, or non-happening of which, limits, modifies or terminates a contractual obligation. In real estate contracts it is common to find *expressed conditions*, that is, conditions formally expressed in the language of the contract. Sometimes, however, a condition is an *implied condition*, a condition whose existence is not formally stated, but inferred from the nature of the promise, or where the law requires such a condition. A buyer might agree to buy your single-family house "to convert it to a duplex," even though you and the buyer both know it is currently zoned for a single-family residence. Such a contract implies that proper land use approval be obtained as a condition to the contract.

Conditions are also classed as conditions precedent, concurrent, and subsequent. A **condition precedent** exists when some event must occur before the duty to perform arises. **Concurrent conditions** exist only when performance by both parties can be simultaneous. This is commonly implicit in real estate sales contracts where the deed and purchase price are to be exchanged at closing. When a contract contains concurrent conditions, neither party may compel performance by the other without first performing his or her side of the bargain.

A *condition subsequent* is a condition which discharges an existing duty. Conditions subsequent abound in real estate sales contracts, especially due to financing requirements. E.g., "I will buy your house for $300,000, provided I can obtain a loan of $240,000" – the duty to buy your house for $300,000 exists as soon as we both agree to the formal contract, but my duty to perform is discharged if the loan cannot be obtained.

Note how critical the financing contingency is to the buyer. Without the contingency the buyer would still be obligated to complete the purchase, even if the loan cannot be obtained. Since the buyer probably is not in a position to pay cash, the buyer would be forced into default. Upon the buyer's default the seller can claim forfeiture of the earnest money or potentially other remedies.

In common real estate parlance, real estate agents use the term **contingency** to describe any type of condition. As a practical matter, this terminology is generally adequate, since it does not usually matter what type of condition it is – it merely matters that the condition can or cannot be met.

Prevention of performance – If one party to a contract prevents the other from performing, the other may be discharged from the contract. This usually occurs in conjunction with a condition. For example, Green offers to buy Brown's house for $400,000, provided that a loan of $300,000 can be obtained. Brown accepts the offer and a contract is formed. But when the bank sends out an appraiser, Brown tells the appraiser that there are hidden structural problems, even though he knows no such problems exist. As a result, the bank refuses to lend the full amount. Green will therefore be discharged from the duty to perform the contract, although Green may compel performance by Brown if he wishes to complete the purchase anyway.

Breach – In bilateral contracts, both parties are obligated to perform. Therefore, a breach by one party may discharge the other's obligation to perform. As a rule, the breach must be a material breach, significant enough that if would cause a reasonable person to question whether full performance would ever be forthcoming.

Repudiation – When one party to a bilateral contract announces that he or she no longer intends to perform the contract, this is called *repudiation*. If the repudiation is announced prior to the time when the performance was called for, it is called *anticipatory repudiation*. If the contract is bilateral, and one of the parties announces an intention not to perform it, the other party may treat this as a breach which excuses his or her performance as well. When anticipatory repudiation is announced, and the other party accepts it, this constitutes *renunciation* and both parties are then discharged.

Time is of the essence – Contracts calling for performance by certain due dates always have a *time is of the essence* clause. Such contracts include mortgages, trust deeds, land sales contracts, leases, and also earnest money agreements and the like – any contract where there is a deadline for performance by one or more of the parties.

The phrase "time is of the essence" is significant not so much for what it means but, rather, what happens if you leave it out of the contract. If the contract does not have the "time is of the essence" clause, then all dates in the contract are suggested dates. If a party fails to perform by a date the other party must notify the party who failed to perform of their failure and give them a demand that they perform within a stated, reasonable time. Only if the party still fails to perform by the end of the time given in the notice can a default be declared. In contrast, placing the "time is of the essence" clause in a contract means that all dates are absolute and no notice is required to declare a default.

Novation – A *novation* occurs when a new party is substituted for one of the original parties to a contract. The new party can substitute for either of the original parties. Novations occur chiefly in debtor-creditor contracts such as mortgages, trust deeds, land sales contracts and leases. In a typical novation, the creditor agrees to accept the new borrower or lessee and relieve the original debtor of the obligation.

Alteration of the contract – If one party to a contract materially alters the contract to the party's benefit, the obligation of the other party is discharged.

Subsequent illegality – If a contract is executory in nature, and during the performance the subject of the contract becomes illegal, both parties' obligations under the contract are discharged.

Impossibility – A contract becomes unenforceable if the contract has become *impossible* to perform. Impossibility of performance excuses a party from a contract only if the situation is such that no one could perform the contract. In other words, personal matters such as financial distress or future incompetence do not discharge a contract. But the destruction of a house by fire just before the closing of a contract of sale discharges the contract because no one could sell the house now. In some circumstances a contract will also be discharged when it is impractical to perform, even though technically possible. Note also that a personal service contract is terminated by the death of either party, due to the fact that it is no longer possible to perform it.

Laches – The principle of *laches* holds that a party to a contract will be barred from asserting any rights under the contract if the party lets too much time elapse before asserting the right. This usually occurs when a court dismisses a complaint because the plaintiff waited too long before filing the suit. Because laches is subjective, there are Statutes of Limitations setting forth the time limit within which suits must be filed. The length of time varies according to the nature of the suit. For example, a suit to recover an interest in real property must be filed within ten years, but a suit arising out of a verbal contract must be commenced within only three years.

Bankruptcy – Bankruptcy discharges most debt obligations. However, debts arising out of fraud or misrepresentation may not be discharged by a bankruptcy. Certain other ongoing obligations, such as child support, are also not dischargeable in bankruptcy. Listing and other agency contracts may be terminated by the bankruptcy of either the principal or the agent.

Mutual rescission – A voidable contract can be rendered unenforceable if the party with the right to rescind elects to do so. A contract can also be rescinded by the mutual agreement of the parties. Remember, however, that a rescission, whether mutual or unilateral, requires the parties be placed in the position they were in before they entered into the contract, as far as possible.

Another matter to note about a mutual rescission is that it is another contract. In fact, it is a contract to end a contract. As such, the law requires that it meet the same formalities as are required of the contract it is ending. So a real estate contract must be in writing and adequately describe the property to be enforceable, therefore a mutual rescission of a real estate contract must also be in writing and adequately describe the property.

Waiver – When one of the parties voluntarily gives up a contract right, this is called a *waiver*. Since implied waiver is a common defense to a suit for breach of contract, it is common for parties to a contract to state that no waiver or modification to the contract is valid unless it is in writing. In many instances there are consumer protection laws (such as the Washington Residential Landlord-Tenant Law, among others) which prohibit a consumer from waiving his or her rights.

Estoppel – Whenever you are barred from asserting a right, whether the right arose from a contract or in another way, this is called an *estoppel*. We would say that you have been estopped. We have seen some of the ways in which parties to contracts are estopped from asserting their rights because the duty of the other party to perform has been discharged. However, the concept of estoppel is a complex area of law. There are many other circumstances which can give rise to estoppel besides the discharge of a duty to perform a contract.

Rule of parol evidence

Stated simply, the **rule of parol evidence** is that oral (parol) testimony to change the terms of a written contract is not permitted. Part of its purpose is to preserve the sanctity of the written contract as the clear expression of the intent of the parties. Thus, if a provision was left out of a written contract, the court would normally disregard the oral testimony of one of the parties that it was his or her intention to include the provision. Another purpose of the rule of parol evidence is to be an object lesson – draft your contracts with care and thought, for later you will have to live with whatever the words say.

Although the following is not an exhaustive list, the rule of parol evidence does not generally apply to
- Contracts which are partly oral and partly written
- Obvious gross clerical and typographical errors
- Defenses of fraud, duress, undue influence or illegal object
- An orally agreed upon condition precedent
- Defining such terms as "customary," "common practice" and the like

In other words, the purpose of the rule is to preserve a written contract as far as possible without creating obvious injustice.

Reformation and interpretation of contracts

Parties to a contract may ask a court to determine the meaning of a contract when they cannot reach mutual agreement between themselves. This is done by filing a suit for **reformation** of the contract. In interpreting the contract, the court will use the rules for interpretation of contracts.

In interpreting the meaning of the language in a written contract, there are numerous rules a court must follow. These are called the rules for interpretation of contracts. The following list is far from complete, but it contains those rules which a real estate agent would find most helpful –
- Technical terms are given their technical meaning, unless the context clearly indicates a different meaning.
- When a provision which ought to be contained in the original contract is missing, that which is good custom in the community prevails. For example a listing which fails to state the commission rate will be presumed to be at the rate which is most common in the area for the kind of property involved in the listing.
- When a printed form is used, typewritten material takes precedence over the printed form; handwritten material takes precedence over both the printed and typed portions.
- Where a public interest is affected, an interpretation is preferred which favors the public interest.
- When there is inconsistency between general provisions and specific provisions, the specific provisions take precedence over the general.
- In construing the meaning of the language of a contract, all circumstances surrounding the contract may be taken into consideration.

- Where there is a series of contracts, the later controls the former. E.g., a listing might exclude the range and refrigerator, but if the seller later accepts an offer which includes them, the earnest money is what the court follows.
- A contract is construed most strenuously against the party who drafted it.

Remedies

Contracts typically stipulate various remedies which one or the other party may seek in the event of a breach by the other. Not all remedies are always available in all contracts. For example, foreclosure is obviously a remedy which can only be used by a lender in a mortgage, trust deed or land sales contract. In the following section we will discuss other remedies which a real estate agent may encounter.

Damages – A suit for damages is one of the most commonly used remedies. Damages can arise through a breach of a contract (*contract damages*), or as a result of a tort (*tort damages*). A *tort* is a civil wrong, such as, for example, an automobile accident. When arising from a tort, damages can be either *punitive damages* or *compensatory damages*. Contract damages are generally limited to compensatory damages.

Punitive damages, as the term would imply, are commonly thought of as punishment. It is true that punishment is one of the purposes of punitive damages. But the modern view of punitive damages also includes the idea that the case should become an object lesson. The idea is that others will realize that the actions which gave rise to the award of punitive damages are not to be condoned.

Compensatory damages, on the other hand, are designed to provide compensation for the loss suffered by the aggrieved party. There are various categories of compensatory damages. *Actual damages*, for example, are simply the exact amount of the loss. But even if a party has not suffered any actual loss, he or she may still sue for damages. In the event the court finds that the defendant breached the contract, but the plaintiff cannot demonstrate any actual damages, the court may award a small sum as *nominal damages*.

Sometimes one party's actions cause a series of events which cause further harm to the other party. In such cases, the other party may be entitled to *consequential damages* (also sometimes called *special damages*). For example, suppose you sell a warehouse. You know the roof leaks, but you deliberately withhold this information from the buyer, even though you know the buyer plans to store furniture in the warehouse. Subsequently, the buyer's furniture is damaged. In this case, the buyer would be entitled not only to actual damages (the cost of the roof repair), but consequential damages as well for the loss of the furniture.

A special problem occurs in some contracts where the dollar amount of the damages would be difficult to determine. The classic example of this is a contract for the sale of real estate (earnest money agreement). Suppose the buyer under an earnest money agreement defaults at the last minute. The seller has been damaged, but how many dollars is the seller's loss worth? In most contracts, the dollar amount of damages is fairly easy to ascertain, but in a case such as this, it can become very difficult. After all, the seller still owns the property. And the seller's real estate agent is the only one who spent actual time and money to advertise and market it. Therefore, in circumstances such as these, the courts will enforce a provision in a contract for a special kind of compensatory damages, called *liquidated damages*. Liquidated damages are a prior agreed upon amount, stipulated in the contract.

In a typical earnest money agreement, the earnest money itself is defined as liquidated damages if the buyer should breach the contract. A liquidated damages clause is also common in a land sales contract, where it stipulates that the buyer's down payment is forfeit as liquidated damages if the buyer fails to perform. Real estate agents should be aware the courts will not likely enforce a liquidated damages clause where the amount of the damages is not reasonable in the light of the circumstances surrounding the contract. Also, since actual damages are more accurate, the courts will also refuse to enforce a liquidated damages clause when actual damages could be determined.

Whenever you have been damaged, you must do everything possible to lessen the amount of the loss. This is called the duty to *mitigate*. You cannot claim any recompense for losses you could have avoided.

Restitution – Although not always granted, an injured party may sometimes seek *restitution* as an alternative to damages. For example, suppose you deed property to a buyer, but after recording your deed, the buyer's check fails to clear the bank. You could sue for damages in the amount of the purchase price, or you could sue for restitution, that is, forcing the buyer to deed the property back to restore your ownership. Restitution is also the remedy sought by a landlord when filing a suit for unlawful detainer.

Specific performance – In most cases, a suit for damages or a suit for restitution are the only remedies available. However, in certain cases the courts will allow the remedy of *specific performance*. A suit for specific performance seeks an order from the court compelling the other party to perform as agreed. As a general rule, the remedy of specific performance is only granted if justice demands that it be applied. Consider the following two cases –

1. You enter into a contract to purchase 100 cases of a certain type of ballpoint pens from a supplier at a price which is below the usual price for that quantity. The supplier defaults and fails to supply the pens as agreed. The same pens are available elsewhere, although at a higher price. If you sue for specific performance, you will lose. The key lies in the fact that the goods were available elsewhere, so you did not need the remedy of specific performance for justice to prevail. You could sue for damages to the extent that buying the pens elsewhere cost you more, i.e. a suit for damages to the extent of the benefit of the bargain would succeed.

2. You contract to buy land from the owner for $100,000 cash, the contract to be closed in escrow in one month. On the closing date, you tender the cash and required documents to the escrow as agreed. The seller thereupon defaults and refuses to close the transaction. In this case you could sue for damages, but specific performance could be granted as an alternative. Your argument is that specific performance is required because the real estate is unique and there is no other property exactly like the property you contracted to buy. Since you cannot obtain an identical substitute at any price, the only remedy that will give you complete justice is specific performance.

As these cases illustrate, ordinary contracts cannot be enforced by specific performance. But real estate sales contracts involve a commodity that is always unique, so contracts involving real property can usually be enforced by specific performance as an alternative to damages.

Real estate agents should also be aware that personal service contracts cannot be enforced by specific performance. These include listings, buyer's service agreements, property management agreements and other broker's employment contracts. In other words, if the seller wants to cancel a listing, the seller can do so at any time. If the seller's cancellation of the listing is wrongful, the agent can sue for damages.

Accord and satisfaction – Suppose you have entered into a contract to buy a property. Just before closing you discover a significant defect. When you contact the seller about the problem the seller agrees to lower the price by $2,000 if you agree to consummate the transaction anyway. If you agree, this is an *accord and satisfaction*, a voluntary recasting of the contract. As long as each of you received something for the new agreement, the courts will enforce the new terms. Think of an accord and satisfaction as a contract to alter a contract.

Assignment and novation

The subject of assignment of contracts is complex. At its simplest, an **assignment** occurs when you name someone else to stand in your position in a contract. But we need to take care here to distinguish between contract *rights* and contract *duties*. In a typical bilateral contract, both parties have rights as well as duties. The rights can be assigned, but the duties can only be delegated.

Take, for example, a land sales contract. The seller has the right to receive the payments, and the duty to deliver the deed when the buyer makes the final payment. The right to receive the payments can be assigned to a third party, but the duty to deliver the deed can only be delegated. Consider what would happen then if the seller assigns his or her rights under the contract, and the buyer then finishes paying the balance due. If the seller's assignee fails to deliver the deed to the buyer, the buyer can take action against the original seller as well as the seller's assignee. Similarly, the buyer has rights of use and enjoyment which can be assigned to a third party, but the buyer's duty to pay can only be delegated.

As discussed previously, a novation is a new contract replacing an old agreement. The distinction between an assignment and a novation is that in an assignment, the assignor is not relieved of the duty to perform, whereas the novation does release the original party from his or her obligations. So if, in our land sales contract example above, the buyer assigns his or her rights to a third party, and thereupon the seller were to release the original buyer from the duty to perform, this would be construed as a substitution of borrower (novation), not an assignment.

Note what happens in a typical **assumption** of a loan. When the buyer assumes the loan, the buyer agrees to become personally obligated for the balance due. The lender has two remedies – foreclosure, or sue the borrower personally to obtain a personal judgment against the borrower for the balance due. To assume creates the same legal obligation as a co-signature. Nevertheless, the buyer's assumption does not relieve the original borrower from the obligation. Now the lender has full obligation to pay from both parties in addition to the right to foreclose.

Many people are unaware that when a buyer assumes their old loan they remain liable. Even if they are aware of it, they think the buyer is "primarily liable" and that they are only "secondarily liable." This is inaccurate. If the buyer defaults the creditor can sue both as co-defendants. There is no "primary" or "secondary" to it. When the lender obtains a judgment it allows the lender to reach assets of either party to satisfy it. The lender has no obligation to attempt to reach the assets of the buyer first and the seller only if the buyer's assets are insufficient. As a practical matter, the lender will go first after the assets that are easiest to reach (e.g., a bank account), without regard to whose assets they are.

The common rule about assignments is that you are generally able to assign your rights under a contract unless the contract prohibits assignment. That is, silence is permission. However, there are certain situations where contract rights cannot be assigned. Rights under a personal service contract, for example, cannot be assigned. As an extreme example, consider the possibility of assigning your interest in a marriage contract. Also, a mere offer cannot be assigned. But if an offeree has given an offeror consideration in exchange for leaving an offer open, then an option has been created. Rights under an option can be assignable.

Uniform Vendor and Purchaser Risk Act

What happens when a property is damaged by fire or other act of God in the middle of a transaction? The **Uniform Vendor and Purchaser Risk Act** addresses this issue. If title has passed to the buyer, or if the buyer has taken possession of the property, even if the transaction has not yet closed, then the buyer is liable for any damages. Otherwise, the seller is liable for the loss. Note that the Uniform Vendor and Purchaser Risk Act has not been adopted by the Washington Legislature, but the Washington Supreme Court referenced and upheld the Act in *Pierce County v. King* (47 Wn 2d 328). Therefore, when the buyer receives possession before closing, the real estate agent should be careful to advise the buyer to obtain casualty insurance immediately on taking possession.

Seller property transfer disclosure

Because failure to disclose material latent defects in the property has become a significant problem, the 1994 Washington Legislature enacted laws (RCW Chapter 64.06) requiring sellers of residential property to complete a property disclosure statement and deliver it to the buyer within five days of entering into a purchase agreement, unless the parties agree to a different period of time. The form of the disclosure statement must be as prescribed by the statute (see form on the following pages).

The seller disclosure requirement applies only to residential properties of one to four units, including sales of mobile homes (whether real or personal), and resales of condominiums and timeshares. Sales by financial institutions of properties acquired by foreclosure are exempt, as are sales of properties by receivers, personal representatives, guardians and conservators. Sales to persons who have held a less than freehold interest in the property for two or more years are also exempt.

Even when the sale is not exempt the buyer can waive the requirement of the disclosure form. In addition, the seller can refuse to give the buyer the completed disclosure form. If the seller gives the buyer the disclosure form the buyer has three days from receipt of it in which to approve the disclosure statement or rescind the purchase contract. If the buyer does nothing within the three days then the buyer is deemed to have approved it and the buyer's right to rescind ends. Similarly, once the buyer has closed the transaction the buyer's right to rescind ends. However, if the seller has not given the buyer the disclosure form and the buyer has not waived it, then the buyer's right to rescind the agreement lasts until three days after closing. Note that it is strictly up to the buyer to decide whether to accept the disclosure form or rescind. The buyer need make no explanation or have any particular reason for the rescission. If the buyer rescinds the buyer is entitled to a full refund of the earnest money deposit.

If the seller discovers an error in the disclosure statement or the condition of the property changes making the statement inaccurate, the seller must give the buyer an amended disclosure form. Upon receipt of the amended form the buyer has three days again to accept and approve of it or rescind. If the seller wishes, the seller can take corrective action instead of giving the buyer the amended disclosure form. If the seller corrects the situation then the buyer does not have an additional right to rescind.

The disclosure form does not constitute a warranty from the seller or the seller's real estate agent to the buyer. The seller and the seller's agent are liable for incorrect statements made on the form only if they had knowledge that the statements were false. Although the disclosure form requirement does not directly involve real estate agents, it is common practice for licensees to take the disclosure form from the seller at the time of taking the listing.

REAL PROPERTY TRANSFER DISCLOSURE STATEMENT
Instructions to the Seller

Please complete the following form. Do not leave any spaces blank. If the question clearly does not apply to the property write "NA". If the answer is "yes" to any * items, please explain on attached sheets. Please refer to the line number(s) of the question(s) when you provide your explanation(s). For your protection you must date and sign each page of this disclosure statement and each attachment. Delivery of the disclosure statement must occur not later than five business days, unless otherwise agreed, after mutual acceptance of a written contract to purchase between a buyer and a seller.

Notice to the Buyer

The following disclosures are made by the seller(s), concerning the condition of the property located at _____ City _____ County _____ ("the property"), or as legally described on attached exhibit a.

Disclosures contained in this form are provided by the seller on the basis of seller's actual knowledge of the property at the time this disclosure form is completed by the seller. You have three business days, unless otherwise agreed, from the seller's delivery of this seller's disclosure statement to rescind your agreement by delivering your separate signed written statement of rescission to the seller, unless you waive this right at or prior to entering into a sale agreement. The following are disclosures made by the seller and are not the representations of any real estate licensee or other party. This information is for disclosure only and is not intended to be a part of any written agreement between the buyer and the seller.

For a more comprehensive examination of the specific condition of this property you are advised to obtain and pay for the services of a qualified specialist to inspect the property on your behalf, for example, architects, engineers, land surveyors, plumbers, electricians, roofers, building in-spectors, or pest and dry rot inspectors. The prospective buyer and the owner may wish to obtain professional advice or inspections of the property and to provide for appropriate provisions in a contract between them with respect to any advice, inspection, defects or warranties.

Seller ❑ is/ ❑ is not occupying the property.

I. Seller's disclosures:

*If "Yes" attach a copy or explain. If necessary use an attached sheet.

1. Title

❑ Yes ❑ No ❑ Don't know   A. Do you have legal authority to sell the property?

❑ Yes ❑ No ❑ Don't know   *B. Is title to the property subject to any of the following?

                    (1) First right of refusal

                    (2) Option

                    (3) Lease or rental agreement

                    (4) Life estate?

❑ Yes ❑ No ❑ Don't know   *C. Are there any encroachments, boundary agreements, or boundary disputes?

❑ Yes ❑ No ❑ Don't know   *D. Are there any rights of way, easements, or access limitations that may affect the owner's use of the property?

❑ Yes ❑ No ❑ Don't know   *E. Are there any written agreements for joint maintenance of an easement or right of way?

❑ Yes ❑ No ❑ Don't know   *F. Is there any study, survey project, or notice that would adversely affect the property?

❑ Yes ❑ No ❑ Don't know   *G. Are there any pending or existing assessments against the property?

❑ Yes ❑ No ❑ Don't know   *H. Are there any zoning violations, non-conforming uses, or any unusual restrictions on the subject property that would affect future construction or remodeling?

❑ Yes ❑ No ❑ Don't know   *I. Is there a boundary survey for the property?

❑ Yes ❑ No ❑ Don't know   *J. Are there any covenants, conditions, or restrictions which affect the property?

2. WATER

    A. Household Water

        (1) The source of the water is ❑ Public ❑ Community ❑ Private ❑ Shared

        (2) Water source information:

❑ Yes ❑ No ❑ Don't know   *a. Are there any written agreements for shared water source?

❑ Yes ❑ No ❑ Don't know   *b. Is there an easement (recorded or unrecorded) for access to and/or maintenance of the water source?

❑ Yes ❑ No ❑ Don't know   *c. Are any known problems or repairs needed?

❑ Yes ❑ No ❑ Don't know   *d. Does the source provide an adequate year round supply of potable water?

❑ Yes ❑ No ❑ Don't know   *(3) Are there any water treatment systems for the property? ❑ Leased ❑ Owned

    B. Irrigation

❑ Yes ❑ No ❑ Don't know   (1) Are there any water rights for the property?

❑ Yes ❑ No ❑ Don't know   *(2) If they exist, to your knowledge, have the water rights been used during the last five-year period?

❑ Yes ❑ No ❑ Don't know   *(3) If so, is the certificate available?

    C. Outdoor Sprinkler System

❑ Yes ❑ No ❑ Don't know   (1) Is there an outdoor sprinkler system for the property?

❑ Yes ❑ No ❑ Don't know   *(2) Are there any defects in the outdoor sprinkler system?

3. SEWER/SEPTIC SYSTEM

    A. The property is served by: ❑ Public sewer main ❑ Septic tank system ❑ Other disposal system (describe)

❑ Yes ❑ No ❑ Don't know   B. If the property is served by a public or community sewer main, is the house connected to the main?

    C. Is the property currently subject to a sewer capacity charge?

    D. If the property is connected to a septic system:

❑ Yes ❑ No ❑ Don't know   (1) Was a permit issued for its construction, and was it approved by the city or county following its construction?

    (2) When was it last pumped:

    _____ , 20 _____ .

❑ Yes ❑ No ❑ Don't know   *(3) Are there any defects in the operation of the septic system?

❑ Don't know   (4) When was it last inspected? _____

    By Whom: _____

❑ Don't know   (5) How many bedrooms was the system approved for? _____ bedrooms

❑ Yes ❑ No ❑ Don't know   *E. Do all plumbing fixtures, including laundry drain, go to the septic/sewer system?

If no, explain: _____

❑ Yes ❑ No ❑ Don't know   *F. Are you aware of any changes or repairs to the septic system?

❑ Yes ❑ No ❑ Don't know   G. Is the septic tank system, including the drainfield, located entirely within the boundaries of the property?

4. STRUCTURAL

❑ Yes ❑ No ❑ Don't know   *A. Has the roof leaked?

❑ Yes ❑ No ❑ Don't know   If yes, has it been repaired?

❑ Yes ❑ No ❑ Don't know   *B. Have there been any conversions, additions, or remodeling?

❑ Yes ❑ No ❑ Don't know   *1. If yes, were all building permits obtained?

❑ Yes ❑ No ❑ Don't know   *2. If yes, were all final inspections obtained?

❑ Yes ❑ No ❑ Don't know   C. Do you know the age of the house? If yes, year of original construction:

❑ Yes ❑ No ❑ Don't know   *D. Do you know of any settling, slippage, or sliding of either the house or other structures/improvements located on the property? If yes, explain:

❑ Yes ❑ No ❑ Don't know   *E. Do you know of any defects with the following: (Please check applicable items)

         ❑ Foundations ❑ Decks ❑ Exterior Walls
         ❑ Chimneys ❑ Interior Walls ❑ Fire Alarm
         ❑ Doors ❑ Windows ❑ Patio
         ❑ Ceilings ❑ Slab Floors ❑ Driveways
         ❑ Pools ❑ Hot Tub ❑ Sauna
         ❑ Sidewalks ❑ Outbuildings ❑ Fireplaces
         ❑ Garage Floors ❑ Walkways
         ❑ Other ❑ Wood Stoves

❑ Yes ❑ No ❑ Don't know   *F. Was a pest or dry rot, structural or "whole house" inspection done? When and by whom was the inspection completed?

❑ Yes ❑ No ❑ Don't know   *G. Since assuming ownership, has your property had a problem with wood destroying organisms and/or have there been any problems with pest control, infestations, or vermin?

5. Systems and fixtures

If the following systems or fixtures are included with the transfer, do they have any existing defects:

❑ Yes ❑ No ❑ Don't know   *A. Electrical system, including wiring, switches, outlets, and service
❑ Yes ❑ No ❑ Don't know   *B. Plumbing system, including pipes, faucets, fixtures, and toilets
❑ Yes ❑ No ❑ Don't know   *C. Hot water tank
❑ Yes ❑ No ❑ Don't know   *D. Garbage disposal
❑ Yes ❑ No ❑ Don't know   *E. Appliances
❑ Yes ❑ No ❑ Don't know   *F. Sump pump
❑ Yes ❑ No ❑ Don't know   *G. Heating and cooling systems
❑ Yes ❑ No ❑ Don't know   *H. Security system ❑ Owned ❑ Leased
                                  *I. Other _____

6. Common interest

❑ Yes ❑ No ❑ Don't know   A. Is there a Home Owners' Association? Name of Association _____
❑ Yes ❑ No ❑ Don't know   B. Are there regular periodic assessments:
                               $ _____ per ❑ Month ❑ Year
❑ Other _____
❑ Yes ❑ No ❑ Don't know   *C. Are there any pending special assessments?
❑ Yes ❑ No ❑ Don't know   *D. Are there any shared "common areas" or any joint maintenance agreements (facilities such as walls, fences, landscaping, pools, tennis courts, walkways, or other areas co-owned in undivided interest with others)?

7. General

❑ Yes ❑ No ❑ Don't know   *A. Is there any settling, soil, standing water, or drainage problems on the property?
❑ Yes ❑ No ❑ Don't know   *B. Does the property contain fill material?
❑ Yes ❑ No ❑ Don't know   *C. Is there any material damage to the property or any of the structure from fire, wind, floods, beach movements, earthquake, expansive soils, or landslides?
❑ Yes ❑ No ❑ Don't know   D. Is the property in a designated flood plain?
❑ Yes ❑ No ❑ Don't know   *E. Are there any substances, materials, or products that may be an environmental hazard such as, but not limited to, asbestos, formaldehyde, radon gas, lead-based paint, fuel or chemical storage tanks, and contaminated soil or water on the subject property?
❑ Yes ❑ No ❑ Don't know   *F. Are there any tanks or underground storage tanks (e.g., chemical, fuel, etc.) on the property?
❑ Yes ❑ No ❑ Don't know   *G. Has the property ever been used as an illegal drug manufacturing site?

8. FULL DISCLOSURE BY SELLERS

    A. Other conditions or defects:

❑ Yes ❑ No ❑ Don't know *Are there any other material defects affecting this property or its value that a prospective buyer should know about?

    B. Verification: The foregoing answers and attached explanations (if any) are complete and correct to the best of my/our knowledge and I/we have received a copy hereof. I/we authorize all of my/our real estate licensees, if any, to deliver a copy of this disclosure statement to other real estate licensees and all prospective buyers of the property.

DATE _____

SELLER _____

SELLER _____

II. BUYER'S ACKNOWLEDGMENT

    A. As buyer(s), I/we acknowledge the duty to pay diligent attention to any material defects which are known to me/us or can be known to me/us by utilizing diligent attention and observation.

    B. Each buyer acknowledges and understands that the disclosures set forth in this statement and in any amendments to this statement are made only by the seller.

    C. Buyer (which term includes all persons signing the "buyer's acceptance" portion of this disclosure statement below) hereby acknowledges receipt of a copy of this disclosure statement (including attachments, if any) bearing seller's signature.

DISCLOSURES CONTAINED IN THIS FORM ARE PROVIDED BY THE SELLER ON THE BASIS OF SELLER'S ACTUAL KNOWLEDGE OF THE PROPERTY AT THE TIME OF DISCLOSURE. YOU, THE BUYER, HAVE THREE BUSINESS DAYS, UNLESS OTHERWISE AGREED, FROM THE SELLER'S DELIVERY OF THIS SELLER'S DISCLOSURE STATEMENT TO RESCIND YOUR AGREEMENT BY DELIVERING YOUR SEPARATE SIGNED WRITTEN STATEMENT OF RESCISSION TO THE SELLER UNLESS YOU WAIVE THIS RIGHT OF RESCISSION.

BUYER HEREBY ACKNOWLEDGES RECEIPT OF A COPY OF THIS REAL PROPERTY TRANSFER DISCLOSURE STATEMENT AND ACKNOWLEDGES THAT THE DISCLOSURES MADE HEREIN ARE THOSE OF THE SELLER ONLY, AND NOT OF ANY REAL ESTATE LICENSEE OR OTHER PARTY.

BUYER _____ DATE _____

BUYER _____ DATE _____

BUYER'S WAIVER OF RIGHT TO REVOKE OFFER

Buyer has reviewed the seller's Real Property Transfer Disclosure Statement. Buyer approves the statement and hereby waives the buyer's right to revoke the buyer's offer.

BUYER _____ DATE _____

BUYER _____ DATE _____

Megan's law – *Megan's law* is a federal law which requires states to make convicted sex offender information available to the public. However, the Washington real estate license laws do not specifically state that real estate licensees are required to disclose such information to buyers or whether or not a sex offender lives in the area. Nevertheless, RCW 18.86.010 (9) (see below) states that the fact that a sex offense occurred on the premises is not a material fact.

Lead-based paint – For residential structures built prior to 1978 the federal ***Residential Lead-Based Paint Hazard Reduction Act of 1992*** requires sellers and landlords to disclose any known lead-based paint hazards, including the location of the problem. If ingested, lead can cause brain, kidney and nervous system damage. Although lead can be found in other products, in housing the most prevalent problem is from flaking paint that was commonly used prior to 1978. The owner or owner's agent must also give the buyer or tenant a lead-based paint disclosure booklet entitled *Protect Your Family from Lead Paint*. However, sellers are not required to remove lead-based paint hazards; the law only requires disclosure. The law does require real estate agents to inform sellers and lessors of their obligation to disclose. The law also requires that buyers be given at least ten days in which to have an inspection made, at the buyer's expense. And there must be a Certification and Acknowledgment of Disclosures in the earnest money agreement or in an addendum to the earnest money agreement.

Normally only sellers and lessors are liable under the law. Real estate agents are liable only if they failed in any of their duties above and a buyer or tenant was injured as a result. Real estate agents are not liable if the seller fails to disclose unless the agent had actual knowledge of the problem. The penalty is severe, however – up to three times the amount of the buyer's or tenant's injuries. In addition, criminal penalties can be imposed in cases of deliberate violation of the law.

Stigmatized housing – Buyers sometimes feel the seller should disclose if the property was the site of a murder or suicide, or even if the property is haunted. RCW 18.86.010 (9) addresses some of these issues and real estate agents should be aware of its provisions –

RCW 18.86.010 (9)
"Material fact" means information that substantially adversely affects the value of the property or a party's ability to perform its obligations in a real estate transaction, or operates to materially impair or defeat the purpose of the transaction. The fact or suspicion that the property, or any neighboring property, is or was the site of a murder, suicide or other death, rape or other sex crime, assault or other violent crime, robbery or burglary, illegal drug activity, gang-related activity, political or religious activity, or other act, occurrence, or use not adversely affecting the physical condition of or title to the property is not a material fact.

Note that the code above says that these matters are not material facts. As discussed previously, if it's not a material fact, it is not necessary to disclose it. Only material latent defects must be disclosed.

Note also that the code does not address the issue of haunted houses in so many words. At first glance it would seem that this is not an issue that real estate agents or property owners need to worry about. After all, proving it would be impossible. But the buyer or lessee does not have to prove the property was haunted to recover damages. All the plaintiff needs to prove is that the property has a reputation in the area as being haunted, and therefore suffers from a loss of market value that the plaintiff was not aware of.

Drafting contracts

Drafting a contract that is legally enforceable is an art. It is not sufficient merely to know the essential elements provided here. Care must be taken to make sure the language is clear and that all the details are covered.

Unfortunately, real estate contracts tend to be highly complex. There is no way any agent could possibly remember all the things that need to be included in even a simple transaction. This is made even more difficult when you consider the pressure you will be under when you have the buyers sitting in front of and you are trying to write up their offer.

Luckily, standard forms are available for most transactions. These forms are designed to cover all the details by providing blanks to fill in. As long as you fill out all the blanks you will cover most of the important issues.

Nevertheless, few transactions these days are sufficiently standard that a printed form will be adequate by itself. It seems that agents are usually called upon to create an addendum or exhibit to the standard form. These are frequently used when the printed form doesn't have enough space, such as, for example, when there is a long legal description. There is a trick to this that is important to keep in mind. Whenever you have a contract that is on multiple pages it is important to tie them together somehow so that anyone picking up an individual page alone can see that it is not the entire agreement. When attorneys draft contracts they usually place a footer on each page that says, for example, "page 1 of 12 … page 12 of 12." This makes it impossible for someone to leave out one of the pages and claim the remainder is the full agreement.

For addendums and exhibits we frequently use a phrase to accomplish the same thing. Just write at the top of the addendum or exhibit "this is addendum (exhibit) A to an earnest money agreement (listing etc.) between _____ as seller and _____ as buyer dated _____." Then on the main contract form be sure you add somewhere "see addendum (exhibit) A to this agreement, by reference made a part hereof." The phrase "by reference made a part hereof" ties the two documents together.

Sometimes agents are confused whether to call it an addendum or an exhibit. Technically, a exhibit is a display or drawing of something, such as a map of property boundaries, blueprints for a house to be constructed, etc. An addendum is additional text of the agreement. But in the real world it doesn't normally matter what you call it. As long as you tie it to the main document as discussed above a court would consider it as part of the contract, which is all that is necessary.

⚷ KEY TERMS

The key to understanding any new field is the vocabulary used in that field. To maximize your comprehension of the material presented in this chapter, be sure you know the meaning and significance of the following terms. Remember that the majority of test questions primarily test knowledge of vocabulary.

Acceptance

Accord and satisfaction

Actual damages

Actual fraud

Actual misrepresentation

Adjudicated incompetents

Anticipatory repudiation

Assignment

Assumption

Bilateral

Cancellation

Caveat emptor

Communication

Compensatory damages

Concurrent condition

Condition precedent

Condition subsequent

Consequential damages

Consideration

Constructive fraud

Constructive misrepresentation

Constructive notice

Contingency

Contract

Contract damages

Counteroffer

Duress

Estoppel

Executed contract

Executory contract

Expressed condition

Expressed contracts

Fraud

Fraud in the inducement

Good consideration

Idem sonans

Implied condition

Implied contracts

Impossible

Incompetent

Innocent misrepresentation

Laches

Latent defect

Legal benefit

Legal detriment

Legal object

Liquidated damages

Material fact

Meeting of the minds

Megan's law

Misrepresentation

Mistake of fact

Mistake of law

Mitigate

Mutual agreement

Mutual assent

Necessary

Negligent misrepresentation

Nominal damages

Novation

Offer and acceptance

Offeree

Offeror

Opinion

Personal service contract

Privity of contract

Puffing

Punitive damages

Ratify

Reformation

Renunciation

Repudiation

Rescind

Rescission

Residential Lead-Based Paint Hazard Reduction Act
    of 1992

Restitution

Right of refusal

Right to rely

Rule of parol evidence

Special damages

Specific performance

Statutes of Frauds

Substitution of mortgagor

Tax parcel (lot) number

Time is of the essence

Tort

Tort damages

Ultra vires

Undue influence

Unenforceable

Uniform Commercial Code

Uniform Vendor and Purchaser Risk Act

Unilateral

Valid

Valid and enforceable

Valuable consideration

Void contract

Voidable contract

Waiver

Chapter

10

Land use regulation

TO PROMOTE the general health, safety and welfare, federal, state and local governments are empowered to create laws regulating the use of land. While these laws are sometimes highly controversial, there are some issues which are no longer a matter for debate. In this chapter we will explore the nature of these regulations and their impact on the practice of real estate in Washington.

As long as a government land use restriction is merely a ***regulation*** on the owner's use of the land, the right to create the restriction is said to be derived from ***police power*** – the right of the government to maintain public order. The majority of such restrictions are ***zoning ordinances***. However, if the restriction is so severe that it deprives the owner of all economic uses of the land, then we say there has been a ***taking***, and the government is exercising its right of ***eminent domain***. The exercise of eminent domain is called ***condemnation***. According to the U.S. Constitution, condemnation requires the government to pay the owner ***just compensation***. The government is also not allowed to condemn property unless it is for a ***public use***. Zoning ordinances are an exercise of police power and not eminent domain according to the decision of the United States Supreme Court in the case of *Village of Euclid v. Amber Realty Company* [272 U.S. 365 (1926)].

However, how far a jurisdiction may regulate before it becomes a taking is sometimes a matter for heated arguments. For example, ***downzoning*** is not always considered a taking. Downzoning occurs when a local jurisdiction re-zones an owner's property for a use which is of less monetary value to the owner. The U.S. Supreme Court stated in *Lucas v. South Carolina Coastal Council* [505 U.S. 1003 (1992)] that a regulation that had the effect of eliminating "all economically viable use of ... land" was a taking and the government had to pay just compensation.

To be constitutional, not only must a land use regulation be enacted to promote the general health, safety and welfare, but it must also meet the constitutional requirements of ***due process*** and ***equal protection***. Due process means that the regulations must have been enacted after public debate, deliberation or election, decisions can be appealed, and that each property owner has the right to his or her day in court. Equal protection means that the regulation must be applied equally and fairly to all owners.

Real estate agents should be careful to distinguish between public land use restrictions such as zoning ordinances, building codes, and so on, and restrictions created by private parties. Private restrictions include conditions, which are discussed in Chapter 3, and covenants, which are discussed in Chapter 4.

Zoning

Zoning ordinances are created by cities and counties to regulate the way land in their jurisdiction is used. Zoning ordinances create a wide variety of limitations. A zoning ordinance describes a particular land use activity in detail. This is called a ***zone designation***, or sometimes also a ***zone classification***, or just ***zone***.

For convenience, the zone designation is given a short name. For example, a zone designation as "R-7" might mean **R**esidential, **7**,000 square feet of lot area required for one single-family dwelling. In similar fashion "M-1" might allow heavy **M**anufacturing, "M-2" might be applied to medium **M**anufacturing, and "M-3" could be reserved for light **M**anufacturing. Each local jurisdiction will create their own unique set of zone classifications. The zoning ordinance will typically go into great detail as to matters such as maximum lot coverage permitted, side, front and back yard setback requirements, height restrictions – even the design of the improvements is sometimes regulated.

Once the zoning designations have been created they are applied to land within the jurisdiction of the city or county. The result of the process is a zoning map of the jurisdiction which shows all the districts in which each zoning designation applies.

When applying the zoning designations to different districts, it is common to create **buffer zones**. A buffer zone is a zone district placed between two incompatible uses. For example, a zone district designated for apartments may be placed between a commercial district and a single-family residential district. Buffer zones are also used along freeways, airports and other noise-producing uses. Even a park can be used as a buffer zone to keep inharmonious uses apart.

When a zoning ordinance is enacted, particularly when property is downzoned, a conflict is frequently created between the new ordinance and land uses already in existence. When this happens, we call the conflicting use a **non-conforming use**, or sometimes a **pre-existing condition**. In order to be legal, the zoning ordinance must allow these uses to continue, at least for a time. The clause in the zoning ordinance which permits non-conforming uses and pre-existing conditions to continue is called a **grandfather clause**.

Of course, if an owner changes the use of the land or discontinues the use (abandonment), the right to continue the use will be in jeopardy. However, a temporary discontinuance of the use, such as where an owner is unable to locate a tenant for a period of time, will probably not result in abandonment. Sometimes the local jurisdiction will require an **abatement** of a non-conforming use. An abatement requires that the owner discontinue the use over a period of time. An abatement is typically required over the remaining economic life of the improvements, so as to avoid the owner's complaint that anything of value was taken.

When the owner wishes to sell a property that is a non-conforming use the question arises whether the new owner can continue the use. Local laws vary on this issue, and in some cases state law applies as well. There may also be additional problems. For example, in some cases the law provides that if the use has been discontinued for a period of time, the right to the use is lost. This makes the question a difficult one for agents to answer accurately, creating a great potential for liability.

If an owner wishes to use a property in a manner which does not comply with the zoning, and the desired use is not a legal non-conforming use, the use can be made legal by obtaining a **zone change** (also frequently called a **rezone**). Obtaining a zone change, however, can be a very expensive and time-consuming process.

Even if the local jurisdiction is willing to grant a zone change, it may not be legal to do so. For example, a **spot zone** occurs where a jurisdiction zones just one or two owners' properties, without any apparent justification, in a manner which is inconsistent with the tenor of the neighborhood. If the spot zone results in loss of market value for adjacent owners, the jurisdiction may even be liable for damages.

Another problem with zone changes is that a zone change may require a change to the **comprehensive plan** which the jurisdiction has adopted. (See *Planning*, later.) This adds another step to the approval process.

Many times what an owner wishes to do with the property does not require a substantive change to the zone, but rather a small exception to the permitted uses. In fact, when zoning ordinances are created, it is customary to anticipate requests for adjustments to prevent a hardship. The permitted adjustments are frequently stipulated in the zoning ordinance itself.

For example, an owner may have a substandard size lot. Since the zoning ordinance is probably specific about the minimum number of square feet required, the property is unbuildable and therefore worthless. To prevent the owner from suffering from such a hardship, the owner could apply for a **variance** to permit building on the lot. Variances are typically granted as title rights (appurtenances) and run with the land. A variance would be used to adjust for setback requirements, height restrictions, lot coverage, and so forth.

Another type of exception to the zoning ordinance is a **use permit**, also sometimes called **special use permit**. A use permit is usually personal to the owner, and not a title right. Use permits frequently have conditions attached, in which case they are called **conditional use permits**.

Permits are not typically used for dimension problems, but rather for more serious exceptions, such as where a different use of the property is required. For example, if an owner wishes to run a small business operation out of a personal residence, this would involve a commercial use in a residential zone, so a permit would be appropriate. Note that running a small home based business in a residential zone is an exception which is commonly asked for, so the zoning ordinance creating the residential zone would probably contain precise rules for when and under what conditions such a permit could be granted. Such permits are frequently called **home occupation permits**.

In an active real estate practice, an agent sells many properties, and each property may be located in a different city or county jurisdiction. Since zoning is created at the city or county level, there is a great deal of difference in the way terms are used from one jurisdiction to the next. What may be a variance in one jurisdiction becomes a conditional use permit in another. Real estate agents find they must learn a completely different set of rules for each jurisdiction in which they work.

Building and housing codes

While zoning ordinances affect what type of improvements are permitted, **building codes** address construction standards. Building codes are adopted by the Washington Building Code Council, but enforced in most areas by cities or counties. In areas where the city or county does not have an agency for enforcement the jurisdiction contracts with an adjacent jurisdiction for enforcement. Cities and counties are also authorized to amend the state code, provided that the amendment does not diminish the standards of the state code.

Many Washington cities have also adopted **housing codes**. In the majority of cases the jurisdiction has adopted the **Uniform Housing Code**, published by the International Conference of Building Officials rather than write their own detailed code. A housing code is applied retroactively to existing structures. As a generalization, a housing code will declare that structures meet the requirements of the housing code if they met the building code which was in force at the time they were constructed. From time to time, however, a city will enact ordinances requiring owners to modify certain conditions which were formerly legal. Housing codes also address issues of maintenance, occupancy standards and nuisances.

Planning

Cities and counties in Washington have been creating and enforcing zoning ordinances for many decades. In recent years, however, the concept of **planning** has become the focus of attention. A zoning ordinance indicates what uses are permitted in an area. Planning, on the other hand, involves decisions about future land use needs.

In theory, planning precedes zoning. For example, we might plan for future economic expansion, resulting in an anticipated number of new jobs, which in turn will result in the need for additional housing, more waste disposal requirements, more transportation corridors, and so forth. Once the plan is determined, then appropriate land areas can be zoned to meet the needs of the plan. Planning impacts more than just zoning, however. Having an effective plan also allows orderly creation of government services at all levels and allows the private sector to plan better as well.

Growth Management Act – In 1990 the Washington Legislature enacted the *Growth Management Act*, a law requiring 18 counties to engage in planning and permitting other jurisdictions to do so as well. In addition to the 18 counties, to date 11 more counties have done so, and over 200 cities as well, representing approximately 95% of the state's population.

One of the goals of the Growth Management Act is to encourage infill in urban areas and discourage sprawl, creating higher urban densities. A strong tool to accomplish this is the creation of an *urban growth boundary*. Communities with an urban growth boundary must review it periodically to ensure an adequate supply of land for development.

Another goal of the Growth Management Act is to identify critical areas that need protection, such as fish and wildlife habitat areas, wetlands, subsurface water recharge areas, as well as areas that are geologically hazardous or subject to flooding. The Growth Management Act also requires that local jurisdictions engage "early and continuous public involvement" in the planning process.

Under the Growth Management Act planning begins at the city or county level; that is, the city or county creates a *comprehensive plan*. In other states a comprehensive plan is sometimes referred to as a *master plan*. The comprehensive plan must be submitted to the state Department of Community, Trade and Economic Development (CTED), but the CTED does not have authority to approve or disapprove of the comprehensive plan. The Growth Management Act assumes that the plan meets the requirements of the Act. If a comprehensive plan does not comply with the Growth Management Act other local governments or citizens directly can contest them before one of the state's three growth management hearings boards.

The comprehensive plan provides overall guidance for 20 years of growth in a community. The Growth Management Act requires that comprehensive plans address land use, transportation, housing, capital facilities (public infrastructure), utilities, and shorelines. For counties it must also address rural concerns. Comprehensive plans also sometimes address economic development, parks and recreation, conservation, energy and recreation.

Local jurisdictions must review and adjust their plans at least once every seven years, but not more often than once each year. The revisions must be in keeping with the Growth Management Act. Local jurisdictions are authorized to levy excise taxes to pay for the cost of implementing and maintaining the comprehensive plan. These taxes are usually in the form of development charges.

Environmental protection

Shoreline Management Act – In addition to identification of critical areas required by the Growth Management Act, the Washington Legislature has created significant restrictions on owners of land adjacent to the shore and waterways with the *Shoreline Management Act*. The Shoreline Management Act applies to cities and counties that have "shorelines of the state." "Shorelines of the state is defined to include all marine waters, streams with greater than 20 cubic feet per second average flow, and lakes of 20 acres or larger. It also applies to "shorelands," which extend back from the high water mark for 200 feet. It also applies to wetlands and river deltas, and some or all of the 100-year floodplain, when any of these are associated with "shorelines of the state." It also defines "shorelands of statewide significance" as all waters of Puget Sound and the Strait of Juan de Fuca, the Pacific coastline and Hood Canal, lakes and reservoirs of 1,000 acres surface area or more, and larger rivers. For management of shorelines of statewide significance it requires that the "interests of the people shall be paramount."

Under the Shoreline Management Act each city and county with shorelines of the state (which includes all counties and over 200 cities) must adopt a *shoreline master program*. The shoreline master program is in many respects similar to a comprehensive plan, but for shorelines. The main enforcement of the provisions of the Shoreline Management Act lies with cities and counties, but some activity, e.g., permits and variances, must be approved by the Department of Ecology.

The Shoreline Management Act was the first state law enacted under the federal *Coastal Zone Management Act*. The Coastal Zone Management Act encourages states to become involved in management of the nation's coastal zones. The Coastal Zone Management Act is a voluntary program that provides funding to states to assist in management of coastal areas.

State Environmental Policy Act – Property owners must also sometimes have to deal with the *State Environmental Policy Act* (SEPA). The State Environmental Policy Act is patterned after the federal *National Environmental Policy Act* (NEPA). SEPA requires that either a *determination of non-significance* or an *environmental impact statement* be created for most projects involving land and development. Some minor matters are defined by the Act as "categorically exempt."

The law applies to actions by government agencies as well as actions by private parties, including matters such as the adoption of zoning and planning ordinances. Whenever an action is contemplated there are usually various agencies involved. In this case one will be designated as the lead agency. The lead agency then decides whether SEPA requires the creation of an environmental impact statement.

Superfund Act – In addition to Washington environmental laws real estate agents sometimes have to deal with federal laws. In 1980 Congress passed the *Comprehensive Environmental Response Compensation and Liability Act* (CERCLA). This law makes owners, operators and lessees of real property strictly liable for expenses of cleaning up hazardous substances. In residential properties the most common hazardous substances are asbestos, radon gas and urea formaldehyde foam insulation.

Direct public ownership as a land use control

When we think of public ownership of land we usually think of government office buildings, transit facilities, and other public installations. Sometimes we think of roads and streets, school buildings and a variety of other structures. But public ownership of land has a great effect on land use as well. For example, if the government does not want the owner of a tideland to develop it for environmental reasons, the government might purchase the land, under condemnation if necessary.

However, outright purchase of the land is expensive. Government would have a hard time justifying the expenditure of scarce funds for the purchase of land. And certainly there would not be enough funds to acquire all lands that the government might like to protect. A common alternative, frequently used in Washington, is to acquire just an easement in the land. The government might, for example, obtain the development rights to land in a scenic area, such that the owners would not be allowed to build in a manner that would harm the view. Such easements are sometimes called negative easements, and are frequently in the form of restrictive covenants.

Dividing land

Any division of land must be reviewed to ensure that it meets all applicable laws and regulations, including the applicable comprehensive plan if the jurisdiction where it is located has created one. Most land division approvals are handled by cities and counties. There is also a possibility that a land division must comply with the requirements of federal law, but this is infrequent (see *Interstate Land Sales Full Disclosure Act*, later in this chapter).

The first step in dividing land is to file a ***preliminary plan*** with the local jurisdiction (city or county). The preliminary plan is a drawing showing the design of the proposed division. Although the local jurisdiction usually requires that the preliminary plan be drawn to certain scale and meet other standards, it does not generally have to be prepared by a surveyor. Ultimately, the division will have to be surveyed, but the expense of a survey can be deferred until such time as the owner knows the division will be approved.

Regardless of what type of division it is, in most jurisdictions it will be reviewed and approval will be granted only if it meets all applicable laws. State law requires the local jurisdiction to review and approve all subdivisions and partitions. The approval ultimately rests in the city or county governing body, but larger jurisdictions use a hearings officer.

Matters which the local jurisdiction will take into account include whether the property is served by utilities and the location of the utilities, flood dangers or high water tables in the area, excessive slope to the land, soil conditions not conducive to building, and many other issues. In similar fashion, the proposed division must also be approved by other local officials such as the fire bureau, roads and public works, water agency, sanitation department, and others. And, of course, the proposed division must comply with existing zoning ordinances and the comprehensive plan for the area.

Real estate agents should be aware that the approval of the preliminary plan can be relatively simple or it can be very time consuming, depending on the type of division which is being proposed. For example, in a larger division, road requirements, location of water and sewer lines and other utilities, street lighting, sidewalks, and a host of other issues will demand greater scrutiny. But in a simple partition where there are no new roads to be built (all the proposed lots have frontage on an existing dedicated street), where there will probably be little need for discussion of utilities and other matters, approval is usually granted with only an informal hearing.

Assuming the preliminary plan is approved, the final step in the process is to create and record a ***final plat*** of the division. The final plat must be created by a registered land surveyor. It must also be approved before recording. The final plat generally carries certifications of all the governing bodies that had to give approval of the preliminary plan. The purpose of recording the final plat is to give constructive notice as to how the land has been divided. If the land is a large division of many lots, the lots will be designated by number, and sometimes grouped into blocks. Once the map has been recorded, it becomes possible to create an adequate legal description for any particular lot just by referring to the lot and block and the name of the subdivision. In other words, the final act of recording the plat map results in the creation of lot and block legal descriptions. (For further discussion and an example of a recorded map with approvals, see Chapter 6.)

Many times the creation of a subdivision or short subdivision will require the establishment of roads or streets on the land to be divided. Larger divisions may even include a new park, school site, or other property which will be owned by the public. In these cases the tentative plan approval will require dedication of the land to the public, including a title report showing that the person or entity granting the dedication owns the land. (For further discussion of dedications, see Chapter 5.) The language of the dedication can be in a separate document, but more commonly it is included right on the plat.

Subdivisions and short subdivisions – A division into five or more lots is a *subdivision*. Divisions into four or fewer lots is a *short subdivision*, also sometimes called a *short plat*. If a city or county wishes it may enact a local ordinance extending the number of lots in a short subdivision to as many as nine.

Binding site plan – A binding site plan is a process for dividing land which is zoned for business, commercial or industrial purposes, or multifamily when the developer wishes to create a condominium project. Binding site plans show the configurations of the lots, road and street improvements, location of utilities, open spaces and other provisions, and restricts development to the use and provisions of the plan. The advantage is that the hearing requirement is waived and approval is granted by staff. Binding site plans must still comply with environmental and other issues, and the final plat must be recorded.

Sales prior to recording of plat – For the protection of the public, if a developer wishes to sell a lot before the final plat has been recorded the buyer's funds must be deposited in an escrow or other trust account (such as a real estate broker's trust account), and may not be turned over to the seller until the final plat is approved and recorded.

Washington Land Development Act

In 1973 the Washington Legislature enacted the *Land Development Act* (RCW Chapter 58.19). The Act was substantially amended in 1992. Currently it applies to all subdivisions of 26 or more lots. The Act exempts subdivisions if –
- All lots are purchased by the same buyer, or
- Each lot is five acres or more, or
- Lots have a residential, commercial or industrial building, or the purchase agreement requires the seller to build such a structure within two years, or
- The buyer is a builder, or
- Fewer than ten lots are offered for sale in any twelve-month period, or
- The subdivision is located in a city incorporated prior to 1974.

The sole purpose of the Land Development Act is to protect the public by requiring full disclosure in the sale of subdivided lands. To accomplish this, when the law applies to a subdivision, it requires that the developer create a *public offering statement* and give a copy to each buyer. RCW 58.18. 055 contains an extensive list of matters which must be included in the public offering statement.

At least two days prior to entering into a sales agreement (not including Saturdays, Sundays or legal holidays) the developer must give a copy of the public offering statement to the buyer. The buyer has the right to cancel the transaction any time within two days after receiving the public offering statement. If the buyer cancels the transaction the seller must return all funds paid by the buyer within 30 days. If the seller fails to deliver the copy of the public offering statement and the buyer is damaged as a result, the seller is liable to the buyer for the damages.

The developer cannot use the public offering statement in advertising, and it must be distributed only in its entirety. The law also provides that the developer cannot imply that the state or any other government entity has approved or endorsed the subdivision.

Many times a developer will need financing on the subdivision. The lender wants all the land to be the collateral for the loan. In such cases it is common practice to make the loan a blanket encumbrance with a lot release clause. A **blanket encumbrance** is a mortgage, trust deed or land sales contract which makes more than one parcel collateral for the loan. The **lot release clause** is a provision in the loan document requiring the lender to release a given lot from the lien upon the payment of a specified amount, typically a portion of the total amount owing. The Land Development Act provides that it is illegal for the developer to sell a lot in a subdivision to which the Act applies when there is a blanket encumbrance unless there is a provision in the encumbrance which allows the buyer to obtain clear title. The Act also requires that the buyer be given title insurance against the blanket encumbrance. In addition, the existence of the blanket encumbrance is one of the items which must be disclosed in the public offering statement.

Interstate Land Sales Full Disclosure Act

The **Interstate Land Sales Full Disclosure Act** is a federal law which regulates the sale of certain subdivided lots when the sales are made in interstate commerce or by use of the mails. Subdivisions are exempt if –
- There are fewer than 25 lots, or
- All the lots are twenty acres or more in size, or
- The lots are improved, or the developer has a contract with the buyer to construct a building on the lot within two years, or
- The project is a low-volume operation (no more than 12 lots sold each year)

A developer should be aware that the above exemptions do not apply in every case. And there are also other exemptions available which apply to certain subdivisions and developers. Moreover, even if the property is exempt, it is a violation of federal law to make false statements about the property in interstate commerce.

The Act is administered by the Office of Interstate Land Sales Registration, an agency of the Department of Housing and Urban Development.

Exemptions from the ILSFDA

❶

❷

❸

❹

When a subdivision is not exempt, to comply with the Act the procedure is to register the subdivision with the Office of Interstate Land Sales Registration and prepare a **property report** which makes full disclosure of facts which buyers should know about the lots. The developer must give a copy of the property report to each buyer and the buyer has a seven-day right to cancel the transaction. Note that the purpose of the property report required by the Interstate Land Sales Full Disclosure Act is the same as the public offering statement required by the Washington Land Development Act, that is, to ensure full disclosure.

🔑 KEY TERMS

The key to understanding any new field is the vocabulary used in that field. To maximize your comprehension of the material presented in this chapter, be sure you know the meaning and significance of the following terms. Remember that the majority of test questions primarily test knowledge of vocabulary.

Abatement

Blanket encumbrance

Buffer zone

Building code

Coastal Zone Management Act

Comprehensive Environmental Response Compensation and Liability Act

Comprehensive plan

Condemnation

Conditional use permit

Determination of non-significance

Downzoning

Due process

Eminent domain

Environmental impact statement

Equal protection

Final plat

Grandfather clause

Growth Management Act

Home occupation permit

Housing code

Interstate Land Sales Full Disclosure Act

Just compensation

Land Development Act

Lot release clause

Master plan

National Environmental Policy Act

Non-conforming use

Planning

Police power

Pre-existing condition

Preliminary plan

Property report

Public offering statement

Public use

Regulation

Rezone

Shoreline Management Act

Shoreline master program

Short plat

Short subdivision

Special use permit

Spot zone

State Environmental Policy Act

Subdivision

Taking

Uniform Housing Code

Urban growth boundary

Use permit

Variance

Zone

Zone classification

Zone designation

Zone change

Zoning ordinance

Chapter

11

The documents of real estate finance

B Y THE TIME a real estate loan has been finalized, the lender's file will contain numerous reports, forms and other documents, each of which is crucial to the lender's security. By far the most important of these documents are those which constitute evidence of the debt and which make the real estate collateral for it. In this chapter we will explore in detail the complexities of the documents which lenders use to perfect their legal rights.

In law, a legal document is called an *instrument*. Therefore, in real estate finance, we refer to mortgages and other loan documents as the *instruments of finance*. When the average lay person thinks of financing documents, the usual instrument that comes to mind is the mortgage. But, although the mortgage is an important instrument of finance, other instruments are more commonly used in modern Washington loan transactions. In fact, today, most lenders rely on standard forms created by the secondary mortgage market. The *secondary mortgage market* consists of lenders who purchase loans originated by local *primary lenders* (discussed in detail in Chapter 12).

Even though a lender may use a standard form, the documents will undoubtedly be one of three possibilities. Lenders in Washington can use either a *note and mortgage*, a *note and trust deed*, or a *land sales contract*. When a lender uses a note and mortgage, the note is the usual evidence of the debt, and the mortgage makes the real estate collateral for the debt by creating a lien on the borrower's real estate. For this reason, we say the mortgage is the *lien instrument*. The same thing happens in a note and trust deed transaction, except that the lien instrument is a trust deed instead of a mortgage.

In a land sales contract, however, the legalities are completely different. For one thing, in a land sales contract, the note and lien instrument are not separate documents. Instead, the buyer promises to pay for the property in installments and the seller agrees to give the buyer a deed when the buyer finishes paying for the property. Note that, since the deed is not delivered to the buyer until the end of the contract, the buyer does not become the legal owner of the property until the loan balance is paid in full. Each of the three loan possibilities will be discussed in detail in this chapter.

Notes

A *note* is also sometimes called a *promissory note* or occasionally, a *bond*. As we observed above, the note is the evidence of the debt and must accompany a mortgage or trust deed. The note is, therefore, central to the loan transaction. Without the note as the evidence of the debt, the mortgage or trust deed would be useless – after all, if there is no debt, the lien instrument would have little purpose.

It is important to understand that in Washington a note can be considered separately from the mortgage or trust deed. That is, it is the borrower's personal pledge, a promise to repay a debt, and can stand alone. In Washington, a lender can sue the borrower on the note and ignore the collateral. This would result in a general judgment against the borrower which the lender can enforce by having the sheriff seize any of the borrower's assets (within certain limits).

A note is similar to a check or a draft, all of which are examples of a category of contracts called *negotiable instruments*, but there are some differences. Of course, we are all familiar with checks. One of the major differences between notes and checks is that checks are due upon presentment, where notes are due on some date in the future. Another difference is that a check is an order to a third party (the bank) to pay the money to the payee, where a note is a promise to pay the money directly to the payee.

In a note the borrower is called the *maker* and the lender is the *payee*. Sometimes there is more than one maker, in which case the terms of the note will obligate the mak-

PROMISSORY NOTE

(Interest Included)

$ _____   (Date) _____

FOR VALUE RECEIVED, _____

promise(s) to pay to _____

or order, at _____

the sum of _____

($ _____) with interest from _____ ,

on unpaid principal at the rate of _____ (_____ %) percent per annum;

principal and interest payable in installments of _____

($ _____) or more on the _____ day of each month, beginning on the _____

day of _____ , and continuing until said principal and interest have been paid.

Each payment shall be credited first on interest then due and the remainder on principal; and interest shall thereupon cease upon the principal so credited. Should default be made in payment of any installment when due, the whole sum of principal and interest shall become immediately due at the option of the holder of this note.

Principal and interest payable in lawful money of the United States.

If action be instituted on this note, Maker agrees to pay such sum as the Court may fix as attorney's fees.

This note is secured by a _____ of even date.

LPB-25 7/97

Promissory note by the Limited Practice Board of the Washington State Bar. The Limited Practice Board creates documents which authorized closing agents can use in real estate transaction.

ers "jointly and severally" – that is each borrower is personally liable for the full amount of the debt, or the lender can recover different portions of the debt from each borrower at the lenders option. When there is a co-signer the co-signer becomes the same as an additional maker and is fully liable. A co-signature is sometimes referred to as the co-signer's *guaranty*.

Notes and checks are called negotiable instruments because the payee can usually transfer his or her interest easily (sell the note) merely by *endorsement*. When a note has been endorsed to another there arises a question of *recourse*. Normally the new payee has recourse against the person from whom it was received, but only if the new payee is a *holder in due course*. A holder in due course is a subsequent payee who accepted a note which was –

- Complete in its terms and appeared to be enforceable, and
- Accepted before it was in default, and
- Accepted in exchange for valuable consideration, and
- Accepted in good faith without knowing or suspecting that it might not be honored.

However, notes are frequently endorsed *without recourse*, that is, the party endorsing the note does not accept any responsibility for payment. When a primary lender sells a loan in the secondary mortgage market, the note is occasionally endorsed without recourse. This means that if a foreclosure becomes necessary, the secondary lender has no recourse to the primary lender and must foreclose on the borrower in order to recover. Naturally, secondary lenders prefer to buy loans endorsed in blank (with full recourse), so that they can simply make the primary lender take the loan back if the borrower defaults.

Investors sometimes use the term "recourse" and "non-recourse" in another way. To an investor these terms refer to whether or not the lender can satisfy the debt from any of the investor's assets (recourse financing), or whether foreclosing on the property being financed is the lender's sole remedy (non-recourse financing).

As noted earlier, a loan file contains numerous documents and, although the note is certainly the most important, there are others that are also critical. When a loan is sold, the usual practice is to endorse the note to the buyer of the loan, but *assign* the interest in the mortgage or trust deed, fire insurance policy, title insurance policy, etc. Most contracts are transferred by assignment; only negotiable interests are transferred by endorsement.

When describing the terms of a note there are various expressions common in the world of finance. A note where the entire principal balance is due at the end of the loan is called a *straight note*. In contrast, real estate loans are more commonly arranged with periodic payments of principal. When the loan is paid off in installments, it is called an *amortized note*. Amortized notes sometimes call for a lump sum payment toward the principal, called a *balloon payment*. Balloon payments are usually used to pay the loan off early, but the term is also used to describe any extra principal payment. For example, a loan with a balloon payment might call for regular payments, but also contain a clause requiring the borrower to pay "the then remaining principal balance" in full at some point. The requirement to pay off the loan early can be structured as a balloon payment or as a *call feature*. A balloon payment requires the borrower to pay the loan off in full at the stated time. A call feature, on the other hand, allows the lender to demand repayment in full any time after some point. Unless the lender calls the loan due, the borrower need not pay it off. The balloon payment is not as flexible as the call feature.

Borrowers should be careful to read the terms of the note. For example, if the loan calls for regular payments, it should also contain the expression "not less than" or "or more," or other language allowing the borrower to pay more than the minimum. If the note does not contain language allowing the borrower to pay extra, then the borrower is said to be *locked in*.

For the lender, probably the most important clause in the note is the *acceleration clause*. Lenders will require an acceleration clause in all installment notes. The acceleration clause allows the lender to call the entire principal balance immediately due in the event the borrower should default. If an installment note does not contain an acceleration clause, then all the lender can do is sue to force the borrower to bring the loan current.

A *demand clause* is similar to an acceleration clause, but allows the lender to call the entire principal balance due in full even if the borrower is not in default. Demand clauses are seldom encountered today in residential lending, but are still common in commercial notes.

Priority of liens

A complete understanding of lien instruments requires knowledge of the priority of liens. Whenever there is a foreclosure the rights of the respective lienholders are determined by their priority. We use the term *junior* or *subordinate* lienholder to describe the lender whose interests are in second or subsequent position. A senior lienholder is a lender who enjoys priority over a junior or subordinate lienholder.

In general, priority is determined by the date the instrument was recorded in the auditor's office. There are certain exceptions, however. The most notable exceptions are judgments, which can be recorded, but which are usually just placed on the court records. Certain other liens, such as city liens and income tax levies are also found in places other than the public records. Regardless of where the record of the lien is found, the date of its creation usually constitutes its priority date, although property tax liens are prior liens regardless of what year they are for. Because the priority date is critical, lenders always make sure their lien instruments are recorded and verified as to priority before they allow the loan funds to be disbursed to the borrower. If a lien is not recorded at all, it is always last in priority.

Normal priority can also be altered if a senior lender agrees to **subordinate** to a junior lienholder. For example, suppose you buy a building lot and the seller carries your note for a portion of the purchase price, secured by a mortgage or trust deed on the lot. Later you go to build on the lot and wish to finance the construction with a bank loan. The bank wants a first lien, but the seller already has a recorded lien. In this case, you could convince the seller to agree to subordinate to the bank. The bank will then have a first lien, even though the bank's mortgage or trust deed will be recorded at a date later than the seller's mortgage or trust deed.

In a foreclosure priority is crucial, as the property will usually be sold at a public auction sale and the proceeds of the sale will be distributed to lienholders according to priority date. Depending on the type of lien instrument, junior lienholders sometimes participate in these proceeds, and sometimes not. Any lienholder can always file a foreclosure when the loan is in default, but junior lienholders must take title subject to the senior liens.

In general, foreclosure by a senior lienholder will extinguish all junior liens, provided the junior lienholder is properly notified of the suit and, in most cases, given the right to protect his or her lien by paying off the senior lien. In some cases, the junior lienholder may save his or her lien merely by bringing the senior lien current to reinstate it, rather than having to pay it off in full. In order to be sure of getting notice of a foreclosure by a senior lienholder, a junior lienholder frequently records a **request for notice of sale**.

It is important to understand that this pecking order of priority is not limited just to financing instruments. Leases, options, earnest money agreements, easements – all other interests are subject to the same rules. If you mortgage your property and then lease it to a tenant, foreclosure by the lender will extinguish the tenant's leasehold. But if the property is already leased when it is mortgaged, the lender must take the property subject to the lease. A wise lender would insist on a subordination from the lessee to the mortgage.

Creation of the mortgage

As we have seen in the preceding discussion, a mortgage is a **lien** on the property, but a mortgage alone is worth little without the note as evidence of the debt. When there is a lien on the property, we say that the title is subject to an **encumbrance**; that is, a lien is a special type of encumbrance which makes the property collateral for a debt.

Encumbrances are said to "run with the land" – if the owner sells the property, the buyer takes title subject to the encumbrance. Therefore, when a lender has a lien on the borrower's property, the borrower cannot get rid of the lien by sale, lease, additional liens, or any other means, short of paying off the debt. This makes a recorded lien an ideal protection for the lender.

Historically, mortgages were the first instruments ever used to make real estate collateral for a debt. Their history goes back to the earliest recorded beginnings of

After recording mail to:

Name

Address

City, State, Zip

Filed for Record at Request of:

_____

MORTGAGE
(Statutory Form)

The mortgagor(s)

mortgage to

to secure payment of the sum of _____ Dollars ($ _____),

according to the terms of promissory note bearing _____ date, the following described

real estate, situated in the County of _____ , state of Washington:

Assessor's Property Tax Parcel/Account Number:

And the mortgagor promise and agree to pay before delinquency all taxes, special assessments and other public charges levied, assessed or charged against said described premises, and to keep all improvements on said described premises insured against loss or damage by fire in the sum of _____

Dollars, (_____) for the benefit of the mortgagee and to deliver all policies and renewals to the mortgagee.

In case the mortgagor shall fail to pay any installment of principal or interest secured hereby when due or to keep or perform any covenant or agreement aforesaid, then the whole indebtedness hereby secured shall forthwith become due and payable, at the election of the mortgagee.

Dated: _____

State of _____)
)-ss
County of _____)

I certify that I know or have satisfactory evidence that _____
(is/are) the person(s) who appeared before me, and said person(s) acknowledged that (he/she/they) signed this instrument and acknowledged it to be (his/her/their) free and voluntary act for the uses and purposes mentioned in this instrument.

Dated:_____
          Notary Public in and for the state of _____
          My appointment expires: _____

                                                                                    LPB-10(i) 7/97

Limited Practice Board statutory mortgage. The Limited Practice Board has created standard real estate documents that qualified closing agents can use.

English common law. Originally, the mortgage was literally a conveyance of the title to the lender. The mortgage operated in a manner similar to a deed. Since the borrower would give the mortgage to the lender, the borrower was called the ***grantor*** and the lender was called the ***grantee***, although the terms ***mortgagor*** and ***mortgagee*** are more common today. (In law, the "-or person" always gives the document to the "-ee person.")

In the earliest mortgages, when the title was conveyed to the mortgagee, the mortgagee took physical possession of the real estate. Later, as mortgage lending became a specialized field and mortgage lenders acquired more than just a few mortgage loans, it became impractical for lenders to oversee their many properties and mortgage instruments were changed to allow the mortgagor to remain in possession.

It is interesting to note that early mortgage instruments were really the conveyance of a ***defeasible fee***. The mortgagor held a ***right of reverter***, that is, the right to recover the title by paying the loan in full. According to the terms of these early mortgages, repayment would cause the title to revert automatically to the mortgagor. The clause setting forth this right was called the ***defeasance*** clause. (See Chapter 3 for a more complete discussion of defeasible titles and rights of reverter.) The right of the borrower to regain clear title after paying off the loan is still called the defeasance clause, even in modern mortgages.

Originally the mortgagee was not required to file a suit to foreclose. If the borrower failed to pay off the loan by the due date, the buyer simply lost the right of reverter and the lender's title to the property would become vested absolutely. As time went by mortgagors gained more and more rights. Eventually mortgagees were required to file a suit and obtain judicial approval to keep the property. This became known as a ***foreclosure***, that is, a suit to foreclose the borrower's interest in the property.

Much later, borrowers gained the right to redeem their property, even after foreclosure. Originally this right lasted for one year. In early England, most people lived close to the land and gained their living from agricultural pursuits. Since most farmers get paid once a year when they sell their crops, if the law is going to give a farmer a second chance, it should be at least one year. Today the time limit for redemption after foreclosure is set by individual state statutes. In Washington the right of redemption today is still one year although in some cases it is eight months. (For further detail about the right of redemption, see *Mortgage remedies* later in this chapter.)

Although borrowers in all states today can count on the right to judicial review of a foreclosure and of a period of time after foreclosure in which to redeem, a few states still follow the old concept that a mortgage is a conveyance of a defeasible title to the mortgagee. These states are called ***title theory*** states. Most states (including Washington and other western states) follow the more modern theory that the mortgage is merely a lien against the borrower's title. Such states are called ***lien theory*** states. A major significance of being in a title theory state is that second mortgages are more difficult. Once the lender is in title to the property, the borrower has little to pledge as collateral for a second mortgage. Title theory states have had to enact special legislation to make a second mortgage possible.

As noted previously, when a mortgage loan has been made the mortgage is recorded to protect the priority of the mortgagee's lien. It is not customary to record the accompanying note, although some lenders incorporate the note into the mortgage document. Since the mortgage has been recorded in the public records, when the borrower pays off the loan, we must record another instrument in order to extinguish the lien created by the mortgage. This document is called a ***satisfaction of mortgage***, or just ***satisfaction***, for short. The term "satisfaction" is also used to describe documents termi-

AFTER RECORDING MAIL TO:

Name

Address

City, State, Zip

Filed for Record at Request of:

_____

SATISFACTION OF MORTGAGE

KNOW ALL PERSONS BY THESE PRESENTS: that _____ ,

_____ the owner and holder of that certain mortgage bearing date _____

executed by _____ to secure payment of the sum of

_____ Dollars ($ _____) and interest, and recorded

in the office of the County Auditor of _____ County, state of Washington, on

_____ , _____ in Volume _____ of Mortgages, at Page _____ being Auditor's

File No. _____ , does hereby acknowledge that the said mortgage has been FULLY SATISFIED AND

DISCHARGED, and does hereby authorize and direct the said County Auditor to enter full satisfaction thereof

of record.

Assessor's Property Tax Parcel/Account Number:

Dated: _____

STATE OF _____)
)-ss
COUNTY OF _____)

I certify that I know or have satisfactory evidence that _____
(is/are) the person(s) who appeared before me, and said person(s) acknowledged that (he/she/they) signed
this instrument and acknowledged it to be (his/her/their) free and voluntary act for the uses and purposes
mentioned in this instrument.

Dated:_____
          Notary Public in and for the state of _____

          My appointment expires: _____

LPB-51(i) 7/97

Limited Practice Board satisfaction of mortgage. The Limited Practice Board has created standard real estate documents that qualified closing agents can use.

nating many other liens – satisfaction of construction lien, satisfaction of judgment, and so forth.

Mortgage remedies

A default is a breach of a contractual promise. When a borrower defaults on a loan agreement, be it a note and mortgage, note and trust deed, or land sales contract, the default is usually a failure to pay when due. However, failure to pay is only one of many possible defaults. There are numerous clauses in any financing instrument, and failure to perform any of these clauses is just as serious a default as failure to pay. For example, the mortgage usually requires the borrower to maintain insurance on the premises and to pay the property taxes when due. Another clause will typically require the borrower to maintain the premises in good condition. Many loans today also contain a clause prohibiting the sale of the property without paying off the mortgage.

If a mortgagor is in default of the mortgage the mortgagee can demand the entire remaining balance at once. If the mortgagor does not pay it, the mortgagee can proceed with foreclosure. If a foreclosure is contemplated legal advice will be necessary, because a mortgage foreclosure must be a *judicial foreclosure*, that is to say, a lawsuit must be filed. Other financing instruments (notably trust deeds) allow for non-judicial foreclosure, where an appointed trustee sells the property at public auction, without judicial review or the necessity of filing suit.

Lenders almost invariably win suits to foreclose; in fact, it is rare for a borrower to win a suit to foreclose. Even if the mortgagor wins, the best that can usually be hoped for is reinstatement of the debt; that is, the acceleration is denied and the mortgagee is required to continue to accept payments. Of course, in order to win reinstatement, the mortgagor would have to be prepared to make up all back payments and cure any other defaults.

When the mortgagee has won, the court will enter a *judgment of foreclosure*. The judgment of foreclosure allows the lender to have the property sold to satisfy the amount owing, which will include not only the balance of the debt, but the costs of foreclosure, unpaid interest and other charges. The judgment of foreclosure is enforced by the sheriff, who will hold a public auction sale of the property.

The sheriff must publish a notice of the impending sale in the county where the property is located. In addition, the sheriff must post a notice by the front door of the courthouse and mail a notice to the debtor. The sheriff (or a deputy) will hold the sale at the front of the courthouse at the appointed time and date.

Anyone may bid at the auction, including the mortgagee, the mortgagor, or any other party claiming an interest in the property, or any member of the public, although the sheriff or deputy holding the sale is not permitted to bid. No one is required to bid. All bids must be for cash, except that the mortgagee may bid up to the total balance owed without paying cash, since the mortgagee already paid that amount when the loan was made. If the mortgagee wishes to bid over the amount owing, the difference must be paid in cash. The mortgagee may also refuse to bid at all.

The successful bidder will receive a *sheriff's certificate of sale*, which will entitle the successful bidder to a *sheriff's deed*, subject to the redemption rights of the mortgagor or junior lienholders (discussed later). The successful bidder is also entitled to immediate possession of the property, unless there is a valid lease which was recorded prior to the mortgage or the property is agricultural or the borrower's *homestead* (place of personal residence). The successful bidder is entitled to collect any income from the property, but if the mortgagor or a junior lienholder later exercises a right of redemption, the net amount goes to the benefit of the mortgagor. The sheriff will turn the proceeds of the sale over to the clerk of the court for final disbursement to the mortgagee. If there is a surplus it must be paid to the mortgagor.

Redemption – The debtor can halt the proceedings at any time prior to the actual sale by paying to the court the full amount due as stated in the judgment of foreclosure together with the lender's costs incurred up to that point. This is called the **equitable right of redemption**. Even after the sale, the mortgagor can still redeem the property. This right is called the **statutory right of redemption**. In Washington the statutory right redemption is one year, unless the lender in filing the suit indicated a waiver of the lender's normal right to a deficiency judgment (see below). If the lender waived the right to a deficiency judgment and the property is not agricultural, the statutory right of redemption is reduced to eight months. However, if the borrower abandoned the property for six months and the property is not used for agricultural purposes, the borrower has no statutory right of redemption. In addition, if the property is the borrower's homestead at the time of the foreclosure, the lender must give the borrower a notice of the impending expiration of their redemption rights at least 40 but not more than 60 days before they expire. If the lender fails to do so, the borrower's redemption rights are extended an additional six months.

In order to exercise this right, the mortgagor must pay to the successful bidder the amount the successful bidder paid for the property, plus interest from the date of the sale, plus any sums the successful bidder paid to keep prior liens current or payments made on property taxes, but less the net income received by the successful bidder. Sums expended for improvements or additions to the property cannot be recovered. If the property is not redeemed, then when all redemption rights have expired, the sheriff will normally deed the property to the successful bidder.

Junior lienholders also have a statutory right of redemption which lasts for 60 days from the date of the sale. Their rights of redemption are substantially the same as the rights of the mortgagor. A junior lienholder who redeems steps into the same position the successful bidder was in, that is, if the mortgagor still has time remaining on the statutory right of redemption, the mortgagor may still exercise it. The only difference is that now the mortgagor would be redeeming from a junior lienholder, rather than from the successful bidder. If there is more than one junior lienholder, then each has a 60-day right of redemption, and if one junior lienholder redeems, the right of redemption of the other junior lienholders is extended to 60 days from the date of the last redemption by a junior lienholder.

Deficiency judgments – Most of the time when a mortgagor borrows money the purpose is to obtain the funds to acquire the property. If the money is borrowed from a third party, such as a bank, then the mortgage is said to be a **hard money mortgage**, because the lender advanced hard cash. On the other hand, maybe the mortgage is carried by the seller rather than a bank. In such a transaction, the seller would deed the property to the buyer, who would then give a note and mortgage back to the seller for part of the purchase money. This is called a **purchase money mortgage**.

What if the property did not sell for enough to satisfy the mortgage debt? In Washington, the mortgagee may then proceed against other assets of the debtor. However, in most states the mortgagee is entitled to this remedy only if the loan was for hard cash (i.e., it was a hard money mortgage). If it was a purchase money mortgage, then the mortgagee lent the equity in the property, and must be satisfied with taking the property back. The right to go after the borrower's other assets is called a **deficiency judgment**.

The terms "purchase money" and "hard money" are applied to other financing instruments as well. In other words, a note and trust deed carried by a seller is called a "purchase money trust deed," but if carried by a third party it is a "hard money trust deed." Land sales contracts are always carried by the seller, so they are always purchase money instruments. Generically, lenders refer to all financing carried by the seller as "purchase money financing" and bank loans as "hard money financing." Similarly, the notes secured by mortgages and trust deeds can be referred to as "purchase money notes" and "hard money notes" respectively.

Upset price – Washington law allows a judge to take notice of economic conditions at the time of a foreclosure and fix a minimum price which the property must be sold for. In auction terms this is sometimes called a *reserve price* or *upset price*. Even if the court does not fix an upset price in the judgment of foreclosure, the court can impose one after the sheriff's sale. In this case the judge can hold a hearing, order an appraisal, and require that the full market value of the property be applied to the debt, regardless of what it sold for. The debtor may use this provision to avoid the possibility of a deficiency judgment.

Trust deeds

The **trust deed** (sometimes called a **deed of trust**) was used occasionally in Washington even before statehood, but did not become common until after the specific rules were established as a part of the Revised Code of Washington in 1965. Today, the modern provisions of the trust deed make it by far the most popular instrument with lenders. In fact, there is hardly a major lender left in Washington who does not use the trust deed to the exclusion of all other instruments.

To understand trust deeds we must first understand the idea of the **trust**. A trust is an arrangement where a person (called a **trustor**), gives something (usually money or property), to someone (called a **trustee**), with the understanding that the trustee is to hold it for the benefit of a third party (called a **beneficiary**). An easy example is what would happen if you placed some assets in trust for your child. You would select a trustee, perhaps the trust department of a bank or a trust company, and transfer the asset to the trustee with instructions for how it is to be managed. Your child is the beneficiary in this arrangement. We use trusts today for dozens of purposes, usually to avoid taxation or legal liability. For example, if you were to set up those assets in trust for your child, a portion the income earned by the assets can become the child's income – not yours – and taxed at the child's tax rates, whose tax bracket is probably not nearly as high as yours. Trusts usually have all three of the parties above, trustor, trustee and beneficiary, and the rights and duties of each is spelled out in the trust agreement.

We will see how we can make use of this concept of the trust in a clever way to create a lien on real property. But first, if you recall, in a note and mortgage transaction the borrower gave a note and a mortgage to the lender. The note was the evidence of the debt, and in fact, could stand alone as an unsecured instrument if desired. The mortgage created the lien on the property –

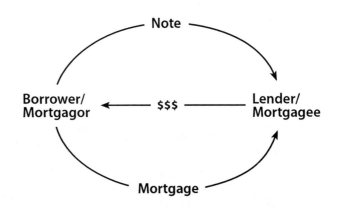

In a mortgage transaction the borrower (called the mortgagor) gives a note to the lender (called the mortgagee). In exchange for the note the lender gives the borrower the cash. The borrower also gives the lender a mortgage which makes the borrower's real estate collateral for the note.

Now, when we substitute a trust deed for the mortgage, things are completely different, although the net result is similar, that is, the lender gets a note, and the lender also gets a lien on the property. However, the way the trust deed creates the lien is unique.

To create a trust deed lien the borrower (owner) deeds a right in the property to the trustee. This right is generally referred to as a limited **power of sale**. This power of sale gives the trustee the right to sell the property, but limited, in that the trustee can sell the property only if the borrower is in default. This power of sale is a title right so it must be conveyed by a deed. Note that the borrower is the grantor of the deed and the trustee is the grantee of the deed. Since the deed creates a trust, we call it a trust deed or deed of trust. And since the lender receives the benefit of the trust, we call the lender the beneficiary.

You can see that the borrower could be called the owner, the borrower, the trustor, or the grantor. The trustee could also be called the grantee. In Washington it is more common to refer to the borrower and the trustee as grantor and trustee, but in other states it is more usual to hear trustor and trustee. The lender is always referred to as the beneficiary.

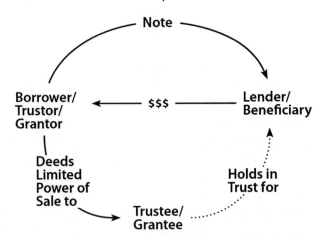

In a trust deed transaction the borrower gives a note to the lender in exchange for the loan funds, the same as in the mortgage transaction on the previous page. The difference is that the lien is created when the borrower deeds a limited power of sale to a third party, called a trustee. The trustee holds the limited power to sell the property in trust for the lender. Since the lender receives the benefit of the arrangement the lender is called the beneficiary.

The best part for the beneficiary is the simplicity of foreclosure. Essentially, a foreclosure can be effected just by telling the trustee that the note is in default and to sell the property at public auction according to the provisions of the statutes. This saves having to file a suit and wait for the cumbersome judicial process to finish. Of course, for the protection of the borrower, the law sets standards which the trustee must follow.

The trustee may not be the same entity as the beneficiary, nor may the trustee be an entity which is a subsidiary of or affiliated with the beneficiary. Washington code specifically states that a trustee may only be a Washington corporation (including a professional corporation), an attorney, a bank or savings and loan, a licensed title insurance company, or an agency of the U.S. government. However, it is important to note that the trustee is not neutral, but rather, owes allegiance to the beneficiary.

Now that you see the basic operation of the trust deed, what would happen when the grantor pays off the note? In a note and mortgage transaction, the mortgagee would give the mortgagor a satisfaction of mortgage to record. However, this time the lien was created by a conveyance of the limited power of sale to the trustee. Logically then, in order to undo the lien, the beneficiary simply orders the trustee to convey the limited power of sale back to the grantor. The document used is called a **deed of reconveyance**.

Trust deed remedies

As we have seen, a beneficiary can foreclose the trust deed just by telling the trustee to sell the property. This is called a **trustee's foreclosure** or **non-judicial fore-**

AFTER RECORDING MAIL TO:

Name

Address

City, State, Zip

Filed for Record at Request of:

_____

Short Form
DEED OF TRUST

THIS DEED OF TRUST, made this _____ day of _____ , _____ , between
_____ , as GRANTOR(S),

whose address is _____ , and
_____ , as TRUSTEE,

whose address is _____ , and
_____ , as BENEFICIARY,

whose address is _____ .

Grantor(s) hereby irrevocably grants, bargains, sells, and conveys to Trustee in trust, with power of sale, the following described property in _____ County, Washington:

Assessor's Property Tax Parcel/Account Number: _____

TOGETHER WITH all the tenements hereditaments and appurtenances, now or hereafter thereunto belonging or in anywise appertaining, and the rents, issues, and profits thereof and all other property or rights of any kind or nature whatsoever further set forth in the Master Form Deed of Trust hereinafter referred to, SUBJECT, HOWEVER, to the right, power and authority hereinafter given to and conferred upon Beneficiary to collect and apply such rents, issues and profits.

THIS DEED IS FOR THE PURPOSE OF SECURING PERFORMANCE of each agreement of Grantor(s) incorporated by reference or contained herein and payment of the sum of _____

DOLLARS ($ _____) with interest thereon according to the terms of a promissory note of even date herewith, payable to Beneficiary or order and made by Grantor(s); all renewals, modifications or extensions thereof, and also such further sums as may be advanced or loaned by Beneficiary to Grantor(s), or any of his/her/their successors or assigns, together with interest thereon at such rate as shall be agreed upon. By executing and delivering this Deed of Trust and the Note secured hereby, the parties agree that all provisions of Paragraphs 1 through 35 inclusive of the Master Form Deed of Trust hereinafter referred to, except such paragraphs as are specifically excluded or modified herein, are hereby incorporated herein by reference and made an integral part hereof for all purposes the same as if set forth herein at length, and the Grantor(s) hereby makes said covenants and agrees to fully perform all of said provisions. The Master Form Deed of Trust above referred to was recorded on the twenty-fifth (25th) day of July, 1968, in the Official Records of the offices of the County Auditors of the following counties in Washington in the book, and at the page designated after the name of each county, to-wit:

Page 1 of 3   LPB-20/Attachment

Limited Practice Board trust deed. The Limited Practice Board has created standard real estate documents that qualified closing agents can use.

COUNTY	BOOK OR VOL.	PAGE NO.	AUDITOR'S	COUNTY	BOOK OR VOL.	PAGE NO.	AUDITOR'S
Adams	2 of Record.Instr	513-16	122987	Lewis	7 of Off. Rec.	839-842	725562
Asotin	Microfilmed	under Aud's	No. 101896	Lincoln	107 of Mort.	776-779	316596
Benton	241 of Off. Rec.	695A-C	592931	Mason	Reel 48 Frame	835-838	236038
Chelan	688 of Off. Rec.	1682-1685	681844	Okanogan	121 of Mort.	517-519A	560658
Clallam	315 of Off. Rec.	195-198	383176	Pacific	213 of Off. Rec.	649-652	55707
Clark	Aud. Microfilm	702859-862	G-519253	Pend Oreille	27 of Mtgs.	8-11	126854
Columbia	49 of Deeds	198-201	F3115	Pierce	1254 of Mtgs.	707-710	2250799
Cowlitz	747 of Off. Rec.	234-237	675475	San Juan	28 of Mtgs.	459-462	69282
Douglas	125 of Mortgages	120-123	151893	Skagit	19 of Off. Rec.	80-83	716277
Ferry	28 of Deeds	413-416	153150	Skamania	47 of Mtgs.	41-44	70197
Franklin	11 of Official Rec.	138-141	309636	Snohomish	233 of Off. Rec.	540-543	2043549
Garfield	Microfilmed	under Aud's	No. 13044	Spokane	14 of Off. Rec.	1048-1051	376267C
Grant	44 of Rec. Doc.	373-376	538241	Stevens	109 of Mtgs.	394-397	390635
Grays Harbor	21 of General	31-34	207544	Thurston	454 of Off. Rec.	731-734	785350
Island	181 of Off. Rec.	710-713	211628	Wakiakum	17 of Mortgage	89-92	24732
Jefferson	4 of Official Rec.	316-319	196853	Walla Walla	308 of Mtgs.	711-714	495721
King	5690 of Mtgs.	436-439	6382309	Whatcom	82 of Off. Rec.	855-858	1047522
Kitsap	929 of Off. Rec.	480-483	934770	Whitman	1 of Misc.	291-294	382282
Kittitas	111 of Mortgages	361-364	348693	Yakima	712 of Off. Rec.	147-150	2170555
Klickitat	101 of Mortgages	107-110	131095				

A copy of such Master Form Deed of Trust is hereby furnished to the person executing this Deed of Trust and by executing this Deed of Trust the Grantor(s) acknowledges receipt of such Master Form Deed of Trust.

The property which is the subject of this Deed of Trust is not used principally or primarily for agriculture or farming purposes.

The undersigned Grantor(s) requests that a copy of any Notice of Default and of any Notice of Sale hereunder be mailed to him at the address hereinbefore set forth.

WITNESS the hand(s) and seal(s) of the Grantor(s) on the day and year first above written.

By _____   By _____

By _____   By _____

By _____   By _____

By _____   By _____

STATE OF _____)

)-SS

COUNTY OF _____)

I certify that I know or have satisfactory evidence that _____

(is/are) the person(s) who appeared before me, and said person(s) acknowledged that (he/she/they) signed this instrument and acknowledged it to be (his/her/their) free and voluntary act for the uses and purposes mentioned in this instrument.

Dated: _____

Notary Public in and for the state of _____

My appointment expires: _____

STATE OF _____)

)-SS

COUNTY OF _____)

I certify that I know or have satisfactory evidence that _____

(is/are) the person(s) who appeared before me, and said person(s) acknowledged that (he/she/they) signed this instrument, on oath stated that (he/she/they) (is/are) authorized to execute the instrument and acknowledged it as the _____ of _____

to be the free and voluntary act of such party(ies) for the uses and purposes mentioned in this instrument.

Dated: _____

Notary Public in and for the state of _____

My appointment expires: _____

I.PB-20 7/97

REQUEST FOR FULL RECONVEYANCE

To be used only when all obligations have been paid under the note and this Deed of Trust.

To: TRUSTEE

The undersigned is the legal owner and holder of the note and all other indebtedness secured by the within Deed of Trust. Said note, together with all other indebtedness secured by said Deed of Trust, has been fully paid and satisfied; and you are hereby requested and directed, on payment to you of any sums owing to you under the terms of said Deed of Trust, to cancel said note above mentioned, and all other evidences of indebtedness secured by said Deed of Trust delivered to you herewith, together with the said Deed of Trust, and to reconvey, without warranty, to the parties designated by the terms of said Deed of Trust, all the estate now held by you thereunder.

Dated: _____

By _____   By _____

By _____   By _____

Mail reconveyance to _____

Do not lose or destroy this Deed of Trust OR THE NOTE which it secures. Both must be delivered to the Trustee before cancellation will be made.

Page 3 of 3

MASTER FORM DEED OF TRUST

Recorded by Washington Mortgage Correspondence Association, a Washington corporation, pursuant to C. 148 L. 1967

The Grantor(s) covenants and agrees as follows:

1. The following described estate, property and rights of Grantor(s) are also included as a security for the performance of each covenant and agreement of Grantor(s) contained herein or in the Short Form Deed of Trust and the payment of all sums of money secured hereby:

(a) All the estate and rights of Grantor(s) in and to said property and in and to land lying in streets and roads adjoining said premises, and all access, rights, and easements appertaining thereto.

(b) All buildings, structures, improvements, fixtures, and articles of property now or hereafter attached to, or used or adapted for use in the operation of, the said premises, including but without being limited to, all heating and incinerating apparatus and equipment whatsoever, all boilers, engines, motors, dynamos, generating equipment, piping and plumbing fixtures, ranges, cooking apparatus and mechanical kitchen-equipment, refrigerators, cooling, ventilating, sprinkling and vacuum cleaning systems, fire extinguishing apparatus, gas and electric fixtures, carpeting, underpadding, elevators, escalators, partitions, mantels, built-in mirrors, window shades, blinds, screens, storm sash, awnings, furnishings of public spaces, halls and lobbies, and shrubbery and plants; and including also all interest of any owner of the said premises in any of such items hereafter at any time acquired under conditional sale contract, chattel mortgage or other title retaining or security instrument, all of which property mentioned in this paragraph shall be deemed part of the realty and not severable wholly or in part without material injury to the freehold.

(c) All and singular the lands, tenements, privileges, water rights, hereditaments, and appurtenances thereto belonging or in anywise appertaining, and the reversion and reversions, remainder and remainders, rents, issues, and profits thereof, and all the estate, rights, title, claim, interest and demand whatsoever of the Grantor(s), either in law or equity, of, in and to the bargained premises. To HAVE AND TO HOLD said premises bargained and described, together with all and singular the lands, tenements, privileges, water rights, hereditaments, and appurtances thereto belonging or in anywise appertaining, and the reversion and reversions, remainder and remainders, rents, issues, and profits thereof, and all of the estate, right, title, claim, and demands whatsoever of the Grantor(s), either in law or in equity, of, in and to the above bargained premises, forever as security for the faithful performance of the promissory note secured hereby and as security for the faithful performance of each and all of the covenants, agreements, terms, and conditions of this Deed of Trust, SUBJECT, HOWEVER, to the right, power, and authority hereinafter given to and conferred upon Beneficiary to collect and apply such rents, issues, and profits.

(d) All of Grantor(s)'s rights further to encumber said property for debt except by such encumbrance which by its actual terms and specifically expressed intent shall be and at all times remain subject and subordinate to (i) any and all tenancies in existence when such encumbrance becomes effective and (ii) any tenancies thereafter created; Grantor(s) hereby (i) representing as a special inducement to Beneficiary to make this loan that as of the date hereof there are no encumbrances to secure debt junior to this Deed of Trust and (ii) covenanting that there are to be none as of the date when this Deed of Trust becomes of record, except in either case encumbrances having the prior written approval of Beneficiary, and all of Grantor(s)'s rights to enter into any lease or lease agreement which would create a tenancy that is or may become subordinate in any respect to any mortgage or deed of trust other than this Deed of Trust.

2. When and if Grantor(s) and Beneficiary shall respectively become the Debtor and Secured Party in any Uniform Commercial Code Financing Statement affecting property either referred to or described herein, or in any way connected with the use and enjoyment of these premises, this Deed of Trust shall be deemed a Security Agreement as defined in said Uniform Commercial Code and the remedies for any violation of the covenants, terms, and conditions of the agreements herein contained shall be (i) as prescribed herein, or (ii) by general law, or (iii) as to such part of the security which is also reflected in said Financing Statement by the specific statutory consequences now or hereafter enacted and specified in the Uniform Commercial Code, all at Beneficiary's sole election. Grantor(s) and Beneficiary agree that the filing of such a Financing Statement in the records normally having to do with personal property shall never be construed as in anywise derogating from or impairing this declaration and hereby stated intention of the parties hereto, that everything used in connection with the production of income from the property that is the subject of this Deed of Trust and/or adapted for use therein and/or which is described or reflected in this Deed of Trust is, and at all times and for all purposes and in all proceedings both legal or equitable shall be, regarded as part of the real estate irrespective of whether (i) any such item is physically attached to the improvements, (ii) serial numbers are used for the better identification of certain equipment items capable of being thus identified in a recital contained in the short form Deed of Trust or in any list filed with the Beneficiary, (iii) any such item is referred to or reflected in any such Financing Statement so filed at any time.

3. To pay all debts and monies secured hereby, when from any cause the same shall become due. To keep the property free from statutory and governmental liens of any kind. That the Grantor(s) is/are seized in fee simple of the property and owns outright every part thereof, that there are no liens or encumbrances against or upon the same and none superior to this Deed of Trust, will be created or suffered to be created by the Grantor(s) during the life of this Deed of Trust, that he has good right to make this Deed of Trust and that he will forever warrant and defend said property unto the Beneficiary, its successors and assigns, against every person whomsoever lawfully claiming or to claim the same or any part thereof. The Grantor(s) upon request by mail will furnish a written statement duly acknowledged of the amount due on this Deed of Trust and whether any offsets or defenses exist against the debt secured hereby.

4. To pay to Beneficiary, if Beneficiary so requires, together with and in addition to the monthly payments of principal and interest payable under the terms of the said note, on the date set forth therein for the making of monthly payments each month, until said note is fully paid, a sum, as estimated by the Beneficiary, equal to the ground rents, if any, and the taxes and special assessments next due on the premises covered by this Deed of Trust, plus the premiums that will next become due and payable on insurance policies as may be required under paragraph 10 hereof, Grantor(s) agreeing to deliver promptly to beneficiary all bills and notices thereof, less all sums already paid therefor, divided by the number of months to elapse before two months prior to the date when such ground rents, premiums, taxes, and special assessments will become delinquent, such sums to be held by the Beneficiary in trust to pay said ground rents, premiums, taxes, and special assessments. All payments mentioned in this paragraph and all payments to be made under said note shall be added together and the aggregate amount thereof shall be paid by the Grantor(s) each month in a single payment to be applied by Beneficiary to the following items in the order set forth: (1) ground rents, if any, taxes, special assessments, fire and other hazard insurance premiums; (2) interest on the note secured hereby; and, (3) amortization of the principal of said note. Any deficiency in the amount of any such aggregate monthly payment shall constitute an event of default under this Deed of Trust. The arrangement provided for in the paragraph 4 is solely for the added protection of the Beneficiary and entails no responsibility on the Beneficiary's part beyond the allowing of due credit, without interest, for the sums actually received by it. Upon assignment of this Deed of Trust by the Beneficiary, any funds on hand shall be turned over to the assignee and any responsibility of the assignor with respect thereto shall terminate. Each transfer of the property that is the subject of this Deed of Trust shall automatically transfer to the grantee all rights of the Grantor(s) with respect to any funds accumulated hereunder.

5. In the event that any payment or portion thereof is not paid within fifteen (15) days commencing with the date it is due, Beneficiary may collect, and the Grantor(s) agree(s) to pay with such payment, a "late charge" of two cents ($.02) for each dollar so overdue as liquidated damages for the additional expense of handling such delinquent payments.

6. If the total of the payments (herein called reserves) made under paragraph 4 hereof relating to reserves for ground rents, taxes, special assessments, and premiums on insurance policies, shall exceed the amount of payments actually made by Beneficiary for the purposes set forth in paragraph 4, plus such amounts as have been reasonably accumulated in such reserves toward payments therefrom next to become due, such excess may, provided no default then exists under the terms of this instrument nor under the terms of the promissory note hereby secured, but not otherwise, be credited by beneficiary in payment of subsequent aggregate, but not partial, payments to be made by Grantor(s) or, at the option of the Beneficiary, refunded to the Grantor(s) or his/her/their successors in interest as may appear upon the records of the Beneficiary. If, however, the monthly payments accumulating such reserves shall not be sufficient to pay the sums required when the same shall become due and payable, the Grantor(s) shall pay to Beneficiary any amount necessary to make up the deficiency within thirty (30) days after written notice to Grantor(s) stating the amount of the deficiency. If there shall be a default under any of the provisions of this Deed of Trust and thereafter a sale of the property in accordance with the provisions hereof, or if the Beneficiary acquires the property otherwise after default, the Beneficiary shall apply, at the time of commencement of such proceedings or at the time the property is otherwise acquired, the balance then remaining in the funds accumulated under paragraph 4, less such sums as will become due and payable during the pendency of the proceedings, as a credit against the amounts secured hereby.

7. To maintain the buildings and other improvements on the property in a rentable and tenantable condition and state of repair, to neither commit nor suffer any waste, to promptly comply with all requirements of the federal, state, and municipal authorities and all other laws, ordinances, regulations, covenants, conditions, and restrictions respecting said property or the use thereof, and pay all fees or charges of any kind in connection therewith. The Beneficiary may recover as damages for any breach of this covenant the amount it would cost to put the property in the condition called for herein. In the event of breach of any requirement of this paragraph, the Beneficiary may, in addition to any other rights or remedies, at any time thereafter declare the whole of said principal sum immediately due and payable. Proof of impairment of security shall be unnecessary in any suit or proceeding under this paragraph. Grantor(s) shall permit Beneficiary or its agents the opportunity to inspect the property, including the interior of any structure at reasonable times and after reasonable notice.

8. To complete or restore promptly and in good workmanlike manner any building or improvement which may be constructed, damaged, or destroyed thereon, and pay when due all costs incurred therefor, and, if the loan secured hereby or any part thereof is being obtained for the purpose of financing construction of improvements on said property, Grantor(s) further agree(s): (a) To commence construction promptly and in any event within thirty (30) days from the date of this instrument, and complete the same in accordance with any agreements relating to construction and plans and specifications satisfactory to Beneficiary within eight months of the date of this instrument. (b) To allow Beneficiary to inspect said property at all times during construction. (c) To replace any work or materials unsatisfactory to Beneficiary, within fifteen (15) calendar days after written notice to Grantor(s) of such fact. (d) That work shall not cease on the construction of such improvements for any reason whatsoever for a period of fifteen (15) consecutive days. The Trustee, upon presentation to it of an affidavit signed by Beneficiary setting forth facts showing a default by Grantor(s) under this numbered paragraph, is authorized to accept as true and conclusive all facts and statements therein, and to act thereon hereunder.

9. No building or other improvement on the property shall be structurally altered, removed, or demolished, without the Beneficiary's prior written consent, nor shall any fixture or chattel covered by this Deed of Trust and adapted to the proper use and enjoyment of the premises be removed at any time without like consent unless actually replaced by an article of equal suitability, owned by the Grantor(s), free and clear of any lien or security interest except such as may be approved in writing by the Beneficiary. 10. To provide to the Beneficiary, at least thirty (30) days prior to expiration of existing insurance, and maintain unceasingly, insurance, with premiums prepaid, on all of the property that is the subject of this Deed of Trust, or hereafter becoming part of said property, against loss by fire and other hazards, casualties, and contingencies, including war damage, as may be required from time to time by the Beneficiary in such amounts and for such period of time, with loss payable clauses (without contribution) in favor of and in form satisfactory to the Beneficiary, and to deliver all policies to Beneficiary, which delivery shall constitute an assignment to Beneficiary of all return premiums. All insurance shall be carried in companies approved by Beneficiary. Beneficiary may at its option require Grantor(s) to maintain said required policies in Grantor(s)'s possession in lieu of delivering said policies to Beneficiary, in which event said policies shall be kept available by Grantor(s) at all times for return to the Beneficiary or for inspection by Beneficiary, its agents

or insurers, and said requirement may be withdrawn by Beneficiary at any time. In event of foreclosure of this Deed of Trust or other transfer of title to the subject property in extinguishment of some or all of the indebtedness secured hereby, all interest of the Grantor(s) in any insurance policies in force shall pass to the purchaser or Grantee to pay to Beneficiary as Beneficiary may require a reasonable fee to cover costs of substituting policies in the event the Grantor(s) replace(s) any policy prior to its expiration. Grantor(s) will reimburse Beneficiary for any premiums paid for such insurance by the Beneficiary upon the Grantor(s)'s default in so insuring the buildings or other improvements or default in assigning and delivering of such policies to the beneficiary so endorsed.

11. To appear in and defend any suit, action, or proceeding that might affect the value of this security instrument or the security itself or the rights and powers of Beneficiary or Trustee; and should Beneficiary or Trustee elect also to appear in or defend any such action or proceeding, be made a party to such by reason of this Deed of Trust or elect to prosecute such action as appears necessary to preserve said value, the Grantor(s) will, at all times, indemnify from, and, on demand reimburse Beneficiary or Trustee for any and all loss, damage, expense, or cost, including cost of evidence of title and attorney's fees, arising out of or incurred in connection with any such suit, action, or proceeding, and the sum of such expenditures shall be secured by this Deed of Trust with interest as provided in the note secured hereby and shall be due and payable on demand. To pay costs of suit, cost of evidence of title and a reasonable attorney's fee in any proceeding or suit brought by Beneficiary to foreclose this Deed of Trust.

12. To pay in full at least thirty (30) days before delinquent all rents, taxes, assessments, and encumbrances, charges or liens with interest, that may now or hereafter be levied, assessed, or claimed upon the property that is the subject of this Deed of Trust or any part thereof, which at any time appear to be prior or superior hereto for which provision has not been made heretofore, and upon request will exhibit to Beneficiary official receipts therefor, and to pay all taxes imposed upon, reasonable costs, fees, and expenses of this Trust. On default under this paragraph Beneficiary may, at its option, pay, or pay out of reserves accumulated under paragraph 4, any such sums, without waiver of any other right of Beneficiary by reason of such default of Grantor(s), and Beneficiary shall not be liable to Grantor(s) for a failure to exercise any such option.

13. To repay immediately on written notice to Grantor(s) all sums expended or advanced hereunder by or on behalf of Beneficiary or Trustee, with interest from the date of such advance or expenditure at the rate of ten percent (10%) per annum until paid, and the repayment thereof shall be secured hereby. Failure to repay such expenditure or advance and interest thereon within ten (10) days of the mailing of such notice will, at Beneficiary's option, constitute an event of default hereunder, or, Beneficiary may, at its option, commence an action against Grantor(s) for the recovery of such expenditure or advance and interest thereon, and in such event Grantor(s) agree(s) to pay, in addition to the amount of such expenditure or advance, all costs and expenses incurred in such action, together with a reasonable attorney's fee.

14. Should Grantor(s) fail to make any payment or to do any act as herein provided, then Beneficiary or Trustee, but without obligation so to do and without notice to or demand upon Grantor(s) and without releasing Grantor(s) from any obligation hereof, may: Make or do the same in such manner and to such extent as either may deem necessary to protect the security hereof, Beneficiary or Trustee being authorized to enter upon the property for such purposes, commence, appear in and defend any action or proceeding purporting to affect the security hereof or the rights or powers of Beneficiary or Trustee; pay, purchase, contest, or compromise any encumbrance, charge, or lien which in the judgment of either appears to be prior or superior hereto, and in exercising any such power, incur any liability, expend whatever amounts in its absolute discretion it may deem necessary therefor including cost of evidence of title, employ counsel, and pay his/her/their reasonable fees.

15. (a) To fully comply with all of the terms, conditions, and provisions of all leases on said property so that the same shall not become in default and to do all that is needful to preserve all said leases in force.

(b) To permit no assignment of any lease, or any subletting thereunder unless the right to assign or sublet is expressly reserved by the lessee under such lease.

(c) That save and except for taxes and assessments provided to be paid by Grantor(s) as specified in paragraph 12 hereof, Grantor(s) will not create or suffer or permit to be created, subsequent to the date of the execution and delivery of this Deed of Trust any lien or encumbrance which may be or become superior to any lease affecting said property.

(d) That if any part of the automobile parking areas included within said property is taken by condemnation, or before said areas are otherwise reduced, Grantor(s) will provide parking facilities in kind, size, and location to comply with all leases, and before making any contract for such substitute parking facilities, Grantor(s) will furnish to Beneficiary satisfactory assurance of completion thereof free of liens and in conformity with all governmental zoning and regulations.

16. Should the property or any part or appurtenance thereof or right or interest therein be taken or damaged by reason of any public or private improvement, condemnation proceeding (including change of grade), fire, earthquake, or other casualty, or in any other manner, Beneficiary may, at its option, commence, appear in and prosecute, in its own name, any action or proceeding, or make any compromise or settlement, in connection with such taking or damage, and obtain all compensation, awards, or other relief therefor. All such compensation, awards, damages, rights of action and proceeds, including the proceeds of any policies or insurance affecting the property, are hereby assigned to beneficiary, which may, after deducting therefrom all its expenses, including attorney's fees, release any monies so received by it, or apply the same on any indebtedness secured hereby or apply the same to the repair or restoration of the property, as it may elect. Grantor(s) further assigns to Beneficiary any return premiums or other repayments upon any insurance at any time provided for the benefit of the Beneficiary, refunds or rebates made of taxes or assessments on said property, and Beneficiary may at any time collect said return premiums, repayments, refunds, rebates, etc., notwithstanding that no sum secured hereby be overdue when such right to collection be asserted. Grantor(s) also agree(s) to execute such further assignments of any such compensation, award, damages, rebates, return of premiums, repayments, rights of action, and proceeds as Beneficiary or Trustee may require.

17. Time is of the essence hereof in connection with all obligations of the Grantor(s) herein or in said note. By accepting payment of any sum secured hereby after its due date, Beneficiary does not waive its right either to require prompt payment when due of all other sums so secured or to declare default for failure so to pay.

18. At any time upon written request of Beneficiary, payment of its fees and presentation of this Deed and said note for endorsement (in case of full reconveyance, for cancellation and retention), without affecting the liability of any person for the payment of the indebtedness Trustee may (a) consent to the making of any map or plat of said property; (b) join in granting any easement or creating any restriction thereon; (c) join in any subordination or other agreement affecting this Deed or the lien or charge thereof; (d) reconvey, without warranty, all or any part of the property. The Grantee in any reconveyance may be described as the "Person or persons legally entitled thereto," and the recitals therein of any matters or facts shall be conclusive proof of the truthfulness thereof. Grantor(s) agrees to pay a reasonable trustee's fee for full or partial reconveyance, together with a recording fee if Trustee, at its option, elects to record said reconveyance.

19. In case of a sale under this Deed of Trust, the said property, real, personal and mixed, may be sold in one parcel.

20. The Grantor(s) shall not, without first obtaining the Beneficiary's written consent, assign any of the rents or profits of the property or collect any rent for more than one month in advance or change the general nature of the occupancy or initiate or acquiesce in any zoning reclassification, or do or suffer any act or thing which would impair the security for said debt or the Beneficiary's lien upon said property or the rents thereof. In the event of breach of any requirement of this paragraph, the Beneficiary may, in addition to any other rights or remedies, at any time thereafter declare the whole of said principal sum immediately due and payable.

21. The holder of this Deed of Trust, in any action to foreclose it, shall be entitled (without notice and without regard to the adequacy of any security for said debt) to the appointment of a receiver of the rents and profits of the property and such receiver shall have, in addition to all the rights and powers customarily given to and exercised by such receiver, all the rights and powers granted to the Beneficiary by the covenants contained in paragraph 23 hereof.

22. As further security for the payment of all indebtedness herein mentioned, all Grantor(s)'s rents and profits of said property and the right, title, and interest of the Grantor(s) in and under all leases now or hereafter affecting said property, are hereby assigned and transferred to the Beneficiary. So long as no default shall exist in compliance with any requirement hereof or of any further instrument at any time executed with respect to this Deed of Trust the Grantor(s) may collect assigned rents and profits as the same fall due, but upon the occurrence of any such default, or at such later time as the Beneficiary in its sole discretion may fix by written notice, all right of the Grantor(s) to collect or receive rents or profits shall wholly terminate. All rents or profits of Grantor(s) receivable from or in respect to said property which it shall be permitted to collect hereunder shall be received by it in trust to pay the usual and reasonable operating expenses of, and the taxes upon, said property and the sums owing the Beneficiary as they become due and payable as provided in this Deed of Trust or in the said note or in any modification of either. The balance of such rents and profits after payment of such operating expenses, taxes, and sums due the Beneficiary, and after the setting aside of accruals to date of such expenses, taxes, and sums, including amortization, shall be Grantor(s)'s absolute property. No lease of the whole or any part of the property involving an initial term of more than three (3)

years shall be modified or terminated without the written consent of the Beneficiary, nor shall the surrender of any such lease be accepted nor any rental thereunder be collected for more than two (2) months in advance without like written consent. In the event of any default hereunder and the exercise by the Beneficiary of its rights hereby granted, Grantor(s) agree(s) that payments made by tenants or occupants to the Beneficiary shall, as to such tenants, be considered as though made to Grantor(s) and in discharge of tenants' obligations as such to Grantor(s). Nothing herein contained shall be construed as obliging the Beneficiary to perform any of Grantor(s)'s covenants under any lease or rental arrangement. Grantor(s) shall execute and deliver to the Beneficiary upon demand any further or supplemental assignments necessary to effectuate the intentions of this paragraph and upon failure of the Grantor(s) so to comply, Beneficiary may, in addition to any other right or remedy it has, declare the maturity of the indebtedness hereby secured.

23. In the event of default in compliance with any requirement of this Deed of Trust or of any further instrument at any time executed with respect to this Deed of Trust, and the continuance thereof for such period as would entitle the Beneficiary to declare said debt due and payable, or for ten (10) days if no such period be applicable, the Beneficiary may, at its option, enter upon and take possession of the said property and let the same or any part thereof, making therefor such alterations as it finds necessary, and may terminate in any lawful manner any tenancy or occupancy of said property, exercising with respect thereto any right or option available to the Grantor(s). From and after the occurrence of any such default, if any owner of said property shall occupy said property or part thereof, such owner shall pay to the Beneficiary in advance on the first day of each month a reasonable rental for the space so occupied, and upon failure so to do the Beneficiary shall be entitled to remove such owner from the property by any appropriate action or proceeding.

24. The entering upon and taking possession of said property, the collection of such rents, issues, and profits, or the proceeds of fire and other insurance policies or compensation, or awards for any taking or damage of the property, and the application or release thereof as aforesaid, shall not cure or waive any default or notice of default hereunder or invalidate any act done pursuant to such notice.

25. All sums secured hereby shall become immediately due and payable, at the option of the Beneficiary without demand or notice, after any of the following occur, each of which shall be an event of default: (a) default by Grantor(s) in the payment of any indebtedness secured hereby or in the performance or observance of any agreement contained herein, or (b) any assignment made by Grantor(s) or the then owner of said property for the benefit of creditors, or (c) any transfer of title made by the Grantor(s) or the then owner of said property to a Grantee or successors in interest without the assumption of all of the terms and conditions herein contained, or (d) any of the following shall occur, with respect to the property, the Grantor(s) or the then owner of said property: (i) the appointment of a receiver, liquidator, or Trustee; (ii) the adjudication as a bankrupt or insolvent, (iii) the filing of any Petition for Bankruptcy or reorganization; (iv) the institution of any proceeding for dissolution or liquidation, (v) if Grantor(s) be unable, or admit in writing an inability to pay his/her/their debts when due; or (vi) a default in any provision of any other instrument which may be held by Beneficiary as security for said note, including the loan agreement and related documents, the terms and covenants of which are incorporated herein by reference as though fully set forth herein. No waiver by Beneficiary of any default on the part of Grantor(s) shall be construed as a waiver of any subsequent default hereunder. In event of such default and upon written request of Beneficiary, Trustee shall sell the trust property, in accordance with the Deed of Trust Act of the State of Washington (RCW Chapter 61.24 as existing now, or hereafter amended) and the Uniform Commercial Code of the State of Washington where applicable, at public auction to the highest bidder. Any person except Trustee may bid at Trustee's sale. Trustee shall apply the proceeds of the sale as follows: (a) to the expense of sale, including a reasonable Trustee's fee and attorney's fee; (b) to the obligation secured by this Deed of Trust; and (c) the surplus, if any, shall be distributed in accordance with said Deed of Trust Act. Trustee shall deliver to the purchaser at the sale its deed, without warranty, which shall convey to the purchaser the interest in the property which Grantor(s) had or had the power to convey at the time of his/her/their execution of this Deed of Trust, and such as he may have acquired thereafter. Trustee's deed shall recite the facts showing that the sale was conducted in compliance with all the requirements of law and of this Deed of Trust, which recital shall be prima facie evidence of such compliance and conclusive evidence thereof in favor of bona fide purchasers and encumbrancers for value. The Power of Sale conferred by this Deed of Trust and by the Deed of Trust Act of the State of Washington is not an exclusive remedy and when not exercised, Beneficiary may foreclose this Deed of Trust as a mortgage. At any time Beneficiary may appoint in writing a successor trustee, or discharge and appoint a new Trustee in the place of any Trustee named herein, and upon the recording of such appointment in the mortgage

records of the county in which this Deed of Trust is recorded, the successor trustee shall be vested with all powers of the Original Trustee. The Trustee is not obligated to notify any party hereto of pending sale under any other Deed of Trust or of any action or proceeding in which Grantor(s), Trustee, or Beneficiary shall be a party, unless such action or proceeding is brought by the Trustee.

26. The property which is the subject of this Deed of Trust is not used principally or primarily for agricultural or farming purposes.

27. In the event of the passage after the date of this Deed of Trust of any federal, state, or local law, deducting from the value of real property for the purpose of taxation any lien thereon, or changing in any way the laws now in force for the taxation of mortgages, deeds of trust, or debts secured thereby, for federal, state or local purposes, or the manner of the collection of any such taxes so as to affect the interest of Beneficiary, then and in such event, Grantor(s) shall bear and pay the full amount of such taxes, provided that if for any reason payment by Grantor(s) of any such new or additional taxes would be unlawful or if the payment thereof would constitute usury or render the loan or indebtedness secured hereby wholly or partially usurious under any of the terms or provisions of the note, or the within Deed of Trust or otherwise. Beneficiary may, at its option, without demand or notice, declare the whole sum secured by this Deed of Trust with interest thereon to be immediately due and payable, or Beneficiary may, at its option, pay that amount or portion of such taxes as renders the loan or indebtedness secured hereby unlawful or usurious, in which event Grantor(s) shall concurrently therewith pay the remaining lawful and non-usurious portion or balance of said taxes.

28. If from any circumstances whatever fulfillment of any provision of this Deed of Trust or said note at the time performance of such provision shall be due shall involve transcending the limit of validity prescribed by the usury statute or any other law, the ipso facto the obligation to be fulfilled shall be reduced to the limit of such validity, so that in no event shall any exaction be possible under this Deed of Trust or under said note that is in excess of the limit of such validity; but such obligation shall be fulfilled to the limit of such validity. The provisions of this paragraph shall control every other provision of this Deed of Trust and said note.

29. In the event that this Deed of Trust is foreclosed as a mortgage and the property sold at a foreclosure sale, the purchaser may, during any redemption period allowed, make such repairs or alterations on said property as may be reasonably necessary for the proper operation, care, preservation, protection, and insuring thereof. Any sums so paid together with interest thereon from the time of such expenditure at the highest lawful rate shall be added to and become a part of the amount required to be paid for redemption from such sale.

30. Grantor(s) shall deliver to the Beneficiary within 20 days after written demand therefor a detailed operating statement in form satisfactory to the beneficiary covering the subject property and certified as correct by the Grantor(s). Grantor(s) shall permit the Beneficiary or its representative to examine all books and records pertaining to the said property, upon prior written demand of not less than ten (10) days. In default thereof Beneficiary shall, in addition to all other remedies, have the option of maturing the indebtedness hereby secured. The Beneficiary shall demand not more than one statement in any calendar year.

31. Beneficiary shall have the right at its option to foreclose this Deed of Trust subject to the rights of any tenant or tenants of the said property and the failure to make any such tenant or tenants a party defendant to any such suit or action or to foreclose his/her/their rights will not be asserted by the Grantor(s) as a defense in any action or suit instituted to collect the indebtedness secured hereby or any part thereof or any deficiency remaining unpaid after foreclosure and sale of the said property, any statute or rule of law at any time existing to the contrary notwithstanding.

32. Upon any default by Grantor(s) and following the acceleration of maturity as herein provided, a tender of payment of the amount necessary to satisfy the entire indebtedness secured hereby made at any time prior to foreclosure sale (including sale under power of sale) by the Grantor(s), its successors or assigns, or by anyone in behalf of the Grantor(s), its successors or assigns, shall constitute an evasion of the prepayment terms of said note and be deemed to be a voluntary prepayment thereunder and any such payment to the extent permitted by law, will, therefore, include the additional payment required under the prepayment privilege, if any, contained in said note or if at that time there be no prepayment privilege then such payment, will to the extent permitted by law include an additional payment of five percent (5%) of the then principal balance.

33. The Beneficiary shall be subrogated for further security to the lien, although released of record, of any and all encumbrances paid out of the proceeds of the loan secured by this Deed of Trust.

34. Grantor(s), from time to time, within fifteen (15) days after request by Beneficiary, shall execute, acknowledge and deliver to Beneficiary, such chattel mortgages, security agreements, or other similar security instruments, in

form and substance satisfactory to Beneficiary, covering all property of any kind whatsoever owned by Grantor(s) or in which Grantor(s) has any interest which, in the sole opinion of Beneficiary, is essential to the operation of the said property covered by this Deed of Trust. Grantor(s) shall further from time to time, within fifteen (15) days after request by Beneficiary, execute, acknowledge, and deliver any financing statement, renewal, affidavit, certificate, continuation statement, or other document as Beneficiary may request in order to perfect, preserve, continue, extend or maintain the security interest under, and the priority of, this Deed of Trust and the priority of such chattel mortgage or other security instrument as a first lien. Grantor(s) further agree(s) to pay to beneficiary on demand all costs and expenses incurred by Beneficiary in connection with the preparation, execution, recording, filing, and refiling of any such instrument or document including the charges for examining title and the attorney's fee for rendering an opinion as to the priority of this Deed of Trust and of such chattel mortgage or other security instrument as a valid first and subsisting lien. However, neither a request so made by Beneficiary nor the failure of Beneficiary to make such request shall be construed as a release of such property, or any part thereof, from the conveyance of title by this Deed of Trust, it being understood and agreed that this covenant and any such chattel mortgage, security agreement, or other similar security instrument, delivered to beneficiary, are cumulative and given as additional security.

35. All Beneficiary's rights and remedies herein specified are intended to be cumulative and not in substitution for any right or remedy otherwise available and no requirement whatsoever may be waived at any time except by a writing signed by the Beneficiary, nor shall any waiver be operative upon other than a single occasion. This Deed of Trust cannot be changed or terminated orally. This Deed of Trust applies to, inures to the benefit of, and is binding not only on the parties hereto, but on his/her/their heirs, devisees, legatees, administrators, executors, successors, and assigns. All obligations of Grantor(s) hereunder are joint and several. The term "Beneficiary" shall mean the holder and owner, including pledgees, of the note secured hereby, whether or not named as Beneficiary herein. Without affecting the liability of any other person for the payment of any obligation herein mentioned (including Grantor(s) should he convey said property) and without affecting the lien hereof upon any property not released, Beneficiary may, without notice, release any person so liable, extend the maturity or modify the terms of any such obligation, or grant other indulgences, release, or reconvey, or cause to be released or reconveyed at any time all or part of the said property described herein, take or release any other security or make compositions or other arrangements with debtors. Beneficiary may also accept additional security, either concurrently herewith or thereafter, and sell same or otherwise realize thereon, either before, concurrently with, or after sale hereunder. This Deed of Trust shall be so construed that wherever applicable, the use of the singular number shall include the plural number, the use of the plural number shall include the singular number, the use of any gender shall be applicable to all genders and shall likewise be so construed as applicable to and including a corporation. The word "note" shall include all notes evidencing the indebtedness secured hereby. If any of the provisions hereof shall be determined to contravene or be invalid under the laws of the State of Washington, such contravention or invalidity shall not invalidate any other provisions of this agreement, but it shall be construed as if not containing the particular provision or provisions held to be invalid, and all rights and obligations of the parties shall be construed and enforced accordingly. Any notices to be given to Grantor(s) by Beneficiary hereunder shall be sufficient if mailed postage prepaid, to the address of the Grantor(s) stated in the Short Form Deed of Trust, or to such other address as Grantor(s) has/have requested in writing to the Beneficiary, that such notices be sent. Any time period provided in the giving of any notice hereunder shall commence upon the date such notice is deposited in the mail.

LPB-20 7/97

closure. The beneficiary should be sure that the note is indeed in default. If the beneficiary wrongfully commences a trustee's foreclosure, the only way the grantor can have a day in court is to bring a suit to enjoin (bar) the trustee from holding the sale.

The first step in foreclosure is always to accelerate the debt. In a trust deed, the second step is normally for the trustee to serve the borrower with a notice of default, which says that if the borrower does not cure the default within 30 days the lender will record and publish a ***notice of sale***. The notice of sale must also be served on the grantor or the grantor's successor in interest, any junior lienholders whose liens are recorded or known to the beneficiary, and on any other person who has recorded a special document called a ***request for notice of sale***. The request for notice of sale is usually recorded by junior lienholders whose liens are small judgments or other liens which are not of record.

The trustee must include in the notice of sale all information pertinent to the foreclosure, including the date, time and place set for the sale. The date for the sale must be a minimum of 120 days from the date of the first notice. During the time between the service and the sale date, the trustee must publish the notice of sale.

A special provision of the law allows the grantor, or any junior lienholder, to cure the default and reinstate the trust deed note, provided that the default is cured before the eleventh day prior to the date set for the sale. In curing the default, the trustee and the attorney for the beneficiary are entitled to reasonable fees for their services in assisting the beneficiary to enforce the trust deed. Of course, all sums due to date, plus late charges, and other costs, must be tendered in order to reinstate the debt. The right of reinstatement essentially bars the lender from enforcing the acceleration until the eleventh day before the sale date. It is a major difference between the trustee's foreclosure and the judicial foreclosure of a mortgage.

If the trust deed is not reinstated prior to the eleventh day before the sale date, then the trustee proceeds to hold the sale. As in a mortgage foreclosure sale, anyone may bid, except that this time it is the trustee who is holding the sale, so the trustee may not bid. All bids must be for all cash, except that the beneficiary may bid up to the balance then due under the note and trust deed without paying cash. If the beneficiary bids more than the amount due, the surplus must be paid in cash. No one is required to place a bid, but it is customary for the beneficiary to start by bidding the total amount due.

Following the sale, the trustee deeds the property to the successful bidder. The deed is called a ***trustee's deed***. There is no right of redemption for the grantor or for junior lienholders. Possession is to be delivered to the successful bidder within 20 days. The trustee will disburse the proceeds of the sale first to the costs of the sale, including the fees of the trustee, second to the beneficiary to the extent of what is due to the beneficiary, and finally, any remaining surplus to the clerk of the court, to whom the grantor can apply for a refund.

If the proceeds of the sale are insufficient to pay the entire trust deed obligation the beneficiary will lose money on the loan if it is on the borrower's personal residence. The beneficiary can sue for a deficiency judgment under a trustee's foreclosure, but only if the trust deed was a commercial loan entered into after June 11, 1998 and the beneficiary can claim that the market value of the property was diminished by waste allowed by the borrower or that the borrower withheld rent, insurance proceeds, or condemnation awards that rightfully belong to the beneficiary.

As you can see, compared to a judicial mortgage foreclosure, the trustee's foreclosure gives a reasonably balanced menu of benefits to both parties. The grantor gains the right to reinstate the loan and, in most cases, freedom from worrying about a deficiency judgment. The beneficiary gains inexpensive and fast foreclosure, and quick possession without having to deal with a possible right of redemption. Most institutional lenders prefer the trustee's foreclosure. After all, they only want to earn interest income on their loans, so if a grantor cures the default and reinstates the loan, so much the better. On the other hand, if the grantor cannot reinstate the loan, then better to have the foreclosure over with as quickly and inexpensively as possible. Of course, the lender must give up the right to a deficiency judgment but, as a practical matter, mortgage lenders rarely get anything out of a deficiency judgment anyway.

However, Washington code states that a beneficiary may foreclose a trust deed "in the same manner as a real property mortgage" [RCW 61.24.100 (8)]. In other words, the beneficiary can simply treat the trust deed as though it were a mortgage and proceed with a judicial foreclosure. This gives the beneficiary the option to accelerate and deny reinstatement. But if the beneficiary takes this route, not only will it likely cost more, but more important, the grantor and junior lienholders have rights of redemption. The beneficiary's hands are tied until the rights of redemption expire. On the other hand, this explains why lenders today prefer the trust deed – a mortgage only has one remedy, where a trust deed could be foreclosed either through a trustee's sale or judicially as a mortgage.

Creating land sales contracts

Even though their histories and the manner in which mortgages and trust deeds are created are very different, still mortgages and trust deeds are similar in major respects. Both create a lien on the borrower's title and both must be supported by a note as evidence of a debt. Not so the **land sales contract**. The land sales contract is also a very commonly used financing instrument, but it involves an entirely different concept.

When we talk of the land sales contract, we have to be sure all the parties know they are talking about the same thing. On occasion, you will hear buyers, sellers and real estate agents use endless synonyms for the land sales contract. Frequently heard are "real estate contract," "conditional sale agreement for real property," "real property contract," "contract for a deed," and the list goes on and on. Probably the most common expressions in Washington are "land sales contract," "real estate contract," or simply "contract."

A contract is usually carried by a seller, so buyers commonly say they are "buying on contract." Unfortunately, buyers and sellers are not ordinarily very sophisticated, so when you investigate such a sale you frequently find that the actual instrument was a purchase money trust deed, or occasionally a purchase money mortgage, not an actual land sales contract. Usually the real estate agent must obtain a copy of the instrument, since it contains important information. For example, whether or not the loan can be assumed is a fact which can only be ascertained for sure by reading the exact language of the instrument.

The expression "contract for a deed" is an interesting synonym for "land sales contract," for that is exactly what it is. Reduced to its essential form, the land sales contract is a contract between an owner and a buyer for the future conveyance of the real estate. The owner agrees to give the buyer a deed to the property when the buyer has finished paying for it. In exchange, the buyer agrees to make the payments called for in the contract. Make special note of the fact that the seller does not usually deed the property to the buyer until the buyer has made the final payment. The seller is said to retain legal title to the property until the buyer has fully performed his or her part of the bargain. Since the buyer's right to a deed is a substantial right, we use the word **equitable title** to describe the buyer's rights. The word "equitable" means "just" or "fair."

Under common law, the rights and responsibilities relating to any parcel of real property are vested in the owner (freeholder). It is always the owner who must pay the

AFTER RECORDING MAIL TO:

Name

Address

City, State, Zip

Filed for Record at Request of:

_____

ANY OPTIONAL PROVISION NOT INITIALED BY ALL PERSONS SIGNING THIS CONTRACT – WHETHER INDIVIDU-
ALLY OR AS AN OFFICER OR AGENT – IS NOT A PART OF THIS CONTRACT.

REAL ESTATE CONTRACT
(RESIDENTIAL SHORT FORM)

1. PARTIES AND DATE. This Contract is entered into on _____ ,

between _____

as "Seller" and _____

as "Buyer."

2. SALE AND LEGAL DESCRIPTION. Seller agrees to sell to Buyer and Buyer agrees to purchase from Seller the fol-

lowing described real estate in _____ County, state of Washington:

Assessor's Property Tax Parcel/Account Number: _____

3. PERSONAL PROPERTY. Personal property, if any, included in the sale is as follows:

No part of the purchase price is attributed to personal property.

4. (a) PRICE. Buyer agrees to pay: $ _____ Total Price

Less ($) _____ Down Payment

Less ($) _____ Assumed Obligation(s)

Results in $ _____ Amount Financed by Seller.

   (b) ASSUMED OBLIGATIONS. Buyer agrees to pay the above assumed Obligation(s) by assuming and agreeing

to pay that certain _____ (Mortgage/Deed of Trust/Contract) dated _____ recorded as

Auditor's File #._____ .

Seller warrants the unpaid balance of said obligation is $ _____ which is payable $ _____

on or before the _____ day of _____ , _____ , _____ (including/plus)

interest at the rate of _____ % per annum on the declining balance thereof; and a like amount on or

before the _____ day of each and every _____ (month/year) thereafter until paid in full.

*Limited Practice Board land sales contract. The Limited Practice Board has created standard real estate docu-
ments that qualified closing agents can use.*

NOTE: Fill in the date in the following two lines only if there is an early cash out date.

NOTWITHSTANDING THE ABOVE, THE ENTIRE BALANCE OF PRINCIPAL AND INTEREST IS DUE IN FULL NOT LATER THAN _____ , _____ . ANY ADDITIONAL ASSUMED OBLIGATIONS ARE INCLUDED IN ADDENDUM

(C) PAYMENT OF AMOUNT FINANCED BY SELLER.

Buyer agrees to pay the sum of $ _____ as follows:

$ _____ or more at buyer's option on or before the _____ day of _____ , _____ , _____ (including/plus) interest from _____ at the rate of _____% per annum on the declining balance thereof; and a like amount or more on or before the _____ day of each and every _____ (month/year) thereafter until paid in full.

NOTE: Fill in the date in the following two lines only if there is an early cash out date.

NOTWITHSTANDING THE ABOVE, THE ENTIRE BALANCE OF PRINCIPAL AND INTEREST IS DUE IN FULL NOT LATER THAN _____ .

Payments are applied first to interest and then to principal. Payments shall be made at _____ _____ , or such other place as the Seller may hereafter indicate in writing.

5. FAILURE TO MAKE PAYMENTS ON ASSUMED OBLIGATIONS. If Buyer fails to make any payments on assumed obligation(s), Seller may give written notice to Buyer that unless Buyer makes the delinquent payment(s) within 15 days, Seller will make the payment(s), together with any late charge, additional interest, penalties, and costs assessed by the Holder of the assumed obligation(s). The 15-day period may be shortened to avoid the exercise of any remedy by the Holder of the assumed obligation(s). Buyer shall immediately after such payment by Seller reimburse Seller for the amount of such payment plus a late charge equal to five percent (5%) of the amount so paid plus all costs and attorney fees incurred by Seller in connection with making such payment.

6. (a) OBLIGATIONS TO BE PAID BY SELLER. The Seller agrees to continue to pay from payments received hereunder the following obligation, which obligation must be paid in full when Buyer pays the purchase price in full: That certain _____ (Mortgage/Deed of Trust/Contract) dated _____ , recorded as Auditor's File # _____ .

ANY ADDITIONAL OBLIGATION TO BE PAID BY SELLER ARE INCLUDED IN ADDENDUM.

(b) EQUITY OF SELLER PAID IN FULL. If the balance owed the Seller on the purchase price herein becomes equal to the balance owed on prior encumbrances being paid by Seller, Buyer will be deemed to have assumed said encumbrances as of that date. Buyer shall thereafter make payments directly to the holders of said encumbrances and make no further payments to Seller. Seller shall at that time deliver to Buyer a fulfillment deed in accordance with the provisions of paragraph 8.

(c) FAILURE OF SELLER TO MAKE PAYMENTS ON PRIOR ENCUMBRANCES. If Seller fails to make any payments on any prior encumbrance, Buyer may give written notice to Seller that unless Seller makes the delinquent payments within 15 days, Buyer will make the payments together with any late charge, additional interest, penalties, and costs assessed by the holder of the prior encumbrance. The 15-day period may be shortened to avoid the exercise of any remedy by the holder of the prior encumbrance. Buyer may deduct the amounts so paid plus a late charge of 5% of the amount so paid and any attorneys' fees and costs incurred by Buyer in connection with the delinquency from payments next becoming due Seller on the purchase price. In the event Buyer makes such delinquent payments on three occasions, Buyer shall have the right to make all payments due thereafter directly to the holder of such prior encumbrance and deduct the then balance owing on such prior encumbrance from the then balance owing on the purchase price and reduce periodic payments on the balance due Seller by the payments called for in such prior encumbrance as such payments become due.

7. OTHER ENCUMBRANCES AGAINST THE PROPERTY. The property is subject to encumbrances including the following listed tenancies, easements, restrictions, and reservations in addition to the obligations assumed by Buyer and the obligations being paid by Seller.

ANY ADDITIONAL NON-MONETARY ENCUMBRANCES ARE INCLUDED IN ADDENDUM.

8. FULFILLMENT DEED. Upon payment of all amounts due Seller, Seller agrees to deliver to Buyer a Statutory Warranty Deed in fulfillment of this Contract. The covenants of warranty in said deed shall not apply to any encumbrances assumed by Buyer or to defects in title arising subsequent to the date of this Contract by, through, or under persons other than the Seller herein. Any personal property included in the sale shall be included in the fulfillment deed.

9. LATE CHARGES. If any payment on the purchase price is not made within ten (10) days after the date it is due, Buyer agrees to pay a late charge equal to 5% of the amount of such payment. Such late payment charge shall be in addition to all other remedies available to Seller and the first amounts received from Buyer after such late charges are due shall be applied to the late charges.

10. NO ADVERSE EFFECT ON PRIOR ENCUMBRANCES. Seller warrants that entry into this Contract will not cause in any prior encumbrance (a) a breach, (b) accelerated payments, or (c) an increased interest rate; unless (a), (b), or (c) has been consented to by Buyer in writing.

11. POSSESSION. Buyer is entitled to possession of the property from and after the date of this Contract or _____ _____ , _____ , whichever is later, subject to any tenancies described in paragraph 7.

12. TAXES, ASSESSMENTS, AND UTILITY LIENS. Buyer agrees to pay by the date due all taxes and assessments becoming a lien against the property after the date of this Contract. Buyer may in good faith contest any such taxes or assessments so long as no forfeiture or sale of the property is threatened as the result of such contest. Buyer agrees to pay when due any utility charges which may become liens superior to Seller's interest under this Contract. If real estate taxes and penalties are assessed against the property subsequent to date of this Contract because of a change in use prior to the date of this Contract for Open Space, Farm, Agricultural, or Timber classifications approved by the County or because of a Senior Citizen's Declaration to Defer Property Taxes filed prior to the date of this Contract, Buyer may demand in writing payment of such taxes and penalties within 30 days. If payment is not made, Buyer may pay and deduct the amount thereof plus 5% penalty from the payments next becoming due Seller under the Contract.

13. INSURANCE. Buyer agrees to keep all buildings now or hereafter erected on the property described herein continuously insured under fire and extended coverage policies in an amount not less than the balances owed on obligations assumed by Buyer plus the balance due Seller, or full insurable value, whichever is lower. All policies shall be held by the Seller and be in such companies as the Seller may approve and have loss payable first to any holders of underlying encumbrances, then to Seller as their interests may appear and then to Buyer. Buyer may within 30 days after loss negotiate a contract to substantially restore the premises to their condition before the loss. If insurance proceeds are sufficient to pay the contract price for restoration or if the Buyer deposits in escrow any deficiency with instructions to apply the funds on the restoration contract, the property shall be restored unless the underlying encumbrances provide otherwise. Otherwise the amount collected under any insurance policy shall be applied upon any amounts due hereunder in such order as Seller shall determine. In the event of forfeiture, all rights of Buyer in insurance policies then in force shall pass to Seller.

14. NON-PAYMENT OF TAXES, INSURANCE, AND UTILITIES CONSTITUTING LIENS. If Buyer fails to pay taxes or assessments, insurance premiums, or utility charges constituting liens prior to Seller's interest under this Contract, Seller may pay such items and Buyer shall forthwith pay Seller the amount thereof plus a late charge of 5% of the amount thereof plus any costs and attorney's fees incurred in connection with making such payment.

15. CONDITION OF PROPERTY. Buyer accepts the property in its present condition and acknowledges that Seller, his/her agents, and subagents have made no representation or warranty concerning the physical condition of the property or the uses to which it may be put other than as set forth herein. Buyer agrees to maintain the property in such condition as complies with all applicable laws.

16. RISK OF LOSS. Buyer shall bear the risk of loss for destruction or condemnation of the property. Any such loss shall not relieve Buyer from any of Buyer's obligations pursuant to this Contract.

17. WASTE. Buyer shall keep the property in good repair and shall not commit or suffer waste or willful damage to or destruction of the property. Buyer shall not remove commercial timber without the written consent of Seller.

18. AGRICULTURAL USE. If this property is to be used principally for agricultural purposes, Buyer agrees to conduct farm and livestock operations in accordance with good husbandry practices. In the event a forfeiture action is instituted, Buyer consents to Seller's entry on the premises to take any reasonable action to conserve soil, crops, trees, and livestock.

19. CONDEMNATION. Seller and buyer may each appear as owners of an interest in the property in any action concerning condemnation of any part of the property. Buyer may within 30 days after condemnation and removal of improvements, negotiate a contract to substantially restore the premises to their condition before the removal. If the condemnation proceeds are sufficient to pay the contract price for restoration or if the Buyer deposits in escrow any deficiency with instructions to apply the funds on the restoration contract, the property shall be restored unless underlying encumbrances provide otherwise. Otherwise, proceeds of the award shall be applied in payment of the balance due on the purchase price, as Seller may direct.

20. DEFAULT. If the Buyer fails to observe or perform any term, covenant, or condition of this Contract, Seller may:
(a) Suit for Installments. Sue for any delinquent periodic payment; or
(b) Specific Performance. Sue for specific performance of any of Buyer's obligations pursuant to this Contract; or
(c) Forfeit Buyer's Interest. Forfeit this Contract pursuant to Ch. 61.30, RCW, as it is presently enacted and may hereafter be amended. The effect of such forfeiture includes: (i) all right, title, and interest in the property of the Buyer and all persons claiming through the Buyer shall be terminated; (ii) the Buyer's rights under the Contract shall be cancelled; (iii) all sums previously paid under the Contract shall belong to and be retained by the Seller or other person to whom paid and entitled thereto; (iv) all improvements made to and unharvested crops on the property shall belong to the Seller; and (v) Buyer shall be required to surrender possession of the property, improvements, and unharvested crops to the Seller 10 days after the forfeiture.

(d) Acceleration of Balance Due. Give Buyer written notice demanding payment of said delinquencies and payment of a late charge of 5% of the amount of such delinquent payments and payment of Seller's reasonable attorney's fees and costs incurred for services in preparing and sending such Notice and stating that if payment pursuant to said Notice is not received within 30 days after the date said Notice is either deposited in the mail addressed to the Buyer or personally delivered to the Buyer, the entire balance owing, including interest, will become immediately due and payable. Seller may thereupon institute suit for payment of such balance, interest, late charge, and reasonable attorney's fees and costs.

(e) Judicial Foreclosure. Sue to foreclose this Contract as a mortgage, in which event Buyer may be liable for a deficiency.

21. RECEIVER. If Seller has instituted any proceedings specified in Paragraph 20 and Buyer is receiving rental or other income from the property, Buyer agrees that the appointment of a receiver for the property is necessary to protect Seller's interest.

22. BUYER'S REMEDY FOR SELLER'S DEFAULT. If Seller fails to observe or perform any term, covenant, or condition of this Contract, Buyer may, after 30 days' written notice to Seller, institute suit for damages or specific performance unless the breaches designated in said notice are cured.

23. NON-WAIVER. Failure of either party to insist upon strict performance of the other party's obligations hereunder shall not be construed as a waiver of strict performance thereafter of all of the other party's obligations hereunder and shall not prejudice any remedies as provided herein.

24. ATTORNEY'S FEES AND COSTS. In the event of any breach of this Contract, the party responsible for the breach agrees to pay reasonable attorney's fees and costs, including costs of service of notices and title searches, incurred by the other party. The prevailing party in any suit instituted arising out of this Contract and in any forfeiture proceedings arising out of this Contract shall be entitled to receive reasonable attorney's fees and costs incurred in such suit or proceedings.

25. NOTICES. Notices shall be either personally served or shall be sent certified mail, return receipt requested, and by regular first class mail to Buyer at _____ . and to the Seller at _____ . or such other addresses as either party may specify in writing to the other party. Notices shall be deemed given when served or mailed. Notice to Seller shall also be sent to any institution receiving payments on the Contract.

26. TIME FOR PERFORMANCE. Time is of the essence in performance of any obligations pursuant to this Contract.

27. SUCCESSORS AND ASSIGNS. Subject to any restrictions against assignment, the provisions of this Contract shall be binding on the heirs, successors, and assigns of the Seller and the Buyer.

28. OPTIONAL PROVISION – SUBSTITUTION AND SECURITY ON PERSONAL PROPERTY. Buyer may substitute for any personal property specified in Paragraph 3 herein other personal property of like nature which Buyer owns free and clear of any encumbrances. Buyer hereby grants Seller a security interest in all personal property specified in Paragraph 3 and future substitutions for such property and agrees to execute a financing statement under the Uniform Commercial Code reflecting such security interest.

SELLER   INITIALS: BUYER

_____   _____   _____

29. OPTIONAL PROVISION – ALTERATIONS. Buyer shall not make any substantial alteration to the improvements on the property without the prior written consent of Seller, which consent will not be unreasonably withheld.

SELLER   INITIALS: BUYER

_____   _____   _____

30. OPTIONAL PROVISION – DUE ON SALE. If Buyer, without written consent of Seller, (a) conveys, (b) sells, (c) leases, (d) assigns, (e) contracts to convey, sell, lease or assign, (f) grants an option to buy the property, (g) permits a forfeiture or foreclosure or trustee or sheriffs sale of any of the Buyer's interest in the property or this Contract, Seller may at any time thereafter either raise the interest rate on the balance of the purchase price or declare the entire balance of the purchase price due and payable. If one or more of the entities comprising the Buyer is a corporation, any transfer or successive transfers in the nature of items (a) through (g) above of 49% or more of the outstanding capital stock shall enable Seller to take the above action. A lease of less than 3 years (including options for renewals), a transfer to a spouse or child of Buyer, a transfer incident to a marriage dissolution or condemnation, and a transfer by inheritance will not enable Seller to take any action pursuant to this Paragraph; provided the transferee other than a condemnor agrees in writing that the provisions of this paragraph apply to any subsequent transaction involving the property entered into by the transferee.

SELLER   INITIALS: BUYER

_____   _____   _____

31. OPTIONAL PROVISION – PRE-PAYMENT PENALTIES ON PRIOR ENCUMBRANCES. If Buyer elects to make payments in excess of the minimum required payments on the purchase price herein, and Seller, because of such prepayments, incurs prepayment penalties on prior encumbrances, Buyer agrees to forthwith pay Seller the amount of such penalties in addition to payments on the purchase price.

SELLER   INITIALS: BUYER

_____   _____   _____

32. Optional provision – periodic payments on taxes and insurance. In addition to the periodic payments on the purchase price, Buyer agrees to pay Seller such portion of the real estate taxes and assessments and fire insurance premium as will approximately total the amount due during the current year based on Seller's reasonable estimate. The payments during the current year shall be $ _____ per _____ . Such "reserve" payments from Buyer shall not accrue interest. Seller shall pay when due all real estate taxes and insurance premiums, if any, and debit the amounts so paid to the reserve account. Buyer and Seller shall adjust the reserve account in April of each year to reflect excess or deficit balances and changed costs. Buyer agrees to bring the reserve account balance to a minimum of $10 at the time of adjustment.

Seller	Initials:	Buyer
_____	_____	_____

33. Addenda. Any addenda attached hereto are a part of this Contract.

34. Entire agreement. This Contract constitutes the entire agreement of the parties and supersedes all prior agreements and understandings, written or oral. This Contract may be amended only in writing executed by Seller and Buyer.

In witness whereof the parties have signed and sealed this Contract the day and year first above written.

Seller _____ Buyer _____

Seller _____ Buyer _____

State of _____)

)-ss

County of _____)

I certify that I know or have satisfactory evidence that _____

(is/are) the person(s) who appeared before me, and said person(s) acknowledged that (he/she/they) signed this instrument and acknowledged it to be (his/her/their) free and voluntary act for the uses and purposes mentioned in this instrument.

Dated: _____

Notary Public in and for the state of _____

My appointment expires: _____

State of _____)

)-ss

County of _____)

I certify that I know or have satisfactory evidence that _____

(is/are) the person(s) who appeared before me, and said person(s) acknowledged that (he/she/they) signed this instrument, on oath stated that (he/she/they) (is/are) authorized to execute the instrument and acknowledged it as

the _____ of _____

to be the free and voluntary act of such party(ies) for the uses and purposes mentioned in this instrument.

Dated: _____

Notary Public in and for the state of _____

My appointment expires: _____

taxes, and who is responsible for the property. The owner is also the party who is entitled to possession, use and enjoyment of the property. When real estate is sold on a land sales contract, the seller retains the legal title, so, logically, the seller retains the right of possession, use and enjoyment. The seller also remains liable for the property taxes and any problems created by the property. But when selling on a land sales contract the owner wishes the buyer to assume the responsibilities, and similarly the buyer wants the rights of possession, use and enjoyment. Thus, a typical land sales contract specifically states that the buyer will pay the taxes and other liens and the buyer will save the seller harmless from any liability regarding the property during the time the buyer is paying for it. Contracts also invariably have clauses giving the buyer the right of possession, use and enjoyment, as long as the buyer is not in default. When essentially all the rights and responsibilities of ownership are given to the buyer, we say that the seller's legal title is reduced to a **naked** or **bare title**.

The above discussion is the common law as it applies to land sales contracts in most states. Washington, however, views the land sales contract in a somewhat different manner. In Washington the land sales contract is deemed to give the buyer legal title to the property, and the seller has a lien interest in it. Thus it is not specifically necessary that the contract contain language giving the buyer possession and enjoyment.

So far we have referred to the parties as the buyer and the seller. Most modern land sales contracts (such as the Limited Practice Board contract on the preceding pages) call them just exactly that, the buyer and the seller. Some more old-fashioned contracts refer to the parties as the **vendor** (seller) and the **vendee** (buyer), but modern attorneys prefer the simplest plain language wherever possible.

As you can see, the seller's security interest during the term of the contract is really the title to the property. You may hear people refer to this as a **vendor's lien** although in reality it is not a lien in the same sense of the word as other liens such as judgments, mortgages, trust deeds, and the like. In most states the land sales contract is really a claim, or possible right, which the buyer has in the seller's title. A **cloud** is what we call a possible interest or claim in another person's real property, so we must conclude that the land sales contract is a cloud. However, the cloud is not on the buyer's title – the buyer does not have a legal title. It is the buyer's equitable title which is a cloud on the *seller's* title.

Previously we saw that when a mortgage was paid in full we recorded a satisfaction of mortgage. And when a trust deed loan was paid off, we used a deed of reconveyance to release the lien from the borrower's title. When a land sales contract is paid off we simply record the deed called for in the contract. This deed is frequently referred to as the **fulfillment deed** since it is in fulfillment of the seller's final obligation to the buyer.

Land sales contract remedies

Where mortgages and trust deeds have either common law or statutory remedies, the only remedies in a land sales contract are those remedies stated in the contract. As a rule, land sales contracts give the seller four remedies – foreclosure as a mortgage, suit for the delinquent payments, forfeiture, and specific performance.

Foreclosure as a mortgage – A suit to **foreclose as a mortgage** is the same as judicial foreclosure of mortgages and trust deeds. When a mortgage or trust deed is foreclosed, the result is an auction sale of the property, with the possibilities of deficiency judgment and right of redemption (see *Mortgage remedies*, previously in this chapter).

Any junior lienholders must also be served and made a party to the foreclosure in order to extinguish their claims. Junior lienholders may also be granted a period of time in which to pay the balance due.

Specific performance – *Specific performance* is a remedy to compel performance of a contract. In the land sales contract the buyer has the obligation to pay, which the seller can enforce by suit for specific performance.

Suit for delinquent payments – A suit asking the court to grant the seller a judgment for the installments in arrears.

Forfeiture – When a land sales contract allows the seller to declare a *forfeiture*, if the buyer defaults, this means that the seller can declare the contract null and void. This remedy would appear to have a great advantage to the seller, because the buyer's rights can be terminated without court action. However, a substantial problem arises when the buyer is still in possession of the property. In order to remove an unwilling buyer, the seller would be required to file a suit for ejectment (similar to an eviction).

Nevertheless, many times the buyer voluntarily leaves, or the property was a rental and the buyer was never in possession at all. In such cases declaring a forfeiture may be the most expedient route. RCW Chapter 61.30 allows the seller to declare a forfeiture without court action. The seller must mail to the buyer, by both certified and first class mail a notice of the nature and amount of the default and the date after which the buyer's rights will be extinguished if the buyer fails to cure the default. The buyer is entitled to at least 90 days in which to cure. If the default is cured within the statutory time limit, the contract is reinstated; if not, the buyer's rights are extinguished. In order to cure the default, the buyer must pay the payments currently due plus the seller's actual expenses incurred. The seller must also mail, in the same manner, a similar notice to all junior lienholders and others claiming an interest in the property, who have the same right to cure and reinstate as the buyer.

In order to regain clear title and extinguish the buyer's interest in the contract, the seller merely records a declaration of forfeiture stating that the default was not cured within the time limit.

Which instrument should the lender choose? Institutional lenders such as banks, savings and loan associations and mortgage bankers may have little choice, since the secondary mortgage market requires a uniform trust deed today. Institutional lenders typically use land sales contracts only if they are selling a property they own themselves, and even then they almost always use a trust deed. However, owners who sell their properties and carry back financing are generally free to choose any of the three instruments, although it is most common for them to use either a standard trust deed or land sales contract. Precisely which instrument you should use depends on whether you are representing the borrower or the lender, as well as the exact language of the instrument in question.

Deed as a mortgage

Have you ever heard someone say "the bank lent me the money, but they made me give them my deed as collateral"? What would happen if a lender literally took a deed to the property instead of a mortgage or other financing instrument? Could the lender then just legally demand possession of the property as the true legal owner?

Normally, the courts will look at the transaction and try to determine the intent of the parties. If the court can find that the borrower truly intended to convey the property to the lender, i.e., the money was given in exchange for the deed and not as borrowed money, then the lender would own the property. However, if the intent was clearly to make the property collateral for a loan, then the court will grant the lender the rights of a normal mortgagee.

Guaranties and collateral agreements

Many times a lender will take a note and trust deed on real property, but will request the borrower give a **collateral agreement** listing certain personal property as additional collateral. Collateral agreements are not commonly used on residential loans where the requirements of the secondary mortgage market dictate that the property alone appraise for sufficient value to support the loan.

However, collateral agreements are found on commercial mortgage loans, typically where a business owner wishes to borrow against real estate owned by a corporation. In these circumstances, bankers frequently request that the borrower give them additional personal property, usually trade fixtures of the business, as collateral.

Do not confuse the collateral agreement with a **personal guaranty**. A personal guaranty is akin to a co-signature. Personal guaranties are used in commercial lending where the lender is lending money to a business, but asks the business owner (or principal stockholders) to guarantee the loan personally. Thus, if the business defaults, the lender can look to the individuals for repayment.

Security agreements

The term **security agreement** is a modern expression for **chattel mortgage**. As the expression "chattel mortgage" would imply, this instrument is used to make personal property (chattels) collateral for a debt. In other words, you would use a mortgage to make real estate collateral for a debt and you would use a chattel mortgage to make chattels collateral for a debt.

If you lend money and take a note and mortgage (or note and trust deed), then your first step would be to record the mortgage or trust deed. As we have seen, recording establishes your priority date. All this is fine for mortgages and trust deeds, but what would you do to give constructive notice and establish priority if you had a note and security agreement? Today you can file a formal **UCC financing statement** in the office of the Washington Department of Licensing. "UCC" stands for the **Uniform Commercial Code**, a set of laws governing commercial transactions that have been adopted by all states in order to create conformity. When the financing statement or security agreement has been filed it establishes the priority of the claim against the personal property.

Real estate agents commonly encounter UCC financing statements on crops, and on fixtures on real property (for example, furnaces, air conditioning units, attached appliances, and so on).

Soldiers and Sailors Civil Relief Act

In rare instances, a lender must consider the **Soldiers and Sailors Civil Relief Act**. This is a federal law which provides relief from foreclosure for those who have been drafted into any branch of the armed forces and, as a result of their military service, are unable to meet their loan obligations.

The law only applies to draftees and not to career military people or those who enlisted voluntarily. In cases where the law applies it provides that the court can delay foreclosure action until 90 days after separation from military service, or if the borrower has already been foreclosed on and has a right of redemption, then the right of redemption extends until separation from the service. All sums due accrue interest at 6% until separation from the service, regardless of the interest rate in the financing instruments.

Alternatives to foreclosure

In some cases a lender may find it expedient to recast a loan agreement or grant concessions to a borrower rather than foreclose if the concessions would make it possible for the borrower to repay the debt. In practice, this occurs most commonly among purchase money lenders who do not want their property back. It is far less common to find institutional lenders granting concessions to borrowers. Institutional lenders generally feel they cannot afford to establish a precedent – if they grant concessions to one borrower, soon all their borrowers will be demanding concessions.

A popular concession is to lower the monthly payments by lowering the interest rate, extending the repayment period, or negative amortization. Or, sometimes the lender will agree to a moratorium, a period of time during which the borrower need not make payments. Unpaid interest can be forgiven or added to the unpaid balance.

In the end, if a satisfactory solution to the default cannot be arranged, the lender must either foreclose or request a **deed in lieu of foreclosure**, also known as an **estoppel deed**. The deed in lieu of foreclosure is called an estoppel deed because it "estops" (bars) the lender from taking any further action against the borrower. The lender agrees to accept the property as full satisfaction of the obligation – if the lender is forced to take a loss on the resale of the collateral, the lender will have no recourse against the borrower, including any right to a deficiency judgment. The savings in legal expense can be significant, but lenders are usually under no requirement to accept a deed in lieu of foreclosure. If the property is not worth the amount owing, and the borrower has other assets that the lender knows about, then the lender commonly refuses to accept a deed in lieu of foreclosure. Lenders accepting a deed in lieu of foreclosure also commonly require a new title insurance policy. If there are judgments against the borrower or the borrower obtained junior financing after the lender's loan, the deed in lieu of foreclosure may be subject to the encumbrances.

The borrower should be aware that an ordinary deed used to convey the title to the lender will not be a release from liability for a deficiency judgment. The borrower should be sure the deed contains the estoppel language.

Typical clauses

A **subordination clause** is sometimes encountered in second lien instruments. Suppose your property already has a first mortgage and you borrowed additional funds on a second mortgage from another lender. If you pay off the first, the second is the only mortgage remaining, so it now automatically becomes a first lien. But you might wish to retain the right to replace the first mortgage without changing the priority position of the second mortgage. You can get this right by having a subordination clause in the second mortgage.

Subordination clauses are also used on occasion in construction financing. A builder may ask the seller of land to carry a purchase money note and trust deed for part of the purchase price. The builder also commonly needs to borrow the construction funds from an institutional lender. The institutional lender will likely require a first position, yet the seller of the land will already have the first position. To solve the

NORMAL LENDER REMEDIES

	MORTGAGE	TRUST DEED			LAND SALES CONTRACT	
	Judicial	Judicial	Trustee's Sale	Forfeiture	Judicial Foreclosure	Specific Performance
Must go to court	YES	YES	NO	NO	YES	YES
Buyer can reinstate	NO	NO	YES	YES	NO	NO
Auction sale	YES	YES	YES	NO	YES	YES [1]
Right of redemption	YES [2]	YES	NO	NO	YES [2]	YES
Deficiency judgment	YES [2]	YES [3]	NO	NO	YES [2]	YES
Time from default to end of foreclosure	3 months to 2 years	3 months to 2 years	4 to 6 months	2 to 5 months	3 months to 2 years	3 months to 2 years

1. Specific performance can result in general judgment, which lender can use to force auction sale of any of debtor's property
2. No right of redemption if lender waived right to deficiency judgment
3. Only if it is a commercial trust deed, entered into after 1998 and the lender can prove waste

dilemma, the builder can ask the seller not only to carry a purchase money note and trust deed, but also to make the instrument junior and subordinate to a mortgage for the construction funds, to be recorded later. The difficulty with this arrangement is that the seller of the land could be in a very poor position in the event of the builder's default.

A junior lien instrument also frequently contains a ***covenant to pay prior encumbrances***. Foreclosure by a first mortgagee would extinguish a second mortgage, so it becomes critical to the second mortgagee to be sure that the first mortgage is kept current. The covenant to pay prior encumbrances typically is worded so a default on the first mortgage is also considered a default on the second. This allows the holder of the second mortgage to cure the default on the first, and then foreclose the second. The second mortgagee can take the title subject to the first without paying it off. However, if the first mortgagee has already accelerated, it may be too late.

When a property is income property (and even on single-family homes today) it is common to find an ***assignment of rents clause*** in the lien instrument. If the property is rented and the borrower defaults, the assignment of rents clause allows the lender to collect the rent directly from the tenant and apply it to the outstanding debt. Without an assignment of rents clause, the lender may still be able to collect the rent from the tenant, but must first obtain a court order appointing a receiver. However, depending on the instrument used Washington code may require a court order to implement the assignment of rents clause anyway.

An ***exculpatory clause*** (also called a ***sole security clause***) is a clause which makes the property the sole source of repayment if the borrower defaults. The legal effect is to block any possibility of a deficiency judgment. Thus, a borrower who has signed a lien instrument with this clause can generally walk away from the property with no further obligations. To be totally effective the clause should block judgments arising from any foreclosure action, including judgments for attorney's fees, and should also block the lender from suing on the note in order to obtain a general judgment.

Many loan instruments today contain index clauses. The ***index clause*** ties the interest rate to a national index, such as the rate paid by the federal government on treasury bills, or the average interest rate on all mortgages purchased by the Federal Home Loan Mortgage Corporation for the previous two weeks. (There are several popular indexes in use by lenders today.) Lenders can change the interest rate on the outstanding loan balance as the index changes.

Usually the index is lower or higher than the rate the lender agrees to, so the loan will contain a ***margin***. The margin is a constant amount, so the actual interest on the loan will be the amount of the index, plus or minus the margin. For example, suppose that you have a loan tied to the treasury bill rate, plus a margin of 2%. Then your interest rate will always be 2% higher than whatever the treasury bill rate is.

An ***escalator clause*** is similar to an index clause, in that it also causes the terms of the loan to change. However, when a loan contains an escalator clause the changes are predetermined and agreed upon by the parties at the time the loan is made. For example, if you and your lender agreed that the interest rate would be 8% the first year, but climb to 9% for the second and subsequent years, this would be an example of an escalator clause. Escalator clauses are also commonly used to change loan terms other than the interest rate. For example, perhaps you agree to make payments which are interest only the first year, the second year you are to pay the interest, plus $50 toward principal, and for the third and subsequent years you are to pay the interest, plus $100 toward the principal. Escalator clauses are typically used in private financing and infrequently in institutional loans.

Lenders on improved real estate need to be sure the insurance is current and that the insurance company has issued a ***loss payable clause*** as a part of the fire insurance policy. The loss payable clause means that the insurance company will pay the proceeds on any loss, first to the lender to the extent of the balance owing, and the surplus, if any, to the borrower. The standard loss payable clause required by most lenders also states that the insurance company will notify the lender of any cancellations and that the insurance will remain in force for ten days after the notice is mailed to the lender. This gives the lender time to contact the borrower and make sure the borrower has obtained a replacement policy, or place their own insurance on the premises.

Real estate lenders also have a special problem with real property taxes. Real property taxes do not follow the normal rules for priority of liens, i.e., in order by recording date. Regardless of when the taxes became a lien on the property or when the mortgage was recorded, real property taxes are a prior lien ahead of private liens. Thus, if the lender forecloses, the lender would have to take the title subject to any unpaid taxes. If the borrower has little equity in the property and the lender allows several years taxes to accrue, the property may actually be overencumbered.

Lenders, therefore, need to be sure the taxes (as well as the fire insurance premiums) are paid by the borrower in timely fashion. Most lenders prefer to handle this by establishing a ***reserve account***, also sometimes called an ***impound*** or ***escrow account***. Simply stated, each month the borrower pays the monthly amount for principal and interest, plus one-twelfth the annual taxes and one-twelfth the annual fire insurance premium. The lender establishes a separate "reserve account" and places the amounts received each month for the taxes and insurance into it. Then when the taxes come due, the lender draws a check against the borrower's reserve account and sends it to the tax collector. Similarly, when the insurance premium comes due, the lender charges the reserve account for the funds to pay the insurance premium. The reserve account may include a reserve for taxes only, for insurance only, or for both. Real estate agents refer to loans where the monthly payment includes principal, interest, taxes and insurance as being paid "PITI." If the payment includes principal, interest and taxes, but not insurance, then the loan is said to be paid "PIT."

In addition, the federal Real Estate Settlement Procedures Act prohibits lenders from setting the monthly amounts for the reserve account higher than would be necessary to cover two additional months worth of the anticipated expense. In other words, a lender knows that property taxes may increase, so establishing the monthly amount a bit higher than $\frac{1}{12}$ of last year's bill is reasonable, just so it is not more than 14 months worth. Further details about the Real Estate Settlement Procedures Act are found in Chapter 14.

Many conventional loans contain a clause requiring a ***prepayment privilege charge*** or ***prepayment penalty***. If the loan instrument contains such a clause, the lender may require the borrower to pay an additional amount in order to pay the loan off ahead of schedule. Prepayment privilege charges are not unusual on conventional loans, but never found on Federal Housing Administration (FHA) loans, Federal Department of Veterans Affairs (VA) loans, or loans made by or with insurance or guaranties from any other state agency. The amount of the prepayment privilege charge varies from lender to lender. Some lenders charge a flat dollar amount, others charge interest on the current balance for several months, yet others charge a flat percentage of the unpaid balance. Some lenders charge only during the first few years of the loan. Other lenders levy the charge any time the loan is paid off ahead of its maturity. Some lenders allow the borrower to pay a certain percentage of the loan balance in any one month without penalty. Other lenders levy the charge only if the loan is paid off in the process of refinancing the property, but forgive the charge if the loan is paid off because the property is sold. The modern practice, even on conventional loans, is not to charge a prepayment penalty at all, since lenders have discovered that it is very unpopular with borrowers.

On rare occasions, a lender may wish to prohibit a borrower from paying off a loan at all before maturity. To do this, the ***not less than*** (or ***or more***) clause should be deleted where the monthly payment is stated, and a ***lock-in clause*** should be stated instead.

Assumptions and novations

When a property is encumbered, the owner can always deed the property to a buyer subject to the encumbrance. This is true regardless of what kind of encumbrance it is – property taxes, leases, mortgages, trust deeds, judgments, clouds – any encumbrance. However, certain lenders in the past have attempted to bar the seller from selling the property subject to the lender's mortgage by placing a ***due on sale clause*** (also sometimes referred to as an ***alienation clause***) in the lien instrument.

These clauses are typical in conventional loans, but do not occur in loans guaranteed by the Department of Veterans Affairs prior to March of 1988 and loans insured by the Federal Housing Administration (FHA) prior to December, 1986. The purpose of the due on sale clause is to force the borrower to pay off a low-interest loan or to force a new buyer to agree to a higher interest rate during a period when interest rates are rising.

In any situation where the buyer takes the title subject to the loan, the lender will want the buyer to ***assume and agree to pay*** the debt. If the buyer assumes and agrees to pay, then the buyer has become personally liable for the debt the same as signing the note personally. If the buyer merely takes the title subject to the loan without assuming and agreeing to pay the debt, then the lender cannot hold the buyer personally liable for the debt. Of course, if the buyer fails to make the payments, the lender can still foreclose. Also, regardless of whether the buyer assumes and agrees to pay the debt or not, the original borrower (the seller) is not relieved of the obligation to pay the debt. So, if the buyer assumes and agrees to pay the debt, the lender has two individuals fully personally liable for the debt. Normally, the buyer assumes and agrees to pay by signing a separate assumption agreement.

Many people mistakenly believe that when the buyer assumes and agrees to pay the seller's old loan the buyer becomes primarily liable and the seller is only secondarily liable. While it is true that the seller will not have to pay as long as the buyer keeps the loan current, when it comes to legal liability, there is no "primary" or "secondary" to the issue. If the lender sues on the debt the lender will name both as co-defendants. Upon obtaining judgment the lender can reach assets of either, and has no obligation to take assets of the seller only if the buyer's assets are insufficient. The lender will typically take whatever assets are easiest to reach, regardless of whose they are.

Is there a way to relieve the seller of liability for the debt when the buyer takes over the loan? Yes, if the lender agrees to a ***substitution of mortgagor***, which is a type of novation. Legally, a novation of a contract occurs where the original contract is canceled and a new one replaces it. If the lender agrees to a substitution of mortgagor, this is deemed to be a novation of the debt agreement, so the original note and lien instrument are canceled. However, it is unusual for a lender to agree to a substitution of mortgagor and, even if the lender does agree, the lender will require the buyer to qualify as thoroughly as if it were a new loan.

Loan types

A ***blanket mortgage*** (or blanket trust deed, blanket land sales contract, blanket encumbrance) encumbers more than one piece of real estate. Loans for development of vacant land and investment loans are kinds of real estate loans which sometimes involve a blanket encumbrance.

A blanket encumbrance typically contains a **lot release clause** (sometimes called a **parcel release clause** or **partial release clause**. The lot release clause allows the borrower to pay a stipulated portion of the debt in exchange for which the lender will give a satisfaction (or deed of reconveyance or fulfillment deed) for a particular parcel. Thus the borrower can get clear title to any given parcel by paying only a portion of the debt. How much the lender demands for each parcel is normally determined by the value of each parcel in relation to the total amount of the debt.

A **package mortgage** (also package trust deed, package land sales contract or package encumbrance) should not be confused with a blanket mortgage. A package encumbrance includes both real property and personal property as collateral. Package encumbrances are typically used by builders who include appliances with a new house, or in seller financing of commercial structures such as apartments and office buildings.

Older real estate agents may still use the expression **budget mortgage** to refer to a loan which is being paid PITI (with a reserve account for taxes and insurance). When amortizing mortgages with equal monthly payments first gained favor with lenders during the 1920s, the payments on a budget mortgage were considered the equivalent in a homebuyer's budget as rent payments were to a renter.

The expression **participation mortgage** has two different meanings. Its more recent meaning is as a synonym for **equity participation loan**. In an equity participation loan, the lender charges a reduced rate of interest, but in exchange is entitled to a share of the profit when the property is sold in the future. In residential lending, these loans are sometimes referred to as **shared appreciation mortgages**. Equity participation loans of this nature have been used for decades in commercial loans such as office buildings and shopping centers, where the lender's future share in the profits is known as an **equity kicker**. However, equity participation loans on single-family residences have been used almost exclusively by private parties rather than institutional lenders. Occasionally the term is used for a loan where the lender actually becomes a co-owner of the property, in which case the lender may share in the ongoing income.

An older meaning for the term "participation loan" is its use in commercial banking. Many times a commercial bank will be called upon to fund a business loan of many millions of dollars for a large corporate customer. If the bank wishes to make the loan, but does not wish to put so many eggs in one basket, the bank may solicit "participation" in the loan on the part of one or more of its competitors. Each bank advances a portion of the loan funds and takes a proportionate share of the interest and risk.

The expression **open mortgage** is a legal term which usually means that the loan has matured and is supposed to be paid off, yet there remains a balance owing. Perhaps this state of affairs was because the borrower missed a payment. More commonly today, the loan had a balloon payment clause requiring the loan to be paid in full at some point and the borrower did not do so. Regardless of the cause, open loans are subject to immediate foreclosure. However, the term open mortgage is rarely used and this definition is virtually unknown in Washington. More commonly, Washington real estate agents use the term to mean a loan that has no prepayment penalty, if they use the term at all.

Do not confuse the open mortgage with an **open end mortgage**, sometimes called a **mortgage for future advances**. An open end mortgage is like a credit line. The lender approves the property and the borrower as being eligible to borrow up to a certain amount. However, the borrower borrows only a portion of the maximum at any one time. From time to time the borrower borrows additional funds (up to the maximum) and from time to time the borrower repays funds previously borrowed. Sometimes this expression is used as a verb – as in "to open-end a mortgage," which occurs when the lender recasts an existing loan in order to advance additional funds to the existing borrower.

Open end mortgages have an advantage in commercial settings, and are particularly common in agricultural financing. Once the lender has the lien instrument recorded and a mortgagee's title insurance policy, these expenses can be avoided on future advances. It is not uncommon, for example, for a borrower to want to pay off the open end mortgage, but leave one dollar still owing, in order to keep the lien instrument still alive.

Wraparound encumbrances (also known as *all-inclusive encumbrances*) have gained a great deal of popularity in recent years. The basic idea is very simple. A seller whose property is encumbered with a loan (which does not contain a due on sale clause) agrees to sell the property to a buyer and carry back a wraparound land sales contract (or trust deed or mortgage). The balance the seller owes is included in the balance the buyer owes the seller. For example, suppose you owe $100,000 on an old FHA loan at 6%. You have a buyer willing to pay $160,000 for your property with $20,000 down, and is willing to give you 8% interest if you will carry a contract for $140,000. If you agree to this, the buyer will make the payments to you on the $140,000 and you, in turn, will continue to make the payments to your lender on the $100,000. Since the buyer will make higher payments to you on the $140,000 than you have to make to the bank on the $100,000, you can pocket the difference. Of course, you gain an additional advantage. The fact is that $100,000 of the $140,000 you lent to the buyer was never your money in the first place. You borrowed that $100,000 from the bank at 6% – and now you are re-lending it to the buyer at 8%. You are getting 2% interest on the bank's money. In fact, because of the interest differential, your yield on that land sales contract is significantly greater than the 8% the buyer is paying you. The exact yield is a complicated calculation and depends on the remaining maturities of the two loans. Financial aspects of wraparound loans are covered in Chapter 16.

A borrower on a wraparound loan needs protection in the event the seller fails to make the payments on the underlying loan. After all, foreclosure by the first lender will extinguish all the buyer's interest. To guard against this, sometimes the buyer and seller agree to use a collection service at a financial institution. The buyer makes the payment to the financial institution, which in turn subtracts the amount due on the underlying loan and remits it to the underlying lender, and then remits the difference to the seller. The buyer would also want to be sure the wraparound encumbrance contained a covenant to pay on prior encumbrances, and that a request for notice of sale was recorded.

O━━ *KEY TERMS*

The key to understanding any new field is the vocabulary used in that field. To maximize your comprehension of the material presented in this chapter, be sure you know the meaning and significance of the following terms. Remember that the majority of test questions primarily test knowledge of vocabulary.

Acceleration clause	*Balloon payment*
All-inclusive encumbrance	*Beneficiary*
Amortized note	*Blanket mortgage*
Assign	*Bond*
Assignment of rents clause	*Budget mortgage*
Assume and agree to pay	*Call feature*

Chattel mortgage

Cloud

Collateral agreement

Covenant to pay prior encumbrances

Deed in lieu of foreclosure

Deed of reconveyance

Deed of trust

Defeasance

Defeasible fee

Deficiency judgment

Demand clause

Encumbrance

Endorsement

Equitable right of redemption

Equitable title

Equity kicker

Equity participation loan

Escalator clause

Escrow account

Estoppel deed

Exculpatory clause

Foreclose as a mortgage

Foreclosure

Forfeiture

Fulfillment deed

Grantee

Grantor

Guaranty

Hard money mortgage

Holder in due course

Homestead

Impound account

Index clause

Instrument

Instruments of finance

Judgment of foreclosure

Judicial foreclosure

Junior

Land sales contract

Lien

Lien instrument

Lien theory

Lock-in clause

Locked in

Loss payable clause

Lot release clause

Maker

Margin

Mortgage for future advances

Mortgagee

Mortgagor

Naked title

Negotiable instrument

Non-judicial foreclosure

Not less than clause

Note

Note and mortgage

Note and trust deed

Notice of sale

Open end mortgage

Open mortgage

Or more clause

Package mortgage

Parcel release clause

Partial release clause

Participation mortgage

Payee

Personal guaranty

Power of sale

Primary lender

Promissory note

Purchase money mortgage

Recourse

Request for notice of sale

Reserve account

Reserve price

Right of reverter

Satisfaction

Satisfaction of mortgage

Secondary mortgage market

Security agreement

Shared appreciation mortgage

Sheriff's certificate of sale

Sheriff's deed

Soldiers and Sailors Civil Relief Act

Sole security clause

Specific performance

Statutory right of redemption

Straight note

Subordinate

Subordination clause

Substitution of mortgagor

Title theory

Trust

Trust deed

Trustee

Trustee's deed

Trustee's foreclosure

Trustor

UCC financing statement

Uniform Commercial Code

Upset price

Vendee

Vendor

Vendor's lien

Without recourse

Wraparound encumbrance

12

Lenders and the loan market

T HE REAL ESTATE and construction industries are what economists call capital intensive businesses. If you think about it, you will realize that a healthy real estate industry uses vast quantities of capital. In fact, no other industry is so dependent on capital as real estate. When credit dries up or becomes expensive, real estate sales drop dramatically, and when interest rates decline and capital is readily available, we prosper. Mortgage loans total over $6 trillion in the United States today. Where this capital comes from, and why the supply and cost of capital are forever changing, is a subject which real estate agents must understand thoroughly in order to survive. Knowing how financial conditions affect the cost and supply of capital is also crucial if a real estate agent is to be able to advise clients properly.

Let us start our discussion by taking a look at the various type of lenders – where you might go to obtain a mortgage loan on real property. Some of these lenders are referred to as *institutional lenders* because they are formal institutions created primarily to lend money. Institutional lenders include commercial banks, savings and loan associations, mutual savings banks, credit unions, mortgage bankers and finance companies.

Commercial banks constitute the single largest source of loan funds in the nation, but historically commercial banks used to shy away from heavy involvement in real estate loans, preferring instead to be providers of short term working capital to business and industry. Today, however, commercial banks are significant lenders in residential real estate.

Savings and loan associations, *mutual savings banks* (known collectively as *thrift institutions*, the *thrift industry*, or just *the thrifts*) for decades were the primary source of residential real estate loans. Unfortunately, most did not survive the bad economic times of the early 1980s. Many today have changed their name to *savings banks*, perhaps in an effort to disassociate themselves from their troubled past, and others have simply reorganized as full service commercial banks. Today there are few true thrifts left in residential lending.

Government loan programs, such as those of the Washington State Housing Finance Commission, sell tax exempt bonds and use the funds to make low-interest loans for special purposes the government wishes to promote. Because the bonds are tax exempt, they can be sold at low interest rates. The savings can be passed on to the borrower in the form of a low interest loan.

A *mortgage banker* is a firm which makes loans using its own funds, and then immediately sells the loans in the secondary market (see *Secondary mortgage market* later in this chapter). The sale of the loans restores the funds so the mortgage banker can make new loans. Mortgage bankers typically make their profit on the loan fees and on fees for *servicing* the loan (collecting the payments) for the secondary lender. Mortgage bankers frequently use the term "mortgage company" in their name.

Finance companies (sometimes called *small loan companies*), like mortgage bankers, do not use capital from depositors, because finance companies do not offer checking and savings accounts. Typically, finance companies borrow their funds from commercial banks or by selling corporate bonds and other corporate securities.

Insurance companies, private and public funds, real estate investment trusts (REITs), real estate mortgage trusts (REMTs) and mortgage brokers are organizations which sometimes become sources for real estate loans. Some people refer to these institutions as *quasi-institutional lenders* because they are institutions, but their primary purpose is not always to make loans, or at least not directly.

For example, insurance companies are organized primarily to provide insurance, not to make real estate loans. But insurance companies have billions of dollars in reserves to pay claims from, and these reserves must be invested. Sometimes insurance companies find real estate mortgage loans to be an excellent investment. Insurance companies invest in real estate mortgages both directly as primary lenders (when they make the loan themselves) and indirectly as secondary lenders (when they purchase pools of loans).

When we use the term *fund* we include pension funds, endowment funds, state government treasuries and private investment groups. While their major investment venues are the stock and bond markets, like insurance companies, these funds sometimes make direct loans on large commercial projects, and sometimes purchase pools of loans as secondary lenders.

Real estate investment trusts (REITs) are **business trusts** in which an investor buys shares of beneficial interest, in much the same way as stockholders buy stock in a corporation. Typically, a REIT is constituted so that the income it earns is not taxed, although the shareholders must pay tax on the earnings when they are distributed. A variant is the *real estate mortgage trust* (REMT), which invests only in mortgages, where the REIT invests primarily by purchasing the real estate as an owner. Both are discussed in more detail later in this chapter.

A *mortgage broker* is a party who locates a borrower and a lender, brings them together and arranges the loan, and collects a fee for the service. Unlike a mortgage banker, a mortgage broker does not service the loan.

Non-institutional lenders include private parties (paper buyers) and sellers who carry land sales contracts and other purchase money instruments. Most of these loans are small loans, frequently second position (junior) loans.

Some of these lenders are referred to as *financial intermediaries* because they act as intermediaries between people who have money (depositors) and people who need money (borrowers). Financial intermediaries include commercial banks, savings and loan associations, mutual savings banks, and credit unions. Mortgage bankers, mortgage brokers, finance companies, pension funds, insurance companies, and similar institutions are not financial intermediaries because they do not have customer deposits.

All financial intermediaries are also referred to as *fiduciary lenders* or *financial fiduciaries* because they have a fiduciary (trust) relationship with their depositors or investors and must follow safe and prudent lending practices to ensure the safety of their depositor's money.

Yet other lenders are referred to as *semi-fiduciary lenders* because they owe some obligations to the persons from whom they obtained their capital, but the obligation is not as strong as it is with a fiduciary institution. Examples of semi-fiduciary lenders are insurance companies, mortgage brokers, REITs and government bond programs.

Finance companies, private parties (paper buyers) and sellers who carry purchase money loans are referred to as *non-fiduciary lenders* because they are lending their own money directly and have no responsibility to anyone but themselves.

In the following section we will discuss in greater detail the real estate loan activity of each of these lenders.

Commercial banks

Of all the institutional lenders, the most prevalent is the commercial bank. The vast majority of lendable funds in the private sector is on deposit at commercial banks. Commercial banks have existed since ancient times, but the commercial bank as we know it today evolved largely from the banks of 17th century England.

In this country commercial banks were mostly unregulated until the National Bank Act of 1863, which required that federally chartered banks be supervised by the

Categories of Real Estate Lenders

Financial fiduciaries	*Financial intermediaries (Have customer deposits)*	Commercial banks Savings and loan associations Mutual savings banks Credit unions	*Institutional lenders*
		Insurance companies Pension funds	
Quasi-fiduciaries		Mortgage bankers Mortgage brokers Trusts (REIT/REMT) Government bond programs Private funds	
Non-fiduciaries		Private lenders Seller financing	*Non-institutional lenders*

Categories of lenders

Comptroller of the Currency. In 1913, the Federal Reserve Act established the **Federal Reserve Bank System** (discussed in greater detail later in this chapter), and most banks today are regulated to some extent by the Federal Reserve Bank.

Commercial banks can be state chartered or federally chartered. While the Federal Reserve Bank System provides most of the regulation of federally chartered banks, state chartered banks are regulated by individual state regulatory agencies. In most states this gives them somewhat greater freedom, although even state chartered banks are subject to some regulation by the Federal Reserve Bank.

Customer deposits in commercial banks are insured up to $100,000 by the **Federal Deposit Insurance Corporation** (FDIC). The FDIC was organized under the provisions of the Banking Act of 1933 and originally insured deposits only in the commercial banks. The purpose of FDIC insurance was to strengthen the credibility of the private commercial banking system of the country.

The FDIC not only insures depositors against losses, but it also supervises member banks in order to prevent improper practices which could lead to failure of the bank. The FDIC conducts regular examinations of the institutions it insures and when it encounters problems, it can take corrective action. Powers of the FDIC include ordering management to change bank policy, lending funds to troubled banks and even requiring a change of bank personnel. When a member bank does fail, the FDIC acts as a receiver and proceeds to collect as much of the failed bank's assets as possible. In some cases the FDIC arranges a merger of the failed bank into a stronger local bank, or in other cases the failed bank is disbanded and the FDIC pays off the depositors directly.

Funds for operations and to pay losses are derived from premiums charged to member institutions. The reserves to pay losses (premiums paid in) comprise the **Bank Insurance Fund** (BIF). The FDIC also insures thrift institutions today, but their premiums are paid into a separate fund call the **Savings Association Insurance Fund** (SAIF). Although the FDIC has jurisdiction over both funds, bank losses can be paid only from the BIF and losses from thrifts can be paid only out of the SAIF. It is important to remember that when you put money on deposit in an insured bank or thrift the institution had to pay the premiums to keep your deposit insured. The premium is generally about ⅓ of 1% of all deposits. For each of the major banks and thrifts doing business in Washington today that expense comes to millions of dollars a year.

Commercial banks are frequently a source of real estate loans for both residential and non-residential properties. Even today, however, commercial banks retain a strong sense that their primary role should be to provide working capital for business and industry, not long term real estate lending. Another hallmark of the commercial bank is their insistence on maintaining a high degree of liquidity. **Liquidity** refers to the ease with which an asset can be converted to cash.

Both of these attitudes are derived from sense of history. Before 1913 there was no Federal Reserve Bank to supply liquidity, and before 1933 there was no Federal Deposit Insurance Corporation to ensure the safety of customer deposits. As a result, runs on banks were common and national financial panics sometimes occurred. Bankers had to be able to convert their loan portfolio to cash (call the loans due) in such circumstances. Long term real estate loans simply could not be called due because, even if the loan instrument contained a demand clause, the borrower did not have the funds anyway. Businesses, on the other hand, could usually pay a loan off, by refinancing at another institution, if necessary. Loans to business and industry are also typically short term, which allows the lender to renegotiate the interest rates periodically in order to maintain the loan portfolio at market rates.

As a result, commercial banks generally only make residential real estate loans which can be sold in the secondary mortgage market. Originally these included only loans insured by the Federal Housing Administration (FHA), or guaranteed by the federal Department of Veterans Affairs (federal GI loans). Today conventional loans can also easily be sold in the secondary market, so commercial banks are now active in the conventional loan market as well. In lender terminology, a **portfolio loan** means either a loan which cannot be sold in the secondary market, or which the lender at least has not yet sold. Portfolio loans are unusual today for any lender, but are less likely to be granted by a commercial bank than by other institutional lenders.

Commercial banks are also a source of temporary construction financing (also called **interim financing**), particularly for commercial construction projects and subdivisions. Loans for home improvements are also commonly available from commercial banks. Note that these loans are not as easily sold in the secondary mortgage market, so a bank will likely insist that they be short term loans.

Commercial banks also participate indirectly in real estate lending by lending funds to other real estate lenders, such as REITs (discussed in more detail later in this chapter), as well as finance companies and mortgage bankers. Also, commercial banks sometimes make real estate loans indirectly by owning a mortgage banking firm, finance company or other lending institution. Many commercial banks have trust departments which manage large sums of money which is part of an estate or employee pension fund. These bank trust departments sometimes make low-risk real estate loans as an avenue to invest these funds.

In recent years one of the most popular real estate loans for commercial banks is the home equity loan – generally short term, small dollar amount, and with above market yields. Notice how such loans fit well with the historical attitude of the commercial bank.

Savings and loan associations

Among thrift institutions, mutual savings banks predominate only in New England. Everywhere else in the country, savings and loan associations outnumber mutual savings banks by a large margin. This is true in spite of the fact that mutual savings banks and savings and loan associations grew up practically side by side.

The first home purchase financed with a loan from a savings and loan association was in 1831 in Philadelphia. Savings and loan associations (originally called ***building and loan associations***) grew slowly but steadily. They were founded on the concept of being a community-based non-profit alternative to the commercial bank – much the same philosophy as is found at credit unions today.

Today, however, there are few mutual non-profit savings and loans; almost all are investor owned for-profit institutions. Today's savings and loan associations typically offer a full range of banking services, but savings accounts and residential mortgages remain their primary business activity.

Savings and loan associations went largely unregulated until 1932 when the Federal Home Loan Bank System was created. Where the Federal Reserve Bank regulates and provides liquidity for member commercial banks, the Federal Home Loan Bank (FHLB) was created to do the same for member thrift institutions. In recent years, however, a great many thrift institutions became insolvent. Although the reasons for this are complex, the result was that regulation of thrift institutions was removed from the FHLB and transferred to a new agency, the Office of Thrift Supervision (OTS), a subsidiary organization under the U.S. Treasury.

Mutual savings banks

Mutual savings banks originated on the east coast during the early and middle 1800s. The vast majority of mutual savings banks are still located in New England states, although occasional mutual savings banks are found in other states. Their original purpose was to provide a place where working people could deposit their savings and be paid attractive interest rates, while at the same time providing consumer loans to the same class of customers, largely for home acquisition.

Note that this is essentially the same philosophy upon which savings and loans are based, which is why real estate agents tend to place mutual savings banks in the same class as savings and loans. The important difference with mutual savings banks is that they are always mutual – that is, the profits are distributed to the depositors as dividends. Today there are practically no true mutual savings banks left. Almost all that survived the financial crisis of the 1980s converted to for-profit regular banks.

Credit unions

Credit unions are always mutual, non-profit organizations. They are insured by the National Credit Union Administration (NCUA) which performs the same role for credit unions as the FDIC does for commercial banks and thrift institutions. Since credit unions are non-profit organizations they are able to offer higher interest rates to depositors and lower interest rates on loans. Because this gives them an advantage over commercial banks and thrifts, their membership is restricted in some manner. They tend to refer to their customers as "members" in order to promote a sense of mutual interests.

Although credit unions make relatively few mortgage loans, they are legally empowered to make any kind of real estate loan. Credit unions are a common source for junior financing, but first mortgage financing is difficult for most credit unions because of their size. Credit unions are generally small organizations and cannot usually afford to hire staff with sufficient expertise to make a first mortgage loan and sell it in the secondary market. Nevertheless, some of the larger credit unions do become active in the first mortgage market, and real estate agents should not overlook even the smaller organizations as sources for junior financing.

Insurance companies

Most life insurance policies are really insurance coupled with an *annuity*. That is, when you buy a typical (whole life) insurance policy you are insured and the full amount of the policy will be paid if there is a claim, but every time you make a premium payment you also build up a *reserve*. Eventually, your policy will be paid up, and then the insurance company will start paying you the money back. In effect, most life insurance is really insurance coupled with a retirement savings account.

Insurance companies must invest these reserves. Most life insurance companies prefer to invest the bulk of their reserves in the bond market. Depending on market conditions, this will range from 30% to 40% of their total assets. However, real estate mortgages are their second most popular type of investment, accounting for 20% to 40% of their assets, again, depending on market conditions. As mortgage lenders, life insurance companies can be very competitive because their cost of funds is very low. They are able to pay rates on the reserves to their policyholders which are much less than the rates the policyholder could get from a savings institution because they are also giving them insurance at the same time. Also, net premiums after claims payments from term insurance (straight insurance without the annuity build-up) must be invested as well, and there is no cost for these funds.

Insurance companies are regulated by the insurance laws and regulations of the states where they do business. These laws and regulations set the loan to value ratios and other lending requirements. However, insurance companies are the least regulated of all institutional lenders.

Insurance companies, primarily life insurance companies, account for relatively few residential loans, but are a frequent source of funds for large commercial projects such as office buildings and shopping centers. Not only do they prefer large commercial projects. but they also prefer loans which are very safe. Typically, a loan from an insurance company would not exceed 80% loan to value ratio and frequently as low as 70% to 75% of the value.

Another common feature in insurance company financing is an *equity kicker* – a low interest rate in exchange for a participation in the equity build-up when the property is sold. If the property is not sold, then the mortgage usually requires an appraisal at some point in the future, at which time the lender's share of the equity build-up is added to the loan balance. Such loans are also referred to as *equity participation loans*, or *shared appreciation loans*.

Many insurance companies service their loans themselves, but most employ mortgage brokers to arrange the loans. Increasingly, however, insurance companies employ the services of a mortgage banker (discussed later) to service loans as well as originate them. Insurance companies also participate in the residential field by purchasing loans as a secondary lender.

Funds

There are various types of funds which operate as mortgage lenders. Some of these are private, such as investment corporations and pension funds for private companies. Other funds are public agencies such as state treasuries, public pension funds, and the like. Their assets range from a few million dollars to hundreds of millions of dollars.

Those funds which are retirement funds are the most heavily involved in real estate lending. The interesting thing about the billions of dollars held in pension funds is the similarity between this pool of money and the funds held in life insurance reserves. Both are paid into the fund in installments over many years and both are very stable with a large dollar amount available for long term investment.

Approximately one-half of all non-government workers are covered by some form of private pension plan (usually company sponsored), other than social security. In addition, about three-fourths of all government personnel are enrolled in private retirement plans. In the past, the pension funds have not contributed directly as real estate lenders, although some (mostly private investment funds) have mimicked the life insurance companies and invest in mortgage loans on large commercial projects. Many people in the real estate field hope to see the pension funds put more of their assets to work in residential real estate. However, the likelihood is that if they begin to invest in residential real estate they will most likely do so as purchasers of securities issued by the secondary mortgage market, not as direct primary lenders.

Mortgage bankers

The term **mortgage banker** sounds as though it means a person who works for a lender and makes mortgage loans. In fact, the term refers to a company, not an individual, which originates mortgage loans and sells the loans to investors. The mortgage banker continues to service the loan – collects the payments, sees that the taxes are paid, and even supervises a foreclosure – which is why they are also occasionally called **loan correspondents**. In many cases, the borrower does not even realize the loan has been sold.

Mortgage banking existed as far back as the turn of the century, but did not become a serious force in mortgage lending until the Federal Housing Administration (FHA) was created in 1934, and the Federal National Mortgage Association (Fannie Mae) was added in 1938. The FHA created standardized loans which meet minimum requirements and which are insured against default by the FHA, an agency of the federal government. The fact that these loans all conform to minimum standards and are insured by the FHA makes them attractive to investors. As a result, Fannie Mae was created to purchase the loans as a secondary lender. Mortgage bankers came into existence to make the FHA loans and service them for Fannie Mae.

Following World War II loans guaranteed by the federal Department of Veterans Affairs (formerly the Veterans Administration) came into being, and mortgage bankers began making "VA" loans as well. Both FHA and VA loans could be sold to Fannie Mae. In more recent years, Fannie Mae and other newer secondary lenders have become the primary purchasers of conventional loans also. As a rule, mortgage bankers must sell the loans they originate because they have limited funds of their own. Since FHA, VA and conventional loans are all salable today, mortgage bankers now make virtually any kind of residential loan. Furthermore, today there are a multitude of secondary mortgage lenders (investors) in addition to Fannie Mae, and practically all of them buy mortgages from mortgage bankers.

It is important to understand that a mortgage banker is not a "banker" in the traditional sense. You cannot go to a mortgage banker and open up a checking or savings account. Mortgage bankers use their own funds (funds invested by stock- and bondholders) to make the loan. The profit in mortgage banking is derived from the loan origination fees and the servicing fees.

In fact, servicing the loan is sufficiently profitable that lenders frequently sell the servicing contracts on their loans. This practice has created a great deal of confusion for borrowers. A borrower may suddenly be told to make future payments to a different lender. This can happen repeatedly, with obvious potential for lost and mis-posted payments. As a result, Congress has enacted legislation to regulate the sale of servicing contracts.

Larger mortgage banking firms supply their own capital to make the loans, and then package them for sale to secondary lenders in large blocks. However, smaller mortgage bankers engage in a practice called **warehousing**. A mortgage banker who does not have the funds to complete the package will go to a commercial bank to borrow the funds, frequently pledging existing loans already on the books as collateral. This suits the commercial bank because their major function is to provide short term working capital. When the mortgage banker completes the package, it is sold in the secondary market and the proceeds of the sale are used to pay back the commercial bank.

Mortgage brokers

The Depository Institution Deregulation and Monetary Control Act of 1980 (DIDMCA) made sweeping changes in the regulations of financial intermediaries. One of these changes is important to note here. Prior to 1980, financial intermediaries were permitted to make mortgage loans only within certain geographical limits, usually only within their state boundaries. The DIDMCA removed most of these geographical restrictions.

This had a profound effect on mortgage lending, for it turned the mortgage market from a local market to a national market practically overnight. Suddenly, local banks, savings and loans, mutual savings banks and mortgage bankers found themselves receiving stiff competition from similar institutions in other states. In retaliation, each institution attempted to gain loans from other areas. Of course, the final result was beneficial for both consumers and lenders. Consumers benefit when there is greater competition, and the lenders benefit from greater diversification in their loan portfolios.

However, this creates a problem. How can you originate a loan in a community unless you have a branch office there? The answer is simple – employ the services of a local **mortgage broker**. The concept of mortgage brokerage has been in existence since practically the day the first loan was created. The basic idea is simple. A mortgage broker brings a borrower and a lender together, collects a fee (commission) for acting as go-between, and departs the scene. Unlike a mortgage banker, the mortgage broker does not service the loan. In fact, mortgage brokers today are as likely to represent mortgage bankers as they are to represent any other kind of lender.

Until the last few years lenders always charged **loan origination fees** (usually called simply **loan fees**) to increase their profitability. On some FHA insured loans and on all federal GI guaranteed loans, the government sets the maximum amount of the loan fee, usually about 1% of the loan balance. On conventional loans, there is no maximum, although competition tended to hold the rate at around 2% of the loan balance. Among commercial banks, thrift institutions and mortgage bankers there has always been an unwritten philosophy that the loan origination fees should pay for maintaining the office and the salaries of the loan officers and staff required to get the loan on the books. Other expenses of operation should be paid out of the profit on the loan – the spread between the cost of the funds (interest paid out) and the interest earned on the loan. Or, if the loan has been sold in the secondary market, the servicing fees should pay for the rest of the expenses and profit.

Now, if a mortgage lender doesn't have to maintain a branch office and pay loan officers' salaries, then all the loan fee is available to pay as a commission to a local mortgage broker. This is exactly what has happened since 1980. We now have mortgage brokers who take applications from borrowers and place the borrower's applications with lenders the broker represents. Since the mortgage broker knows each lender's particular requirements, the broker can match the borrower with the lender most likely to make the loan. The lender allows the broker to retain the loan fee as a commission.

Starting a few years ago lenders realized that loan fees were unpopular with borrowers, especially with borrowers who are seeking a refinance loan. As a result most lenders have dropped the loan origination fee and raised the interest rate on the loan to compensate. The concept that part of the revenue on the loan should pay the broker remains; the difference today is that it tends to come from interest and other earnings on the loan instead of an up-front loan fee.

Of course, mortgage brokers also broker loans other than residential loans. In fact, only since 1980 have mortgage brokers been active in residential loans. In the past, mortgage brokers tended to specialize in certain types of loans, usually loans for large commercial projects, vacant land, or other less common situations, and some mortgage brokers still provide these services.

Real estate trusts

Real estate trusts come in two main categories – *real estate investment trusts* (REITs), and *real estate mortgage trusts* (REMTs), although there are also real estate trusts which are called *combination*, or *hybrid trusts*, which take on aspects of both types of trust.

Real estate investment trusts invest in real estate equities, that is to say, they purchase properties for investment. A REMT lends money as a mortgage lender. Combination trusts sometimes invest as owners and sometimes as mortgage lenders. A REIT which invests solely as purchaser of real estate is called an *equity REIT*.

Real estate trusts came into being as a result of the enactment of the Real Estate Investment Trust Act of 1960, which allowed the creation of trusts to invest in real estate equities and/or real estate mortgages as tax-exempt entities. In this respect, REMTs and REITs operate in much the same way as mutual funds do in the stock and bond markets. For example, a mutual fund invests shareholders' funds and distributes the profits to the shareholders by way of dividends. If the mutual fund meets the criteria required by the law, the mutual fund is tax-exempt – so all the profits are passed through directly to the shareholders. Of course, the shareholders must pay tax on their earnings, but double taxation is avoided. Real estate trusts operate the same way. As long as the trust qualifies, it pays no income taxes.

Real estate mortgage trusts have had a significant impact in financing of commercial projects. A typical REMT attracts capital not only by selling shares to investors, but also by borrowing from a commercial bank, or even sometimes from a REIT. It is not uncommon for a commercial bank or a REIT to sponsor or even own the REMT. Real estate mortgage trusts require higher interest rates than other mortgage lenders, partly because their investors demand a higher return and also because capital borrowed from commercial banks must be at market prime rate. Lending by real estate trusts is generally short term and usually as junior financing, primarily for large commercial projects.

In order to qualify as a REIT or REMT, the trust must meet various requirements, including the following –
- The trust may own real property, but not as a dealer for resale,
- There must be at least 100 investors,
- The top five investors must not own more than 50% of the total shares,

- The trust must be organized as a business trust which issues shares of beneficial interest, and not as a corporation which issues shares of stock,
- 95% of the trust's income must be derived from investments,
- 75% of the trust's income must be derived from real estate investments (equities or mortgage loans),
- A maximum of 30% of the annual income can come from securities held for less than twelve months, or real estate held for less than four years, and
- Each year the trust must pay out at least 95% of its profits to the shareholders.

Mortgage bonds

With some exceptions, state governments are allowed to borrow money by issuing bonds which are exempt from federal income tax. That is to say, investors who buy the tax-exempt bonds do not pay federal income tax on the interest income. If the state passes a statute exempting a bond issue from state income taxes as well, then the interest income will be what investors call *double tax-exempt*. Because the interest income is double tax-exempt, the issuing agency can sell the bonds at very low rates.

If the funds from the bond sale are used to fund mortgage loans, the interest rate on the loans can be correspondingly low. States commonly use bond issues to make low-interest mortgage loans available to promote special government purposes such as urban renewal, low-income housing, and so forth. Of course, bondholders eventually have to be repaid, so the bond issue will structured in a manner to ensure that the revenue generated from loan repayments will be sufficient to repay the bonds. In Washington the agency which sells bonds to provide loans such as these is the Washington State Housing Finance Commission. The details about its operations are covered in Chapter 13.

Private lenders

Financing can sometimes be arranged from private lenders. Private lenders can generally be grouped into those who are private parties (who usually buy loans originated by sellers, rather than lend directly themselves) and those which are more institutional in nature, such as finance companies and other small loan companies.

These lines of distinction become somewhat gray, because some private paper buyers become large enough to have an office and start looking fairly institutional. And some finance companies not only make loans themselves, but also buy real estate paper generated by others. Finance companies in Washington must be licensed, so there is some regulation. However, even though licensed, they are largely unregulated as to the type of loan which they can make. Most finance companies prefer junior liens in small dollar amounts, although some commercial banks have spawned fairly large finance companies as subsidiaries for the express purpose of lending on junior liens for large commercial projects, as well as residential loans. The true private party lender is, of course, totally unregulated, but usually likes to limit exposure to 80% of the value of the property. Both private parties and finance companies insist on very high yields.

Seller financing

The seller of the property is a common source of funding for a real estate purchase. The percentage of transactions which involve seller financing varies dramatically with market conditions. Usually the seller would prefer to be cashed out, but some properties are just not amenable to outside financing. For example loans to finance vacant land, and loans to finance unique special purpose properties are difficult to place with outside lenders.

The seller will likely have to discount the sales price dramatically to attract an all-cash buyer. Also, in difficult times when interest rates are high, the seller may find it expedient to carry the loan, in fact, it may be the only way to sell the property. Seller financing involves every conceivable kind of instrument – land sales contracts, purchase money trust deeds, junior liens, wraparounds, balloon payments, sale leasebacks – and every other creative device that real estate agents have been able to conjure up. This area is so complex that all of Chapter 16 is devoted to it.

Real estate cycles

The real estate market tends to run in cycles of boom and bust. For the most part, these cycles are caused by the availability and cost of mortgage funds. When mortgage funds are in short supply and interest rates are high, not as many buyers can qualify for the monthly payments necessary to amortize the debt. This causes fewer sales. Conversely, when interest rates are low, the real estate market picks up and sales volume is good.

General economic conditions can also contribute to the cycle. To take one example, the wood products industry is one of Washington's major industries. When it is in a slump due to a national slowdown in the demand for its products or due to extreme competition, Washington's entire economy slows down. Even if mortgage funds are readily available and interest rates are reasonable, it will be difficult to have a good real estate market under these conditions. Of course, in Washington we have a double problem with interest rates, for when interest rates are high in Washington, they are also high in the rest of the country. This causes the real estate market in the rest of the country to be slow also. This, in turn, causes there to be fewer construction starts nationwide, which further lowers the demand for wood products.

What causes these cycles of high and low interest rates? Why can't we just have a set interest rate that varies only a little over the years? This would be an ideal, but in a free market economy, it is difficult to achieve. These are some of the questions to which we will turn our attention next.

The supply and cost of loan funds is determined by various complex institutions and their reactions to economic conditions. Not the least of these institutions is Congress and the Office of the President, both of whom want nothing but good economic times, particularly in an election year.

Every year Congress and the President create a budget for the coming fiscal year. In response to budgetary considerations, Congress and the President also change the tax rates from time to time. We all know that this process frequently creates a deficit. How big the deficit is, how it is funded, how high the tax rates are, are all controlled by Congress and the President. The Federal Treasury is charged with the responsibility of managing not just the deficits, but the entire national debt. This is referred to as *fiscal policy*, and is an important force in determining the course of the economy.

However, a more powerful force is the Federal Reserve System. In theory, the Federal Reserve System is supposed to manipulate and control the economy to smooth out the effects of fiscal policy. This is called *monetary policy*. Other institutions which have some effect on mortgage lending (but not on lending in general) are the Federal Home Loan Bank, the Office of Thrift Supervision, and the institutions of the secondary market (Fannie Mae, Freddie Mac, and Ginnie Mae, among others).

The Federal Reserve System

The Federal Reserve System was established by the Federal Reserve Act of 1913. As the nation's central bank, it attempts to ensure that the growth of money and credit over the long run is sufficient to provide a rising standard of living for Americans.

Over the short run, the Federal Reserve Bank System seeks to adapt its policies in an effort to combat deflationary or inflationary pressures. And as a lender of last resort, it is responsible for making and adjusting policy decisions as necessary to forestall national liquidity crises and financial panics.

The Federal Reserve System (sometimes called the Federal Reserve Bank, but usually referred to by bankers as "the Fed") is a central banking system composed of twelve federal reserve districts, each of which contains a federal reserve bank. The operations of the twelve federal reserve banks are coordinated and governed by a seven-member Board of Governors.

The Federal Reserve System is comprised of 12 Federal Reserve Banks, some of which have branches. The twelfth district (shaded on this map) is served by the Federal Reserve Bank of San Francisco. The Federal Reserve Bank of San Francisco has branches in Los Angeles, Portland, Salt Lake City and Seattle. Note that the twelfth district is geographically the largest district. This is because the districts were apportioned roughly according to population as it existed in 1913 when the system was created. Federal Reserve Banks are also located in Atlanta, Boston, Chicago, Cleveland, Dallas, Kansas City, Minneapolis, Richmond, St. Louis, New York and Philadelphia. The Board of Governors meets in Washington, D.C.

All federally chartered banks are required to be members of the Federal Reserve System. In addition, some state chartered commercial banks and some thrifts are members. In order to join, a member bank must agree to the regulations of the Federal Reserve System, and must purchase capital stock in the Federal Reserve Bank equal to 3% of the institution's net worth. Banks receive many benefits from membership, but one of the most important is that the Federal Reserve Bank will lend them money.

The monetary policy of the Federal Reserve System includes three major functions (called ***instruments of credit policy***). These functions are the regulation of the reserve ratios of member banks (percentage of the bank's deposits that it must keep invested in federal securities), adjustment of the discount and federal funds rates (the rate charged when a member bank borrows from the Federal Reserve Bank or from another bank) and open market activity (purchase and sale of federal securities). These are discussed in detail below.

One of the requirements the Federal Reserve imposes on all banks (not just its members) is to maintain a ***reserve ratio***. Part of the purpose of the reserve ratio is to ensure that the bank remains solvent and has enough funds available to serve depositors' ordinary day-to-day banking needs. However, this is no longer the main purpose of the reserve requirement. Today, the Federal Reserve System changes the reserve requirement as a means of manipulating the economy. If the percentage is raised by, say, one percent, then one percent of the funds in all member banks would suddenly have to be invested in federal securities, and unavailable for loans to customers. If the supply of lendable funds shrinks, with no change in demand, interest rates will go up, which in turn will slow down the economy.

But, while it would slow down the economy, it would also have the side effect of increasing unemployment rates. So, perhaps it would be politically better to lower the reserve ratio. The effect of lowering the reserve ratio would be to increase the funds member institutions have available for lending. Assuming no change in demand, interest rates would go down. This would stimulate the economy. However, in an economy in which there is an excess of demand, merchants and suppliers are able to charge more, and this translates into inflation. So the Federal Reserve System changes the reserve ratio with care, and in conjunction with the other instruments of credit policy, to keep the economy on an even keel. The reserve ratio varies from about 3% for long term deposits to 22% for checking accounts.

When the Federal Reserve Bank lends funds to a member bank, it charges interest on those funds. The rate the Federal Reserve Bank Board of Governors sets on these funds is called the ***discount rate***. Changes in the discount rate affect the interest rates that the borrowing bank must charge its customers. Of course, this has a profound effect on the nation's economy. Lowering the discount rate lowers interest rates member banks charge their customers, and heats up the economy, and raising the discount rate will slow down the economy because member banks will have to charge their customers more.

If the Federal Reserve Bank raises the discount rate a member bank in need of additional funds will be stimulated to seek the funds elsewhere. A logical alternative is to borrow from another bank. Most commercial banks have borrowing relationships with other banks, usually banks in a different region – after all, you wouldn't want to owe money to a competitor across the street. When a bank borrows from another bank it is called borrowing ***federal funds***. Note that this process nullifies the effects the discount rate. If the Fed raises the discount rate, banks will just borrow from each other instead. So, in order to use the interest rate on borrowings by commercial banks as a tool to manipulate the economy, the Fed also manipulates the rates banks charge each other on federal funds. Today the Fed almost always maintains the rate on federal funds lower than the discount rate, so the real regulation is the federal funds rate. The purpose of setting the federal funds rate lower than the discount rate is to encourage banks to borrow from each other instead of borrowing from the Federal Reserve Bank.

Prime rate – Every bank establishes its own ***prime rate***, which is the rate it charges its best corporate customers. While the discount rate and the federal funds rate have an influence on a bank's prime rate, there is no direct relationship. Banks are free to set their own prime rate as they wish. Of course, every bank feels intense competition from other banks, so when one bank changes its prime rate other banks in the community generally follow suit immediately. For this reason it may appear to the public that the prime rate is somehow set by a regulatory body, but that is not the case.

The third instrument of credit policy is ***open market activity***. This is controlled by the Federal Open Market Committee (FOMC). The FOMC is made up of the Board of Governors of the Federal Reserve System (all seven members), plus four of the presidents of the twelve district banks, and the President of the Federal Reserve Bank of New York.

Open market activity consists of buying and selling federal securities, such as treasury bills, notes and bonds and bond issues of federal agencies.

The FOMC meets monthly to decide when, how many, and which kind of federal securities the Federal Reserve System should sell. When the Federal Reserve System sells securities it absorbs money from the private banking system – that is, banks will buy the securities rather than invest in loans. If the Federal Reserve System buys securities back, it pumps money into the banking system. Selling securities slows down the economy, and buying securities heats it up.

The U.S. Treasury

While the Federal Reserve System is responsible for monetary policy, the Treasury is responsible for fiscal policy – including management of the federal debt, as well as day-to-day operations. The Treasury's funds come from tax receipts. These funds are kept on deposit in the twelve Federal Reserve Banks and in private banks which are members of the Federal Reserve System. In fact, these institutions act as agents for the Treasury in the collection of employers' withholding taxes.

The Treasury issues three basic types of security – ***treasury certificates***, which have maturities from five to ten years, ***treasury notes***, with maturities of from one to five years, and ***treasury bills***, which have maturities of three months, six months, and sometimes one year. The total national debt is made up of a mix of these securities. How the Treasury funds the debt, which securities it issues and when, can have a major effect on the supply of lendable funds in the private sector. In theory, selling securities should remove money from the economy and slow things down, while repaying securities as they come due should pump money into the economy and heat things up.

In real life, the decisions of the Treasury are not always motivated by economic considerations. For example, if there is a huge deficit, the Treasury has no choice but to borrow additional funds (issue more securities). Thus it becomes the task of the Federal Reserve Bank to minimize the effect of this borrowing. The Federal Reserve System would probably do so by buying some or all of the securities itself. To do so, it might issue its own federal reserve notes (print currency) to raise some or all of the funds. Unfortunately, this would increase the money supply, which ultimately will result in inflation.

Another important function of the Treasury has been to supply the initial funds to start many of the institutions on which we depend today to create stability in real estate lending. The Federal Home Loan Bank (FHLB), the Federal National Mortgage Association (Fannie Mae) and a few other institutions, are capital stock organizations (i.e., owned by stockholders). The initial stock subscription was purchased by the Treasury in order to get these organizations going. Without the initial investment by the Treasury, these organizations would not exist today.

The Federal Home Loan Bank System

In 1932 Congress created the Federal Home Loan Bank System (FHLBS). The purpose of the FHLBS was, and remains, to provide financial stability for member institutions. Savings and loans, mutual savings banks and life insurance companies may be members of the FHLBS.

The FHLBS is patterned after the Federal Reserve Bank System. There are 12 Federal Home Loan Banks, each serving the needs of one of the twelve Federal Home Loan Bank districts (although the boundaries are not the same as the boundaries of the twelve federal reserve districts). The system is governed by a three-member board, plus the Federal Savings and Loan Advisory Council, composed of 18 members, twelve of whom are elected (one from each district) and four of whom are appointed by the Board. The Council advises the Board on policy decisions.

All federally chartered savings and loans must be members of the FHLBS. State chartered institutions, mutual savings banks and life insurance companies may also join. Even state chartered institutions in Washington are likely to be members of the FHLBS. Membership in the FHLBS requires that the institutions purchase FHLBS capital stock equal to 3% of their total assets.

The FHLBS provides regulation and liquidity to its member institutions, in much the same way as the Federal Reserve Bank System does for commercial banks. Regulations include a reserve ratio, which is adjusted from time to time as market conditions dictate. However, the percentage of reserves required is lower than the percentage the Federal Reserve System requires of commercial banks, because accounts in savings institutions are more stable and for longer terms.

In addition to the funds from the sale of capital stock to its members, the FHLBS raises money by selling securities to investors. These securities are sold for the FHLBS through the open market activity of the Federal Reserve System. Member institutions may borrow from their district Federal Home Loan Bank. Most Federal Home Loan Bank lending is to enable a member institution to forestall insolvency by restructuring the organization.

For real estate lenders, one of the most significant actions of the FHLBS was the creation of the Federal Home Loan Mortgage Corporation (Freddie Mac), a subsidiary of the FHLBS. Freddie Mac purchases loans as a secondary lender. It also publishes a journal in which it publishes various interest rates. Many lenders use these interest rates as indexes for variable and adjustable rate loans. Other operations of Freddie Mac are discussed in greater detail later in this chapter.

The secondary mortgage market

When a lender sells a loan, the originating lender is called the primary lender and the lender who buys the loan is called the secondary lender. As a group, secondary lenders make up what is called the secondary mortgage market.

When a primary lender sells the loan to the secondary lender someone still has to do the loan servicing, and it is usually done by the primary lender. In other words, a primary lender makes the loan, sells it to the secondary lender, but continues to collect the payments, which are remitted to the secondary lender as they are received from the borrower. Of course, loan servicing is not free – the secondary lender must agree to a servicing fee. Today, servicing fees run about ⅜ of 1%. So, a secondary lender buying an 8½% loan, really only receives an 8⅛% yield, the remaining ⅜ of 1% is retained by the primary lender for servicing the loan.

Before the great depression of the 1930s, the idea of a secondary market was really only a dream. Occasionally, a primary lender would be able to sell a block of loans to a secondary lender – for example, a commercial bank might sell a block of loans to an insurance company. But this practice was infrequent. The idea of selling loans to investors was an attractive idea to lenders, but investors were not interested in loans without uniform standards. One bank might do an excellent job of making loans, but another bank might do a terrible job. How was an investor to know whom to buy loans from?

The problem was eventually solved when the Federal Housing Administration (FHA) was created in 1934. The FHA is a government-owned insurance company. With rare exceptions, the FHA does not lend money. Instead, the FHA insures loans against default. The loans are actually made and funded by private lenders such as commercial banks, mutual savings banks and mortgage bankers. In FHA terminology, these lenders are called **participating lenders**, because they have been approved to participate in the FHA mortgage insurance program. The FHA will bear the loss if the loan must be foreclosed and the property does not sell for enough to cover the balance due, so the FHA insists that each loan meet certain minimum standards.

Since the FHA is huge, it insures millions of loans. And each loan meets minimum standards. Once the FHA was underway, many investors were attracted to FHA insured loans as an investment, and a true secondary mortgage market became possible.

Fannie Mae

Within a short time it became apparent that, in spite of FHA standardization and insurance, there were just not enough investors available to purchase all the loans that participating lenders wished to sell.

So, in 1938, a federal secondary lender was established. Its original name was the National Mortgage Association of Washington, which was later changed to the **Federal National Mortgage Association** (FNMA). It quickly gained the nickname "**Fannie Mae**" among investors. Today, FNMA has adopted the name "Fannie Mae" as its official corporate name, although it also goes by "Federal National Mortgage Association."

Fannie Mae grew quickly. Originally the idea was to sell federal securities to secure funds and then either lend these funds as direct loans under FHA Section 207 (construction loans for small apartment buildings), or to purchase other types of FHA loans originated by primary lenders. Originally only FHA loans would be purchased; conventional loans would not be added until the 1970s.

During this time the FHA set (and changed from time to time) the maximum interest rates that a lender could charge on FHA loans. This rate was always a little below market, which meant that secondary lenders would discount the loans (pay less than face value for it) in order to raise their yield. However, Fannie Mae's cost of funds was below market, since its source was the sale of federal securities, which are not only direct federal obligations, but also exempt from state income taxes. Fannie Mae was able to buy the FHA loans at face value, and still make a profit for the government. Thus Fannie Mae became an indispensable partner for the success of the FHA program.

At the close of Word War II, Congress enacted the GI Bill, one of whose provisions was the authority of the Department of Veterans Affairs (at that time organized under the Department of Defense) to guarantee home loans for eligible veterans. In 1948, Fannie Mae was authorized to purchase these popular new VA guaranteed loans.

Fannie Mae continued to grow, fueled by the post-war housing and construction boom. Finally, in 1954, Fannie Mae was completely reorganized and Congress granted Fannie Mae a new charter. The Charter of 1954 was designed to turn Fannie Mae eventually into a private organization. For its ownership interest (100% at that time), the Treasury was issued preferred stock. Common stock was authorized also, to be issued to private investors. Primary lenders doing business with Fannie Mae were required to purchase a portion of the common stock. Today, these primary lenders hold about 10% of Fannie Mae's outstanding stock. In addition to selling stock, Fannie Mae was authorized to sell bonds and other corporate debt securities publicly in order to raise capital to buy mortgages. And the Charter of 1954 discontinued Fannie Mae's authority to make direct loans. From then on Fannie Mae would be strictly a secondary lender.

The Charter of 1954 specified three functions for Fannie Mae. First, Fannie Mae was charged with continuing its secondary market activities in order to stabilize and provide liquidity to the mortgage market. This included not only being a mortgage buyer, but now Fannie Mae would be able to sell loans from its portfolio as well. Second, Fannie Mae would continue to manage and collect for all FHA and VA loans acquired prior to 1954. And third, Fannie Mae would be the vehicle through which Congress could create special housing assistance programs. All three of these functions were kept in separate departments.

The Charter of 1954 also allowed Fannie Mae to buy mortgages at whatever yield was necessary to provide an adequate return to the investors in Fannie Mae. Since FHA and VA interest rates were still set slightly below market, this meant that Fannie Mae would start buying these loans at a discount. The private investors in Fannie Mae also began to insist on other changes. Not being satisfied with the standards of the FHA and of the VA, Fannie Mae announced that only loans which met Fannie Mae's somewhat more stringent credit requirements would be purchased. Eventually, the FHA and the VA raised their standards to Fannie Mae's standards.

One of the most significant functions of the "new" Fannie Mae would be the special housing assistance programs which Congress wished to begin. Programs were developed to encourage mortgage lending in geographic areas where mortgage loans were normally not available. There were also programs to fund projects such as urban renewal, disaster relief, low-income housing, and many other programs considered to be in the national interest.

Fannie Mae continued its functions under the Charter of 1954, growing stronger and helping to make the American dream of homeownership a reality. However, 1967 and 1968 were difficult years for real estate. In response, Congress enacted the Housing and Urban Development Act in 1968, which changed Fannie Mae's Charter once again. Under the Charter of 1968, Fannie Mae became a totally private organization. Fannie Mae was authorized to issue a large block of common stock, which was sold to the public. The proceeds of the stock sale were used to buy back the preferred stock held by the Treasury.

Fannie Mae still operates today under the Charter of 1968 (amended) as a private corporation. It is governed by a Board of Directors consisting of 18 members. Although Fannie Mae is now completely privately owned, it is still heavily government controlled. After all, it is only authorized to do what its charter allows, and its charter is issued by Congress. Congress has the authority to amend or even revoke its charter at will. Furthermore, of the 18 members of the Board of Directors, 13 are elected by the stockholders, but the other five are appointed by the President. These five members must be chosen from the mortgage banking, construction and real estate industries.

Another significant change resulting from the Housing and Urban Development Act of 1968 was the creation of the ***Government National Mortgage Association*** (GNMA), or as it is more commonly called, ***Ginnie Mae***. Ginnie Mae immediately took over two of Fannie Mae's departments – collection of pre-1954 FHA and VA loans, and buying mortgages for special assistance programs. After 1968, Fannie Mae would no longer be required to buy mortgages created for special assistance programs without receiving a market rate of return. Future secondary markets for these programs would be provided by Ginnie Mae.

Fannie Mae was also given some additional authorities. In order to fund Ginnie Mae's continuing mortgage purchases, the government wished for it to be able to sell securities. Fannie Mae's Charter of 1968 granted it authority to buy the securities issued by Ginnie Mae. The new Charter also gave Fannie Mae the authority to issue securities which were backed by specific blocks of mortgages in Fannie Mae's portfolio. These are called *mortgage-backed securities*. Investors buying these securities could be assured that, even if Fannie Mae went broke, they still had the value of the mortgages which had been pledged by Fannie Mae as collateral. And in 1970, Congress gave Fannie Mae the authority to purchase mortgages other than just FHA and VA mortgages. By 1972, Fannie Mae was using this new authority to buy conventional loans.

In order to sell loans to Fannie Mae, an approved Fannie Mae lender calls Fannie Mae to find the current commitment rates. Fannie Mae posts several rates, which change as often as daily. The best rate is for a 10-day commitment – that means that the lender is willing to commit to deliver the loans to Fannie Mae within 10 days. There are also 30-day, 60-day and 90-day commitment rates. Fannie Mae will buy as few as one loan at a time (minimum $25,000.00), or as large a block as Fannie Mae has capital available.

Today, Fannie Mae buys FHA (all types), VA, and conventional loans. Conventional loans can be fixed rate or adjustable and can be first mortgages or second mortgages. Fannie Mae buys loans for all kinds of residential property, including condominiums and multifamily housing. In addition, if a lender wishes to make loans which do not meet any of Fannie Mae's current programs, Fannie Mae may create a special program to buy loans from that lender. Fannie Mae also offers a unique program for public housing agencies who sell tax-exempt bonds and use the proceeds to make mortgage loans for special targeted areas and borrower groups. Fannie Mae will buy the loans these agencies have made by exchanging them for Fannie Mae mortgage-backed securities. The public housing agency can then pledge the mortgage-backed securities as collateral for the bonds.

Ginnie Mae

The Housing and Urban Development Act of 1968 divested Fannie Mae of two of its programs, collection of pre-1954 FHA and VA loans, and special housing assistance. These were picked up by the Government National Mortgage Association (Ginnie Mae), created at the same time, under the provisions of the Urban Development Act of 1968. Ginnie Mae operates under the supervision of the Department of Housing and Urban Development (HUD). (The FHA is also organized under HUD.) Unlike Fannie Mae and Freddie Mac, Ginnie Mae is wholly government owned.

Ginnie Mae has helped fund loans for urban renewal, housing for the elderly, below-market loans for low-income borrowers (mostly FHA 235 and 236 loans), and experimental housing projects, among other special assistance programs. Most of these loans are either below market rate or involve higher than market risk, and so are unsalable in the normal secondary market. Ginnie Mae has the full authority of the federal government, so Ginnie Mae guarantees the payments on risky loans to make them salable to other secondary lenders, chiefly Fannie Mae.

Ginnie Mae has also received grants of money from Congress to subsidize below market rate loans. When possible, these loans would be sold directly to investors. However, when money became tight, Ginnie Mae would sell these below-market mortgages to Fannie Mae under the *tandem plan*. Under the tandem plan, the primary lender received a commitment from Ginnie Mae to buy the mortgage at par (face value without discount). This assured the primary lender a market for the mortgage. By previous arrangement, Fannie Mae agreed to buy the mortgage from Ginnie Mae, but at a discount, since Fannie Mae must have a market yield to satisfy its stockholders. When the primary lender had funded the loan, it would be sold directly to Fannie Mae, and

Ginnie Mae would pay Fannie Mae the discount. Since Ginnie Mae only had to come up with enough money to pay the discount, this stretched Ginnie Mae's funds available for special assistance loans. New special assistance programs were discontinued in 1984, although mechanisms such as the tandem plan could be revived if desired in the future.

Ginnie Mae's most significant activity has been its mortgage-backed security program. A primary lender can issue and sell securities directly to investors to raise capital to make loans. In order to make the securities attractive, the primary lender pledges a pool of mortgages, which it already holds in portfolio, as collateral for the securities. The mortgages must be FHA-insured or VA-guaranteed. Loans guaranteed by Department of Agriculture programs are also eligible, but are not commonly used.

The securities to be sold will equal the dollar value of the mortgages. When the primary lender has the details worked out, application is made to Ginnie Mae to guarantee the securities. Ginnie Mae reviews the application and, if the pool qualifies, issues its guaranty. The GNMA guaranty carries the full faith and credit of the U.S. Government. Principal and interest payments on the mortgages are funneled through to the investors, since it is these principal and interest payments which will pay back their investment. When the primary lender has sold the securities, the sales proceeds will replenish the lender's cash reserves, the same as if the mortgages had been sold directly to Ginnie Mae.

These securities are called ***pass-through securities*** because the principal and interest pass directly through to the investors. Ginnie Mae guarantees that the investor will receive both the principal and interest. In the original GNMA program the securities were sold in denominations of $15,000 – in other words, if you bought one of these securities, you bought a $15,000 participation in the pool. Since the early Ginnie Mae pools were usually $1 million pools, your share would be 1½% of the pool ($15,000 ÷ $1,000,000 = 0.015). Each month you would receive 1½% of the total principal and interest payments due from the borrowers. Your $15,000 investment would be evidenced by a ***participation certificate***.

Ginnie Mae securities are considered among the safest investments possible, and are therefore favored by pension funds, insurance companies and other conservative lenders. There are various kinds of Ginnie Mae pass-through securities – some are backed by fixed rate mortgages only, others are backed by adjustable rate mortgages. The dollar amounts of the pools also vary. Because of the variety, it is difficult for private individuals to participate directly, so mutual funds and other investment vehicles have been developed to allow investment in Ginnie Mae securities with professional fund management.

Freddie Mac

The Emergency Home Finance Act of 1970 created the **Federal Home Loan Mortgage Corporation** more commonly referred to as **Freddie Mac**. Its original purpose was to provide a secondary market for savings and loan associations which are members of the Federal Home Loan Bank System. Freddie Mac is supervised by three members of the Federal Home Loan Bank Board of Governors, but is nevertheless a private capital stock organization whose stock is largely owned by member thrift institutions.

The years 1967–1968 saw financial intermediaries in a state of crisis. Loan demand was strong, and at the same time the Treasury found it necessary to sell a large dollar volume of federal securities to fund a larger than usual federal deficit. Meanwhile, inflationary trends made the Federal Reserve Bank decide to curtail the creation of new money. The resulting crunch caused interest rates on federal securities to rise to (at that time) unheard of levels. When these rates climbed, people withdrew money from their savings accounts to buy federal securities. This process is called ***disintermediation*** (money flowing out of financial intermediaries). Hardest hit were the thrifts, who found themselves with practically no funds to make new mortgage loans.

Freddie Mac was formed to solve this problem. As a secondary lender, it could buy existing portfolio loans from the thrifts that were members of the Federal Home Loan Bank System in order to pump cash back into these institutions. To get the funds to buy the mortgages, the twelve district Federal Home Loan Banks bought the initial stock subscription. Freddie Mac was authorized to sell securities in order to raise additional cash. Freddie Mac would buy mortgages and pledge them as collateral for the securities issues. In addition, the securities would be guaranteed by Ginnie Mae.

Since thrift institutions deal mainly in conventional loans, the most important function of Freddie Mac became the purchase of conventional loans. Fannie Mae was also granted authority in 1970 to purchase conventional loans, and began doing so in 1972. Today, the majority of the secondary market for conventional loans is shared by Freddie Mac and Fannie Mae, who compete with each other for the mortgage production of primary lenders. Freddie Mac and Fannie Mae are also authorized to buy FHA and VA loans, but most of the loans they buy today are conventional loans.

At the time Freddie Mac began purchasing conventional loans, standards had existed for FHA and VA loans for decades, but there were few standards among conventional lenders. The first major effect Freddie Mac had on mortgage lending was the creation of standardized instruments – uniform notes, trust deeds/mortgages, credit application and appraisal forms, and so on. In addition, uniformity in underwriting standards (loan approval requirements) was totally lacking. Although they compete with each other, Fannie Mae and Freddie Mac have agreed to use the same uniform instruments, and most of their underwriting standards are also the same. This enables a primary lender today to make a conventional loan, knowing that it will be salable to either Fannie Mae or Freddie Mac.

Fannie Mae and Freddie Mac have also taken a leaf out of Ginnie Mae's book. Ginnie Mae, technically speaking, does not buy loans, but rather issues a guaranty for a mortgage-backed securities issue. This is called ***securitizing*** the loans. Fannie Mae and Freddie Mac today engage heavily in the same practice, although both make direct purchases of loans as well.

From a historical standpoint we have changed the mechanisms and in the process freed up more capital for housing, but housing is still funded mostly from the same basic pool of capital. Before the advent of FHA and the secondary market in the 1930s, people provided for their retirement by putting their money into savings accounts in banks and thrift institutions. These financial intermediaries would use these funds to make mortgage loans. Today, people provide for their retirement by investing primarily in insurance annuities and public and private pension funds. These funds, in turn, invest heavily in secondary market mortgage-backed securities, which provides the funds for mortgage loans.

Federal Agricultural Mortgage Corporation

The ***Federal Agricultural Mortgage Corporation***, more commonly known as ***Farmer Mac***, was formed by the Agricultural Credit Act of 1987 to securitize pools of agricultural loans. In this respect it functions similarly to Ginnie Mae. Once a pool of loans has been underwritten by Farmer Mac investors in the pool enjoy a federal guaranty the same as investors in a pool of residential loans underwritten by Ginnie Mae.

While a securities issue by Fannie Mae or Freddie Mac may be securitized with hundreds of individual loans, pools underwritten by Farmer Mac may have only a handful of loans. The reason is that agricultural loans usually run into many millions of dollars. It doesn't take many such loans to make a pool of a substantial amount.

Real Estate Mortgage Investment Conduits

The Tax Reform Act of 1986 created **Real Estate Mortgage Investment Conduits** (REMICs), which have a feature in common with mutual funds and REITs – they are created to avoid double taxation. They can issue pass-through securities collateralized with real estate mortgages, where only the investor who owns the securities is liable for the tax on the income. These securities are issued in **tranches**, which are participations in **multiclass securities**.

Multiclass securities are securities which are collateralized with various types of loans, unlike the older Ginnie Mae, Fannie Mae and Freddie Mac securities, which generally had to be collateralized with loans of all the same type. For example, a loan pool could contain a mixture of adjustable rate loans, fixed rate loans, multifamily loans, and many other types. This allows much greater flexibility and has attracted a lot of investor capital to secondary market investments.

Loan discounting

Suppose a loan were made at a below-market rate, and then sold to a secondary lender at a discount. If the secondary lender bought the loan for, say, 96¢ on the dollar, then the discount was 4%. The 4% discount was calculated on the loan balance, so if the loan balance in our example was $100,000, the discount would be $4,000 ($100,000 × 0.04 = $4,000). The secondary lender actually invested only $96,000, but is getting a return on the investment as though the investment were the full $100,000. After all, the secondary lender's purchase of the loan does not change the borrower's obligation to repay the full $100,000. This effectively raises the secondary lender's yield on the $96,000 investment.

To keep from confusing the percentage of discount with the percentage of interest (interest rate) on the loan, we refer to the interest on the loan with the word "percent," as in "eight percent interest"; but we refer to percentage of discount with the term **points**. In other words, the 4% discount in the above example would more commonly be stated as "four points" or "four points discount."

Real estate agents have a rule of thumb about discount points. Lenders have more sophisticated methods of calculating the discount, but real estate agents have discovered that there will usually be between six and eight points of discount (6% to 8% discount) charged for each whole percent of difference between the loan interest rate and market interest rate. In other words, if a lender makes a loan at 6% interest, but secondary lenders demand a rate of 7%, the secondary lender will discount the loan about six to eight points. Similarly, if the differential between the note rate and market rate is ½ of 1%, then you can anticipate about three to four points discount, and so on. The higher market interest rates at the time the higher the rule of thumb will be. At market rates of 6% to 7% the discount rule of thumb will be about six points. If market interest rates are hovering about 8% to 9%, the rule of thumb will be closer to eight points.

Of course, the primary lender will suffer a loss when the loan is sold in the secondary market. In our example above where a $100,000 loan was sold for 96¢ on the dollar, the loss would be $4,000. Obviously, the lender would decline to make such a loan unless someone agreed to reimburse the lender for this loss. The logical candidate would be the borrower, since the borrower is getting the benefit of the below-market interest rate. But making the borrower pay an additional loan discount would not further the seller's goal of making the house affordable, so many times the seller agrees to pay the discount.

Loan discounting today is complex and involves the use of computer programs to calculate exactly what the discount will be. Selling a loan at a discount to raise the yield to the secondary lender is a way to buy the loan down for the buyer. For further discussion of buydowns as they are used in contemporary lending, see Chapter 13.

KEY TERMS

The key to understanding any new field is the vocabulary used in that field. To maximize your comprehension of the material presented in this chapter, be sure you know the meaning and significance of the following terms. Remember that the majority of test questions primarily test knowledge of vocabulary.

Annuity

Bank Insurance Fund

Building and loan associations

Business trusts

Combination trust

Commercial banks

Discount rate

Disintermediation

Double tax-exempt

Equity kicker

Equity participation loan

Equity REIT

Fannie Mae

Farmer Mac

Federal Agricultural Mortgage Corporation

Federal Deposit Insurance Corporation

Federal funds

Federal Home Loan Mortgage Corporation

Federal National Mortgage Association

Federal Reserve Bank System

Fiduciary lender

Finance company

Financial fiduciary

Financial intermediary

Fiscal policy

Freddie Mac

Fund

Government National Mortgage Association

Hybrid trust

Institutional lenders

Instruments of credit policy

Interim financing

Liquidity

Loan correspondent

Loan fee

Loan origination fee

Monetary policy

Mortgage banker

Mortgage broker

Mortgage-backed securities

Multiclass securities

Mutual savings banks

Non-fiduciary lender

Non-institutional lender

Open market activity

Participating lender

Participation certificate

Pass-through securities

Points

Portfolio loan

Prime rate

Quasi-institutional lenders

Real estate investment trust (REIT)

Real Estate Mortgage Investment Conduit

Real estate mortgage trust (REMT)

Reserve ratio

Reserves

Savings and loan associations

Savings Association Insurance Fund

Savings banks

Securitizing

Semi-fiduciary lender

Servicing

Small loan company

Tandem plan

Thrift industry

Thrift institutions

Tranch

Treasury bill

Treasury certificate

Treasury note

Warehousing

13

Loan programs

AMERICA HAS DEVELOPED the highest level of home ownership of any country in the world, and in Washington the percentage of homeowners is near the top of the national average. The success of financing programs over the last seven decades is a large part of the reason.

Although non-government loans provide financing for most residential borrowers today, real estate agents would make far fewer sales if the various government financing options were not available. Even more important, government loan programs have made home ownership possible for millions of Americans who could not have qualified without them. Furthermore, since their beginnings in the 1930s, government loan programs have provided experimentation and innovation which lenders in the private sector later copied. It is only fitting that we begin our discussion of loan programs with government loans.

A government loan is any loan that is insured, guaranteed, made directly by, or funded by the federal, state or local government. In contrast, conventional loans are private contracts strictly between the lender and the borrower without any government involvement of any sort other than regulation of the lender.

Among government loan agencies, the largest and oldest is the Federal Housing Administration (FHA). On a national level, loans to veterans guaranteed by the federal Department of Veterans Affairs are the second largest source of government loans. For rural properties loans through various federal agencies such as the Farm Service Agency and Rural Housing Service are also important sources of mortgage funding. The Washington State Housing Finance Commission is a state agency which provides financing for special housing needs including below-market rate loans for first time home buyers and buyers of homes in specially targeted areas. The various programs offered by these agencies with specific purposes and qualifying requirements are what we will explore next.

The Federal Housing Administration

The ***Federal Housing Administration*** (FHA) was created under the provisions of the National Housing Act of 1934. Its original purpose was to create jobs by stimulating housing construction and also to upgrade the nation's housing stock by promoting loans for home improvement. Under the original provisions of the National Housing Act, Title I was for home improvement loans and Title II spelled out the programs for home acquisition and refinance loans. Later many other titles were added to the original Act, creating programs for rent and interest rate subsidies, among a multitude of other purposes.

Real estate agents owe a great deal to the FHA. Although the FHA is not technically a lender, no other institution in the field of residential lending is as large. FHA loans are responsible for approximately 800,000 home purchases every year. Over the years as the largest government loan agency, the FHA is the source of most new approaches to residential lending. The FHA pioneered minimum property standards and established standard qualifying procedures. And most importantly, FHA loans made the secondary market possible, without which real estate lending would be at the mercy of local economic conditions.

Today, the FHA loan program is operated by the Department of Housing and Urban Development (HUD) in Washington, D.C. For purposes of administering FHA loans, HUD has divided the nation into ten regions, and each region has area offices in major cities. Washington is in Region 10, whose headquarters are in Seattle with area offices in Portland, Spokane, Anchorage and Boise.

Although the FHA has been a direct lender on occasion in the past, it functions today almost exclusively as an insurer of loans. As a federal agency, it places the credit of the U.S. Government behind the borrower by insuring the borrower's loan against default. The loan itself is made by an institutional lender (called a ***participating lender*** in FHA terminology), such as a bank, thrift institution, mortgage banker, or any other organization that wishes to make totally secure loans. In the event of a default, the lender can recover losses from the FHA insurance pool.

The FHA insurance is called ***mutual mortgage insurance***, to distinguish it from insurance provided by private insurance companies for conventional loans, called private mortgage insurance. Premiums for the mutual mortgage insurance are paid by the borrower and are calculated to be sufficient to cover anticipated losses and overhead. The FHA insurance program is designed to be self-liquidating and cost the taxpayers nothing.

The beauty of FHA insurance is that it entices lenders to make riskier loans with higher loan to value and more liberal income to debt ratios than they would otherwise be willing to make. Although anyone can get an FHA loan, FHA programs are structured primarily for first time buyers.

Throughout most of the history of the FHA the mutual mortgage insurance premium was ½ of 1% (0.5%) per annum of the principal balance. The borrower would pay ¹⁄₁₂ of this annual premium with each payment. Lenders would collect the premium and place it in a reserve account for the borrower. Each year the lender would remit the premium to the FHA to continue the insurance for the coming year. Millions of loans were made this way, a few of which remain on the books even today.

In 1983 the method for collecting the mutual mortgage insurance was changed. Instead of paying ¹⁄₁₂ of ½ of 1% of the loan balance monthly, the borrower would pay 3.8% of the principal balance at the beginning of the loan, which provides insurance for the entire first ten years. No additional amounts are collected on these loans. However, 3.8% of the principal balance is a lot of money for most borrowers, so FHA rules allow the lender to increase the loan amount by adding the premium to the balance due. Since the loan balance is higher, the monthly payments are higher, but then, the total monthly payment is probably not significantly different from what it would have been under the old system.

In 1991 calculation of the mutual mortgage insurance was modified again. The borrower paid the 3.8% premium in advance *plus* the monthly ¹⁄₁₂ of ½ of 1% of the loan amount. Although this made the program somewhat unattractive, we must bear in mind that the program is designed to be self-liquidating. The same economic conditions which caused the massive failures of savings and loan associations during the 1980s also caused the FHA mutual mortgage insurance fund to suffer fairly serious losses for several years. Raising the premiums was the only way to ensure the solvency of the FHA program.

Because the high premium charges made the program undesirable, the up-front premium was subsequently lowered to 2¼% of the loan balance for loans over 15 years, which is the vast majority of FHA loans. For borrowers in central cities who complete a 16-hour home buyer education program the up-front fee is reduced to 1½% of the loan balance. The borrower still pays the ¹⁄₁₂ of ½ of 1% as well.

If a borrower pays the loan off early, there will be a partial refund of that portion of the premium which was prepaid (the 1½ or 2¼%). Similarly, if a borrower sells the property and the new buyer takes over the borrower's loan, it is customary for the new buyer to reimburse the original borrower for the portion of the premium which remains prepaid.

Real estate agents should be aware that a lender with an FHA insured loan will never lose money on the loan, but will also never profit from a foreclosure. If the lender

NOTES

forecloses on an FHA loan, the FHA usually requires the lender to open the bidding at the foreclosure sale with the total amount owed. All bidders other than the lender must pay all cash, so if the lender is outbid, this means the lender will be cashed out, and there is no further need for the FHA insurance. If the lender wins the bidding, the lender will receive title to the property. The lender then trades the property to the FHA for FHA bonds which mature at the same term as the remaining term on the loan, and bear the same interest rate as the original note. The lender does not receive cash, which could then conceivably be used to make a new loan at a higher rate to someone else. Because there is no way to profit from a foreclosure, the lender sees a foreclosure only as a last resort. As a result, lenders usually demonstrate greater forbearance with FHA loans than with conventional loans.

The FHA has many different programs, but for all FHA programs there is a maximum loan amount. The FHA changes the maximum amounts from time to time, and the maximums also vary from county to county. Of course, the FHA has different loan to value ratios for different programs, so the actual maximum loan amount can vary. To determine the current maximum loan amount requires consultation with a participating lender.

Traditionally, a borrower wanting an FHA loan would make application at a participating lender. Originally, the lender would gather all the documents necessary to approve the loan – the verification of employment, credit report, copies of the earnest money agreement, and so forth – and send the documents to the area FHA office for **_underwriting approval_**. The term "underwriting" is used here as a synonym for "insurance." In other words, since the ultimate risk is being carried by the FHA, it is the FHA which will want to be sure the borrower and the property qualify for the loan.

Today, most FHA loans are processed in a different manner. FHA now tells lenders what is required to approve an FHA loan. A lender can apply to be a **_direct endorsement_** lender, which allows the lender to approve the loan without sending the paperwork to the FHA for underwriting approval. To ensure compliance with FHA standards the FHA conducts spot audits of lenders' loan files. However, even direct endorsement lenders are not allowed to approve all loans. If a loan does not meet direct endorsement standards, it must be sent to the FHA for underwriting approval. Nevertheless, direct endorsement allows almost all FHA loans to be approved without waiting for FHA approval.

Another recent innovation to the FHA program is the possibility of co-insurance. Co-insurance, as the term would imply, means that the lender shares any losses with the FHA. The advantage to the lender is that the FHA gives the lender complete authority over loan approval. The disadvantage is the potential for greater losses in the event of a downturn in the economy that causes defaults.

The FHA sets maximums on the amount lenders can charge for borrower expenses such as loan origination fees, credit report fees, appraisals, and the like. Until 1983, the FHA also set a maximum interest rate that a lender could charge on an FHA loan. This interest rate was almost always set a little below market. After all, the goal of the FHA was to make housing affordable, and keeping the interest rate down would further that goal.

However, setting a maximum interest rate which was below market created a problem when the primary lender tried to sell the loan in the secondary market. Secondary market investors demand a market rate, so the loans had to be sold at a discount. But FHA prohibited charging the buyer, so the seller ended up having to pay the discount. This made FHA loans unpopular with sellers. Sellers would, quite naturally, try to raise the price of the house to cover the anticipated discount. Sometimes this worked, although other times the appraisal would not come back high enough to allow the seller to recover the discount.

As a result, in 1983 FHA changed the rules. There is no longer a maximum interest rate on most FHA loans. Therefore, if the borrower agrees to pay a market rate, there will be no discount. On the other hand, the seller could agree to pay a certain number of points to buy the interest rate down for the borrower. A seller might agree to do this as a sales incentive. At the same time the FHA also rescinded the rule that borrowers were not allowed to pay the discount. So if a borrower wants a lower interest rate and the seller will not pay the discount, the borrower is now free to do so.

Not only do FHA loans provide more liberal qualifying terms for the borrower, they also have another great advantage. Unlike most conventional loans, all FHA loans are assumable. The rules on assumptions have changed, however, and the assumption requirements today depend on when the loan was originated.

When a buyer "assumes" a loan the buyer enters into an ***assumption agreement*** with the lender. In this case the seller (original borrower) remains liable, and the buyer also takes personal responsibility to pay the loan. Think of an assumption as being the equivalent of the new buyer co-signing the note. A buyer could also take title subject to the loan without entering into an assumption agreement with the lender, in which case the buyer would incur no personal obligation to pay. The lender could still foreclose, but if the property failed to sell for enough at the foreclosure sale, only the original borrower could be held liable for any deficiency.

Of course, lenders want the buyer to enter into an assumption agreement and they want the buyer to submit to credit approval as well. As a result, it became common practice to offer the original borrower an incentive to get the new buyer to submit to credit approval and to assume the loan. The inducement is to offer to release the original borrower from liability if the new buyer will submit to credit approval and assume the loan.

When a buyer takes title without entering into an assumption agreement, real estate agents call this taking title ***subject to*** the loan. Technically speaking, the buyer takes title subject to the loan when the buyer enters into an assumption agreement as well, but real estate agents generally refer to this as an ***assumption***. When the buyer assumes without going through credit approval, this is commonly called a ***blind assumption*** or sometimes a ***simple assumption***. When a buyer assumes, goes through credit approval, and the original borrower is released from liability, this is called a ***substitution of mortgagor***, or in terms of contract law, a ***novation***.

In the past, all FHA loans could be taken over by a buyer, with or without assuming, and the FHA made no requirements of the buyer. Starting with loans originated after December 1, 1986, the loan documents require a new buyer to submit to credit approval and enter into an assumption agreement if the loan is taken over during the first two years of the loan. After the loan was two years old, the old rules applied and the lender could no longer require the new buyer to assume or submit to credit approval. And even if the loan was assumed during the first two years, the lender could not require a change in the interest rate.

In March of 1989 the rules were changed again. For loans made after that date, the new buyer only needed to submit to credit approval and assume the loan if it was taken over during the first year of the loan. And both the original borrower and the new buyer would be equally personally obligated for five years, after which the original borrower would be released from liability. And as before, even if the loan was assumed during the first year, the lender could not require a change in the interest rate.

Then the rules changed yet again. For all loans originated after December 15, 1989, the new buyer must always submit to credit approval and enter into an assumption agreement; blind assumptions are no longer possible. Both the original borrower and the new buyer remain fully liable until the entire loan is paid in full. Furthermore, the new buyer must agree to occupy the property; investor assumptions are prohibited. The only advantage is that the lender still cannot require a change in the interest rate.

When taking over an FHA loan it is important to know when the loan was made. Whatever the rules were when the loan was made are the rules which govern its assumption. This is because the rules were written into the note and trust deed, so neither the lender nor the FHA can change them after the fact.

Another advantage of FHA loans (and all government loans) is that there is never a prepayment penalty. The borrower can pay the loan off at any time without extra charges. This is not always true on conventional loans.

Federal Housing Administration programs

Over its history, the FHA has developed dozens of different loan programs. Many of these programs are no longer being used. Others are programs to finance large residential complexes, frequently to provide elderly, handicapped and low-income housing. A complete discussion of all FHA loan programs is beyond our scope here, but we should examine at least the more commonly encountered programs.

The most popular FHA program is the **Section 203 (b) Loan Program**. This is the primary program and many other programs are based on it. Any resident of the United States can obtain an FHA 203 (b) loan, whether a citizen or not. An FHA 203 (b) loan is a fixed rate loan with a term of up to 30 years. Lenders sometimes limit the term to 20 or 25 years if the property has a short remaining economic life. Many lenders also offer a 15-year term at a slightly lower interest rate, even if the property has a long remaining life. But those are individual lender requirements; the program itself allows loans up to 30 years. Section 203 (b) loans can be used to buy or refinance one- to four-family properties. Manufactured housing also qualifies if the borrower will own the land. To acquire a home, the borrower must agree to occupy the property.

For most FHA loan programs, the maximum loan to value ratio is a complicated calculation, and 203 (b) loans are no exception. FHA allows the borrower to finance some of the **allowable closing costs**. The allowable closing costs vary according to the amount of the purchase price. FHA has created a chart of maximum allowable closing costs which is based on their estimate of what the actual average closing costs ought to be. The chart is available from area FHA offices or from local lenders. Note that the borrower will ultimately pay the actual closing costs at closing; the purpose of the chart is just to estimate the closing costs for purposes of calculating the maximum loan amount.

The calculation is to add the financeable portion of the allowable closing costs to the sales price. If this comes to more than $50,000, then the maximum loan amount is 97% of the first $25,000 and 95% of the rest.

The borrower can also ask the seller or third party to pay all or part of the allowable closing costs. In this case, the procedure to calculate the maximum loan amount will be slightly different because some or all of the allowable closing costs cannot be added, although the loan to value ratio will still be very high, sometimes over 100% loan to value ratio.

Since the goal of the FHA is to make housing affordable, it should come as no surprise that there are rules establishing maximum amounts that can be charged to the borrower. For example, the maximum loan fee the borrower is allowed to pay is one percent. In addition, the borrower may not be charged for document preparation, notary services, and a number of other charges that lenders like to pass on to borrowers.

An FHA **Section 203 (b) (2)** loan is a special type of 203 (b) loan for eligible veterans. Real estate agents sometimes call these "FHA/VA" loans, but note that they should not be confused with loans guaranteed by the federal Department of Veterans Affairs. Section 203 (b) (2) loans are the same as regular 203 (b) loans except that only single-family properties (including manufactured housing on owned land) are acceptable, and the loan to value ratio is more liberal. For most properties the loan to value ratio will be 100% of the first $25,000, including allowable closing costs, and 95% of the balance. For new construction less than one year old, or manufactured housing which has been in place for less than one year, the maximum loan to value ratio is 90%. Of course, the borrower must be a qualified veteran who has served at least 90 days of continuous active duty (longer for peacetime duty) and has obtained a Certificate of Veteran's Status from the federal Department of Veterans Affairs.

Section 203 (h) loans provide special terms for victims of disasters.

Section 203 (i) loans are similar to 203 (b) loans, but for outlying areas.

Section 203 (k) loans are designed to allow the borrower to obtain a fixed or adjustable rate loan to acquire and rehabilitate a home. Most lenders are unwilling to make 203 (k) loans because of the extensive documentation required. Extra paperwork is necessary because the loan can be closed and funds disbursed to acquire the property, but the remainder of the loan must remain in escrow to be disbursed as work is completed. One important advantage of this program is that the up-front mortgage insurance premium is waived.

Section 221 (d) (2) loans are not commonly encountered today because the maximum loan amounts are too stringent. This program was originally created to assist people displaced by the freeway construction projects of the late 1950s and 1960s, but continues today and is available for all borrowers who qualify for its special provisions.

Section 222 provides lower down payment loans for career military personnel.

Section 223 (e) loans are loans for properties in older, declining areas.

Section 234 (c) provides loans to acquire a unit in a condominium which is being converted from apartments, by a renter in the building.

Section 237 is a special program for borrowers who are poor credit risks.

Section 245 (a) loans are graduated payment loans (GPMs) with a fixed interest rate for the acquisition of a single-family home only. Graduated payment loans are not popular today, but during periods of high interest they can be a useful financing tool. A GPM loan has monthly payments at the beginning which are deliberately calculated to be too low even to cover the interest, let alone repay (amortize) the debt. This results in **negative amortization**, a situation where the balance owing increases over the first years of the loan. The amount of the monthly payment is increased each year, so that eventually the negative amortization is reversed and the borrower starts paying off the loan. Of course, GPM loans will be popular only when borrowers believe that increasing property values will cover the increasing debt. In any other kind of market, a GPM loan is potentially a disaster.

Section 234 (c) is a section of the National Housing Act that makes special provisions for condominium loans under the other programs. Section 234 (c) provides that condominium loans can be made only in complexes that have been approved by FHA, the federal Department of Veterans Affairs, or Fannie Mae. To gain approval, the bylaws and operations of the homeowners' association must be scrutinized and the ratio of owner occupied units to rental units must meet minimum standards.

Section 251 allows loans under Section 203 (b), 203 (k) and 234 (c) to be made with adjustable interest rates, using the one year Treasury Constant Maturities Index to determine interest rate changes, with an annual cap of 1% and a lifetime cap of 5%.

The above programs are for single-family dwellings up to four-plexes. Although less popular, there are additional programs for properties in excess of four units. These include a wide variety of purposes, including rental housing for the elderly, people with disabilities, single room occupancy projects, projects in urban areas targeted for revitalization, mobile home parks, as well as ordinary rental investments.

Federal Department of Veterans Affairs

Hard on the heels of World War II victory, Congress passed the Servicemen's Readjustment Act of 1945, more popularly called the "GI Bill," and now officially referred to as Title 38 U.S. Code. The GI Bill provided medical benefits, pensions, educational opportunities and many other advantages to promote the welfare of returning veterans. For real estate agents, the most significant of these other benefits is the right to borrow money for a home and have the federal government guarantee the loan.

Most real estate agents call these loans *federal GI* loans or *federal VA* loans, although the latter term is no longer technically correct. The loans originally were obtained through the Veterans Administration, an agency under the Department of Defense. In 1988 the Veterans Administration was elevated to its own cabinet post and renamed the *U.S. Department of Veterans Affairs* (DVA), so "federal VA" should probably be changed to "federal DVA," although it's not likely people will stop using the old term.

Federal GI loans are similar to FHA loans in one respect – like the FHA, the U.S. Department of Veterans Affairs does not ordinarily lend money. Instead it entices private banks, thrift institutions, mortgage bankers and others to make loans to eligible veterans by guaranteeing the loan against default. There is one major difference, however. Where the FHA *insures* the loan against default, the Department of Veterans Affairs *guarantees* the loan. The technical difference is significant. The word "insurance" implies that a premium is paid, which is definitely the case with FHA loans. A "guaranty" is like a co-signature, for which there is no charge.

Officially there is no charge for the guaranty. Today, however, the DVA charges a *funding fee*. Currently the funding fee is 2% of the loan amount for a loan with no down payment. This is reduced to 1½% of the loan balance if the veteran borrower makes a 5% down payment, and to 1¼% for a 10% down payment. The funding fee is ¾ of 1% higher for reservists. The funding fee may be added to the loan amount, even if this would cause the loan amount to be greater than the appraised value of the property.

Unlike other loan programs, the DVA requires no down payment. Nor does the DVA set any maximum loan amount. There is, however, a maximum *guaranty* or *entitlement*. In 1945 the original entitlement was $2,000, but today is an amount determined by the sales price, but not to exceed $60,000.

The interesting thing about the entitlement is that lenders will treat it the same as down payment, from a security standpoint. The most important reason for a down payment is to protect the lender in the event of a foreclosure. Since properties rarely sell for their highest market value when they are sold for cash in a forced auction sale, lenders want a cushion for protection. Traditionally, lenders have considered that a 75% loan to value ratio is safe and prudent.

Now, if the U.S. Department of Veterans Affairs will guarantee a maximum of the top $60,000, a lender will generally consider that guaranty the same as down payment from a security standpoint. Therefore, the question is, how big a loan will a lender be willing to make if the top 25% of the loan is $60,000? The answer is simple – four times the $60,000, or $240,000. In other words, at a loan of $240,000, the top 25% of the loan is $60,000.

As a practical matter then, lenders will not make federal GI loans over $240,000. Note that this maximum is set by the *lender*, not by the DVA. The DVA sets no maximum loan amount. And, in fact, in high cost areas of the country, it is customary to find lenders willing to exceed the $240,000 maximum. However, they will exceed the $240,000 only if the veteran borrower makes a down payment of 25% of the amount of the purchase price which exceeds $240,000. Such a down payment keeps the lender from exceeding the 75% risk level. Note that it is not the original lender who makes the rule – the rule is from secondary mortgage market investors who buy securities backed by federal GI loans. To make a loan over $240,000 requires the primary lender to find an alternate market.

Of course, the loan also cannot exceed the amount of the sales price or appraised value, whichever is less, plus the funding fee. The DVA will have the property appraised and the appraisal report is called a ***certificate of reasonable value***, or just **CRV** for short. Note that the veteran is free to pay more for the property than the appraised value – it is only the loan amount that cannot exceed the appraised value plus funding fee.

The DVA does allow junior financing, but only as long as the total of the DVA guaranteed first lien and the junior lien does not exceed the amount of the CRV. Although loans can be as high as 100% loan to value ratio, there may be lenders unwilling to lend the full 100%, therefore junior financing can sometimes occur. The second lien document must be approved by the DVA, the interest rate cannot exceed the rate on the first, it must be amortized over at least five years, and there can be no balloon payments.

Occasionally the question comes up if a veteran who already used his or her entitlement can obtain another loan. There are several ways this can be done. If the veteran has sold the property and the loan is either paid in full or assumed by another veteran who uses his or her own entitlement, the original borrower can apply to the DVA for a complete restoration of entitlement. Or a veteran could get an additional DVA loan if the veteran has not used all of his or her entitlement. For example, suppose a veteran bought a home years ago when the entitlement was lower. Since Congress has raised the entitlement, now the veteran may have unused entitlement. Since lenders will generally lend four times the amount of the entitlement without requiring a down payment, it may be possible for many veterans to obtain a second federal GI loan. Veterans may also have their complete loan entitlement restored for purposes of refinancing an existing federal GI loan in order to obtain a lower interest rate.

To qualify for a federal GI loan the borrower's first step is to request a Certificate of Eligibility from the Department of Veterans Affairs. The eligibility requirements are complex and most real estate agents find it is more convenient to have a potential veteran buyer go or write directly to the Department of Veterans Affairs and let them determine the veteran's eligibility. After, all the veteran has to get the Certificate of Eligibility sooner or later, so why not get it before even beginning to look for a home? Washington is served by a DVA regional office in Seattle, so it is not difficult for most veterans to do this.

However, there are certain persons who are entitled to a federal GI loan guaranty even though they are not technically "veterans." For example, service personnel currently on active duty who have been on continuous active duty for at least 90 days are entitled to a federal GI loan. Unmarried surviving spouses of veterans who died from service connected injuries also qualify, as well as spouses of service persons who have been missing in action or prisoners of war for at least 90 days. The Department of Veterans Affairs will even grant a Certificate of Eligibility to U.S. citizens who served in the armed forces of another country which was a U.S. ally during World War II.

Many lenders who make federal GI loans are qualified as ***automatic lenders***. This is the equivalent of an FHA direct endorsement lender, in fact, FHA direct endorsement lenders probably also qualify as federal GI automatic lenders. Automatic lenders are allowed to approve the loans themselves, and the Department of Veterans Affairs spot audits their loan files to ensure that they are following required underwriting standards.

Federal GI loans are always assumable but, like FHA loans, the rules have changed over the years. Loans made before March 1, 1988 had no due on sale clause, and any buyer, whether a veteran or not, could take title subject to the loan with or without assuming and with or without qualifying. As with FHA loans, lenders would sometimes offer to release the original veteran borrower from liability if the buyer would assume and submit to credit approval. Loans made after March 1, 1988 have a due on sale clause which requires the buyer to be qualified for the credit and assume the loan. However, the lender cannot use the due on sale clause to raise the interest rate, as is common on conventional loans.

As with FHA loans, there is never a prepayment penalty on a federal GI loan. The borrower can pay the loan off at any time without extra charge.

Federal GI loans can be used to acquire or refinance a one- to four-family property, but the veteran must occupy the property — investor loans are not available. A veteran can also use his or her federal GI entitlement to finance a manufactured dwelling, including a manufactured dwelling on rented land. Condominiums can also be financed with federal GI loans.

The federal Department of Veterans Affairs has several different loan programs. The original program is a traditional fixed rate loan amortized up to 30 years. This remains the most popular program today. Many lenders also offer shorter terms if the borrower desires to pay the loan off more quickly. It is also common for a lender to require a down payment, even if the DVA makes no such requirement.

Growing equity mortgages are also available under the federal GI guaranty. A **growing equity mortgage** (GEM) loan is a loan which may start out with payments lower than even the monthly interest charge (resulting in negative amortization similar to a graduated payment mortgage), but with regular increases to the payment over the entire life of the loan. The federal Department of Veterans Affairs does not allow their GEM loan to have negative amortization and the amount of the payment increases must be reasonable so the veteran borrower can handle them without difficulty.

The third federal GI loan program is a **graduated payment mortgage** (GPM). The payments are initially set below the amount necessary to cover the interest, resulting in negative amortization. The payments increase by a certain percentage each year, usually for the first five years, and then remain the same for the remaining term of the loan, which can be up to 30 years. Federal DVA graduated payment loans require a down payment equal to the highest amount the negative amortization will climb to at the end of the fifth year. The final payment once the annual increases end is higher than if the loan were a regular 30-year mortgage, in order to compensate for the lower payments the first years.

The DVA recently moved to allow **hybrid mortgage loans**. A hybrid loan starts out as a fixed rate loan for the first few years (usually three years or five years), and then converts to an adjustable rate mortgage for the remainder of the loan.

In connection with most loans the DVA also allows the seller or someone else to buy down the loan for the veteran. For example, the seller may agree to pay a lump sum at closing in order to gain the veteran a lower interest rate.

Agricultural credit

The **Farm Service Agency** (FSA) is organized under the Department of Agriculture. It has a number of rural loan programs, including loans for –

- Purchase of land, farms and ranches
- Construction and rehabilitation of farm homes and outbuildings, and
- Beginning farmers to acquire farms and for operating expenses.

Some programs have a maximum loan amount of $200,000 and others can be up to $782,000. Loans can be made by institutional lenders and guaranteed by the Farm Service Agency or, in some cases, direct loans. For some beginning farmer loans the Farm Service Agency makes direct loans for 40% of the purchase price and the remainder (up to 90% loan to value ratio) will be funded by an institutional lender, whose share of the loan will be guaranteed by the Farm Service Agency. Beginning farmer loans have a maximum maturity of 15 years, but other programs offer maturities up to 40 years. Interest rates are typically very attractive, usually one percent or more below market. The Agency uses federal funds for its direct lending, which are frequently exhausted and the applicant has to wait for additional appropriations. Part of the annual appropriation is reserved for loans to socially disadvantaged farmers and ranchers (subject to racial, ethnic or gender prejudice). Farm Service Agency loans can be sold in the secondary market, generally through Farmer Mac (see below).

Rural Housing Service is another agency of the Department of Agriculture that provides rural real estate lending. It offers programs for –

- Home ownership,
- Housing rehabilitation and preservation,
- Housing for farm labor, and
- Assistance to developers of multifamily projects, including assisted housing for the elderly and disabled.

Like Farm Service Agency, some of Rural Housing Service loans are direct loans and others are guaranteed. Loans generally must be in rural areas or towns with a population of 20,000 or less, although farm labor housing can be in urban areas. For home ownership, loans can be direct loans at below-market interest rates, or by an institutional lender up to 100% loan to value ratio and guaranteed by Rural Housing Service. Loans are also available for people to provide their own labor to build a home, up to 65% of the work. There are also grants and loans for home repairs for low income families and persons with disabilities.

Farm Service Agency has offices in several locations throughout Washington. Rural Housing Service maintains an office in Olympia.

Farm Credit System

The **Farm Credit System** holds over $60 billion in loans to more than half a million farmers, ranchers and rural homeowners, among others. The Farm Credit System is made up of six regional Farm Credit Banks, one Bank for Cooperatives, and one Agricultural Credit Bank.

Banks within the Farm Credit System do not take customer deposits. Instead, they raise funds by selling bonds and notes in the primary capital markets. Selling the securities is a function of the Federal Farm Credit Banks Funding Corporation. Although government-sponsored and regulated by the federal Farm Credit Administration, the banks within the system are customer-owned entities. The system provides loans for all kinds of agricultural needs, including long term mortgages to farmers and ranchers.

The Agricultural Credit Act of 1987 created the **Federal Agricultural Mortgage Corporation** (Farmer Mac) to provide a secondary market for agricultural loans. It functions in this manner the same as Ginnie Mae – that is, it provides a government guaranty for mortgage-backed securities issued by the originating lender.

NOTES

Washington State Housing Finance Commission

The ***Washington State Housing Finance Commission*** has federal authority to sell tax-exempt bonds to promote housing for first time borrowers whose income does not exceed the median income for the area. Borrowers must not have owned a home during the preceding three years and must agree to occupy the home they are financing under the program. For most programs only single-family homes qualify and there are limits on the purchase price, which generally cannot exceed the median purchase price for homes in the area. Maximum income and purchase price figures are adjusted periodically for inflation. For specially targeted areas higher purchase prices are allowed and the requirement that the borrower not have owned a home in the preceding three years is waived. In most cases the borrower must attend a home buyer seminar where they learn about home maintenance, the importance of maintaining good credit, and other matters. For home ownership there are several programs –

House Key program – Buyers can obtain a below-market 30-year fixed rate loan through FHA, DVA, Rural Housing Service or it can be a Fannie Mae conventional. The Commission uses funds from the sale of tax-exempt bonds to purchase the loans from local lenders throughout the state at face value. In essence, the Commission acts as a secondary lender, but unlike normal secondary lenders, being able to sell tax-exempt bonds gives the Commission a source of low interest funds so it can buy loans at rates well below market. If the borrower sells the home during the first nine years of the loan there is the possibility that the borrower will have to pay a recapture tax.

House Key Teacher program – Similar to the House Key program except the cash out of pocket can be less and the qualifying ratio can be higher. Loans must be conventional only. Borrower must be an employee of a public school or private school recognized by the state.

House Key Plus program – A down payment assistance program through which borrowers can obtain a second mortgage up to $5,000 at very low interest and a ten-year repayment term.

House Key Plus Seattle program – A down payment assistance program through which borrowers can obtain a down payment assistance loan up to $45,000 at 3% interest with no payments due over the first eight years. Over the eight years there is a shared appreciation provision which reduces by 2% per year starting in the ninth year.

Tacoma Open Door program – A second mortgage up to $5,000 for down payment and closing costs through Fannie Mae. The borrower's first mortgage cannot be a House Key program loan funded by tax-exempt bonds.

HomeChoice program – A down payment assistance program for buyers who are low or moderate income and have a disability. Buyers can borrower up to $15,000 on a second mortgage with payments deferred up to 30 years.

House Key Extra program – A down payment assistance program consisting of grants up to $7,500 which can be forgiven pro-rata over five years. Buyers must not have over $5,000 in assets and must have a disability. The home must be in a rural area or a city with a population under 25,000.

The Commission also provides a ***low income tax credit*** for persons and entities which invest in low-income housing. The credit is apportioned to the state each year based on the state's population, so the amount is not unlimited. The Commission determines how much credit to authorize for a given project on a case-by-case basis.

The Commission can also sell bonds for a specific project of a qualified tax-exempt organization. Eligible projects include land and structures for things like day care centers, job training sites, athletic facilities, independent schools, research facilities, and many others. The benefit is obtaining funds at rates typically one or two percent below market. In addition, qualified tax-exempt organizations can use funds from bonds sold by the Commission to fund non-profit housing developments such as assisted living units, group homes, nursing homes, housing for the homeless, emergency shelters, and similar projects. Organizations that are not tax-exempt can also finance multifamily projects from bond sales provided a percentage of the units are reserved for low-income persons.

Conventional financing

In the early days of real estate finance the term "conventional loan" did not exist. All real estate loans were simply called "mortgage loans." But in 1934 the Federal Housing Administration (FHA) came into being and a new breed of mortgage loan became available. The FHA was created to insure loans and these loans needed to be distinguished from regular mortgage loans. As a result the term ***conventional loan*** was coined to differentiate ordinary mortgage loans from FHA insured loans. A conventional loan is any loan which is not insured or guaranteed by a government agency, or made directly by a government body.

Later many other government loan programs were created. Loans guaranteed by the Veterans Administration, direct loans from the Washington State Housing Finance Commission, farm loans from the Farm Service Agency and the Rural Housing Service – all were added to the list of government loan programs. Through it all, the conventional loan retained a solid market share.

Today conventional loans comprise the vast majority of all new loan originations in spite of some of the advantages of government loans. For one thing, not everyone qualifies for government programs. And even those who qualify, may not need the extra assistance that government programs offer and prefer what they perceive as better service in the private sector. Until FHA loans came on the scene, residential mortgage lending was largely a function of the commercial banks, although the thrift industry was making serious inroads into their business. During the depression, however, real estate lending by all lenders dropped to a trickle. Commercial banks took to the new FHA loans because of the liquidity they offered – the fact that FHA loans all met minimum standards and were insured made them salable, so a secondary market could be developed. The thrifts were less concerned with liquidity and so conventional loans became their standard. Many thrifts did make FHA loans, but the majority of thrift lending was on a conventional loan basis.

When the Federal National Mortgage Association (Fannie Mae) was created in 1938, a dependable secondary market was finally available. At this time mortgage bankers sprang up all over the country. Mortgage bankers do not have customer deposits to lend, so they are completely dependent on the existence of a secondary market. At that time Fannie Mae was a government agency, and did not buy anything but government loans. Therefore, there was no secondary market for conventional loans.

This situation did not change until the early 1970s. The result was that from 1934 until the 1970s, commercial banks hardly ever made conventional loans and mortgage bankers never did. Commercial banks insisted on the liquidity of the secondary market. Mortgage bankers had no choice but to make government loans only, because they were completely dependent on the secondary market as a source of funds. This left the conventional market to the thrift institutions. Most thrifts in Washington made nothing but conventional loans until very recent years. Even today, the conventional loan still comprises the bulk of the loan activity at thrift institutions.

NOTES

Starting in the early 1970s, however, Fannie Mae and the (then) newly created Freddie Mac, began buying conventional loans. Suddenly a secondary market for conventional loans opened up. And the result was that commercial banks and mortgage bankers started making conventional loans as well as government insured and guaranteed loans. Nevertheless, there is a strong sense of history in the lending business, and when a thrift institution makes a real estate loan today it is most likely a conventional loan. Still, thrifts have lost a lot of market share in the past several years, and real estate agents place far more conventional loans with commercial banks and mortgage bankers today than they do with thrift institutions.

Mortgage insurance

The Federal Deposit Insurance Corporation, the Federal Reserve Board, the Comptroller of the Currency, and the Office of Thrift Supervision have established uniform maximum loan to value ratios for different kinds of property that apply to the various kinds of lenders they regulate.

For land acquisitions, the maximum is 65% and for land development, 75%. For multifamily and commercial properties the maximum is 80%. And for one- to four-family properties the maximum is 85% loan to value ratio. For residential loans the maximum is waived, as long as the amount of the loan over 85% is insured against default.

Government insurance and guaranties have allowed lenders to make loans with little or no down payment for a long time. To allow conventional loans to compete with government loans, *private mortgage insurance* (PMI) has been developed by various private insurance companies. Although lenders can make residential loans up to 85%, as a rule, lenders require private mortgage insurance for all loans over 80% loan to value ratio, and some lenders even insure loans over 75% loan to value ratio.

Borrowers pay the premiums for the private mortgage insurance. The premium varies considerably according to the risk. For example, loans with buydowns, adjustable interest rates, and other features which allow the amount of the payment to change will be more likely to go into default than loans with fixed payments. Similarly, the lower the down payment, the greater the risk and the higher the premium.

The premium to insure the loan over its entire life can be paid up front at closing or it can be paid monthly with just the first month's premium at closing. Some lenders also allow the borrower to pay the entire premium at closing by borrowing it and adding it to the principal balance. Many lenders include it in the cost, and then charge a higher interest rate for insured loans as opposed to uninsured loans. For a home buyer, the latter is desirable, as the interest is tax deductible.

Once the loan balance drops to 80%, the borrower can ask the lender to discontinue the insurance. After all, the private mortgage insurance company no longer has any liability, so paying the premiums is pointless. Lenders used to follow secondary market guidelines regarding when to allow cancellation of the mortgage insurance, but today everyone follows the requirements of the Private Mortgage Insurance Act, discussed in more detail in Chapter 14.

Conforming and non-conforming financing

The secondary market establishes the maximum loan amount for the various types of conventional loans. Loan limits are adjusted in January each year according to changes in the national average house price as published by the Federal Housing Finance Board.

Conventional lenders are happy to lend up to the maximum, and such loans are called **conforming loans**. Loans which exceed the maximum are **non-conforming loans**, and must be sold to alternative secondary markets or kept in the lender's own portfolio. Non-conforming loans are less desirable for lenders, so the yield they demand tends to be slightly higher. Many lenders call a non-conforming loan a **jumbo mortgage**.

Fixed rate loans

The fixed rate conventional mortgage loan (FRM) remains the most popular conventional loan, by far. While the interest rates for a FRM will be higher than for an adjustable rate mortgage loan (ARM), many borrowers are willing to pay the higher rates in exchange for the security of knowing that the principal and interest will not change.

Why are interest rates higher for fixed rate loans? Very simply, lenders are hedging their bets. Being able to change the interest rate in the future helps the lender remain profitable in periods when interest rates increase.

Throughout most of its history, the **amortization** (payoff through periodic payments) of a fixed rate loan has been 30 years. In recent years, however, lenders have offered amortization terms of 20 years, 15 years and 10 years as well. Although 30-year amortization remains the most popular with borrowers, amortization over 15 years is the second most popular. The reason for its popularity is really very simple – enormous interest savings. The following chart shows the interest that would be paid on a loan amortized to the full term over various terms on a $200,000 loan at 7% –

Term	Monthly payment	Total interest over life of loan
30 years	$1,330.61	$279,017.80
25 years	$1,413.56	$224,967.52
20 years	$1,550.60	$172,143.49
15 years	$1,797.66	$123,578.18

Of course, the borrower has to be able to afford the higher payments to take advantage of the interest savings on a 15-year loan. However, there is an additional savings on the 15-year loan. The fact that the term is shorter means that the lender is less concerned with inflation and increasing interest rates in the future. Therefore, it is not uncommon for lenders to offer 15-year loans at about ¼ of 1% below the rate for 30-year loans. If you consider the interest at 6¾% on the 15-year loan in the example on the preceding chart, the monthly principal and interest payment would be slightly less ($1,769.82) and the total interest over the life of the loan would be only $118,567.41.

Of course, if you are clever you have already perhaps thought, "why not just get a 30-year loan, and make extra principal payments when you can?" This would give borrowers the greatest flexibility – in tough times they could make just the minimum payment, and when times are good, they could pay extra on the mortgage. In principle this sounds good. In practice, there are several drawbacks, not the least of which is the loss of the preferential interest rate of the short term loan. Furthermore, the notes required by secondary lenders today provide that if the borrower prepays, the prepayment must be an amount equal to an entire payment. The borrower cannot just add an extra little amount to the payment. In addition, the terms state that, even if the borrower does prepay an amount equal to an entire payment, this does not excuse the borrower from making the next payment. In other words, the extra amount will be subtracted from the principal balance and the borrower will end up paying less interest over the life of the loan, but the borrower is not ahead a payment. And another reason borrowers consider the 15-year amortization is that they know they are less likely to adhere to a plan of making higher payments unless they are forced to do so.

A few lenders offer **bi-weekly loans**. The idea is fairly simple, the repayment is structured with payments every two weeks instead of once a month. Other than the convenience of having a house payment come due exactly on payday, the borrower would ordinarily find no significant advantage to a bi-weekly loan. However, if we look at the way bi-weekly mortgages are structured, the borrower can end up paying the loan off significantly earlier. Calculating the payments on a monthly amortization and dividing it by two would mean 24 payments every year. However, there are 52 weeks in a year, so with a biweekly mortgage, 26 payments are made. If we keep the amount of the payment half as much as the monthly payment, an extra payment gets made every year with the bi-weekly mortgage. The extra payment starts a snowballing effect and the result is a significantly faster payoff. A loan of $100,000 at 8% for 30 years would have monthly payments of $733.76 and total interest of $164,155.24 over the life of the loan. Dividing the payment in half means the payments would be $366.88, but making 26 per year means the loan would be paid off in only 23 years, nine months, and the total interest cost would be only $117,926.72.

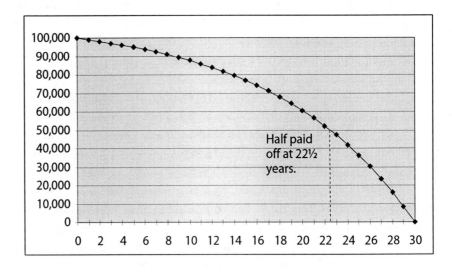

Payoff of an ordinary 30-year mortgage loan of $100,000 with 360 equal monthly payments of 733.76. The halfway mark is reached at approximately 22½ years.

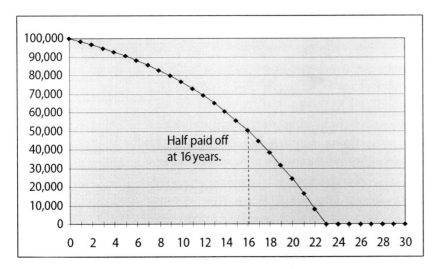

Payoff of a bi-weekly mortgage loan of $100,000 with equal payments of 366.88 every two weeks. By making bi-weekly payments each of which is half of the payment for the 30-year mortgage above, the borrower makes one extra payment each year. The halfway mark is reached at approximately 16 years instead of 22½ years for the 30-year loan.

As you can see, biweekly loans offer the borrower a payoff better than six years sooner, with a substantial interest savings over the life of the loan. And all of this can be done fairly painlessly, since most borrowers wouldn't notice the slight increase in total principal and interest payment.

Some conventional lenders offer loans with **balloon payments**, or a **call feature**. A balloon payment means that the entire remaining principal balance must be paid in full at some point in the future (usually five years or seven years). Some balloon payment mortgages contain a **rollover clause** , which allows the borrower to continue the loan. A balloon payment loan with a five-year rollover clause would be called a "5/25 convertible mortgage." Similarly, a seven-year rollover clause would make it a "7/23 convertible mortgage."

Balloons and call features are, quite naturally, unpopular with borrowers. What would you do if the due date arrived and you were unable to refinance or sell the property to pay off the loan? The potential for foreclosure is great. Lenders usually lose money on foreclosures, so balloon payment loans are not popular with secondary market investors either. In order to make balloon payment loans more palatable, they are generally made at a slightly lower than market interest rate. They also commonly contain a rollover clause. Even then, the borrower is required to meet certain tests in order to exercise the rollover privilege, and the rollover is usually at a rate slightly higher than the lender's current rate for new loans. The idea is to give the borrower an escape route, but make it less attractive than refinancing.

Adjustable rate loans

When the interest rate on the loan is tied to an index, we call it an **adjustable rate mortgage** (ARM). Adjustable rate mortgages are more popular with lenders than with borrowers, although many borrowers also find plenty of advantages in ARM loans.

The chief benefit to the lender is a hedge against inflation and interest rate increases in the future. The lender is so thrilled with this benefit that the borrower may find the lender offering very enticing interest rates – two to three percent below the rate for fixed rate mortgages is not uncommon. So enticing, in fact, that ARMs score very high in the area of affordability. When the buyer cannot qualify for a fixed rate loan high enough to buy the property, an ARM frequently saves the sale.

There are also **hybrid loans** which combine the features of a fixed rate and an adjustable rate loan. Usually these loans start out with a fixed rate for the first seven or ten years, then switch to an adjustable rate. This kind of loan is sometimes called an **introductory rate ARM**.

Lenders tie their ARM loans to all kinds of different **indexes**. There are many published interest rate indexes and each lender will have a favorite. Some of the more popular are –

One-year, three-year and five-year treasury indexes – Averages of U.S. government bills and bonds adjusted to a constant one-year maturity. Published by the Federal Reserve Bank.

Six month treasury bill index –Based on the results of the weekly auction of 180-day treasury bills, quoted as a bank discount basis.

Cost of Funds Index (COFI) – The average monthly cost of deposits and other funds for thrifts. Some indexes are compiled for individual Federal Home Loan Bank districts. By far the most popular among Washington lenders is the 11th District Cost of Funds Index, published by the Federal Home Loan Bank of San Francisco. The 11th District is comprised of thrifts in Arizona, California and Nevada.

Regardless of the index, the loan must also stipulate the adjustment period. Most lenders today prefer to adjust the interest rate once every six months, although one-year adjustments are also common. Lenders offer ARMs with a wide range of adjustment period options. At one extreme a few lenders offer adjustments at three years and five years; and at the other end of the spectrum there are lenders who adjust as often as monthly. A **two-step mortgage** is a special kind of ARM that is adjusted just once during its lifetime; usually at the fifth or seventh year.

Although ARMs offer the lowest interest rates of all conventional loans, lenders still charge more than the index rate. For example, suppose the lender wants 7%, but the index is at, say 4½%. In this case the note will call for interest to be charged at the index rate plus the **margin** – in this case 2½%. The margin is a constant and does not vary over the life of the loan. Now, if the margin is 2½% and the index climbs to, say 6%, the borrower's interest rate will be adjusted to 8½% (6% + 2½% = 8½%). The index rate plus the margin is called the **fully indexed rate**.

Of course, if market interest rates were to skyrocket, borrowers with adjustable rate loans would be in deep trouble, indeed. It is common practice to adjust the payment every time the interest rate changes. A 30-year ARM loan of $200,000 at an initial rate of 6% would have monthly payments of $1,199.10. If the index rate goes up 2% six months later, the new interest rate will be 8%. The monthly payment would then be recalculated to amortize the loan over its remaining term (29½ years), or $1,473.56. This could cause what lenders call **payment shock**.

To guard against the inevitable defaults this would cause, lenders offer a variety of safeguards in the form of **caps**. A cap is a ceiling, usually on the interest rate. For example, a **lifetime cap** is a maximum amount the interest rate can increase to over the life of the loan. An ARM loan at 5% initially with a 7% lifetime cap can never increase to more than 12%. An **interim cap**, also called **adjustment cap** or sometimes **annual cap**, is the maximum amount the loan interest can increase in any one period. If the adjustment period is annual, then it is called an annual cap, and so on. There are loans with interim caps as long as three years, and as short as monthly. The longer the period, the less the gamble. Lenders prefer shorter adjustment periods. But if rates are falling, borrowers would benefit from shorter adjustment periods too.

Another kind of cap is a **payment cap**. Some lenders agree not to raise the payment by more than a certain percentage in any one year (7½% is common). Then, if the interest rate increases and the increase would cause the payment to exceed this percentage, the lender accepts the lower payment and adds the unpaid interest to the principal balance. This is called **negative amortization**. Lenders use payment caps in order to calm a borrower's fears about an ARM loan, yet not be constrained to very restrictive interest caps. Needless to say, payment caps are not popular with borrowers.

In fact, this is really a type of **graduated payment adjustable rate mortgage** (GPARM) – essentially the same as a GPM (see above), but where the interest rate is tied to an index. In the past many lenders offered formal GPARM loans with payment caps for the first five or ten years. Quite a few were made. But because they can easily create negative amortization, GPARMs are no more popular than GPMs and, hence, rare today. On the other hand, it is still not uncommon for lenders to offer a **teaser rate**. A teaser rate is a special below-market rate used for the first year – an additional incentive for the borrower to choose an ARM loan.

Some ARM loans have a **conversion privilege**. A conversion privilege allows the borrower to convert the ARM to a FRM. The exact terms of the conversion privilege vary dramatically from one lender to the next. Most of the time the borrower can only exercise the conversion privilege during the first few years of the loan. In most cases, the interest rate at conversion will be the lender's (then) current rate for new fixed rate loans. In most cases, interest rates would have to decline substantially before exercising the conversion privilege would make sense.

Growing equity mortgages

A **growing equity mortgage** (GEM) is a special kind of 15-year fixed rate loan. Unlike regular 15-year FRMs it has graduated payments like a GPM. Most GEMs have payment caps, so there is negative amortization. The major difficulty with GEM loans is that the payments start too low, which means they have to increase to rather high amounts later in order to complete the amortization in 15 years.

Most lenders list GEM loans as available, but there are few actually written today. Some lenders refer to an ordinary 15-year FRM as a GEM, although that is not technically a correct usage, since a GEM is supposed to have graduated payments, at least according to the standard definition.

Buydowns

What do you do when the buyer cannot qualify for the loan? If the buyer fails to qualify because the payments are too high, it may be possible to save the day with a buydown. A **buydown** is a lump sum paid to the lender up front, in exchange for which the lender agrees to lower the interest rate. In effect, it is prepaid interest. In fact, buydowns are the same as discount points (see Chapter 12 for additional discussion of loan discounting), although they don't always work exactly the same way.

The first thing to remember about buydowns on conventional loans is that it generally does not matter who pays the buydown. Typically it is the seller, but it is also common for friends or relatives of the borrowers to pay it. There are qualifying restrictions, however. Lenders want to see the borrower pay some of his or her own funds to buy the property, so if too much of the down payment or amounts to buy the loan down come from the seller or as gifts, this can cause the loan to be denied.

The second thing to bear in mind about buydowns is that they can be used with either fixed rate mortgages or adjustables. Of course, if the interest rate on an adjustable is bought down, it is really the margin that is bought down. For example, with an index that started at 4½% and a margin of 2½%, the initial interest rate is 7%. If the interest rate is bought down 1%, it is the margin that is reduced from 2½% to 1½%.

In conventional financing there are two kinds of buydowns – **permanent buydowns** and **temporary buydowns**. A permanent buydown operates precisely the same as loan points to lower the interest rate over the life of the loan. A temporary buydown, on the other hand, lowers the interest rate only for the first year or first few years of the loan.

In conventional financing permanent buydowns are not nearly as common as temporary buydowns. The main reason for this is the cost. As discussed in Chapter 12, the rule of thumb for buydowns is six to eight points for every percent the loan is bought down. So to buy a FRM down permanently from 8% to 7% would require a discount of six to eight points (6% to 8% of the loan balance). On a $200,000 loan, this is going to cost someone – probably the seller – $12,000 to $14,000.

But a temporary buydown may be sufficient. Buydowns are commonly used only when the borrower cannot qualify because the payments are too high. So if the lender will qualify the borrower on the initial, lower payments, then a temporary buydown should be all that is necessary. Lenders will not always agree to qualify the borrower on the initial payment, however. Temporary buydowns commonly run for one, two or three years.

If a temporary buydown is for more than one year, it can be a flat rate or it can be graduated. A **flat rate buydown** is a buydown where the amount of the buydown remains constant. For example, suppose you bought a loan down 2% for each of the first three years of the loan. This would be a flat rate buydown. But suppose instead that you bought the rate down 3% the first year, 2% the second year, and 1% the third year. This would be an example of a **graduated rate buydown**. Some lenders offer a **flex fixed rate temporary buydown** – the same as an ordinary buydown but where the rate increases every six months instead of every year.

Regardless of whether a temporary buydown is flat rate or graduated, it is very easy to get an approximation of what the lender would charge. Just add up the interest that the lender is losing each year because of the buydown. However, this is only an estimate. In reality, the lender is getting the money up front and can reinvest it and earn interest on it, so the actual cost tends to be slightly less than the estimate. For example, a 3–2–1 buydown would cost the lender 3% interest (3% of the loan balance) the first year, 2% the second year, and 1% the third year. Therefore, the total interest the lender would lose is 6%, so someone has to pay 6% of the loan balance (six points). But by getting the money up front, the lender may be willing to discount the six points to, say, 5¾ points. Buydowns are commonly used when the property is being sold by a corporation due to an employee relocation. The corporation will agree to pay the buydown in order to facilitate their employee's transfer.

As an alternative to charging someone points to buy the loan down, lenders today also offer to lower the interest rate for the first few years, in exchange for a higher interest rate over the remaining term of the loan. For example, in a market where FRMs are going for 7½%, a 3–2–1 buydown could be cast at an initial rate of 5¼%, a second year rate of 6¼%, a third year rate of 7¼%, and a rate of 7¾% for the fourth through the 30th year. The extra ¼ of 1% for the last 26 years allows the lender to recover the interest lost the first three years.

Graduated payment mortgages

A **graduated payment mortgage** (GPM) is a type of FRM where there is a special reduced payment for the first few years (usually five years). This results in **negative amortization**, that is, the payment is not even high enough to cover the interest, so the unpaid interest is added to the principal balance. In today's market, negative amortization is no more popular with lenders than it is with borrowers.

There is an additional difficulty with GPMs. For a five-year GPM, the payment would be higher for years five through 30 than if it were an ordinary FRM. This is necessary to pay back the negative amortization incurred during the first five years. To lessen the amount of negative amortization, the payment are scheduled to increase every year. Theoretically, there is no limit to how low the first year's payments can be made. But if they are made too low, the annual payment increases can cause payment shock. Secondary market investors do not like loans where the payments can increase more than 7½% a year, so most lenders structure GPMs with 7½% as the maximum annual increase.

Graduated payment mortgages are useful mostly in a market with rapid property appreciation. In such a market the GPM allows the borrower greater purchasing power. However, if future appreciation does not materialize as expected and the borrower needs to move during the adjustment period, the GPM can be a disaster.

Assumability

Where government loans are always assumable (although the buyer is usually asked to qualify), conventional loans usually are not. Adjustable loans are the major exception. Since the lender has a means to maintain the interest rate close to market, it becomes less important to enforce the due on sale clause on ARM loans.

Still, there are occasional fixed rate mortgages which do not have a due on sale clause. Real estate agents should always verify from the actual documents whether or not the loan is assumable and, if so, under what terms. Over the last 20 years there have been many different lien documents used and policies followed. For conventional loans, there are no standards when it comes to due on sale clauses. It is also not uncommon to find lenders' employees giving incorrect information about assumability of a loan. The only way to be sure is to get a copy of the recorded document.

Construction financing

Of all the different kinds of mortgage financing, construction lending entails the greatest risk to the lender. In fact, a common rule of thumb is to add an extra 2% to the rate for ordinary real estate loans if the loan is for construction purposes. The reasons for this are many, but one reason is simply because a half-finished structure makes pretty poor collateral.

Although in the past there have been government programs for construction financing, today these programs are virtually non-existent. Practically all construction financing today is conventional lending.

Construction financing (also called *interim financing*) is short term (not usually more than a couple of years at the most) and designed to be replaced by a new loan to be taken out by the eventual buyers. The new loan is called the *permanent loan* or *takeout loan*. The term "takeout loan" refers to the fact that the permanent financing "takes out," or pays off the construction financing. A few lenders have made available a one-stage construction loan where the borrower is the eventual buyer, the interest rate is at the higher "construction" rate until the construction is completed, and then the rate is reduced to the mortgage prime rate and the loan is amortized over the usual term. To be sure that permanent financing is available the construction lender sometimes issues a *standby commitment* to the builder, usually at a specific interest rate. The builder must pay for a standby commitment, so they are used only in circumstances where the builder fears rapidly rising interest rates.

A major problem with construction financing is the possibility of *mechanic's liens* and *materialman's liens*. Such liens are placed by a worker who claims that a bill for labor or materials was not paid. The problem is that, under Washington law, the priority of a construction lien is prior in right to all other liens that were recorded after construction was begun or materials supplied. This could create a problem for a lender. Suppose a bank lends funds to the builder and the documents were recorded on April 1. However, unknown to the lender, one of the builder's subcontractors began work on March 15. If the subcontractor is not paid and files suit to enforce a construction lien, the subcontractor's lien will be ahead of the bank's mortgage.

To guard against this happening construction lenders use a number of safeguards. First, they carefully scrutinize the contractor's financial ability. But most important, they need to be sure that all the workers, subcontractors and materials suppliers are paid. Construction lenders commonly disburse the loan proceeds in stages as the construction progresses. These are called *construction draws*. And the money is usually disbursed directly to the workers, subcontractors and materials suppliers. These people bring their bills to the general contractor who approves them for payment, and then the lender issues checks to pay the bills. The lender uses an endorsement on the checks where the endorser waives the right to a construction lien. Note that this process takes considerably more paperwork than an ordinary mortgage loan. This is probably the greatest reason construction loans are more expensive than permanent financing.

The possibility of construction liens not only makes the construction financing hazardous, it also frequently creates problems for the permanent loan. If the buyers want to close their purchase right after the construction is complete, the lender has to remember that workers, subcontractors and materials suppliers have up to 90 days after substantial completion in which to file their claims. Due to the priority of construction liens, these claims would predate the new permanent mortgage. The usual solution is to pay an extra premium for an *early issue* lender's title insurance policy to cover this possibility.

Another construction problem occurs when a property owner orders improvements built. The owner needs to be sure the builder will finish the project. A common solution is for the owner to insist that the contractor obtain a *completion bond* from an insurance company.

Loan underwriting

For real estate agents, understanding how to qualify the borrower is just as important as knowing about loan programs and financing arrangements. After all, it makes little sense to sell a house only to have the sale fall through because the buyer cannot get the necessary financing.

In lending circles, the process of credit qualification is called *underwriting*. Buyers, sellers and real estate agents complain about the convolutions that are required to gain loan approval. Yet, we also have to remember that the average mortgage loan today is a substantial amount of money. Lenders would be foolish to approve such loans without careful scrutiny of the borrower's ability to repay the debt, as well as the borrower's past credit history, and the quality of the collateral.

Lenders have an old saying – "you've got to have the three C's of credit to qualify." The three C's of credit are *collateral*, *character* (or *credit*), and *capacity*. Collateral refers to the value of the property being offered as security for the debt. Character (credit) refers to the borrower's past credit history. And capacity refers to the borrower's income and ability to meet the payments necessary to amortize the debt.

The quality and value of the collateral is demonstrated by an appraisal report. In real estate, if the appraisal is not high enough, the loan will usually be approved for a lesser amount which meets the lender's standards for security. In the final analysis, the collateral is the most important consideration in granting the loan because the lender must be prepared for the worst possible outcome. For the lender, that would be a foreclosure, so the lender must be sure to limit the risk to the amount that could be recovered by taking title to the property at the foreclosure sale and reselling it. Lenders normally apply the loan to value ratio to the lesser of the appraised value or the sales price.

An appraisal will not only tell the lender the market value of the property, but appraisal reports also give the remaining economic life of the improvements. Since it would be imprudent to lend for a term which exceeds the time over which the improvements will have a useful life, lenders must be concerned with their economic life. For most residential properties, this is seldom an issue. Usually it the economic life becomes a matter of concern only of the property is residential, but zoned for commercial use, or there is some other reason to believe the improvements have a limited remaining life. Economic life and other appraisal topics are complex concepts which are discussed in detail in Chapter 15.

Character refers to the borrower's credit rating. Lenders start with a credit report from standard credit reporting agencies. There are three national agencies –

- Equifax, P.O. Box 740256, Atlanta, Georgia 30374-0256, 800-997-2493, www.consumer.equifax.com.
- Experian (formerly TRW), P.O. Box 9595, Allen, Texas 75013-0036, 888-397-3742, www.experian.com
- TransUnion, P.O. Box 1200, Chester, Pennsylvania 19022, 800-916-8800

The ***Fair Credit Reporting Act*** requires credit reporting agencies to furnish a borrower with a copy of their credit report at no charge if the borrower was declined for a loan. Borrowers who have not been turned down can also obtain a copy of their credit report for a nominal charge. Credit reporting agencies are required to verify and correct any errors on a borrower's credit report when the borrower advises them of the error. In addition, borrowers have the right to have a statement included with their credit report to explain derogatory information. Real estate agents should begin their relationship with new buyers by having a frank discussion of these issues and having them make sure their credit report is as clean as it can be. For further discussion of the Fair Credit Reporting Act, see Chapter 14.

The borrower's credit rating has to meet secondary market requirements for the loan. It used to be that the secondary market had only one standard – all borrowers had to have impeccable credit or the loan was not salable. Today there are many options, including loans for persons with impaired credit. For less than perfect credit, the interest rate is increased, unless there are offsetting factors such as a very high down payment. Loans rated less than perfect also take much longer to close, as it will take a lot longer to find a lender willing to make the loan. Very highly rated loans can be approved and funded within a few days, since they can be immediately sold to Fannie Mae and Freddie Mac investors.

In gauging a borrower's credit history, there are always exceptions to every rule. Even a past bankruptcy is not necessarily a bar to getting a real estate loan, provided the cause of the bankruptcy is not likely to be repeated. Suppose, for example, that the borrower was found at fault for an accident that resulted in a large personal injury judgment. Or suppose a family member died of cancer after years of medical expenses. Such catastrophes could force a person into bankruptcy, but after re-establishing good credit history, the bankruptcy need not be a bar to obtaining new credit.

Of course, not only do different lenders have different requirements, but the rules change according to the loan type as well. For example, it is common knowledge among real estate professionals that FHA and federal VA loans offer fairly liberal qualifying standards.

Determining the borrower's capacity is, in the final analysis, an art, not a science. Nevertheless, lenders have rules and guidelines and real estate agents should be aware of them. In times past, real estate agents were taught to find the maximum price home the buyer could afford just by multiplying the buyer's gross annual income by two and a half Such simplistic rules are not adequate in today's lending market.

Lenders today qualify the borrower by placing their major emphasis on two ratios. The first is the ratio of the borrower's monthly housing costs to total gross income (commonly called the ***housing cost ratio,*** or sometimes the ***front-end ratio***. Monthly housing costs include the amounts necessary for principal and interest, one-twelfth the annual property taxes and one-twelfth the annual fire insurance premiums, plus the amount needed each month for association dues (required in condominiums and some subdivisions). Most lenders insist that the ratio not exceed 28%, although FHA will allow up to 29%. The following example of a typical borrower demonstrates the calculation –

Assume buyers with $54,000 annual gross income, buying a home for $170,000 with a $20,000 down payment. The loan will be a fixed rate conventional, and market interest rates at the time are 7%. Property taxes on the home will be $2,400 per year and the annual premium for the homeowner's insurance policy will be $480. There are no homeowners' association dues.

Monthly principal and interest on $150,000 at 7% for 30 years	$998
One-twelfth annual property taxes ($2,400 ÷ 12)	200
One-twelfth annual insurance premium ($480 ÷ 12)	40
Total monthly housing cost	$1,238

Gross monthly income ($54,000 ÷ 12) = $4,500
Ratio of monthly housing expense to gross income ($1,238 ÷ $4,500) = 27.5%

The second factor is the ratio of the borrower's total debt payments (including the proposed mortgage loan) to the borrower's gross monthly income. This ratio is frequently called the ***total debt service ratio***, or sometimes the ***back-end ratio*** Total debt payments include car payments, credit cards, alimony and child support, student loans – everything that the borrower is obligated to pay each month. The FHA and the federal Department of Veterans Affairs will go as high as 41%, and most conventional lenders will allow the ratio of total debt payments to gross income to go as high as 43%, although some are more strict.

Assume the same buyer as in the previous example, and assume that the buyer has a monthly car payment of $220 and monthly credit card and other installments of $320.

Total monthly housing costs (from above example)	$1,238
Car payment	220
Credit card payments	320
Total debt service	$1,778

Gross monthly income ($54,000 ÷ 12) = $4,500
Ratio of total monthly debt service to gross income ($1,778 ÷ $4,500) = 39.5%

In the preceding examples, the borrower qualified comfortably on both ratios. In the real world, it is not uncommon for lenders to encounter a borrower who qualifies comfortably on one ratio, but does not quite qualify on the other. Depending on the circumstances, lenders may bend the rules by a percent or two on one ratio if the borrower qualifies well on the other.

Lenders also take into account the reliability and stability of the borrower's income. Length of time on the job and the type of occupation all have a bearing on underwriting. Overtime pay and bonuses, for example, may be included if they are sufficiently regular that they can be counted on. In some cases, the law requires lenders to include certain income. For example, the Equal Credit Opportunity Act (see Chapter 14) requires that both incomes be counted when the borrowers are husband and wife.

Both the debt ratios above are modified somewhat when the initial interest rate is lowered, as in a GPM loan, an ARM loan, or a loan with a buydown. Lenders are aware that the payment may increase, so the qualifying ratios tend to be slightly higher.

In addition to the ratios above, lenders typically verify that the borrower has the funds to close. If the source of the down payment and closing costs will be a gift or other source, the source must be identified. Not only do lenders insist on knowing where the funds to close are coming from, they also typically expect to see the borrower have enough cash left over after closing equal to two months payments.

Credit scoring

Most lenders today use credit scoring, a system of assigning point values to aspects of the borrower's profile. Credit scoring started in the last half of 1970s when the Equal Credit Opportunity Act went into effect. The Act prohibited discrimination against borrowers, and lenders were initially afraid they would be sued if they turned a loan down. Point scoring was seen as a way to neutralize the loan approval process and safeguard the lender against discrimination claims. (For more information about the Equal Credit Opportunity Act, see Chapter 14.)

Although lenders are now comfortable with discrimination issues, credit scoring has become the norm because it avoids personal attitudes of the loan officer from coloring the approval process. The majority of residential loans today are brokered, and the mortgage broker receives no compensation unless the loan is made. Therefore, the institution making the loan knows the broker will try to present the loan in the best light possible. Credit scoring helps balance the broker's excess enthusiasm.

The score looks at past delinquencies, derogatory payment behavior, current debt level, length of credit history, types of past credit and the number of inquiries. For example, if the borrower has a past history of a loan from a finance company or other high-risk lender, this has a negative impact on the score. Similarly, if the borrower has a lot of recent credit inquiries from other lenders, it is a caution sign – the borrower may be attempting to solve financial problems by seeking additional loans.

Point scoring today is based on a statistical analysis system developed by Fair, Isaac Company (commonly called the FICO score). All three of the above national credit bureaus do it the same way, although they call it by different names. Equifax calls it the "Beacon," TransUnion calls it "Empirica," and Experian uses the original name "Fair, Isaac." The score is reported in a range from 350 to 900 points. A score of zero means there was insufficient data in the credit file to generate a score. The following chart gives an idea of what most lenders consider in credit scoring. Notice that even an A+ loan can have a couple of revolving past dues and one installment past due –

Credit Score	Debt Ratio	Max LTV	Mortgage Past Dues			Revolving Past Dues			Installment Past Dues		
			30	60	90	30	60	90	30	60	90
A+	670+	36%-	95%	0	0	0	2	0	0	1	0	0
A	660	45%	95%	1	0	0	3	1	0	2	0	0
B	620	50%	85%	2	1	0	4	2	1	3	1	0
C	580	55%	75%	4	2	1	6	5	2	5	4	1

Borrowers with a score above 670 will qualify for an A+ loan. Credit approval will be completed within minutes, probably through a computerized automated underwriting system. The loan can be closed as soon as the appraisal is complete, usually within a few days. Interest will be at the best rates current in the market. A score of 660 to 670 (an A rating) will probably also gain a good interest rate, but the approval process will take longer, as the lender will have to take a look at supplemental credit information. The borrower should expect inquiries to explain the delinquencies, and the responses may need further verification.

Borrowers with a B rating will not qualify for Fannie Mae and Freddie Mac guidelines, so the loan originator will have to find an alternative secondary market for the loan. It may take some time before a suitable market is found, and investors in such markets demand rates one to two percent higher than prime mortgage rates.

Here are some samples to demonstrate how the statistics work out –
- Scores below 601 yield eight good loans for each bad one
- Scores between 700 and 729 yield 129 good loans for each bad one
- Scores above 800 yield 1,292 good loans for each bad one

Creditors, of course, receive the full statistical breakdown from the credit reporting agency so they can assess the exact odds that a given score will be loan.

Among professional lenders, however, "FICO" has come to be distrusted. Its purpose is just to alert the lender that more investigation is in order. Unfortunately, a lot of lenders just go by the score and little else.

Professional lenders know that the FICO score is just statistics and nothing more. The Fair, Isaac Company created their models based on various criteria, but those issues don't necessarily apply in all cases. For example, although the Fair, Isaac Company maintains their statistical models as proprietary, they have recognized that they use five categories –
- Previous credit history
- Current amount of debt
- Amount of time the borrower has used credit
- How often the borrower has made application for credit
- Types of credit available

Looking at these criteria it's easy to see inconsistencies and faults. For example, look at how often the borrower has made application for credit. This could be an indication that the borrower is desperately trying to borrow money in order to stave off defaults on other obligations. Or it could mean that the borrower is shopping for the best loan terms. Or it might mean absolutely nothing at all. The problem is that the credit agency furnishes the lender with the final FICO score with no explanation of how it was derived. Professionals know that the score is not necessarily a correct indicator.

Fannie Mae and Freddie Mac publish guidelines for loans they will purchase or securitize. In addition to credit qualifications and income to debt ratios above, these guidelines include –
- Loans greater than 80% loan to value ratio must be insured for the amount of the loan exceeding 80% by an insurance company outside of the lender's control.
- Buydowns are permitted for all loans except ARMs.
- The seller cannot contribute toward the borrower's closing costs more than the lesser of 6% of the sales price or appraised value on 90% loans, and 3% on loans over 90% loan to value ratio.
- The borrower may receive gifts for most loan programs, but only from relatives and, if the loan is over 80% loan to value ratio, the borrower must have a personal investment of at least 5%. Gift funds must be documented with a gift letter stating that the funds need not be repaid, and must be verified to be sure the donor did not secretly borrow the money.
- Co-borrowers, cosigners and guarantors do not need to take title to the property. Their income is considered, providing they sign the promissory note. If the loan is over 90% loan to value ratio, the co-borrower must occupy the property to have his or her income considered.

Prequalification and preapproval

These days residential agents find it is imperative for the buyer to have inquired about financing before they begin shopping for a home. Some lenders offer prequalification, and others provide preapproval.

Prequalification means the lender has issued a letter stating that, based on the income the potential borrower has stated, the person should be able to obtain a loan of a certain amount. Preapproval means the lender has run the credit report as well as the potential borrower's credit history. The result is a letter stating that the person should be approved for a loan of a certain amount, subject only to the appraisal.

No-doc and low-doc loans

Many borrowers have a difficult time demonstrating their income. Perhaps they are self-employed, receive income irregularly from commissions, or live off investments. Other borrowers insist on maximum privacy. For such borrowers there are options that may be preferable to the standard loan process with its reams of paperwork and intrusive investigations.

There are three kinds of loans borrowers like this might wish to consider –

Stated income loan – A *stated income mortgage* is good for a borrower who works, but doesn't draw regular wages or salary from an employer, such as a self-employed borrower or someone who makes a living off commissions. The borrower on a stated income mortgage must disclose annual earnings, usually for the past two years, by showing tax returns, bank statements, assets and debts, and possibly other documentation. The borrower must also list debts so the lender can determine the debt to income ratio. A stated income mortgage would cost anywhere from one eighth of a percentage point above the conventional rate to more than a whole percentage point higher.

No-ratio loans – A *no-ratio* loan is a loan where the usual debt and income ratios are ignored. The borrower is expected to list assets, however. The interest is generally about a half a percent to two percent higher than mortgage prime. For the lender to remain secure, loan to value ratios are 80% or less; for non-owner occupied property 70% loan to value ratios are common. No-ratio loans are favored by real estate investors who would otherwise have very high debt ratios.

No-doc loans – *No-doc* or *NINA* (no income/no asset verification) mortgages are for creditworthy people who want maximum privacy and are willing to pay for it. Interest rates are generally one to three percent higher than mortgage prime. No-income/no-asset verification mortgages require the least documentation. In some cases the borrower provides his or her name, social security number, the amount of the down payment and the address of the property. The lender gets a credit report and a property appraisal and that's all. The borrower does need to have an excellent credit report.

Forms

On the following pages you will find three of the dozens of forms that a residential borrower must complete at time of loan application –

Uniform Residential Loan Application, Form 1003
Fannie Mae Request for Verification of Employment, Form 1005
Fannie Mae Request for Verification of Deposit, form 1006

⚿ KEY TERMS

The key to understanding any new field is the vocabulary used in that field. To maximize your comprehension of the material presented in this chapter, be sure you know the meaning and significance of the following terms. Remember that the majority of test questions primarily test knowledge of vocabulary.

Adjustable rate mortgage	Federal VA
Adjustment cap	Flat rate buydown
Allowable closing costs	Flex fixed rate temporary buydown
Amortization	Front-end ratio
Annual cap	Fully indexed rate
Assumption	Funding fee
Assumption agreement	Graduated payment mortgage
Automatic lender	Graduated rate buydown
Back-end ratio	Growing equity mortgage
Balloon payment	Guaranty
Bi-weekly loans	Housing cost ratio
Blind assumption	Hybrid mortgage loan
Buydown	Index
Call feature	Interim cap
Cap	Interim financing
Certificate of reasonable value	Introductory rate ARM
Character	Jumbo mortgage
Collateral	Lifetime cap
Completion bond	Low income tax credit
Conforming loan	Materialman's lien
Construction draw	Mechanic's lien
Construction financing	Mutual mortgage insurance
Conventional loan	Negative amortization
Conversion privilege	NINA loan
Credit	No-ratio loan
Capacity	No-doc loan
CRV	Non-conforming loans
Department of Veterans Affairs	Novation
Direct endorsement	Participating lender
Early issue	Payment cap
Entitlement	Payment shock
Fair Credit Reporting Act	Permanent buydown
Farm Credit System	Permanent loan
Farm Service Agency	Private mortgage insurance
Federal Agricultural Mortgage Corporation	Rollover clause
Federal GI	Rural Housing Service
Federal Housing Administration	Section 203 (b)

Uniform Residential Loan Application

This application is designed to be completed by the applicant(s) with the Lender's assistance. Applicants should complete this form as "Borrower" or "Co-Borrower", as applicable. Co-Borrower information must also be provided (and the appropriate box checked) when ☐ the income or assets of a person other than the "Borrower" (including Borrower's spouse) will be used as a basis for loan qualification or ☐ the income or assets of the Borrower's spouse will not be used as a basis for loan qualification, but his or her liabilities must be considered because the Borrower resides in a community property state, the security property is located in a community property state, or the Borrower is relying on other property located in a community property state as a basis for repayment of the loan.

I. TYPE OF MORTGAGE AND TERMS OF LOAN

Mortgage Applied for:	☐ VA ☐ Conventional ☐ Other: ☐ FHA ☐ FmHA	Agency Case Number	Lender Case Number

Amount $	Interest Rate %	No. of Months	Amortization Type:	☐ Fixed Rate ☐ GPM	☐ Other (explain): ☐ ARM (type):

II. PROPERTY INFORMATION AND PURPOSE OF LOAN

Subject Property Address (street, city, state & zip code)	No. of Units

Legal Description of Subject Property (attach description if necessary)	Year Built

Purpose of Loan	☐ Purchase ☐ Construction ☐ Other (explain): ☐ Refinance ☐ Construction-Permanent	Property will be: ☐ Primary Residence ☐ Secondary Residence ☐ Investment

Complete this line if construction or construction-permanent loan.

Year Lot Acquired	Original Cost $	Amount Existing Liens $	(a) Present Value of lot $	(b) Cost of Improvements $	Total (a + b) $

Complete this line if this is a refinance loan.

Year Acquired	Original Cost $	Amount Existing Liens $	Purpose of Refinance	Describe Improvements ☐ made ☐ to be made Cost: $

Title will be held in what Name(s)	Manner in which Title will be held	Estate will be held in: ☐ Fee Simple ☐ Leasehold (show expiration date)

Source of Down Payment, Settlement Charges and/or Subordinate Financing (explain)	

III. BORROWER INFORMATION

Borrower	Co-Borrower
Borrower's Name (include Jr. or Sr. if applicable)	Co-Borrower's Name (include Jr. or Sr. if applicable)

Social Security Number	Home Phone (incl. area code)	Age	Yrs. School	Social Security Number	Home Phone (incl. area code)	Age	Yrs. School

☐ Married ☐ Separated ☐ Unmarried (include single, divorced, widowed)	Dependents (not listed by Co-Borrower) no. ages	☐ Married ☐ Separated ☐ Unmarried (include single, divorced, widowed)	Dependents (not listed by Borrower) no. ages

Present Address (street, city, state, zip code) ☐ Own ☐ Rent No. Yrs:	Present Address (street, city, state, zip code) ☐ Own ☐ Rent No. Yrs:

If residing at present address for less than two years, complete the following:

Former Address (street, city, state, zip code) ☐ Own ☐ Rent No. Yrs:	Former Address (street, city, state, zip code) ☐ Own ☐ Rent No. Yrs:

Former Address (street, city, state, zip code) ☐ Own ☐ Rent No. Yrs:	Former Address (street, city, state, zip code) ☐ Own ☐ Rent No. Yrs:

IV. EMPLOYMENT INFORMATION

Borrower	Co-Borrower
Name & Address of Employer ☐ Self Employed	Years on this job: Years employed in this line of work/profession:	Name & Address of Employer ☐ Self Employed	Years on this job: Years employed in this line of work/profession:

Position/Title/Type of Business	Business Phone (incl. area code)	Position/Title/Type of Business	Business Phone (incl. area code)

If employed in current position for less than two years or if currently employed in more than one position, complete the following:

Name & Address of Employer ☐ Self Employed	Dates (from - to): Monthly Income $	Name & Address of Employer ☐ Self Employed	Dates (from - to): Monthly Income $

Position/Title/Type of Business	Business Phone (incl. area code)	Position/Title/Type of Business	Business Phone (incl. area code)

Name & Address of Employer ☐ Self Employed	Dates (from - to): Monthly Income $	Name & Address of Employer ☐ Self Employed	Dates (from - to): Monthly Income $

Position/Title/Type of Business	Business Phone (incl. area code)	Position/Title/Type of Business	Business Phone (incl. area code)

V. MONTHLY INCOME AND COMBINED EXPENSE INFORMATION

Gross Monthly Income	Borrower	Co-Borrower	Total	Combined Monthly Housing Expense	Present	Proposed
Self Empl. Income *	$	$	$	Rent	$	
Overtime				First Mortgage (P & I)		$
Bonuses				Other Financing (P & I)		
Commissions				Hazard Insurance		
Dividends/Interest				Real Estate Taxes		
Net Rental Income				Mortgage Insurance		
Other (before completing, see the notice in "describe other income," below)				Homeowner Assn. Dues		
				Other:		
Total	$	$	$	Total	$	$

* Self Employed Borrower(s) may be required to provide additional documentation such as tax returns and financial statements.

	Describe Other Income	Notice: Alimony, child support, or separate maintenance income need not be revealed if the Borrower (B) or Co-Borrower (C) doesn't choose to have it considered for repaying this loan.	Monthly Amount
B/C			$
			$
			$

VI. ASSETS AND LIABILITIES

This Statement and any applicable supporting schedule may be completed jointly by both married and unmarried Co-Borrowers if their assets and liabilities are sufficiently joined so that the Statement can be meaningfully and fairly presented on a combined basis; otherwise separate Statements and Schedules are required. If the Co-Borrower section was completed about a spouse, this Statement and supporting schedules must be completed about that spouse also.

Completed ☐ Jointly ☐ Not Jointly

ASSETS Description	Cash or Market Value	Liabilities and Pledged Assets. List the creditor's name, address and account number for all outstanding debts, including automobile loans, revolving charge accounts, real estate loans, alimony, child support, stock pledges, etc. Use continuation sheet, if necessary. Indicate by (*) those liabilities which will be satisfied upon sale of real estate owned or upon refinancing of the subject property.		
Cash deposit toward purchase held by:	$	LIABILITIES	Monthly Payt. & Mos. Left to Pay	Unpaid Balance
		Name and address of Company	$ Payt./Mos.	$
List checking and savings accounts below				
Name and address of Bank, S & L, or Credit Union				
		Acct. no.		
		Name and address of Company	$ Payt./Mos.	$
Acct. no.	$			
Name and address of Bank, S & L, or Credit Union				
		Acct. no.		
Acct. no.	$	Name and address of Company	$ Payt./Mos.	$
Name and address of Bank, S & L, or Credit Union				
		Acct. no.		
Acct. no.	$	Name and address of Company	$ Payt./Mos.	$
Name and address of Bank, S & L, or Credit Union				
Acct. no.	$			
Stock & Bonds (Company name/number & description)	$	Acct. no.		
		Name and address of Company	$ Payt./Mos.	$
Life Insurance net cash value Face amount: $	$			
Subtotal Liquid Assets	$	Acct. no.		
Real estate owned (enter market value from schedule of real estated owned)	$	Name and address of Company	$ Payt./Mos.	$
Vested interest in retirement fund	$			
Net worth of business(es) owned (attach financial statement)	$	Acct. no.		
Automobiles owned (make and year)	$	Name and address of Company	$ Payt./Mos.	$
Other Assets (itemize)	$	Acct. no.		
		Alimony/Child Suppport/Separate Maintenance Payments Owed to	$	
		Job Related Expense (child care, union dues, etc.)	$	
		Total Monthly Payments	$	
Total Assets a.	$	Net Worth (a minus b) $	**Total Liabilities b.**	$

VI. ASSETS AND LIABILITIES (cont.)

Schedule of Real Estate Owned (if additional properties are owned, use continuation sheet.)

Property Address (enter S if sold, PS if pending sale or is it rental being held for income)	Type of Property	Present Market Value	Amount of Mortgage & Liens	Gross Rental Income	Mortgage Payments	Insurance, Maintenance, Taxes & Misc.	Net Rental Income
		$	$	$	$	$	$
	Totals	$	$	$	$	$	$

List any additional names under which credit has previously been received and indicate appropriate creditor name(s) and account number(s):

Alternative Name	Creditor Name	Account Number

VII. DETAILS OF TRANSACTION | VIII. DECLARATIONS

VII. DETAILS OF TRANSACTION		VIII. DECLARATIONS				
		If you answer "Yes" to any questions a through i, please use continuation sheet for explanation.	Borrower Yes	No	Co-Borrower Yes	No
a. Purchase price	$	a. Are there any outstanding judgements against you?	☐	☐	☐	☐
b. Alterations, improvements, repairs		b. Have you been declared bankrupt within the past 7 years?	☐	☐	☐	☐
c. Land (if acquired separately)		c. Have you had property foreclosed upon or given title or deed in lieu thereof in the last 7 years?	☐	☐	☐	☐
d. Refinance (incl. in debts to be paid off)		d. Are you a party to a lawsuit?	☐	☐	☐	☐
e. Estimated prepaid items		e. Have you directly or indirectly been obligated on any loan which resulted in foreclosure, transfer of title in lieu of foreclosure, or judgement? (This would include such loans as home mortgage loans, SBA loans, home improvement loans, educational loans, manufactured (mobile) home loans, any mortgage, financial obligation, bond, or loan guarantee. If "Yes," provide details, including date, name and address of Lender, FHA or VA case number, if any, and reasons for the action.)	☐	☐	☐	☐
f. Estimated closing costs						
g. PMI, MIP, Funding Fee paid in cash						
h. Discount (if Borrower will pay)						
i. otal costs (add items a through h)		f. Are you presently delinquent or in default on any Federal debt or any other loan, mortgage, financial obligation, bond, or loan guarantee? If "Yes," give details as described in the preceding question.	☐	☐	☐	☐
j. Subordinate financing		g. Are you obligated to pay alimony, child support or separate maintenance?	☐	☐	☐	☐
k. Borrower's closing costs paid by Seller		h. Is any part of the down payment borrowed?	☐	☐	☐	☐
l. Other Credits (explain)		i. Are you a co-maker or endorser on a note?	☐	☐	☐	☐
		j. Are you a U.S. citizen?				
		Are you a permanent resident alien?				
		l. Do you intend to occupy the property as your primary residence? If "Yes," complete question below.	☐	☐	☐	☐
m. Loan amount (exclude PMI, MIP, Funding Fee financed)		m. Have you had an ownership interest in a property in the last three years?				
n. PMI, MIP, Funding Fee financed		(1) What type of property did you own -- principal residence (PR), second home (SH), or Investment Property (IP)?			___	
o. Loan amount (add m & n)		(2) How did you hold title to the home -- solely by yourself (S), jointly with your spouse (SP), or jointly with another person (O)?			___	
p. Cash from/to Borrower (subtract j, k, l & o from i)						

IX. ACKNOWLEDGEMENT AND AGREEMENT

The undersigned specifically acknowledge(s) and agree(s) that: (1) the loan requested by this application will be secured by a first mortgage or deed of trust on the property described herein: (2) the property will not be used for any illegal or prohibited purpose or use; (3) all statements made in this application are made for the purpose of obtaining the loan indicated herein; (4) occupation of the property will be indicated above; (5) verification or reverification of any information contained in the application may be made at any time by the Lender, its agents, successors and assigns, either directly or through a credit reporting agency, from any source named in this application, and the original copy of this application will be retained by the Lender, even if the loan is not approved; (6) the Lender, its agents, successors and assigns will rely on the information in the application and I/we have a continuing obligation to amend and/or supplement the information provided in this application if any of the material facts which I/we have represented herein should change prior to closing; (7) in the event my/our payments on the loan indicated in this application become delinquent, the Lender, its agents successors and assigns, may, in addition to all their other rights and remedies, report my/our name(s) and account information to a credit reporting agency; (8) ownership of the loan may be transferred to successor assign of the Lender without notice to me and/or the administration of the loan account may be transferred to an agent, successor or assign of the Lender with prior notice to me: (9) the Lender, its agents, successors and assigns make no representations or warranties, express or implied, to the Borrower(s) regarding the property, the condition of the property, or the value of the property.

Right to Receive Copy of Appraisal. I/We have the right to a copy of the appraisal report used in connection with this application for credit. To obtain a copy, I/We must send Lender written request at the mailing address Lender has provided. Lender must hear from me/us no later than 90 days after Lender notifies me/us about the action taken on this application, or I/we withdraw this application.

Certification: I/We certify that the information provided in this application is true and correct as of the date set forth opposite my/our signature(s) on this application and acknowledge my/our understanding that any intentional or negligent misrepresentation(s) of the information contained in this application may result in civil liability and/or criminal penalties including, but not limited to, fine or imprisonment or both under the provisions of Title 18, United States Code, Section 1001, et seq. and liability for monetary damages to the Lender, its agents, successors or assigns, insurers and any other person who may suffer any loss due to reliance upon any misrepresentation which I/We have made on this application.

Borrower's Signature	Date	Co-Borrower's Signature	Date
X		X	

X. INFORMATION FOR GOVERNMENT MONITORING PURPOSES

The following information is requested by the Federal government for certain types of loans related to a dwelling, in order to monitor the Lender's compliance with equal credit opportunity, fair housing and home mortgage disclosure laws. You are not required to furnish this information, but are encouraged to do so. The law provides that a Lender may neither discriminate on the basis of this information, not on whether you choose to furnish it. However, if you choose not to furnish it, under Federal regulations this Lender is required to note race and sex on the basis of visual observation or surname. If you do not wish to furnish the above information, please check the box below. (Lender must review the above material to assure that the disclosures satisfy all requirements to which the Lender is subject under applicable state law for the particular type of loan applied for.)

BORROWER

Race/National Origin:
☐ I do not wish to furnish this information
☐ American Indian or Alaskan Native
☐ Asian or Pacific Islander
☐ White, not of Hispanic origin
☐ Black, not of Hispanic origin
☐ Hispanic
☐ Other (specify)

Sex: ☐ Female ☐ Male

CO-BORROWER

Race/National Origin:
☐ I do not wish to furnish this information
☐ American Indian or Alaskan Native
☐ Asian or Pacific Islander
☐ White, not of Hispanic origin
☐ Black, not of Hispanic origin
☐ Hispanic
☐ Other (specify)

Sex: ☐ Female ☐ Male

To be Completed by Interviewer This application was taken by:	Interviewer's Name (print or type)	Name and Address of Interviewer's Employer
☐ face-to-face interview	Interviewer's Signature Date	
☐ by mail		
☐ by telephone	Interviewer's Phone Number (incl. area code)	

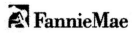

Request for Verification of Employment

Privacy Act Notice: This information is to be used by the agency collecting it or its assignees in determining whether you qualify as a prospective mortgagor under its program. It will not be disclosed outside the agency except as required and permitted by law. You do not have to provide this information, but if you do not your application for approval as a prospective mortgagor or borrower may be delayed or rejected. The information requested in this form is authorized by Title 38, USC, Chapter 37 (if VA); by 12 USC, Section 1701 et. seq. (if HUD/FHA); by 42 USC, Section 1452b (if HUD/CPD); and Title 42 USC, 1471 et. seq., or 7 USC, 1921 et. seq. (if USDA/FmHA).

Instructions: Lender — Complete items 1 through 7. Have applicant complete item 8. Forward directly to employer named in item 1.
Employer — Please complete either Part II or Part III as applicable. Complete Part IV and return directly to lender named in item 2.
The form is to be transmitted directly to the lender and is not to be transmitted through the applicant or any other party.

Part I — Request

1. To (Name and address of employer)	2. From (Name and address of lender)

I certify that this verification has been sent directly to the employer and has not passed through the hands of the applicant or any other interested party.

3. Signature of Lender	4. Title	5. Date	6. Lender's Number (Optional)

I have applied for a mortgage loan and stated that I am now or was formerly employed by you. My signature below authorizes verification of this information.

7. Name and Address of Applicant (include employee or badge number)	8. Signature of Applicant

Part II — Verification of Present Employment

9. Applicant's Date of Employment	10. Present Position	11. Probability of Continued Employment

12A. Current Gross Base Pay (Enter Amount and Check Period)

☐ Annual ☐ Hourly
☐ Monthly ☐ Other (Specify)
$ _____ ☐ Weekly

12B. Gross Earnings

Type	Year To Date	Past Year 19___	Past Year 19___
Base Pay	Thru _____ 19__ $	$	$
Overtime	$	$	$
Commissions	$	$	$
Bonus	$	$	$
Total	$	$	$

13. For Military Personnel Only

Pay Grade

Type	Monthly Amount
Base Pay	$
Rations	$
Flight or Hazard	$
Clothing	$
Quarters	$
Pro Pay	$
Overseas or Combat	$
Variable Housing Allowance	$

14. If Overtime or Bonus is Applicable, Is Its Continuance Likely?

Overtime ☐ Yes ☐ No
Bonus ☐ Yes ☐ No

15. If paid hourly — average hours per week

16. Date of applicant's next pay increase

17. Projected amount of next pay increase

18. Date of applicant's last pay increase

19. Amount of last pay increase

20. Remarks (If employee was off work for any length of time, please indicate time period and reason)

Part III — Verification of Previous Employment

21. Date Hired	23. Salary/Wage at Termination Per (Year) (Month) (Week)
22. Date Terminated	Base _____ Overtime _____ Commissions _____ Bonus _____
24. Reason for Leaving	25. Position Held

Part IV — Authorized Signature - Federal statutes provide severe penalties for any fraud, intentional misrepresentation, or criminal connivance or conspiracy purposed to influence the issuance of any guaranty or insurance by the VA Secretary, the U.S.D.A., FmHA/FHA Commissioner, or the HUD/CPD Assistant Secretary.

26. Signature of Employer	27. Title (Please print or type)	28. Date
29. Print or type name signed in Item 26	30. Phone No.	

Fannie Mae
Form 1005   July 96

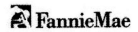

Request for Verification of Deposit

Privacy Act Notice: This information is to be used by the agency collecting it or its assignees in determining whether you qualify as a prospective mortgagor under its program. It will not be disclosed outside the agency except as required and permitted by law. You do not have to provide this information, but if you do not your application for approval as a prospective mortgagor or borrower may be delayed or rejected. The information requested in this form is authorized by Title 38, USC, Chapter 37 (If VA); by 12 USC, Section 1701 et.seq. (If HUD/FHA); by 42 USC, Section 1452b (If HUD/CPD); and Title 42 USC, 1471 et.seq. or 7 USC, 1921 et.seq. (If USDA/FmHA).

Instructions: Lender — Complete Items 1 through 8. Have applicant(s) complete item 9. Forward directly to depository named in Item 1.
Depository — Please complete Items 10 through 18 and return DIRECTLY to lender named in Item 2.
The form is to be transmitted directly to the lender and is not to be transmitted through the applicant(s) or any other party.

Part I — Request

1. To (Name and address of depository)	2. From (Name and address of lender)

I certify that this verification has been sent directly to the bank or depository and has not passed through the hands of the applicant or any other party.

3. Signature of lender	4. Title	5. Date	6. Lender's No. (Optional)

7. Information To Be Verified

Type of Account	Account in Name of	Account Number	Balance
			$
			$
			$

To Depository: I/We have applied for a mortgage loan and stated in my financial statement that the balance on deposit with you is as shown above. You are authorized to verify this information and to supply the lender identified above with the information requested in Items 10 through 13. Your response is solely a matter of courtesy for which no responsibility is attached to your institution or any of your officers.

8. Name and Address of Applicant(s)	9. Signature of Applicant(s)

To Be Completed by Depository
Part II — Verification of Depository

10. Deposit Accounts of Applicant(s)

Type of Account	Account Number	Current Balance	Average Balance For Previous Two Months	Date Opened
		$	$	
		$	$	
		$	$	

11. Loans Outstanding To Applicant(s)

Loan Number	Date of Loan	Original Amount	Current Balance	Installments (Monthly/Quarterly)		Secured By	Number of Late Payments
		$	$	$	per		
		$	$	$	per		
		$	$	$	per		

12. Please include any additional information which may be of assistance in determination of credit worthiness. (Please include information on loans paid-in-full in Item 11 above.)

13. If the name(s) on the account(s) differ from those listed in Item 7, please supply the name(s) on the account(s) as reflected by your records.

Part III — Authorized Signature
- Federal statutes provide severe penalties for any fraud, intentional misrepresentation, or criminal connivance or conspiracy purposed to influence the issuance of any guaranty or insurance by the VA Secretary, the U.S.D.A., FmHA/FHA Commissioner, or the HUD/CPD Assistant Secretary.

14. Signature of Depository Representative	15. Title (Please print or type)	16. Date
17. Please print or type name signed in item 14	18. Phone No.	

Fannie Mae
Form 1006   July 96

Chapter

14

Lending regulations

L ENDERS IN TODAY'S WORLD must deal with a multitude of laws and rules. While many regulations involve government organizations which insure and guarantee loans, such as FHA and the Department of Veterans Affairs, even lenders who make nothing but conventional loans have to deal with rules. The secondary mortgage market, for example, dictates what kind of loans they will buy. In addition, to these rules, there are a variety of consumer protection laws that lenders must observe. In this chapter we will explore those consumer laws which affect lending practices.

Truth in Lending Act

Of all consumer protection laws, the most significant for lenders is the **Consumer Protection Act of 1968**. This law is so large it is divided into various separate areas. Title I of the Consumer Protection Act includes the **Truth in Lending Act**, a thorough knowledge of which is not only essential today for lenders, but for real estate agents as well.

The Truth in Lending Act empowers the Board of Governors of the Federal Reserve Bank to create reasonable regulations as are necessary to implement the purposes of the Act. The resulting rules are called Federal Reserve Regulation Z, and have the force and effect of law. You may hear lenders refer to these laws just as "Truth in Lending" or just as "Regulation Z," but in fact lenders use either term loosely to refer to both the Act and the Regulation together.

The concept of the Truth in Lending Act and Regulation Z is simple – lenders must disclose loan terms to prospective borrowers so the borrowers can shop for credit more easily. There are endless ways to calculate interest, most of which the average consumer does not understand. Furthermore, lenders might make a loan at a low interest rate, but make up for the low rate by requiring loan fees, discount points and other charges. Prior to the Truth in Lending Act and Regulation Z it was virtually impossible for consumers to know which lender offered the best terms. Now, not only must loan terms be disclosed, but all lenders must use the same rules when calculating the actual cost of the financing.

One thing the Truth in Lending Act and Regulation Z do not affect is the interest rate and the fees lenders are allowed to charge. Many states set the maximum interest rates for different types of loans. These are called usury rates. However, there are no federal usury laws. Washington usury laws are discussed later in this chapter. The point to understand is that the Truth in Lending Act and Regulation Z are strictly disclosure laws. Lenders can charge whatever they want; they just have to disclose it in meaningful ways as required by the law.

Although Regulation Z was created by the Federal Reserve Bank Board of Governors, both it and the Truth in Lending Act are enforced by other federal agencies. For non-institutional lenders and real estate agents, the Federal Trade Commission has the responsibility to ensure compliance. Intentional violations can result in a fine of up to $5,000 and/or imprisonment for up to one year. Unintentional violations are a civil matter between the lender and the borrower. The borrower can sue the lender for actual damages, and in addition, punitive damages equal to twice the amount of the finance charge (minimum $100, maximum $1,000), and the borrower is also entitled to recover reasonable attorney's fees. The $1,000 maximum does not apply to class action suits.

Who must comply – Only persons and entities who regularly extend credit (creditors) or who arrange credit (arrangers of credit) must comply with the Truth in Lending Act and Regulation Z. For residential real estate, Regulation Z defines such a person or entity as one who has made five loans during the current or preceding year. Note that real estate agents regularly arrange credit, so every real estate agent must know how to comply with the Truth in Lending Laws.

However, certain loans are exempt. Business, commercial and agricultural credit is exempt. Loans to corporations and entities other than natural persons are exempt. Loans over $25,000 on personal property are exempt, although this exemption does not apply if the loan is secured by real estate. Loans are also exempt if they are to be repaid in four or fewer installments (in addition to the down payment). A loan where no finance charge is made is exempt; but if a creditor gives discounts for cash to buyers of the same merchandise, the cash discount normally granted to such buyers is considered a finance charge for those who elect to use credit.

How to comply – There are various disclosures required under the Truth in Lending Act. Not all disclosures must be made in all situations. In general, the law distinguishes between disclosures required in the actual extension of credit, and disclosures required when advertising the availability of credit. Real estate agents arrange and advertise credit, but do not usually extend credit, so agents generally need to be concerned only with disclosures required when advertising the availability of credit.

Note, however, that if a real estate licensee takes a loan application for a lender, the licensee is acting as agent of the lender, and will probably be required to make disclosures on behalf of the lender.

Before making disclosures to the borrower, the annual percentage rate, finance charge and total amount financed must be calculated. These are discussed below.

The Annual Percentage Rate (APR) – When interest rates are stated, they must usually be stated as an ***annual percentage rate***, although in advertising, the term may be abbreviated to "APR."

Although there are exceptions, the general rule for stating the annual percentage rate is that it should be stated as an annual rate, not as a periodic rate (for example, "12% APR," not "1% per month APR." The rate must be accurate to within ⅛ of 1%.

The idea of the annual percentage rate is to divide the total finance charge (see below) by the number of years the loan will be in force, and again by the amount financed. However, this does not work for loans with more than one payment. For real estate loans, which typically involve many payments on a declining principal balance, calculating the annual percentage rate involves extremely complex formulas. In some cases it may be possible for a real estate agent to calculate the annual percentage rate with a financial calculator, but in most cases it is best to get the lender to make the calculations.

Disclosing the annual percentage rate is a special problem for adjustable rate loans. In this case, disclosure must be made that the rate can increase, whether or not there are caps, and if there are caps, how high the maximum rates are. Also, if the initial rate is a "teaser rate" not related to the index, then the method by which the increases or decreases are calculated must be disclosed. The usual way to do this is to show a range of payments for the high and low possibilities.

Calculating the total finance charge – Lenders and arrangers of credit must disclose the ***total finance charge*** when offering or extending credit. Obviously, interest usually constitutes the bulk of the total finance charge, however, certain other charges must be included as well –

- Service charges, transaction charges and activity charges
- Points paid by the buyer, including loan fees and assumption fees
- Appraisal and credit report fees in non-residential loans
- Mortgage insurance premiums, including FHA and private mortgage insurance on conventional loans

The following items are *not* included in the total finance charge –

- Application fees, if they are charged to all applicants, whether or not credit is actually extended

- Late payment, return check and similar penalty charges
- Points paid by the seller
- Title insurance premiums
- Document preparation fees, including notarization and recording
- Amounts required to be paid into reserves for taxes and fire insurance
- Appraisal and credit report fees on a residential real estate loan

Certain other items must be included only in special cases. For example, premiums for credit life and/or disability insurance must be included as part of the total finance charge if the lender requires the borrower to carry it. Premiums for fire insurance must be included only if the lender requires the borrower to obtain the fire insurance from an agent of the lender's choosing. And fees for services rendered by third parties need not be included if the lender does not require the service and if the lender does not retain the fees.

Calculating the total amount financed – The total amount financed is the original loan balance plus other amounts financed by the lender which are not part of the total finance charge, less any prepaid finance charges.

For example, suppose a lender makes a $200,000 residential home loan. As we have seen above, the appraisal and credit report fees are not part of the total finance charge. So if the borrower pays these items separately at closing, then no disclosure need be made. But if the lender pays for the appraisal and credit report and then increases the loan amount to cover them, they must be included when calculating the total amount financed.

Prepaid finance charges must be subtracted in figuring the total amount financed. A prepaid finance charge is any part of the finance charge which the borrower pays directly to the lender or to a third party. A prepaid finance charge also includes any part of the loan amount which is withheld from the loan proceeds (not disbursed to the borrower).

Prepaid finance charges are common in real estate loans. For example, it is normal practice for lenders to require the payments to be due on the first of the month, with a full month between each payment. If a real estate loan closes on, say, April 16, then the lender will require that the borrower pay 15 days interest on closing (for the 16th through the 30th of the month), so the interest will be paid to May 1. The first monthly payment will be due June 1. The June 1 payment will include the interest which accrues during May.

What must be disclosed (in extending credit) – Although the following list is not exhaustive, lenders must usually disclose –

- The interest rate as an annual percentage rate
- The identity of the creditor
- The total finance change
- The loan amount, stated as the total amount financed
- The payment schedule
- The total of all payments

And where applicable, lenders must also disclose –

- If the loan is secured, and a description of the collateral
- The amount of any prepayment privilege charge (prepayment penalty)
- The date the finance charge begins, if different from the note
- The amount of any late charges or other penalties for default
- Whether or not the loan is assumable, and under what conditions
- The amount of any discounts or prepaid interest
- The amount of any tax and insurance reserve requirements
- Any other of the repayment terms

What must be disclosed (in advertising credit) – Full disclosure is required in advertising credit terms only if the advertisement contains specific statements about any of the following –

- The amount of the down payment
- The number of payments or the period of repayment
- The amount of any of the periodic installments
- The amount of any of the components of the total finance charge

General statements such as "low down payment" or "no down payment," "budget terms," "monthly payment terms" and the like do not trigger full disclosure. Also, stating the annual percentage rate does not trigger full disclosure, such as "9% APR loan available." Examples of statements which trigger full disclosure are "only 5% down," "pay off in 15 years," "only $825 per month" or "total move-in costs only $1,500."

Full disclosure requires that the advertising include at least the following –

- The annual percentage rate
- The down payment required
- The terms of repayment

The terms of repayment generally include the total finance charge as well as the number of payments, the amount of each payment and the period of payments (e.g., "360 equal monthly payments of $1,300"). However, if there are special terms such as irregular payments, balloon payments, call features, adjustable rates and the like, these terms must also be disclosed.

There is considerable latitude in the exact language used, as long as the disclosure is clear. For example, if the purchase price is $200,000 and the down payment is $40,000, this could be stated as a dollar amount ("$40,000"), as a percentage ("20% down") or even as a loan to value ratio ("80% financing").

Sometimes the annual percentage rate will be different from the actual rate on the note. This happens when there are loan fees and other charges which raise the annual percentage rate above the actual rate. In this case, it is acceptable to state the note rate, as long as the annual percentage rate is also stated, e.g., "Note rate 9% (9.5% APR)."

ADVERTISING REQUIREMENTS SUMMARY

Triggering Items
- Down payment
- Number of payments
- Term of the loan
- Amount of the payment
- Any part of the total finance charge

Items Which Do Not Trigger
- General statements
- The cash price
- That there is no down payment
- The annual percentage rate

Usual Advertising Requirements if Full Disclosure Triggered
- The annual percentage rate
- The down payment required
- The total finance charge
- Number, amount and period of payments
- Any additional special terms

NOTES

Right of rescission – In some credit transactions, borrowers may have a three-day **right of rescission**. This means the borrower can notify the lender in writing of the borrower's intent not to go through with the transaction. The parties then return to their original position; the lender's security position is void and any loan funds which have already been disbursed must be returned to the lender. If the right of rescission applies, the lender must give the borrower notice of this right.

The right of rescission applies only if the loan will result in a lien on the borrower's principal residence. However, loans for the *acquisition* of a personal residence are exempt from the right of rescission because at the time of obtaining the loan the property was not yet the borrower's residence. Also, even a loan to refinance a principal residence is exempt if the lender is also the existing creditor. Loans for business purposes are also exempt from the right of rescission, even if they result in a lien on the borrower's existing principal residence.

Miscellaneous – The Truth in Lending Act and Federal Reserve Regulation Z are very complicated laws. The material presented here should be considered a simplified overview of the subject. We have deliberately concentrated on real estate loans and largely ignored special requirements for unsecured loans and loans secured by personal property. Furthermore, you should always bear in mind that changes are constantly being made to reflect new loan programs. Real estate agents should always be careful to check with appropriate reliable sources before making loan disclosures.

Required advertising disclosures

❶

❷

❸

❹

❺

The Real Estate Settlement Procedures Act

During the early 1970s, the Department of Housing and Urban Development (HUD) conducted a study of the costs of closing a residential loan transaction. The study revealed that closing costs varied significantly, not just from one area to another, but even within the same community there were frequently large differences in closing costs required by different lenders.

The Department concluded that some lenders were successful in charging more for their services, largely because of the ignorance of consumers. To remedy this situation, HUD asked Congress to pass the **Real Estate Settlement Procedures Act** (RESPA). The law was originally passed in 1974 and substantially amended in 1979. Its purpose is to require lenders to disclose closing costs to borrowers, to encourage competition among lenders and to eliminate referral fees and kickbacks.

Real estate agents should take careful note that RESPA is similar to the Truth in Lending laws, but where the Truth in Lending Act and Federal Reserve Regulation Z require lenders to disclose *credit* costs, RESPA requires lenders to disclose *closing* costs associated with the purchase – that is costs such as prorates for taxes, escrow and recording fees, title insurance charges, etc.

The Real Estate Settlement Procedures Act applies only to first mortgage loans incurred to acquire a one to four-family personal residence made by a **federally related lender**. A "federally related lender" means any lender which –

- Is federally chartered, or
- Is federally regulated, or
- Has accounts which are federally insured, or
- Makes loans under a federal program such as FHA, Farm Service Agency, DVA, etc., or

- Sells loans to Fannie Mae, Freddie Mac or Ginnie Mae, or
- Makes more than $1 million worth of real estate loans per year.

Notwithstanding the above, the following loans are exempt –

- Loans to acquire land of 25 acres or more
- Junior financing (not a first lien)
- Loans for vacant land unless acquired as a site for a mobile home or for construction of a residence
- Construction loans where the borrower already owns the lot
- Transactions where the buyer takes title subject to an existing loan, unless the lender charges an assumption fee over $50 or the terms of the loan are modified (e.g., raising the interest rate).

What lenders must do to comply – Compliance with RESPA does not usually involve real estate agents directly. Lenders, escrow agents and, to a lesser extent, title insurers are more directly concerned with RESPA. However, anything which affects these parties will also indirectly affect real estate agents, so it is good for real estate agents to be aware of the basic provisions of the law. In addition, as real estate agents become more and more involved in computerized loan origination, an understanding of RESPA promises to become more and more important.

When RESPA applies to a loan, the closing statement must be on a form created by HUD called a ***Uniform Settlement Statement*** (HUD-1). Within three days of obtaining a loan application the lender must give the borrower (at no additional charge) a ***good faith estimate*** of the closing costs, which must reference the lines on the Uniform Settlement Statement so the borrower can compare to the final settlement statement at closing. (See the samples on the following pages.) If the borrower requests it, the borrower is entitled to review a copy of the final settlement statement not less than one day before the closing, again, on the Uniform Settlement Statement. The idea is that everything must refer to the Uniform Settlement Statement so the borrower can compare the actual costs with the original estimate, line by line. The closing agent is not allowed to charge extra for the preview of the statement, nor may the lender charge for the good faith estimate.

Under RESPA a reserve account is referred to as a ***escrow account*** (which is also sometimes referred to as an ***impound account***). Within 45 days of closing the lender or closing agent (escrow) must also provide the borrower with an ***Initial Escrow Statement***. The Initial Escrow Statement itemizes the estimated taxes, insurance premiums and other charges anticipated to be paid from the escrow account during the first twelve months of the loan. It lists the escrow payment amount and any required extra amounts. Thereafter loan servicers must deliver to borrowers an ***Annual Escrow Statement*** once a year. The annual escrow account statement summarizes all escrow account deposits and payments during the servicer's twelve month computation year. It also notifies the borrower of any shortages or surpluses in the account and advises the borrower about what the servicer is doing about any shortages or surpluses. Any excess of $50 or more must be returned to the borrower.

During the course of the loan a lender may not charge excessive amounts for the escrow account. Each month the lender may require a borrower to pay into the escrow account no more than $\frac{1}{12}$ of the total of all disbursements payable during the year (usually just taxes and insurance), plus an amount necessary to pay for any shortage in the account. In addition, the lender may require a ***cushion***, not to exceed an amount equal to two months worth of the total disbursements for the year.

Within three days of the loan application, the lender must give the borrower a copy of a settlement costs booklet which has been published by HUD. The booklet is de-

GOOD FAITH ESTIMATE
(Not a Loan Commitment)

This Good Faith Estimate is being provided by a mortgage broker and no lender has yet been obtained

The information provided below reflects estimates of the charges which you are likely to incur at the settlement of your loan. The fees listed are estimates – actual charges may be more or less. Your transaction may not involve a fee for every item listed.

The numbers listed beside the estimates generally correspond to the numbered lines contained in the HUD-1 or HUD-1A settlement statement which you will be receiving at settlement. The HUD-1 or HUD-1A settlement statement will show you the actual cost for items paid at settlement.

HUD-1	DESCRIPTION OF CHARGES	AMOUNT
801	Loan Origination Fee @ % + $	
802	Loan Discount Fee @ % + $	
803	Appraisal Fee	
804	Credit Report	
805	Inspection Fee	
806	Mortgage Insurance Application Fee	
807	Assumption Fee	
808	Mortgage Broker Fee @ % + $	
809	Tax Related Service Fee	
810	Processing Fee	
811	Underwriting Fee	
812	Wire Transfer Fee	
813	Application Fee	
814	Commitment Fee	
815	Lender's Rate Lock-in Fee	
901	Interest @ /day for days	
902	Mortgage Insurance Premium	
903	Hazard Insurance Premium	
904	County Property Taxes	
906	Flood Insurance	
1001	Hazard Ins. @ /mo. for months	
1002	Mortgage Ins. @ /mo. for months	
1004	Tax & Assmt. @ /mo. for months	
1006	Flood Insurance @ /mo. for months	
1008	Aggregate Escrow Adjustment	
1101	Settlement or Closing/Escrow Fee	
1102	Abstract or Title Search	
1103	Title Examination	
1105	Document Preparation Fee	
1106	Notary Fee	
1107	Attorney's Fee	
1108	Title Insurance	
1201	Recording Fee	
1202	City/County Tax/Stamps	
1203	State Tax/Stamps	
1204	Intangible Tax	
1301	Survey	
1302	Pest Inspection	

"S"/"B" designates those costs to be paid by Seller/Broker   "A" designates those costs affecting APR.

"F" designates financed costs.

These estimates are provided pursuant to the Real Estate Settlement Procedures Act of 1974, as amended (RESPA). Additional information can be found in the HUD Special Information Booklet which is to be provided to you by your mortgage broker or lender, if your application is to purchase residential property and the Lender will take a first lien on the property.

Mailing Address   Property Address

Proposed Loan Amount   Loan Type   Estimated Interest Rate
Preparation Date   ☐ FHA ☐ VA ☐ Conventional   Loan Number

_____   _____
Date   Date

_____   _____
Date   Date

Page 1 of 1   GFE 3/95

Good Faith Estimate required by RESPA. Note the line numbers which match the HUD-1 form to the right.

A. Settlement Statement

U.S. Department of Housing
and Urban Development

OMB Approval No. 2502-0265

B. Type of Loan

1. ☐ FHA 2. ☐ FmHA 3. ☐ Conv. Unins. 4. ☐ VA 5. ☐ Conv. Ins.	6. File Number:	7. Loan Number:	8. Mortgage Insurance Case Number:

C. Note: This form is furnished to give you a statement of actual settlement costs. Amounts paid to and by the settlement agent are shown. Items marked "(p.o.c.)" were paid outside the closing; they are shown here for informational purposes and are not included in the totals.

D. Name & Address of Borrower:	E. Name & Address of Seller:	F. Name & Address of Lender:

G. Property Location:	H. Settlement Agent:	
	Place of Settlement:	I. Settlement Date:

J. Summary of Borrower's Transaction		K. Summary of Seller's Transaction	
100. Gross Amount Due From Borrower		**400. Gross Amount Due To Seller**	
101. Contract sales price		401. Contract sales price	
102. Personal property		402. Personal property	
103. Settlement charges to borrower (line 1400)		403.	
104.		404.	
105.		405.	
Adjustments for items paid by seller in advance		*Adjustments for items paid by seller in advance*	
106. City/town taxes to		406. City/town taxes to	
107. County taxes to		407. County taxes to	
108. Assessments to		408. Assessments to	
109.		409.	
110.		410.	
111.		411.	
112.		412.	
120. Gross Amount Due From Borrower		**420. Gross Amount Due To Seller**	
200. Amounts Paid By Or In Behalf Of Borrower		**500. Reductions In Amount Due To Seller**	
201. Deposit or earnest money		501. Excess deposit (see instructions)	
202. Principal amount of new loan(s)		502. Settlement charges to seller (line 1400)	
203. Existing loan(s) taken subject to		503. Existing loan(s) taken subject to	
204.		504. Payoff of first mortgage loan	
205.		505. Payoff of second mortgage loan	
206.		506.	
207.		507.	
208.		508.	
209.		509.	
Adjustments for items unpaid by seller		*Adjustments for items unpaid by seller*	
210. City/town taxes to		510. City/town taxes to	
211. County taxes to		511. County taxes to	
212. Assessments to		512. Assessments to	
213.		513.	
214.		514.	
215.		515.	
216.		516.	
217.		517.	
218.		518.	
219.		519.	
220. Total Paid By/For Borrower		**520. Total Reduction Amount Due Seller**	
300. Cash At Settlement From/To Borrower		**600. Cash At Settlement To/From Seller**	
301. Gross Amount due from borrower (line 120)		601. Gross amount due to seller (line 420)	
302. Less amounts paid by/for borrower (line 220)	( )	602. Less reductions in amt. due seller (line 520)	( )
303. Cash ☐ From ☐ To Borrower		**603. Cash ☐ To ☐ From Seller**	

Section 5 of the Real Estate Settlement Procedures Act (RESPA) requires the following: • HUD must develop a Special Information Booklet to help persons borrowing money to finance the purchase of residential real estate to better understand the nature and costs of real estate settlement services; • Each lender must provide the booklet to all applicants from whom it receives or for whom it prepares a written application to borrow money to finance the purchase of residential real estate; • Lenders must prepare and distribute with the Booklet a Good Faith Estimate of the settlement costs that the borrower is likely to incur in connection with the settlement. These disclosures are manadatory.

Section 4(a) of RESPA mandates that HUD develop and prescribe this standard form to be used at the time of loan settlement to provide full disclosure of all charges imposed upon the borrower and seller. These are third party disclosures that are designed to provide the borrower with pertinent information during the settlement process in order to be a better shopper.

The Public Reporting Burden for this collection of information is estimated to average one hour per response, including the time for reviewing instructions, searching existing data sources, gathering and maintaining the data needed, and completing and reviewing the collection of information.

This agency may not collect this information, and you are not required to complete this form, unless it displays a currently valid OMB control number.

The information requested does not lend itself to confidentiality.

Previous editions are obsolete   Page 1 of 2   form **HUD-1** (3/86)
 ref Handbook 4305.2

Uniform Settlement Statement (HUD-1) required by RESPA.

L. Settlement Charges

	Paid From Borrowers Funds at Settlement	Paid From Seller's Funds at Settlement
700. Total Sales/Broker's Commission based on price $ @ % =		
Division of Commission (line 700) as follows:		
701. $ to		
702. $ to		
703. Commission paid at Settlement		
704.		
800. Items Payable In Connection With Loan		
801. Loan Origination Fee %		
802. Loan Discount %		
803. Appraisal Fee to		
804. Credit Report to		
805. Lender's Inspection Fee		
806. Mortgage Insurance Application Fee to		
807. Assumption Fee		
808.		
809.		
810.		
811.		
900. Items Required By Lender To Be Paid In Advance		
901. Interest from to @$ /day		
902. Mortgage Insurance Premium for months to		
903. Hazard Insurance Premium for years to		
904. years to		
905.		
1000. Reserves Deposited With Lender		
1001. Hazard insurance months@$ per month		
1002. Mortgage insurance months@$ per month		
1003. City property taxes months@$ per month		
1004. County property taxes months@$ per month		
1005. Annual assessments months@$ per month		
1006. months@$ per month		
1007. months@$ per month		
1008. months@$ per month		
1100. Title Charges		
1101. Settlement or closing fee to		
1102. Abstract or title search to		
1103. Title examination to		
1104. Title insurance binder to		
1105. Document preparation to		
1106. Notary fees to		
1107. Attorney's fees to		
(includes above items numbers:)		
1108. Title insurance to		
(includes above items numbers:)		
1109. Lender's coverage $		
1110. Owner's coverage $		
1111.		
1112.		
1113.		
1200. Government Recording and Transfer Charges		
1201. Recording fees: Deed $; Mortgage $; Releases $		
1202. City/county tax/stamps: Deed $; Mortgage $		
1203. State tax/stamps: Deed $; Mortgage $		
1204.		
1205.		
1300. Additional Settlement Charges		
1301. Survey to		
1302. Pest inspection to		
1303.		
1304.		
1305.		
1400. Total Settlement Charges (enter on lines 103, Section J and 502, Section K)		

Uniform Settlement Statement (HUD-1) required by RESPA.

signed to explain the Uniform Settlement Statement and to inform the borrower about all the costs which might be involved in purchasing a home. The booklet also encourages the borrower to shop for the services needed.

Also within three days of loan application the lender must give the borrower a *Mortgage Servicing Statement*. This is required only if the provisions of the loan allow the lender to sell the loan servicing. But since practically all loans today give the lender the right to sell the servicing of the loan, the Mortgage Servicing Statement is almost always required.

If the loan servicer sells or assigns the servicing rights to another loan servicer, a *Servicing Transfer Statement* must be given to the borrower. Generally, the loan servicer must notify the borrower 15 days before the effective date of the servicing transfer. As long the borrower makes a timely payment to the old servicer within 60 days of the servicing transfer, the borrower cannot be penalized. The notice must include the name and address of the new servicer, toll-free telephone numbers, and the date when the new servicer will begin accepting payments.

A principal feature of RESPA is that kickbacks and referral fees are prohibited. If a fee is charged, a service must have been provided. Moreover, if anyone involved in the transaction (including a real estate agent) refers a buyer to another company, and the referring party has an ownership interest in the entity to which the buyer is referred, the ownership interest must be disclosed to the buyer using an *Affiliated Business Arrangement Disclosure*. For example, a real estate brokerage company may offer a package of services such as title insurance, escrow, insurance, mortgage lending, home inspections, etc., as long as the package is offered by an independent business organization. Such an arrangement is called a *Controlled Business Arrangement* (CBA). When an agent refers a borrower to a CBA the agent must ensure that the borrower understands the relationship between the agent and the CBA and that the borrower may wish to shop for the services elsewhere. The agent cannot receive a referral fee from the CBA, although the agent is entitled to participate in any profits made by the CBA, the same as any owner of a business.

When RESPA applies to a transaction, the buyer cannot be required to obtain financing from any particular lender, nor may the buyer be required to secure title insurance from any particular title insurance company. Note that the seller and the real estate agent cannot require the buyer to secure these services from a particular provider, but there is nothing wrong with the seller or the agent making suggestions or giving the buyer price and quality information relative to providers of financing and title insurance.

The Equal Credit Opportunity Act

In 1974 Congress passed the *Equal Credit Opportunity Act* (ECOA) as Title VII of the Consumer Credit Protection Act. Similar to the Truth in Lending Act, ECOA authorizes the Board of Governors of the Federal Reserve Bank to create such reasonable regulations as are necessary to implement the purposes of the Act. Pursuant to this authority, the Board created Federal Reserve Regulation B. Lenders must comply with both the Equal Credit Opportunity Act and with Federal Reserve Regulation B.

The Equal Credit Opportunity Act requires the extension of credit without regard to race, color, religion, national origin, sex, marital status, age (provided the applicant is of legal age), the fact that all or part of the applicant's income is derived from public assistance, or that the applicant has in good faith exercised any rights under the Consumer Credit Protection Act.

Discrimination under the Equal Credit Opportunity Act includes not only refusal to grant credit, but also discouraging an applicant to apply for credit because the applicant falls into one of the protected categories listed above.

When creditors file reports with a credit reporting agency, if the account is a joint account of a husband and wife, the report must be made in both names and the credit reporting agency must maintain separate files for each spouse. Creditors are not permitted to ask the borrower's marital status and credit applications must be neutral as to sex and marital status. When creditors use loan rating systems, they cannot include sex or marital status as factors.

When an applicant is married, or formerly married, creditors cannot ask for credit information about the applicant's spouse, unless the applicant is relying upon child support or alimony from the spouse. If an applicant who receives child support or alimony does not wish to reveal it to the creditor, the creditor cannot require that it be disclosed, or discriminate if it is not disclosed. However, if it is not revealed, then the creditor need not count it as income in making the credit decision.

Creditors cannot ask an applicant about child-bearing plans or birth control practices. If the applicant, or the spouse of an applicant is of child-bearing age, the creditor violates the law by assuming that the applicant might experience even a temporary interruption in income as a result of child bearing. However, the creditor may ask about the number and ages of the applicant's children and other dependents.

If a credit application is denied, the creditor must give notice to the applicant and the notice must state the specific reason. Statements such as "failed to score high enough on our point scoring system" or "we have changed our loan policy" are not sufficient.

The Equal Credit Opportunity Act contains specific provisions prohibiting real estate agents from discriminating or discouraging applications because the applicant is a member of a protected category.

The Home Mortgage Disclosure Act

The Fair Housing Act (see Chapter 22) prohibits *redlining*. This is the practice where lenders refuse to lend in certain areas or to certain persons on the basis of their race, color, religion, national origin, sex, mental or physical handicap or familial status. To assist in enforcing this provision of the act, in 1975 Congress passed the **Home Mortgage Disclosure Act**. To implement the purposes of the Act the Federal Reserve Bank Board of Governors issued Federal Reserve Regulation C. The Act and the regulation require lenders to file with federal agencies an annual report of all loans made during the year. The report must break the loans down by area, so that cases of redlining will be easily visible. In 1977 Congress passed the **Community Reinvestment Act**, which requires further reporting. For more detailed discussion the Home Mortgage Disclosure Act and the Community Reinvestment Act, see Chapter 22.

The Fair Credit Reporting Act

The **Fair Credit Reporting Act** was enacted in 1970. Its purpose is to ensure fair practices in credit reporting. As a result of its passage, consumers now have the right to know the contents of their credit file. Consumers may also make a statement disputing or explaining derogatory information in their file and the credit bureau must include the statement in any reports it issues.

The Fair Credit Reporting Act differentiates between a **credit report** and an **investigative report**. A credit report is ordinary computerized credit information, where an investigative report includes information gained by specific inquiries made by the reporting agency. A credit report can be ordered on anyone, with or without their permission, provided the person ordering the report has a legitimate business purpose. An investigative report, on the other hand, cannot be ordered without notice to the loan applicant and their permission.

Washington usury laws

The maximum amount of interest which a lender is allowed to charge is the ***usury rate***. Usury rates are always state laws. Each state sets maximum rates for different kinds of lending, e.g., credit cards versus mortgage loans, and so on. Although many states still set usury rates, many have been discontinued in Washington. The rationale for eliminating usury laws is that they discourage venture capital and loans to marginal borrowers. If a lender cannot obtain a yield commensurate with the risk, then the lender will not make the loan. Venture capital is essential for the production of new jobs and industry. Therefore, usury laws hurt working people more than any other group.

Washington's usury laws establish the maximum rate at 12% or a rate equal to the rate on the most recent sale of 26-month treasury bills, plus four percent, whichever is higher. Thus, if the rate on the treasury bills is, say, 5%, adding 4% makes it 9%, but 12% is still higher, so 12% is the usury rate.

There are many exemptions to the usury laws in Washington. All loans for commercial, agricultural or business purposes are exempt, for example. In addition, federal law exempts all residential real estate loans from state usury statutes if the loan is made by a federally chartered lender or were insured or guaranteed by the federal government. Thus, the majority of loans that the usury law in Washington apply to are conventional loans made by mortgage bankers, or seller-carried financing when the buyer will occupy the property.

Legal rate – The ***legal rate*** is the rate that applies when interest is called for, but the parties failed to specify a rate in their agreement. Revised Code of Washington defines it as 12% (RCW 19.52.005).

The Private Mortgage Insurance Act

The ***Private Mortgage Insurance Act*** was passed on July 29, 1999 and requires that lenders inform borrowers at closing that they have private mortgage insurance (PMI), what the insurance is, and how and when the borrower can cancel it. After that, the borrower must be notified annually by the lender about when the borrower can cancel the PMI.

The law applies only to loans made after July 29, 1999. However, both Fannie Mae and Freddie Mac have adopted the policy that the borrower is entitled to cancellation of the PMI once the midpoint of the loan is reached, even for loans made prior to July 29, 1999.

For loans made after July 29, 1999 the law states that after the borrower has paid off 20 percent of the original value of the house the borrower can contact the lender and ask to have the PMI canceled. And once there is 22 percent equity in the house the lender must automatically cancel the PMI coverage. Loans insured by the FHA are exempt from the law.

There are two ways to prove that the equity in the property is high enough to cancel the PMI. The simplest is when the loan balance has been paid down to the 78% level. There is no way the lender can argue about this – the loan has been paid down to that level and the borrower is entitled to cancellation of the PMI by law.

As an alternative, the borrower can prove that the equity is high enough by hiring an appraiser to prove that the value has increased. Note that the law allows the lender to choose the appraiser, so the borrower is advised to contact the lender and obtain a list of approved appraisers before incurring the expense of an appraisal.

Nationwide there are only eight insurers who provide PMI. The existence of these insurers has made low down payment mortgage loans available for millions of buyers who would never have been able to save a large enough down payment to purchase their first home. Private mortgage insurance has been a godsend to the real estate and mortgage lending industries. The purpose of the Private Mortgage Insurance Act is to ensure that lenders use it fairly and wisely.

KEY TERMS

The key to understanding any new field is the vocabulary used in that field. To maximize your comprehension of the material presented in this chapter, be sure you know the meaning and significance of the following terms. Remember that the majority of test questions primarily test knowledge of vocabulary.

Affiliated Business Arrangement	Impound account
Annual Escrow Statement	Initial Escrow Statement
Annual percentage rate	Investigative report
Community Reinvestment Act	Legal rate
Consumer Protection Act of 1968	Mortgage Servicing Statement
Controlled Business Arrangement	Private Mortgage Insurance Act
Credit report	Real Estate Settlement Procedures Act
Cushion	Real Estate Settlement Procedures Act
Disclosure	Redlining
Equal Credit Opportunity Act	Right of rescission
Escrow account	Servicing Transfer Statement
Fair Credit Reporting Act	Total finance charge
Federally related lender	Truth in Lending Act
Federally related lender	Uniform Settlement Statement
Good faith estimate	usury rate
Home Mortgage Disclosure Act	

15

Real estate valuation

THE STUDY OF APPRAISAL is essential for anyone associated with real estate. Real estate agents not only need to understand how market forces affect the value of their listings, but they must also be sufficiently conversant with appraisal theory and practice to be able to interpret professional appraisal reports to their clients. This short introduction presents an overview of real estate appraisal sufficient to meet the needs of a beginner, and to point the direction for additional study for those who wish to appraise professionally.

In any introductory work on appraisal, the first need is to define what an appraisal is. A synonym for *appraisal* is *valuation*. That is, the function of a professional appraiser is to estimate the value of the property. Note that appraisers do not "set" value, nor do they determine or create value. Only the activity of buyers and sellers in the open market can create value. Appraisers merely estimate the value of a property from the evidence they find in the marketplace and report their findings to the client.

The public perceives of an appraiser as being hired by buyers or sellers. Although buyers and sellers are certainly common appraisal clients, the vast majority of appraisal assignments today are ordered by financial institutions. Because most appraisals are required by financial institutions and by government agencies, many appraisers work as full-time employees. Yet others, including many of those who appraise for lending institutions, operate independently. Appraisers who take appraisal assignments independently are sometimes called *fee appraisers* or *independent fee appraisers.*

When an appraiser works independently, the relationship with the client is usually that of *principal* and *agent*. A principal hires an agent because of the agent's special expertise, and frequently grants the agent authority to perform tasks on behalf of the principal. Because of this special relationship, the agent is held to a high standard of loyalty toward the principal – to the exclusion of all others. This is commonly referred to as the agent's *fiduciary* duty to the principal. Fiduciary duties include such obligations as full disclosure, confidentiality and due diligence.

While an appraiser usually acts as an agent, there is a special difference between an appraisal agency and a normal agency relationship. For example, a real estate broker is usually the agent of the seller or the buyer, and represents the client's best interests. If the broker represents the seller, then the broker has a duty to obtain the highest price and best terms possible from the buyer. This is called *advocacy*. An appraiser is also an agent, but does not advocate the position of any of the parties when reporting the opinion of value. The value conclusion must be impartial without regard to the best interests of the client. Note that the appraiser is still obligated to the other aspects of the agency relationship – confidentiality, due diligence and full disclosure.

Definitions of value

Since the function of an appraiser is to report value to the client, the first issue is to clarify the definition of value. To say that value is elusive is an understatement, considering the effort appraisers make in its specifying its meaning with precision. There are numerous kinds of value, all of which would result in different dollar amounts.

Appraisers generally recognize two categories of value – *value in use* and *value in exchange*. Value in use is the value a commodity has to the owner. This may be subjective, as the result of emotion or other personal considerations. It may also relate to a property which was custom made for a specific purpose.

Value in exchange, on the other hand, is a value that an ordinary, informed buyer would pay in comparison to other choices available in the marketplace. As such, value in exchange is objective. Although there are numerous definitions of *market value*, market values are always values in exchange.

Example – An owner builds a large and expensive home, but with only one bedroom. The value to the owner may equal what the owner paid for construction of the home (cost), but the average buyer would probably want more than one bedroom in such a home, and would therefore likely be unwilling to pay as much as the owner. The market value (value in exchange) is less than the value in use.

Example – You buy some land and have a commercial building constructed at a cost of $500,000, custom built to suit your needs. Later you go to sell the property, but discover that many of the features of the building are useless to a typical buyer. As a result, the price an ordinary buyer would pay for this property is only $250,000. We would say then, that the value in use was $500,000, but the value in exchange was only $250,000.

It is true that either owner in the above examples may be able to sell the property for what it cost if the owner can find the one-in-a-million buyer for whom the special features had value. But appraisers ordinarily define market value as the value to the typical or average buyer who can be found after a reasonable marketing time.

Market values are representative of trends. For example, if a comparable property was recently sold for $200,000, this does not prove that the property being appraised will sell for $200,000. But it does start a *trend*. Suppose now the appraiser locates several other recently sold comparable properties, and their sales prices corroborate the trend. The market value becomes clear when the trend is evident.

Appraisers consider that any commodity has value only when four factors are present –

- Utility
- Scarcity
- Effective purchasing power
- Demand (Desire)

For example, if a commodity has no *utility* (is useless), it will have no value, regardless of the other factors. Similarly, the greater the *scarcity* of a commodity, the greater the value. Buyers must also have the ability to buy, or no sales will occur, so *effective purchasing power* is an essential element of value. (Some texts refer to effective purchasing power as *transferability*.) And finally, there must be *demand* (also sometimes stated as *desire*) for a commodity before it can possess value. If any one of the above elements of value is completely lacking, the commodity has no value at all.

Assuming that the above four elements of value are present, the value of the commodity is also affected by the four great forces which affect the value of all real property. These forces are –

- *Social*
- *Governmental*
- *Economic*
- *Environmental*

Elements of value		
❶		
❷		
❸		
❹		

Sometimes these forces – social forces, for example – are not rapid. Attitudes towards minorities in this country, for example, have improved steadily, although slowly over recent years. As a result, values of properties in areas where minorities predominate have tended to increase in value faster than properties in other areas. On the other hand, some of these forces have an almost overnight effect. For example, if the local government decides to rezone an area, the governmental influence can change the value of properties in the affected area in the time it takes for the news media to break the story. Economic and environmental forces can also change values relatively quickly. (Some texts refer to environmental forces as ***physical*** forces.)

Clearly, the appraiser's normal task is to report the market value (value in exchange) of the property, not its value in use. Yet, even the way appraisers define market value varies according to the circumstances and the needs of the client. In other words, there is no such thing as "the" market value. One of the most common is the definition used in the Uniform Residential Appraisal Report (URAR), a form required by secondary lenders today –

"The most probable price which a property should bring in a competitive and open market under all conditions requisite to a fair sale, the buyer and seller, each acting prudently, knowledgeably and assuming the price is not affected by undue stimulus. Implicit in this definition is the consummation of a sale as of a specified date and the passing of title from seller to buyer under conditions whereby: (1) buyer and seller are typically motivated; (2) both parties are well informed or well advised, and each acting in what he considers his own best interest; (3) a reasonable time is allowed for exposure in the open market; (4) payment is made in terms of cash in U.S. dollars or in terms of financial arrangements comparable thereto; and (5) the price represents the normal consideration for the property sold unaffected by special or creative financing or sales concessions granted by anyone associated with the sale."

Note that the basis of this definition is the "willing buyer, willing seller" concept. The essence of this definition is that the value of a property is its ability to command something else (usually money) in exchange.

Another aspect of value is that it is dependent upon the anticipated future benefits which the owner could derive from the property. In other words, the greater the anticipated benefits of ownership, the more a buyer would be willing to pay and the more a seller would demand in exchange for the property. This concept becomes crucial in appraising income properties, where the anticipated benefit of ownership is the income potential of the property.

But not all clients want the appraiser to report the value according to the URAR definition above. In many cases the request is not for the "most probable" price the property would bring, but rather the highest price possible. Yet other clients might want the most probable price, but also want to know what they could expect to get for the property within the constraints of a short marketing time. Or a seller might want to know how much could be obtained for their property if special financing concessions were offered to the buyer. All of these are variations on the definition of "market value," and each would result in a different value to report.

There are also various other types of value which are important in certain contexts. A partial list includes –

Assessed value – The ***assessed value*** is a percentage of the true cash value used for property tax purposes. The county treasurer multiplies the tax rate by the assessed value to find the amount of the tax bill. See also "true and fair value" below.

Book value (also sometimes called depreciated value) – ***Book*** or ***depreciated value*** is the value of a property as carried on the books of a business. Property held for business or income use is subject to cost recovery (depreciation) expense for income tax purposes. Every year the cost recovery claimed must be deducted from the cost on the books of the business. The result at any given time is the remaining book value of the property. Book value is generally a fiction created for accounting purposes and has little relation to market value.

Insurance value – The amount the improvements should be insured for is called the ***insurance value***. In theory, insurance value is the reproduction cost of the improvements without subtracting an allowance for depreciation. This is because (1) the land cannot be destroyed, so only the value of the improvements need be insured and, (2) the insurance company is generally required to reproduce the structure, not just replace it with another with similar utility located elsewhere. Older properties tend to be insured for amounts far in excess of their market value. At the same time, newer properties can be reproduced for about their market value, but because insurance value does not consider land value, the total market value tends to be higher than the insured value.

Intrinsic value – The ***intrinsic value*** of a commodity is the value of the thing in and of itself, without regard to market forces. Intrinsic value is the utility value alone, even if demand, scarcity and effective purchasing power are not present. Many appraisers consider it to be a misuse of the word "value," since value cannot exist without the presence of the other factors in addition to utility. Certainly, intrinsic value is not market value.

Liquidation (liquidated) value – What a property would sell for at auction, under distress conditions or with limited exposure in the marketplace is the ***liquidation value***.

Loan value – Lenders refer to the ***loan value*** as the value of a property for mortgage loan purposes. Greater reliance is placed on the earnings potential of the property and its liquidation value in the event of a foreclosure.

Salvage value (also sometimes called residual value) – When a property has been fully depreciated (see "book value" above), the remaining value is its ***salvage value*** or ***residual value***. For example, an owner of an apartment building can claim cost recovery as a deductible expense, but only on the structure, not on the portion of the cost attributable to the land. Thus, when the building has reached the end of its useful life and has been fully depreciated, its book value will be zero. The book value of the property will then be just the land value. In this case the land value is the salvage or residual value.

True and fair value – ***True and fair value*** is the value for property tax purposes. Revised Code of Washington requires the county assessor to value all property for its true and fair value, which is more or less a market value. However, the assessor uses mass appraisal techniques and, in some counties, does not reappraise the property every single year. Thus, the true and fair value may not be the same value as an independent appraiser would find.

In our discussion of value we have occasionally used the term ***cost***. Cost, as would seem obvious, is what an owner paid for a property. The cost was paid either as a purchase price or as the sum of the land and construction expenses. What is not so obvious to lay persons is that cost does not equal value. What an owner paid for a property could easily have been a value in use, rather than a value in exchange, and therefore not market value. Market prices change with market conditions too, so even if an owner paid market value for the property, its cost would have little to do with its market value at some point in the future. Furthermore, an owner could pay $200,000 to build certain improvements, but even though brand new, a bad design might cause the market value of the improvements to be substantially less than the cost.

Another term we have already used is ***price***. Appraisers use the word "price" to mean the amount an owner is or was asking for a property, or the amount a buyer paid for a property. Naturally, the price an owner is asking for a property does not establish its value. Even the price a buyer paid for a property does not indicate anything more than a value in use for that property. However, the prices paid for various comparable properties do establish a trend, and therefore is indicative of market value for a comparable property.

Principles of value

Various principles of value are fundamental to the appraisal concept of value. Although many of these principles are derived from general theories of economics, here they are applied to a particular economic unit – a parcel of real property. As a result, appraisers sometimes employ these concepts differently than an economist would –

Highest and best use – The *highest and best use* of the property is basic to the appraisal process. To determine the highest and best use of the property the appraiser applies four tests; that is, the proposed use must be –

- Physically possible,
- Legal, or can be made legal,
- Financially feasible, and
- That which maximizes benefits to the owner.

For example, soil which will not support a proposed structure makes that use physically impossible, therefore the proposed structure cannot be the highest and best use of the land. Similarly, zoning and availability of financing at reasonable rates to support the project are necessary if the proposed use is to be the highest and best use. Because of the first three of these constraints, the highest and best use of a developed property (land with improvements already in place), is usually the current use. In fact, zoning constraints alone are usually sufficient to dictate the highest and best use.

Of greater difficulty, however, is determining the highest and best use of property where many uses may be legal, physically possible and financially feasible. Such is frequently the case with undeveloped land. Even improved property may require substantial effort to determine the highest and best use, such as where the current use of the structure is coming to an end and the improvements will have to be converted to a new use.

In these cases the appraiser must determine which use will maximize the benefit to the owner. Benefits are not always financial; for example, the benefit of owning a house is use and enjoyment (shelter), not financial reward. Even where the benefits are financial it is not always an easy task to determine the highest and best use. You might think that when the rewards are financial, the highest and best use is simply that use which provides the greatest net return. On the face of it, this would seem to be so, but what if all the proposed uses would bring in the same net revenue, but one shows greater potential for stability or longevity of the income than others? An appraiser must take all these factors into account when analyzing the highest and best use of a property.

A highest and best use analysis is most problematic when the property is vacant land. Economists speak of the *four agents in production* – land, labor, capital, and entrepreneurial expertise (management). In classic economic theory, all four are necessary to produce income, but not always in the same proportion, and the amounts of each can be changed according to prevailing economic conditions. If labor becomes more expensive, for example, management will attempt to compensate by utilizing the other factors in different ways. Of the four agents in production, land is the most passive, therefore, the income allowed to it us usually last after the others have been paid. We sometimes speak of the income attributable to the land as residual income.

Substitution – Simply stated, the principle of *substitution* is that no prudent and knowledgeable buyer would pay more for a commodity than it would cost to acquire an identical substitute, assuming the buyer is acting in his or her own best interests and not under undue pressure. In real life, the available substitutes are never identical, but the principle still holds. For example, if there is a shortage of potatoes and they become very expensive, people will eat bread or rice – equivalent, if not identical substitutes.

Anticipation – According to the principle of ***anticipation***, buyers pay and sellers demand more or less for properties in direct proportion to the anticipated future benefits of ownership. While this is true of all properties, it is especially true of income-producing properties. Note that the buyer is motivated by anticipated future benefits, not past performance of the investment. Buyers rely on the past only as a guide to what they can expect in the future.

Example – You are listing an apartment building. The owner has not raised the rents for some time, so the rents are half of what they should be. You must value the property using the market rent, not the existing rent. (You should, however, subtract a small allowance from your final estimate to compensate a buyer for vacancies and inconvenience which could occur when the new owner raises the rents.)

What effect does the anticipation of inflation have on property values? In general, it will drive dollar values up because investment in real estate is a classic hedge against inflation. However, inflation will generally drive the values of all properties up more or less equally, since the inflation rate will affect all properties in much the same way.

Externalities – The principle of ***externalities*** holds that value is affected by outside forces (extrinsic factors) as well as features of the property itself (intrinsic factors). For example, if the property is in poor condition, this is an intrinsic problem. But if the property is in a poor neighborhood, then the neighborhood is causing the property to lose value, not the property itself; therefore we say the property lost value due to externalities. Because of its inherent immobility, real estate is at the mercy of externalities more than any other commodity.

There are many, many forces which have an effect on property values. In fact, externalities are generally more powerful forces than intrinsic factors. External forces can be international, national, regional or local in scope. Interest rates, for example, are national and international in scope today, and have a profound effect on market values. Or consider that the same house will sell for more in San Francisco than in Seattle. The externality in this case is regional supply and demand forces. On the other hand, forces such as zoning decisions would be local externalities. An externality can be as narrow in focus as the fact that the neighbors do not maintain their property well.

Change – ***Change*** is constant and unavoidable. Because of this we say that an appraisal report is valid for the date of the report only. In fact, we should be even more precise and say that it is valid for the moment it is delivered to the client. Events occurring after that time may easily change the value. And since future events are unforeseeable, it is impossible to appraise a property for what it will be worth on a future date. It is, however, possible to appraise a property for a past date, simply by using historical data.

When the principle of change is applied to analysis of a neighborhood it becomes evident that neighborhoods go through stages. The first stage is ***growth***, during which improvements are constructed. At some point the neighborhood is fully built and relatively little further change occurs. This is called the period of ***stability*** or ***equilibrium***. There is no set time period over which this period will last, nor is it tied to the age of the improvements. Many older residential neighborhoods, for example, are extremely stable and show no signs of impending change; yet many newly constructed developments may be in imminent danger of being razed to make way for some other use. When a neighborhood reaches the stage where properties are being torn down or converted for other uses, then we say that the period of stability has ended and ***decline*** has begun.

Note that the declining stage really merges with the growth of the next use pattern. Although different neighborhoods change in different ways, a common change is for a residential neighborhood to give way to commercial or industrial use. Thus, when a house is torn down to make way for a shopping center, the decline of the residential use pattern is merging with the growth of the commercial use. Some appraisers refer to this as revitalization.

Revitalization, however, should not be confused with **gentrification**. Gentrification is the process where older neighborhoods are salvaged and reborn with the same use pattern. Revitalization, in contrast, occurs when the use pattern shifts, as where a residential neighborhood goes commercial.

Conformity – The principle of **conformity** simply means that property values are maximized when a neighborhood is composed of structures which are generally of the same character. This does not mean that the structures are the same to the point of monotony, but rather that they are generally the same; for example, all single family detached residences.

When a neighborhood has a high degree of conformity, the neighborhood will be able to withstand change better. The better the neighborhood can withstand change, the longer will be the period of stability, so the useful life of the structure will be longer. Logically, the longer the anticipated remaining useful life of the structure, the greater its value, hence, the greater the conformity, the greater the market value.

Progression and regression – Properties which do not conform because they are under-improved in relation to other properties in the neighborhood frequently benefit in value by **progression**. For example, a small home in a neighborhood of larger homes will command a higher price than if the same home were located in a neighborhood of similar small homes. Conversely, a property which does not conform because the owner has overbuilt suffers from **regression**. In this case, the owner may never be able to recover the cost.

Balance – According to the principle of **balance**, a property will bring the highest value when all of its components – land and structure – are in optimum equilibrium with each other. For example, a new five-bedroom house with only one bath is in disequilibrium and its value will suffer, perhaps to the point where its value is less than the cost of construction. The principle of balance also requires that the land and structure be appraised for the same use.

Example – Suppose an owner wishes you to take a listing on a home which is located on a 100 × 100 foot commercially zoned lot. The owner feels that the structure (as a house) is worth $200,000, based on the value of similar structures in the area. The owner also feels that the land is worth $200,000, based on the value of nearby similar commercial lots. Therefore, the owner wishes you to take a listing at $400,000.

However, the reality is that the owner has appraised the structure according to its residential value and the land according to its commercial value. Suppose the residential value of the land is only $80,000? Adding this to the residential value of structure gives a market value of $280,000. If we appraise the property according to its commercial value, the land is worth $200,000, but suppose the structure requires $60,000 worth of alterations to bring it up to commercial code. Then the value for commercial purposes is $340,000 ($200,000 land value + $200,000 structure value – $60,000 cost of alterations = $340,000).

Clearly, the highest and best use of this property is for commercial use, but its value as such is only $340,000, not the $400,000 the owner thinks it is worth. The owner's appraisal is incorrect because the owner misapplied the principle of balance in valuing the land for one purpose and the structure for another.

Contribution – According to the principle of **contribution** all components of the property – land and structures – contribute to the overall value of the whole, but not necessarily in direct proportion to their cost. For example, a **plottage increment** is an increase in value that can occur when smaller parcels are joined. Sometimes the value of the large parcel is greater than the total of the value of the smaller pieces from which is was made up. Or consider the owner of a house in Washington who spends $20,000 to install an in-ground swimming pool on an $160,000 house. It is doubtful that buyers will pay a great deal extra for the swimming pool, so the amount the swimming pool contributes to the overall value is far less than its cost. People who rehabilitate properties for resale need to keep the principle of contribution uppermost in mind.

Competition – The market value for any commodity is established by **competition**. However, if there is little competition, there is likely to be excessive profit. Excessive profit, on the other hand, attracts competition, which dilutes the profit. In fact, excess profit usually attracts too much competition which ultimately becomes ruinous. In a free market these forces always equalize themselves within a short period of time.

Surplus productivity – A measure of the value of any commodity is its productive capacity. In other words, the more productive an item, the greater its desirability, and therefore the greater its value. We can derive a portion of the productivity attributable to one component of an investment and calculate the value of that one component separately from the whole. This is an example of determining the value of one segment of the property by the **surplus productivity** applicable to that segment.

For example, suppose an income property produces an annual net operating income of $50,000 (income after all expenses but before payments on debt). Assume further that there is a $400,000 mortgage with interest payments of $40,000 per year. The net income attributable to the owner's equity is, therefore, $10,000. We can now ascertain the value of that $10,000 annual projected income, and thereby determine the value of one component of the property – the value of the owner's equity.

Overview of the appraisal process

In conducting an appraisal the first step is to define the task. This usually means creating a clear understanding with the client as to the definition of market value the client desires and the client's reason for ordering the appraisal. On the other hand, it could mean that the appraiser must first complete a highest and best use analysis before the actual valuation can begin, or perhaps extensive discussions with the client will be necessary to determine precisely what the client's needs are.

In an ordinary request for the simple appraisal of a single-family home – such as where the appraisal is ordered by a lender – determining the appraisal task is fairly routine. Lenders are sufficiently sophisticated that they know exactly what to ask for and can communicate their needs easily. And the highest and best use of most improved property is constrained by the zoning, so determining the appraisal task becomes relatively simple.

The second step in the appraisal process is to gather the necessary data. Data required will include information about the region and the neighborhood as well as the property itself. After all available data has been collected, the appraiser is ready to apply the data to the property. In doing this, there are three recognized **approaches to value** – the market approach, the cost approach and the income approach. Each of these approaches will be the subject of extensive discussion later.

Not all of these approaches may be suitable for a given property and, even when appropriate, the appraiser usually finds that the results of one or two of the approaches are more reliable or credible than the results of the other(s). To ensure optimum accuracy, the appraiser uses a process called **reconciliation** or **correlation** to make the final estimate of market value. Reconciliation or correlation means taking a weighted average of the results of the approaches which were used.

For example, in the appraisal of a 20-year old single-family dwelling, the market approach is usually the most accurate, although the cost approach can sometimes be used with fair accuracy. The income approach, however, is less reliable. Therefore, to reconcile the value estimates derived from each of the three approaches, the appraiser might take 75% of the value from the market approach, 25% of the value from the cost approach, and 0% of the value from the income approach. Reconciliation or correlation is a matter of judgment, dependent on the appraiser's skill and experience.

Having made the final value estimate, it is time to complete the appraisal report. Most appraisal reports today are made on the **Uniform Residential Appraisal Report** (URAR), which is the form required by most secondary market lenders. In addition, all appraisers must adhere to the **Uniform Standards of Professional Appraisal Practice** (USPAP), which dictate the minimum requirements for appraisal reports. The USPAP allows an appraiser to report on a self-contained appraisal report, a summary appraisal report or a restricted use appraisal report. The difference in the three types of reports lies in the amount of detail included in the report. The URAR is considered a summary report.

Regardless of the form in which the report is made, the Revised Code of Washington provides that appraisals can only be made by persons licensed or certified by the Department of Licensing –

RCW 18.140.020 Use of title by unauthorized person.

(1) No person other than a state-certified or state-licensed real estate appraiser may receive compensation of any form for a real estate appraisal or an appraisal review. However, compensation may be provided for brokers price opinions prepared by a real estate licensee, licensed under chapter 18.85 RCW.

(2) No person, other than a state-certified or state-licensed real estate appraiser, may assume or use that title or any title, designation, or abbreviation likely to create the impression of certification or licensure as a real estate appraiser by this state.

(3) A person who is not certified or licensed under this chapter shall not prepare any appraisal of real estate located in this state, except as provided under subsection (1) of this section.

...

(5) This chapter does not preclude an individual person licensed by the state of Washington as a real estate broker or as a real estate salesperson from issuing a brokers price opinion. However, if the brokers price opinion is written, or given as evidence in any legal proceeding, and is issued to a person who is not a prospective seller, buyer, lessor, or lessee as the only intended user, then the brokers price opinion shall contain a statement, in an obvious location within the written document or specifically and affirmatively in spoken testimony, that substantially states: "This brokers price opinion is not an appraisal as defined in chapter 18.140 RCW and has been prepared by a real estate licensee, licensed under chapter 18.85 RCW, who (is/is not) also state certified or state licensed as a real estate appraiser under chapter 18.140 RCW." However, the brokers price opinion issued under this subsection may not be used as an appraisal in conjunction with a federally related transaction.

...

Note that the statute specifically exempts real estate brokers from having to be licensed or certified provided the "appraisal" work is performed in the course of taking a listing or making a sale and is in the nature of a competitive market analysis.

The market data approach to value

Appraisers most commonly call this approach the **market data approach**, although it is also sometimes just called the **market approach**, and sometimes also called the **sales comparison approach**. The market data approach is the easiest to explain to lay people because it echoes exactly what buyers and sellers do in the marketplace. Buyers and sellers simply compare one property in the marketplace to others.

Although all principles of value are used in all approaches, the market data approach relies most heavily on the principle of substitution. A buyer will simply not offer to pay more than it would cost to get another property of equal desirability and a seller will not accept less than what other similar properties are selling for.

Needless to say, the market data approach requires the availability of adequate comparable properties. Whenever possible these should be properties which have been sold, and the sales must have been **arms length transactions**. An arms length transaction occurs when the property was exposed in the open market for a reasonable period of time, both parties were knowledgeable and both parties acted prudently in their own self-interest without undue stimulus. Note that the definition of an arms length transaction contains essentially the same elements as the definition of market value.

Example – A property is very comparable to the subject property in all respects, but sold the day it was listed. The appraiser must conclude that the transaction locates the bottom of the market for the value of the subject property. Clearly it might have sold for much more if it had been exposed to a greater range of potential buyers.

Example – You find an excellent comparable for the property you are appraising. When you research the data relating to the sale, you note the seller's name is Georges LeRoux and the buyer's name is Etienne LeRoux. Can you use this sale as a comparable? The parties are obviously related, therefore love and affection may have been part of the consideration, so the price reflected on the deed is not necessarily representative of the market.

Example – A sale of a comparable property was recorded 120 days after the property was listed. The grantee on the deed was the Perpetual Savings and Loan Association and the consideration is stated as $172,369.42. If further investigation reveals that this was a deed in lieu of foreclosure, or a sheriff's or trustee's deed, then the transaction was under undue stimulus and is not representative of the market.

The most serious problem with the market data approach occurs when there are few or no comparable properties. Obviously, the better the comparables, the more accurate the results of the market data approach. Appraisers refer to a market with high activity level as an **efficient market**. Real estate markets tend to be inefficient in comparison to markets for other commodities.

When there are no comparable sold properties, can an appraiser use comparable properties currently listed for sale? Properties on the market are generally not used by appraisers because there is no guarantee that the property will ultimately command the price the owner is asking. On the other hand, if the property has been on the market for a time and has not sold at its asking price, one fact becomes clear – the asking price must be higher than market value. Therefore appraisers do occasionally use listed properties as comparables, but use the data only as evidence of the upper limit of value.

Lack of good comparables is also typical of **single-purpose properties**, also called **single-use properties**. A single-purpose property is a property which was specially built for just one use. Examples include properties such as gymnasiums, schools, library buildings, bowling alleys, theaters, churches, among many others.

If you determine that conversion to another use is the highest and best use of a single-use property, then you can use **appraisal by anticipated use** (also sometimes called **appraisal by development cost**) as a technique to appraise the existing structure. To appraise by anticipated use, simply find comparables for the property *as it will be when converted*. This should yield the market value after conversion. Then subtract the anticipated cost of conversion, which will give the present value of the property in its current condition.

The "Sales Comparison Analysis" section of the Uniform Residential Appraisal Report (URAR) has been reproduced on the following page. To illustrate our discussion of the market data approach, it has been completed with appropriate adjustments as an appraiser would have filled it out for a sale as described in the narrative below.

Sales Comparison Narrative

Subject property is a three-bedroom ranch style house of 1,500 ☐ (☐ means "square feet"), built 15 years ago on a 70 × 100 lot (7,000 ☐). It is in average condition and has two full baths, one fireplace and a double garage. The neighborhood is average as is the quality of construction. There is no basement or unusually large front porch, but there is a 10 × 20 foot deck off the back of the house. There are no other special amenities or recent remodeling.

Comparable #1 sold two weeks ago for $169,900. It is in the same block as the subject and was built by the same builder at the same time. Its amenities are the same as the subject and are in the same condition, except that the structure is 1,510 ☐. Its lot is slightly irregular, but totals 7,000 ☐. There are no other special amenities or recent remodeling.

Comparable #2 sold three months ago for $171,000. It is located two blocks from the subject property in the same subdivision and was built by the same builder at the same time. Its amenities are the same as the subject, but they are in superior condition, although the structure is only 1,450 ☐. Investigation of the sale revealed that the seller paid $3,000 to a bank to buy the interest rate down for the buyer.

Comparable #3 sold six months ago for $175,950. It is located four blocks from the subject property in the same subdivision and was built by the same builder at the same time. Its amenities are the same as the subject property and in the same condition, but there is no fireplace and the structure is 1,475 ☐. A major difference is that the lot is 100 × 100 (10,000 ☐).

Because the comparable properties above are not identical to the subject property, adjustments must be made. Note that all the adjustments were made *to the comparables*. The adjustments must be made in order to find out how much each comparable would have sold for if it had been identical to the subject. This means that if the comparable is larger or better, the adjustment must be subtracted, and vice-versa.

Note also in this report that the appraiser reconciled the results from the three properties into the final value conclusion by taking a weighted average of the results. In this case the appraiser weighed 100% on Comparable #1 and gave no weight to Comparables #2 and #3. This judgment appears to be justified from the nature and reliability of the data in this report.

ITEM	SUBJECT	COMPARABLE NO. 1		COMPARABLE NO. 2		COMPARABLE NO. 3	
Address 120 S.W. Lois Lane		123 S.W. Lois Lane		345 S.W. Lois Lane		678 S.W. Lois Lane	
Proximity to Subject		Across street		Two blocks		Four blocks	
Sales Price	$	$	169,900	$	171,000	$	175,950
Price/Gross Liv. Area	$	$ 112.52		$ 117.93		$ 119.29	
Data and/or Verification Source			MLS		MLS		MLS
VALUE ADJUSTMENTS	DESCRIPTION	DESCRIPTION	+(-)$ Adjustment	DESCRIPTION	+(-)$ Adjustment	DESCRIPTION	+(-)$ Adjustment
Sales or Financing Concessions		None		Seller buydown	-3,000	None	
Date of Sale/Time		Current		3 months	+2,600	6 months	+5,300
Location	Average	Average		Average		Average	
Leasehold/Fee Simple	Fee	Fee		Fee		Fee	
Site	7,000	7,000		7,000		10,000	-25,000
View	None	None		None		None	
Design and Appeal	Ranch/Avg	Same		Same		Same	
Quality of Construction	Average	Average		Average		Average	
Age	15/15 effective	Same		Same		Same	
Condition	Average	Average		Superior	-5,000	Average	
Above Grade	Total 7 Bdrms 3 Baths 2	Total 7 Bdrms 3 Baths 2		Total 7 Bdrms 3 Baths 2		Total 7 Bdrms 3 Baths 2	
Gross Living Area	1,500 Sq. Ft.	1,510 Sq. Ft.	-1,100	1,450 Sq. Ft.	+5,900	1,475 Sq. Ft.	+3,000
Basement & Finished Rooms Below Grade	None Average	None Average		None Average		None Average	
Functional Utility	Standard	Standard		Standard		Standard	
Heating/Cooling	FAGas	FAGas		FAGas		FAGas	
Energy Efficient Items	Standard	Standard		Standard		Standard	
Garage/Carport	2/None	2/None		2/None		2/None	
Porch, Patio, Deck, Fireplace(s), etc.	One fireplace 10 x 20 deck	Same No deck	+2,000	Same No deck	+2,000	Same No deck	+2,000
Fence, Pool, etc.	None	None		None		None	
Net Adj. (total)		X + ☐ - $	900	X + ☐ - $	2,500	☐ + X - $	14,700
Adjusted Sales Price of Comparable		$	170,800	$	173,500	$	161,250

Comments on Sales Comparison (including the subject property's compatibility to the neighborhood, etc.):   Due to uncertainty of effect of buydown on Comparable #2, and of effect of oversized lot on Comparable #3, weight was placed 100% on Comparable #1. Value change per Marshall and Swift.

ITEM	SUBJECT	COMPARABLE NO. 1		COMPARABLE NO. 2	COMPARABLE NO. 3
Date, Price and Data Source, for prior sales within year of appraisal	7/9/__ MLS	7/1/__ MLS	4/2/__ MLS	1/10/__ MLS	

Analysis of any current agreement of sale, option, or listing of the subject property and analysis of any prior sales of subject and comparables within one year of the date of appraisal.

INDICATED VALUE BY SALES COMPARISON APPROACH .... $	170,800

In other situations, an appraiser may have comparables where the appraiser feels each should be given at least partial weight. Still, the least reliable comparable should receive the least weight. This is why appraisers try to use at least three, but not usually more than six comparables. Additional comparables would create a substantial amount of extra work and, since they would be given decreasing weight, would not significantly influence the appraiser's final value conclusion.

The cost approach to value

Like the market data approach, the cost approach to value relies primarily on the principle of substitution. Unlike the market data approach, however, in the cost approach the appraiser uses the cost to reproduce the property as a measure of the upper limit of value. In other words, if a buyer could have the property reproduced for a certain amount, then by the principle of substitution the buyer would not pay any more than that amount.

Example – A builder offers you a brand new house on a lot in a new subdivision for $250,000. You contact other builders and determine that you can have the house reproduced (identical in all respects) for $150,000 total construction costs. There are also vacant lots, equivalent to the site on which the builder's house is situated, still available in the subdivision at a price of $60,000. Obviously then, you can get an identical substitute for $210,000, so there would be no point in paying the builder the asking price of $250,000. The reproduction cost of the structure, plus the land value, equals the upper limit of value.

Note that the cost approach can be used only on the improvements. The cost approach assumes either reproduction or replacement, and land cannot be reproduced or replaced. Therefore, to complete the appraisal of a property by the cost approach the appraiser estimates the reproduction or replacement cost of the improvements, and then adds the land value. The land value is ascertained by other approaches, usually simply by comparison with sales of similar vacant parcels (market data approach).

Of course, in the above example we used a brand new structure. It is easiest to explain the cost approach by beginning with a brand new structure. But most improvements are not new. And clearly, the value of a used structure is not as high as a new structure of exactly the same size and style. To account for this most appraisers use *replacement cost* when appraising a used structure rather than *reproduction cost new* (*cost to reproduce new*). Replacement cost is the cost of acquiring a structure which offers the same utility and amenities, but with modern materials, construction techniques and floorplans. Reproduction cost, on the other hand, requires calculation of the cost to create an identical reproduction of the structure. For most properties, especially older properties, this would be very time-consuming, and usually adds nothing to reliability or accuracy.

But even if an appraiser uses replacement cost, the structure may have suffered from *depreciation*. Depreciation is defined as a loss in value from any cause. There are three types of depreciation –

- Physical deterioration
- Functional obsolescence
- Economic (external) obsolescence

Physical deterioration means what it sounds like – maintenance has been deferred, so the building is in poor condition. In contrast, *functional obsolescence* refers to those conditions which render the structure outmoded. For example, if the gutters are falling off, this is physical deterioration. But if the property has four bedrooms and only one bath, the property is out of date by today's standards, so this is functional obsolescence. *Economic obsolescence* (sometimes called by its newer name *external obsolescence*) is caused by outside forces (externalities). Poor economic conditions in the region, for example, would cause economic obsolescence.

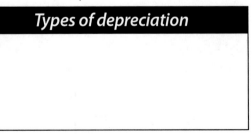

Types of depreciation

❶

❷

❸

Regardless of the type of depreciation, it causes the improvements to lose value, so it must be subtracted from the cost to reproduce or replacement cost. The complete theory of the cost approach is now apparent. The following diagram captures its essence –

Replacement (or Reproduction) Cost
Less Accrued Depreciation

Value of Improvements (Upper Limit)
Plus Land Value (by Market Approach)

TOTAL VALUE (Upper Limit)

Calculating cost – Determining the replacement or reproduction cost of the improvements is the first step in appraising a property with the cost approach. There are three commonly recognized methods for calculating cost –

- Quantity survey
- Unit in place
- Comparative unit

The ***quantity survey method*** is the most comprehensive and accurate method of estimating cost. It essentially repeats what a contractor would do to make a construction bid. Determining the cost by quantity survey means the appraiser must determine the cost of all materials and labor which would be required to replace or reproduce the structure. Because this is time-consuming, the quantity survey method is used only in unusual circumstances.

Measuring costs by the ***unit in place method*** means that the cost of each whole component of the structure is calculated separately. For example, suppose that an appraiser determines that a typical foundation costs a certain number of dollars per cubic yard of concrete used when it is poured (cost factor per cubic yard). Then the cost to reproduce any typical foundation can be estimated easily just by measuring its volume in cubic yards and multiplying the results times the cost factor per cubic yard. Similar techniques can be developed to determine the cost to reproduce other components such as the roof, flooring, siding, and so on.

While quantity survey and unit in place are used occasionally, the most commonly used method to determine cost is by a ***comparative unit***. For example, suppose you are appraising a warehouse. Warehouses have high ceilings, but the height of the ceiling may vary from one warehouse to the next. Therefore, the reproduction or replacement cost would be more closely related to the volume than to the floor area, so cubic footage would be an appropriate comparative unit. To determine the overall cost, an appraiser needs to determine only the cost per cubic foot, and then multiply this cost by the number of cubic feet in the subject property.

The unit of comparison can be any unit, but cubic foot and square foot are the most commonly used units. In residential and office structures, ceilings tend to be of fairly uniform height, so square footage is the most commonly used comparative unit. If a property has high ceilings (i.e., vaulted ceilings) which would increase the cost, the appraiser can just adjust the cost per square foot. Measurements of square footage for appraisal purposes are generally based on the outside dimensions.

Cost factors per square foot are readily available. Appraisers subscribe to commercial cost service bureaus which provide detailed information with periodic updates. The most popular of these is the *Marshall Valuation Service* published by Marshall and Swift Publication Company. Two sample pages from their *Residential Cost Handbook* are reproduced on the next page. Most appraisers today automate the process by using the online or the computerized edition.

Measuring Depreciation – Depreciation is said to be ***curable*** or ***incurable***. Curable depreciation is a loss in value which is repairable, from a practical standpoint. Incurable depreciation includes problems which either cannot be remedied at all, or which are impractical to repair or remedy.

ONE STORY
Square Foot Costs
Average Quality

RESIDENCE

STUD FRAMED

Total Area	Plywood or Hardboard	Metal or Vinyl Siding	Stucco	Wood Siding	Wood Shingles	Synth. Plaster (EIFS)
600	$58.41	$59.53	$59.49	$59.61	$59.74	$61.26
800	55.35	56.38	56.34	56.45	56.57	57.97
1000	53.08	54.05	54.01	54.12	54.23	55.54
1200	51.30	52.22	52.18	52.29	52.39	53.64
1300	50.54	51.43	51.40	51.50	51.60	52.82
1400	49.84	50.72	50.68	50.78	50.88	52.07
1500	49.20	50.06	50.03	50.13	50.22	51.39
1600	48.61	49.45	49.42	49.52	49.61	50.76
1700	48.06	48.89	48.86	48.95	49.05	50.17
1800	47.55	48.37	48.33	48.43	48.52	49.62
1900	47.07	47.87	47.84	47.93	48.02	49.11
2000	46.62	47.41	47.38	47.47	47.56	48.63
2100	46.20	46.98	46.95	47.03	47.12	48.18
2200	45.80	46.57	46.54	46.62	46.71	47.75
2400	45.06	45.81	45.78	45.86	45.95	46.96
2600	44.39	45.12	45.09	45.17	45.25	46.25
2800	43.78	44.49	44.46	44.54	44.62	45.59
3000	43.22	43.91	43.89	43.97	44.04	44.99
3200	42.70	43.38	43.35	43.43	43.51	44.44

STUD FRAMED / MASONRY

Total Area	Rustic Log	Masonry Veneer	Concrete Block	Stucco on Block	Common Brick	Poured Concrete (SIP) Forming
600	$65.28	$65.62	$61.75	$63.57	$69.02	$65.62
800	61.52	61.84	58.40	59.97	64.88	61.87
1000	58.75	59.06	55.94	57.31	61.85	59.11
1200	56.59	56.88	53.99	55.23	59.48	56.94
1300	55.66	55.95	53.16	54.34	58.46	56.02
1400	54.82	55.10	52.41	53.53	57.54	55.17
1500	54.04	54.32	51.71	52.79	56.70	54.40
1600	53.33	53.60	51.07	52.10	55.92	53.69
1700	52.67	52.94	50.47	51.46	55.19	53.02
1800	52.05	52.32	49.92	50.87	54.52	52.41
1900	51.47	51.74	49.40	50.32	53.89	51.83
2000	50.93	51.19	48.91	49.79	53.30	51.29
2100	50.42	50.68	48.45	49.30	52.75	50.78
2200	49.94	50.19	48.01	48.84	52.22	50.30
2400	49.05	49.30	47.21	47.99	51.26	49.41
2600	48.25	48.50	46.49	47.21	50.38	48.61
2800	47.52	47.76	45.82	46.51	49.59	47.87
3000	46.85	47.09	45.22	45.86	48.86	47.20
3200	46.23	46.46	44.65	45.27	48.19	46.58

SQUARE FOOT ADJUSTMENTS

ROOFING:
Composition shingle or
   Built-up, small rock ...... (base)
Clay tile .... + $4.57
Concrete tile .... + 2.82
Metal, preformed .... + .89
Wood shake .... + 1.38
Wood shingle .... + 1.19
Composition roll .... – .66

ENERGY ADJ: Mod. Climate (base)
Mild climate .... – $.78
Extreme climate .... + 1.29
Superinsulated .... + 2.77
FOUNDATION ADJ: Mod. Climate (base)
Mild climate .... – $1.66
Extreme climate .... + 3.05
Hillside, moderate slope .. + 1.53
Hillside, steep slope ...... + 4.58

Add for SEISMIC ZONES (Z)/HURRICANE (Wind) ADJ.: See Intro–9; maps. D–12.
Frame (Z2) +$1.04, (Z3–4/wind) +$1.82   Masonry (Z2) +$.73, (Z3–4/wind) +$1.51

See Pages Avg–27 & Avg–28 for other Sq. Ft. Adjustments, Basements, Porches, Garages, etc.

REFINEMENTS
Square Foot Costs
Average Quality

SQUARE FOOT ADJUSTMENTS

SUBFLOOR:
Wood subfloor .... (base)
Concrete slab .... – $1.86
Asphalt (for garage or carport) – 1.37

FLOOR INSULATION:
Mild climate .... + $ .62
Moderate climate .... + .78
Extreme climate .... + 1.00

PLASTER INTERIOR: .... + $2.29

FLOOR COVER:
Allowance (if not itemized) + $2.33
Carpet and pad .... + 2.03
Ceramic tile .... + 8.01
Wood flooring .... + 7.29
  Parquet blocks .... + 7.63
Terrazzo .... + 7.79
Vinyl comp. sheet or tile .. + 1.47
Vinyl sheet .... + 2.68

HEATING/COOLING:
Forced air .... (base)
  Oil-fired .... + $ .51
Floor or wall furnace ...... – 1.19
Electric, radiant .... – .28
  Baseboard or panel .... – .19
Hot water, baseboard .... + 1.33
Warm and cooled air .... + 1.37
Heat pump .... + 1.79
Evap. cooling w/ducts .... + 1.68
Air-to-air exchange system + 1.06

LUMP SUM ADJUSTMENTS

PLUMBING: 8 fixtures + rough-in (base)
Per fixture .... + or – $770
Per rough-in .... + or – 285

BUILT-IN APPLIANCES:
Allowance (if not itemized) + $2,100
Dishwasher .... + 525
Exhaust Fan or Bath Heater + 125
Garbage Disposer .... + 190
Hood and Fan .... + 205
Oven .... + 690
Oven, microwave combo .. + 1,350
Range and Oven .... + 1,075
Range top .... + 375
Radio Intercom .... + 730
Refrigerator or Freezer .... + 675
Res. security sys., wireless + 1,025
Trash compactor .... + 470
Vacuum cleaner system ... + 1,400

DORMERS: per linear foot
Hip or gable roof $97.50
Shed roof 82.50

FIREPLACES:
Single one story ... $1,975 – $2,425
Single two story .... 2,450 – 3,000
Single three story .. 2,925 – 3,575
Double one story ... 2,625 – 3,550
Double two story ... 3,225 – 3,950
Double three story . 5,100 – 6,250

BASEMENTS

Unfin. basements	200	400	800	1200	1600	2000	2400
Concrete walls 6"	$20.50	$15.56	$12.48	$11.04	$10.31	$10.01	$ 9.59
8"	22.00	16.61	13.25	11.66	10.85	10.52	10.03
12"	24.50	18.38	14.53	12.68	11.75	11.38	10.78
Conc. block walls 6"	18.66	14.26	11.54	10.29	9.64	9.38	9.04
8"	19.93	15.15	12.19	10.81	10.10	9.82	9.42
12"	22.26	16.80	13.38	11.76	10.94	10.61	10.11
Add for fin., minimal	4.86	4.35	4.05	3.91	3.84	3.81	3.76
partitioned	20.48	17.92	15.79	15.30	15.05	14.48	14.33

Outside Entrance: $775 – $1,075   For radon removal fan and alarm, add $245.

PORCH/BREEZEWAYS

Square Feet (Each)	FLOOR STRUCTURE:			WALL ENCLOSURE:			Add For Roof	Add For Ceiling
	Open Slab	Open W/Steps	Wood Deck	Screen Only	Knee Wall W/Glass	Solid Walls		
25	$4.36	$11.78	$18.82	$11.76	$43.20	$26.38	$9.58	$3.94
50	3.98	9.86	16.88	7.84	28.80	17.59	8.43	3.11
75	3.88	9.06	14.30	6.53	24.00	14.66	8.14	2.83
100	3.78	8.27	11.73	5.88	21.60	13.19	7.85	2.69
150	3.71	7.83	10.53	4.57	16.80	10.26	7.56	2.55
200	3.65	7.38	9.32	3.92	14.40	8.79	7.27	2.48
300	3.53	6.49	6.91	3.27	12.00	7.33	6.69	2.41

For example, an older house with no garage suffers from functional obsolescence today. Normally, the owner can add a garage, in which case we would say that the depreciation is curable. But if there is no place on the site to put a garage, then the problem is incurable. Physical deterioration and functional obsolescence can be curable or incurable. However, economic (external) obsolescence is, by its very nature, outside of the owner's control, and therefore always incurable.

The measurement of curable depreciation is most accurate when the appraiser determines the ***cost to cure*** — that is, how much it will cost to repair the problem. A more difficult problem is measurement of incurable depreciation. Obviously, if the problem is incurable there cannot be a cost to cure. For example, a residence located next to a used car lot suffers from economic obsolescence, but measuring the loss of value in dollars is difficult because the problem cannot be cured. Appraisers have various techniques for estimating the amount of incurable depreciation. These techniques rely on the concepts of ***economic life*** and ***physical life***.

Economic life and physical life – The concept of "life" as used in real estate appraisal can only be applied to the improvements. To speak of the life of the land is meaningless, since the land is indestructible, immovable and perpetual. Every improvement has both a physical life and an economic life. The physical life is the length of time it could actually remain in existence, and is normally longer than the economic life. The economic life, on the other hand, is the *useful life* of the improvements. When the improvements no longer produce a benefit beyond the benefit which could be derived if the land were unimproved, then we say the improvements have reached the end of their economic life.

In real life, the only time the physical life turns out to be shorter than the economic life is in the event of a catastrophe which results in the destruction of the improvements (end of the physical life) before the end of their economic life. This principle is exemplified by the saying "more houses are torn down than fall down." That these concepts are true is proved by what happens when there is a catastrophe – if the improvements are destroyed, but still had remaining economic life at the time of their destruction, the owner will use the insurance money to rebuild. If the improvements were at the end of their economic life anyway, the owner will probably just put the insurance money in the bank and sell the vacant lot. When there are vacant lots in a neighborhood where the improvements have been destroyed and not rebuilt, this is a symptom that the structures in the area are reaching the ends of their economic lives.

Example – You own a single-family residence in a blighted area. The land has been rezoned for general commercial use. You are able to rent the property as a residence for $1,000 per month ($12,000 per year), which nets you $9,000 per year after expenses. However, due to its zoning, the land value alone is $120,000. If you tore the house down and sold the land, you could place the $120,000 realized from the sale of the land into another investment. If the rate available for an alternative investment is 9%, then you could realize $10,800 per year. This is greater than what you are currently getting from the land and the building together, so keeping the building on the land is a diseconomy and a violation of the appraisal principles of balance and highest and best use. In this case the building is past the end of its economic life.

Chronological (actual) age and effective age – The ***chronological age*** of the improvements is simply the number of years since they were first constructed. A building which was built 70 years ago has a chronological age of 70 years. However, the ***effective age*** may be more or less than the chronological age, depending on the remaining economic life.

For example, consider a structure which would have a projected economic life of 50 years if new today with today's amenities, style and design. If the structure currently has a remaining economic life of 30 years, then it is 20 years old effectively –

Economic
Life if
New Today
50 Years

| Remaining Economic Life 30 Years |
| Effective Age 20 Years |

If the chronological age of the building in the drawing above is 70 years, we can conclude that there is some condition which has made the effective age (20 years) dramatically less than the chronological age (70 years). Perhaps the owner has rehabilitated the structure, perhaps it is of a historic style that is in great demand, or perhaps there is a shortage of similar properties in the area.

The effective age is frequently incorrectly thought of as being determined by the manner in which the improvements have been maintained. A longer economic life generally means a shorter effective age (and greater value). But the remaining economic life is determined more by externalities than by factors intrinsic to the property.

For example, it is possible to find properties which have been maintained in excellent condition, even though the owner knew the property would likely be torn down soon to make way for a different land use. If we judge the economic life from the condition, we would erroneously conclude that the improvements have a long remaining economic life. Even more common is the opposite – a property in poor condition located in an excellent neighborhood. When a property in a good neighborhood has been poorly maintained it does not mean that the remaining economic life of the property is shorter than its neighbors. The proof can be seen if the poorly maintained property is offered for sale. The buyer will usually restore the structure, or if it has deteriorated to the point where it cannot be restored, the owner will tear it down and replace it with a new structure of similar utility. This is because the new owner senses that the economic life is sufficiently long to justify the expense of rehabilitation or rebuilding. Notice that it was the externalities – the area surrounding the property, that determined the economic life, not the condition of the property itself.

However, appraisers do tend to equate good maintenance with a shorter (younger) effective age, and poor maintenance with a longer (older) effective age. As a rule, this tends to work, because owners usually maintain their properties in good condition if the remaining economic life is long enough to justify it. But care must be taken to remember that effective age is related to the remaining economic life of the structure, not to its condition. The current condition of the improvements is merely a symptom or indication of the probable remaining economic life.

Using the concepts of life and age, an appraiser can determine the dollar amount of accrued depreciation. Take the property in the previous graphic, for example. If a new property with today's amenities, style and design would have a projected economic life of 50 years, and the subject property has a remaining economic life of 30 years, then the effective age is 20 years, and we can conclude that 20 years of the economic life is used up. In other words, depreciation on this structure – from all sources – is $^{20}/_{50}$, or 40%. Now, if the appraiser has determined that the cost to reproduce the structure would be $200,000, then the current depreciated value can be computed by subtracting 40%, that is, $200,000 – $80,000 = $120,000 current value.

The problem with the above method is that it requires accurate judgment as to the remaining economic life and the projected economic life if the property were new. This is not possible. Appraisers, therefore, try to arrive at the amount of accrued depreciation in more scientific ways. One way is by ***observed condition***. This means that the appraiser rates different components of the property to determine their condition and arrives at conclusions as to the remaining economic life and effective age from the results. The problem, however, is that observed condition still assumes that the remaining economic life is tied to the condition of the property, which we know is not always the case.

Another technique used by appraisers is to observe the amount of difference between the market value of different types of properties and their replacement or reproduction cost. If an appraiser can determine from studying market transactions that bungalow style houses in a certain neighborhood tend to depreciate at a rate of, for example, ½ of 1% per year, then this fact can be used the next time the appraiser has an assignment to appraise a similar property. This technique requires experience to use effectively, but in most cases is probably the most accurate.

Regardless of the technique used to calculate the amount of accrued depreciation, it is not easy to be accurate. The result is that the more accrued depreciation in the improvements, the less reliable the cost approach. Measuring accrued depreciation is the weak link in the cost approach. Therefore, when correlating the results of the three approaches, the results of the cost approach should be weighted heavily as an indication of the upper limit of value if the property is a newer property with little or no incurable depreciation. The older the property, however, the less the results of the cost approach should be relied upon.

The income approach to value

The ***income approach to value*** (also sometimes called the ***income capitalization approach to value*** or just the ***capitalization approach***) rests squarely on the principle of anticipation. That is, the greater the anticipated future benefits the property will produce, the greater the present value.

The income approach is the most powerful approach for income properties such as office and apartment buildings, warehouses, and even going businesses. Even if a property does not currently produce an income, such as, for example, an owner occupied residence, a potential income can be imputed on which to base the value.

The first step in appraising a property by the income approach is to determine the income the property can produce. To find this, the appraiser must determine the ***market*** or ***economic rent***. Market rent is the income the property could and should be producing, and is determined by comparison with other similar income-producing properties in the area. The process of finding the market rent is called a ***market (economic) rent survey***.

Market rent must be contrasted with ***contract rent***. Contract rent is the rent the owner is currently receiving from the property. If the investment is properly managed, the contract rent should be the same as market rent. But it is certainly possible for the contract rent to be higher or, more likely, lower than the market rent. However, if the property is leased at a fixed rate (flat lease), then the contract rent is the market rent because the owner does not have the option to raise the rents.

If the rent is payable in installments, the appraiser computes what the total annual income would be. This is called the ***potential gross income*** (PGI). Similarly, all expense figures are also computed on an annual basis. Keeping all figures on an annual basis helps avoid computational errors.

The potential gross income is the first figure on the appraisers ***projected operating statement***, also sometimes called a ***pro-forma***. The projected operating statement is the appraiser's estimate of the amount of income the property will produce, net of expenses, in the current economic climate, under optimum management.

It is easier to understand the income approach if we take it from the standpoint of a specific property. Look at the projected operating statement for the Barkdust Apartments on the next page.

The Barkdust Apartments consist of a 15-unit complex located in an average metropolitan neighborhood. The structure is 12 years old and in generally good condition. All units have two bedrooms, one bath and no other unusual amenities. A market rent survey has disclosed that the units should be rented for $900 per month. The tax assessed value is $1,215,000 and the tax rate is $15 per thousand. All other expenses on the projected operating statement were verified by the appraiser personally from independent sources.

BARKDUST APARTMENTS
Projected Operating Statement

Income
Potential Gross Income (**PGI**)
15 Units × $900 per month = $13,500; × 12 months = $162,000
Less Vacancy and Credit Loss $8,100
Effective Gross Income (**EGI**)   153,900

Operating Expenses
Fixed Expenses
    Property taxes   18,500
    Fire and liability insurance   2,500
    Subtotal   21,000
Variable Expenses
    Management (@10% of PGI)   16,200
    Utilities (water/sewer, outside lights, trash)   6,000
    Normal maintenance   5,500
    Reserves for replacements   6,500
    Advertising   500
    Miscellaneous (accounting, landscaping, etc.)   1,000
    Subtotal   35,700
Total Operating Expenses   (56,700)

Net Operating Income (NOI) $97,200

    Notes to Projected Operating Statement *Vacancy and credit loss from market at 5% of PGI. Property taxes based on current tax assessed valuation of $1,215,000 at current tax rate of $15.00 per thousand. Normal maintenance includes ongoing expenses for ordinary repairs. Reserves for replacement is allowance for replacement or maintenance of major structural items, such as roof, exterior paint, appliances, carpeting and the like. All income and expense figures obtained from sources deemed to be reliable.*

The Projected Operating Statement – Referring to the projected operating statement above, note that the appraiser has deducted 5% of the potential gross income as an allowance for **vacancy and credit loss**. In order to reflect the real world as accurately as possible the appraiser must adjust for the fact that a certain vacancy factor is inevitable. *The vacancy and credit loss factor is not an arbitrary percentage; it must be derived from the market.* If the appraiser calculates projected rents as derived from the market area surrounding the subject property, then an owner who rents the units at the market rent will experience the same vacancy factor as is being experienced by owners of other properties in the area. The gross income after subtracting vacancy and credit loss is currently called the **effective gross income** (EGI), although some older texts may still refer to it as the **gross operating income**.

    Operating expenses are those expenses which are required for the property to produce an income, exclusive of principal and interest on loans or owner's income taxes. (Why these items are excluded is discussed later.) Many appraisers prefer to categorize expenses as those which are **fixed expenses** and those which are **variable expenses**. Fixed expenses are those expenses which the owner would incur whether all units are rented or the building is completely vacant. Variable expenses, on the other hand, are expenses which increase with occupancy. For example, if the management company charges their management fee on the rent *as collected*, then their fees are variable with the rate of occupancy. If their fees are based on the potential gross income, whether collected or not, then their fees are a fixed expense.

After subtracting all expenses, the result is called the ***net operating income*** (NOI). The net operating income is the amount the owner could expect to realize net of all expenses attributable to the property, exclusive of principal and interest on loans. Note that the net operating income also represents what the property would net if completely managed, assuming the owner's investment is totally passive.

Principal and interest on loans are disregarded at this point because the purpose of the projected operating statement is to determine what income the property would produce if the investment were all cash. At the same time, complete management expense has been duly subtracted. While it is true that in the real world many properties are financed, and it is also true that many owners manage their own properties, at this point in the appraisal we wish to disregard these factors. The reason is that we now wish to use the principle of substitution and compare the income potential of this investment with investments in the marketplace other than real estate. And most other investments – stock, bonds, certificates of deposit – are all cash, completely passive investments. Structuring the projected operating statement to determine what net income the apartment building could produce if it were an all cash and completely passive investment allows us to make it as comparable to these other investments as possible.

The capitalization process – Now that we understand the purpose of the projected operating statement, we can proceed with the process of finding what an owner would pay for the investment, based on the projected net operating income. This process is called ***capitalization***.

The investment marketplace is full of investment opportunities, each with its particular advantages and disadvantages. For our purposes, however, it does not matter which type of investment we choose, because they are all competing with each other continually. Since they all constantly seek their own level with each other, by comparing the apartment building investment to any one type of non-real estate investment, we automatically compare to all. It is common practice, therefore, to compare to the simplest non-real estate investment, usually a deposit at a financial institution.

Before we can begin the comparison, we must learn a few formulas. If you invest $100 in a bank deposit for one year, the amount of interest (income) you will receive is determined by the interest rate. In other words, if the bank will pay, say, 9%, then at the end of the year you will have earned $9.00. This is expressed by the formula

$$\textit{Income} = \textit{Rate} \times \textit{Investment}$$

Of course, we can also calculate the rate an investor is getting on an investment. The formula is

$$\textit{Rate} = \textit{Income} \div \textit{Investment}$$

For our purposes, there is another formula that is the most important – the formula to compute the amount of the investment when the rate and income are known. This formula is

$$\textit{Investment} = \textit{Income} \div \textit{Rate}$$

Of course, these formulas are used primarily by investors. Appraisers need to change the terminology slightly. An appraiser would recast the investment formula as

$$\textit{Value} = \textit{Income} \div \textit{Rate}$$

Now we are ready to think about what a buyer would pay for the Barkdust Apartments. We already know the net operating income is $97,200, so if a buyer were willing to accept a rate of, say, 8%, our formula above indicates the buyer must be willing to pay $1,215,000 ($97,200 ÷ .08 = $1,215,000).

Of course, depending on the current market interest rates, a given investor may be happy with an 8% rate on a bank deposit, but would the same investor be satisfied with 8% on the apartment investment? If not, then an adjustment must be made. Consider the following chart showing what happens to the value of the apartments as rates demanded by investors change –

$97,200	÷	8.00%	=	$1,215,000
$97,200	÷	8.25%	=	$1,178,182
$97,200	÷	8.50%	=	$1,143,529
$97,200	÷	8.75%	=	$1,110,857
$97,200	÷	9.00%	=	$1,080,000
$97,200	÷	9.25%	=	$1,050,811
$97,200	÷	9.50%	=	$1,023,158
$97,200	÷	9.75%	=	$996,923
$97,200	÷	10.00%	=	$972,000

The above chart shows what happens when the rate demanded by investors changes. As the rate increases, the value decreases, and vice-versa. If you think about the bank account – our point of comparison – this makes sense. The higher the interest rate, the less you have to put on deposit to get the same annual interest income. Therefore, if the bank will pay 10% interest, it would take a deposit of only $972,000 to get an annual interest income of $97,200. Because the income from the apartment building is constant at any point in time, we would expect an investor to be unwilling to pay more for the apartment building than $972,000.

Think of the relationship among the rate, the income and the value like a teeter-totter. At any point in time the net operating income (NOI) is unalterable, so as the rate changes the value changes in the opposite direction –

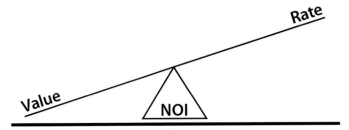

Even having made the net operating income (NOI) appear as similar as possible to the return on other investments – all cash and completely passive – we must still adjust the rate. Appraisers recognize that investors may be willing to accept a certain rate on a bank deposit, but the same investor may demand a different rate for an investment in an apartment building.

There are several reasons the rate must be adjusted. Most obvious is that the investment in the bank account is generally regarded as safer than the investment in the apartment building. Furthermore, real estate investments have a reputation of being less liquid – harder to sell for cash – than other investments; certainly less liquid than the bank deposit. Less obvious, but still important, is the fact that investment in improved real property offers an investor income tax advantages which would not be available if the money were invested in a bank account.

One of the most important differences between an investment in a bank deposit and a real estate investment is the potential for capital gain. In other words, if you put your money in a bank account for a number of years and then withdraw it, the money has lost purchasing power because of inflation. But if you put your money into a real estate investment, when you sell the investment years later, your will get more dollars in return. Even though the dollars you get back when you sell the investment are not worth as much, you get sufficiently more of them to make up for their lost value. This is called a **hedge against inflation**.

Special note – Although unsophisticated investors do not usually understand the difference, professionals know that "hedge against inflation" is not the same as "appreciation." Hedge against inflation occurs when you invest in a hard asset such as real estate, gold, classic cars, art, and the like, and then sell the asset for more, albeit cheaper, dollars later. Inflation raises the number of dollars you can get for the investment, and does so equally for all investments, but does not raise the real value.

Appreciation occurs when some unforeseen event raises the value of an investment more than the value of other similar investments. If you buy an apartment building for $1,000,000 and later sell it for $2,000,000 because the dollar has devalued to half its former value, you have benefited from a hedge against inflation. If you buy an apartment building for $1,000,000 and are later able to sell it for $2,000,000 because a shopping center was built next door making the apartment building more desirable to an investor, you have benefited from appreciation. Some appraisers use the older term **unearned increment** to describe both appreciation and hedge against inflation. Sophisticated investors know that true appreciation accounts for little of the increase in market value. Properties almost always increase in market value over time, but mostly from the effects of inflation, not appreciation.

To summarize the adjustments we need to make, let us suppose the banks are currently offering about 7% on deposits. Appraisers call this the **safe rate**, or sometimes **bank rate**, **guaranteed rate** or **annuity rate**. Let us further suppose that investigation of market data leads us to the conclusion that we should further adjust the safe rate as follows –

Safe rate	7%	
Add for additional risk	+ 1%	
Add for lack of liquidity	+ 1%	
Subtract for tax shelter benefits	− 1%	
Subtract for hedge against inflation	− 4%	
Adjusted return on investment required	6%	(Yield Rate)

The above adjustments were not meant to be accurate; they were made solely for the purpose of illustration. Therefore, the conclusion that an investor would accept 6% return on the apartment building investment when banks are paying 7% on deposits, is not necessarily correct. Later in our discussion we will discover a technique which allows appraisers to determine an accurate and reliable rate. However, there is another factor which must be considered first.

When an investor will get the entire principal back at the end of the investment period, such as when the money is deposited in a bank account, the proper rate to use is a **yield rate** (as above), also sometimes called a **return on the investment**.

But in some investments, the amount invested is used up over the life of the investment. For example, if you invest in an oil well, the investment becomes worthless as the oil is pumped out and sold. When the well is dry, it is worth only the value of the used pumping equipment and whatever the land will bring – little or nothing in comparison to the original value of the well. At the end of the bank account investment, however, the investor will get back the entire amount of the principal invested. The bank account does not become worthless over its term. (Note that we have already adjusted for loss of market value due to inflation in the adjustments above.) If an investor were comparing the rate of return required for the bank account with the rate of return required for an oil well, it would be necessary to add an additional percentage to account for **recapture** of the oil well investment over its useful life. The rate for recapture is also sometimes called the **return of the investment**.

Assets such as oil wells are referred to as **wasting assets** because they are used up and become worthless over their economic lives. Wasting assets include not only oil wells, but real estate as well. If you recall from the discussion of economic life, we discovered that a structure has an economic life, and the value of the structure at the end of its economic life is zero. So if an additional percentage should be added to the bank rate to adjust it for an oil well, an additional percentage should also be added when comparing the bank deposit to a real estate investment.

The next question to be determined is how much the recapture adjustment should be. Apartment buildings usually have a fairly long useful life, so let us assume the Barkdust Apartments have a remaining economic life of 40 years. If the structure will become worthless over the next 40 years, then we must recapture 2½% each year (100% ÷ 40 years = 2.5% per year).

But there is another important fact to consider. Only the building will become worthless at the end of its useful life; there is no economic life for land, so recapture of the land is not necessary. For the sake of the discussion, let us assume that the structure accounts for 80% of the total investment and the land represents the other 20%. In other words, if an investor paid $1,000,000 for the investment, this was really $800,000 (80%) for the improvements, and $200,000 (20%) for the land.

Therefore, we only need to recapture 80% of the total investment. And if we have a 40-year economic life in which to do this, the recapture rate should be 2% (80% ÷ 40 years = 2% per year). Now our adjustments look like this –

Safe rate	7%	
Add for additional risk	+ 1%	
Add for lack of liquidity	+ 1%	
Subtract for tax shelter benefits	− 1%	
Subtract for hedge against inflation	− 4%	
Adjusted return *on* investment required	6%	(Yield Rate)
Return *of* investment required	+ 2%	(Recapture Rate)
Capitalization rate	8%	

Note that the rate above is now called the **capitalization rate**. To an accountant or an appraiser, a capitalization rate is a rate which includes a yield on the investment plus a rate for recapture of the investment. Non-wasting assets such as bank accounts, bonds, and the like, must be considered in terms of a yield rate; wasting assets such as buildings, oil wells, mines and the like, must be valued with a capitalization rate.

Now it appears that, if all our assumptions and adjustments are accurate, an investor should demand a return of 8% for the Barkdust Apartments. In fact, however, there is no way to be sure that our figures are accurate. If you recall from our previous discussion, raising or lowering the rate has a dramatic effect on the value. On a net operating income of $97,200, if we change the rate by a mere ¼ of 1%, the difference in value is almost $37,000 –

$97,200 ÷ 8.00% = $1,215,000
$97,200 ÷ 8.25% = $1,178,182

It is apparent that appraisers cannot use the income approach properly without an accurate capitalization rate, and the process we just used is likely to be far from accurate. The theory we used is correct, but it is impossible to be accurate about the assumptions and adjustments we made.

To derive an accurate capitalization rate appraisers usually apply a more direct method called *market extraction*. If you recall, we can calculate the rate of return an investor is getting on an investment with the formula –

Rate = Income ÷ Investment

To recast this for appraisal purposes, just change the names of the terms –

Capitalization Rate = Net Operating Income ÷ Value

In other words, appraisers can find the capitalization rate which an investor is getting just by dividing the net operating income (NOI) by the market value of the property. We know that investors base a great deal of the investment decision on the anticipated rate of return. Therefore, an appraiser uses this formula to extract the capitalization rates from several recently sold comparable properties, and correlates the resulting rates to derive an overall market capitalization rate for similar properties. Using market extraction to find the capitalization rate is highly reliable, since it is based directly on the market.

Of course, if appraisers can simply find an accurate overall capitalization rate by market extraction, it would seem that dissecting the capitalization rate into components such as safe rate, risk factor, recapture, and the like, is a pointless academic exercise. Even though the theory of the capitalization rate is not usually very helpful in real world appraising, the theory is nevertheless correct. In fact, capitalization theory is useful in another way, because it lets us understand better what happens in the marketplace.

For example, at any given point in time, should we use the same capitalization rate on all properties? If you understand the adjustments we made in discussing the theory of the capitalization rate, you will realize that different properties entail different risk and liquidity considerations, and have different remaining economic lives. A new property in an excellent neighborhood will have comparatively little risk and a long remaining economic life, so its capitalization rate should be low. On the other hand, an older property in a poorer neighborhood may entail substantial risk, lack of liquidity and have a short remaining economic life. For such a property, a much higher capitalization rate is needed.

Investors also benefit from understanding capitalization rates. For example, what would happen to the values of properties if interest rates increase? Increasing interest rates would be translated immediately into higher capitalization rates demanded by investors. And higher rates mean lower values. Or what would happen if there is suddenly an anticipation of increased inflation? Or an increase in tax benefits of owning real estate? Both of these are benefits, so investors would lower the capitalization rates they demand, and there would be a corresponding increase in market values.

Gross rent multipliers – Let us consider again the Barkdust Apartments. The potential gross income (PGI) was $162,000 and the net operating income (NOI) was $97,200. If market extraction tells us the proper capitalization rate to use is 8%, then the value is $1,215,000 ($97,200 ÷ .08 = $1,215,000).

If this is an accurate reflection of the market, then we can conclude another fact – that the property ought to sell for about 7.5 times its potential gross income (PGI). The number "7.5" here is called a ***gross rent multiplier*** (GRM), or sometimes ***gross income multiplier*** (GIM). Gross rent multipliers are extracted from the market in much the same way as capitalization rates. To find the gross rent multiplier for a recently sold comparable, just divide the sales price at which the comparable sold by the potential gross income of the property when it sold. The formula is

Gross Rent Multiplier = Sales Price ÷ Potential Gross Income

In other words, $1,215,000 divided by $162,000 is 7.5 – ($1,215,000 ÷ $162,000 = 7.500), so the market value is 7.5 times the potential gross income. If we had several recently sold comparable properties, all of which corroborate the fact that such properties tend to sell for about 7.5 times their potential gross income, the number "7.5" could be considered a market gross rent multiplier for all such similar properties.

Using a gross rent multiplier is an easy way to determine the market value of an income property – just multiply the subject property's potential gross income by a multiplier extracted from the market, and you have the market value. But there are several dangers in using a gross rent multiplier.

Gross rent multipliers are derived from the potential gross income (PGI), not the net operating income (NOI). If you wish to use a gross rent multiplier accurately, then you must derive it from properties that are very similar. Whether a property is older or newer, in a poorer or better neighborhood, among many other factors, has great bearing on the ratio of expenses to income, and this ratio must be identical for the gross rent multiplier to be used accurately.

In the Barkdust Apartments, the total operating expenses were $64,800, which is 40% of the potential gross income ($64,800 ÷ $162,000 = .40). If the Barkdust Apartments had been older, in poorer condition, or suffered from some other detriment, the expenses would likely have been much higher, and therefore the ratio of expenses to potential gross income would have been higher. Since gross rent multipliers are based on the potential gross income, not the net income, their use presumes that the subject property will have the same ratio of expenses to potential gross income as the properties from which the gross rent multiplier was derived. The danger in using a gross rent multiplier is that many novices take the shortcut too quickly and do not verify that the gross rent multiplier is correct for the property they are appraising.

Most appraisers today consider a gross rent multiplier effective as a quick estimating tool, but not a satisfactory method for serious appraisal of an income property. Considering that the income approach is the most powerful approach for an income property, it makes little sense to use a questionable technique. However, gross rent multipliers are commonly used by brokers and their customers and clients in establishing an asking or offering price for a property.

Forms

On the following pages you will find one of the many forms that an appraiser would use in a residential appraisal –
Uniform Residential Appraisal Report,
(Fannie Mae Form 1004, Freddie Mac Form 70)

O━🔑 KEY TERMS

The key to understanding any new field is the vocabulary used in that field. To maximize your comprehension of the material presented in this chapter, be sure you know the meaning and significance of the following terms. Remember that the majority of test questions primarily test knowledge of vocabulary.

Actual age

Advocacy

Agent

Annuity rate

Anticipation

Appraisal

Appraisal by anticipated use

Appraisal by development cost

Approaches to value

Arms length transactions

Assessed value

Balance

Bank rate

Book value

Capitalization approach to value

Capitalization rate

Change

Chronological age

Comparative unit

Competition

Conformity

Contract rent

Contribution

Correlation

Cost

Cost to cure

Cost to reproduce new

Curable depreciation

Decline

Demand

Depreciated value

Depreciation

Economic forces

Economic life

Economic obsolescence

Economic rent

Effective age

Effective gross income

Effective purchasing power

Efficient market

Environmental forces

Equilibrium

External obsolescence

Externalities

Fee appraiser

Fiduciary

Fixed expenses

Four agents in production

Functional obsolescence

Gentrification

Governmental forces

Gross income multiplier

Gross operating income.

Gross rent multiplier

Growth

Guaranteed rate

Hedge against inflation

Highest and best use

Income approach to value

Income capitalization approach

Incurable depreciation

Independent fee appraiser

Insurance value

Intrinsic value

Liquidation (liquidated) value

Loan value

Market data approach

Market extraction

Market rent survey

Market value

Neighborhood

Net operating income

Observed condition

Physical deterioration

Physical forces

Physical life

Plottage increment

Potential gross income

Price

Pro-forma

Progression

Projected operating statement

Quantity survey method

Recapture

Reconciliation

Regression

Replacement cost

Reproduction cost

Residual value

Return of the investment

Return on the investment

Revitalization

Safe rate

Sales comparison approach

Salvage value

Scarcity

Single-use property

Social forces

Stability

Substitution

Surplus productivity

Transferability

Trend

True and fair value

Unearned increment

Uniform Residential Appraisal Report

Uniform Standards of Professional Appraisal Practice

Unit in place method

Utility

Vacancy and credit loss

Valuation

Value in exchange

Value in use

Variable expenses

Wasting assets

Yield rate

FNMA 1004

Property Description

UNIFORM RESIDENTIAL APPRAISAL REPORT   File No.

SUBJECT

Property Address	City	State Zip Code
Legal Description		County
Assessor's Parcel No.	Tax Year R.E. Taxes $	Special Assessments $
Borrower Current Owner	Occupant	Owner Tenant Vacant
Property rights appraised Fee Simple Leasehold Project Type PUD	Condominium (HUD/VA only)	HOA$ /Mo.
Neighborhood or Project Name	Map Reference	Census Tract
Sale Price $ Date of Sale	Description and $ amount of loan charges/concessions to be paid by seller	
Lender/Client Address		
Appraiser Address		

NEIGHBORHOOD

Location	Urban	Suburban	Rural	Predominant occupancy	Single family housing		Present land use %	Land use change
					PRICE $(000)	AGE (yrs)		
Built up	Over 75%	25-75%	Under 25%				One family ___	Not likely Likely
Growth rate	Rapid	Stable	Slow	Owner	Low		2-4 family ___	In process
Property values	Increasing	Stable	Declining	Tenant	High		Multi-family ___	To: ___
Demand/supply	Shortage	In balance	Over supply	Vacant (0-5%)	Predominant		Commercial ___	
Marketing time	Under 3 mos.	3-6 mos.	over 6 mos.	Vacant (over 5%)				

Note: race and the racial composition of the neighborhood are not appraisal factors.

Neighborhood boundaries and characteristics:_____

Factors that affect the marketability of the properties in the neighborhood (proximity to employment and amenities, employment stability, appeal to market, e
_____
_____
_____
_____

Market conditions in the subject neighborhood (including support for the above conclusions related to the trend of property values, demand/supply, and marketing ti
-- such as data on competitive properties for sale in the neighborhood, description of the prevalence of sales and financing concessions, etc.):
_____
_____
_____
_____
_____
_____

PUD

Project Information for PUDs (If applicable) -- Is the developer/builder in control of the Home Owner's Association (HOA)?   Yes No

Approximate total number of units in the subject project_____ Approximate total number of units for sale in the subject project_____

Describe common elements and recreational facilities:_____

SITE

Dimensions		Topography	
Site area	Corner Lot Yes No	Size	
Specific zoning classification and description		Shape	
Zoning compliance Legal Legal nonconforming (Grandfathered use) Illegal No Zoning		Drainage	
Highest & best use as improved: Present use Other use (explain)		View	

Utilities	Public	Other	Off-site Improvements	Type	Public	Private	
Electricity			Street				Landscaping
Gas			Curb/gutter				Driveway Surface
Water			Sidewalk				Apparent easements
Sanitary sewer			Street lights				FEMA Special Flood Hazard Area Yes No
Storm sewer			Alley				FEMA Zone ___ Map Date ___
							FEMA Map No.

Comments (apparent adverse easements, encroachments, special assessments, slide areas, illegal or legal nonconforming zoning use, etc.):_____

DESCRIPTION OF IMPROVEMENTS

GENERAL DESCRIPTION	EXTERIOR DESCRIPTION	FOUNDATION	BASEMENT	INSULATION
No. of Units	Foundation	Slab	Area Sq. Ft.	Roof
No. of Stories	Exterior Walls	Crawl Space	% Finished	Ceiling
Type (Det./Att.)	Roof Surface	Basement	Ceiling	Walls
Design (Style)	Gutters & Dwnspts.	Sump Pump	Walls	Floor
Existing/Proposed	Window Type	Dampness	Floor	None
Age (Yrs.)	Storm/Screens	Settlement	Outside Entry	Unknown
Effective Age (Yrs.)	Manufactured House	Infestation		

ROOMS	Foyer	Living	Dining	Kitchen	Den	Family Rm.	Rec. Rm.	Bedrooms	# Baths	Laundry	Other	Area Sq. Ft.
Basement												
Level 1												
Level 2												

Finished area **above** grade contains:____ Rooms;____ Bedroom(s);____ Bath(s);____ Square Feet of Gross Living Area

INTERIOR	Materials/Condition	HEATING	KITCHEN EQUIP.	ATTIC	AMENITIES	CAR STORAGE
Floors		Type	Refrigerator	None	Fireplace(s) # ___	None
Walls		Fuel	Range/Oven	Stairs	Patio	Garage # of cars
Trim/Finish		Condition	Disposal	Drop Stair	Deck	Attached
Bath Floor		COOLING	Dishwasher	Scuttle	Porch	Detached
Bath Wainscot		Central	Fan/Hood	Floor	Fence	Built-In
Doors		Other	Microwave	Heated	Pool	Carport
		Condition	Washer/Dryer	Finished		Driveway

COMMENTS

Additional features (special energy efficient items, etc.):_____

Condition of the improvements, depreciation (physical, functional, and external), repairs needed, quality of construction, remodeling/additions, etc.:_____
_____
_____

Adverse environmental conditions (such as, but not limited to, hazardous wastes, toxic substances, etc.) present in the improvements, on the site, or in
immediate vicinity of the subject property.:_____

Freddie Mac Form 70 6-93   Fannie Mae Form 1004 (6-93)

UNIFORM RESIDENTIAL APPRAISAL REPORT

Valuation Section   File No.

COST APPROACH

ESTIMATED SITE VALUE .... = $

ESTIMATED REPRODUCTION COST-NEW-OF IMPROVEMENTS:

Dwelling _____ Sq. Ft. @ $ _____ = $ _____
_____ Sq. Ft. @ $ _____ = _____
= _____
Garage/Carport _____ Sq. Ft. @ $ _____ = _____
Total Estimated Cost New .... = $ _____
Less   Physical   Functional   External
Depreciation _____ = $ _____
Depreciated Value of Improvements .... = $ _____
"As is" Value of Site Improvements .... = $ _____
INDICATED VALUE BY COST APPROACH .... = $ _____

Comments on Cost Approach (such as, source of cost estimate, site value, square foot calculation and for HUD, VA and FmHA, the estimated remaining economic life of the property):

Est Rem Econ Life: yrs

SALES COMPARISON ANALYSIS

ITEM	SUBJECT	COMPARABLE NO. 1	COMPARABLE NO. 2	COMPARABLE NO. 3
Address				
Proximity to Subject				
Sales Price	$	$	$	$
Price/Gross Liv. Area	$	$	$	$
Data and/or Verification Source				
VALUE ADJUSTMENTS	DESCRIPTION	DESCRIPTION +(-)$ Adjustment	DESCRIPTION +(-)$ Adjustment	DESCRIPTION +(-)$ Adjustment
Sales or Financing Concessions				
Date of Sale/Time				
Location				
Leasehold/Fee Simple				
Site				
View				
Design and Appeal				
Quality of Construction				
Age				
Condition				
Above Grade Room Count	Total Bdrms Baths	Total Bdrms Baths	Total Bdrms Baths	Total Bdrms Baths
Gross Living Area	Sq. Ft.	Sq. Ft.	Sq. Ft.	Sq. Ft.
Basement & Finished Rooms Below Grade				
Functional Utility				
Heating/Cooling				
Energy Efficient Items				
Garage/Carport				
Porch, Patio, Deck, Fireplace(s), etc.				
Fence, Pool, etc.				
Net Adj. (total)		+ - $	+ - $	+ - $
Adjusted Sales Price of Comparable		$	$	$

Comments on Sales Comparison (including the subject property's compatibility to the neighborhood, etc.):

ITEM	SUBJECT	COMPARABLE NO. 1	COMPARABLE NO. 2	COMPARABLE NO. 3
Date, Price and Data Source, for prior sales within year of appraisal				

Analysis of any current agreement of sale, option, or listing of the subject property and analysis of any prior sales of subject and comparables within one year of the date of appraisal

INDICATED VALUE BY SALES COMPARISON APPROACH .... $ _____
INDICATED VALUE BY INCOME APPROACH (If Applicable) Estimated Market Rent $ _____ /Mo.x Gross Rent Multiplier _____ =$ _____

This appraisal is made ☐ "as is" ☐ subject to the repairs, alterations, inspections or conditions listed below ☐ subject to completion per plans and specifications
Conditions of Appraisal:

Final Reconciliation:

RECONCILIATION

The purpose of this appraisal is to estimate the market value of the real property that is subject to this report, based on the above conditions and the certification, contingent and limiting conditions, and market value definition that are stated in the attached Freddie Mac Form 439/Fannie Mae Form 1004B (Revised _____).
I (WE) ESTIMATE THE MARKET VALUE, AS DEFINED, OF THE REAL PROPERTY THAT IS THE SUBJECT OF THIS REPORT, AS OF _____
(WHICH IS THE DATE OF INSPECTION AND THE EFFECTIVE DATE OF THIS REPORT) TO BE $ _____

APPRAISER:	SUPERVISORY APPRAISER (ONLY IF REQUIRED):	
Signature	Signature	☐ Did ☐ Did Not
Name	Name	Inspect Property
Date Report Signed	Date Report Signed	
State Certification #	State Certification # State	State
Or State License # State	Or State License #	State

DEFINITION OF MARKET VALUE: The most probable price which a property should bring in a competitive and open market under all conditions requisite to a fair sale, the buyer and seller, each acting prudently, knowledgeably and assuming the price is not affected by undue stimulus. Implicit in this definition is the consummation of a sale as of a specified date and the passing of title from seller to buyer under conditions whereby: (1) buyer and seller are typically motivated; (2) both parties are well informed or well advised, and each acting in what he considers his own best interest; (3) a reasonable time is allowed for exposure in the open market; (4) payment is made in terms of cash in U.S. dollars or in terms of financial arrangements comparable thereto; and (5) the price represents the normal consideration for the property sold unaffected by special or creative financing or sales concessions* granted by anyone associated with the sale.

*Adjustments to the comparables must be made for special or creative financing or sales concessions. No adjustments are necessary for those costs which are normally paid by sellers as a result of tradition or law in a market area; these costs are readily identifiable since the seller pays these costs in virtually all sales transactions. Special or creative financing adjustments can be made to the comparable property by comparisons to financing terms offered by a third party institutional lender that is not already involved in the property or transaction. Any adjustment should not be calculated on a mechanical dollar for dollar cost of the financing or concessions but the dollar amount of any adjustment should approximate the market's reaction to the financing or concessions based on the appraiser's judgment.

STATEMENT OF LIMITING CONDITIONS AND APPRAISER'S CERTIFICATION

CONTINGENT AND LIMITING CONDITIONS: The appraiser's certification that appears in the appraisal report s subject to the following conditions:

1. The appraiser will not be responsible for matters of a legal nature that affect either the property being appraised or the title to it. The appraiser assumes that the title is good and marketable and, therefore, will not render any opinions about the title. The property is appraised on the basis of it being under responsible ownership.

2. The appraiser has provided a sketch in the appraisal report to show approximate dimensions of the improvements and the sketch is included only to assist the reader of the report in visualizing the property and understanding the appraiser's determination of its size.

3. The appraiser has examined the available flood maps that are provided by the Federal Emergency Management Agency (or other data sources) and has noted in the appraisal report whether the subject site is located in an identified Special Flood Hazard Area. Because the appraiser is not a surveyor, he or she makes no guarantees, express or implied, regarding this determination.

4. The appraiser will not give testimony or appear in court because he or she made an appraisal of the property in question, unless specific arrangements to do so have been made beforehand.

5. The appraiser has estimated the value of the land in the cost approach at its highest and best use and the improvements at their contributory value. The separate valuations of the land and improvements must not be used in conjunction with any other appraisal and are invalid if they are so used.

6. The appraiser has noted in the appraisal report any adverse conditions (such as, needed repairs, depreciation, the presence of hazardous wastes, toxic substances, etc.) observed during the inspection of the subject property or that he or she became aware of during the normal research involved in performing the appraisal. Unless otherwise stated in the appraisal report, the appraiser has no knowledge of any hidden or unapparent conditions of the property or adverse environmental conditions (including the presence of hazardous wastes, toxic substances, etc.) that would make the property more or less valuable, and has assumed that there are no such conditions and makes no guarantees or warranties, express or implied, regarding the condition of the property. The appraiser will not be responsible for any such conditions that do exist or for any engineering or testing that might be required to discover whether such conditions exist. Because the appraiser is not an expert in the field of environmental hazards, the appraisal report must not be considered as an environmental assessment of the property.

7. The appraiser obtained the information, estimates, and opinions that were expressed in the appraisal report from sources that he or she considers to be reliable and believes them to be true and correct. The appraiser does not assume responsibility for the accuracy of such items that were furnished by other parties.

8. The appraiser will not disclose the contents of the appraisal report except as provided for in the Uniform Standards of Professional Appraisal Practice.

9. The appraiser has based his or her appraisal report and valuation conclusion for an appraisal that is subject to satisfactory completion, repairs, or alterations on the assumption that completion of the improvements will be performed in a workmanlike manner.

10. The appraiser must provide his or her prior written consent before the lender/client specified in the appraisal report can distribute the appraisal report (including conclusions about the property value, the appraiser's identity and professional designations, and references to any professional appraisal organizations or the firm with which the appraiser is associated) to anyone other than the borrower; the mortgagee or its successors and assigns; the mortgage insurer; consultants; professional appraisal organizations; any state or federally approved financial institution; or any department, agency, or instrumentality of the United States or any state or the District of Columbia; except that the lender/client may distribute the property description section of the report only to data collection or reporting service(s) without having to obtain the appraiser's prior written consent. The appraiser's written consent and approval must also be obtained before the appraisal can be conveyed by anyone to the public through advertising, public relations, news, sales, or other media.

APPRAISER'S CERTIFICATION: The Appraiser certifies and agrees that: File No.

1. I have researched the subject market area and have selected a minimum of three recent sales of properties most similar and proximate to the subject property for consideration in the sales comparison analysis and have made a dollar adjustment when appropriate to reflect the market reaction to those items of significant variation. If a significant item in a comparable property is superior to, or more favorable than, the subject property, I have made a negative adjustment to reduce the adjusted sales price of the comparable and, if a significant item in a comparable property is inferior to, or less favorable than the subject property, I have made a positive adjustment to increase the adjusted sales price of the comparable.

2. I have taken into consideration the factors that have an impact on value in my development of the estimate of market value in the appraisal report. I have not knowingly withheld any significant information from the appraisal report and I believe, to the best of my knowledge, that all statements and information in the appraisal report are true and correct.

3. I stated in the appraisal report only my own personal, unbiased, and professional analysis, opinions, and conclusions, which are subject only to the contingent and limiting conditions specified in this form.

4. I have no present or prospective interest in the property that is the subject to this report, and I have no present or prospective personal interest or bias with respect to the participants in the transaction. I did not base, either partially or completely, my analysis and/or the estimate of market value in the appraisal report on the race, color, religion, sex, handicap, familial status, or national origin of either the prospective owners or occupants of the subject property or of the present owners or occupants of the properties in the vicinity of the subject property.

5. I have no present or contemplated future interest in the subject property, and neither my current or future employment nor my compensation for performing this appraisal is contingent on the appraised value of the property.

6. I was not required to report a predetermined value or direction in value that favors the cause of the client or any related party, the amount of the value estimate, the attainment of a specific result, or the occurrence of a subsequent event in order to receive my compensation and/or employment for performing the appraisal. I did not base the appraisal report on a requested minimum valuation, a specific valuation, or the need to approve a specific mortgage loan.

7. I performed this appraisal in conformity with the Uniform Standards of Professional Appraisal Practice that were adopted and promulgated by the Appraisal Standards Board of The Appraisal Foundation and that were in place as of the effective date of this appraisal, with the exception of the departure provision of those Standards, which does not apply. I acknowledge that an estimate of a reasonable time for exposure in the open market is a condition in the definition of market value and the estimate I developed is consistent with the marketing time noted in the neighborhood section of this report, unless I have otherwise stated in the reconciliation section.

8. I have personally inspected the interior and exterior areas of the subject property and the exterior of all properties listed as comparables in the appraisal report. I further certify that I have noted any apparent or known adverse conditions in the subject improvements, on the subject site, or on any site within the immediate vicinity of the subject property of which I am aware and have made adjustments for these adverse conditions in my analysis of the property value to the extent that I had market evidence to support them. I have also commented about the effect of the adverse conditions on the marketability of the subject property.

9. I personally prepared all conclusions and opinions about the real estate that were set forth in the appraisal report. If I relied on significant professional assistance from any individual or individuals in the performance of the appraisal or the preparation of the appraisal report, I have named such individual(s) and disclosed the specific tasks performed by them in the reconciliation section of this appraisal report. I certify that any individual so named is qualified to perform the tasks. I have not authorized anyone to make a change to any item in the report; therefore, if an unauthorized change is made to the appraisal report, I will take no responsibility for it.

SUPERVISORY APPRAISER'S CERTIFICATION: If a supervisory appraiser signed the appraisal report, he or she certifies and agrees that: I directly supervise the appraiser who prepared the appraisal report, have reviewed the appraisal report, agree with the statements and conclusions of the appraiser, agree to be bound by the appraiser's certifications numbered 4 through 7 above, and am taking full responsibility for the appraisal and the appraisal report.

ADDRESS OF PROPERTY APPRAISED: _____

APPRAISER: **SUPERVISORY APPRAISER**   (only if required):

Signature: _____   Signature: _____
Name: _____   Name: _____
Date Signed: _____   Date Signed: _____
State Certification #: _____   State Certification #: _____
or State License #: _____   or State License #: _____
State: _____   State: _____
Expiration Date of Certification or License: _____   Expiration Date of Certification or License: _____
                                                   ❏ Did   ❏ Did Not Inspect Property

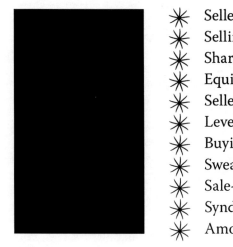

Chapter 16

Alternative financing and principles of investing

I N MOST REAL ESTATE TRANSACTIONS the buyer pays cash for the property. Of course, most buyers do not have the cash in the bank, but they can get the cash from an outside lender – so the seller still receives the entire purchase price in cash at closing. There are cases, however, where this is not possible or even desirable. For example, the seller may wish to create an installment sale in order to spread out a large capital gain. (Details about income tax issues in real estate are covered in Chapter 17.) In this chapter we will explore several alternatives to traditional all-cash transactions.

The most obvious circumstance in which the seller does not receive cash for the entire purchase price is where the buyer takes over the seller's old loan and just pays cash for the seller's equity. Or the buyer could take over the seller's old loan and the seller could carry paper for part or all of the equity. The latter is commonly referred to as "carrying a second mortgage" (or trust deed). A popular alternative is for the seller to carry the entire unpaid balance on a contract (land sales contract or purchase money trust deed). Of course, even where the seller carries a second or a contract, the seller could still cash out by selling the second or the contract to a third party. Because these techniques are very common in real estate practice, we will discuss them in detail.

We will also look into other alternative financing concepts such as equity sharing (equity participation), sweat equity (work credits), equity kickers (shared appreciation), seller refinances, buying with no money down and use of leverage in real estate investment, ways in which investments can be syndicated, and sale-leaseback arrangements. From time to time all of these can be useful concepts in real estate transactions.

Seller carried financing

When the seller wishes to carry paper, whether it is a mortgage, trust deed or land sales contract, or a junior lien such as a second trust deed, the first and most obvious issue to address is whether or not there is an underlying loan. If there is an underlying loan, you must scrutinize it carefully to see if it has a ***due on sale clause*** (also sometimes called an ***alienation clause***).

A due on sale clause, as the term would imply, allows the lender to accelerate (call the loan due in full) if the seller (original borrower) should convey title to the property. To keep a seller from getting around a due on sale clause, lenders today phrase the clause to prohibit sales on land sales contracts, options and long term leaseholds as well as transactions where fee title is conveyed.

What kinds of loans have due on sale clauses? Most (but not by any means all) conventional loans have due on sale clauses. For FHA loans, however, the rules vary. If the loan was taken out prior to December 1, 1986, there is no due on sale clause. For loans made after December 1, 1986 there is a due on sale clause, but it can only be used to force the new buyer to meet credit approval and to take personal liability for the debt. federal Department of Veterans Affairs loans had no due on sale clause until March, 1988. Loans made after March, 1988 have a due on sale clause. But as with FHA loans, the lender cannot use the due on sale clause to force an increase in the interest rate – only to require the buyer to be approved and qualify for the loan, and to take personal liability for it. As for private trust deeds and land sales contracts, you will find that most contain a due on sale clause, but many do not. As you can see, whether or not a loan has a due on sale clause is complicated. In most cases, the best approach is to obtain a copy of the financing documents every time you take a listing, and read them carefully.

Of course, the advantage of a loan which does not have a due on sale clause is that it allows the seller greater flexibility in selling the property. This is particularly true if the interest rate on the seller's old loan is below market, as we shall see later.

Even when the loan does not contain a due on sale clause, the buyer must consider the difference between taking title to the property subject to the encumbrance or taking title subject to the encumbrance and assuming and agreeing to pay it (***assumption***). If the buyer takes title subject to the encumbrance, and also enters into an ***assumption agreement*** with the lender, then the buyer has agreed to be personally obligated for the debt. Whether the buyer assumes or not, the seller is not relieved of the responsibility to pay (unless there is a ***novation***), so the only issue is whether the buyer would also become personally obligated. Becoming "personally obligated" means that the lender can reach all the buyer's assets in the event that a foreclosure sale does not yield enough to satisfy the obligation. If the lender chooses to sue on the note, ignoring the collateral, again only the seller would be obligated unless the buyer has assumed the debt. A novation, of course, extinguishes the seller's liability. These concepts are covered in more detail in Chapter 13.

The following chart will help clarify the issue of which party is normally liable when a buyer takes over a seller's old loan –

Lender remedy	*Assumption*	*No Assumption*	*Novation*
Foreclose on the collateral	Yes	Yes	Yes
Deficiency judgment against buyer	Yes	No	Yes
Deficiency judgment against seller	Yes	Yes	No
Judgment on note against the buyer	Yes	No	Yes
Judgment on note against the seller	Yes	Yes	No

Many real estate agents feel that it is in the seller's best interest for the buyer to take title subject to the seller's old loan and also assume it. Since the seller is not relieved of liability, this is of questionable value to the seller. The only course which would really benefit the seller is a novation, which lenders generally will not agree to. On the contrary, lenders will attempt to insist on an assumption whenever possible, since they gain an additional person obligated to pay the debt.

Now let us look at some actual cases. Assume that you have a seller who has listed a house for $200,000 and there is an assumable loan in the amount of $100,000. The loan is at 6% fixed rate and has 20 years remaining at monthly payments of 716.43. But suppose the market rate for such loans has risen and would be closer to 9% today. Suppose further that you have a buyer for this house and that the buyer has $20,000 cash for a down payment. For various reasons, the buyer wishes to ask the seller to carry the financing for the $80,000 difference between the balance of the underlying loan, and the balance after the down payment (180,000 – $100,000 = $80,000). The seller is to carry the balance as a second trust deed at 10% interest with a 15-year amortization and monthly payments of 859.69, with a balloon payment (payoff) at seven years. (See graphic on the next page.)

There are several ways the buyer can make this offer. The easiest is to have the buyer take title subject to the seller's old loan (assume it or not), and have the seller carry a second trust deed for $80,000, as shown in the graphic on the next page. The repayment terms on the second trust deed can be as creative as you wish. You can create –

- Adjustable interest rates, tied to an index, with or without caps
- Interest only, for a period of time or for the life of the loan
- Graduated (escalating) payments, with or without negative amortization
- Balloon payments (refinance clause)
- Different interest rates on different portions of the loan
- Additional real or personal property as collateral (blanket or package trust deed)

In short, you can be as creative with the second trust deed as required in order to reach an agreement between the parties.

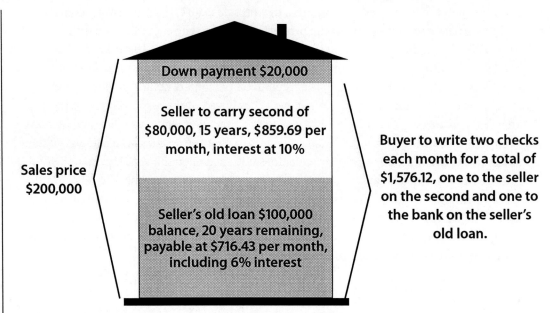

A popular alternative is for the seller to carry the entire balance ($180,000) on a land sales contract or trust deed. In this case the buyer will write one check to the seller for the principal and interest on the $180,000 contract, and the seller will continue to make the payments on the old loan. In our first example the buyer took over the seller's old loan, so the buyer would be writing two checks every month – one to the seller on the $80,000 second and one to the bank on the $100,000 loan. Suppose the seller carries a contract or trust deed on the balance of $180,000 at 8% for 30 years, with a balloon payment (payoff) at seven years – then the transaction would look like this –

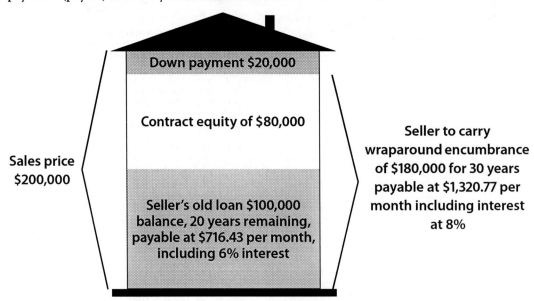

In the second example, notice that the balance of the contract ($180,000) includes the seller's old loan ($100,000). The buyer did not take over the seller's old loan in this case. Since the seller is carrying a contract or trust deed which encompasses the underlying loan, this is called a **wraparound** encumbrance, or just "wrap loan" for short.

Wraparound loans are sometimes better for both the buyer and the seller. The seller can offer a lower interest rate and still receive a good return because the seller is re-lending the underlying loan to the buyer. In the wraparound example, the seller borrowed the underlying $100,000 from the bank at 6% interest, and is now re-lending it to the buyer at 8%. The 2% difference in rates is pure profit to the seller, which effectively raises the yield on the wraparound loan. The following chart demonstrates the seller's first year yield on the $80,000 contract equity –

```
First year interest income on $180,000
(Calculated with a financial calculator)      $14,345.66
Less first year interest paid on $100,000
(Calculated with a financial calculator)        5,727.51
Net profit                                     $8,618.15
Profit ÷ Investment = Yield
$8,618.15 ÷ $80,000 = 10.77%
```

Note that the seller's investment is $80,000 whether the seller carries a second (first example) or a wraparound (second example). But in the first example, the seller's yield is just the rate on the second (10%), where the wraparound increases the seller's yield to 10.77% because the seller gets the 2% override between the first and the contract.

At the same time that the wraparound increases the seller's yield, it is easy to structure it so that the buyer's monthly payment is the same, or even less. If the seller carries a second trust deed (first example), the seller will typically want the repayment to be fairly fast – which tends to make the buyer's monthly payment high. In our example above, the buyer's total payments will be $1,576.12 ($716.43 on the first and 859.69 on the second). But in a wraparound transaction (second example), the seller is usually more amenable to longer repayment terms, so the buyer's total payment can be lower. In our example of the $180,000 wraparound at 8% with 30-year amortization the payment is only $1,320.78 – $255.34 lower.

Both examples require a few extra considerations. If the buyer takes over the seller's old loan and the seller carries a second (first example), then the buyer is in control of the first loan. The seller needs protection to ensure that the buyer will keep the underlying loan current. After all, a foreclosure of the underlying loan will extinguish the seller's second trust deed. Therefore, it is common practice for the seller to record a ***request for notice of sale***. A request for notice of sale requires the underlying lender to notify the seller in the event of a default, so the seller can take steps to bring the first current and avoid a foreclosure. The second trust deed must also have a clause stipulating that a default on the first will also be considered a default on the second.

In the wraparound transaction (second example) there are different considerations. Now the seller retains control of the underlying loan, so the buyer needs protection to ensure that the seller will keep it current. A typical wraparound instrument provides that the seller will keep the first current, and if the seller fails to do so, the buyer can make the payments due on the first and deduct the sums so paid from the amounts due on the wraparound.

The buyer would also want to be sure that the seller did not pay off the underlying loan any faster than required. Since the interest rate on the first is below market, the buyer would like the option of paying the seller the balance of the wraparound down to the balance of the underlying loan, and then taking over the underlying loan. If the seller pays off the underlying loan ahead of schedule, the buyer will be denied this benefit.

Selling paper

Many times a seller will need to carry paper from a buyer, but need to raise more cash in the transaction than the buyer is giving as down payment. For example, in either of the two preceding examples, the seller will receive only $4,000 to $6,000 out of the buyer's $20,000 down payment after deductions for a commission, title insurance, escrow fees and other closing expenses. If the cash normally generated by the transaction is not sufficient for the seller's needs, the seller could generate additional cash by selling the paper to an investor.

Investors might pay face value (par) for the paper, but more commonly it is sold at a discount. To calculate the discount, investors start with the yield they desire. **Seasoned paper** (paper with a good payment history) is more desirable than **green paper** (brand new paper). Referring to the first of the preceding examples (seller carries a second trust deed for $80,000), assume that the investor (paper buyer) wants a yield of 14%. The $80,000 second trust deed was written at 10% interest with a 15-year amortization and the monthly payments were $859.69.

Now, to calculate what an investor would pay for this second trust deed, just use an amortization chart or financial calculator to find out what could be the principal balance of a loan with 180 payments (15 years) of $859.69 at 14% interest. This is the present value of the second trust deed to an investor who wants a 14% yield. The answer is $64,553.82. In other words, the investor will buy the paper for a discount of $15,446.18 ($80,000.00 − $64,553.82 = $15,446.18).

Of course, the preceding calculation does not take into account the fact that the second trust deed has a balloon payoff at seven years. Using a financial calculator or a loan amortization chart, you can find the payoff at the end of seven years (the 84th payment) to be $45,969.05. In this case an investor would make two calculations in order to decide how much to pay for the paper. The first would be similar to the preceding case, except that the investor would assume a loan of 83 payments of $859.69 at 14% interest (we have to use 83 payments because the 84th payment is the balloon). The principal balance of such a loan would be $45,550.08, so that is what the investor would be willing to pay for the 83 payments.

The investor would make a separate calculation for the value of the balloon payment. To calculate it, the investor must calculate what amount would have to be put on deposit if the interest rate is 14%, compounded monthly, and the deposit is to mature to $45,969.05. Using a financial calculator or present value (present worth) table, you can calculate this to be $17,350.84. Therefore, the investor would pay for this paper –

Present value of 83 payments of $859.69 at 14% yield	$45,550.08
Present value of balloon payment of $45,969.05 at 14% yield	17,350.84
Total value of $80,000 second	$62,900.92

Note that the total value comes to slightly less than the example without the balloon. The interesting point, however, is that the seller could sell to the investor a participation in the paper by selling just the payments (for $45,550.08) or just the balloon (for $17,350.84). Or any other participation could be sold. The seller could also simply borrow money from the investor and pledge the paper as collateral for the loan.

Calculating what an investor would pay for a wraparound loan is more complicated. In a wraparound loan, the benefits are the difference between the payments and the interest rate difference. In the wraparound loan above (second example), the buyer is scheduled to make 360 payments of $1,320.78 to amortize the $180,000 balance at 8% interest. If an investor buys the loan, the investor will receive these payments. But the investor will also have to make the payments on the underlying loan. The underlying loan has a remaining term of 20 years (240 payments) at 6%, and the monthly payments on it are $716.43. Considering that our example has a balloon at seven years (the same as the first example), the balloon will pay off both the wraparound loan and the underlying first. Therefore, the investor will calculate the benefit of receiving the difference between $1,320.78 and $716.43 (which is $604.35) for 83 payments, and then add the present value of the net amount received in the balloon. Using a financial calculator, the calculation would look like this –

Present value of 83 payments of $604.35 at 14% yield		$32,021.07
Payoff amount on wraparound loan at 84th month	$166,458.97	
Less payoff amount on underlying first in 84th month	$77,475.28	
	88,983.69	
Present value of 88,983.69 received in 84th period at 14% yield		33,586.55
Total value of wraparound		$65,607.62

Note that the amount which can be realized from the sale of the wraparound loan is greater than for the second trust deed. This is simply because the wraparound had a higher yield (10.77%) than the second (10.00%), therefore the discount is less.

Shared appreciation loans

A common technique in commercial lending, the concept of a ***shared appreciation loan*** is also possible in residential financing. (A shared appreciation loan is also sometimes referred to as a loan which has an ***equity kicker***.) In a shared appreciation loan, the lender agrees to an interest rate or other terms which are less than market, in exchange for a share in the future increase in market value. For example, if interest rates are about 8%, a lender might agree to lend at only 6%, if the borrower will agree to pay one-half the first five years increase in market value to the lender.

In this example, the amount of the first five years increase in market value could be determined at the end of the five years either by a sale of the property, or by an appraisal. If the borrower wished to keep both the property and the loan at the end of the five years, the amount of increase in market value, as determined by the appraisal, could be added to the principal balance. The exact terms of a shared appreciation loan will be different for each transaction.

Shared appreciation loans are common in commercial settings where market interest rates might be too high to make a project financially feasible. A lower interest rate might make it possible for the project to proceed. In residential financing, shared appreciation loans are most common with seller financing. A seller may feel there is great potential for future appreciation, and therefore be reluctant to sell. Having the seller carry a shared appreciation loan can be a useful tool in this situation. Institutional lenders, however, do not make residential shared appreciation loans because there is no secondary market for them.

Equity sharing loans

Because they are similar, many people get the terms "shared appreciation" (discussed above) and "equity sharing" confused. An ***equity sharing loan*** (also sometimes called ***equity participation***) is an arrangement where a buyer teams up with an investor to buy the property together. Using the investor's money, the pair can cash out the seller.

Understanding an equity sharing loan may be easier with an example. Let us suppose you wish to buy a property for $200,000 and you only have $5,000 for a down payment and closing costs. Since this is not enough for most ordinary loan programs, you approach an investor to become your partner in the purchase. The investor will put up $195,000 and you will put up the other $5,000.

At closing you and the investor will become tenants in common. By separate agreement, you will have the right of possession, but also the responsibility to pay for all maintenance. When you go to sell the property, the investor will become entitled to a predetermined percentage share of the increase in market value. It is also common for the buyer to make some small monthly payment to the investor, in which case the investor will be entitled to a lesser share of the potential appreciation. The exact terms, of course, are worked out by negotiation between the parties.

In an equity sharing arrangement it is also common for the parties to obtain outside financing. In our preceding example, your $5,000 would be inadequate as down payment for practically any kind of outside loan. But if the investor would add $35,000 (plus some additional amount for closing costs) you would jointly have $40,000 for a down payment. This would allow you to get an 80% conventional loan. You would still become tenants in common, but you would also become co-borrowers on the new loan. Of course, you and the investor would have a separate agreement as to which of you would make the payments (typically, you), perform maintenance (typically, you), and be entitled to possession of the property (typically, you). Again, by negotiation, you and the investor would agree to share the potential increase in market value.

Seller refinances

Either as a separate technique, or in conjunction with other financing, the seller could refinance the property prior to the sale. The buyer could then assume the seller's loan. The refinance could be either a new first trust deed or it could be junior financing. Regardless of how the seller refinances, the seller will receive a substantial portion of the equity in cash as loan proceeds. The advantage is that the seller is now in a better position to accept a low down payment from the buyer. The disadvantage of the refinance is that the lender(s) will probably not permit the buyer to take over the seller's loan(s).

However, there are cases where this technique may be useful. Again, an illustration may help to make things understandable. Suppose the seller has a commercial property which is in need of substantial rehabilitation, although it has a current market value of $500,000 in its present condition. There is a buyer who wishes to rehabilitate the property, but does not have any significant amount of cash to put into the transaction, although the buyer would agree to a $100,000 down payment if the cash for it were available.

Here's how the sale could be structured. First, the seller refinances the property for 50% of its market value ($250,000). To do this, go to a commercial lender, not a residential lender. Arrange the loan as a short term loan, which means that the seller should be able to get the lender to agree to waive the typical due on sale clause for at least one subsequent sale. Suppose the proceeds of the refinance (after loan fees and other costs) equals $242,000. The loan proceeds are disbursed to the escrow where the property is being sold to the buyer. Out of the $242,000 loan proceeds, the escrow will disburse $100,000 to the seller as "down payment." The escrow will retain the other $142,000 for the buyer.

The buyer will buy the property for a sales price of $750,000 ($500,000 market value, plus the new encumbrance of $250,000). The buyer will buy on a contract with a balance of $650,000 after the "down payment" of $100,000. The buyer will submit bills for the rehabilitation to the escrow for payment out of the $142,000. When the buyer has finished rehabilitating the property, the buyer can either sell it or refinance it in order to cash out the seller's refinance loan and the contract balance.

Notice how this transaction allowed the seller to gain $100,000 of equity in cash immediately, yet allowed the buyer to obtain the property and rehabilitation expenses with no cash up front. However, there is a grave danger for the seller if the transaction does not leave the $142,000 in the escrow. If the $142,000 is disbursed to the buyer directly, there is the possibility that the buyer could simply leave town with it, never to be seen again. For the seller's protection it is imperative that the funds remain in the escrow to be disbursed only as the rehabilitation proceeds.

Leverage

In real estate investment **leverage** is a tool which can greatly multiply an investor's return. Leverage (also sometimes called **trading on the equity**) is the practice of buying a property with as little cash as possible, then reaping great profit when the property increases in dollar value.

Let us take two examples to illustrate this principle. Assume you have $200,000 cash to invest. In both examples, assume that you invest the $200,000 in real estate and hold the real estate for 10 years. During the ten years, assume a 5% per annum inflation in property value. In the first example, you will use no leverage. In the second example, you will buy with moderately high leverage.

Example 1 – You buy a duplex for $200,000 cash. The monthly rent is $1,000 per unit, but the taxes and insurance are $4,000 per year. Maintenance and other expenses total $5,000 additional per year. Assuming no change in income or expenses, your return on investment would look like this –

Income: $1,000 × 2 units × 12 months × 10 years	$240,000	
Less tax and ins., $4,000 × 10 years	40,000	
Less other expenses, $5,000 × 10 years	50,000	
Income net of expenses		$150,000
Sales price on resale, @ 5% per annum inflation	300,000	
Less original invested amount	200,000	
Profit on resale		100,000
Total net profit		$250,000

$250,000 profit is for ten years; average annual profit is $25,000.
Original investment is $200,000
Profit ÷ Investment = Yield
$25,000 ÷ $200,000 = **12.5%** average annual return on investment

Example 2 – You use the $200,000 to buy ten duplexes identical to the duplex in Example 1, making a down payment of $20,000 on each and financing the balance of $180,000 at a bank at 8% interest. All other considerations remain the same. Your investment would now look like this –

Income: $1,000 × 20 units × 12 months × 10 years	$2,400,000	
Less tax and ins., $4,000 × 10 duplexes × 10 years	400,000	
Less other expenses, $5,000 × 10 duplexes × 10 years	500,000	
Less interest on loans for 10 years	1,363,974	
Income net of expenses		$136,026
Plus sales price on resale, @ 5% per annum inflation	3,000,000	
Less loan balance on payoff	1,579,038	
Less original invested amount	200,000	
Net profit on resale		1,220,962
Total Profit		$1,356,988

$1,356,988 profit is for ten years; average annual profit is $135,699
Original investment is $200,000
Profit ÷ Investment = Yield
$135,699 ÷ $200,000 = **67.85%** average annual return on investment

Notice that use of leverage can make a vast improvement in the investor's return. The reason for the increase in return is that the interest on the bank loan is 8%, but the net operating income from the investment is an even greater return. In other words, if you have an investment that you are reasonably certain will produce a certain rate of return, then it makes sense to borrow the money to acquire the investment, as long as the cost of the borrowed money is less than the anticipated return on the investment.

Investors who use the leverage principle frequently **pyramid** their investment. Pyramiding simply means cashing out of the investment, and immediately reinvesting the profits in another, larger investment, using leverage again. In Example 2 above, the investor started with $200,000, but when the duplexes were sold, realized an immediate cash flow of $1,207,924 (sales price of $3,000,000 less loan payoff of $1,592,075 = $1,207,924). Using leverage, the investor should be able to use that $1,207,924 to buy 50, 60 or more units.

Of course, there is a downside to leverage. In the preceding examples, a significant portion of the income the properties generated was in the increased market value on resale. What would have happened if there had been no inflation? Or worse yet, what if the properties had declined in dollar value over the ten-year holding period? The answer is simple. The investor would make little return, or possibly suffer a serious loss.

In fact, if the dollar value of the properties is not increasing, then it is likely that economic conditions are generally poor and there is a high vacancy factor in the rental market. This means that the leveraged investor will not be able to make the loan payments, and will likely lose the entire investment in a foreclosure. The non-leveraged investor, on the other hand, will be able to weather the storm and hold out for better days. Therefore, while leverage is usually the investor's friend, in a down market, it can be the investors undoing. Each investor should tailor an investment to his or her personal situation and accept only that amount of risk which the investor can comfortably handle.

Buying with nothing down

The less the down payment, the greater the leverage, so buying with nothing down is the ultimate in leverage. Of course, as we noted above, the greater the leverage, the greater the risk, especially for the lender. Still, buying with nothing down may be the right decision in certain cases.

Today we have television real estate course marketers who promise to teach us how to get rich in real estate. Their most popular technique is to buy with nothing down and reap the rewards of leverage. But transactions with no down payment are difficult to structure. Nevertheless, since real estate agents encounter such offers, let us look at some practices which can make a "nothing down" transaction more attractive.

Since the party with the greatest risk is the lender, let us look first at ways the lender can be protected. When the buyer puts nothing down on a property bought for investment, the lender is most likely to be the seller, so we will assume that it is a purchase money financing arrangement. How then, can the seller gain better protection? A lender's position is enhanced by additional sources for repayment. The two traditional sources are the borrower's income, or a sale of the property itself. Therefore, co-signature(s) or additional collateral, or both, would enhance the lender's position. For first time buyers on a residential sale, co-signatures of relatives is the usual solution. For seasoned investors, additional collateral is more likely.

Looking at a "nothing down" transaction from the borrower's viewpoint, there is also significant risk. The borrower needs protection from the possibility that property values will decrease. A borrower will therefore want to include a **sole collateral clause** in the financing documents. A sole collateral clause states that the property is the sole collateral and the lender cannot obtain a judgment against the borrower, even if the property is sold at a sheriff's or trustee's sale and fails to realize enough to cover the debt.

Negotiating between these opposing interests and desires is what makes it difficult to put together a "nothing down" transaction. In spite of this, most real estate agents can tell you about cases where a "nothing down" sale made sense for the parties involved.

Sweat equity

A time-honored alternative for a down payment is for the buyer to perform work on the property and receive credit for the work. Officially, this is called a **work credit**, but everyone calls it **sweat equity**.

Many lenders recognize a work credit, and FHA even has a formal program. Most lenders, however, prefer not to make such loans because they involve a great deal of extra paperwork. Another problem with a work credit is that the borrower, the seller and the lender have frequent disputes over the quality of the work done and the timeliness with which the buyer completed it. Nevertheless, a property which is run-down is a likely candidate for a work credit financing arrangement, particularly when economic conditions are poor.

Sale-leasebacks

A financing technique which is common in commercial transactions is the **sale-leaseback**. A sale-leaseback is exactly what the term would imply – the seller sells the property (usually to cash out), and then leases the property back from the buyer. The sale-leaseback allows an owner to obtain cash for all the equity in the property, yet retain possession.

In commercial transactions the sale-leaseback is popular, particularly with retailers. A retailer wants a building constructed exactly to their specifications, yet wants to use their available capital for merchandise and promotion, not tie it up in the real estate. Therefore, they will build the store, and immediately turn around and sell it to an investor, while leasing it back on a long term lease.

A sale-leaseback transaction is especially valuable in a commercial transaction because the lease payments are a deductible business expense. Ownership of the real estate also produces a tax benefit in the form of cost recovery, but only on the improvements; the Internal Revenue Code does not allow cost recovery on the land. And the investor also gains because there is an assured rate of return from a creditworthy payer.

In some sale-leaseback transactions there is a **buy-back option**, that is, the seller/lessee has an option to buy the property back from the buyer/lessor at some date in the future, either at an agreed-upon price or at a price to be established by independent appraisal.

Syndicates

Many people think that a **syndication** is a type of business organization, the way a corporation is a specific type of legal entity. However, this is not true. The term "syndication" (or "syndicate") merely means any investment in a common enterprise. The vehicle for the syndication is commonly a limited partnership, although when the purpose of the investment is to acquire real estate, a simple tenancy in common is also frequently used. Today, the limited liability company is also popular.

NOTES

For tax reasons, the corporate form of ownership is not as common for ownership of real estate, although Subchapter S corporations are sometimes encountered. Syndicates are frequently created to provide financing for large commercial projects. Real estate agents should be aware that when the syndicate is a passive investment, it is probably subject to registration and regulation as a security.

The most important consideration in choosing the form of organization is income tax liability. A regular corporation must pay income taxes, and when the after-tax profits are distributed to the investors, they are taxed yet again. To avoid this double taxation, investors could choose to be a Subchapter S corporation. Subchapter S corporations pay no income taxes, so the tax liability (or tax benefit in the case of real property investments) is passed through to the investors. Limited liability companies offer the same pass-through tax benefits, and have some additional flexibility in the number of investors that can be allowed.

KEY TERMS

The key to understanding any new field is the vocabulary used in that field. To maximize your comprehension of the material presented in this chapter, be sure you know the meaning and significance of the following terms. Remember that the majority of test questions primarily test knowledge of vocabulary.

Alienation clause	*Pyramid*
Assumption	*Request for notice of sale*
Assumption agreement	*Sale-leaseback*
Buy-back option	*Seasoned paper*
Due on sale clause	*Shared appreciation loan*
Equity participation loan	*Sole collateral clause*
Equity kicker	*Sweat equity*
Equity sharing	*Syndication*
Green paper	*Trading on the equity*
Leverage	*Work credit*
Novation	*Wraparound loan*

Amortization Chart

This chart shows the monthly payment for a loan of $1,000 at varying interest rates for one to 30 years. For loans greater than $1,000, multiply the factor below by the number of thousands in the loan. For example, a $258,000 loan at 7% interest for 30 years would use the factor $6.65. This is the amount for a $1,000 loan, so for a $258,000 loan, multiply by 258. The payment is therefore $1,715.70 ($6.65 × 258 = $1,715.70).

Years	6%	7%	8%	9%	10%	11%	12%	13%	14%	15%
1	86.06	86.53	86.99	87.45	87.92	88.38	88.49	89.32	89.79	90.26
2	44.32	44.77	45.23	45.68	46.15	46.61	47.07	47.54	48.01	48.49
3	30.42	30.88	31.34	31.80	32.27	32.74	33.21	33.69	34.18	34.67
4	23.49	23.95	24.41	24.89	25.36	25.85	26.33	26.83	27.33	27.83
5	19.33	19.80	20.28	20.76	21.25	21.74	22.24	22.75	23.27	23.79
6	16.57	17.05	17.53	18.03	18.53	19.03	19.55	20.07	20.61	21.15
7	14.61	15.09	15.59	16.09	16.60	17.12	17.65	18.19	18.74	19.30
8	13.14	13.63	14.14	14.65	15.17	15.71	16.25	16.80	17.37	17.95
9	12.01	12.51	13.01	13.54	14.08	14.63	15.18	15.75	16.33	16.92
10	11.10	11.61	12.13	12.67	13.22	13.78	14.35	14.93	15.53	16.13
11	10.37	10.88	11.42	11.96	12.52	13.09	13.68	14.28	14.87	15.51
12	9.76	10.28	10.82	11.38	11.95	12.54	13.13	13.75	14.37	15.01
13	9.25	9.78	10.33	10.90	11.48	12.08	12.69	13.31	13.95	14.60
14	8.81	9.35	9.91	10.49	11.08	11.69	12.31	12.95	13.60	14.27
15	8.44	8.99	9.55	10.14	10.75	11.37	12.00	12.65	13.32	14.00
16	8.11	8.67	9.25	9.85	10.46	11.09	11.74	12.40	13.08	13.77
17	7.83	8.40	8.98	9.59	10.21	10.85	11.51	12.19	12.87	13.58
18	7.58	8.16	8.75	9.36	10.00	10.65	11.32	12.00	12.70	13.42
19	7.36	7.94	8.55	9.17	9.81	10.47	11.15	11.85	12.56	13.28
20	7.16	7.75	8.36	9.00	9.65	10.32	11.01	11.72	12.44	13.17
21	6.99	7.58	8.20	8.85	9.51	10.19	10.87	11.60	12.33	13.07
22	6.83	7.43	8.06	8.71	9.34	10.07	10.78	11.50	12.24	12.99
23	6.69	7.30	7.93	8.59	9.27	9.97	10.69	11.42	12.17	12.92
24	6.56	7.18	7.82	8.49	9.17	9.88	10.60	11.34	12.10	12.86
25	6.44	7.07	7.72	8.39	9.09	9.80	10.53	11.28	12.04	12.81
26	6.34	6.97	7.63	8.31	9.01	9.73	10.47	11.22	11.99	12.76
27	6.24	6.88	7.54	8.23	8.94	9.67	10.41	11.17	11.95	12.73
28	6.15	6.80	7.47	8.16	8.88	9.61	10.37	11.13	11.91	12.70
29	6.07	6.72	7.40	8.10	8.82	9.57	10.32	11.09	11.88	12.67
30	6.00	6.65	7.34	8.05	8.78	9.52	10.29	11.06	11.85	12.64

In times past real estate agents carried around small booklets of loan amortization tables, similar to the chart above, but broken down by quarters of a percent. Today, agents simply use an inexpensive financial calculator. For beginners, the Texas Instruments BA-35 is one of the most popular. The keystrokes to compute the monthly payment necessary for a $258,000 loan at 7% for 30 years on the BA-35 are –

258,000 **PV** 7 **2nd** **%i** (hit the **%i** key twice) 30 **2nd** **N** (hit the **N** key twice) **CPT** **PMT**

Display: 1,716.48

Note that the answer from the calculator is a few cents off from the results by using the chart. The reason is because the figures in the chart are rounded to the nearest cent, whereas the calculator holds the decimal to many places of accuracy. The factor used above for a 7% loan of 30 years is given as $6.65 in the chart, but the calculator uses the whole decimal ($6.653024953).

The nice thing about the financial calculator is that it allows quick what-if scenarios. If the client asks what the payment would be if the interest rate were 8% instead of 7%, all you have to do is enter the new percentage rate, then hit **CPT** **PMT** and the calculator will recalculate the payment. The calculator remembers what was entered in the **%i** and **N** registers.

Chapter

17

Income taxation and real estate

EDERAL INCOME TAXES have a great impact on real estate financing and on buy-sell decisions. Tax benefits are frequently one of the principal motivations for buying real estate. Even where the tax benefits are not the most important reason for buying, they still influence the amount and nature of the buyer's offer. Sellers also must consider the tax impacts of a sale. When capital gains tax rates are high, sellers may prefer not to sell, or may decide to sell on installment sales or use exchanging instead of selling for cash. The tremendous impact of income taxes on real estate makes it essential for all real estate agents to have a knowledge of income tax basics.

That income taxes are based on income is obvious. What is not so clear is when the income becomes taxable. Wages, interest, dividends, and other income received, generally becomes taxable when received. Gain on the sale of property is also taxable, but does not ordinarily become taxable until the gain is realized. **Realization** of the gain normally occurs when the property is sold. In other words, if you buy a property and its value increases, no gain is recognized and no tax is due until you sell the property.

Capital gains

The increase in value of an asset is called a **capital gain**. For real estate agents, how taxes are levied on capital gains is the most important part of the Internal Revenue Code. A capital gain should be thought of as profit realized on the sale of the asset. A more complete definition would be "net profit," because taxes are not levied on the costs incurred in making the profit. For example, a brokerage fee incurred in acquiring the property is part of the acquisition cost, and a brokerage fee paid on selling the property is part of the sales expense to be deducted from the selling price.

The Internal Revenue Code also provides that **capital improvements** are not part of the gain. A capital improvement adds something to the property which was not there when it was purchased. For example, suppose you buy a personal residence, and during your ownership you add a bedroom at a cost of $10,000. The cost of the bedroom will be excluded from the sales price when calculating gain on a sale, because it is actually part of what you paid for the property.

Capital improvements are contrasted with repair or maintenance expenses. If you paint your kitchen, this is maintenance, not a capital improvement. But the distinction between capital improvements and maintenance items is not always clear. For example, painting the kitchen is maintenance, but if it is part of an extensive kitchen remodeling project, it would be considered part of a capital improvement.

The contrast between capital improvements and maintenance items is subjective. In general, if it is a large expense in relation to the total value of the asset, and if it will have a long remaining economic life, it will likely be considered a capital improvement, not maintenance. For example, most tax counsel considers that a new roof is a capital improvement. But re-roofing just part of the structure is generally considered a maintenance item.

To calculate the capital gain, first you must determine your **adjusted sales price**. The adjusted sales price is the price you sold the asset for, less the costs of the sale. Among other expenses, the costs of the sale include title insurance, escrow and recording fees, as well as the brokerage fee (commission) paid by the seller. Last-minute fix-up expenses are also generally considered costs of the sale.

Next, you must calculate your **cost basis**. The cost basis is the purchase price, plus your costs of acquisition, and any capital improvements. To find the capital gain, subtract the cost basis from the capital gain. The following example shows the calculation of capital gain for the sale of a personal residence for $240,000, which was purchased for $198,000, incurring acquisition costs of $700, a capital improvement of $20,000, and sales expenses of $17,400.

Sales price	$240,000
Less sales expenses	– 17,400
Adjusted sales price	222,600
Less purchase price	– 198,000
Less cost of acquisition	– 700
Less capital improvement	– 20,000
CAPITAL GAIN	$ 3,900

Tax is due on the amount of the capital gain. To calculate the amount of the tax, Congress has contemplated various schemes. Central to the debate over capital gains taxes is the fact that a capital gain realized by the taxpayer is not completely profit; in many cases it is just the effect of inflation. In other words, if you bought the house in the above example for $198,000 (plus $20,000 capital improvement) and sold it for $240,000, the "profit" is just caused by the fact that the dollars you sold it for were cheaper dollars than the dollars you used to buy it. The house you sold was the same house you bought (including the capital improvement) so, in reality, there was no "profit" at all.

Of course, sometimes the profit does come from true appreciation. If you buy property and the local jurisdiction changes the zoning in your favor, the resulting increase in value is not due to inflation.

The difficult part is trying to determine how much of the profit is just from inflation and how much is from appreciation. In recognition of this problem, tax rates usually exclude a portion of the gain from taxation. In times past this percentage has been as high as 60%. An alternative philosophy is to index the acquisition cost to the inflation rate, so the taxpayer will pay tax on 100% of the actual profit after inflation. Still another concept is to tax the gain at different arbitrary percentages according to how long the owner held the asset. Since Congress changes the tax laws constantly, you should check with your instructor for the rules currently in effect.

Cost recovery

Under the Internal Revenue Code there are four categories of real property – *personal use property*, *trade or business property*, *investment property* and *dealer property*. Personal use property is the taxpayer's personal residence. Trade or business property is property used to produce income in a trade or business. Investment property is property used to produce income by being rented to another or by being held for speculation, such as vacant land. And dealer property is property held as inventory for resale.

These definitions are fairly straightforward, but observe what happens when a taxpayer involved in an incorporated trade or business buys a property. If the taxpayer takes title personally and rents the property to the corporation, it is the taxpayer's investment property. If the corporation buys the property, it is trade or business property of the corporation. Such a taxpayer should always consult with appropriate counsel before acquiring the property to determine the way to take title in order to maximize the tax advantages.

When a taxpayer buys real property, the category in which it falls becomes of great importance. The Internal Revenue Code allows the owner of trade or business property and the owner of investment property to claim an annual expense for loss of market value of the improvements due to depreciation. In real estate appraisal, depreciation is defined as a loss of market value over the economic life of the improvements. (For more detail see Chapter 15.) Note that this deduction applies only to trade or business property or to investment property; but no deduction can be claimed for depreciation of a personal residence. Since land does not have an economic life, vacant land, even the land on which trade or business property and investment property is built, also does not produce a deduction for depreciation. The improvements on trade or business property and investment property are sometimes referred to as **depreciable** assets.

When appraising property, appraisers try to calculate the amount of the depreciation as accurately as possible. For income tax purposes, however, an arbitrary amount is typically used. Because of this, depreciation for income tax purposes is now officially called **cost recovery**, although in the past it was just called "depreciation" and many people still refer to it as depreciation. Note that cost recovery springs from the same concept as depreciation – the improvements are declining in value over their economic life.

Now let us see how the use of cost recovery can benefit an investor. Suppose that you bought an apartment building (investment category) for $500,000, and that $400,000 of the purchase price was the value of the improvements and $100,000 was the value of the land. Let us also assume that the Internal Revenue Code allows a 20-year economic life for this type of asset. (From time to time Congress changes the allowable economic life. Check with your instructor for the current allowable life.)

If you paid $400,000 for the depreciable portion (improvements), and they have a life of 20 years, then the amount of cost recovery allowed would be $20,000 per year ($400,000 ÷ 20 years = $20,000). Let us further suppose that the potential gross income is $96,000, the vacancy and credit loss is 5% ($4,800), and the total expenses before principal and interest are $38,000. This would leave a net operating income of $53,200 –

Potential Gross Income	$96,000
Less vacancy and credit loss	− 4,800
Effective Gross Income	91,200
Less operating Expenses	− 38,000
Net operating income	$ 53,200

Now let us suppose that you borrow $450,000 at an interest rate of 9% in order to buy the property. This means that your interest expense for the year will be approximately $40,500 ($450,000 × .09 = $40,500). (In reality your interest expense will be slightly less than $40,500 due to amortization, but $40,500 is close enough for purposes of our illustration.) This means that your **net spendable income** would be $12,700 –

Potential gross income	$96,000
Less vacancy and credit loss	− 4,800
Effective gross income	91,200
Less operating expenses	− 38,000
Net operating income	53,200
Less interest expense	− 40,500
Net spendable income	$ 12,700

For income tax purposes, the interest is fully deductible, so your taxable income would be $12,700. However, if the Internal Revenue Code allows you to claim an additional $20,000 expense for the loss of market value of the improvements, then you have a tax loss of $7,300 ($12,700 − $20,000 = −$7,300). *This tax loss can be applied on your tax return to offset other taxable income,* but only if you actively manage the property yourself. Tax losses from passive investments cannot generally be used to offset active income. Investors can structure investment in depreciable property so the cost recovery will create paper losses. Some investors are able to escape almost all income tax liability. This is commonly called **tax shelter**.

Of course, the shorter the economic life of the property, the higher the dollar amount of cost recovery. Therefore, investors prefer property with a short economic life. Until 1981, individual taxpayers found themselves constantly battling the Internal Revenue Service over the economic life of the improvements. Today, however, the Internal Revenue Code simply stipulates an arbitrary number of years for the economic life, and both taxpayers and the IRS must use this number of years. The number of years of economic life is the product of politics, and is not intended to reflect reality or even some imaginary average property.

In order to claim cost recovery at a faster pace, investors have developed some creative ways of calculating depreciation. If the law requires the economic life to be 20 years, then you would ordinarily expect to claim 5% of the value of the improvements each year (100% ÷ 20 years = 5% per year). This is another way to perform the calculation we used in the example above –

$$\$400,000 \div 20 \text{ years} \quad = \quad \$20,000 \text{ per year}$$
$$\$400,000 \times 5 \text{ percent} \quad = \quad \$20,000 \text{ per year}$$

When the cost recovery is the same amount each year, as in this example, we say the cost recovery is being calculated on a **straight line** basis.

Suppose, however, you calculate the depreciation at twice the straight line rate (10% per year instead of 5% per year). And suppose you subtract the amount you claim each year from the basis and recalculate the cost recovery each year on the new basis. This is called **double declining balance** (or sometimes **200% declining balance**) depreciation. Using the same property as above, the following example will illustrate this –

	Straight line	*Double declining*
First year	$20,000	$40,000
Second year	$20,000	$36,000
Third year	$20,000	$32,400
Fourth year	$20,000	$29,160
etc.		

Notice that the amount of cost recovery claimed the first year under double declining balance depreciation is twice the straight line amount, but in the second year the amount is less than twice the straight line amount. This is because "declining balance" depreciation means that the amount claimed each year is deducted from the basis, so the percentage (10%, in our example) is applied to an ever-decreasing basis.

In the preceding chart, the original basis was $400,000, so the first year's depreciation by double declining balance method was $40,000 ($400,000 × .10 = $40,000). Subtracting the $40,000 from the original basis leaves a remaining basis of $360,000 ($400,000 − $40,000 = $360,000). Multiplying the $360,000 by the rate (10%) gives us the second year's cost recovery ($360,000 × .10 = $36,000). To find the third year's cost recovery, subtract the second year's cost recovery from the remaining basis ($360,000 − $36,000 = $324,000) and multiply by the rate. The result is $32,400 ($324,000 × .10 = $32,400). The $32,400 must then be subtracted to find the basis for the fourth year, and so on.

Double declining balance depreciation will never depreciate the property completely to zero because, even after many years, there will always be a small amount left over. Its advantage is that it allows an investor to gain more tax shelter in the early years of the investment. Of course, mathematically speaking, an investor does not have to calculate the depreciation at double the straight line rate – depreciation could be calculated at any percentage of the straight line rate. Commonly used percentages include ***125% declining balance*** and ***150% declining balance*** depreciation. In fact, an investor could calculate the depreciation at any multiple of the straight line rate. For example, if the straight line rate is 5% (as in our previous examples), a rate of ten times the straight line rate would result in a first year cost recovery of $200,000!

In addition to the various declining balance depreciation schedules, investors have sometimes used a technique called ***sum of the years' digits***. To calculate depreciation by the sum of the years' digits, first add up the numbers for the years in the economic life. For a 20-year economic life, write down the numbers 1 through 20, and add them up, e.g., 1 + 2 + 3 + 4 ... + 20. This comes to a total of 210. Now create fractions working backwards with 20 as the denominator and 210 as the numerator for the first fraction, i.e., $\frac{20}{210}$ and lowering the numerator down to 1; e.g., $\frac{20}{210}$, $\frac{19}{210}$, $\frac{18}{210}$, $\frac{17}{210}$ ... $\frac{1}{210}$. Each fraction represents the portion of the depreciable basis which the investor can claim each year, starting with $\frac{20}{210}$ the first year, and ending with $\frac{1}{210}$ the 20th year. At the end of the 20th year, the investor will have claimed $\frac{210}{210}$, or 100% of the value. Notice that sum of the years' digits depreciation is also much faster than straight line and has not always been allowed.

Because investors could gain immense short term tax shelter by using any multiple of the straight line rate or by using sum of the years' digits depreciation, Congress enacted legislation setting the maximum rate at which investors can claim the cost recovery. In the past the rate has been as high as double the straight line rate, but you should check with your instructor for the current maximum allowable rate. Depreciation schedules which are faster than straight line are called ***accelerated depreciation***.

Effect of cost recovery on capital gains

As we have outlined above, investors commonly structure a real estate investment so the cost recovery makes it produce a paper loss. The paper loss can then be used to shelter their other income. But there is a downside to cost recovery. Owners of depreciable real property must claim at least straight line cost recovery, whether they need the tax shelter it creates, or not. And every year the investor claims cost recovery, *the investor's cost basis in the property is reduced by the cost recovery claimed*. This means that when the investor sells the property, the capital gain will be higher.

If you owned the apartment building we used in our example above, held it for ten years, and then sold it for $750,000, this is what your capital gain might look like (costs are estimated) –

Sales price	$750,000
Less sales expenses	– 60,000
Adjusted sales price	690,000
Less purchase price	– 500,000
Less costs of acquisition	– 5,000
Less capital improvement	0
Plus cost recovery	+ 200,000
CAPITAL GAIN	$385,000

The $200,000 cost recovery above was calculated at $20,000 per year for ten years. Note that payment of tax on $385,000, all received in one year, would create a tax disaster for most taxpayers. Because of this, many investors use various techniques to avoid payment of capital gains taxes. These techniques will be discussed next.

Avoiding capital gains

A common technique to avoid capital gains tax is simply not to sell the property. If no sale occurs, no gain is realized, so no tax is due. However, for investment property, this creates a drawback. Investors typically want to sell the property after they have built up a certain amount of equity. For example, recall the apartment building in our previous example –

Potential gross income	$96,000
Less vacancy and credit loss	– 4,800
Effective gross income	91,200
Less operating expenses	– 38,000
Net operating income	53,200
Less interest	– 49,500
Net spendable income	3,700
Less cost recovery	– 20,000
Tax loss	$ (16,300)

The potential gross income may be projected at $96,000 when the investor buys the property, but the investor would certainly expect the income to increase with inflation. Although expenses will increase at the same rate of inflation, the dollar amount is less, so the net operating income will increase. As the net operating income increases, the investor's tax shelter (tax loss in the example above) will decrease. Eventually, the property will be producing taxable income. How long this will take depends on a multitude of factors, so an investor's holding period is different for each property.

A common technique to prolong the holding period is simply to borrow additional money against the property. After all, if the net operating income is higher, the value would normally be higher, so the property can support additional financing. The added financing could be in the form of a junior lien or refinance loan. Additional debt will increase the interest expense, thereby reducing the net spendable income, and restoring the tax loss. By judiciously borrowing additional funds against the property, the investor can maintain the tax loss position indefinitely, or at least as long as the economic life under the Internal Revenue Code. What makes this technique especially attractive to investors is that, under normal circumstances, borrowed money is not taxable.

Eventually, of course, the owner will die and leave the property to heirs. The owner's estate must pay estate taxes, but capital gains are not recognized in an estate. The estate taxes are levied on the total value of the owner's estate, which includes the net equity in the property at the time of the owner's death. The equity, of course, is the difference between the value of the property (estate value) and the outstanding loan(s) at the time of the owner's death. Real estate agents should be aware that the Internal Revenue Code allows a substantial exemption from estate taxes, so an ordinary investor's estate will owe no estate taxes. An additional benefit is that the heirs will take title to the property at its new estate valuation, and can claim cost recovery all over again from the beginning, as though they had just purchased the property

Installment sale – Another common method to escape payment of capital gains tax is to defer the payment of the tax by an ***installment sale***. In an installment sale the owner sells the property and receives part of the sale price in at least two different tax years. For example, if you sell your property with 20% down, and the buyer pays the balance over a period of years, then you received "part of the sales price in at least two different tax years," so you are eligible for installment sale treatment. Installment sale treatment can be used on any type of property, whether personal residence, trade or business property, or investment property. The Internal Revenue Code does not specify what kind of financing instrument is used – all that is required is that you carried the paper on the property.

If the sale qualifies for installment sale treatment, then you pay tax on the gain only as you receive it. The following example shows a taxpayer who sold a property with $40,000 down on an installment contract for an adjusted sales price of $200,000 in which the taxpayer had a cost basis of $100,000. The taxpayer is in the 28% tax bracket and the interest on the contract is 10% –

Year	Principal Received	Gain Received	Tax on Gain	Interest Received	Tax on Interest	Total Tax Due
1	40,462	23,232	6,504	15,980	4,474	10,978
2	508	254	72	15,930	4,460	4,532
3	564	282	78	15,876	4,446	4,524
4	622	312	88	15,818	4,430	4,518

In the above chart, note that the "Gain Received" is one-half of the "Principal Received." This is because the taxpayer's basis in the example was $100,000, but the adjusted sales price was $200,000. Therefore, for every dollar of the sales price that is received, half is gain and half is simply return of basis. Return of basis is not taxable gain.

The preceding chart also presumes that the gain is 100% taxable at the taxpayer's ordinary rate of 28%. The interest figures are calculated assuming the balance of $160,000 is being amortized at 360 equal monthly payments of $1,370.04 which include principal and interest at 10%.

Selling a property on an installment contract spreads the payment of tax out over the life of the contract, so the taxpayer can avoid being thrown into a high bracket in the year the property is sold. But it does not usually occur to the average seller to think about what would happen if the buyer were to pay the contract off suddenly. In this case, the tax law is clear – the tax on the rest of the gain would be due for the tax year in which the seller received it. To avoid this dilemma, sellers who plan ahead sometimes insist on a clause in the contract providing that only a certain percentage of the principal can be paid in any one year.

Tax-deferred exchange – For property held for trade or business or for investment property, Section 1031 of the Internal Revenue Code allows an owner to avoid capital gains tax through a **tax-deferred exchange**, also called a **like-kind exchange**. Tax-deferred exchanges are also sometimes called **tax-free exchanges**, although this term is misleading and should not be used. The exchange is not tax-free; payment of the tax on the gain is merely deferred until such time as the substitute property received in exchange is finally sold.

To qualify as a tax-deferred exchange, there are two requirements – the exchange must be of like property for like property, and the exchange must be "simultaneous." Both of these concepts are discussed in detail below.

It is of important to understand that anyone can exchange anything for anything. No tax law can stop you from making any trade you wish. What the tax law means when it says that the properties must be "like for like" is that if one or more of the properties in the exchange do not qualify as "like for like," then the exchange will not be entirely tax deferred. Note also that either party can bring as few as one property to the exchange, or as many as that party owns. The number of properties on each side of the exchange is irrelevant; what is significant is that they must all qualify as like property for the exchange to be completely tax deferred.

Property qualifies as like property if it is of the same nature and character as the property received in exchange. This is interpreted fairly broadly. For example, land can be exchanged for improved property, apartments can be exchanged for commercial space, farm property can be exchanged for urban property, and so forth.

Some types of property are always unlike property. A personal residence, jewelry, cash, property held as inventory (dealer property), and paper (notes, mortgages, trust deeds, land sales contracts) – never qualify as like property. When property which does not qualify as like property is used in an exchange, it is called **boot**. If a party to an exchange receives boot, that party will have at least some recognizable gain.

Beginners in exchanging frequently become confused by the fact that the properties are usually of dissimilar values. Actually, the values of the properties are irrelevant. In fact, standard exchange contracts do not ordinarily have a place to write in the prices of the properties. The fact is, it is the equities which the owners have in their respective properties which must be equal, not the values. For example, if you trade a free and clear $100,000 property for your neighbor's property worth $500,000, the trade is balanced if it turns out that your neighbor's property is encumbered with a $400,000 mortgage.

Originally, the Internal Revenue Code required the exchange to be "simultaneous," which was ordinarily interpreted to mean that the documents had to be recorded at the same time. However, a 1979 decision [*Starker v. United States*, 602 F2d 1341 (CA9, 1979)] resulted in a taxpayer being able to take up to 60 months to find substitute property, under certain circumstances. Subsequently. Congress amended the Internal Revenue Code so that a taxpayer may create a tax deferred exchange provided the substitute property is identified within 45 days and the transaction is closed within 180 days. When one of the parties has to located substitute property the exchange usually involves the service of a *facilitator*. A facilitator is a third party who steps in to complete the exchange.

Capital losses – Another possible way to avoid tax on a capital gain is to offset the capital gain with a *capital loss*. As the term would imply, a capital loss occurs when the owner sells a property for less than the cost basis. This could easily happen if the property goes down in value. An important fact to remember is that a capital loss can be used only to offset a capital gain – a capital loss cannot be used to offset ordinary taxable income.

Personal residences – The foregoing discussion has concentrated mainly on investment properties and the methods investors use to avoid or defer capital gains taxes on them. Although installment sale and other methods described above can be used on a personal residence, tax-deferred exchanging can be used on trade or business property and investment property only. However, owners of personal residences have a huge benefit that is not available for other kinds of property. Owners who wish to sell their personal residence may exclude up to $250,000 of gain ($500,000 for married taxpayers filing jointly). To qualify, the property must be used exclusively as the taxpayer's personal residence for an aggregate of at least two of the five years prior to the sale. The exclusion may be taken as many times as desired, but not more than once every two years. If a personal residence is sold prior to the two year period, the amount of gain is prorated. For example, if you sold a property at a gain of $50,000 nine months after buying it, 9/24 of the $50,000 may be excluded from income.

Income taxes and the real estate agent

Most real estate agents act as ***independent contractors*** under the terms of the Internal Revenue Code. The alternative is to act as an ***employee***. If you are an independent contractor your employer need not withhold for income taxes or social security. Of course, you must still pay the tax, but you will take the responsibility for paying it yourself. If you are an independent contractor you are required to file an estimated tax return quarterly. Employees, on the other hand, are subject to withholding. For more discussion of the rules regarding independent contractor versus employee status, see Chapter 18.

Whether they are independent contractors or employees, real estate agents are entitled to deduct as legitimate business expenses those costs which they incur in producing or attempting to produce an income. These include, travel expenses (including auto expenses), multiple listing service dues, REALTOR® dues, license fees, and the like. Education is also deductible, but only if it is required by the employer and where the purpose is to enhance your abilities. Costs of education to enter a field (such as prelicense classes) are not generally deductible.

A special mention should be made of automobile expenses and expenses of an office in your home. Both of these items are commonly scrutinized by the IRS when they audit your tax return. The IRS may disallow deductions for which you do not have adequate records, so it is imperative that you check with your tax advisor to be sure your auto log and other expense records will withstand an audit.

Dealer status – Property held for resale is considered dealer property. Gain on the sale of dealer property is considered ordinary income, not capital gains. Although Congress changes the rates periodically, capital gains tax rates have always been lower than rates for ordinary income. Thus, it would be far better to have property classified as investment property instead of as dealer property. Furthermore, dealer property does not produce tax shelter because cost recovery cannot be claimed.

Real estate licensees who buy investment property occasionally have a difficult time convincing the IRS that their acquisition was an investment, not a property purchased for resale. Because you are licensed you must take extra care to structure your acquisitions to avoid it being classified as a dealer transaction.

Foreign Investment in Real Property Tax Act – In the past it was popular for foreigners to sell real estate assets owned in the U.S. and ignore the capital gains tax. As a result, in 1980 Congress passed the ***Foreign Investment in Real Property Tax Act***. The Act requires closing agents to withhold for the capital gains tax due unless the seller furnishes the closing agent with a certification that the seller is a U.S. resident and exempt from the withholding requirement. The closing agent must then remit the tax withheld to the IRS.

🔑 KEY TERMS

The key to understanding any new field is the vocabulary used in that field. To maximize your comprehension of the material presented in this chapter, be sure you know the meaning and significance of the following terms. Remember that the majority of test questions primarily test knowledge of vocabulary.

Accelerated depreciation

Adjusted sales price

Boot

Capital gain

Capital improvements

Capital loss

Cost basis

Cost recovery

Dealer property

Depreciable

Double declining balance

Employee

Facilitator

Foreign Investment in Real Property Tax Act

Independent contractor

Installment sale

Investment property

Like-kind exchange

Net spendable income

125% declining balance

150% declining balance

Personal use property

Realization

Straight line

Sum of the years' digits

Tax shelter

Tax-deferred exchange

Tax-free exchange

Trade or business property

200% declining balance

Chapter 18

The law of agency

ALTHOUGH REAL ESTATE AGENTS must be conversant with many laws, the most important is the law of agency, for it is the law of agency that governs the day to day relationships that the agent forms with sellers, buyers, and practically everyone the agent comes in contact with.

The law of agency is not unique to real estate – there are many fields in which the law of agency is important. We are all familiar with travel agents, insurance agents, entertainers' agents, among others. All of these agents operate under much the same set of rules as real estate agents. However, the rules for real estate agents are somewhat specialized and more complex than for other types of representation. Worse, the public does not always understand their relationships with real estate agents. The result is that the Washington Legislature created Chapter 18.86 of RCW to clarify matters. Chapter 18.86 does not negate the common law and other general concepts related to agency, but does modify it in some respects. However, since Chapter 18.86 was created to expand and modify the common law, it will make much more sense if you understand the history of agency law before looking at the way Chapter 18.86 changed it. Therefore, in the first part of this chapter we will discuss common law concepts, followed by the specifics of Chapter 18.86.

Common law definition of an agent

As a generalization, an **agent** is one who is authorized to represent the interests of another (called a **principal**) in negotiations or dealings with third parties. Because there is always a principal as well as the agent, the **law of agency** is frequently called the law of **principal and agent**.

The key idea in the agency relationship is the authority. The agent is simply someone to whom the principal has given authority. In fact, the whole purpose of the law of agency is to allow people to expand the scope of their activity. Because of the law of agency, you can hire unlimited numbers of persons to represent you, and even to enter into contracts on your behalf with third parties. And if you authorize your agent to hire his or her own agents, the number of people representing you can multiply indefinitely. You can see that the law of agency creates endless possibilities.

There are two central concepts in practically any agency relationship. One is that the principal relies on the agent as an expert for specialized advice. The other is that the agent has a high standard of responsibility toward the principal's best interests. This responsibility is called the agent's **fiduciary** duty to the principal.

An easy way to look at agency is to examine a common agency relationship that most people are familiar with – a power of attorney. If you give someone a power of attorney, you become the principal, and you give the other party authority to do something on your behalf, such as signing a document for you. The party you authorize is called an **attorney in fact** (as opposed to an attorney at law). The attorney in fact is your agent and you will be bound by the document he or she signed on your behalf provided, of course, that the attorney in fact acted within the scope of the authority you granted.

Now that we have a basic grasp of the purpose of the law of agency, let us turn our attention to its real estate application. If an agent is one who is authorized to represent another, and sometimes authorized to enter into a contract with another on behalf of a principal, then in a typical real estate transaction, who is the principal and who is the agent? The answer is not simple. In a traditional sale of real estate, the seller lists the property with the broker. In effect, the seller hires the broker as an agent. Therefore, the seller is the principal, the broker is the agent, and the broker has a fiduciary duty to the seller.

Nevertheless, it is perfectly possible for the broker to represent the buyer, and today representing buyers is just as common as representing sellers. And, of course, in other types of real estate activity, brokers represent different parties. In property management real estate licensees commonly represent owners in their negotiations with renters and lessees. Here again, while licensees would most likely represent the owner, it is also perfectly possible for them to represent a potential tenant. We will discuss the issue of buyer brokerage and tenant brokerage in more detail later.

So far we have discussed only the role of the owner's agent, i.e., the listing broker. But brokers may hire other licensees. What happens if the broker hires another broker or a salesperson? Then the broker or salesperson who acts as the employee of a broker becomes the agent of the employing broker. As we noted above, the principal can authorize the agent to hire his or her own agents, and this is precisely what happens in a lot of real estate transactions – the owner hires the broker as an agent, and grants the broker the authority to hire other persons as agents for the broker. The broker then hires other brokers and/or other salespersons as agents of the broker. The broker's employees in this situation are frequently referred to as subagents. Subagency will also be covered in greater detail later.

Many agents use the words *client* and *customer* with special meanings. Agents commonly refer to the principal as a client, and to third parties as customers. While these are not legal definitions, and not all agents use them as we have defined them here, these are nevertheless common definitions.

Types of agents

As we noted above, you become an agent when the principal grants you *authority*. The authority may be to represent the principal in a single task, various tasks, or may even be unlimited authority.

An agent who is given authority to represent the principal for just one task is called a *special agent*. Most of the time real estate brokers act as special agents. For example, a seller will hire the broker to sell the property. This is just one task.

An agent who is given various or several tasks, or more commonly, a category of tasks, is a *general agent*. Property managers, for example, would be general agents, since the owner gives them authority to show and rent vacant property, arrange for repairs and maintenance, make mortgage payments, and take care of many other matters relating to the owner's investment. In the case of the property manager, the owner grants the agent authority for the entire category of tasks, so it is a general agency. The relationship between a broker and brokers or salespersons licensed under the broker is another example. The broker gives the affiliated agents the authority to handle any of the properties the broker has listed, including showing property, writing offers and getting them accepted, the authority to take new listings, possibly the authority to engage in property management, and so on. Since this is a category of tasks, the agency is general.

An agent who is granted unlimited authority is called a *universal agent*. An unlimited power of attorney would be a common example of a universal agency. Guardians and conservators of minors and incompetents are also usually universal agents. A universal agent in real estate would be rare.

Special income tax considerations

Although not properly a discussion of agency, mention must be made of the issue of withholding taxes. Under the Internal Revenue Code, wages, salaries and the like are subject to withholding, and the employer is subject to certain payroll taxes. Of course, regardless of whether or not there is withholding, if you earn money you must pay tax on it. The issue is whether your broker withholds for your income taxes, or whether there is no withholding and you pay your taxes yourself. Note that, even if there is no withholding, in most cases you will have to file and pay estimated taxes quarterly. But at least, without withholding, you get the use of the money until filing time. It also simplifies the bookkeeping for a broker who has subagents. In the Internal Revenue Code, taxpayers whose income is subject to withholding are called **employees**. Taxpayers whose income is not subject to withholding are called **independent contractors**.

Real estate agents have zealously guarded their right to be independent contractors. In the past, the Internal Revenue Service attacked this right at every opportunity. As a result REALTORS® lobbied Congress for clarification of this issue. The outcome was the "Safe Harbor Rules" which have been made a part of the Internal Revenue Code. Under the Safe Harbor Rules, a real estate agent is an independent contractor for federal tax purposes if several conditions exist:

- The agent is a real estate licensee,
- The agent's income is almost entirely based on production rather than on hours worked, i.e., the agent's income is at risk,
- The agent provides at least some of the materials and equipment required (e.g., an automobile), and
- There is a written contract which specifies that the agent is an independent contractor and not an employee.

In real estate sales today, practically all agents act as independent contractors. In other types of real estate activity, such as property management, commercial leasing, appraisal and the like, most agents are still independent contractors, but it is less unusual to find employees.

Agent's compensation

An agent's compensation is determined strictly by negotiation with the principal. There is no set fee. If any organization set fees it would be in restraint of trade and a violation of anti-trust laws, both state and federal.

However, an individual agent may set his or her own standards. And a real estate brokerage firm may set minimums for the company which all brokers and salespersons working for the company must adhere to. What is illegal is if one real estate company conspires with other companies to set minimum fees. To avoid claims of price fixing most real estate companies instruct their brokers and salespersons never even to discuss company fee policies with agents from other companies.

Creating agency relationships

An agency relationship is created when the principal grants the agent authority, as we have seen above. At first blush this would simply appear to be an ordinary contract. Yet the agency relationship is not contractual in the strict sense of the word. A better term to describe it would be "consensual," since it is derived from the consent of the principal. Also, unlike most contracts, consideration is not required to create an agency relationship.

There are three ways that agency relationships are normally created. The most common is where the consent to be represented is stated orally or in writing, in which case we say it is an **expressed agency**. If the agency involves real estate, the Washington

Statute of Frauds requires it to be in writing. Besides listing agreements, typical agency contracts in real estate include property management agreements, appraisal orders, buyer brokerage agreements, escrow instructions, and the like. Note that an earnest money agreement is not an agency agreement. The only real estate contracts that are agency contracts are those where someone hires someone else to provide a service.

An agency can also be created where the principal agrees to the agent's actions after the agent has acted. In this case, we say the agency was created by ***ratification***, that is, that the principal ratified the agency. For example, suppose you know an owner wishes to sell his or her real estate, but has not yet given anyone a listing agreement. Suddenly you have a prospective buyer who might be interested in the property, but there is no time to go to the owner and obtain a listing agreement prior to showing it, so you show it to the prospective buyer anyway, without an expressed agency. After showing it to the prospect, you have time to contact the owner and obtain the owner's consent for you to represent the owner. If you obtain the owner's consent after performing the task, the owner is now bound by the fact that you are his or her agent, retroactively to the beginning of the act.

The previous example can also serve to illustrate another point about ratification. Suppose you were able to secure an offer from the prospective buyer and the owner were to accept the offer. It is fundamental in agency law that when a principal accepts the benefit of the agent's actions, the principal ratifies those actions, even though there was no expressed ratification. In other words, the principal cannot accept the benefit of your actions as his or her agent without recognizing you as an authorized agent.

Since an agency relationship frequently involves many authorities, it sometimes occurs that only one particular authority is ratified, the rest having been expressed. For example, suppose you take a listing agreement on a property (creating an expressed agency), but in the agreement the owner insists that there be no sign on the property. However, you proceed to place a sign on the property anyway. Since this exceeds your authority, this action could have dire consequences, as we will discuss later. But if the owner then agrees that the sign can stay, the owner ratifies your authority to place a sign on the property. Similarly, if the sign produces a buyer and the owner knows you put the sign on the property, and the owner accepts the offer from the buyer, then the owner has accepted the benefit of the wrongful action, and is thereby deemed to have ratified the authority.

Less commonly, an agency is sometimes created where one party leads someone to believe that an agency exists. Under the right circumstances, this can result in an agency by ***estoppel***. We call it an agency by estoppel because the party who led the other to believe an agency exists is estopped (barred) from denying the existence of the agency.

For example, suppose a property owner allows a friend to take care of various business matters such as writing checks to pay the owner's bills, purchasing supplies on behalf of the owner, and so on. A broker knows that the friend has done these things for the owner over a period of time. The friend (not the owner) then gives the broker an agreement to secure a buyer for the owner's property. In good faith, the broker shows the property to a prospective buyer and secures an offer to buy, which the owner then accepts. Must the owner pay the brokerage fee? Assuming that a court would agree that the broker had the right to rely on the circumstances, the owner would be estopped from denying that the friend was authorized to act on the owner's behalf. An agency by estoppel was created.

A common agency created by estoppel occurs where an owner has not hired the agent formally, but nevertheless allows the agent to show the owner's property to a potential buyer. If the owner takes no action to correct the impression of the buyer that the agent is authorized, then the agency becomes established and both the agent and the third party may rely upon it.

This can be even more direct, such as where the owner leads the agent to believe that the agent is authorized to represent the owner. In this case, however, the agent will have a more difficult time collecting compensation because the owner can raise the defense of the Statute of Frauds, which requires agency agreements in Washington to be in writing.

An important point about agencies created by estoppel is that either party can create the belief in the other. In other words, the owner can lead an agent to believe that the owner authorizes the agent, thus creating an agency by estoppel. But in similar fashion, the agent can lead the owner to believe that the agent is representing the owner, in which case an agency has also been created by estoppel. Or an agent could lead a third party to believe the agent was representing the third party, such as where a real estate agent leads a prospective buyer to believe that the agent is representing the buyer. These are sometimes referred to as *accidental* or *unintentional agencies*. Creating an accidental agency with the buyer can have far-reaching implications when the broker is already representing the owner under an expressed listing agreement. These are some of the problems that Chapter 18.86 RCW addresses, and will be discussed in more detail later.

The scope of the agent's authority is usually expressed in the agreement which creates the agency. For example, a listing agreement for a home would likely grant the agent authority to show the property, to place a for sale sign on the property, to advertise the property, to hire additional agents (other licensees), to cooperate with agents in other real estate companies, and so forth. However, an owner may not wish a sign, or may wish to withhold some other authority. This is generally accomplished simply by modifying the standard listing agreement form.

Property management agreements usually present a completely different set of authorities to the agent than you find in real estate sales. Where a listing agreement for the sale of a property would authorize the agent to secure offers, it would generally not authorize the agent to accept the buyer's offer on behalf of the seller. Of course, it is possible for a listing to grant the agent the authority to accept an offer, but most agents would feel that such authority might create more liability than the agent cares to accept. In property management agreements, however, the agent usually does accept the authority to enter into contracts with third parties (tenants) on behalf of the owner. A property management contract might typically authorize the agent to set rental rates, advertise the property for rent or lease, show the property, take applications from tenants, check credit and other references and make credit decisions, and then enter into rental agreements on behalf of the owner.

As you can see, the agency contract usually contains extensive provisions expressing the authority of the agent. All such provisions are called *expressed actual authority*. But there is almost always another kind of authority that is created. Where the listing, buyer service agreement, property management agreement, or other document creates all sorts of specific authorities, it can never express every detail or conceivable circumstance that might occur during the agent's performance of the agreement. For example, a listing contract may stipulate that the agent may show the property during reasonable hours, but it may not stipulate what hours are reasonable, or whether the agent is authorized to use the agent's personal automobile to bring the prospective buyers to the property, and so on. Nevertheless, even though these authorities are not expressed, they are *implied*. The law refers to such authority as *implied actual authority*, defined as the authority which is necessary to the performance of the expressed authority.

In addition to expressed and implied actual authority, the law also recognizes *apparent* or *ostensible authority*. This is the authority granted when the agency is created by estoppel.

PRINCIPAL   *Grants by*   **Agreement**
- **Expressed**
- **Implied**
- **Ratified**

Estoppel
- **Apparent (ostensible)**

   Authority to   **AGENT**

The usual ways in which an agency can be created

Another important point about agency relationships is that, at common law, the principal is liable to third parties for the actions of the agent when the agent is acting within the scope of the authority granted by the principal, whether the authority is expressed or implied. At common law the liability of the principal for the actions of the agent is called the legal principal of *respondeat superior* (let the employer respond). For example, suppose a broker takes a listing agreement from an owner where the owner authorizes the broker to say something about the property in advertising the property to buyers. If the owner has specifically authorized the ad, then the owner is liable for any misrepresentations. However, if the owner did not specifically authorize the ad matters become more confusing. As we will see later, this is another area where Chapter 18.86 RCW clarifies matters.

However, when a third party (such as a buyer) deals with an agent, the third party is required to make a reasonable attempt to determine the scope of the agent's authority. Since the third party can only hold the principal to representations and actions of the agent if the agent was acting within the scope of the agent's authority, then knowledge of the agent's authority is crucial to the third party. Courts also generally recognize disclaimers in contracts where the principal agrees to be responsible for representations made by the agent only if the representations are contained in the contract.

What would be the penalty to the agent if the agent should exceed the authority granted by the principal? There are various liabilities the agent might incur, depending on the circumstances. For one, if the agent exceeds the authority granted by the principal, it gives the principal just cause to revoke the authority and cancel the agency agreement. As we shall see later, a principal may always revoke the authority, but if the principal revokes the authority without just cause, the agent can hold the principal liable for damages. However, if the agent has exceeded the authority granted by the principal then the principal has just cause to revoke the authority without liability for damages.

If the principal suffers a loss as a result of the agent having exceeded the agent's authority, then the principal has cause for damages. For example, suppose the agent takes an agreement to sell the principal's office building. The principal stipulates that there be no sign on the property. However, the agent places a for sale sign on the property anyway. Unknown to the agent, the principal was negotiating with a potential tenant. The tenant sees the for sale sign suddenly appear, and decides to break off negotiations. The principal has lost the tenant and the agent could be held liable for the principal's losses.

If the agent exceeds the authority granted by the principal, and as a result a third party is damaged, then the third party may have cause of action against the agent. For example, suppose a broker takes a management agreement from the owner to manage the owner's building. But the owner insists that the owner alone will sign any leases; the agent will not have the right to sign leases with prospective tenants. The agent locates a prospective tenant and wrongfully signs a lease with the tenant. In reliance on the agent's apparent authority, the tenant purchases furniture and moves into the premises. When the owner discovers what has happened, the owner refuses to acknowledge the lease. Since the agent acted outside of the scope of the authority granted by the owner, the tenant cannot enforce the lease on the owner. However, the tenant has cause to recover damages from the agent.

Of course, another potential liability to the agent who exceeds his or her authority is loss of the agent's real estate license. And finally, an agent who exceeds his or her authority also loses the right to collect the agent's compensation.

Agent's fiduciary obligations

As mentioned earlier, the agent has a fiduciary duty to the principal. This fiduciary duty includes various obligations. At the top of the list we could place *loyalty*. In fact, we could go further and say "utmost loyalty," since the agent must be loyal to the principal to the exclusion of all other interests, including the interests of the agent. That is to say, if there is a conflict between the interests of the principal and the interests of the agent, the interests of the principal come first.

And clearly, the interests of the principal also come ahead of the interests of third parties. Normally, when the agent takes a listing agreement from the owner the agent cannot also represent the prospective buyer, since the agent cannot advocate both positions at the same time. An exception occurs in a dual agency, which we will discuss later. And there are also certain statutory obligations of agents under Chapter 18.86 RCW, which will also be discussed later.

The agent's duty of loyalty includes the obligation of *confidentiality*. Obviously, if the agent is to be loyal to the principal the agent cannot disclose confidential information to a third party if the information would be harmful to the position of the principal. The obligation of confidentiality goes further than just not disclosing sensitive information to the other side. It should be viewed more in the same sense that a doctor or attorney must maintain confidentiality – i.e., private matters should not be disclosed to anyone unless there is authority to do so. Again, Chapter 18.86 RCW clarifies the duty of confidentiality, which we will discuss later.

In addition to loyalty, an agent owes the principal a duty of *full disclosure*. On its face, the obligation of full disclosure would seem to be a direct contradiction to the obligation of confidentiality. But we are dealing with different matters – we must keep the principal's affairs confidential from third parties; but we must make full disclosure to the principal of anything we know about the third party. Full disclosure to the principal includes matters such as –

- The fair market value of the property,
- Any relationship the agent has with third parties (conflicts of interest),
- A prospective buyer's financial condition (if representing a seller),
- That a fee will be paid to another broker or property manager,
- All offers and counteroffers as soon as received,
- If there is a deposit or earnest money, what kind (cash, check, etc.),
- The legal provisions of any offer, and
- Any other material fact.

The agent could even be held responsible for disclosing facts which the agent should have known, even if the agent did not actually know. This would include matters which the agent, with the agent's special expertise should be aware of, such as matters of law relating to provisions of the earnest money agreement, local housing and zoning codes, etc. Again, Chapter 18.86 clarifies these issues, as well will see later.

Suppose the agent wishes to buy the property that the agent has listed. Obviously, real estate agents have the right to buy property the same as anyone else. But when the agent is the third party as well as the agent, then the agent clearly has a duty to disclose that fact to the principal. Using someone else as a **straw man** to keep the principal from knowing that the real party of interest is the agent is a clear violation of the law of agency. It would also be a violation of the license law. Similarly, any **secret profit** the agent makes at the expense of the principal is a violation of the agent's fiduciary obligations to the principal and of the license law.

The agent also owes the principal a duty of **obedience**. Naturally, this does not mean that the agent may break the law, even if the principal instructs the agent to do so. For example, if the owner knows of a material defect in the property, this must be disclosed to the prospective buyer. Failure to disclose a material fact is fraud. Therefore, if the owner instructs the agent to keep quiet about the defect, the agent need not keep quiet and, in fact, must disclose it to the prospective buyer.

In cases where the agency itself is dependent upon following illegal instructions of the principal, the agent may not accept the agency. However, where a legitimate agency relationship exists, and thereafter the principal gives the agent illegal instructions, the agent is not required to withdraw from the agency (although doing so may be wise). In this case, the agent may continue as the principal's agent, as long as the agent refuses to obey the illegal instructions. For example, if an owner, when giving an agent a listing agreement, stipulates that the agent is not to show the property to minorities, the agent must refuse the entire agency agreement. But if the principal has already given the agent an ordinary listing agreement, and later instructs the agent to discriminate illegally, the agency may continue – the agent merely ignores the illegal instructions.

The principal is also entitled to a complete **accounting** for all funds and property coming into the agent's possession on behalf of the principal. In a sale transaction this is normally accomplished when the closing statement is given to the owner. In cases where deposits or other funds are collected but the transaction falls through (i.e., no final closing statement), the principal is still entitled to a complete accounting.

Not only must the agent make a complete accounting, the agent must also follow accepted practices with principal's funds and property. Mixing the principal's funds with the agent's own funds is called **commingling**, and is a violation of the license law. If the agent goes so far as to use the funds for his or her own purposes, this is called **conversion**. Either usually results in immediate revocation of the agent's license.

The agent's fiduciary responsibilities to the principal also include a duty of **due diligence**. There are many aspects to due diligence. First, the agent should not accept tasks for which the agent does not possess the necessary skills and abilities. Due diligence implies that the agent has enough knowledge of real property and related laws to advise the principal to seek the advice of appropriate counsel when necessary to protect the interests of the principal. Due diligence also includes the agent's obligation to investigate to discover material facts which affect the interests of the principal. And, of course, real estate agents are expected to have an expert knowledge of values and marketing methods.

In addition to having the ability to perform the task with reasonable care and skill, the agent must exert his or her best efforts to perform the task quickly and efficiently. An agent who fails to work on the property in the usual fashion – signs, normal advertising, showing the property – as appropriate to the property and the task assigned, is surely in violation of the obligation of due diligence to the principal. Again, as we will see later, Chapter 18.86 RCW modifies and clarifies the duty of due diligence.

If an agent fails to honor the agent's fiduciary obligations to the principal the consequences can be severe. Such failure is a **tort** (civil wrong) which entitles the principal to recover from the agent any damages the principal has suffered. In addition, it is just cause for the principal to revoke the authority without being liable to the agent for the agent's compensation. And it could result in revocation or suspension of the agent's license, or other sanction from the Department of Licensing.

Obligations of the agent to third parties

In a traditional real estate agency relationship the broker or property manager is the agent of the property owner and owes a duty to the owner as the owner's fiduciary. This is the same whether the agent was hired to sell the property or to manage it for the owner. But even though the agent owes a fiduciary duty to the owner as the principal, the agent still has obligations to other parties in the transaction.

An agent representing the owner owes the prospective buyer or tenant common law obligations of honesty, good faith, fair dealing, competence and full disclosure, in addition to duties specified in Chapter 18.86 RCW. Of these duties, the most common failure lies in failure to disclose. In Washington the courts have consistently ruled it unlawful if anyone makes any kind of false representation about real property.

In addition, the 1994 Washington Legislature enacted laws (RCW Chapter 64.06) requiring sellers of residential property to complete a property disclosure statement and deliver it to the buyer. This law applies to sales only, not rentals and leases. Nevertheless, it would also be good practice for property managers to make disclosures about the condition of the property to prospective tenants. (For more detail about the property disclosure statement and other matters related to fraud and misrepresentation, see Chapter 9.)

Obligations of the principal to the agent

Of course, in an agency relationship, the agent is not the only party with responsibilities. The principal has various duties toward the agent and to third parties as well. The chief duty of the principal to the agent is to pay the compensation as agreed and in a timely fashion. If the agent has performed as agreed, and has not exceeded the authority granted by the principal or breached the agent's fiduciary obligations to the principal, then the agent is usually entitled to his or her compensation. However, it may be possible for the principal to avoid this obligation if the agent was not properly licensed at the time the agent claimed to have earned the fee, or if the agency agreement itself was not in writing or was otherwise defective.

The principal also must reimburse the agent for the agent's expenses if the agent was authorized to pay expenses in advance to others. And the principal is responsible to the agent for any losses the agent suffers as a result of the principal's wrongful acts. For example, suppose an owner gives an agent a listing agreement to sell the owner's property. The agent secures a buyer, who makes an offer, and the owner accepts. When the transaction is about to be finalized, it is discovered that there is an unrecorded lien against the property which the owner failed to disclose to the agent. The lien causes the transaction to fall through. Nevertheless, the principal must pay the commission to the agent, since the failure of the transaction was caused by the negligence of the principal, not the agent.

Obligations of the principal to third parties

The fact that the agent is required to disclose to third parties does not relieve the principal of the same obligation. In other words, if the third party is damaged, he or she has cause of action against the party or parties who caused the harm. Usually this includes the principal but it only includes the agent if, as we noted above, the agent is also negligent.

Of course, the chief obligation of the principal to third parties is to honor the actions of the agent, assuming the agent was acting within the scope of the agent's authority. Thus, if the agent was authorized to sign a rental agreement with a tenant, then the principal is bound to honor the rental agreement. At common law (modified by Chapter 18.86 RCW) the principal is also responsible to third parties for the agent's actions, even if the actions are wrongful, as long as the agent was acting within the agent's authority. The principal is not responsible to third parties for the wrongful acts of the agent if the agent acts outside of the scope of the agent's authority.

Since the agent is the representative of the principal, at common law the principal is deemed to be given notice of anything the third party communicates to the agent. This is called *imputed notice*. In other words, if a prospective buyer wishes to put the seller on notice, the buyer does not have to tell the seller directly; telling the seller's agent is deemed to be the same as telling the seller. Imputed notice is another issue addressed in Chapter 18.86 RCW.

Terminating agency relationships

General principles of contract law could create situations where an agency agreement becomes unenforceable. For example, if one of the parties enters into the agreement in reliance upon fraud, misrepresentation, mutual mistake of fact, undue influence, or was temporarily incompetent, then the agreement is voidable at the option of the damaged party. Similarly, if the agreement is not in writing, does not contain an adequate description of the property, or is for an illegal act, the agreement is void. Agency agreements also become unenforceable due to impossibility beyond the control of one of the parties, among many other possibilities. However, in real estate sales, agency relationships are normally terminated by expiration or by one of the parties unilaterally terminating it.

Notwithstanding an expiration clause, an agency contract is not necessarily terminated immediately when the expiration date arrives. Even though the agency contract has expired, if the principal continues to encourage the agent to work on behalf of the principal the principal will likely be held to have waived the expiration date. Even if the principal does not actively encourage the agent to continue, if the principal is aware of the agent's continuing efforts and permits the agent to proceed, the agency relationship will not be severed.

Expiration dates are also ineffective if the agent is able to rely on a safety clause in the agreement. A *safety clause* (sometimes called an *extender clause* or a *carry-over clause*) is a clause that extends an agreement for anyone the agent showed the property to during the term of the agreement. Its purpose is to prevent an unscrupulous owner from going around the agent by waiting to sell the property after the listing agreement expires. For example, suppose you have a listing agreement, which is set to expire on July

15. Shortly before the agreement expires you show the property to a prospective buyer. The owner and the buyer conspire to avoid paying your commission by waiting to execute a sale agreement until after the listing agreement expires. If you have a safety clause which lasts long enough to cover the time when the sale finally occurred, the owner still owes you the commission.

Agency agreements, the same as any agreement, can be mutually canceled or rescinded. That is, the principal and the agent can simply agree to terminate the relationship. It is not uncommon in ordinary real estate practice for the principal to have a change of plans so he or she no longer wishes to sell the property. When this happens, agents try to protect themselves from an unscrupulous owner who may claim to have a change of plans, but in reality has found a buyer and wishes to sell the property without paying the commission. To keep the principal honest, most agents ask the principal, as a condition of canceling the agency agreement, to sign an agreement that if the property is sold during a period of time after the cancellation, the owner will pay the commission anyway, and if the owner enters into a new listing agreement for the property, that it will be listed with the agent.

Agency agreements fall into a special category of contracts called *personal services contracts*. There are various special rules which apply to personal services contracts. First, personal services contracts cannot be assigned, so an agent must perform the task himself or herself, although the agent may hire employees and assistants. If the principal authorizes the agent to use employees, assistants and other agents, then at common law the principal is responsible for the employees, assistants and other agents. The agent can hire employees, assistants and other agents even if the principal does not authorize it, but then the principal is not responsible for their actions. Again, Chapter 18.86 RCW clarifies these concepts for real estate agents.

Another feature of personal services contracts is that they are terminated by the death, incompetence or bankruptcy of either the principal or the agent. For example, if you take a management agreement on a property and the owner dies during the term of the agency, the agency agreement is extinguished. Contrast this with an ordinary, non-agency contract, such as selling a property on a land sales contract. If either the seller or the buyer dies, the estate of the deceased person must still perform the contract. Of course, in an agency contract, if the agent dies, the agency is terminated the same as if the principal had died. This is the reason that most real estate companies (both brokerage and property management) are incorporated. If the owner gives a management agreement for the property to the corporation, the death of the broker or property manager does not terminate the agency relationship, because the broker or property manager was not the agent in the first place; the agent was the corporation.

Personal services contracts cannot be enforced by specific performance. **Specific performance** is a pleading asking a court to order a party to a contract to perform it as agreed. So if the owner wishes to withdraw the authority, or if the agent wishes to renounce the agency, neither can stop the other. However, while specific performance is not possible, a suit for damages is. So if the principal withdraws the authority wrongfully, the agent has grounds to recover damages. Note that it is not a wrongful revocation of the authority if the agent has exceeded the agent's authority or breached the fiduciary obligations to the principal.

The rule that the principal cannot be stopped from revoking the authority has a major exception. If the agent has an interest in the property we say it is an *agency coupled with an interest*. In this case the principal may not revoke the authority without cause. For example, if the principal grants the agent a management agreement on the property, and an option to buy the property as well, then the agent has an interest in the property (the option) and the principal cannot revoke the authority. The interest can be any interest – e.g., the agent could have a leasehold, be holding a mortgage, have an easement, etc.

Agency agreements are frequently **unilateral contracts**. That is, only one party can be compelled to perform; performance by the other is optional. For example, the terms of an open listing agreement to sell a property provide that the owner promises to pay the agent if the agent secures a buyer, but the agent makes no promise that the agent will actually find a buyer – that is, performance by the agent is optional. Therefore, in most cases, the agent can renounce the agency at will, without fear of demand for damages from the principal.

However, not all agency agreements are unilateral. Suppose a broker takes a listing from a seller and guarantees that if the broker cannot sell the property the broker will buy it for a certain price. (Brokers commonly call this a "guaranteed sale program" and use it as a marketing tool.) Notice that both parties have made promises to the other, so each has the ability to force the other to perform. This agreement is now bilateral, and the agent is not permitted to renounce the agency without being liable to the principal for damages.

Subagency

In a traditional listing or management arrangement, the owner is the principal and the broker is the agent. Typical agreements provide authority for the agent to hire the agent's own agents (**subagents**) to assist in discharging the agent's duties. Brokers may hire other licensed brokers and salespersons.

Real estate agency relationship. Subagent represents agent who, in turn, represents the owner. Thus indirectly the subagent is working for the owner the same as the agent.

In the above diagram, the owner is the principal, the broker is the agent, and the contract between them is a listing or management agreement. The broker, in turn, has hired a subagent. The contract between the broker and the subagent is another employment agreement. The listing or management contract between the owner and the broker probably grants numerous authorities to the agent, including the right to show the property to prospective buyers or tenants, to place a sign on the property, to advertise the property, to hire subagents, and to seek the cooperation of other brokers.

But the contract between the broker and his or her subagents contains authorities of a more general nature. Typically, it authorizes the subagents to secure new listing or management agreements for the broker, secure offers on existing properties that are available, present offers to owners and secure their acceptances, show and sell, or rent or lease, properties listed by other brokers who have requested the assistance of the broker, and so forth. Normally there is also an extensive discussion of the amount of the subagent's compensation.

Subagents should take care to note that they are authorized to take listing or management agreements and other business only on behalf of the employing broker. When the subagent takes a listing or management agreement, for example, the agreement is the personal property of the broker, not of the subagent who obtained it. Therefore, if the subagent wishes to leave the broker, he or she cannot take any listing or management agreements, since they are not his or her agreements in the first place. The subagent's employment agreement may even stipulate that if the subagent leaves, he or she earns no compensation, even if the property is sold, rented or leased after the subagent leaves.

The arrangement above with one broker and his or her subagent(s) is typical. However, many times there is another brokerage or property management firm involved. And this second brokerage or property management firm may have its own subagents, as well. In a normal, traditional transaction, this second firm is also an agent of the first broker, and a subagent of the owner.

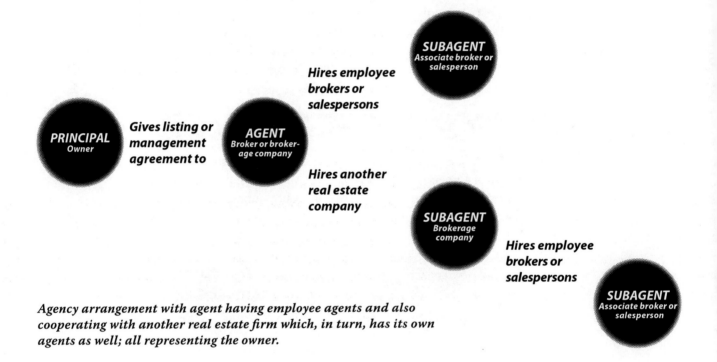

Agency arrangement with agent having employee agents and also cooperating with another real estate firm which, in turn, has its own agents as well; all representing the owner.

In the scheme above, the first brokerage or property management firm originally took the listing or management agreement, or one of the firm's brokers or salespersons took it on the firm's behalf. It is the personal property of the first firm. The first firm is under no obligation to cooperate with the second firm, although if the second firm belongs to the National Association of REALTORS®, their code of ethics may require the firm to cooperate with other members. If the first brokerage or property management firm agrees to cooperate with the second brokerage or management firm, the second firm becomes another agent of the first firm. In other words, the first firm has two agents, its own subagent, and the second firm. The contract between the first firm and the second firm is called a ***cooperation agreement***, or "coop agreement," for short.

The second firm, in turn, has hired a subagent. If the second firm's broker is the one who procured the offer from the buyer or tenant, then he or she is the subagent of the second broker (and sub-subagent, if you wish, of the first broker). Ultimately, all have a fiduciary duty to the owner.

What then of the buyer or tenant? Who is representing the third party in this typical transaction? In the majority of cases, the third party is simply without representation. Of course, a broker, either directly or via his or her subagents, may represent a buyer or a tenant instead of an owner. This is called ***buyer brokerage*** or ***tenant brokerage***. Or a broker may represent both the owner and the third party. This is called ***dual agency***. Both buyer or tenant brokerage and dual agency have their good points and their bad points, as we shall see below.

Buyer brokerage

Buyer brokerage, as the term would imply, is when the agent represents the buyer rather than the seller. A parallel situation would exist if a broker represented a prospective tenant in a management setting. Both are not the traditional manner in which agents acted in the past, but are very common today. Representing a buyer or a tenant is a time-honored way of doing business in commercial real estate. It is not uncommon, for example, for a company to engage the services of a local real estate broker to locate property for them and to represent them in negotiations with the owner and the owner's agent. Today it has become a common alternative in the residential field as well especially in the light of Chapter 18.86 RCW, which creates a legal presumption of buyer brokerage in most transactions.

Single agency with buyer or tenant representation. Each principal has a separate agent

Consider the diagram above and note how it is different from the preceding diagrams. This time we have the second broker and his or her subagent representing the buyer. Although the preceding diagram, showing both brokers representing the owner, is the more traditional arrangement, this chart showing buyer brokerage is more common today. To many real estate buyers and agents, buyer brokerage seems more logical.

In the past, buyer brokerage was used almost exclusively in commercial settings. With the rise in popularity of buyer brokerage in residential transactions, we have a solution to problems that used to occur. Suppose your sister wishes to buy a home and, quite naturally, expects you to find her one. In the past, residential agents represented only sellers. Would you seriously try to represent the seller's best interests when the buyer is your sister? Clearly, you want to advocate your sister's best interests, so buyer representation in this situation is the only practical and honest alternative.

Dual agency

There is yet another alternative to explore. Under the law of agency, it is also possible to represent both parties. This is called ***dual agency***. However, there are some special rules for dual agency. First, there must be full disclosure to, and written permission from both parties. Considering that most brokers take listing and management agreements which only provide for **single agency** (representing just one side of the transaction), you would have to notify and secure written permission from each owner before showing their property.

The second problem is that all fiduciary duties are suddenly owed to both. Of course, this means that the duties must be altered. For example, you cannot have "utmost loyalty" to two different parties, so the duty becomes closer to "equal loyalty." Similarly, at common law "full disclosure" means that you cannot keep confidences from either party – whatever one party tells you must be disclosed to the other, and vice-versa. In the past, because of these problems, most agents found that dual agency was not normally the answer. Today, however, Chapter 18.86 RCW solves most of the problems of dual agency.

Of course, you can act as a single agent to perform certain tasks for one party, while acting as a single agent to perform other non-conflicting tasks for the other. This may appear to be a dual agency, but in reality is two separate single agencies. For example, suppose the owner gives you a listing agreement on a house, but the agreement does not authorize you to take a deposit from the buyer. (Most listing agreement forms do authorize this, but for the sake of the example, let us suppose that you have one that does not.) Now suppose you find a buyer who wishes to make an offer and also wishes to tender a $5,000 earnest money deposit. If you take the $5,000 from the buyer, you are representing the buyer as to the act of taking the deposit, but you are still representing the best interests of the owner as to the task the owner has given you. Most agents avoid these situations. As you can imagine, making sure that the task you have accepted from one party does not conflict with your duties to the other is very difficult.

Who represents whom?

As you can see, the issue of who the agent represents is far from simple. And if you think it is confusing for agents to understand, imagine how the average buyer and seller see their relationships with their agents. In fact, in residential sales, the typical buyer is frequently convinced that the agent who is showing the property is representing his or her interests and not the interests of the seller.

The confusion is made worse by the ease with which agency contracts can be created. Remember, an agency contract need not be in writing for the third party to rely on it. Nor do agency agreements require a consideration. All that is required is that the principal consent to being represented.

Consider the case of a real estate agent who has been showing property to a buyer for some time. As the agent shows property after property to the buyer, the agent is very helpful with information about the neighborhood, including recent sales prices, location of schools, and so forth. And while showing property, the agent is careful to point out latent defects, possible violations of land use laws, and other material facts which the agent wants to be sure to disclose to the buyer. When the buyer finally makes an offer, does this buyer think the agent is representing his or her best interests, or the interests of the seller?

Remember that an agency agreement can be created by estoppel. If the principal leads the agent to believe that he or she will honor an agency relationship, or if the agent acts so as to induce the principal into believing that the agent is representing him or her, an agency by estoppel may be created. In the above example, does the buyer have justification to believe that the agent was representing his or her best interests? Does "being helpful" create an agency the buyer is entitled to rely upon? If a court made such a finding, the agent would be in big trouble indeed. For if the agent were found to have been representing the buyer, after agreeing in writing to be the agent of the owner (through the listing agreement), then the agent is a dual agent. And in this case, the dual agency is undisclosed and without the consent of both parties. We refer to this kind of situation as an **unintentional** or **accidental dual agency**.

An agent of the seller may generally do any of the following for the buyer without creating an agency with the buyer –

- Give information about comparable sales in the area
- Make disclosure of material defects
- Give the buyer information and assistance with financing
- Give information about the neighborhood
- Entertain the buyer and cultivate his or her good will
- Advise the buyer to seek legal or tax counsel

The reason these are acceptable is that the primary goal of an agent representing the seller is to secure an offer for the seller. As long as the agent's actions lead in that direction, and as long as there is no direct conflict of interest, it does not matter if the actions also benefit the buyer.

However, what if the agent starts advocating the buyer's position? The agent makes statements such as "If you want to buy this property, I would start by offering $ _____ ." These are examples of actions which would justify the buyer in believing that the agent is on the buyer's side.

But what if the agent, when beginning to work with a new buyer, stated that the agent was representing the best interests of the seller? Now that the buyer has been put on legal notice of the agent's position, it will be very difficult for the buyer to claim that the agent was acting on his or her behalf. Today, the majority of states, including Washington, require that the agent make some form of disclosure as to whom they represent. These requirements are contained in Chapter 18.86 RCW and will be discussed later.

Undisclosed principals

Although unusual, sometimes a buyer will ask a broker for representation and the buyer will not want the broker to disclose the buyer's identity to sellers. This usually happens in a commercial setting, perhaps where a company wishes to acquire property in an area but doesn't want it to be known that they are contemplating the move. After all, if word got out that a large company was looking for property in the area, it could increase asking prices.

When a broker works for an **undisclosed principal** there are some special issues to consider. Note that the usual authority of the agent in this case will be to enter into the sales contract on behalf of the principal. In the example of a large company acquiring property in the area, the seller would assume that the broker is the buyer, since the broker cannot disclose to the seller that the broker is acting as agent of the real buyer. In this case the seller can hold the real buyer to the bargain as well as the broker.

Alternatives to agency

Some real estate brokers feel that the law of agency does not fit the role they want to take in a real estate transaction. They view their job as being that of a **facilitator**, not an agent (sometimes also called a **transaction broker**). Washington law does not specifically prohibit this. Nothing says that a real estate broker must operate under the law of agency. If a broker wants to be a facilitator instead of an agent, it is permitted as long as the broker follows the statutory obligations to the parties contained in Chapter 18.86 RCW.

Nevertheless, being a facilitator is potentially more fraught with problems than being an agent. In an agency relationship the common law of agency and statutory requirements spell out exactly what the agent's duties are. If you are a facilitator you will have to create your own contract. Furthermore, over the past ten to twenty years the public has come to expect that real estate brokers are agents. People are accustomed to the relationship and deviating from it may be more trouble than it's worth.

Statutory obligations of the agent

Because of past misunderstandings of who represents whom, effective in 1985 Washington licensees were required to disclose which party the licensee was representing.

Today the statutory obligations of the agent are contained in Chapter 18.86 RCW. All exam applicants should study the complete text of these statutes and rules. A copy can be obtained from the Department of Licensing (DOL) by calling (360) 664-6488, or you can download them from the website for the Real Estate program of the Business and Professions Division of the DOL at http://www.dol.wa.gov/realestate/refront.htm.

Unfortunately, the requirement did not work well. Selling agents, for example, gave buyers a disclosure form that they were representing the seller under a subagency, and then proceeded to work as through they were really representing the buyers anyway. At the same time, some licensees began to work officially as buyers agents, but ran into problems with listing brokers, mostly because the listing broker felt that sharing the commission with a buyer's agent would violate their duty to the seller. And there were also problems with many multiple listing services which, at the time, had rules that a selling agent had to work as subagent of the seller.

Eventually the Washington Association of REALTORS® formed a task force to study the problem and come up with solutions. The result was Chapter 18.86 RCW, enacted by the Legislature in 1996.

Presumption of agency – Chapter 18.86 provides certain legal presumptions about who the licensee represents. If the licensee provides services for which a license is required (see Chapter 19 for a discussion of real estate activity which requires a license), to a buyer or tenant, then the licensee is presumed to be representing the buyer or the tenant unless –

- The licensee is the listing agent or has a management agreement with the owner or
- The licensee has a written subagency agreement with the seller's or owner's agent, or
- The licensee has a written dual agency agreement with both parties, or
- The licensee is the owner or one of the owners of the property, or
- The parties agree otherwise in writing (e.g., the licensee agrees to work as a facilitator (transaction broker) instead of under the law of agency).

The result is that most of the time the licensee showing the property and writing up the buyer's or tenant's offer will be representing the buyer or the tenant and not the seller. The seller's sole agent will be the listing agent.

If this is the state of affairs that the licensees want, then no formal disclosure forms need be given to the parties, although many licensees do so voluntarily. Licensees representing buyers find a number of advantages to using a buyer agency agreement. For one, it can provide for payment of the licensee's fee even if the buyer wishes to buy a property that is not listed. In addition, it can provide for a minimum fee in the event the seller declines to allow the listing commission to be shared with the buyer's agent, as is customary practice. And it also protects the agent's fee in the event the buyer purchases a property through someone else that the licensee showed to the buyer.

While the legal presumption of buyer agency goes a long way toward resolving questions as to whom the licensee represents, there is a problem when the listing agent and the selling agent work for the same firm. Under the law, when a salesperson or broker works for another broker or brokerage firm, their activity is always on behalf of the employing broker or firm. In other words, when you take a listing, the listing is the property of your broker or firm. Your broker or firm is actually the seller's agent, and you are the seller's subagent. Similarly, if you show a house to a buyer and the buyer makes an offer, it is really your broker or firm that is representing the buyer. Again, you are the subagent.

This creates a legal dilemma. If the listing and the selling agent work for the same firm, then the firm is actually a dual agent. (Sometimes this is called a *split* or *assigned agency*.) Dual agency is legal, but only with the prior written permission of both principals. Chapter 18.86 addresses this problem by stating that the employing broker is a dual agent, and the individual licensees are single agents, each representing just one party to the transaction. The broker must still have the prior written permission of both parties, but this is simple to obtain by putting language in the listing and buyer service agreements to that effect.

Agent's duties – Until very recently the common law obligations of agents to their principals is all the guidance the law gave real estate brokers. Chapter 18.86 RCW clarifies and modifies those common law duties, as well as common law obligations regarding condition of the property under principles of contract law.

All licensees, regardless of whom they represent, owe all parties certain duties, including –

- To exercise reasonable skill and care,
- To deal honestly and in good faith.
- To present all written offers and communications in a timely fashion, regardless of whether the seller has already accepted an offer to sell or a buyer is already under contract to buy a property,
- To disclose all material facts known by the licensee and not apparent or readily ascertainable by a person, but the licensee has no duty to investigate matters unless the licensee has agreed to do so,
- To give the parties a complete accounting.
- To provide a pamphlet on agency before the party signs a listing or an offer, consents to dual agency, or waives any rights (see *Disclosure pamphlet*, later),
- To disclose in writing whom the licensee represented in the transaction, either in the contract between the parties or in a separate document.

A buyer's agent owes extra duties to the buyer –

- To be loyal to the buyer by taking no action adverse or detrimental to the buyer,
- To disclose to the buyer any conflicts of interest,
- To advise the buyer to seek expert advice on matters that are beyond the agent's expertise,
- Not to disclose confidential information, even after termination of the agency relationship,
- After supplying the pamphlet, to make a continuous effort to locate a property for the buyer, except after the buyer has already entered into a contract to buy. However, a buyer's agent has no obligation to show properties to a buyer where there is no written agreement to pay the agent's compensation.

A buyer's agent may show a property that the client is interested in to other buyers without automatically violating the duty to the client. And if a broker has two affiliated agents each representing a different buyer, where the buyers are both interested in a property the broker has listed, this does not create an automatic conflict of interest for the broker.

A seller's agent also owes extra duties to the seller. Note that these duties are parallel to the extra duties of a buyer's agent –

- To be loyal to the seller by taking no action adverse or detrimental to the seller,
- To disclose to the seller any conflicts of interest,
- To advise the seller to seek expert advice on matters that are beyond the agent's expertise,
- Not to disclose confidential information, even after termination of the agency relationship,
- After supplying the pamphlet, to make a continuous effort to locate a buyer for the seller's property, except after the seller has already entered into a contract to sell.

A seller's agent may show other properties to a buyer without automatically violating the duty to the seller. And if a broker has two affiliated agents each representing a different seller, where there is one buyer who is interested in both properties, this does not create an automatic conflict of interest for the broker.

And Chapter 18.86 also lists additional duties for a dual agent –

- To be take no action adverse or detrimental to either party,
- To disclose to the both parties any conflicts of interest,
- To advise both parties to seek expert advice on matters that are beyond the agent's expertise,
- Not to disclose confidential information about either party, even after termination of the agency relationship,
- After supplying the pamphlet, to make a continuous effort to locate a buyer for the property, except after the seller has already entered into a contract to sell, and after supplying the pamphlet, to make a continuous effort to locate a property for the buyer, except after the buyer has already entered into a contract to buy. However, a buyer's agent has no obligation to show properties to a buyer where there is no written agreement to pay the agent's compensation.

A dual agent may show other properties to a buyer without automatically violating the duty to the seller. A dual agent may also show a buyer more than one listed property.

And if a broker has two affiliated agents each representing a different seller, where there is one buyer who is interested in both properties, this does not create an automatic conflict of interest for the broker.

Compensation – In the past there was always a fear that if a buyer's agent shared in the commission paid by the seller, it would create a conflict of interest. After all, the commission is usually stated as a percentage of the sales price, so the more the buyer pays for the property, the greater the compensation of the buyer's agent. Chapter 18.86 resolves this problem by providing that a buyer's agent or a dual agent may receive compensation based on the purchase price without violating any of the agent's duties to the buyer. Furthermore, it provides that paying compensation does not establish an agency relationship. And if the parties agree, the seller's agent can share in compensation paid by the buyer and the buyer's agent can share in compensation paid by the seller.

Disclosure pamphlet – Chapter 18.86 requires the agent to give the prospective principal a pamphlet on agency relationships and specifies the format, down to the point size of the type. The pamphlet must contain almost the entire text of Chapter 18.86. (See sample on the following pages.) Most agents use forms (listing, earnest money, etc.) which contain a clause acknowledging receipt of the pamphlet.

However, since the law does not require the agent to give a disclosure form to the principal in most cases, to ensure that the agent informed the party of which role the agent took in the transaction, Chapter 18.86 provides that the final agreement must contain a disclosure as to the agent's role in the transaction (i.e., represented the buyer, the seller, both, or neither). Thus, if the agent was acting for the seller but failed to tell the buyer that fact, the buyer would likely become angry at the time of seeing in the contract that the agent was acting for the seller. The law presumes that the agent would avoid this problem by making disclosure up front.

Imputed notice – Under the common law a principal was deemed to have knowledge of anything communicated to the agent. Chapter 18.86 removes this rule. Not only does this apply to principals who are members of the public (e.g., buyers and sellers), but to agents within a firm as well. In other words, if someone tells something to a salesperson licensed under a broker, the broker is not automatically deemed to have notice of it.

Respondeat superior – Chapter 18.86 also modifies the common law responsibilities of the principal to third parties (called *vicarious liability* in the RCW). At common law the principal is liable for wrongful acts of the agent as long as the agent was acting within the scope of the agent's authority. Of course, a principal would not authorize an agent to break the law, so the principal's liability is usually only for errors and omissions of the agent. Still, this could be expensive for the principal. And, while the principal has recourse against the agent to recover the loss, if the agent does not have the resources to pay the damages the principal may end up footing the whole bill.

To protect principals Chapter 18.86 provides that principal is liable for the agent's wrongful acts only if the principal "participated in or authorized the act, error, or omission," or "the principal benefited from the act, error or omission" and even then only if it appears to a court that the claimant would be unable to enforce a judgment against the agent [RCW 18.86.090 (1)]. Note how this modifies the common law principle of respondeat superior.

Many years ago real estate agents were only dimly aware of the law of agency. No one ever disclosed anything to anyone. But as time went on brokers discovered that they are more respected by the public when they are open and forthright about their relationship with their clients and customers. In the final analysis, fairness and honest dealings will make for the most successful and profitable real estate practice.

KEY TERMS

The key to understanding any new field is the vocabulary used in that field. To maximize your comprehension of the material presented in this chapter, be sure you know the meaning and significance of the following terms. Remember that the majority of test questions primarily test knowledge of vocabulary.

Accidental agency	Buyer brokerage
Actual authority	Carry-over clause
Actual fraud	Client
Agency coupled with an interest	Commingling
Agency by estoppel	Complete accounting
Agent	Confidentiality
Apparent authority	Conversion
Assigned agency	Cooperation agreement
Attorney in fact	Customer
Authority	Dual agency

Due diligence

Employee

Estoppel

Expressed actual authority

Expressed agency

Extender clause

Facilitator

Fiduciary

Fraud

Full disclosure

General agent

Implied authority

Imputed notice

Independent contractor

Law of agency

Loyalty

Obedience

Ostensible authority

Personal service contract

Principal

Principal and agent

Ratification

Respondeat superior

Safety clause

Secret profit

Single agency

Special agent

Specific performance

Split agency

Statute of Frauds

Straw man

Subagent

Tort

Transaction broker

Undisclosed principal

Unilateral contract

Unintentional dual agency

Unintentional agency

Universal agent

Vicarious liability

The Law of Real Estate Agency

This pamphlet describes your legal rights in dealing with a real estate broker or salesperson. Please read it carefully before signing any documents.

The following is only a brief summary of the attached law:

Sec. 1. Definitions. Defines the specific terms used in the law.

Sec. 2. Relationships between Licensees and the Public. States that a licensee who works with a buyer or tenant represents that buyer or tenant – unless the licensee is the listing agent, a seller's subagent, a dual agent, the seller personally or the parties agree otherwise. Also states that in a transaction involving two different licensees affiliated with the same broker, the broker is a dual agent and each licensee solely represents his or her client – unless the parties agree in writing that both licensees are dual agents.

Sec. 3. Duties of a Licensee Generally. Prescribes the duties that are owed by all licensees, regardless of who the licensee represents. Requires disclosure of the licensee's agency relationship in a specific transaction.

Sec. 4. Duties of a Seller's Agent. Prescribes the additional duties of a licensee representing the seller or landlord only.

Sec. 5. Duties of a Buyer's Agent. Prescribes the additional duties of a licensee representing the buyer or tenant only.

Sec. 6. Duties of a Dual Agent. Prescribes the additional duties of a licensee representing both parties in the same transaction, and requires the written consent of both parties to the licensee acting as a dual agent.

Sec. 7. Duration of Agency Relationship. Describes when an agency relationship begins and ends. Provides that the duties of accounting and confidentiality continue after the termination of an agency relationship.

Sec. 8. Compensation. Allows brokers to share compensation with cooperating brokers. States that payment of compensation does not necessarily establish an agency relationship. Allows brokers to receive compensation from more than one party in a transaction with the parties' consent.

Sec. 9. Vicarious Liability. Eliminates the common law liability of a party for the conduct of the party's agent or subagent, unless the agent or subagent is insolvent. Also limits the liability of a broker for the conduct of a subagent associated with a different broker.

Sec. 10. Imputed Knowledge and Notice. Eliminates the common law rule that notice to or knowledge of an agent constitutes notice to or knowledge of the principal.

Sec. 11. Interpretation. This law replaces the fiduciary duties owed by an agent to a principal under the common law, to the extent that it conflicts with the common law.

RCW 18.86.010 Definitions.

Unless the context clearly requires otherwise, the definitions in this section apply throughout this chapter.

(1) "Agency relationship" means the agency relationship created under this chapter or by written agreement between a licensee and a buyer and/or seller relating to the performance of real estate brokerage services by the licensee.

(2) "Agent" means a licensee who has entered into an agency relationship with a buyer or seller.

(3) "Business opportunity" means and includes a business, business opportunity, and goodwill of an existing business, or any one or combination thereof.

(4) "Buyer" means an actual or prospective purchaser in a real estate transaction, or an actual or prospective tenant in a real estate rental or lease transaction, as applicable.

(5) "Buyer's agent" means a licensee who has entered into an agency relationship with only the buyer in a real estate transaction, and includes subagents engaged by a buyer's agent.

(6) "Confidential information" means information from or concerning a principal of a licensee that:
    (a) Was acquired by the licensee during the course of an agency relationship with the principal;
    (b) The principal reasonably expects to be kept confidential;
    (c) The principal has not disclosed or authorized to be disclosed to third parties;
    (d) Would, if disclosed, operate to the detriment of the principal; and
    (e) The principal personally would not be obligated to disclose to the other party.

(7) "Dual agent" means a licensee who has entered into an agency relationship with both the buyer and seller in the same transaction.

(8) "Licensee" means a real estate broker, associate real estate broker, or real estate salesperson, as those terms are defined in chapter 18.85 RCW.

(9) "Material fact" means information that substantially adversely affects the value of the property or a party's ability to perform its obligations in a real estate transaction, or operates to materially impair or defeat the purpose of the transaction. The fact or suspicion that the property, or any neighboring property, is or was the site of a murder, suicide or other death, rape or other sex crime, assault or other violent crime, robbery or burglary, illegal drug activity, gang-related activity, political or religious activity, or other act, occurrence, or use not adversely affecting the physical condition of or title to the property is not a material fact.

(10) "Principal" means a buyer or a seller who has entered into an agency relationship with a licensee.

(11) "Real estate brokerage services" means the rendering of services for which a real estate license is required under chapter 18.85 RCW.

(12) "Real estate transaction" or "transaction" means an actual or prospective transaction involving a purchase, sale, option, or exchange of any interest in real property or a business opportunity, or a lease or rental of real property. For purposes of this chapter, a prospective transaction does not exist until a written offer has been signed by at least one of the parties.

(13) "Seller" means an actual or prospective seller in a real estate transaction, or an actual or prospective landlord in a real estate rental or lease transaction, as applicable.

(14) "Seller's agent" means a licensee who has entered into an agency relationship with only the seller in a real estate transaction, and includes subagents engaged by a seller's agent.

(15) "Subagent" means a licensee who is engaged to act on behalf of a principal by the principal's agent where the principal has authorized the agent in writing to appoint subagents.

RCW 18.86.020 Agency relationship.

(1) A licensee who performs real estate brokerage services for a buyer is a buyer's agent unless the:
    (a) Licensee has entered into a written agency agreement with the seller, in which case the licensee is a seller's agent;
    (b) Licensee has entered into a subagency agreement with the seller's agent, in which case the licensee is a seller's agent;
    (c) Licensee has entered into a written agency agreement with both parties, in which case the licensee is a dual agent;
    (d) Licensee is the seller or one of the sellers; or
    (e) Parties agree otherwise in writing after the licensee has complied with RCW 18.86.030(1)(f).

(2) In a transaction in which different licensees affiliated with the same broker represent different parties, the broker is a dual agent, and must obtain the written consent of both parties as required under RCW 18.86.060. In such a case, each licensee shall solely represent the party with whom the licensee has an agency relationship, unless all parties agree in writing that both licensees are dual agents.

(3) A licensee may work with a party in separate transactions pursuant to different relationships, including, but not limited to,

representing a party in one transaction and at the same time not representing that party in a different transaction involving that party, if the licensee complies with this chapter in establishing the relationships for each transaction.

RCW 18.86.030 Duties of licensee.

(1) Regardless of whether the licensee is an agent, a licensee owes to all parties to whom the licensee renders real estate brokerage services the following duties, which may not be waived:

 (a) To exercise reasonable skill and care;

 (b) To deal honestly and in good faith;

 (c) To present all written offers, written notices and other written communications to and from either party in a timely manner, regardless of whether the property is subject to an existing contract for sale or the buyer is already a party to an existing contract to purchase;

 (d) To disclose all existing material facts known by the licensee and not apparent or readily ascertainable to a party; provided that this subsection shall not be construed to imply any duty to investigate matters that the licensee has not agreed to investigate;

 (e) To account in a timely manner for all money and property received from or on behalf of either party;

 (f) To provide a pamphlet on the law of real estate agency in the form prescribed in RCW 18.86.120 to all parties to whom the licensee renders real estate brokerage services, before the party signs an agency agreement with the licensee, signs an offer in a real estate transaction handled by the licensee, consents to dual agency, or waives any rights, under RCW 18.86.020(1)(e), 18.86.040(1)(e), 18.86.050(1)(e), or 18.86.060(2) (e) or (f), whichever occurs earliest; and

 (g) To disclose in writing to all parties to whom the licensee renders real estate brokerage services, before the party signs an offer in a real estate transaction handled by the licensee, whether the licensee represents the buyer, the seller, both parties, or neither party. The disclosure shall be set forth in a separate paragraph entitled "Agency Disclosure" in the agreement between the buyer and seller or in a separate writing entitled "Agency Disclosure."

(2) Unless otherwise agreed, a licensee owes no duty to conduct an independent inspection of the property or to conduct an independent investigation of either party's financial condition, and owes no duty to independently verify the accuracy or completeness of any statement made by either party or by any source reasonably believed by the licensee to be reliable.

RCW 18.86.040 Seller's agent – Duties.

(1) Unless additional duties are agreed to in writing signed by a seller's agent, the duties of a seller's agent are limited to those set forth in RCW 18.86.030 and the following, which may not be waived except as expressly set forth in (e) of this subsection:

 (a) To be loyal to the seller by taking no action that is adverse or detrimental to the seller's interest in a transaction;

 (b) To timely disclose to the seller any conflicts of interest;

 (c) To advise the seller to seek expert advice on matters relating to the transaction that are beyond the agent's expertise;

 (d) Not to disclose any confidential information from or about the seller, except under subpoena or court order, even after termination of the agency relationship; and

 (e) Unless otherwise agreed to in writing after the seller's agent has complied with RCW 18.86.030(1)(f), to make a good faith and continuous effort to find a buyer for the property; except that a seller's agent is not obligated to seek additional offers to purchase the property while the property is subject to an existing contract for sale.

(2) (a) The showing of properties not owned by the seller to prospective buyers or the listing of competing properties for sale by a seller's agent does not in and of itself breach the duty of loyalty to the seller or create a conflict of interest.

 (b) The representation of more than one seller by different licensees affiliated with the same broker in competing transactions involving the same buyer does not in and of itself breach the duty of loyalty to the sellers or create a conflict of interest.

RCW 18.86.050 Buyer's agent – Duties.

(1) Unless additional duties are agreed to in writing signed by a buyer's agent, the duties of a buyer's agent are limited to those set forth in RCW 18.86.030 and the following, which may not be waived except as expressly set forth in (e) of this subsection:

 (a) To be loyal to the buyer by taking no action that is adverse or detrimental to the buyer's interest in a transaction;

 (b) To timely disclose to the buyer any conflicts of interest;

 (c) To advise the buyer to seek expert advice on matters relating to the transaction that are beyond the agent's expertise;

(d) Not to disclose any confidential information from or about the buyer, except under subpoena or court order, even after termination of the agency relationship; and

(e) Unless otherwise agreed to in writing after the buyer's agent has complied with RCW 18.86.030(1)(f), to make a good faith and continuous effort to find a property for the buyer; except that a buyer's agent is not obligated to: (i) Seek additional properties to purchase while the buyer is a party to an existing contract to purchase; or (ii) show properties as to which there is no written agreement to pay compensation to the buyer's agent.

(2) (a) The showing of property in which a buyer is interested to other prospective buyers by a buyer's agent does not in and of itself breach the duty of loyalty to the buyer or create a conflict of interest.

(b) The representation of more than one buyer by different licensees affiliated with the same broker in competing transactions involving the same property does not in and of itself breach the duty of loyalty to the buyers or create a conflict of interest.

RCW 18.86.060 Dual agent – Duties.

(1) Notwithstanding any other provision of this chapter, a licensee may act as a dual agent only with the written consent of both parties to the transaction after the dual agent has complied with RCW 18.86.030(1)(f), which consent must include a statement of the terms of compensation.

(2) Unless additional duties are agreed to in writing signed by a dual agent, the duties of a dual agent are limited to those set forth in RCW 18.86.030 and the following, which may not be waived except as expressly set forth in (e) and (f) of this subsection:

(a) To take no action that is adverse or detrimental to either party's interest in a transaction;

(b) To timely disclose to both parties any conflicts of interest;

(c) To advise both parties to seek expert advice on matters relating to the transaction that are beyond the dual agent's expertise;

(d) Not to disclose any confidential information from or about either party, except under subpoena or court order, even after termination of the agency relationship;

(e) Unless otherwise agreed to in writing after the dual agent has complied with RCW 18.86.030(1)(f), to make a good faith and continuous effort to find a buyer for the property; except that a dual agent is not obligated to seek additional offers to purchase the property while the property is subject to an existing contract for sale; and

(f) Unless otherwise agreed to in writing after the dual agent has complied with RCW 18.86.030(1)(f), to make a good faith and continuous effort to find a property for the buyer; except that a dual agent is not obligated to: (i) Seek additional properties to purchase while the buyer is a party to an existing contract to purchase; or (ii) show properties as to which there is no written agreement to pay compensation to the dual agent.

(3) (a) The showing of properties not owned by the seller to prospective buyers or the listing of competing properties for sale by a dual agent does not in and of itself constitute action that is adverse or detrimental to the seller or create a conflict of interest.

(b) The representation of more than one seller by different licensees affiliated with the same broker in competing transactions involving the same buyer does not in and of itself constitute action that is adverse or detrimental to the sellers or create a conflict of interest.

(4) (a) The showing of property in which a buyer is interested to other prospective buyers or the presentation of additional offers to purchase property while the property is subject to a transaction by a dual agent does not in and of itself constitute action that is adverse or detrimental to the buyer or create a conflict of interest.

(b) The representation of more than one buyer by different licensees affiliated with the same broker in competing transactions involving the same property does not in and of itself constitute action that is adverse or detrimental to the buyers or create a conflict of interest.

RCW 18.86.070 Duration of agency relationship.

(1) The agency relationships set forth in this chapter commence at the time that the licensee undertakes to provide real estate brokerage services to a principal and continue until the earliest of the following:

(a) Completion of performance by the licensee;

(b) Expiration of the term agreed upon by the parties;

(c) Termination of the relationship by mutual agreement of the parties; or

(d) Termination of the relationship by notice from either party to the other. However, such a termination does not affect the contractual rights of either party.

(2) Except as otherwise agreed to in writing, a licensee owes no further duty after termination of the agency relationship, other than the duties of:

(a) Accounting for all moneys and property received during the relationship; and

(b) Not disclosing confidential information.

RCW 18.86.080 Compensation.

(1) In any real estate transaction, the broker's compensation may be paid by the seller, the buyer, a third party, or by sharing the compensation between brokers.

(2) An agreement to pay or payment of compensation does not establish an agency relationship between the party who paid the compensation and the licensee.

(3) A seller may agree that a seller's agent may share with another broker the compensation paid by the seller.

(4) A buyer may agree that a buyer's agent may share with another broker the compensation paid by the buyer.

(5) A broker may be compensated by more than one party for real estate brokerage services in a real estate transaction, if those parties consent in writing at or before the time of signing an offer in the transaction.

(6) A buyer's agent or dual agent may receive compensation based on the purchase price without breaching any duty to the buyer.

(7) Nothing contained in this chapter negates the requirement that an agreement authorizing or employing a licensee to sell or purchase real estate for compensation or a commission be in writing and signed by the seller or buyer.

RCW 18.86.090 Vicarious liability.

(1) A principal is not liable for an act, error, or omission by an agent or subagent of the principal arising out of an agency relationship:

(a) Unless the principal participated in or authorized the act, error, or omission; or

(b) Except to the extent that: (i) The principal benefited from the act, error, or omission; and (ii) the court determines that it is highly probable that the claimant would be unable to enforce a judgment against the agent or subagent.

(2) A licensee is not liable for an act, error, or omission of a subagent under this chapter, unless the licensee participated in or authorized the act, error or omission. This subsection does not limit the liability of a real estate broker for an act, error, or omission by an associate real estate broker or real estate salesperson licensed to that broker.

RCW 18.86.100 Imputed knowledge and notice.

(1) Unless otherwise agreed to in writing, a principal does not have knowledge or notice of any facts known by an agent or subagent of the principal that are not actually known by the principal.

(2) Unless otherwise agreed to in writing, a licensee does not have knowledge or notice of any facts known by a subagent that are not actually known by the licensee. This subsection does not limit the knowledge imputed to a real estate broker of any facts known by an associate real estate broker or real estate salesperson licensed to such broker.

RCW 18.86.110 Application.

This chapter supersedes only the duties of the parties under the common law, including fiduciary duties of an agent to a principal, to the extent inconsistent with this chapter. The common law continues to apply to the parties in all other respects. This chapter does not affect the duties of a licensee while engaging in the authorized or unauthorized practice of law as determined by the courts of this state. This chapter shall be construed broadly.

The real estate license law

HARDLY ANY WASHINGTON real estate agents today remember when you could deal in a client's real estate without a license. But then, in the old days real estate transactions could be taken care of by a handshake. Today's complex transactions would put both agents and the public in grave peril without modern licensing regulations.

Although the world has not always enjoyed the benefits of an organized real estate profession, by the end of the 1800s most real estate was being sold through the services of an agent. In the early days, without real estate licensing, you could just hang out your shingle and you were in business. In an attempt to create some regulation, responsible real estate agents in many communities began to create local real estate boards. In 1908 many of these boards banded together to form the National Association of Real Estate Boards (NAREB, later to be called the National Association of REALTORS®). Although NAREB created a code of ethics, membership was not required, so shady operators simply did not join.

It remained for legislative action to utilize the police power of the government to regulate real estate agents. California passed the first real estate licensing law which became effective in 1919, followed by Oregon, Michigan and Tennessee. Today every state, the District of Columbia, Guam and Puerto Rico have licensing laws. In addition, all Canadian provinces and many other countries have followed suit. Washington was one of the earliest states to enact a licensing law in 1925.

> *Today the statutory obligations of licensees are contained in Chapter 18.85 and 18.235 RCW, plus licensees are expect to know and follow administrative rules contained in Washington Administrative Code 308-124 to 308.124H All exam applicants should study the complete text of these statutes and rules. A copy can be obtained from the Department of Licensing (DOL) by calling (360) 664-6488, or you can download them from the website for the Real Estate program of the Business and Professions Division of the DOL at http://www.dol.wa.gov/realestate/refront.htm.*

Under the original licensing law there was no educational requirement, or even an experience requirement. In other words, you could walk in off the street, obtain a brokers license and immediately open up a brokerage business. Temporary permits for brokers were soon discontinued, but many Washington licensees remember that temporary salesperson permits were available as late as 1977.

Under current licensing law the Director of the Department of Licensing (appointed by the Governor) is the person with enforcement authority, although most activity is performed by staff. The Director relies on the advice of the Real Estate Commission, consisting of six Commissioners who are also appointed by the Governor. The Commissioners serve for six-year terms staggered so one position is vacated each year. The Commissioners must be experienced in real estate and must be appointed from areas so the geographic diversity of the state is represented. In addition to advising the Director the Commissioners have authority over license exams.

It is significant to note that every change made to the licensing laws, and even the original statute of 1925, was originally directed strictly at sales work. Appraisal activity was originally unregulated, and property management was not originally considered activity for which a license was required. Today appraisal requires certification under Chapter 18.140 RCW, although licensed brokers are permitted to do broker's price opinions in the course of sales work.

Who must be licensed

The license laws today requires you to obtain a license in all cases where you conduct **real estate activity**. Real estate activity is any real estate activity done for another and for compensation. In other words, to sell your friend's real estate without charge, you need no real estate license because you did not perform any real estate activity. Nor is it real estate activity which requires a license when a person sells his or her own property.

Activities which come within the scope of real estate activity include selling, listing, buying or selling for another and all negotiations involved in these activities. Business opportunities are also covered. A business opportunity is any existing business. The statutes are thorough in their scope of what you cannot do without a license. If it involves the real estate of another, and you do it for compensation, you probably need a license. In the definitions at the beginning of the license law it states that a broker is anyone who –

"(a) Sells or offers for sale, lists or offers to list, buys or offers to buy real estate or business opportunities, or any interest therein, for others;

(b) Negotiates or offers to negotiate, either directly or indirectly, the purchase, sale, exchange, lease, or rental of real estate or business opportunities, or any interest therein, for others;

(c) Negotiates or offers to negotiate, either directly or indirectly, the purchase, sale, lease, or exchange of a manufactured or mobile home in conjunction with the purchase, sale, exchange, rental, or lease of the land upon which the manufactured or mobile home is, or will be, located;

(d) Advertises or holds himself or herself out to the public by any oral or printed solicitation or representation that he or she is so engaged; or

(e) Engages, directs, or assists in procuring prospects or in negotiating or closing any transaction which results or is calculated to result in any of these acts" (18.85.010 RCW).

While a license is not required for someone to sell his or her own property, 18.85.010 RCW states that a broker as defined above includes a "licensee under this chapter while acting in his or her own behalf." In other words, an unlicensed person can sell his or her own property without worrying about the license law, but if you have a license, any transactions you enter into regarding your own property must be handled according to the same rules and requirements as for transactions involving property of clients and customers.

Nevertheless, the statutes also provide for certain exemptions. Most of the exemptions deal with a specific type of activity, such as –

• A person buying or selling real estate or a business opportunity for a group of which the person is a member,

• A secretary, bookkeeper or other office staff who does not engage in real estate activity,

• Property management by a member of the family of an owner of rental property or by a resident manager in a residential complex,

• Property management by someone who manages residential property on an incidental basis and where the person does not advertise to the public as being in the property management business,

• Management of a self-service storage facility,

• A person acting under a power of attorney without compensation,

• An attorney at law, dealing in the real property of a client where the real estate activity is in the normal course of the attorney's law practice. For example, an attorney is handling an estate and there is property to be sold. But an attorney cannot go out and take listings and make sales without obtaining a license,

• A receiver, guardian, executor, administrator, trustee in bankruptcy or personal representative acting under a trust agreement, trust deed, or will,

• A person acting under court order,

The license law provides a fine up to $5,000 for conducting real estate activity without a license. In addition, the Director can issue a cease and desist order. The law also prohibits anyone from suing to collect a commission if the person did not have a license when the commission was earned.

Note that real estate activity includes a **broker's price opinion**, but not an appraisal. A broker's price opinion (sometimes called a **competitive market analysis**) is similar to an appraisal, but cannot generally be used for financing. If required for financing an **appraisal** is required, which must be done by an appraiser certified separately from the licensing requirements for real estate activity.

Types of licenses

Today the Department of Licensing issues two main types of real estate licenses – brokers, and salespersons. In addition, brokers can be designated brokers or associate brokers. All are "real estate licenses," but each type enjoys different privileges and restrictions. You can hold only one real estate license at a time. For example, you cannot hold a salesperson license and a brokers license at the same time.

Most people start with a **salespersons license**. Although some licensing requirements can be waived, to become a salesperson the license law and administrative rules normally require you to complete a 60-hour course in Real Estate Fundamentals. Salespersons must also pass the national and state salespersons exams.

A salesperson can perform any type of real estate activity. However, a salesperson cannot supervise other real estate licensees and cannot function independently. A salesperson must be licensed under a broker (see below). "Being licensed under" is sometimes referred to in the license law and administrative rules as "affiliated with." The broker is responsible for everything and the salesperson becomes the agent of the broker. When the salesperson takes an earnest money or a listing it must be turned over to the broker. Everything the salesperson does is done in the name of the broker. A salesperson can be affiliated with only one broker at a time. Salespersons must also receive all commissions, even bonuses and other compensation, through the broker under whom they are licensed.

The **brokers license** is unrestricted as to real estate activity. To become a broker requires two years experience licensed as a salesperson, plus additional courses in Brokerage Management, Real Estate Law, Business Management, and one elective course, each of at least 30 hours. Broker applicants must also pass the national and state brokers exam and must hold at least a high school degree or equivalent. The experience must be demonstrated by either 40 hours per week spent in licensed activity, or that the applicant derived a major portion of his or her income from real estate activity during the period.

A broker can do anything that a salesperson can do and, in addition, can supervise other licensees. A broker can also operate independently as a sole practitioner, but the usual reason for obtaining the brokers license is to be able to operate a real estate brokerage firm and supervise other licensees. A real estate company that has multiple licensees working for it needs at least one broker to supervise the activity of the other licensees.

While the basic idea of the brokers license is to be able to supervise the real estate activity of other licensees, a brokers license is not required in order to own a real estate company. A salesperson, for example, can have an ownership interest in a real estate company as long as there is a broker to supervise. In fact, even an unlicensed individual can own a real estate company. But, while you don't need any license at all to own the real estate company, you cannot set policy or dictate how licensees conduct real estate activity. The broker must be the one in control of the real estate activity of licensees. In addition, a broker violates the license law by allowing someone to use of his or her license without actively supervising the real estate activity of licensees. A broker who does this is sometimes called a *fee broker*.

If the broker loses his or her license for whatever reason, the license of a licensee affiliated with the broker is immediately suspended until the broker's license is restored, or until the licensee affiliates with a new broker. This works in the other direction too – not only can licensees not be licensed under a broker whose license is inactive, suspended or revoked, but brokers violate the license law if they permit a licensee whose license is not active to engage in real estate activity.

Under the license law and administrative rules a corporation, partnership, limited liability partnership and limited liability company can be issued a brokers license. When you think about it, this makes sense. After all, the organization is conducting the real estate activity, so it should have a license. However, someone still has to supervise the real estate activity of affiliated licensees. To accomplish this, one of the officers of the corporation (or partners in a partnership, or members in a limited liability company) must be named as the *designated broker* for the organization. The designated broker has all the responsibilities of an individual broker. When a broker operates under his or her own name or an assumed business name, then the broker is called an *individual broker*.

Sometimes a licensee will be qualified as a broker, but will choose to work for another broker instead of operating as an individual broker or designated broker. In such cases the broker will be an *associate broker*. Think of an associate broker as someone who could be an individual broker or designated broker, but has stepped into the shoes of a salesperson. All the limitations that apply to a salesperson apply to an associate broker.

The broker or designated broker for a real estate firm is responsible for all the real estate activity of the licensees affiliated with the broker. This includes legal liability to clients and customers for damages they might suffer as a result of the actions of an affiliated licensee.

If an affiliated licensee violates the license law or administrative rules, the broker or designated broker could be subject to disciplinary action as well as the affiliated licensee, if the broker or designated broker failed to supervise adequately. However, the administrative rules provide that the broker or designated broker will not be responsible for inadequate supervision if –

- The violation of the affiliated licensee was in contravention to the broker's written policies or instructions, and
- There were reasonable procedures to verify that adequate supervision was being performed, and
- The broker attempted to prevent or mitigate the damage as soon as the broker learned of it, and
- The broker did not participate in the violation, and
- The broker did not avoid learning of the violation.

A *temporary brokers permit* is a license issued to a person who must wind up the affairs of a deceased or incapacitated broker. As discussed in Chapter 18, the death of either the principal or the agent terminates an agency relationship, so when an individual broker dies, all listings are terminated. Nevertheless, the transactions currently in closing must be consummated, and to do so is "real estate activity," done "for another" and "for compensation," so the person winding up the affairs of the deceased broker must have a license. Even if the broker is a corporation or other organization, there must be a designated broker. The license law and administrative rules allow the Director to issue a temporary brokers permit to someone for this purpose. Typically it will be issued to the

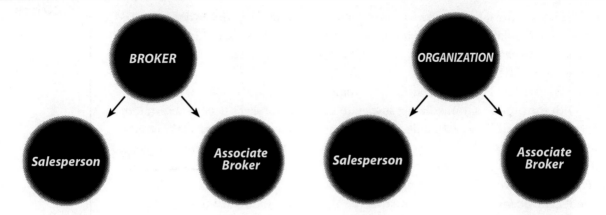

Who can hire whom

Brokers can work as individual brokers or can be the designated broker for a corporation or other organization acting as a broker. Salespersons must be licensed under either an individual broker or organization acting as a broker. Brokers can also be licensed under an individual broker or organization acting as a broker, in which case they are called associate brokers.

personal representative of the broker's estate, or to a senior salesperson in the office. The temporary broker's permit can be issued for up to four months. A temporary broker cannot take new business – no new listing or management agreements, for example.

Each **branch office** can be established only with the permission of the Director, who will issue a license for the branch office. The license for the branch office will show the location of the branch office on the license and must be displayed in the branch office. A broker can establish as many branch offices as desired, but can have a maximum of three branch offices under names other than the name of the main firm. If different names are used the name of the main office must appear on the sign as well. All branch offices must be managed by a branch manager who must be an associate broker.

A branch office is any office which is open to the public, but does not include an office in a subdivision, provided the subdivision is within 35 miles of a licensed office.

All licenses must be available for examination in the office where they work (i.e., the main office or a branch office). Brokers licenses and designated brokers licenses are mailed to the broker, but associate broker and salespersons licenses are sent to the employing broker, who maintains custody and control of them. The broker or designated broker must return the license of an affiliated licensee to the Department of Licensing promptly when requested. Failure to do so can result in forfeiture of the broker's or designated broker's license. If the license has been lost an affidavit of lost license must be filed. The affiliated licensee cannot have his or her license reissued until the original or the affidavit is received. In the event the broker sends in the license of an affiliated agent because the licensee violated the license law or administrative rules, the broker must send a statement outlining the details along with the license.

The license will be accompanied by a **pocket identification card**. This is a small card designed to fit in a wallet like a drivers license. Its purpose was initially to provide identification as a real estate licensee in the event a homeowner was afraid to admit the broker. Most states have eliminated the identification card after discovering that licensees never use them, but Washington still provides them.

Many real estate licensees find a tax advantage in becoming a **professional corporation** (P.C.). An individual in certain licensed professions, including real estate, is permitted under Washington law to create a professional corporation. A real estate licensee acting as a professional corporation is normally one sole individual. A licensee acting as a professional corporation is still regulated and bound in every way as though they were ordinary licensees. A licensee acting as a professional corporation must create the professional corporation through the Secretary of State.

Washington licensees should be aware that the license category "real estate broker" exists in all states. Practically all states have a "salesperson" category also. As in Washington, a salesperson is typically not allowed to operate independently but, rather, must be licensed under a broker. Most states also have "associate brokers," however, the terminology is sometimes slightly different, i.e., what we call an "associate broker" may be an "affiliate broker," "assistant broker" or other similar term. What we call a "salesperson" is frequently called a "salesman" or some other term in another state. Also, some states do not license property management activity or business opportunity brokerage (sales of going businesses), both of which require a real estate license in Washington.

To further confuse the issue, a few states have recently adopted *single licensing*. Single licensing means that the salesperson category is eliminated and everyone must be a broker.

Because the license laws vary somewhat from state to state, test questions regarding licensing laws and regulations are on the state (Washington) portion of the exam.

Non-resident and reciprocal licenses

The term "reciprocity" is commonly used when determining whether it is legal for an out of state agent to conduct real estate activity in Washington, or for Washington licensees to deal in real estate in other states. Unfortunately, this term is highly confusing, as there are several levels of "reciprocity."

Persons who are not residents of Washington may be entitled to license as a broker or salesperson. Such a license grants to the holder the same privileges as a Washington resident with the same license would have. To obtain the license, you must meet the same requirements as a person who lives in Washington would have to meet for the same license – all the same competencies and examinations, except that if you also hold a license in another jurisdiction the national exam and some or all of the education may be waived.

A broker licensed in another jurisdiction must maintain a Washington address where the license is to be displayed and where records relating to the broker's Washington real estate activity must be maintained. When the Department of Licensing sends the broker an audit notice the broker must appear at the office of the Department of Licensing in person to sign the audit report.

Washington law provides that a real estate broker may accept compensation, including referral fees, from any broker in another state, provided the other state has no prohibition on their brokers paying fees to out of state agents. Since all states have essentially the same provision in their license laws, it is common practice for licensees to pay referral fees to each other across state borders. Washington places no restriction on paying or accepting compensation (fee-sharing) with agents in other states, except, of course, that all funds must be paid through a supervising broker.

Active and inactive licenses

Except for temporary licenses, all Washington real estate licenses are issued for a two-year term which expires on the licensee's birthday. Brokers licenses issued to corporations and other organizations expire on the two-year anniversary of their first issuance. When any license is up for renewal, the licensee has a one-year grace period to pay the renewal fee. Until the license is reissued, of course, the licensee is not permitted to engage in real estate activity. If the license is renewed during the one-year grace period the licensee must pay a late renewal charge in addition to the regular renewal fee. After the one-year grace period, the license is canceled. However, the licensee may apply for reinstatement up to two years after cancellation by paying an additional fee of $100 and completing 60 hours of approved additional course work. Thereafter, the only way to get the license back is to meet all the initial licensing requirements, including the examination.

Whenever a real estate license is returned to the Department it automatically goes *inactive*. A license can remain inactive indefinitely, provided the licensee pays the fee for renewal of the inactive license. When a license is inactive the licensee is not permitted to engage in real estate activity. The agency relationship between the broker and the person affiliated with the broker is not terminated until the license has been returned to Department.

Continuing education

To renew a license the licensee must provide evidence of attendance at 30 clock hours of *continuing education*. three hours of which must be in approved *core curriculum*. The Department defines core curriculum according to the needs of the industry.

Except for the core curriculum, 15 hours can be carried forward from the previous renewal period, although they must have been taken within 36 months of the renewal date for which they are used. In other words, a licensee may have taken 45 hours in one renewal period, but needs only 30 to renew. The remaining 15 hours can be carried forward provided they were taken within 36 months of the renewal for which the licensee desires to use them.

In addition, all newly licensed salespersons must complete a 30-hour course in Real Estate Practices prior to their first renewal.

Handling funds

The license law and administrative rules contain extensive provisions dealing with situations where an agent must handle funds belonging to others. One obvious source of funds belonging to others is earnest money deposited on offers to purchase. But real estate agents frequently hold other funds belonging to their clients and customers. For example, real estate brokers who engage in property management frequently handle many thousands of dollars in rent each month which belongs to the owners of the properties being managed.

An agent might also sometimes collect an *advance fee*, sometimes also called a *retainer fee*, from a client or customer. An advance fee is a fee for services which have not yet been rendered, but which are anticipated in the future. For example, suppose you agree to represent a prospective buyer. The prospective buyer agrees to pay you directly, but also agrees to an hourly rate as a minimum, whether a property is found or not. You might then take an advance fee from the buyer, to ensure that you will be paid your hourly fee.

Funds that do not belong to the agent are subject to special requirements. A licensee cannot mix these funds with his or her own funds or company funds. It is called *commingling* to deposit funds which do not belong to you in your personal or company account. It is also commingling to do the reverse – deposit personal or company funds in with clients' funds (sometimes called *reverse commingling*).

Commingling is a sufficiently serious infraction that it merits an almost automatic and immediate license suspension or revocation. However, ***conversion*** is even worse. Conversion occurs when you convert the funds to your own use. It is called commingling when you put the client's funds in your personal account; if you spend the funds, it becomes conversion. Not only is conversion a violation of the license law, it makes you subject to criminal prosecution. Conversion carries essentially the same penalties as theft.

To ensure the safety of clients' funds, a broker must keep a ***real estate trust bank account***, commonly just called a ***trust account***, or sometimes an ***escrow account***. The account may be in a commercial bank, savings and loan, mutual savings bank, or credit union, provided the institution is located in Washington. An important feature of any real estate trust bank account is that the funds are exempt from execution and garnishment by creditors of the licensee. Also, the mere fact that the account is labeled "trust account" creates prima facie evidence that the funds are not the property of the signer on the account. Therefore, if a broker were to die the clients could have immediate access to their funds and would not have to convince a probate judge that the money was not part of the licensee's estate.

Washington license law and administrative rules provide different procedures for funds derived from sales activity (e.g., earnest money deposits) and funds for property management and contract collection activity (e.g., rent or mortgage payments received for a client). For sales activity the trust funds must be placed in an interest-bearing account if the amount is $10,000 or less. The interest earned must be remitted to the Department of Licensing, which turns it over to the state treasurer. The treasurer, in turn, gives 25% of it to the real estate education account to be used for courses and materials for licensees. The remaining 75% is turned over to the Washington Housing Trust Fund, to be used to promote low-income housing and housing for persons with special needs.

If the funds are over $10,000 the parties may direct that the funds be placed in a separate account, with the interest to go to the benefit of the parties. Or the parties may agree to let the broker place the funds in the regular account so the interest earned will go to the education account and Housing Trust Fund.

On cooperative transactions between two brokers (where one is the listing broker and the other is the selling broker), the broker who receives the funds is the one who must maintain custody and control of the funds. Normally, that would be the selling broker. However, as an alternative to placing clients' funds in a clients' trust account, a licensee may turn the funds over to a neutral escrow in Washington or to the seller.

Sometimes in sales transactions the buyer gives a note instead of a check or cash for earnest money. When the broker transfers a note to an escrow or to the seller the broker is required to keep records and proof of the transmittal, normally by taking a receipt for the note from the party to whom it is transferred.

The administrative rules also address the problem of earnest money deposits on rejected offers. If the broker deposits the check immediately into the trust account, the funds cannot be returned to the prospective buyer until the check has cleared, which may take a week or longer. But if the earnest money agreement signed by the buyer and the seller authorizes it, the broker can hold a check without depositing it until the seller accepts or rejects the buyer's offer. If the seller accepts the offer, then the check must be deposited by the close of business of the next banking day. If the seller rejects the offer, then the broker may return the check to the buyer.

For property management activity or mortgage collection accounts there are different procedures. First, the broker need not use an interest-bearing account and, even if the broker does use an interest-bearing account, it is exempt from the requirement that the interest go to the education account and the Housing Trust Fund. For example, if the management agreement with an owner provides for an interest-bearing account, the interest must go to the owner, although the owner can assign it to the broker.

If a broker engaging in property management takes a residential security or damage deposit the funds must be maintained in the account until the termination of the tenancy or an event occurs for which the rental agreement allows them to be used. They cannot be used for other expenses.

Regardless of where they are placed, the funds must be deposited or turned over to whomever is to receive them by the close of business of the first banking day following receipt. This means the first banking day following receipt by the licensee, or the licensee's agent. In other words, anyone affiliated with a broker is required to turn over the funds to his or her broker promptly, because the broker must deposit the funds by the close of business of the first banking day after the person affiliated with the broker received the funds.

Balancing, auditing and recordkeeping requirements for clients' funds are strict. A broker must balance the account monthly and must maintain all trust account records. Checks used for the real estate trust bank account must be consecutively numbered so that they can easily be accounted for. Deposit slips must contain the file number of the transaction.

Normally you may not pay any part of the clients' trust funds to yourself before you have earned it. For sales activity, this means not before the transaction is closed. And for property management, you cannot pay the management fees to yourself until you have gained the right to collect them. But property management fees may become "earned" at different times. Theoretically, every time a tenant gives the manager a rent check, a management fee has been earned. To simplify this situation, the administrative rules require that the broker deduct a management fee from the clients' trust account and pay it to himself or herself only once every month.

What to do with trust funds

Earnest money
- *$10,000 or under –*
  Must be placed in pooled interest-bearing account; interest goes to state
- *Over $10,000 –*
  Place in pooled interest-bearing account (interest goes to state), or in separate account, according to agreement of parties. If in separate account, interest goes to seller or buyer.

Property management
- *Can go in non-interest bearing account or interest-bearing account. If interest-bearing, interest goes to owner, who can assign it to the broker*
- *If security deposit on residential property must be maintained in the account until termination of the tenancy; can be used only for purposes as defined in rental agreement*

When a sale closes and the broker has earned the commission there are different procedures, depending on how the transaction was closed. If the transaction was closed in an escrow the broker probably turned the earnest money over to the escrow prior to closing. After closing the escrow wrote a check to the broker for the commission. The broker then deposited the total commission check to the broker's business operating account, and used that account to pay shares of the commission due to affiliated licensees. Some brokers prefer to hold the commission out of the earnest money and send just the surplus (if any) to the escrow. After closing the broker then writes a check to the company operating account and further disburses any shares due to affiliated licensees. However, most brokers consider this a bad accounting practice. Furthermore, any time a check from the trust account is payable to the broker or the broker's company, it invites additional audit scrutiny. A better practice would be to make all checks from the trust account payable to a neutral escrow, whenever possible.

Washington brokers are permitted to close transactions in the office provided no fee is charged for the service. When the broker closes the transaction in the office the broker has no choice but to use the trust account for all disbursements. In this case the broker will write a check for the full commission to the company operating account. Checks for shares of the commission due to affiliated licensees will be paid from the company operating account. Brokers should never pay affiliated licensees directly from the trust account.

Recordkeeping requirements

The license law requires all brokers to maintain records of all real estate activity for three years. For rental and lease agreements, this means three years after the termination of the tenancy and for management agreements it is three years after the expiration or termination of the agreement. These records must be kept in the main office or branch office if the broker has a licensed branch office, but all the records must be in one location. The reason is so that when the Department wishes to audit a broker's real estate activity everything will be in one place.

Records of a real estate licensee include anything in which the licensee was involved, even listings which never sold and offers which were never accepted, plus all rental activity, including leases, rental agreements and property management agreements with owners. Obviously, anything which a customer or client signed must be retained, but you must also retain copies of vouchers, bills, receipts, closing statements, property management monthly accountings, trust account records and bank statements, and so on.

Prohibited acts

The license law prohibits certain acts and provides sanctions such as license revocation, suspension, reprimand or fine if the licensee engages in those acts. While most of these are obvious matters such as fraud, conversion, and the like, others are not so obvious. Disciplinary action can be taken against a real estate licensee for –

- Fraud, misrepresentation, making or advertising false statements.
  Note that the party to whom the false statement must act on it to their detriment before the statement is legally considered fraud. However, merely making a false statement, while not grounds for a damage suit from the customer or client, is nevertheless grounds for disciplinary action, even if the customer or client was never harmed. The license law is detailed in its definition – "concealment, conspiracy, collusion, trick, scheme or device" and "advertising that is false, deceptive or misleading" in addition to fraud, misrepresentation and false statements.

- Accepting compensation from or representing someone other than the broker with whom affiliated, or if a broker, paying a commission to someone not licensed under the broker.
  Exception (1): If a licensee leaves the firm, but a transaction closes afterwards, the original broker may pay the compensation directly to the licensee even though he or she is now affiliated with a different broker or is inactive. Exception (2): A broker may share commissions with licensed brokers in Washington or other states, and may share a commission with a Washington licensed manufactured housing retailer if the transaction also involves the sale of land.

- Conversion or failing to return any "money contract, deed, note, mortgage or abstract, or other evidence of title" to the rightful owner.
  Failing to do so within 30 days after receiving demand from the owner is considered prima facie evidence of conversion.

- Failing to disclose to a seller and place the fact in the earnest money agreement if the earnest money is in a form other than cash.
- Acting as a vehicle dealer without first obtaining a vehicle dealer's license or if, when dealing in a mobile home sale, failing to ensure that the title is transferred to the buyer.
  I.e., selling a mobile home without land, in which case it is considered personal property and a dealer's license is required.
- Making a secret profit at the expense of the principal or obtaining a kickback from a mortgage lender to whom the licensee refers his or her principal.
  Note: See also provisions regarding kickbacks under the Real Estate Settlement Procedures Act in Chapter 14.
- Violating federal or Washington laws relating to discrimination in real estate sales, rentals or in hiring.
- Misrepresenting membership in any real estate association.
  I.e., calling yourself a REALTOR® when you are not a member of the National Association of REALTORS®.
- Using a straw man when dealing in real estate for the licensee's own account (self-dealing) to avoid disclosing that the licensee is the real principal.
  I.e., buying property for your own account without disclosing in writing that you have a license.
- Advertising property for sale without disclosing in the ad the name of the broker.
  Exception: If advertising property you own yourself you need disclose only that you have a license.
- Accepting compensation from more than one party in a transaction without full disclosure to all parties in the transaction,
  For example, you sell your own listing so you are representing the seller and the buyer is aware of that fact, yet the buyer wishes to give you a bonus for your excellent service. You must disclose the bonus to the seller before accepting it.
- Failing to deliver to the parties copies of contracts to the parties at the time they sign them.
- Failing to supervise adequately (only applies to brokers who have licensees affiliated with them).
- Violating the provisions of an order of the Director stating objections to a plan of selling, or any other order of the Director.
- Failing to disclose information or provide copies of documents to, or to cooperate with the Director's authorized representatives, or to interfere with any investigation by misrepresenting facts or harassing or paying inducements to witnesses.
  E.g., if an auditor from the Department asks for you to send a letter explaining your actions in a transaction, you must do so and the facts must be truthful.
- Failing to maintain records of transactions and trust account activity for three years.
- Making a broker's value opinion (competitive market analysis), where the licensee's employment or compensation is contingent upon the reporting of a predetermined value or where the licensee had an interest in the property which was not disclosed.
- Committing or being convicted of, or entering a plea of guilty or nolo contendere to an act involving moral turpitude, dishonesty or corruption relating to the practice of real estate, including being convicted of a gross misdemeanor or felony with regard to real estate activity.

- Concealment of material facts or fraud in an application for, or renewal of, a license.
- Helping a person without a license to operate any business for which a license is required.
- Exceeding the scope of what a licensee is allowed to practice under the license law and administrative rules.
- Demonstrating bad faith, dishonesty, negligence, incompetence, malpractice or untrustworthiness.

  Note: It is a violation even if an act has not occurred, if it appears that there is a risk that someone may be harmed.
- Having any professional license suspended, revoked or restricted by any other state, federal or foreign authority.
- Violating any other provision of the license law or administrative rules or of the timeshare regulation law, campground regulation law, land development act, or Chapter 18.86 regarding broker agency relationships.

The above violations of the Real Estate License Law are grounds for revocation or suspension of a license or for a reprimand or, in some cases, a fine. In addition, the Director can refuse to reissue a license. The Director can also issue a cease and desist order. Violations are also a gross misdemeanor, for which criminal prosecution is possible.

In addition to the above, the Director may suspend a license if the licensee defaults or fails to pay an educational loan or scholarship, or if the licensee fails to comply with a support order. Reinstatement is automatic as soon as the licensee provides the Director with proof of payment or compliance.

Office requirements

Real estate brokers must maintain a sign at their main office and at each branch office. The branch office sign must include the name of the firm as licensed and the fact that it is a branch office. The sign must be visible to the public, although there are no specific requirements as to size. If the business name includes a franchise, the name of the company as licensed must be included as well. The office must meet all local zoning requirements. In other words, if a broker wishes to operate out of the broker's house which is zoned residential, the broker must obtain a proper home occupation permit from the local jurisdiction and comply with their requirements.

If desired, two or more brokers can use the same office, provided each is separated physically within the office and identified so as to make it clear to the public. A broker may also operate other non-real estate businesses from the same office is desired, provided records relating to the real estate business are maintained separately from the other business.

The broker's license and licenses of all affiliated agents must be displayed in the office whose address is on their license.

Special document requirements

Not only must the licensee give a copy of any contract to the party signing it, the administrative rules prescribe certain additional requirements for earnest money agreements (offers). Not only must the licensee give a copy of to the offeror when the offer is made, but also to the offeree when it is accepted. And then the licensee must then tender to the offeror a copy showing the offeree's signature. Finally, the broker must maintain a copy in the transaction file for the required three years.

In practice licensees frequently note on the earnest money form not only the date of the offer, but the time of day as well. And when the seller accepts or rejects the offer, it is a good practice to note the date and time again. This becomes especially important in a sellers' market where multiple offers on the same property are common.

A licensee may not conduct property management without first obtaining a signed property management agreement from the owner. The property management agreement must specify the agent's compensation, what kind of property it is and how many units, or the square footage if non-residential, whether the agent is authorized to collect security deposits or rent and, if so, what the agent is authorized to disburse the funds for. The agreement must also stipulate how often the licensee is to furnish statements to the owner.

The periodic statements (called *summary statements*) as provided in the management agreement must include the total rent receipts for the period, any owner contributions, any other receipts, an itemization of expenses paid, and the ending balance. It must also show the number of units rented, or the square footage rented if non-residential.

Sometimes a broker doing property management will take a listing on the property as well. Brokers also frequently provide maintenance and other additional services besides the management. In these cases the amount of fees charged and the relationship of the broker must be disclosed to the owner. The owner must give permission for the additional services.

Closing transactions

Real estate transactions in Washington are sometimes closed in a neutral escrow company. It is also common for them to be closed in the office of a bank or other lender providing the financing for the transaction. It is also not unusual for a broker to close the transaction in the broker's office, especially in rural areas of the state.

A license from the Department of Financial Institutions is required under RCW 18.44.021 to conduct escrow activity in Washington, but there are a few common exemptions –

- A bank or most other financial institutions,
- A title insurance company, or
- A real estate broker, provided the broker charges no fee for the service.

When a broker closes a transaction the broker must provide the buyer and the seller each with a detailed closing statement regarding their side of the transaction. The broker must retain copies of these closing statements as other records of real estate transactions. The closing statements must show in all cases the closing date, the purchase price, and an itemization of debits and credits to each party and the names of the parties involved in each item.

Whether it is preparing the closing statement or other activity involved in closing a transaction, the broker must do everything as expeditiously as possible. Delays that are intentional or due to negligence are considered a violation of the license law.

Report of litigation

Whenever a real estate licensee is involved in legal action or proceeding as defendant involving a criminal complaint, indictment, including a plea of guilty or nolo contendere, the licensee must report the matter to the real estate program director. Reports must also be made for civil cases involving real estate or business activity of the licensee, but only if the licensee loses the case, and regardless of whether or not the licensee files an appeal. Whether it is a criminal or civil case, the report must be made within 20 days.

Agency disclosure

Since the early 1980s the real estate profession has been struggling with the problem of what the role of the real estate agent should be. The traditional role was to represent just the seller, via a formal listing agreement, although (especially in commercial real estate) buyer agency was practiced occasionally. Regardless of which role the agent took, the public never understood the issue clearly. Today these issues are covered in Chapter 18.65 RCW, Real Estate Brokerage Relationships. Details of this and the common law of agency are covered in Chapter 18.

Washington Center for Real Estate Research

The Washington Center for Real Estate Research was created in 1989 by Washington State University. Its activities are currently funded by a $10 surcharge on license fees.

The Center has various purposes –
- Conduct studies on affordable housing, rural and urban economics and economically isolated communities and disseminate it and other information,
- Provide educational expertise and research results to the Real Estate Commission,
- Prepare and make available information to consumers about real estate,
- Encourage economic development and growth,
- Support professional development and continuing education of licensees,
- Recommend changes to real estate licensing laws, and
- Develop a vacancy rate standard for low-income housing.

Land development representatives

In addition to licenses for brokers, designated brokers, associate brokers and salespersons, the license law provides for registration of a *land development representative*. A land development representative must be registered to a real estate broker and can be registered to only one broker at a time. Registrations are valid for one year, or until the relationship with the broker is terminated.

Land development representatives are permitted to disseminate information, make sales calls, and transport prospective purchasers to the site. Land development representatives may not engage in any other sales activity such as writing up contracts, taking money or engaging in negotiations.

To become a registered development representative all that is required is to be 18 years of age or older and demonstrate to the Director that the applicant is honest, of good reputation, and the applicant's identity, for which the Directory is authorized to require fingerprinting.

Multiple listing service entrance requirements

In the past many real estate brokers, especially those operating independently or running small firms, had a difficult time meeting the entrance requirements of local multiple listing services. Especially in larger cities it was not uncommon for several very large companies to form a multiple listing service and deliberately exclude smaller brokers from membership. In some cases the three or four largest companies in the city controlled the majority of the listings. During the 1970s there were many anti-trust suits filed by the Federal Trade Commission to halt these practices.

Nevertheless, problems still occur even today. For example, many multiple listing services are run by the local association of REALTORS®, who require that members of the multiple listing service also be members of the association. As a result, the Washington Legislature enacted 18.85.400 RCW which addresses these issues.

Under 18.85.400 a *multiple listing association* (as it is referred to in the statute) can only require that a member –

- Be licensed as a broker,
- Maintain liability insurance to cover possible theft of the contents of an owner's home due to the fact that members have access to the keys,
- Pay an initiation fee, which cannot exceed five times the book value of the association divided by the number of members,
- Have been a broker in the area for one year or be an associate broker with one year experience in the area and one year experience in another area of the state.
- Follow the rules of the association which all other members must follow, provided the rules are legal under state and federal law (i.e., not deemed to be in restraint of trade – see *Anti-trust laws affecting licensees*, below).

Anti-trust laws affecting licensees

Anti-trust laws are designed to insure competition in the marketplace. Everyone knows that the public receives the best quality at the lowest price when competition is unrestrained. Thus, the purpose of anti-trust laws is to prevent *restraint of trade*.

The first major anti-trust law was the Sherman Anti-Trust Act of 1890, which is still the backbone of anti-trust legislation. In the past several decades real estate agents have had to become aware of practices that used to be common and are now considered violations.

For example, *price-fixing* is illegal. Price-fixing means conspiring to set prices. Real estate brokers for two competing firms in an area might make an agreement that neither will charge less than a certain commission rate. Similarly, local organizations such as multiple listing services and associations of REALTORS® may not set minimum fee amounts or the percentages of commission splits. All compensation is to be set by negotiation with the client. However, an individual broker may set a company policy that all affiliated agents must follow with regard to commission rates.

The licensee must be careful not to state or imply to a potential client that there is a "going rate" or "standard commission," as such actions could be construed as price-fixing. Some even suggest placing a statement in a listing or buyer agency agreement where the client acknowledges that the fee they agreed to pay was negotiated at arms length.

Licensees should also avoid even discussing the fees they charge with agents from other companies. Just mentioning such things could be held to be an invitation to price-fixing. Brokers should also never discuss their plans for their business with competing brokers.

Group boycotting is also illegal. For example, real estate firms in an area may agree not to cooperate on listings held by a local cut-rate firm. This could be more subtle, however. For example, brokers for two large firms might be having lunch during a meeting of the local association. During the conversation one mentions to the other that his brother in law is starting a home inspection service. The two brokers then agree that each will send all their home inspection business to the brother in law. In effect, they are agreeing to boycott other inspection service companies in the area.

It is also illegal for brokers to enter into an agreement for the **allocation** of customers or market areas. For example, two brokers, each on a different side of town, might agree not to take listings or show properties in the other's area. The allocation does not have to be geographic; for example it could involve agreeing that each will work only on a specific type of property, or properties in a certain price range.

Tying agreements are also illegal. A **tying agreement** is an arrangement where a party will sell a product only if the buyer will also purchase a tied product. The tied product is typically less desirable. For example, suppose a real estate firm creates a subdivision and refuses to sell the lots except to builders who will agree to list the homes they build back with the brokerage firm. The listing service is the tied product and this may be considered an illegal tying agreement.

There are severe fines for violations of anti-trust laws and even the possibility of jail time. In addition, a consumer harmed by the anti-trust activity may be entitled to

O══ KEY TERMS

The key to understanding any new field is the vocabulary used in that field. To maximize your comprehension of the material presented in this chapter, be sure you know the meaning and significance of the following terms. Remember that the majority of test questions primarily test knowledge of vocabulary.

Advance fee	Individual broker
Allocation	Land development representative
Appraisal	Multiple listing association
Associate broker	Pocket identification card
Branch office	Price-fixing
Broker's price opinion	Professional corporation
Brokers license	Real estate activity
Commingling	Real estate trust bank account
Competitive market analysis	Restraint of trade
Continuing education	Retainer fee
Conversion	Reverse commingling
Core curriculum	Salespersons license
Designated broker	Single licensing
Escrow account	Summary statement
Fee broker	Temporary brokers permit
Group boycotting	Trust account
Inactive	Tying agreement

Chapter

20

Listing agreements

H ARDLY ANY OTHER TYPE of sales endeavor works the same way as the real estate business. In most businesses, the sales staff never has a problem with the supply of goods to be sold. If a car dealer runs short of cars to sell, the factory will be delighted to send another shipment immediately. Not so in real estate. For when you run out of listings, you are out of business until you get more. And getting more is not just a matter of a phone call to the factory. Each listing is itself a sale.

In fact, it could be said that every real estate sale is really two sales – someone had to sell the company's services to the seller, and then someone had to sell the property to the buyer. This is why most brokerage firms pay a "listing commission" and a separate "sales commission." In many firms the percentage paid for getting a listing is about the same as for making a sale.

The listing is the document that creates the agency relationship between the property owner and the broker or brokerage firm. The listing is the personal property of the broker or firm, even though it was taken by an affiliated licensee. Affiliated licensees frequently refer to a listing they have taken themselves as "my listing," but it still belongs to the broker or firm they are affiliated with.

The affiliated licensee is the agent of the broker or firm, and is typically granted the authority to enter into agency (listing or property management) agreements with owners, subject to the broker's approval. Therefore, if an affiliated licensee leaves the firm, the listings remain with the firm. Of course, the broker can give them back to the seller so the seller can relist with the affiliated licensee's new firm, but this is rarely done.

Because of the importance of listings, brokers place great emphasis on them. In most firms, there is more effort put into getting the listing than in making the sale. After all, once you have the listing, you have control over the sale of the property. If you have the majority of the listings in your area, you will control the market.

This inevitably leads to a great deal of competition for listings. And the competition leads to a great variety of marketing strategies. Some brokers try to compete by offering something the other brokers do not. For example, you can usually find brokers who work on flat rate commissions, brokers who work on reduced commissions in exchange for which the seller does some of the sales work, not to mention brokers who take no listings and work as buyers' brokers. Commission rates vary widely, not only according to property, but also according to how keenly a broker feels the competition. There is no minimum or a maximum commission that a broker can charge.

What is a listing

Central to the idea of a listing is that it grants the broker authority to offer the property for sale. The authority which the broker typically accepts is that authority which is required to secure offers from potential buyers. Normally a broker takes authority to show the property, to advertise it, to accept an earnest money deposit from a buyer, to place the property in the multiple listing service, and to seek the subagency or cooperation of other brokers (cooperative sales).

Special note should be made of the authority to accept a deposit. According to the terms of most standard form listing agreements the seller grants the agent the authority to accept a deposit from a buyer. However, if the seller does not grant the authority to take a deposit, and the agent nevertheless takes a deposit from the buyer, then the agent represented the buyer as to the specific task of holding the deposit.

Although it is possible, it would be unusual for a broker to take the authority to accept an offer for a principal. Usually the listing limits the broker's authority merely to securing offers to present to the seller.

Of course, brokers do occasionally take additional authority beyond what an ordinary listing agreement would grant. For example, suppose you have brought about a sale which is about to close, but the seller must be away on the closing date. It is not uncommon for the seller to grant an agent a power of attorney to sign the closing papers. Note that a power of attorney and a listing both create agency relationships and are really closely related documents.

Remember too that a listing is not an offer to sell. All the listing does is create the agency relationship by granting authorities to the broker. If a seller lists a property with a broker, it has no effect on buyers. Since the listing is not an offer to sell, a buyer cannot agree to pay the listed price and then assume that a contract of sale has been created.

For example, suppose a seller lists a house with you for $300,000 and in the listing agrees to accept 20% down and carry the balance on a land sales contract at 8% interest. You locate a creditworthy buyer who makes an offer to the seller of $300,000, with $60,000 down and the balance at 8% interest – exactly the terms the seller was asking for. Now suppose the seller suddenly refuses to sell. If the buyer attempts to force the seller to sell, the buyer will lose. The buyer will lose because there has never existed a contract between the buyer and the seller. The buyer merely made an offer which was not accepted. The purpose of the listing was just to hire the broker; it was not an offer to sell.

Notwithstanding the foregoing, if the broker has secured an offer at the listed price and terms, then the broker has performed his or her duty. The seller now owes the broker the commission, whether the seller agrees to sell the property or not.

Creating a listing

There are numerous legal requirements for a listing to be valid and enforceable. Chief among these is the Statute of Frauds, which requires all contracts involving real property to be in writing lest they be void (except a lease for a year or less). Although many states do not require a listing to be in writing, Washington law makes it clear that an agent with a verbal or implied listing will normally receive little sympathy in court.

Another requirement is that the parties must be aware of the property which is the subject of the agreement. Normally, this is accomplished by placing a legal description, or other adequate description in the listing agreement itself. Sometimes the exact description of the property is not available at the time the seller signs the listing so the agent writes "legal to follow" on the form, then adds the legal description later. Washington courts have generally held that this does not constitute a valid legal description unless the listing agreement specifically authorized the agent to add the legal description.

The agent must also have held a valid real estate license at the time the agent alleges the commission was earned. In other words, without a license, you cannot prevail in a suit to collect a commission. You should also note that taking a listing is considered "real estate activity" for which a license is required. Thus if you take a listing without a license, not only can you not collect the commission in court, but you are also in violation of the license law and subject to being fined by the Department of Licensing.

Interestingly, although a seller can assert the defense that the agent was not licensed, this protection does not extend to the buyer. Suppose that a buyer wished to rescind a purchase agreement. The buyer learned that the agent was not licensed at the time the agent brought about the sale. Can the buyer use the agent's lack of a license as an excuse to avoid the purchase agreement. The answer is no. The fact that the agent was not licensed benefits only the seller, and only to the extent that the seller can avoid paying the commission.

Of course, in order to enforce a listing, it must constitute a valid agency agreement. This is normally created by an expressed agreement, although in actual real estate practice it is occasionally created by ratification. In rare circumstances an agency agreement may be created by estoppel. In addition, the agent cannot have violated the fiduciary and statutory obligations of an agent to a principal.

One of the most important requirements to enforce a listing is that the broker must have done what the seller hired the broker to do. For example, if the buyer cannot or will not close the transaction, then the agent has not performed and will not be able to collect the commission. The usual legal expression is that the buyer must be ***ready, willing and able*** or just ***ready and able***. In this context, "ready" and "willing" means that the buyer has signed the necessary documents. "Able" means that the buyer had the cash or credit necessary to pay for the property.

Therefore, if the transaction does not close, the agent has not performed and will not be able to collect a commission. However, it is possible that the buyer was ready, willing and able, yet the transaction does not close because the seller cannot or will not perform. In this case, the agent has performed, so the seller owes the commission, even if the sale never closes.

Even then, the agent must have brought the seller an offer that was exactly at the price and terms on the listing agreement. For example, if the listing states the terms as "$300,000" and no other provisions, an offer at a lesser price or an offer where the seller is to carry a contract do not comply with the terms of the listing and the agent has not earned the commission.

There is yet one more legal requirement in order to be able to enforce collection of a commission. The agent must be the ***procuring cause*** of the sale. This means that the sale would not have been brought about without the efforts of the agent. Law books say the broker must have set in motion the chain of events leading to the sale. But what that means is not always legally clear. For example, publishing a circular for buyers listing properties for sale would probably not be sufficient. But showing a property to a buyer undoubtedly would be adequate.

Part of the reason this is a gray area in the law is that there is little case law on the subject. Disputes between brokers as to who was the procuring cause of the sale are usually handled through professional arbitration, rather than court actions. And disputes between brokers and sellers are not common because brokers today take mostly the exclusive right to sell listing, in which case the broker will be paid regardless of who sells the property (see further discussion under *Legal forms of listing agreements* on the following pages).

LEGAL REQUIREMENTS TO COLLECT COMMISSION
- Agency agreement
- In writing
- Adequate description of the property
- License
- Buyer ready, willing and able
- Procuring cause of the sale

The license law and the administrative rules also require the agent to give a copy of a listing to the principal at the time the principal signs it. Failing to adhere to this requirement, however, would not necessarily result in an unenforceable listing agreement, but would nevertheless result in potential disciplinary action against a real estate licensee by the Director.

Termination of listings

Most of the general principles of contract law apply to agency agreements. Therefore, a listing would be unenforceable if it was entered into in reliance on fraud, misrepresentation, or mistake of fact. It would also be rendered unenforceable due to impossibility of performance, mutual rescission, conditions not met, and countless other reasons that contracts are held to be unenforceable. (For a more thorough discussion of factors which render a contract unenforceable, see Chapter 9.)

There are, however, a few special rules that apply just to agency contracts. First, an agency contract is a contract for personal services, and as such is not generally enforceable by *specific performance*, a special suit to compel performance of a contract, as an alternative to a suit for damages. So a listing is enforceable only by a suit for damages.

Second, non-exclusive listing agreements are *unilateral*, that is, performance by one of the parties is optional. In many listings, the seller promises to pay the broker if the broker is successful in selling or leasing the property. The broker, on the other hand, does not promise that the broker will find a buyer, so performance by the broker is optional. In other words, in such a listing, while the agent can hold the seller to his or her end of the bargain, the seller cannot force the agent to continue as agent. The agent can simply renounce the agency at any time. However, in Washington an exclusive right to sell listing is held to be bilateral, thus the seller can conceivably force the broker to continue to perform until the expiration of the listing.

But since an agency contract cannot be enforced by specific performance, the principal can also usually terminate the listing at any time, simply by revoking the authority. The exception is that the principal cannot revoke the authority if the agent has an interest in the property. Even if the agent does not have an interest in the property, the principal must have just cause to do so without being liable for damages.

Let us summarize this situation. The broker can renounce a non-exclusive agency at any time, with or without cause, and can not generally be held liable for damages. If the listing is exclusive the broker cannot renounce without just cause, but if the broker refuses to perform the seller can only sue for damages. And the seller would be hard pressed to demonstrate a dollar amount of loss, since the seller could easily relist the property with another broker. The principal can also revoke the authority at any time, but if the principal does so wrongfully the agent is entitled to damages. In other words, if the seller gives you a listing for 180 days, the seller is still free to revoke the listing at any time. But if the seller revokes the authority wrongfully before the end of the 180 days, you are entitled to damages.

Another special rule which does not generally apply in ordinary contract situations is that an agency contract is terminated by the future death, incompetence or bankruptcy of either principal or agent. And finally, an agent may find himself or herself with an unenforceable listing if the agent violates the agent's fiduciary obligations to the principal. A principal's defense to paying the commission is to maintain that the agent failed to disclose a material fact, failed to give a complete accounting, violated the agent's duty of confidentiality or did not maintain loyalty to the principal.

Legal forms of listing agreements

There are many preprinted listing forms available for real estate brokers today. All of them, however, fall into one of just three categories. The simplest to understand is the *open listing*. An open listing authorizes the agent to act on behalf of the seller in bringing about a transaction, and promises a commission if the agent is successful.

Now, we must always bear in mind that any rights in the owner's bundle of rights which the owner has not granted to another, the owner must still have. (The concept of the bundle of rights is covered in Chapter 3.) So now let us consider just what sales rights the seller has granted the agent. With an open listing, the agent has the right to sell the property, and probably various additional authorities such as the right to show the property, and so on. But can the seller grant a similar right to another agent? And can the seller sell the property by his or her own efforts without paying the agent? Since an open listing does not mention these matters the seller clearly retains those rights. In other words, if a seller grants an open listing to an agent, the seller can grant additional open listings to as many brokers as the seller finds desirable, and if one of the other brokers sells the property the seller pays only that broker. Furthermore, if the seller is the one who sells the property, no one is entitled to a commission.

Let us now go one step further. Let us suppose that the seller grants an open listing, and adds one additional right. Suppose the seller agrees that the broker will be the only one with the right to sell the property. In this case we say the agent has an *exclusive agency listing*. It is called an exclusive agency listing, because the broker is the seller's exclusive agent; there will be no others. But note that the seller has said nothing about paying the agent if the seller is the one who sells the property. Therefore, in an exclusive agency listing, the broker will be paid the commission in all cases, unless the seller sells the property by his or her own efforts without the broker's assistance.

Going one step further, now suppose the seller were to add one more right. Not only will the seller pay the broker if the broker is successful (open), and agree not to grant the right to sell the property to any other agents (exclusive agency), but the seller now agrees to pay the broker a commission even if the seller sells the property by his or her own efforts. This is called an *exclusive right to sell listing*.

When discussing listing agreements, there are two other terms that are commonly encountered. An *exclusive listing* is any listing where the seller can only have one agent. Therefore, both exclusive agency and exclusive right to sell listings are said to be exclusive. And if that is the definition of an exclusive listing, then a *non-exclusive listing* is one where there can be many agents. In other words, non-exclusive listing is, practically speaking, just another term for open listing. It is a term used by agents when they wish to stress the fact that the owner can give listings to as many agents as the owner wants – it is "not exclusive."

While the above is the legal meaning of "exclusive," real estate agents, especially in Washington, have used it for many years as a synonym for "exclusive right to sell." Thus, Washington agents refer to listings as "exclusive," "exclusive agency," and "open."

Now that we can see the different types of listings, it seems that the open listing is better for the seller, and the exclusive right to sell listing is better for the agent. At first glance, this may appear to be so, but on closer examination, the exclusive right to sell listing may be better for both. That it is better for the agent is obvious – the agent has far greater assurance of earning a commission if the listing is exclusive right to sell. Yet, it is precisely this reason that the exclusive right to sell listing is usually the best for the seller. The seller will obtain the best service from the agent when the agent is motivated. An agent who must worry about the seller, as well as many other agents, beating the agent to the sale will not be motivated to exert a great marketing effort.

Of course, while it is true that the open, exclusive agency, and exclusive right to sell are the three basic formats for listings, there are still many variations on the theme.

For example, consider the seller who is willing to give you an exclusive right to sell listing, but wishes to wait because a neighbor is interested in the property. You could easily overcome this objection just by taking an exclusive right to sell listing from the seller, and then excluding the neighbor from the listing for a short period of time – that is, just give the seller one of the sales rights back. In similar fashion, you can modify any listing to meet the special needs of any client.

Other types of listings

A *multiple listing* is a popular arrangement with buyers and sellers, as well as agents. The term would lead you to believe that the seller grants individual open listings to multiple brokers, but this is not the case.

Multiple listings are possible when a group of real estate brokers get together and form a *multiple listing service*. This may be a non-profit or for-profit organization. Its business is to serve as a medium where brokers can expose their listings to other member brokers. Each broker takes (normally) exclusive right to sell listings, and then submits the listings to the multiple listing service. The service then publishes the listings. Originally the listings were published in a book format with a new book published every week or two, but today it is more common to use just electronic means to make the listings available to the brokers. The purpose of placing a listing in the multiple listing service is to seek the subagency of the other member brokers or seek offers from brokers working as buyer's agents.

Multiple listing services have extensive rules and bylaws. Each broker agrees to abide by these rules and bylaws as a condition of joining the organization. The rules and bylaws generally require a member broker to submit all listings, and to do so within a certain time limit. They also govern the manner in which appointments are made to show property, how offers are presented, and the like. Since multiple listing services are generally local rather than state-wide, state licensing examinations cover only general concepts that are normally true of all multiple listing services.

One-party listings are occasionally encountered by real estate agents. A one-party listing is a listing which is valid only for one buyer. If an broker has a buyer for a property, but the seller does not wish to grant a regular listing, the broker may nevertheless take a listing valid only for the broker's buyer. Most agents refuse to accept one-party listings, since the agent can work better on the property when it can be exposed to all the buyers in the marketplace. If the seller does not wish to tie up the property with a full listing, a better practice would be to take a normal exclusive right to sell listing, but for a shorter period of time. Note that a one-party listing can be open, exclusive agency, or an exclusive right to sell listing.

A *net listing* is a listing arrangement where the broker's compensation is to be the amount the property sells for over and above a net amount to the seller. For example, suppose a seller has a property worth about $300,000, on which there is a current loan balance of $120,000. The seller tells the agent "just get me $150,000 for my equity, you can have everything the property sells for above that for your commission." If the broker accepts the listing on this basis, then the broker can potentially earn a $30,000 commission if the property sells for its full value of $300,000 ($300,000, less $120,000 loan equals seller's equity of $180,000; less $150,000 net to seller, equals $30,000 for the broker's commission).

There are various difficulties with net listings. First, the agency relationship between the seller and the broker would require the broker to make full disclosure of how much the broker expects to earn. The broker and the seller must also have a clear understanding of the price at which the property is to be offered. After all, the higher the price, the longer it will take to attract a buyer – certainly an important fact for the seller. And when an offer is finally received, the broker must disclose at the time of presenting the offer the amount of commission the broker will earn if the seller accepts the offer.

The biggest problem with net listings is that it may leave the seller feeling cheated. When the seller sees the broker earn a large commission it may breed a suspicion that the broker has breached his or her fiduciary obligations. In fact because net listings create a temptation for a broker to place his or her own interests ahead of the interests of the principal, they are illegal in many states. They are also a violation of the code of ethics of the National Association of REALTORS®. As a result, even though net listings are legal in Washington, agents practically always avoid them.

While brokers may wish to avoid a net listing arrangement, often a seller will propose something similar to the example we quoted above. Of course, the seller does not realize the pitfalls in a net listing agreement, so it is up to the broker to steer the seller into a traditional listing on a percentage or flat fee basis. Considering the above example then, at what price should the agent take the listing if the seller is to realize the goal of $150,000 and the agent is to receive a commission of, say, 6% of the sales price?

You can calculate this easily. The question is asking for the price at which you must list the property. Note that we want the full listing price (100% of the listing price). Therefore, let us use "100% of LP" to stand for the amount we must find.

Now, you can easily see that "100% of LP" has to include the loan balance ($120,000), and the amount the seller is to net ($150,000), plus the commission. Therefore, we can create the following formula –

100% of LP = $120,000 + $150,000 + Commission

Another way to state the commission is "6% of LP," since the commission is to be 6% of the listed price. Let us therefore substitute the term "6% of LP" for "Commission" in the above formula:

100% of LP = $120,000 + $150,000 + 6% of LP

Let us also simplify the formula by combining terms. Adding the two dollar figures on the right side of the formula gives us:

100% of LP = $270,000 + 6% of LP

Now we are ready to solve the problem. You may recall from high school math that when you deal with formulas, you can do anything to the formula and still have a true statement, as long as you do the same thing to both sides of the formula equally. Therefore, let us subtract "6% of LP" from both sides of the formula. This leaves us:

94% of LP = $270,000

Now let us state the formula in more conventional notation:

.94 × LP = $270,000

The expression ".94 × LP" really means ".94 times Listing Price." Any number divided by itself gives the answer 1. So if we divide ".94 times Listing Price" by .94, we will get just "LP" standing alone. Let us then divide both sides of the formula by .94. This gives us:

LP = $270,000 ÷ .94

And now we are ready to make the final calculation. When we use the calculator to divide $270,000 by .94, we find the result is $287,234.04. In other words, if the commission is to be 6%, and the seller is to net exactly $150,000, we must list the property at $287,234.04.

You can prove this just by taking 6% of $287,234.04 away from $287,234.04. It will leave the exact amount we must have after the commission in order to satisfy the seller:

$$\begin{array}{r} \$\ 287{,}234.04 \\ \times\ \ .06 \\ \hline \$\ \ \ 17{,}234.04 \end{array}$$

As you can see, 6% of $287,234.04 is $17,234.04. Subtracting $17,234.04 from $287,234.04 leaves us exactly the $270,000 we need ($287,234.04 − $17,234.04 = $270,000). Now we know the correct answer is $287,234.04.

Note that we cannot get the right answer by adding 6% onto $279,000.

$$\begin{array}{r} \$\ 270{,}000.00 \\ \times\ \ .06 \\ \hline \$\ \ \ 16{,}200.00 \end{array}$$

As you can see, 6% of $270,000 is $16,200. When we add the two together we get a listed price of only $286,200, which is not quite enough.

However, you can shortcut this arithmetic. It is not necessary to go all the way through the formula each time you need to calculate a listing price from a net listing situation. If you refer back to the second stage of our original formula, "100% of LP = $120,000 + $150,000 + 6% of LP," you will note that the commission is stated as "6% of LP." What would happen if the commission were 7%? We would just replace "6% of LP" with the expression "7% of LP." Following down to the end of the formula, we would end up dividing the $270,000 by .93 instead of by .94. In similar fashion, if the commission were 8%, we would divide the $270,000 by .92, and so on. In other words, regardless of the commission rate, just subtract the commission rate from 100% and divide the result into the total you have to net.

Agent's remedies

Earlier we discussed what an agent must be able to prove in order to prevail in a legal action to collect a commission. Now we must turn our attention to certain other situations which may give rise to the agent's right to damages from the principal.

Although not an everyday circumstance, it is not unusual for a seller to attempt to avoid paying a broker the commission. Sellers frequently believe that the broker did little to earn the commission, so they feel morally justified in trying to avoid paying it. After all, the agent comes to the property, spends an hour or two taking the listing, then shows up when an offer is obtained and spends another hour or two presenting it. All the seller sees is a commission amounting to thousands of dollars for what seems to be a few hours work. Of course, the seller does not see the fact that the commission is frequently divided up to four ways. And the seller does not see the advertising bills, the car expenses, the multiple listing service dues, and the countless other bills that the agent must pay to stay in business, not to mention the time spent showing dozens of properties to a buyer before finding one the buyer likes.

A common way for the seller to attempt to avoid paying the commission is to conspire with the buyer to wait until the listing expires. After all, the seller may reason, if the property is sold after the listing expires, the broker is not entitled to a commission. Of course, the buyer's motivation to agree to this is that the seller may be willing to lower the price if there is no commission to pay.

Naturally, the broker wishes to avoid this. In order to stop the seller from going around the broker and conspiring with the buyer, the broker normally places a special clause in the listing agreement. The clause is usually called a **safety clause**, although it is also called a ***carry-over clause*** or an ***extender clause***. A typical listing agreement might state the owner's agreement to pay the commission in the manner used in the Washington Association of REALTORS® form (see the full form at the end of this chapter) –

"... Further, if Seller shall, within _____ days (180 days if not filled in) after the expiration of this Agreement, sell the Property to any person to whose attention it was brought through the signs, advertising or other action of Broker, or on information secured directly or indirectly from or through Broker, during the term of this Agreement, then Seller will pay Broker the above commission. Provided, that if a commission is paid to a member of MLS in conjunction with a sale, the amount of commission payable to Broker shall be limited to the amount of commission which would have been payable pursuant to this Agreement less any commission so paid to another member of MLS."

In the above clause, note that the agent is entitled to the commission if the property is sold during the term of the listing or within a certain number of days thereafter. In other words, if the broker introduced the seller to a buyer, the broker is entitled to the commission if the property is sold to that buyer even up to stipulated number of days after the listing expires. Of course, the broker must maintain records to demonstrate that the buyer was introduced to the property during the term of the listing.

Different listing forms provide for different time periods for the safety clause, such as "a term equal to the original term of this listing," or "one year." Some forms even provide that the seller owes the commission to the agent if the property is ever sold to someone the agent showed the property to during the term of the listing.

Unfortunately, this could create a problem if the seller relists the property with a different broker right after the expiration of the first broker's listing, and the second broker ends up selling the property to someone the first broker showed the property to. Both brokers have the right to the full commission. To avoid subjecting the seller to two full commissions many multiple listing services create a rule stipulating that the second broker is entitled to the full commission. But this creates a loophole for a clever seller. A seller and a buyer could wait out the first listing, then the seller could relist the property with a second broker who offers very low fees in exchange for the seller doing a lot of the sales work. When the seller sells to the buyer the seller can pay the reduced commission to the second broker and use the second listing as protection against the claims of the first broker. To get around this many listing forms use language like the Washington Association of REALTORS® form that says the first broker is still entitled to the full commission but it will be reduced by the amount paid to a subsequent broker.

Another problem that occasionally arises is a missing signature on the listing. Most commonly this happens when the property is owned by husband and wife as community property, although it can happen any time there is a concurrent tenancy. What if both parties are in title, only one signs the listing agreement, and then the other party refuses to close a subsequent sale?

There are two possible outcomes. If the broker did not know that there were two or more co-owners, then the party who signed the listing owes the broker the commission. After all, this person hired the broker to procure a buyer, and the broker performed the task. But if the broker knew there was more than one owner, and proceeded without the agreement of the other owners, then the broker did so at his or her own peril and cannot claim a commission. On the other hand, sometimes the agency with the co-tenant can be implied. If a co-tenant knew that the other co-tenant listed the property and did nothing to stop the broker, the co-tenant who did not sign may be estopped (barred) from denying the agency.

The seller may also be liable to the broker for damages if the seller prevents the broker from performing the agreed task. A common example of this occurs where the seller lists the property for sale, and then leases the property to a tenant on a long term lease. Although the property can be sold subject to the lease, the owner no longer has the same interest to sell, since the title is now severely encumbered. The existence of the lease greatly hampers the broker's ability to attract a buyer at the same price and terms as originally listed, therefore the seller would be held to have prevented the broker from performing. If the seller prevents the broker from performing, the seller would likely be held liable to the broker for the commission as though earned.

If a seller refuses to pay a commission, the broker may have little recourse but to sue the seller for it. The broker should be careful not to attempt to collect the commission by interfering with the closing of the transaction. To do so may be construed by a court as harming the principal for the agent's personal gain, which is a violation of the broker's fiduciary obligation to the principal. And if a broker violates the fiduciary duty to the principal, one possible penalty is forfeiture of the commission.

However, the Washington *Commercial Real Estate Broker Lien Act* provides an alternative remedy for a broker when the property is commercial. Commercial property means any property other than a one- to four-family dwelling, or land zoned for a one- to four-family dwelling, a residential condominium, or agricultural property.

The Act allows the broker to record a claim of lien against the net proceeds of the sale. The lien is on the proceeds of the sale, not the real estate itself. The lien does not become effective for 30 days after recording. The broker must give the owner a notice of the claim within ten days of recording. The owner can contest the claim in court and the broker must appear and explain the reason why the broker is entitled to the claim. If the broker does not appear the court will order the claim released. Or the seller can post with the court an amount equal to one and one-quarter the amount of the claim and the court will automatically order a release.

Sales considerations

There's an old saying in real estate – "you've got to list to last." Some agents become very successful doing nothing but selling, but the majority of agents who prosper at real estate do so by concentrating on listing.

Obtaining a listing is a sale. You are selling your services to the owner. If the owner does not feel you and your company can do the job, you are not going to get a signature on the listing form. Convincing the owner to list with your company requires real sales ability. New agents typically go through sales training classes where they learn techniques to make them more effective. Still, even the best agent will strike out more often than not. You need a constant supply of new listings, and that means continually seeking new business.

There are several classic sources for listings –

Expired listings – Checking with data from the multiple listing service and contacting owners of properties whose listings have expired is an excellent way to get new listings. But bear in mind that if you do the same thing as the original listing agent you will get the same results – an expired listing. The secret to taking expired listings is to resolve the problem that caused the listing to expire in the first place. Also bear in mind that the seller will be wary of you. The first agent promised the moon and delivered nothing.

Referrals – Every new agent needs to cultivate his or her friends, acquaintances and relatives (some agents call these their "FARs"). Other books on sales methods refer to them as your "sphere of influence." Whatever you call them, you must keep them constantly aware that you are in real estate and would appreciate referrals. You can also advertise for referrals from certain groups. For example, attorneys are constantly dealing with estates, foreclosures and other cases involving real estate. A small constant ad in the local bar journal will yield slow, but steady referrals.

For sale by owners – Many agents love to work the for sale by owners. Others hate them. Under normal market conditions five to ten percent of all residential sales are for sale by owners. However, far more than that start out trying to sell the property themselves. Most give up and list the property at some point. If you were the agent who respected their efforts and were available to help, you may be the one to end up with the listing.

Cold calling – Cold calling is going out of favor these days, but some agents still do it. The public is becoming extremely averse to receiving telemarketing calls. The fact that you represent a local company they have heard of doesn't stop them from being annoyed. And laws regulating telemarketing calls are making it more and more difficult. Furthermore, in many communities it is becoming hard to find lists of phone numbers by geographic location, like a list of phone numbers for the houses up and down a street. Many agents today find that going up and down the street in person is more effective and far less annoying to the public.

Listing ads – Placing an ad that says "Listings Wanted" will probably get zero results. But placing an ad that says "Four-bedroom Home in Rockmont Needed" will get calls. The key is to advertise for a property with specific features. Of course, it would be misrepresentation and a violation of the license law unless you are actually working with a buyer who needs that particular type of property.

Open houses – The public assumes the purpose of an open house is to sell the house. Certainly the agent holding an open house would not turn down an offer, but there are other purposes for an open house as well. One of them is to find people who need to sell their home. Half the people coming to a typical open house already have a home and need to sell it in order to buy a new one.

Farming – Probably the single most powerful source of listings is a listing farm. A residential farm might be an area consisting of 50 to 100 blocks, or more, typically an identifiable geographic area in the community. The agent works the farm using various methods – door to door (especially at first), newsletters, direct mail, and even by promoting neighborhood needs. Eventually the agent's name becomes a household word in the community and most of the for sale signs bear the agent's name. Once established, the farm provides a lifetime of business for the agent.

A farm doesn't have to be residential. For example, an agent who specializes in apartment complexes could establish a farm consisting of all multi-family properties in the city. Just because they are scattered all over town doesn't mean the agent's name can't become the one every owner of a multi-family property thinks of when it's time to sell.

Other listing considerations – When taking the listing the agent must bear in mind that the seller is depending on the agent's knowledge and expertise. This includes advice about what price to ask and how to make the property more attractive to buyers in order to command a better price. The final decision in such matters is the seller's, but an agent who does not give the seller the benefit of the agent's experience is derelict in his or her duties to the seller. Agents should normally arrive at the listing appointment with a competitive market analysis and a checklist of possible property improvements the seller can make. These should be discussed openly and frankly so both the seller and the agent know what to expect of each other.

New agents not only need to consider where they are going to get listings, but what to do after they take one. In real estate we refer to this as *servicing the listing*. Servicing the listing means more than just advertising and showing it. It means constant communication with the seller. Even if your ads are pulling no calls and no one wants to see the property, you must call the seller often, usually at least once a week. If you have nothing to say, then call the seller and say you have nothing to say. Almost all legal and sales problems with sellers would never have occurred if the agent had taken the time to communicate with the seller.

Forms

To see how the principles discussed in this chapter apply, read through the sample exclusive right to sell listing agreement, reproduced with the kind permission of the Washington Association of REALTORs® on the following pages.

KEY TERMS

The key to understanding any new field is the vocabulary used in that field. To maximize your comprehension of the material presented in this chapter, be sure you know the meaning and significance of the following terms. Remember that the majority of test questions primarily test knowledge of vocabulary.

Carry-over clause

Commercial Real Estate Broker Lien Act

Exclusive right to sell listing

Exclusive agency listing

Exclusive listing

Extender clause

Multiple listing service

Multiple listing

Net listing

Non-exclusive listing

One-party listing

Open listing

Procuring cause

Ready, willing and able

Safety clause

Servicing the listing

Specific performance

Unilateral contract

W.A.R. Form No. L-102-R
NWMLS Form No. 1A
Exclusive Sale
Rev. 12/96
Page 1 of 2 pages

EXCLUSIVE SALE AND LISTING AGREEMENT

The undersigned Seller ("Seller") hereby grants to _____, ("Broker")
from date hereof until midnight of _____ , _____ , the sole and exclusive right to submit offers
to purchase, and to receipt for deposits in connection therewith, the real property ("the Property") commonly known as _____
_____ in the City of _____ , County of _____ , State of Washington, Zip _____ ;
and legally described as: LOT _____ , BLOCK _____ , DIVISION _____
_____ VOL _____ , PAGE _____

1. **DEFINITIONS.** For purposes of this Agreement: (a) "MLS" means the _____ Multiple
   Listing Service/Association/Bureau; and (b) "sell" includes a contract to sell; an exchange or contract to exchange; an option to
   purchase; and/or a lease with option to purchase.

2. **AGENCY/DUAL AGENCY.** Seller authorizes Broker to appoint _____ to act as Seller's
   Listing Agent(s). It is understood and agreed that this Agreement creates an agency relationship with Listing Agent(s) and Broker
   only, not with any other sales associates of Broker. Any broker or salespersons, other than Broker or Listing Agent, who procures
   a prospective buyer for the Property will not be representing Seller and may represent the Buyer. Accordingly, for the purposes of
   this Agreement, the term "Broker" means Listing Agent(s) and Listing Agent's Broker or Designated Broker, unless expressly stated
   otherwise

   Seller agrees that if the Property is sold to a buyer represented by one of Broker's salespersons other than Listing Agent(s), then
   Seller consents to Broker acting as a dual agent. Seller further agrees that if the Property is sold to a buyer who Listing Agent also
   represents, then Seller consents to Listing Agent(s) and Broker acting as dual agents. Seller acknowledges that a dual agent
   represents both parties to a transaction; that the parties' interest in the transaction may differ and that a dual agent is not permitted
   to give advice to either party to the detriment of the other party, promote or advocate the interest of either party over the other
   party, or disclose to either party confidential information from or concerning the other party. If this Agreement is executed on or
   after January 1, 1997, then Seller acknowledges receipt of the pamphlet entitled "The Law of Real Estate Agency".

   If Broker acts as a dual agent, then Broker shall be entitled to the entire commission payable under this Agreement plus any
   additional compensation Broker may have negotiated with the Buyer.

3. **COMMISSION.** If (a) Broker procures a Buyer on the terms in this Agreement, or on other terms acceptable to Seller; or (b) Seller
   directly or indirectly or through any person or entity other than Broker, during the term hereof, sells the Property; then Seller will
   pay Broker a commission of (fill in one and strike the other) _____ % of the
   sales price, or $ _____ . Further, if Seller shall, within _____ days (180 days if not filled in) after the expiration of
   this Agreement, sell the Property to any person to whose attention it was brought through the signs, advertising or other action of
   Broker, or on information secured directly or indirectly from or through Broker, during the term of this Agreement, then Seller will
   pay Broker the above commission. Provided, that if a commission is paid to a member of MLS in conjunction with a sale, the
   amount of commission payable to Broker shall be limited to the amount of commission which would have been payable pursuant to
   this Agreement less any commission so paid to another member of MLS. Provided further, that if Seller cancels this Agreement
   without legal cause, Seller may be liable for damages incurred by Broker as a result of cancellation, regardless of whether Seller
   pays a commission to another MLS member.

4. **KEYBOX.** Broker is authorized to install a keybox on the Property. Such keybox may be opened by a master key held by all
   members of MLS and their salespeople. A master key also may be held by affiliated third parties such as inspectors and
   appraisers who cannot have access to the Property without Broker's prior approval which will not be given without Broker first
   making reasonable efforts to obtain Seller's approval.

5. **SELLER'S WARRANTIES AND REPRESENTATIONS.** Seller warrants that he/she has the right to sell the Property on the terms
   herein and that the Property information on the additional pages to this Agreement is correct. Further, Seller represents that to the
   best of Seller's knowledge, there are no structures or boundary indicators that either encroach on adjacent property or on this
   Property. Seller understands that Broker and other members of MLS will make representations to prospective buyers based on the
   Property information on the additional pages to this Agreement. Seller agrees to indemnify and hold Broker and other members
   of MLS harmless in the event the foregoing warranties and representations are incorrect.

6. **CLOSING COSTS.** Seller agrees to furnish and pay for a buyer's policy of title insurance showing marketable title to the Property.
   Seller agrees to pay real estate excise tax and one-half of any escrow fees or such portion of escrow fees and any other fees or
   charges as provided by law in the case of FHA or VA financed sale. Rent, taxes, interest, reserves, assumed encumbrances,
   homeowner fees and insurance are to be prorated between Seller and Buyer as of the date of closing.

7. **MULTIPLE LISTING.** Broker shall cause this listing to be published by MLS. Broker may refer this listing to any other multiple listing service at Broker's discretion. Broker shall cooperate with all other members of MLS, or of the multiple listing service to which this listing is referred, in working toward the sale of the Property. Regardless of whether a cooperating MLS member is the agent of the Buyer, the Seller, neither or both, the member shall be entitled to receive the selling office's share of the commission. SELLER UNDERSTANDS AND AGREES THAT THE PROPERTY INFORMATION ON THE ADDITIONAL PAGES TO THIS AGREEMENT WILL BE GIVEN TO PROSPECTIVE BUYERS AND TO OTHER COOPERATING MEMBERS OF MLS WHO DO NOT REPRESENT THE SELLER AND, IN SOME INSTANCES, MAY REPRESENT THE BUYER. IT IS UNDERSTOOD THAT MLS IS NOT A PARTY TO THIS AGREEMENT AND ITS SOLE FUNCTION IS TO FURNISH THE DESCRIPTIVE INFORMATION ON THE ADDITIONAL PAGES OF THIS LISTING TO ITS MEMBERS, WITHOUT VERIFICATION AND WITHOUT ASSUMING ANY RESPONSIBILITY FOR SUCH INFORMATION OR IN RESPECT TO THIS AGREEMENT.

8. **DISCLAIMER/SELLER'S INSURANCE.** Neither Broker, MLS, nor any members of MLS or of any multiple listing service to which this listing is referred shall be responsible for loss, theft, or damage of any nature or kind whatsoever to the Property and/or to any personal property therein, including entry by the master key to the keybox and/or at open houses. Seller is advised to notify Seller's insurance company that the Property is listed for sale and ascertain that the Seller has adequate insurance coverage. If the Property is to be vacant during all or part of the term of this listing, Seller should request that a "vacancy clause" be added to Seller's insurance policy.

9. **BROKER'S RIGHT TO MARKET THE PROPERTY.** Seller shall not commit any act which materially impairs Broker's ability to market and sell the Property under the terms of this Agreement. In the event of breach of the foregoing, Seller agrees to pay Broker a commission in the above amount, or at the above rate applied to the listing price herein, whichever is applicable. Broker shall be entitled to show the Property at all reasonable times. Broker need not submit to Seller any offers to lease, rent, execute an option to purchase, or enter into any agreement other than for immediate sale of the Property.

10. **REAL PROPERTY TRANSFER DISCLOSURE STATEMENT.** Unless Seller is exempt under RCW 64.06, Seller shall provide to Broker as soon as reasonably practicable a completed and signed "Real Property Transfer Disclosure Statement" (W.A.R. Form D-5 or NWMLS Form 17). Seller agrees to indemnify, defend and hold Broker harmless from and against any and all claims that the information Seller provides on W.A.R. Form D-5 or NWMLS Form 17 is inaccurate.

11. **DAMAGES IN THE EVENT OF BUYER'S BREACH.** In the event Seller retains earnest money as liquidated damages on Buyer's breach, any costs advanced or committed by Broker on Seller's behalf shall be paid therefrom and the balance divided equally between Seller and Broker.

12. **ATTORNEYS' FEES.** In the event either party employs an attorney to enforce any terms of this Agreement and is successful, the other party agrees to pay reasonable attorneys' fees. In the event of trial, the successful party shall be entitled to an award of attorneys' fees and expenses; the amount of the attorneys' fees and expenses shall be fixed by the court. The venue of any suit shall be the county in which the property is located.

DATED THIS _____ DAY OF _____ , _____. Are the undersigned the sole owner(s)? ☐ YES ☐ NO

BROKER (COMPANY) _____ SELLER _____

BY_____ SELLER _____

Chapter 21

Earnest money agreements

P ROBABLY NO OTHER DOCUMENT in real estate is as complex as the earnest money agreement. Although the listing is the beginning of a sale, the earnest money receipt has greater potential for creating problems. Yet that is also its challenge. For the knowledgeable real estate agent, the earnest money receipt is a place to demonstrate their creativity in bringing about a meeting of the minds.

The earnest money agreement goes by as many synonyms, it seems, as there are real estate agents. **Earnest money receipt** or **earnest money agreement** are the most common. It is also occasionally called a **binder**, especially in the eastern United States. Other expressions to describe the earnest money receipt include **deposit receipt and sales agreement**, **purchase contract and earnest money receipt**, **conditional sales agreement and receipt for deposit**, and endless others. Several of these terms point out an interesting feature of the earnest money agreement – it really has two functions. On the one hand, it is a receipt for the actual **earnest money** (also occasionally referred to as the **hand money**). And it is the contract between the buyer and the seller for the sale of the property. The fact that it is a receipt for the earnest money is why the selling agent should sign it and the reason the license law and administrative rules require the agent to give a copy of it to the buyer at the time the buyer signs it.

Of course, a purchase contract need not contain an earnest money deposit. A buyer and seller can simply agree to a contract for the sale of the property. In fact, the buyer and seller can simply exchange the cash and deed on the strength of a verbal contract if they wish. But modern transactions sometimes take a long time to close. For the seller, the fact that the buyer put up funds as earnest money, which will be forfeit if the buyer defaults, is some assurance that the transaction will, indeed, close. Naturally then, the more earnest money the buyer puts up, the better the seller's position.

But if a sales contract does not include earnest money, does it not fail for lack of consideration? A contract for the sale of real estate, the same as most contracts, must be supported by consideration. But the earnest money is not the whole consideration. Remember that the earnest money agreement is a contract for the sale of the property. Therefore it stipulates the purchase price, and it is that agreed purchase price of the property which is the consideration. The earnest money itself is described as deposit money (good faith money) to be credited to the buyer at closing. So the earnest money is part of the consideration, but the real consideration for the contract is the agreed price.

Anatomy of an earnest money agreement

Suppose you sold a property to a buyer and prepared a complete, formal earnest money receipt on a standard form. The terms of the earnest money agreement were that the buyer would pay $300,000 for the property, on account of which the buyer was putting down $30,000 as earnest money, which would be forfeit if the buyer did not complete the transaction. The buyer was to pay the balance of $270,000 in installments of $2,580.26 per month which include interest at 8% over the next 15 years. At the end of the 15 years, assuming the buyer made all the payments promptly as agreed, you would be obligated to close the transaction and deliver a free and clear deed to the buyer.

Is this an earnest money agreement? Or is it a land sales contract? Does an earnest money receipt have to close sooner than 15 years? For that matter, if we take a standard land sales contract and provide that the buyer will pay it in full in a month or two, does it become an earnest money agreement? What is, after all, the real difference between a land sales contract and an earnest money agreement?

In both contracts the buyer promises to pay for the property at some later date. There is no provision of contract law which states a minimum or maximum term for either contract. And in both contracts, the seller promises to give the buyer a deed when the buyer finishes paying for the property.

The fact that the $30,000 in our example above is called "earnest money" in one contract, and "down payment" in the other, is not really a difference. In either case, if the buyer defaults, the seller can declare a forfeiture and retain the $30,000.

Perhaps the issue of possession would clarify the matter. A land sales contract in Washington grants the buyer possession during the term of the contract, but it doesn't have to if the parties agree otherwise. Looking at a typical earnest money agreement, the buyer does not get possession. However, it certainly is possible (although dangerous real estate practice) for the buyer to move in before closing. Therefore, in the land sales contract, the buyer usually gets possession, but might not; in the earnest money agreement, the buyer usually does not get possession, but frequently does. In other words, which party is in possession does not prove conclusively that the contract is a land sales contract or that it is an earnest money agreement.

Let us look then at the responsibilities of the parties. If the agreement is a land sales contract, then the buyer pays the taxes, maintains insurance, and is generally responsible for the property. Under an earnest money agreement, these matters fall to the seller. Unfortunately, that is not necessarily always true. Again, it depends on the language of the contract. It is possible, although not common, for the buyer in a land sales contract not to be responsible for taxes, insurance or to agree to accept responsibility. And, under the **Uniform Vendor and Purchaser Risk Act**, if the buyer has taken possession, even if the possession is granted by an earnest money agreement, then the buyer is legally responsible for the property. Again, we fail to find a clear distinction between the two contracts.

Perhaps the difference is in recording. A land sales contract is almost always recorded, whereas an earnest money agreement is not generally recorded. While this is true, there are exceptions. Many times parties will enter into a land sales contract and not record it. And an earnest money contract certainly can be recorded if the parties desire. Once again, we fail to find a concrete difference.

There is, however, perhaps one significant difference between the earnest money agreement and a land sales contract. Although not necessarily required, it would be an unusual land sales contract that did not provide for foreclosure as a remedy for default by the buyer. Similarly, it would be a strange earnest money contract if this remedy were included. Strange enough, that perhaps we should call such an earnest money agreement a land sales contract instead.

Now that we have seen the similarity between the earnest money agreement and the land sales contract, it should come as no surprise to learn that the buyer's interest under an earnest money agreement is called **equitable title** – the same term used for the buyer's interest in a land sales contract.

License law obligations

The license law and administrative rules create certain additional requirements for earnest money agreements. Note that failing to adhere to these requirements may not invalidate the agreement, but would result in disciplinary action by the Department of Licensing.

Copies – As with practically all contracts the agent enters into with the public, the agent must give a copy of an earnest money agreement to the party signing it. This means that the agent must give a copy of the offer to the buyer at the time the buyer makes the offer. Then the agent must leave a copy with the seller after presenting the offer. And finally, if the seller accepted the offer, the agent must deliver a copy of it with the seller's signature on it to the buyer. Of course, the agent must keep a copy as well, so the agent usually reserves the original for the office copy.

The license law and the administrative rules do not require that these copies be "carbon copies" or "originally signed" – photocopies are perfectly acceptable. However, most agents find that stopping to make photocopies of the document at each stage in the negotiations is inconvenient. Therefore, most standard form earnest money agreements are prepared as snap-out carbon forms.

Many times the preprinted earnest money form does not contain sufficient space for all the information necessary. For example, what would you do if the earnest money form contains three blank lines for the legal description, but the property is described by a metes and bounds description which is two-thirds of a page long? The simple solution is to use any of several **addendum** or **exhibit** forms which are commercially available. Like the earnest money agreements, these are usually preprinted in snap-out carbon format, and in fact, the copies are typically color-coded to match the colors of the various copies of the earnest money agreement.

A special note should be made of the modern practice of transmitting documents by facsimile machine. The authenticity of a document transmitted by facsimile is still subject to legal challenge. Therefore, if it is important to be able to prove that a signature on a facsimile is really the signature of the party who signed it, then an acknowledgment or attestation to the signature by a third party is in order. Although this is probably not called for in the ordinary course of negotiating, when the negotiations are finally complete, the agent should be sure that there exists at least one copy of the final agreement, originally signed by each of the parties.

The administrative rules also require the agent to tender to the offeree each offer or counteroffer. In addition, the agent should maintain a written record of the date and time of the presentation. Most popular earnest money forms in use today have a place for the date and time. A good practice is to maintain a record of the date and time of the offer as well. For example, most earnest money agreements provide that the buyer agrees to leave the offer open "for _____ days." How would you be able to prove when this time period was over, if you had no record of the date and time the offer was made? This becomes especially crucial in a market where multiple offers are likely to be received. And, as noted above, if the offer is accepted, the agent must deliver a copy of the accepted offer to the offeror.

Note that the administrative rule requires that the form in which the earnest money is received be stated on the form, i.e., check, draft, note, etc., unless it is cash. As a practical matter, most earnest money forms simply have blanks for all common forms, including cash, so the agent ends up disclosing the form in which the earnest money was taken even if it is cash. The reason for this rule is that the agent must make full disclosure to his or her principal, and is liable for any damages resulting from failure to disclose a material fact such as the form in which the earnest money was received. For example, if the agent receives a note as earnest money, and fails to disclose to the principal that the earnest money is a note, the agent could be held liable to the seller for the amount of the earnest money if the note later cannot be collected.

Of course, the license law and administrative rules also contain provisions regarding the handling of the actual earnest money deposit (funds). All funds must be deposited either to a trust account maintained by the broker or designated broker, unless the terms of the earnest money agreement dictate otherwise. Typical earnest money forms contain a special section covering this matter.

Of special importance is the right of the buyer to a refund of the earnest money when the buyer is entitled to it. There is no grace period, although, if the buyer gave a check for earnest money which has been deposited, the broker is entitled to wait until it has cleared before refunding the money. There may also be other legitimate delays. For example, today it is common practice to obtain releases from all the parties before refunding the earnest money.

Because the buyer might have to wait to get a refund of the earnest money the rules permit a broker to hold an earnest money check without depositing it until the seller accepts the buyer's offer or some other specific event occurs, as long as the parties direct the broker to do so in the agreement. And if the seller does not accept the offer, the agent is allowed to return the buyer's check directly without having to deposit it first. In cases where the broker gives the buyer's check back to the buyer it would be a good practice for the broker to obtain a receipt from the buyer for the returned check. A simple but effective way to do this would be to make a photocopy of the check and have the buyer just write on the photocopy "received [date]" and sign it. Keep the copy in the transaction file and you will have a clear record of what happened to the earnest money check.

To whom does the earnest money belong? Clearly, the earnest money does not belong to the licensee. This is, after all, why it must normally be placed in a trust account. The earnest money belongs to the buyer until such time as the buyer's offer has been accepted and communicated – that is, until there is a binding contract between the buyer and seller. At that time, it becomes the property of the seller. Of course, regardless of which party it technically belongs to at any given moment, the other party always has a contingent interest in the funds. Since it does not ever belong to the broker, the broker holds it "in trust" for the parties.

If a broker places clients' funds in a personal or business account, it is called ***commingling***. To guard against the possibility of this happening by mistake, it is a good practice to ask the clients to make the check payable to the broker or firm, adding the words "Trust Account," as in "pay to the order of ABC Realty, Inc., Trust Account." Not only does this practice help avoid errors, but writing the phrase "Trust Account" on the check puts the buyer more at ease and is a good sales practice.

Contingencies

Some ***contingencies*** are so common that they occur in almost all earnest money agreements. An example is to make the offer subject to the buyer obtaining a certain loan. Another contingency (which agents prefer to avoid) is to make the contract subject to the prior sale of another property. And apartment properties are frequently sold "subject to satisfactory interior inspection" as a contingency, in order to avoid having to give notice to tenants before showing the property.

Agents also sometimes use contingencies to avoid a potential misrepresentation. When the agent is not sure about the condition of the property or some other matter which must be disclosed, rather than risk being guilty of negligent misrepresentation, the agent just makes the buyer's offer subject to inspection, verification, or whatever is required to ascertain the truth. And, of course, contingencies are commonly used to obtain approvals of others, such as where the offer is made subject to the approval of a spouse, attorney, accountant, and so on. (For further discussion of contingencies, see Chapter 9.)

Typical provisions of earnest money agreements

We should begin our discussion with the question of what may be suitable for earnest money. As a principle of contract law, anything the parties find to be of value is acceptable as earnest money. Remember that the earnest money is only part of the

NOTES

consideration – the stated full price of the property is the consideration that makes the contract enforceable. The most common types of earnest money are checks, notes and cash, and occasionally a draft. Less common, but still possible are chattels such as cars, jewelry and equipment, or even another parcel of real estate. Of course, tangible property creates an inherent difficulty as earnest money. If the buyer offered to give you a car as earnest money, what would you do with it? You certainly can't deposit it to your trust account. Most agents try to avoid accepting tangible personal property. The usual form is a check or note. Drafts and cash are used less frequently.

> *Note: You may find it helpful to refer to an actual earnest money agreement, such as the one at the end of this chapter. Or you can ask your instructor what forms are available and commonly used in your area.*

There are special considerations if a note is to be used for earnest money. The note must be drafted in a manner that is enforceable on the buyer. A note is legally defined as "a promise to pay a sum certain on a date certain." This means that there must be an ultimate due date for the note to be valid. You can state any due date you and the buyer want, but there must be some kind of date stated. For example, you might say "due on closing, but not later than February 25, 200x, whichever occurs first." If you leave off the date then, if there is no closing, the buyer can argue that the note never became due.

How much earnest money should a broker try to obtain from the buyer? And which form of earnest money is the best sales practice? Does cash impress a seller more than a check? Or would a cashier's check be better? How about a note?

The first thing you consider when thinking about these questions is whether you are representing the seller (listing agent) or whether you are representing the buyer (a buyer's agent). If you are representing the seller, then clearly the more earnest money, the better. But is the converse true as well? If you are representing the buyer as a buyer's agent, should you try to see how little earnest money the buyer can get away with?

The fact is that the seller will likely be unimpressed with a small earnest money deposit. If the buyer wants the seller to accept the offer, then a decent amount of earnest money is essential. In fact, giving a large earnest money deposit may actually be in the buyer's best interests. Suppose the buyer offered a low price but sweetened the deal by giving a very large earnest money deposit. The buyer will be spending the earnest money at closing in a short time anyway. Why not use it to enhance the buyer's bargaining position? Although for different reasons, a large earnest money deposit is usually in the best interests of both parties.

In similar vein, a seller will usually be most impressed with earnest money in the form of a check rather than a note. While a note for earnest money is very common today, it should be avoided when possible.

Legal description – All earnest money agreement forms have a space for the legal description. On many earnest money forms the space for the legal description is followed by the phrase "commonly known as _____ ." Defining the property by its legal description, and then referencing that description to the street address allows the property to be described later just by its street address, rather than having to repeat the complete description.

Real estate agents should remember that a contract involving real property is legally unenforceable without an adequate description of the property. Worse, using an incorrect description can have disastrous consequences. Consider the case of a seller who already sold half of a farm and is now selling the remainder. What if the agent took a legal description from an old document which actually described the entire farm? The point is that it is not sufficient just to copy a description blindly. You must read the description to make sure it is the right property as well.

What is a good place to obtain an accurate description of the property? Probably the best place would be the owner's title insurance policy. But if this is not available, then the owner's deed is also an excellent source. Both these documents were carefully double-checked for accuracy before being prepared, so it would be unusual to find an error in either of them. Ditto that for a copy of the seller's loan documents (mortgage, trust deed, contract). An earnest money agreement should also reference the tax parcel number.

The above sources for the legal description are fine for the seller's agent, but what if you are writing up an offer for the buyer and you are a subagent or a buyer's agent? Then all you usually have available is what is in the multiple listing data. If the listing agent did not put a good description in the listing data then you may have a problem. In this case you should call the listing agent to see if there is a better description in their office. Or you can call a title insurance company's customer service department. Title insurance companies are happy to supply correct legal descriptions for real estate agents at no charge. They would rather you get it right from the beginning than have to straighten out a mess later when closing the transaction.

In the real world things are not always as easy as textbooks would have you believe. Occasions do arise where you need to write up an offer and you do not have a legal description or even the tax parcel number. As noted in Chapter 6, a street address will fail as a legal description. But if that is all you have, then you have no choice but to use it. Many agents have been taught to add the phrase "legal to follow" to the agreement. Washington courts have upheld the authority of an agent to add the legal description to an agreement after the client signs it, but the authority must be clearly stated. "Legal to follow" does not specifically authorize the agent to add the legal description.

Financial information – Every earnest money agreement must contain a section for financial information. This includes recitals of the down payment and how the balance will be paid. Typical matters which would also be covered here include loan fees, discount points, maximum interest rates the buyer will accept, and so on. And there must also be a contingency regarding the financing here. If you leave out the financing contingency then the buyer will be obligated to pay cash even if the buyer cannot obtain the loan. Since the buyer probably cannot do so, this would force the buyer to default. The major terms of a land sales contract or other purchase money financing instrument is also something that would be stated in the financial section.

The financial information can be very detailed, making it easy for an agent to forget a necessary provision. As a result most standard forms currently in use in Washington provide pre-printed addendums for financing. Most of these provisions are handled by checking boxes and filling in blanks.

Title evidence – All earnest money forms have a section discussing the evidence of title the buyer will be entitled to. It is not sufficient just to say that the buyer will receive title insurance. There is a problem to resolve here. Normally, the buyer would not want the escrow or closing agent to deliver the funds for the purchase price to the seller until the seller has delivered the deed and title insurance. The title insurance is the problem. A title insurance company cannot issue title insurance which insures that the buyer is in title, until the buyer is, indeed, in title. This will not happen until the seller's deed is recorded. Now we have a problem with the seller. The seller will not want the deed recorded until the seller has received the funds for the sales price. This brings the parties to an impasse.

We eliminate the problem in a simple way. Prior to closing, the title insurance company will issue a ***preliminary title report***, sometimes called just a ***title report***, or ***preliminary title commitment***, or even just "PTR." This document is not insurance.

Yet it does contain a statement of the condition of the seller's title. If the preliminary title report shows the title as the seller represented it to be, the buyer agrees to close the transaction and deliver the funds to the seller on the strength of the title report. The title insurance policy will be mailed to the buyer a few days after closing.

The earnest money agreement must also stipulate the title insurance company. If the Real Estate Settlement Procedures Act applies to the transaction, the choice of title insurance company is the buyer's. To avoid misunderstandings all pre-printed forms specify that the seller will pay the premium for a standard form buyer's policy. In some forms there are options in the main form or a pre-printed addendum form where the party responsible for paying for the policy can be changed. Sometimes a buyer may want an extended coverage policy or an endorsement, which can also be specified by checking boxes or filling in blanks on most standard forms.

The condition of the title is a more complex discussion. Obviously, the seller cannot convey the title to the buyer free and clear of governmental restrictions such as zoning, building restrictions and the like. And it was not uncommon in the early days for a federal patent to exclude the mineral rights, so many property owners in Washington have never owned the mineral rights. Therefore, the buyer must accept these restrictions on the title. In addition, most forms provide for the buyer to accept the title subject to easements (usually stated as "beneficial easements" only). There is a legal term for a title which is free and clear except for these encumbrances. We call such a title a ***marketable title*** or sometimes ***insurable title***.

Inclusions and exclusions – The earnest money contract must also deal with personal property and fixtures which the seller is including with the real estate. Usually there is a list of such items that is already in the printed form. It also contains a space to add any items the seller agrees to include but which are not already contained in the printed form. And there is also a space for items of real property which the seller will be allowed to remove. Personal property which the seller will leave behind are referred to as ***inclusions***. Items of real property which the seller will remove are called ***exclusions***.

Dates – All real estate transactions have three dates that must be specified in the earnest money agreement. They are the closing date, the prorate date and the possession date. The ***closing date*** is the day the escrow or closing agent records the documents and disburses the funds. Some agents find the term "closing date" to be unclear. It is not uncommon for the parties to sign the papers on different dates, and this can easily give rise to an argument as to when the closing actually happened. As a result, most forms today define closing date to mean the date the documents are recorded and the seller can pick up the check for the sales proceeds.

The ***prorate date*** is the date as of which the expenses of the property are apportioned between the buyer and the seller. For example, as of the prorate date forward the buyer will be responsible for the taxes, and prior to the prorate date the taxes are the seller's responsibility. Taxes, interest on loans assumed, occasionally rent, sometimes fire insurance premiums and utility charges are the types of expenses which are commonly prorated. The prorate date is normally defined to be either the closing date or the possession date (see below), although it could be defined to be any date the parties agree to. Calculating prorates is covered in Chapter 23.

Washington law allows some utility providers a lien against the property for unpaid utility charges. As a result Chapter 60.80 RCW requires the seller to furnish the closing agent with the names of utility providers and account numbers for the property. The parties can request that the closing agent handle payment of the utility charges, or they can waive the requirement. Whether the closing agent is to handle utility charges must be provided for in the earnest money agreement.

The term ***possession date*** is self-explanatory. It is common practice among real estate agents to grant the buyer possession on closing, or a few days thereafter. If the seller is allowed to retain possession for a significantly longer time after closing, the buyer will likely start thinking about charging the seller rent. Because no one can tell for sure exactly when a transaction will close, it is also common practice to define the possession date in terms of the closing date, e.g., "possession to be delivered five days after recording of deed." Setting a fixed date for possession date is a dangerous practice.

Notice that all three dates could be the same date, all three could be different dates, or any two of the three could be the same with the third one different. And any can be either before or after any of the others. For example, the possession date is normally on or after closing, but it could be before closing as well (although a dangerous practice).

Computation of dates – Under Washington law when counting dates and grace periods the first day doesn't count. For example, if payments are due on the first of the month and there is a 15-day grace period, then payment through the close of business on the 16th of the month satisfies the requirement. However, most people are unaware of this feature of the law, so most earnest money forms express it in writing.

All standard form earnest money agreements also contain a ***time is of the essence*** clause. This phrase is poorly understood. It does not mean exactly what it appears to mean. For example, it does not require the parties to perform as fast as possible. But it does mean that the dates in the contract are not suggested dates. It also means that if either party fails to perform by any date set in the contract, neither party has to give notice to the other in order to declare a default.

Deadline for seller's acceptance – In some older earnest money forms, the form provided that the buyer would leave the offer open for a certain period of time, during which time the buyer could not revoke the offer. In most cases, however, the buyer could revoke the offer at any time, regardless of how long it said the offer had to remain open. Of course, the offer would automatically expire after the termination of the stated time period. In modern earnest money forms, the clause simply states that the offer will expire if not accepted within a stated time period. Regardless of the language, the buyer can usually withdraw the offer as long as it has not yet been accepted and notice of the acceptance delivered to the buyer. An exception would be an offer which required the seller to expend effort or money in determining whether to accept the offer or not. Once the seller begins the process, the buyer cannot revoke such an offer.

Although unusual, once in a while the buyer's offer will state that the buyer will leave it open for a stated period of time if the seller gives the buyer something in return, e.g., "offer to remain open for 30 days if the seller tenders $100 to the buyer." In this case, if the seller tenders the $100 to the buyer, then the buyer cannot withdraw the offer. This is because it is no longer an offer; it is a contract. The buyer has entered into a contract with the seller to leave an offer open and the seller has paid consideration for the right to accept the offer any time in the next 30 days. In effect, the offer is now an option to sell.

Agency disclosure – Chapter 18.86 RCW requires the agents in the transaction to disclose which party they represented in the transaction –

RCW 18.86.030

... (g) To disclose in writing to all parties to whom the licensee renders real estate brokerage services, before the party signs an offer in a real estate transaction handled by the licensee, whether the licensee represents the buyer, the seller, both parties, or neither party. The disclosure shall be set forth in a separate paragraph entitled "Agency Disclosure" in the agreement between the buyer and seller or in a separate writing entitled "Agency Disclosure."

Forms in common use today handle this by creating a simple statement with boxes the agent can check.

Inspections – Most buyers request an inspection today. The earnest money should stipulate the rights of the parties with respect to the inspection. For example, if the inspection report indicates a problem, does the buyer have the right to cancel the transaction? What if the seller agreed to repair the problem? Standard earnest money forms in use today typically come with optional addendum forms that the agent can use to clarify these and other questions relative to the inspection.

Assignment – Whether or not the parties can *assign* their rights under the contract must also be part of the agreement. Most forms do not restrict the seller's right to assign but the buyer is required to obtain the seller's permission or may not be allowed to assign at all. This is because, from the buyer's standpoint, it makes little difference if the seller assigns his or her rights. But it may make a great deal of difference to the seller if the buyer assigns to a new buyer. For example, if the seller agreed to carry a note and trust deed or land sales contract from the buyer, the seller would definitely want to approve any substitute buyers. Even if the buyer is paying cash, if the buyer needs to obtain a loan to do so, it's possible a new buyer would not be able to qualify. Exactly how the buyer is restricted varies. On some forms the buyer must always get the seller's permission to assign. On other forms it says the buyer cannot assign without the seller's permission if the seller is carrying financing for the buyer, but otherwise is free to assign.

Title – The manner in which the buyers are to take title also should to be stipulated in the earnest money agreement. When there is more than one buyer, the question of which concurrent tenancy they should use becomes a major issue. Concurrent tenancies are discussed in Chapter 3.

Foreign Investment in Real Property Tax Act – Under income tax laws a seller may be required to pay tax on capital gains. In the past foreigners would ignore U.S. tax laws when selling property in the U.S. As a result, Congress passed the ***Foreign Investment in Real Property Tax Act,*** which requires the closing agent to obtain the seller's certification that the seller is not a foreign person as defined in the law. If the seller is a foreign person, then the closing agent must withhold from the proceeds and remit the amount to the Internal Revenue Service. The earnest money agreement should contain a provision where the seller agrees to sign the certification or be subject to the withholding.

Disclosures – In residential transactions today the seller must give the buyer the residential real property transfer disclosure statement required by Chapter 64.06 RCW. In addition, the seller may be required to give the buyer a lead-based paint disclosure form. There may also be other disclosure forms required as well. Most earnest money agreements today reference these forms and some provide that the buyer receipts for a copy of the disclosure form.

Earnest money – Earnest money agreements always contain a section which stipulates what the agent is to do with the earnest money. By default, the earnest money is to be held by the selling broker unless the parties agree otherwise. In many transactions today the agents prefer to have the earnest money held by an escrow or other closing agent. All earnest money forms used today also contain check boxes or blanks where the agent can specify the form in which the earnest money is received.

Since the license law and administrative rules permit a broker to hold the earnest money undeposited if the agreement so stipulates, earnest money forms contain a provision stipulating exactly when or under what conditions the broker is to deposit the earnest money. For example, a form might stipulate that the broker is to hold a check for earnest money until the seller accepts the offer. Some forms even provide for the buyer not to tender the earnest money to the broker at all until the seller has accepted the offer.

The earnest money agreement should also discuss the requirement that the broker place earnest money of $10,000 or less into a pooled account and that the interest will go to the state treasurer. The broker cannot waive this requirement, but putting it in the earnest money agreement makes the buyer aware of it and eliminates questions. Of course, if the earnest money is over $10,000, the buyer can elect otherwise, and this must be clarified in the agreement as well.

Breach and remedies – Next come two related issues. What will happen if the buyer breaches the contract and what will happen if the seller breaches the contract? All forms provide that if the seller never accepted the buyer's offer, or even if the seller did accept the offer, if the seller is unable or unwilling to close the transaction, the buyer is entitled to a refund of the earnest money. Most forms, either explicitly, or by their silence, provide that the buyer may also take action against the seller for specific performance, or in the alternative, for damages caused by the seller's breach, assuming the seller did accept the buyer's offer. Some forms, however, distinguish as to the reason the seller breached the agreement. For example, a form might provide that if the seller is unable to close because of title problems that cannot be cleared, the buyer's sole remedy is refund of the earnest money, but if the seller's failure to close because the seller has a change of heart, the buyer may use other remedies.

If the buyer defaults the seller may declare a forfeiture of the earnest money as *liquidated damages*. Damages are referred to as liquidated when they are pre-agreed upon. A liquidated damages provision is typical of contracts such as the earnest money agreement, where the dollar amount of the damages would be difficult to determine. The seller's remedies must be stated on the form because of 64.04.005 RCW –

RCW 64.04.005

(1) (a) A provision in a written agreement for the purchase and sale of real estate which provides for the forfeiture of an earnest money deposit to the seller as the seller's sole and exclusive remedy if the purchaser fails, without legal excuse, to complete the purchase, is valid and enforceable, regardless of whether the seller incurs any actual damages, PROVIDED That:

(i) The total earnest money deposit to be forfeited does not exceed five percent of the purchase price; and

(ii) The agreement includes an express provision in substantially the following form: "In the event the purchaser fails, without legal excuse, to complete the purchase of the property, the earnest money deposit made by the purchaser shall be forfeited to the seller as the sole and exclusive remedy available to the seller for such failure."

(b) If the real estate which is the subject of the agreement is being purchased by the purchaser primarily for the purchaser's personal, family, or household purposes, then the agreement provision required by (a)(ii) of this subsection must be:

(i) In typeface no smaller than other text provisions of the agreement; and

(ii) Must be separately initialed or signed by the purchaser and seller.

(2) If an agreement for the purchase and sale of real estate does not satisfy the requirements of subsection (1) of this section, then the seller shall have all rights and remedies otherwise available at law or in equity as a result of the failure of the purchaser, without legal excuse, to complete the purchase.

Thus, whether (1) or (2) applies to the transaction must be specified in the form. All forms in use in Washington handle this with simple boxes the agent can check.

If (2) is the election of the parties, then the seller may declare the earnest money forfeit, may sue for damages or may sue the buyer for specific performance.

Counteroffers

In common real estate practice earnest money forms take a good deal of time to complete properly, so it is not unusual for an agent not to wish to take the time to draft an entire new contract each time an offer or *counteroffer* is made. After all, many sales involve numerous offers and counteroffers between the parties. As a result, preprinted counteroffer forms exist to assist the agent to keep things clear. These forms make reference to the original offer, have a large blank space to state the desired changes, and then stipulate that the offeree accepts all the other provisions of the original offer.

The requirements of the administrative rules regarding earnest money forms apply as well to counteroffers. That is, the broker must give a copy to the person making the counteroffer, leave a copy with the person to whom the counteroffer was made, and when a counteroffer is finally accepted and a completed contract has been made, give a copy with the accepting signature on it to the other party. Also, it is good practice for the agent to keep a record of the time the counteroffer was presented and the party's response to it.

Many times there are multiple offers on a property at the same time, especially in residential sales. Of course, the seller can accept only one offer. But many times the seller will desire to keep another buyer's offer as a backup in case the first one falls through. To do this the seller must usually make a counteroffer. The second buyer's original offer probably did not contemplate it being a backup contract. So when the seller accepts it and marks the acceptance as creating a *backup offer* the agent must then take this back to the second buyer for acceptance.

Although less common, sometimes a backup offer will be made when the backup buyer knows that there is already an existing contract of sale in progress. In this case the second buyer can make the offer as a backup offer to begin with, in which case the seller's acceptance is not a counteroffer. As with counteroffers, some providers of earnest money forms also make available specific forms for backup offers.

Options

Options are not often used by real estate agents because it is difficult to structure a commission when the buyer takes an option instead of buying the property outright. The amount of money paid for the option is not generally sufficient to cover a commission. And the seller would probably prefer to see the agent get paid only if the option is exercised. Furthermore, if the broker has a listing on a property, the broker does not want to tie it up with an option which will typically last longer than the expiration of the listing. If the option is not exercised, the broker will end up with neither a commission nor a listing.

Nevertheless, brokers occasionally use options, particularly when selling their own property. Options are also sometimes useful in commercial transactions, especially development land where the buyer (a developer) needs time to perform studies before making a firm commitment. The developer may need to investigate the condition of the soil, do marketing and feasibility studies, and check zoning and development costs. All of this can take months and cost a lot of money. The developer needs to be sure that the seller will not sell to anyone else while the developer is working on the project.

When a seller grants an option to a buyer, the seller is the **optionor** and the buyer is the **optionee**. The option must be supported by consideration. There must also be a stated time limit. Unless the instrument creating the option states otherwise, the presumption is that the optionee need not close the transaction within the time limit, but rather only has to agree to exercise the option.

While an option is most commonly granted by a property owner to a prospective buyer, it can be the reverse as well. That is, there is nothing wrong with a buyer giving the seller the right to sell the property to the buyer – an option to sell instead of an option to buy.

Whether it is an option to buy or an option to sell, the option must be signed by at least the optionor. This is similar to the rule for deeds and leases. Since it creates an equitable interest in real estate, it must be signed by the party who has the right to create such an interest. Also, the same as for deeds and most other documents, an option need not be recorded to be enforceable between the parties, although recording it would better protect the interests of the optionee, especially in the case of an option to buy.

A significant problem which the person drafting an option must address is the manner in which the optionee will close the transaction when the optionee elects to exercise the option. For example, suppose you grant an option to buy your property to someone for an option price of $350,000. The optionee notifies you within the stated time limit that the option will be exercised. Later you go to the closing, only to discover that the optionee bought the property with a loan which requires the seller to pay discount points and various other expenses. To avoid disagreements over such issues, the option should have stated the specific price and terms. In fact, the option should have been as detailed as a typical earnest money agreement would be.

An option is a unilateral contract. Sometimes this is called a **standing offer**. This makes sense when you think about how an option comes about. An option is created when one of the parties, for consideration, promises to leave an offer open for the other to act on it any time during the option period.

Note then, that since the option needs to be as detailed as an earnest money agreement, it is really the same as an earnest money agreement, except that the earnest money agreement is a bilateral contract and the option is unilateral. That is, in the earnest money agreement each party has made promises that the other can enforce, while in the option the optionee may elect not to perform.

Options, the same as most ordinary contracts, can be assigned unless the instrument says that it cannot. This creates an interesting potential for a creative real estate transaction. A buyer could take an option, and then assign the option to a new party for a profit. Real estate investment experts sometimes teach this as a technique for making quick profits in real estate. Of course, anyone can buy a property and quickly resell it for more. But using an assignable option avoids the expense of actually closing a transaction to buy a property. Moreover, while earnest money agreements usually state that the buyer cannot assign his or her rights without the permission of the seller, many sellers and their agents might not notice if the prohibition on assignment was left out of an option.

Lease-options

A **lease-option** is just what the term sounds like. It is a lease, as well as an option to buy – two contracts in one. The important issue is whether the lease and the option are tied together, or whether they are separate instruments.

This can be crucial. Suppose you grant a two-year lease-option on your property to a party you hope will buy the property. One year later, the optionee defaults on the lease and moves out. Six months thereafter, with six months yet remaining on the option, the optionee informs you that the option will be exercised. Did the default on the lease extinguish the option as well? Not unless there was some language in the agreement to stipulate that the option was dependent on the lease. Otherwise, the law might hold them to be separate agreements.

In a lease-option, the consideration for the option can be the lease (right to possession). Most lease-option agreements state the consideration in this way, rather that stating some additional dollar amount.

Lease-options are popular with buyers who are short on funds for a down payment or who are not sure if they really want to stay in the area. Buying a house and then selling it a very short time later can result in financial loss if the buyers haven't owned the house long enough for it to increase in market value sufficiently to cover the costs of selling. Lease-options can also be advantageous to sellers because they can usually get a top price for the property, plus it is easier to get high lease payments.

People looking for a property to lease-option frequently misunderstand what the owner is likely to agree to. It is not unusual for the potential lease-optionee to think that they get credit for the entire lease amount toward their down payment. From the owner's viewpoint this is unrealistic. The owner feels that the amount to be credited toward the down payment should be only that portion of each payment above what ordinary market rent would be for the property. After all, the owner has all the expenses of ownership which continue during the lease, and has an investment in the property which the owner feels entitled to a return on. Therefore, it is customary for the lease payments to be higher than market rent, with the extra amount being credited to the lease-optionee if the option is exercised. Sometimes a lease-option does not give the optionee credit for any part of the lease payments.

Rights of refusal

A ***right of refusal*** is created when an owner promises to offer the property to one person before selling it to anyone else. As such it does not necessarily state a price and terms, although it might. In many respects a right of refusal is similar to an option. One difference is that an option states the purchase price, where a right of refusal need not. The idea of a right of refusal is that the seller must notify the holder when an offer is received and allow the holder to match it. Another difference is that an option must state an expiration date, where a right of refusal can be indefinite.

Occasionally a seller may wish to give rights of refusal to different persons. In this case, the first person would receive a ***first right of refusal***, the second would have a ***second right of refusal***, and so on. The holder of the second right of refusal could exercise the right only if the holder of the first right of refusal decides not to buy, and so on for as many rights of refusal as exist.

Although usually they try to avoid doing so, real estate brokers sometimes create rights of refusal in real estate transactions. This frequently occurs when the buyer must sell another property in order to complete the purchase of the new property. It would be preferable if the buyer had adequate financial resources to buy the new property without having to sell the old one first, but there are occasions where this is not possible and the buyer has no choice but to make the offer subject to the sale of the old property.

An offer to buy subject to the sale of another property is not likely to be agreeable to the seller of the new property. After all, the seller of the new property has no control over the buyer's old property, so why would the seller be willing to take his or her property off the market while waiting for the buyer to sell the old property?

This is easier to understand with an example. Suppose a broker has a buyer who has a home now, but wishes to make an offer to buy a new home subject to the sale of the old home. The seller of the new home may, understandably, refuse this offer, since the seller does not want to have his or her property tied up. Nevertheless, while the seller of the new home may refuse the buyer's offer, the seller may grant this buyer a first right of refusal, assuming the buyer's offer is otherwise acceptable. The right of refusal allows the seller of the new property to keep it on the market and solicit additional buyers.

It is common to create such a right of refusal with the stipulation that if the seller finds another buyer, the seller will give the original buyer a certain amount of time in which to perform – 72 hours being a typical time period. In other words, when the seller finds another buyer, the seller gives the first buyer 72 hours to remove the contingency relating to the buyer's old home, or the seller will sell the property to the new buyer. Many agents refer to this as the **72-*hour contingency***. It is also commonly called the ***bump period***. However, it is legally a right of refusal, and the time period does not have to be 72 hours.

Note that the buyer does not have to close the transaction within the 72 hours in the above example. The only requirement is that the buyer agree to remove the contingency regarding the sale of the old property.

Creating the earnest money and right of refusal documentation when the buyer must sell another property first involves a great many details. For example, should the buyer give the seller notice when the buyer does finally obtain an offer? Should the seller have any say in whether the offer is acceptable and likely to close? There are so many things to consider that most agents use standard pre-printed forms to use as an addendum to a standard earnest money form.

Forms

Apply the knowledge gained in this chapter by reading through the sample earnest money forms on the following pages, reproduced with the kind permission of the Washington Association of REALTORS®.

🗝 KEY TERMS

The key to understanding any new field is the vocabulary used in that field. To maximize your comprehension of the material presented in this chapter, be sure you know the meaning and significance of the following terms. Remember that the majority of test questions primarily test knowledge of vocabulary.

Addendum	Contingency
Assign	Counteroffer
Backup offer	Deposit receipt and sales agreement
Binder	Earnest money
Bump period	Earnest money receipt
Closing date	Earnest money agreement
Commingling	Equitable title

Exclusions

Exhibit

First right of refusal

Foreign Investment in Real Property Tax Act

Hand money

Inclusions

Insurable title

Lease-option

Liquidated damages

Marketable title

Optionee

Optionor

Possession date

Preliminary title report (commitment)

Prorate date

Purchase contract and earnest money receipt

Right of refusal

Second right of refusal

72-hour contingency

Standing offer

Time is of the essence

Title report

Uniform Vendor and Purchaser Risk Act

RESIDENTIAL PURCHASE and SALE AGREEMENT
THIS CONTRACT CONTROLS THE TERMS OF THE SALE OF THE PROPERTY
(Please read carefully before signing)

No. _____

_____, Washington, _____, _____

AGENCY DISCLOSURE: At the signing of this Agreement, the Selling Agent (insert name of selling agent) _____ _____

_____ represented ❑ Buyer, ❑ Seller, ❑ Both

parties, ❑ Neither party and the Listing Agent (insert name of listing agent) _____

_____ represented ❑ Seller, ❑ Both Parties. Buyer and Seller both confirm that prior oral and/or written disclosure of agency was provided to each of them in this transaction. If Selling Agent and Listing Agent are different licensees affiliated with the same broker, then both parties consent to that broker acting as a dual agent. If Selling Agent and Listing Agent are the same person representing both parties, then both parties confirm their consent to that agent and his/her broker acting as dual agents. Both parties acknowledge receipt of a copy of the pamphlet entitled "The Law of Real Estate Agency."

1. PARTIES: This RESIDENTIAL PURCHASE and SALE AGREEMENT ("Agreement") is made between _____

_____ as "Buyer",
and _____ as "Seller". Buyer agrees to purchase Seller's property on the following terms and conditions.

2. PROPERTY: Common Address _____
City:_____ County:_____ State of Washington,
Zip:_____ (Tax Parcel Number) _____
Legal Description:_____

❑ If Legal Description is not attached at final acceptance of this Agreement, Buyer shall have three (3) business days after receiving the Legal Description to approve the Legal Description as accurately reflecting the Property which the parties intend to be the subject of this Agreement. Failure to give written disapproval shall be deemed to be approval.

3. PURCHASE PRICE/FINANCING: The Purchase Price is ($ _____), payable as follows:
❑ All cash at closing (not conditioned on buyer obtaining a loan).
❑ Proceeds of Buyer Financing (attach a Financing Addendum).
❑ Other (attach a Method of Payment Addendum).
Buyer Representation: Buyer represents that Buyer has sufficient funds available to close this sale in accordance with this Agreement, and is not relying on any contingent source of funds unless otherwise set forth in this Agreement.

4. EARNEST MONEY: The amount of Earnest Money is: ($ _____). Selling Agent acknowledges receipt of

Earnest Money from Buyer in the form of: ❑ a check for $_____, ❑ cash of $_____,

❑ note for $ _____, due as stated in the note (copy attached), and/or ❑ Other $ _____
in the form of:_____ . These funds shall be deposited into the selling broker's trust account or _____ to be credited to Buyer at closing. Selling Licensee shall deposit any check to be held by Selling Broker, or deliver any Earnest Money to be held by Closing Agent within three days of receipt or mutual acceptance, whichever occurs later. The parties instruct Closing Agent to : 1) provide written verification of receipt of the Earnest Money and notice of dishonor of any check to the parties and licensees at the addresses and/or fax numbers provided herein; and 2) commence an interpleader action in the Superior Court for the county in which the Property is located within 30 days of a party's demand for the Earnest Money unless the parties agree otherwise in writing.

5. ADDITIONAL CONTINGENCIES: This Agreement is contingent on:
❑ The sale of Buyer's property (attach Sale of Buyer's Property Contingency Addendum).
❑ Inspections (attach Inspection Contingency Addendum).
❑ Other:

6. CONVEYANCE OF TITLE: Conveyance of fee title shall be by ❑ statutory warranty deed ❑ other:_____
_____ (statutory warranty deed if not filled in).
Buyer and Seller understand that the form of the deed may affect significant legal rights as to which a real estate licensee is not licensed to give advice. If this Agreement provides for the sale and transfer of the vendee's interest under an existing real estate contract, Seller shall convey Seller's interest by an assignment of contract and deed sufficient in form to convey after acquired title.

7. CLOSING: Closing shall be within ten (10) days after satisfaction or waiver of all contingencies and "subject to's", but not earlier than _____ , nor later than _____ , the latest of which shall be the termination date of this Agreement. Closing shall mean the date on which all documents are recorded and the net sales proceeds are available for disbursement to Seller. Buyer and Seller shall deposit, when notified and without delay, in escrow with the closing agent all instruments, monies, and other documents reasonably required to complete the closing of the transaction in accordance with the terms of this Agreement.

8. POSSESSION: Buyer shall take physical possession of the Property (and all existing keys to locks and alarms, and any portable control devices for accessing the Property):
❑ on closing
❑ other (specify) _____
Seller shall maintain the property in its current condition until Buyer takes possession.

9. ESCROW/CLOSING COSTS: Closing shall occur at _____ , who shall act as the escrow/closing agent unless the parties agree in writing otherwise. Unless limited by law or modified by the terms of this Agreement, Buyer and Seller shall pay at closing all customary and usual closing costs and fees, including but not limited to the following: Seller shall pay the Seller's excise tax, the cost of the owner's standard form of title insurance, recording fees, and Seller's half share of escrow fees (unless Buyer obtains VA financing in which case Seller shall pay all escrow fees); Buyer shall pay all costs and fees associated with the financing, any other costs agreed to under the terms of this Agreement, and Buyer's half share of the escrow fees (unless prohibited by government regulation).

Buyer's Initials _____ _____   Seller's Initials _____ _____

Taxes for the current year, rents, interest, association or homeowner's fees, if any, shall be pro-rated as of the date of closing. Except as described in Paragraph 10(b) of this Agreement, all utility charges shall be paid and/or pro-rated outside escrow directly between Buyer and Seller.

10.SELLER'S DISCLOSURE AND REPRESENTATIONS: If Buyer has any questions regarding the following, Buyer should make Buyer's offer subject to relevant inspections and reports.

(a)**Utilities:** The Seller represents that the Property is served by the following utilities: ❑ private/community water system, ❑ private well, ❑ community well, ❑ private irrigation system, ❑ septic system, ❑ natural gas, ❑ telephone, ❑ cable TV, ❑ public water, ❑ electricity, ❑ sewer, ❑ other _____ .

(b)**Governmental Utilities:** Pursuant to RCW 60.80, Buyer and Seller ❑ do request ❑ do not request (If neither box is checked, then "do request" applies) the escrow/closing agent to administer the disbursement of closing funds necessary to satisfy unpaid utility charges affecting the Property. Seller represents that the Property is served by the following utilities operated by the state, county, city or other governmental agencies which have lien rights against the Property. The parties authorize the Listing Agent or the Selling Agent to insert, over their signatures, the name and addresses of the following utility providers:

Name of Provider	Address		Name of Provider	Address
❑ Sewer _____	_____	❑ Electricity	_____	_____
				_____
❑ Storm Water ____	_____	❑ Garbage	_____	_____
Drainage	_____			_____
❑ Water	_____	❑ Irrigation	_____	_____
	_____			
		❑ Special Districts	_____	
		(LID's and ULID's)		

Seller will pay for all utilities through the date of closing and keep all utilities/services presently connected until closing or occupancy by the Buyer, whichever is sooner, except: _____

Shares in light and/or water companies and associations, if any, ❑ will ❑ will not be included in the sale. If the Property is served by a septic system, Seller ❑ will ❑ will not have the septic tank pumped prior to closing. If the Property is served by a septic system, Seller ❑ will ❑ will not provide a septic system inspection report from the controlling regulatory authority, or a private inspector approved by the controlling regulatory authority. If the Property is served by an individual private well, Seller ❑ will ❑ will not provide a basic water test (bacteriological test) of well water, ❑ will ❑ will not provide a quantity test, and Seller ❑ will ❑ will not provide an additional water test (primary inorganic chemical test) of well water which meets State Department of Health Services standards. If Buyer wishes any additional type of water test, Buyer should make such request in an addendum attached to this Agreement.

(c)**Leased Fixtures:** The following fixtures presently are leased: ❑ furnace, ❑ gas conversion burner, ❑ hot water heater, ❑ soft water unit, ❑ security/fire alarm system, ❑ propane tanks, ❑ other _____ . Buyer ❑ does ❑ does not agree to assume such lease(s) at closing. If Buyer does not agree to assume such leases, or if Buyer cannot assume such leases because of the requirements of the lessor or a lender providing financing, then ❑ Buyer ❑ Seller shall purchase such fixtures and they shall be included in this sale.

(d)**Property Maintenance:** Seller will perform ordinary maintenance on the Property and yard as presently exists until closing or as otherwise agreed. Seller will remove all of Seller's personal property, trash, debris, and all articles not agreed to be left at closing.

(e)**Boundaries/Square Footage:** Seller makes no representations regarding the locations or length of the boundary lines, size of lot, or the square footage of the house and other improvements. Buyer has personally observed the property and has reached Buyer's own conclusions as to the adequacy and acceptability of the Property based upon such personal inspection.

(f) **Lead Based Paint:** If the Property includes a house built before 1978, then the addendum entitled "Disclosure of Information on Lead-Based Paint and Lead-Based Paint Hazards" must be attached to this Agreement.

11.SELLERS LEAD-BASED PAINT DISCLOSURE If Seller is required to provide Buyer a "Disclosure of Information on Lead-Based Paint and Lead-Based Paint Hazards", and has not done so prior to mutual execution of this Agreement, then Buyer shall have the unconditional right to terminate this Agreement for three days following Buyer's receipt of the Disclosure. In addition, Buyer shall have ten days following receipt of the Disclosure to conduct an inspection for lead-based paint hazards.

12.INCLUDED ITEMS: All fixtures and fittings that are attached to the Property are included, free of liens, in the purchase price including, plumbing and light fixtures and bulbs (except floor, standing, and swag lamps), attached television antenna, satellite dish and equipment, all attached floor coverings, trees, plants and shrubs in the yard, built-in appliances, shades, blinds, curtain rods, window treatments, bathroom fixtures, awnings, attached heating and cooling systems, attached irrigation equipment, screens, shutters storm windows, screen doors, fireplace inserts, attached fireplace screens, electric garage door openers, wall to wall carpeting, gas logs and lighters, and all oil or other fuel on hand at the time of possession and _____

except _____ .

13.TITLE:

(a)**Title Insurance to be Issued by:** _____ .
Title insurance provided at closing shall be ❑ Standard Title Insurance ❑ Extended Title Insurance. (If no box is checked, Standard Title Insurance shall be provided.) Seller will pay the cost of Standard Title Insurance. If Buyer requires Extended Title Insurance, Buyer agrees to pay all costs in excess of those charged for the standard form including, without limitation, increased premiums and survey costs. If a survey is required, Buyer shall order the survey within three (3) business days of receiving notice from the title company that a survey is required and Buyer shall pay the estimated cost of the survey prior to performance of any survey work or Buyer can waive requirement for an extended policy and accept standard title insurance.

(b)**Title Insurance Commitment:** Within five (5) days of mutual acceptance, Seller shall arrange for the ❑ Listing Agent or ❑ Closing Agent, at Seller's expense, to apply for a preliminary commitment ("Commitment") for an ALTA form Owner's policy of title insurance ("Policy") as described in subparagraph (a) above, with homeowner's additional protection and inflation protection endorsements, if available at no additional charge, to be issued by the above title company. Seller shall pay title insurance cancellation fees.

Buyer's Initials _____ _____   Seller's Initials _____ _____

(c) **Extended Title Insurance:** Buyer acknowledges that the coverage afforded by a standard form policy of title insurance provides limited or no coverage for loss by reason of conflicts in boundary lines, shortage in area, encroachments, or any other matters which an accurate survey would disclose. More extensive coverage through an extended policy of title insurance may be available for an additional charge and subject to additional requirements imposed by the title company including a survey.

(d) **Title Insurance Exceptions and Exclusions:** The title policy shall contain no exceptions to or exclusions from coverage other than those generally provided in the specified title policy form and those which are consistent with subparagraph (e) below. If title cannot be made so insurable by closing, and if Buyer does not elect to waive any exceptions to coverage which are not consistent with this subparagraph and subparagraph (e) below, this Agreement shall terminate at Buyer's option.

(e) **Condition of Title:** Unless otherwise specified in this Agreement, title to the Property at closing shall be free of all encumbrances and defects provided that presently recorded reservations, covenants, conditions and restrictions, easements and existing building or zoning regulations or restrictions, reserved oil and/or mining rights, and rights reserved in federal patents or state deeds which do not interfere with Buyer's intended use of the Property shall not be considered encumbrances or defects. Monetary obligations not assumed by Buyer shall be paid from Seller's funds at closing.

14. **ASSIGNMENT:** Buyer may not assign Buyer's interest in this Agreement without Seller's prior written consent.

15. **DEFAULT/TERMINATION:** If this Agreement is terminated for any reason, any costs authorized under this Agreement to be advanced from the earnest money deposit shall be deducted before the remaining earnest money is refunded to the Buyer or forfeited to Seller. If a dispute should arise regarding the disbursement of any earnest money, the party holding the earnest money may interplead the funds into court and that party shall recover all costs and attorney fees associated with the interpleader action from the earnest money before any other disbursements are made. Furthermore, if either Buyer or Seller defaults, the non-defaulting party may seek specific performance or damages, except that the Seller's remedy shall be limited as follows if the box below has been checked.

   ❑ In the event the Buyer fails, without legal excuse, to complete the purchase of the property, the earnest money deposit made by the Buyer shall be forfeited to the Seller as the sole and exclusive remedy available to the Seller for such failure. Furthermore, if the earnest money deposited exceeds five percent (5%) of the sale price, Seller may retain as liquidated damages and as Seller's sole remedy earnest money equaling only five percent (5%) of the purchase price; any additional earnest money shall be refunded to Buyer. If the earnest money is forfeited as liquidated damages, the money shall be divided fifty percent (50%) to Seller, twenty-five percent (25%) to the listing broker, and twenty-five percent (25%) to the selling broker provided, however, that the amount paid to the real estate brokers shall not exceed the agreed brokerage fee.

16. **ATTORNEYS FEES/COSTS AND MEDIATION:** If the Buyer, Seller, or any real estate licensee or broker involved in this transaction is involved in any dispute relating to this transaction, any prevailing party shall recover reasonable attorney's fees and costs (including those for appeals) which relate to the dispute. In the event of a dispute, it is recommended (but not required) that the parties engage in mediation in an effort to resolve the dispute without the need for a lawsuit. The Washington Association of REALTORS® does offer a mediation service. For information, call 1-800-562-6024.

17. **FIRPTA COMPLIANCE:** If Buyer does not intend to use the property as a principal residence, or if the purchase price exceeds $300,000.00, this sale may be subject to the withholding and reporting requirements of the Foreign Investment in Real Property Tax Act (FIRPTA), unless Seller furnishes to Buyer an affidavit of non-foreign status. Seller and Buyer agree to comply with FIRPTA, if applicable.

18. **CASUALTY/LOSS:** If, prior to closing, the Property or improvements on the Property are destroyed or materially damaged by fire or other casualty, Buyer may elect to terminate this Agreement, and the earnest money shall be refunded to Buyer.

19. **COMPUTATION OF TIME:** Unless specified otherwise herein, any periods of time referenced in this Agreement shall start on the day following the event commencing the period and shall expire at 9:00 p.m. (Pacific Time Zone) of the last calendar day of the specified time period, unless the last day is a Saturday, Sunday, or legal holiday as prescribed in RCW 1.16.050, in which event the specified period of time shall expire at 9:00 p.m. (Pacific Time Zone) on the next business day. Any specified period of three (3) days or less shall include business days only.

20. **PROFESSIONAL ADVICE:** Buyer and Seller each acknowledge that it is advisable to have the terms and conditions of this Agreement reviewed by independent legal counsel and/or a tax advisor, as the terms and conditions affect the parties' rights and may have tax implications. Each party is specifically aware that issues such as form of deed used for conveyance, agency representation, financing documents, liquidated damages, title insurance and seller representations are complicated and that the parties may require advice that a real estate licensee is not licensed to give and for which the parties should contact their own attorney or accountant. Furthermore, Buyer and Seller agree that: (a) they are not relying on any representations or advice by the real estate licensees involved in this transaction; and, (b) they have satisfied themselves as to the terms and conditions of this sale.

21. **GENERAL PROVISIONS:**

   (a) **Notices:** Unless otherwise specified in this Agreement, any notice required or given under the terms of this Agreement must be written. Receipt of any notice shall be defined as the earlier of: three (3) business days following the postmark date; or the date the notice is actually received by the party or at the office of the Listing Agent for Seller and Selling Agent for Buyer regardless of the agency relationships involved. For the purposes of this Agreement, receipt by the appropriate agent (as set forth above) of a copy of a Real Property Transfer Disclosure Statement, Condominium Public Offering Statement and Condominium Resale Certificate or any other documents related thereto, as applicable, shall constitute receipt by the party. Seller must keep the Listing Agent advised of the Seller's whereabouts, and Buyer must keep the Selling Agent advised of Buyer's whereabouts. The Listing Agent's responsibility to the Seller and the Selling Agent's responsibility to the Buyer for delivery of notices is limited to calling the party and if the party is not available by phone, mailing the notice to the party's last known address.

   (b) **Faxes and Counterparts:** Facsimile transmission of any signed original document, and retransmission of any signed facsimile transmission shall be the same as delivery of an original. At the request of either party, or the closing agent, the parties will confirm facsimile transmitted signatures by signing an original document. This Agreement may be signed in counterparts.

   (c) **Integration:** There are no verbal agreements or understandings which modify this Agreement. This Agreement constitutes the full understanding between Buyer and Seller.

   (d) **Time is of the Essence:** Time is of the essence as to all terms and conditions of this Agreement.

   (e) **Home Protection Plan:** Buyer and Seller have been informed that home protection plans may be available. These plans may provide additional protection and benefit to Seller or Buyer. Cost of coverage may vary.

   (f) **Backup Offers:** Buyer is aware that during the term of this Agreement, Seller may continue to market the Property and solicit and accept backup offers.

Buyer's Initials _____ _____   Seller's Initials _____ _____

(g)**Venue/Applicable Law:** This Agreement shall be interpreted and construed according to the laws of the state of Washington; venue shall be in the county in which the Property is located.

(h)**Survival:** All terms of this Agreement, which are not satisfied or waived prior to closing, shall survive closing. These terms shall include, but not be limited to, representations and warranties, attorney's fees and costs, disclaimers, repairs, rents and utilities, etc.

22.**ADDITIONAL TERMS AND CONDITIONS:** _____

23.**ADDENDA/ATTACHMENTS:** At the time of Buyer's offer, the following addenda/attachments are part of this Agreement: _____

Buyer and Seller may only amend this Agreement by mutual written consent.

24.**AGREEMENT TO PURCHASE:** Buyer offers to purchase the Property on the above terms and conditions. Buyer hereby acknowledges receipt of a copy of this Agreement. Seller shall have until _____ ☐ a.m./ ☐ p.m., _____, _____ to accept this offer unless sooner withdrawn by delivering a signed copy to Buyer or Selling Agent's office. Acceptance shall not be effective until a signed copy hereof is actually received by Buyer or at the office of the Selling Agent.

_____ _____ _____
Buyer's Signature   Date   Selling Broker (Name)

_____ _____ _____ _____
Buyer's Signature   Date   Selling Agent's (Name)   Date

_____   _____
Buyer's Phone (work)/(home)   Selling Agent's Phone (work)/(home)

                                     _____
                                     Selling Agent's FAX Number

_____   _____
Buyer's Address   (City, State, Zip)

25.**SELLER'S ACCEPTANCE:** Subject to Seller's counteroffer or modifications, if any, Seller agrees to sell the Property on the terms and conditions specified herein. Upon Buyer's and Seller's mutual acceptance of terms, Seller confirms by signing this Purchase and Sale Agreement that the Listing Agent has performed Listing Agent's obligations to Seller by procuring a buyer, and has earned the compensation described in the listing agreement referenced by MLS number _____. Seller confirms that Broker(s) is entitled to collect Broker's compensation directly from the escrow agent at closing from proceeds of the sale. Seller acknowledges receipt of a copy of this Purchase and Sale Agreement, signed by both parties. ☐ Seller's Counteroffer or modifications are made a part of this Agreement. Buyer shall have until _____ ☐ a.m./ ☐ p.m., _____ , _____ , unless sooner withdrawn within which to accept same. Acceptance shall not be effective until a signed copy hereof is actually received by Seller or at the office of the Listing Agent.

_____ _____ _____
Seller's Signature   Date   Listing Broker (Name)

_____ _____ _____ _____
Seller's Signature   Date   Listing Agent's (Name)   Date

_____   _____
Seller's Phone (work)/(home)   Listing Agent's Phone (work)/(home)

                                     _____
                                     Listing Agent's FAX Number

_____   _____
Seller's Address   (City, State, Zip)

_____   _____
Mortgagee's Name   Seller's Loan Number

_____   _____
Mortgagee's Phone Number   Mortgagee's Address

There are _____ additional mortgages on this property.

26. **BUYER'S RECEIPT:** A true copy of the foregoing signed by Seller, is hereby received on: _____

_____   _____
Buyer   Buyer

Buyer's Initials _____ _____   Seller's Initials _____ _____

Purchase and Sale Agreement No. _____

Addendum No. _____

FINANCING ADDENDUM

This Financing Addendum ("Addendum") is entered into this _____ day of _____ , _____ between
_____ ("Buyer")
and _____ ("Seller")
and modifies and supplements that Purchase and Sale Agreement between the Buyer and the Seller dated _____
_____ ("Agreement").

The Buyer and The Seller Agree As Follows:

1. **Type Loan/Down Payment:** The agreement is contingent upon Buyer obtaining a purchase loan with the following terms: the Buyer shall pay ❑ $ _____ or ❑ % _____ down, including receipted earnest money and the balance of the sale price from a ❑ conventional ❑ FHA ❑ VA ❑ private loan for not less than $ _____ at an interest rate of not more than _____ percent (_____%) for a term of not less than _____ years (30 years if not filled in).

2. **Loan Application – Buyer's Duty To Act In Good Faith:** The Buyer shall make application for the loan within _____ days (3 days if not filled in) of mutual acceptance of this Addendum. The Buyer shall use best efforts and act in good faith to obtain financing in a timely manner under this contingency. Buyer shall provide a letter from lender within _____ days of mutual acceptance (7 days if not filled in) showing that lender has reviewed Buyer's credit and that Buyer's credit is sufficient to obtain the loan described in paragraph 1 above.

3. **Financing Deadline/Seller Termination Notice:** If within _____ days (30 days if not filled in) of mutual acceptance of this Addendum the Buyer has not given written notice that Buyer has waived this contingency, the Seller may elect to terminate the Agreement upon three (3) days notice to the Buyer. If the Buyer does not waive this contingency within three (3) days of Seller's notice, the Agreement shall terminate and the earnest money shall be returned to the Buyer.

4. **Inspections/Repairs:**
   A. Inspection May Be Required. The Seller shall permit access for any inspections required to process the Buyer's loan application, including, but not limited to general structural, hazardous waste, pest, heating, plumbing, roof, electrical, septic system and well water. The lender, as a result of such inspections, may require that the Property comply with the housing code and other governmental requirements of the city or county in which the Property is located.

   B. Inspection Cost. The cost of any inspections required by the lender, FHA or VA as a condition of loan approval shall be paid by the ❑ Buyer ❑ Seller, unless otherwise required by governmental regulations, not to exceed $ _____ .

   C. Work Orders. If the Buyer's loan is conditioned on Property repairs or pest control measures, the Seller agrees to perform such repairs or measures prior to closing and pay up to $ _____ . (If this blank is not filled in, the amount is zero.) If the cost of repairs is equal to or less than the stated amount, Seller may hire contractors, at the Seller's discretion, to complete the repairs. If the cost of repairs exceeds the stated amount, and the Buyer and the Seller fail to negotiate a mutually acceptable resolution within _____ days (7 days if not filled in) from the Buyer's receipt of work orders, the Agreement shall terminate, and the earnest money shall be returned to the Buyer. If necessary, the Closing Date shall be extended by a period necessary to allow completion of negotiation plus an additional _____ days (3 days if not filled in).

   D. Seller's Obligation to Repair. The Seller acknowledges that the Seller may be required to complete repairs imposed by the city or county housing code as a result of any inspection(s).

5. **Low Appraisal:**
   A. Seller's Option. If the lender's appraisal of the Property is less than the sale price, then Buyer must provide the Seller with written notice of the low appraisal within three (3) days of Buyer's receipt of notification of the low appraisal. The Seller shall have _____ days (10 days if not filled in) from receipt of Buyer's notice of the low appraisal to: 1) obtain at Seller's expense a reappraisal by the same appraiser or another appraiser acceptable to the lender in an amount not less than the sale price; or 2) consent in writing to reduce the sale price to equal the higher of the appraisal or reappraisal; or 3) refuse to lower the sale price to the appraised value.

   B. Buyer's Response. Upon the earlier of: 1) the Seller's written notice of an unacceptable reappraisal or refusal to accept a purchase price equal to the appraisal to the Buyer; or 2) the expiration of the Seller's time to obtain a new appraisal, the Buyer may elect, within _____ days (3 days if not filled in) to (i) terminate the Agreement upon notice to the Seller, and obtain a refund of the earnest money less the costs for appraisal fee, credit report, and cancellation fees, if any or (ii) pay the difference between the sale price and the highest appraisal in cash at closing.

Buyer's Initials _____ _____   Seller's Initials _____ _____

Purchase and Sale Agreement No. _____

Addendum No. _____

C. Buyer's Obligation/Closing Date. The Buyer shall be obligated to purchase at the reduced price unless this Agreement is conditioned upon FHA/VA financing in which case the applicable FHA/VA regulations shall control. The Closing Date shall be extended up to sixteen (16) days to allow for the foregoing notice periods plus an additional _____ days (3 days if not filled in) if the sale is not terminated.

OPTION:

☐ **6. FHA/VA Provisions:**

A. FHA/VA Loan Costs. If this sale is conditioned on the buyer obtaining a FHA or VA loan, the Seller agrees to pay such portion of buyer's loan costs as Buyer is prohibited from paying under applicable FHA/VA regulations together with a loan discount fee, not to exceed ☐ _____% of Buyer's loan amount (including the mortgage insurance premium) or ☐ $ _____ with an initial interest rate of _____% per annum.

B. FHA/VA - Appraisal Certificate. If this Agreement is conditioned on Buyer obtaining FHA or VA financing, the Buyer shall not be obligated to complete the purchase of the Property unless the Buyer is in receipt of a written statement issued by FHA or VA stating that the appraised value of the Property (excluding closing costs) is not less than the purchase price.

C. FHA/VA Low Appraisal. Notwithstanding any other provision of the Agreement, Buyer shall not be obligated to complete the purchase of the Property or to incur any penalty by forfeiture of earnest money deposit or otherwise unless Buyer has been given in accordance with HUD/FHA or VA requirements a written statement by the Federal Housing Commissioner, Department of Veterans Affairs, or a Direct Endorsement lender setting forth the appraised value of the Property of not less than the purchase price. The Buyer shall have the privilege and option of proceeding with consummation of the Agreement without regard to the amount of the appraised valuation. The appraised valuation is arrived at to determine the maximum mortgage that FHA or VA will insure and is not intended to warrant the value nor the condition of the Property. Buyer should satisfy himself/herself that the purchase price and condition of the Property are acceptable.

Note: This Addendum supersedes any conflicting terms in the Agreement, and all other terms of the Agreement which have not been modified or superseded by this Addendum are ratified and shall remain in full force and effect.

Buyer: **Seller:**

_____   _____

_____   _____

Date: _____   **Date:** _____

Prepared By:

_____

Chapter 22

Civil rights laws

P ROBABLY THE FASTEST WAY to lose a potential client or customer today
is to engage in discriminatory practices. Not only is it likely to be illegal
and subject an agent to potential financial loss, but it will also result in
loss of sales. Professional real estate agents realize that discrimination is counterproductive to sales and has no place in a real estate sales or management organization.

Actually, everyone discriminates continuously all day long. Each day we make continual choices about who our friends will be, where we will live, what foods we like to eat, what brand of car we will drive, and endless other choices. All of these discriminatory acts are, of course, perfectly legal. It is illegal discrimination that can get us into trouble.

Note, however, that even if a certain discriminatory act is legal, it may be socially unacceptable by modern standards in Washington. For example, except in a few local communities, it is legal to refuse to sell or rent to persons who are homosexuals. Yet, most of us would feel uncomfortable in a social setting where someone is making jokes about gay people. And we certainly wouldn't expect it from a real estate agent.

The fact is, when people attempt to belittle another group, it is usually an attempt to make themselves look better in comparison. Unfortunately, all they accomplish is to make themselves look foolish and uneducated.

There are thousands of laws in the United States covering the issue of discrimination. Of these, only a handful deal with real estate in Washington, so we will limit our discussion to just those few.

Civil Rights Act of 1866

The earliest discrimination law goes back to shortly after the Civil War – the ***Civil Rights Act of 1866***. This act states –

"... citizens of every race and color ... shall have the same right, in every State and Territory of the United States, as is enjoyed by white citizens thereof, to inherit, purchase, lease, sell, hold, and convey real and personal property ..." (42 U.S.C. Section 1982)

The act is based on the 13th Amendment to the U.S. Constitution, which prohibits slavery. Although the Act was largely unused for nearly a century after its enactment, in 1968 the U.S. Supreme Court reaffirmed the scope and the constitutionality of the act in the case of *Jones v. Mayer*, (392 U.S. 409, 1968). In this case it was claimed that the Civil Rights Act of 1866 was an unconstitutional restraint on the rights of a property owner. The Supreme Court disagreed, and ruled that this act "prohibits all racial discrimination, private as well as public, in the sale and rental of property." In a 1988 decision, the Court took this act yet one step further when it decided a case brought by Jewish students who had been discriminated against. The court declared that the terms "race and color" includes persons who were not thought of as "white" according to the way the terms were used by common persons in 1866.

While the Civil Rights Act of 1866 does offer redress to persons who are the victims of racial discrimination, race is its sole focus, not any of the other categories we normally think of today. And even with respect to race issues, it does not provide for any assistance from government agencies and the complainant must file the suit themselves directly.

Executive Order 11063

In 1962 President John Kennedy signed ***Executive Order 11063***, which became binding on all federal agencies. The order prohibited federal agencies from discriminating in housing related matters on the basis of race, color, creed or national origin. Executive Order 11063 has been amended over the years, but it remains in force today.

Executive Order 11063 applies if the property is residential, or vacant land for residential development, and is –

(i)   owned or operated by the federal government, or

(ii) provided in whole or in part with the aid of loans, advances, rents, or contributions hereafter agreed to be made by the federal government, or

(iii) provided in whole or in part by loans hereafter insured, guaranteed, or otherwise secured by the credit of the federal government, or

(iv) provided by the development or the redevelopment of real property purchased, leased, or otherwise obtained from a state or local public agency receiving federal financial assistance for slum clearance or urban renewal with respect to such real property under a loan or grant contract hereafter entered into ...

Civil Rights Act of 1964

Very little additional occurred in the way of legislation to prohibit discrimination in real estate transactions until after the great protest March on Washington in 1963. Although it did not immediately impact ordinary persons in most housing transactions, in 1964 Congress passed the *Civil Rights Act of 1964*. Title VI of this act prohibits discrimination in programs which receive federal assistance. In many respects the Civil Rights Act of 1964 echoes the provisions of Executive Order 11063.

Civil Rights Act of 1968

The *Civil Rights Act of 1968* went much further in prohibiting housing discrimination. Title VIII of this act, called the *Fair Housing Act* created the first national, comprehensive law banning discrimination in virtually any transaction involving housing. The preamble to the act states that "it is the policy of the United States to provide, within constitutional limitations, for fair housing throughout the United States."

The act covers discrimination in transactions involving housing and any vacant land offered for residential construction or use. Although it does not cover other real estate transactions, remember that race issues are covered by the Civil Rights Act of 1866. In addition, Washington state law would cover other types of transactions. Discrimination under the Fair Housing Act includes actions based on a protected category such as –

- Refusing to sell, rent, negotiate or deal with a person,
- Different terms or conditions,
- Advertising that a property is not available,
- Denying that property is available when, in fact, it is available,
- Advertising a preference or intent to discriminate,
- Blockbusting, defined as for profit, inducing owners to sell their property by implying that minorities are moving into the area,
- Redlining by lenders, defined as refusing to lend or creating different terms for loans in certain areas or for certain persons,
- Discrimination in services such as brokerage and management services, membership in multiple listing services, and so on.

• Coercion, intimidation, threats or interference with someone because of the person's enjoyment of their rights under the Act, or because the person assisted or encouraged another to assert their rights under the Act.

The Fair Housing Act prohibits discrimination based on race, color, religion, sex, national origin, familial status or that the person is mentally or physically handicapped. Each of these is referred to as a ***protected category***. Note that certain other laws include other protected categories which are not included here. For example, the Equal Credit Opportunity Act bars discrimination based on marital status and age, among others. However, age is not covered under federal housing discrimination laws.

Mental or physical handicap includes persons who have AIDS, or who are mentally handicapped as a result of drug or alcohol abuse. However, you do not have to sell or rent to persons who are still abusing these substances, nor do you have to sell or rent to persons who are a clear and present danger to themselves or others. It is also not illegal to discriminate against a person because the person has been convicted of illegal manufacture or distribution of drugs. And, of course, you are entitled to insist that the sale or rental agreement be binding. So if the person is not competent, you are entitled to insist that the contract be signed by a guardian or conservator with appropriate authority to sign.

If a handicapped person requires modifications to a rental property the landlord is not required to provide them. However, the handicapped person has the right to make alterations if the person agrees to pay for them and is willing to agree to restore the premises at the end of the tenancy.

Housing Amendments Act of 1988

The ***Housing Amendments Act of 1988*** (generally effective March 12, 1989), provided for new construction to meet certain requirements for the handicapped. New residential projects of four or more units, completed under building permits issued on or after January 13, 1990 must be wheelchair accessible for units which are adaptable to the handicapped. If the building has an elevator, all units must be adaptable, which means doors, faucets, switches and the like must be reachable and the walls must be reinforced for grab bars. If there is no elevator, then only units on the ground floor must be adaptable.

The term ***familial status*** refers to whether or not the individual has children. Recently added to the list of protected categories, this category ensures that a person will not be discriminated against solely because they have children. In other words, "all-adult" buildings are generally illegal. Familial status includes whether an individual is pregnant or is in the process of securing custody of a minor.

There are several exceptions to the familial status category. Obviously you can refuse to rent to someone who has too many children for the size of the apartment or house. Reasonable occupancy standards are legitimate exceptions. Second, if at least 80% of the properties or units are occupied by at least one person 55 years of age or older and the project was developed to meet the needs of seniors, children can be excluded. Children can also be excluded if all the units are intended for and occupied by persons 62 years of age or older. Properties developed under any government elderly assistance program are also exempt.

For all protected categories under the Fair Housing Act and the Fair Housing Amendments Act of 1988, an exemption exists for the sale, rental or leasing of single-family residences. An owner is exempt if –

• The owner does not employ the services of an agent,
• No discriminatory advertising is used,

- The owner owns three or fewer homes at one time, and
- The owner only sells one home per two-year period, unless the owner was the most recent occupant of the home.

An exemption also exists for the rental of certain owner occupied properties. This exemption is sometimes called the **Mrs. Murphy exemption**, or the **Mother Murphy exemption**. An owner is exempt from the Fair Housing Act in renting a room or a unit provided –

- The owner occupies one of the units,
- No discriminatory advertising is used, and
- The owner does not employ the services of a real estate agent.

Religious organizations are permitted to discriminate, or even refuse to sell or rent at all, in the sale or rental of dwellings owned by the organization. The only requirement is that membership in the organization is available to all regardless of race, color, national origin, sex, mental or physical handicap, or familial status.

Private clubs who own residential property which they hold for non-profit and non-commercial purposes may rent or sell the property exclusively to their members without violating the law.

Note that these exemptions avoid liability for compliance with the Fair Housing Act and the Fair Housing Amendments Act of 1988. But they do not exempt the owner from complying with the Civil Rights Act of 1866, nor do they exempt the owner from complying with Washington state laws. As we will see later, Washington state laws have very limited exemptions.

In times past it was common practice in many communities to encourage or discourage persons to buy or rent in certain areas based on the person's race, color, religion, or national origin. Doing so today on the basis of any of the protected categories is called **steering** and is prohibited by the Fair Housing Act.

Steering can be very subtle. For example, if a real estate agent leads an owner to believe that the agent will aid and abet the owner in controlling the character of the neighborhood, this is steering. If a real estate broker assigns clients to the agents in the office based on the fact that the client and the agent are of the same protected category, this is also steering.

Occasionally, a client will ask an agent about the race, color, religion, or national origin of the other party to a transaction. For example, suppose you have shown a house to a prospective buyer. The buyer makes an offer and now you are presenting the offer to the seller. The seller asks you what nationality (or race, color, religion, etc.) the buyer is. If you answer the seller, you may be an accomplice to steering, or you may be guilty of blockbusting (see below).

Blockbusting is the illegal practice of inducing **panic selling** for the profit of the perpetrator. There are many ways to do this. Suppose you started a rumor in a neighborhood that minorities were moving into the area. Then you went out and listed properties for sale. You are guilty of blockbusting. Or you could start the rumor, buy the houses at distress prices, then later resell them at a profit. This is another example of blockbusting. Note that you cannot tell an owner that minorities are moving into an area even if it is true. To do so would make it appear that you were attempting to engage in blockbusting.

What if you bought a house in a white area and then rented it to a minority? Is this blockbusting? No, this is **integration**, and the law is designed to encourage it. It would not be blockbusting because you did not attempt to create panic selling and profit thereby.

In 1972 Congress amended the Fair Housing Act and added an additional requirement for real estate agents and developers. The amendment requires brokers, developers

NOTES

and mortgage lenders to display a poster called the Equal Housing Opportunity Poster. It must be displayed in real estate offices, model homes, lending offices and any other locations where these persons conduct business. The poster also displays prominently the Equal Housing Opportunity Logo. The logo must also be included in real estate advertising sections of newspapers.

The Equal Housing Opportunity Logo

EQUAL HOUSING
OPPORTUNITY

A person who feels he or she has been discriminated against (called a ***complainant***) in violation of the Fair Housing Act may file a complaint with the Office of Equal Opportunity at the Department of Housing and Urban Development (HUD). The complaint must be filed within 180 days of the discriminatory act.

Upon receipt of the complaint, HUD will investigate it. To lower the work load, if the complaint is also a violation of a state or local law, the normal process is to refer the complaint to the state or local agency. If the state or local agency does not take appropriate action, HUD will ask to have jurisdiction returned to HUD. When HUD has jurisdiction over a complaint, HUD usually starts by attempting to obtain a confidential agreement to comply from the other party (called the ***respondent***).

As an alternative, a complainant may file suit directly in U.S. District Court. However, the court will generally turn the matter over to the Office of Equal Opportunity for attempt at conciliation before proceeding with the case.

There are several penalties a wrongdoer may suffer for violation of the Fair Housing Act. First, the court may enter an injunction against completing the sale or rental of the property to another if the owner is found to have refused to sell or rent to the complainant in violation of the law. The court may also simply order compliance, and find the wrongdoer guilty of contempt if he or she continues to refuse to comply.

In addition, monetary penalties are possible, including the complainant's actual damages (including the cost of alternative housing), attorney's fees, and the possibility of punitive damages up to $10,000.

An additional penalty for a real estate agent could be loss of the agent's real estate license. The license law provides for disciplinary action for a violation of any state or federal discrimination law. In addition, the administrative rules create additional prohibited discriminatory acts (see Washington civil rights laws later).

Real estate agents should be aware that Congress makes federal funds available for testing compliance. For example, a person speaking with the accent of a minority might call a real estate office to ask if a property is available. If the tester is told that it is no longer available, a short time later someone else will call using an ordinary accent. If this person is told the property is available further investigations will ensue.

While the Fair Housing Act is designed to punish those who would deny equal opportunity in housing, at the same time, there are very few such individuals. Except for the new familial status issue incidents of fair housing complaints are relatively infrequent in Washington today. Yet many agents are concerned about dealing with minorities for fear that if they say the wrong thing, they may end up having to defend themselves from a fair housing complaint. But if you perceive the language and the intent of the law, there is no need to fear minorities if you simply treat them the same as anyone else.

U.S. Department of Housing and Urban Development

EQUAL HOUSING OPPORTUNITY

We Do Business in Accordance With the Federal Fair Housing Law

(The Fair Housing Amendments Act of 1988

It is Illegal to Discriminate Against Any Person Because of Race, Color, Religion, Sex, Handicap, Familial Status, or National Origin

- ■ In the sale or rental of housing or residential lots

- ■ In advertising the sale or rental of housing

- ■ In the financing of housing

- ■ In the provision of real estate brokerage services

- ■ In the appraisal of housing

- ■ Blockbusting is also illegal

Anyone who feels he or she has been discriminated against may file a complaint of housing discrimination.
　1-800-669-9277 (Toll-free)
　1-800-927-9275 (TDD)

**U.S. Department of Housing and Urban Development
Assistant Secretary for Fair Housing and Equal Opportunity
Washington, D.C. 20410**

Previous editions are obsolete

form HUD-928.1 (8/93)

Real estate brokers and property mangers are required by federal law to display the Equal Housing Opportunity poster in their offices. To obtain a free copy contact the Northwest/Alaska Regional Office at 800-877-0246.

Home Mortgage Disclosure Act

The Fair Housing Act prohibits *redlining*. This is the practice where lenders refuse to lend in certain areas or to certain persons on the basis of their race, color, religion, national origin, sex, mental or physical handicap or familial status. To assist in enforcing this provision of the Act, in 1975 Congress passed the *Home Mortgage Disclosure Act*. To implement the purposes of the Act the Federal Reserve Bank Board of Governors issued Federal Reserve Regulation C. The Act and the regulation require lenders to file with federal agencies an annual report of all loans made during the year. The report must break the loans down by area, so that cases of redlining will be easily visible. In 1977 Congress passed the *Community Reinvestment Act*, which requires further reporting.

During the enactment of the Home Mortgage Disclosure Act and subsequent legislation, lending institutions lobbied successfully for a provision that the data supplied would be kept confidential and not available to the public. Lenders also successfully argued that it was not a violation or discriminatory practice to refuse to make loans under certain dollar amounts, due to the fact that such loans are not profitable. Real estate agents quickly learned that this practice caused disadvantaged areas of urban areas to be the object of de facto discrimination because property values were too low in these areas to substantiate the minimum loan amount requirements of local lenders.

As a result, in 1993 the Federal Reserve Bank Board of Governors revised Regulation C to make reporting data available to the public. Lending institutions were immediately hit with adverse publicity when the press reported their practices. As a result most lenders have revised their loan policies. Many lenders have also taken steps to encourage lending in disadvantaged areas.

It should also be noted that the *Equal Credit Opportunity Act* prohibits discrimination in lending. The Equal Credit Opportunity Act is discussed in detail in Chapter 14.

Affirmative action

Beginning in 1972, the Department of Housing and Urban Development began a program of *affirmative marketing* by developing regulations designed to attract minorities into the housing market. The regulations require developers of federally assisted or insured housing to –

- Establish and maintain an equal opportunity hiring policy,
- Display the HUD logo in all printed material,
- Post the HUD Equal Opportunity Statements at all project sites,
- Submit to HUD for approval a marketing plan outlining the target minority group and how the developer plans to attract the members of the group, and
- Submit copies of advertising and media exposure for approval.

In addition, HUD will review the developer's sales staff for their experience and ability to market to the target group.

Real estate agents in Washington have subscribed to affirmative marketing plans entered into by their local real estate associations. Membership in the local association involves agreement to abide by the plan.

Americans with Disabilities Act

The *Americans with Disabilities Act* (ADA) is a federal law enacted in 1990. It is divided into five titles, each of which addresses different aspects of discrimination with respect to the estimated 43 million Americans with disabilities. Under the Act a ***disability*** is any physical or mental impairment that substantially limits the individual's life activities. The titles are –

Title I – Hiring and employing persons with disabilities

Title II – State and local activities, plus public access issues in public and private transportation

Title III – Access in places of public accommodation, including private businesses

Title IV – Telecommunication access

Title V – Miscellaneous provisions

Title III of the Act is the portion with the most impact on real estate agents. Title III affects access to facilities in a real estate office, such as rest rooms, doorways and other such matters. It also affects access in commercial rental property. Existing properties must be modified if the modification is "readily achievable." Not only does this include the offices of a real estate brokerage firm, it also includes an on-site office for property management, including a residential management office. Factors which are taken into account when determining if a modification is readily achievable include –

- The nature and cost of the modification,
- Financial resources available,
- The effect on expenses and resources, and
- Safety requirements.

New construction, of course, must meet higher standards. In most cases a structure built after 1990 can be assumed to comply. However, agents listing or selling non-residential properties built before 1990 should be sure the buyer is aware of the possibility that modifications may be required. Even if the structure is currently being used for commercial purposes, the buyer's business may impose additional modification requirements.

Washington civil rights laws

In addition to the preceding federal laws, the Washington legislature has enacted several statutes prohibiting discrimination in real estate transactions. The purpose is summarized in 49.60.010 RCW –

"The legislature hereby finds and declares that practices of discrimination against any of its inhabitants because of race, creed, color, national origin, families with children, sex, marital status, age, or the presence of any sensory, mental, or physical disability or the use of a trained dog guide or service animal by a disabled person are a matter of state concern, that such discrimination threatens not only the rights and proper privileges of its inhabitants but menaces the institutions and foundation of a free democratic state."

The bulk of Washington laws prohibiting discrimination are contained in Chapter 49.60 RCW. The original versions of these laws were enacted in 1949, many years before most federal laws. Washington laws prohibit discrimination in practically any real estate transaction, including the providing of brokerage services. The protected categories are sex, marital status, race, creed, color, national origin, families with children status, the presence of any sensory, mental or physical disability, or the use of any trained dog guide or service animal by a disabled person. The terms "mental or physical handicap" are given the same definitions as under federal laws (see previous discussion).

The law also makes it unlawful to coerce, intimidate, threaten, or interfere with anyone because the person exercised their rights, or to do so to someone who assisted another in exercising their rights. In addition, discriminatory provisions based on the above protected categories in deeds and other real estate contracts are void and unenforceable.

It is not uncommon for developers to create restrictive covenants when creating a subdivision. These covenants deal with issues such as setback requirements, height of fences, placement of utilities and so on. The covenants are typically recorded as an encumbrance on the title, and then each deed is made subject to the covenants.

In times past it was not uncommon for these covenants to restrict occupancy or sale of the property to minorities. Washington law provides that such covenants are void and unenforceable today (49.60.224 RCW). However, you should note that only the covenants which constitute illegal discrimination are void; the rest of the covenants normally remain in full force and effect.

Any person who believes he or she has been discriminated against illegally under Washington state law may file a complaint with the Washington State Human Rights Commission. The complaint must be filed within six months of the act giving rise to the complaint. If the Commission cannot resolve the matter by conciliation and persuasion, the complaint will be heard before an administrative law judge. The judge can issue a cease and desist order, and can also enter an order requiring the perpetrator to do other things, such as report on future activities. The judge can award damages to the victim of up to $1,000 each for violation of the victim's civil rights and for mental suffering and humiliation.

If desired, the victim can have the attorney general file a suit against the perpetrator. The results of such a suit could be damages in excess of the amounts in a case heard before an administrative law judge.

Penalties can also include fines up to $50,000 if the perpetrator is a real estate licensee, in addition to the victim's actual damages and an injunction to cease discriminating.

In addition, the requirements of Chapter 49.60 are more or less echoed in the administrative rules of the Department of Licensing (WAC 308-124D-070). Violation of an administrative rule is grounds for disciplinary action against the licensee, including license revocation. Violation of the license law is also a gross misdemeanor.

Washington Fairness in Lending Act

In addition to the above, Chapter 30.04 RCW, the **Washington Fairness in Lending Act** prohibits discrimination by lenders –

RCW 30.04.510 Fairness in lending act – Unlawful practices.
Subject to RCW 30.04.515, it shall be unlawful for any financial institution, in processing any application for a loan to be secured by a single-family residence to:
(1) Deny or vary the terms of a loan on the basis that a specific parcel of real estate offered as security is located in a specific geographical area, unless building, remodeling, or continued habitation in such specific geographical area is prohibited or restricted by any local, state, or federal law or rules or regulations promulgated thereunder.
(2) Utilize lending standards that have no economic basis.

However, lenders are not prohibited from making loan decisions based on the willingness and financial ability of the borrower to repay the loan, the market value of the collateral, or diversification of the lender's portfolio.

After reading this chapter most students are surprised at what the discrimination laws do not cover. For example, the majority of the public assumes that you cannot discriminate on the basis of age, yet now you know that age applies only in certain areas, most of which do not involve real estate sales and rentals. Similarly, there are no laws prohibiting discrimination on many other issues – you can discriminate against fat people, thin people, education level, taste in music, and thousands of other categories. A few, such as sexual orientation are controversial, but most are not.

The point, however, is not whether it is legal to discriminate, but whether you should, even where the law allows it. Suppose you are showing a house in a luxury neighborhood to a buyer. You make a derogatory comment about a poorer part of town. And what happens if the buyer has a son or daughter who lives in that poorer neighborhood? Making buyers angry isn't a good way to get them to buy from you.

By the time they reach adulthood most people have learned that putting down other people is a sad attempt to make themselves look better in comparison but that, in reality, all they accomplish is to make themselves look pathetic. Professionals know that the saying they learned from their mothers is still true – "if you can't say something nice, don't say anything at all." Your sole job is to handle the real estate transaction for the client. Veteran agents ignore everything else.

🔑 KEY TERMS

The key to understanding any new field is the vocabulary used in that field. To maximize your comprehension of the material presented in this chapter, be sure you know the meaning and significance of the following terms. Remember that the majority of test questions primarily test knowledge of vocabulary.

Affirmative marketing
Americans with Disabilities Act
Blockbusting
Civil Rights Act of 1866
Civil Rights Act of 1964
Civil Rights Act of 1968
Community Reinvestment Act
Complainant
Disability
Equal Credit Opportunity Act
Executive Order 11063
Fair Housing Act

Fair Housing Amendments Act of 1988
Familial status
Home Mortgage Disclosure Act
Integration
Mrs. Murphy exemption
Panic selling
Protected category
Redlining
Respondent
Steering
Washington Fairness in Lending Act

Chapter

23

Closing real estate transactions

I N THE EARLY DAYS a real estate transaction was concluded without anything more complicated than the seller delivering the deed to the buyer. Of course, you can still close a real estate transaction that way today, but unless the buyer records the deed there is no protection of constructive notice, the buyer has no evidence that the seller really owns the property, and there is no one to handle the prorating of expenses and tend to the other myriad of details required in a modern real estate transaction.

Today, the closing of most Washington real estate transactions is handled by escrow agents. This is not necessarily the case in other regions. For example, in eastern states, it is customary for the transaction to be closed by an attorney. Furthermore, the closing takes place across a closing table, where the buyer and seller meet to sign the papers at the same time. In contrast, in most Washington transactions a closing agent arranges for the parties to come in at different times, to avoid possible confrontations.

Although escrow agents close the majority of transactions, there are other persons and entities who can and do conduct real estate closings. While relatively few transactions in Washington are closed by attorneys, it is certainly possible, and not even unusual, to close transactions in an attorney's office, especially if the transaction involves a large commercial property. Banks, savings and loan associations and other financial institutions also frequently act as the closing agent in transactions where they are acting as lender. And licensed real estate brokers may also act as closing agents in Washington, provided the broker does not charge any extra fee for the closing services. In rural areas of the state it is not uncommon for brokers to close transactions.

Regardless of who does the closing, the license law and administrative rules require the broker to facilitate the closing. Administrative rule 308-124D-030 states "A real estate licensee shall perform all acts required of the licensee by a real estate agreement as expeditiously as possible. Intentional or negligent delays in such performance shall be considered detrimental to the public interest in violation of RCW 18.85.230 (26)." The administrative rules also require a broker to furnish a complete, detailed closing statement to each party in the transaction and to retain a copy in the broker's transaction file for three years. Closing statements must show "the date of closing, the total purchase price of the property, an itemization of all adjustments, money, or things of value received or paid showing to whom each item is credited and/or to whom each item is debited. The dates of the adjustments shall be shown, together with the names of the payees, makers and assignees of all notes paid or made or assumed" (WAC 308-124D-020). Throughout this chapter we will see some of the issues involved and how closings are conducted.

When we refer to the closing of a transaction we refer to the process where the parties each perform their respective obligations under a contract. In real estate, the contract is usually an earnest money agreement, but it can also be a lease, option, right of refusal, or virtually any other agreement. In most transactions funds normally change hands, and so each party receives a closing statement showing the sources and uses of their funds. This process is also frequently called settlement, and the closing statements are commonly called settlement statements. The license law and administrative rules require a real estate broker to ensure that each party to a transaction received a complete written accounting of all funds belonging to the party. Delivery of the closing statements to the parties discharges this obligation.

Why do the parties decide to close their transaction with the services of an escrow? The escrow handles all the prorating and recording, a large task in itself. But the most important reason is simply that the parties cannot trust each other with the large sums involved in a typical real estate transaction. Suppose the buyer gave the cash to the seller, expecting the deed, but the seller simply took off with the money? Use of an escrow as a stakeholder eliminates this problem.

As we noted, the closing is most commonly handled by an escrow agent in Washington. An escrow agent is a neutral party who acts as agent for all the parties to the escrow. The parties (called principals) are normally a buyer and a seller, although the principals might also include a lender, or they might be a lessor and a lessee, optionor and optionee, or any other party to a contract which is being finalized in escrow.

It is important to note that an escrow agent is an agent in every sense of the word. (For a more complete discussion of the law of agency, see Chapter 18.) That is to say, the agent is a fiduciary and is said to have a fiduciary duty to the principals. In fact, an escrow agent acts in a special type of agency relationship called a dual agency. In most agency relationships, the agent represents just one party, and owes utmost loyalty to that party to the exclusion of all others. In a dual agency, the loyalty is equal and impartial to both.

Therefore, an escrow agent must remain neutral. In order to avoid compromising this neutrality, an escrow agent does not generally negotiate. Whenever an escrow agent is presented with an impasse or disagreement between the parties, the agent's usual reaction is simply to return all documents and funds and instruct the parties to come back when they have settled their differences.

If the parties cannot come to terms, and the principals enter into a lawsuit, the escrow frequently finds itself in the middle of the dispute. While the argument continues, the escrow agent may find itself legally unable to return the funds and documents because the escrow agent cannot determine who the funds or documents belong to. In this case, the escrow may file an interpleader. This is a legal action where the escrow agent deposits everything with the court and asks the court to determine the final disposition of the funds and documents.

Because escrow agents must handle other people's money, frequently in large amounts, escrow agents must maintain one or more trust accounts. The rules for handling funds are similar to the rules real estate agents must follow with respect to maintaining records, including records of the trust account, giving closing statements to the parties, and so on.

Like real estate brokers, escrow agents are required to keep records of all transactions they handle. But, while real estate brokers must maintain their records for three years, escrow agents must maintain them for six years.

One very important rule is that an escrow agent may not accept an escrow without written *escrow instructions*. Each principal to the transaction must give the escrow separate instructions. The escrow instructions constitute the contract between the escrow agent and the principal. Many times, in transactions with multiple parties, there will be several sets of escrow instructions, which can become very involved, depending on the complexity of the transaction.

For example, suppose a seller were selling a house to a buyer. But the seller owes money on a first trust deed, and the buyer will be obtaining a new loan so the seller's old loan will be paid off at closing. In this transaction there would commonly be four separate and different sets of escrow instructions, since there are four principals – the seller, the buyer, the seller's lender, and the buyer's lender.

The seller's deed to the buyer will accompany the seller's instructions, which will authorize the agent to record the deed as soon as the agent has received full performance from the buyer. The buyer's funds and loan documents will be mentioned in the buyer's instructions, which will authorize the agent to disburse the funds to the seller when the seller has delivered the deed as agreed. And the two lenders each give the escrow instructions in reference to their respective loans.

Note that all instructions to the escrow must be in harmony. Suppose the seller gives the escrow instructions not to record the deed to the buyer until the buyer has paid the sum of $300,000. But the buyer's instructions call for a purchase price of $280,000. Closing can occur only when all instructions of each party have been, or can be, complied with. Since the instructions do not mesh in this case, there is no way to close the transaction. We would say that this escrow is deadlocked.

Notice that there are several requirements for a valid escrow. First, there must be a contract between two or more principals which the principals wish to close in an escrow. Second, there must be an escrow agent (whether licensed or exempt). And third, there must be sets of escrow instructions, setting forth the contracts between the escrow agent and the principals, and the instructions must be without conflict.

Once the escrow has been created, it can be terminated or rendered unenforceable in all the usual ways that agency contracts can be terminated. These include death, future incompetence, or bankruptcy of any of the principals or of the agent. However, a special circumstance develops in an escrow agency. Once the escrow instructions have been signed and the seller has delivered the deed to the agent – that is, once the agent has arrived at the point where the agent can close at any time – the escrow is complete. From this point on, death, incompetence or bankruptcy of the seller will not terminate the escrow. The legal principal behind this is that the date of the delivery of a deed relates back to the point when it was delivered to the escrow, not the point at which the escrow agent finally recorded it or handed it to the buyer.

Even if the escrow is terminated by death, incompetence or bankruptcy, this does not mean that the deceased, incompetent or bankrupt principal will necessarily be able to avoid performance of the contract which underlies the escrow. For example, a typical earnest money contract in Washington is binding on the heirs of the parties. Suppose that prior to delivery of all documents to the escrow agent, the seller dies. The escrow may be terminated, but assuming the earnest money is binding upon the heirs of the seller, the seller's estate must still proceed to perform the earnest money agreement and deed the property to the buyer when the buyer finishes performing.

Washington Escrow Agent Registration Act

Anyone wishing to act as an escrow agent in Washington must first be licensed by the Washington State Department of Financial Institutions, although most enforcement is by the Department of Licensing, including suspension and revocation of the license. However, title insurance companies, attorneys, and most lenders are exempt. Real estate brokers are also exempt, provided no fee is charged for the closing services. In effect, most of the licensed escrow agents are independent escrow services. Regardless of whether transactions are closed by a licensed agent or someone exempt from licensing, it is useful to real estate agents to be aware of the statutory requirements for licensed escrow agents.

In Washington an *escrow agent* is the company, not the individual performing the service. In other words, it is normally a corporation, partnership, or limited liability company. The individuals who perform the closing services must be licensed as *escrow officers*. Every escrow agent that is an organization must have a *designated escrow officer* who must be one of the officers of the organization. The designated escrow officer is responsible for the escrow activity of the escrow agent. A company licensed as an escrow agent is referred to as a *certified escrow agent*.

To obtain a license as an escrow officer, the applicant must pass an examination. In addition, unlike other real estate agents, escrow agents (i.e., the companies) are required to post a bond, cash, or other deposits in a substantial amount. Escrow agents must also have errors and omissions insurance to protect the public.

It is also important to distinguish between a title insurance company and an escrow agent. Title insurance companies issue various types of title insurance policies, and also commonly operate an escrow service as a separate function. Because title insurance companies also operate escrow services, many people become confused between the two operations. You should bear in mind that the escrow services rendered by the title insurance company are a separate department within the company.

What a closing agent does

At some point in the closing of a real estate transaction one of the parties needs to open the escrow. This means that the escrow agent receives the escrow instructions. As we noted earlier, an escrow can be used to finalize any contract. However, in real estate practice, the most common contract is a simple sale agreement (earnest money agreement). In the following discussion, we will see how a typical uncomplicated sale is handled.

Today the licensee normally uses an earnest money form which states who the closing agent will be. On some forms the default is to allow the buyer to stipulate the closing agent later. In either event, if the Real Estate Settlement Procedures Act applies to the transaction, the closing agent is the buyer's choice. (The Real Estate Settlement Procedures Act is covered in more detail in Chapter 14.) In most transactions today the closing agent will be an escrow, a title insurance company, or a lender who is supplying financing for the transaction. In a few cases transactions are closed by the broker. Even if the transaction is not closed by a company licensed as an escrow agent (e.g., a lender or a title insurance company, which are exempt), the closing agent will take on the functions of an escrow agent. It is common to refer to the closing process as the escrow, even if the closing agent is not licensed as an escrow agent.

Normally, the broker is the one who does the legwork of opening the escrow. The broker does not open the escrow, however, until all contingencies in the transaction have been removed. For example, most real estate sales are subject to the buyer being able to obtain financing. There is no point, therefore, in opening an escrow until the loan commitment from the lender is firmly in hand.

Once the escrow has been opened, the closing agent usually orders a preliminary title commitment, also called a preliminary title report, or just "PTR" or "prelim" for short. This is not a title insurance policy, but rather a report of the condition of the title. Preliminary title commitments show the person in title (the seller), and the condition of the seller's title. The preliminary title commitment also includes the results of a judgment search, since a judgment is a lien against the real property. Normally, the preliminary title commitment shows only encumbrances which were already expected, and which the seller planned to take care of at closing. Occasionally a surprise occurs, such as a judgment for back child support, an IRS levy, or other unforeseen encumbrance.

Depending on local market conditions, the preliminary title commitment will generally take a couple of days to prepare. While waiting for it, the closing agent will also order a payoff letter from the seller's lender. If the seller's old loan is to be paid off, the agent must have a written statement from the lender as to the balance, net of any reserve accounts, which the lender demands. The escrow agent also needs the appropriate release instrument (satisfaction of mortgage or deed of reconveyance, or fulfillment deed if the loan is a land sales contract) properly signed and acknowledged so that it can be recorded at the proper time. Since the lender is handing the closing agent documents which will cancel its lien on the property, the lender becomes another principal to the escrow and should give instructions to the escrow agent.

On occasion, a buyer will take over the seller's old loan. Although the majority of loans today contain a due on sale clause, many do not. Even if the loan does contain a due on sale clause, the parties may have been able to negotiate with the lender for a waiver of the clause. The buyer usually takes title subject to the loan, which the buyer typically assumes and agrees to pay. In this case, the closing agent must order an assumption letter from the lender, rather than a payoff letter. The assumption letter is essentially the same as the payoff letter, but will not be net of the reserve account since the lender will not generally give up the right to maintain reserves. Note that the reserve account is the seller's money, so when the closing agent makes up the closing statement, the closing agent must have the buyer reimburse the seller for the reserve account. Also, an assumption letter will usually contain a demand that an assumption fee be paid. Unless the parties agree otherwise, the buyer is usually charged for the assumption fee.

Whenever the closing agent is dealing with the seller's old loan(s), the agent must be sure to have a written statement from the lender(s) as to the balance(s). Payoff letters and assumption letters both contain this type of information. Once the bank has sent a written statement, the bank can generally be held responsible for any errors it made in preparing the statement. Even a borrower can usually hold the lender responsible for preparing a correct annual loan reduction statement. The legal principle is that the lender will be estopped (barred) from asserting that a larger amount is due. As a result, all of these various types of statements issued by lenders have much the same effect and are frequently referred to generically as ***estoppel certificates***.

With respect to new loan funds being advanced to a buyer, the closing agent cannot close the transaction until these have been received. In addition, the buyer's lender will insist on giving the escrow instructions relative to the funds. The lender's check for the loan proceeds will be accompanied by the loan papers. These may or may not include auxiliary documents such as Truth in Lending disclosure statements and the like, but they most definitely will include the note and trust deed or other documents the buyer must sign to evidence the debt and the lien on the property.

Handling the buyer's new loan can be very complicated. Not only will the lender frequently charge a loan fee, but the lender will also charge interest from the date the check is negotiated, while at the same time insisting that the payments fall due on the first of the month. Thus, the closing agent must collect from the borrower interest from the closing date (normally somewhere in the middle of the month) until the end of the month. Then the borrower will make the first payment on the first of the second month after closing, with subsequent payments due on the first of each month thereafter. The interest from the middle of the month until the end of the month is commonly called ***prepaid interest***.

Notice that the borrower will be paying a payment on the first of the month, but that each payment will include the interest charge for the preceding month. It is customary on real estate (as well as most consumer loans) to make the interest payments at the end of the period, not in advance. This means that a payment due on April 1 (for example), includes the interest which accrued during March.

Once the loan papers and title report have been received and are in good order the closing agent is ready to work up the closing statement. To do this, the prorates must be calculated. To prorate means to apportion the expenses of the property between the parties to the escrow. For example, the seller may have paid the property taxes in full, which means that the bill has been paid through December 31. If the transaction closes before December 31, then the buyer takes title to a property with taxes already paid on it for a time. To be fair, the closing agent will calculate the value of the prepaid taxes, debit the buyer for that amount, and credit the seller for the same amount. Thus, the buyer will end up reimbursing the seller for the prepaid taxes (See *Prorating* later for a more thorough discussion of prorating procedures).

When the closing statement is finished and the papers are ready to be signed, the principals are called in to finalize the transaction. The buyer is asked to bring the total amount necessary to close. This includes not only the down payment, but all the buyer's other expenses, less any credits due the buyer. The seller usually is to receive a check after closing for the sales proceeds, including any credits due the seller, but less any expenses charged to the seller.

At the time the buyer makes the original offer to buy the real estate agent normally gives the buyer an estimate of the total amount of cash the buyer will need to close. Similarly, the agent normally gives the seller an estimate of how much the seller can expect to net after closing. While these figures are only estimates, nevertheless, the agent should give copies of these estimates to the closing agent. The closing agent will then know how much the parties were expecting, and can avoid surprises.

Once the parties have signed, the closing agent is ready to record. This is a simple process, but it can also be crucial. For example, with some exceptions, the priority of a lien is determined by the time of recording. Therefore, if there is more than one loan, they must be recorded in the right order so the priority will be what the lenders contracted for.

After recording the documents, there is generally a short delay before the closing agent will finally disburse the funds. This is to allow the title insurance company to double-check the recording. In most recording offices today, the documents are filmed or scanned by high-speed equipment. It is not uncommon to lose a document or to have a machine malfunction which caused it not to be imaged.

Limited practice officers

Note that the escrow agent may secure the signatures of the parties to the documents, may even fill in the blanks on forms at the request of the parties (i.e., act as a **scrivener**, but not as a lawyer), and may record them as necessary to protect the interests of the parties, but the closing agent does not practice law. That is, the escrow agent does not review the documents for accuracy or for their legal adequacy.

However, this creates a problem. Sometimes there is a fine line between acting as a scrivener and the practice of law. In the past, to protect themselves from being charged with unauthorized practice of law, closing agents would refuse even to fill out standard forms. The parties had to secure the services of an attorney, which added expense and delay to the closing.

To solve this problem, at the request of the real estate industry, the Washington State Bar created a certification as a **limited practice officer**. A limited practice officer is a lay person who has passed an examination given by the Bar and is qualified to handle certain real estate documents commonly used in closing transactions. Along with the certification, the Bar created a Limited Practice Board, one of whose duties is to create standard form documents for use by limited practice officers. Limited practice officers can use only these forms, but they are adequate for the closing of the vast majority of real estate transactions in Washington today.

Double and chained escrows

Many times a property is sold, and then immediately resold. For example, suppose a real estate broker took a property in trade in order to sell the owner another property. Unless the broker has some use for the property, the broker probably needs to resell it. But there is a simpler way to handle this situation.

If the broker actually buys the property, the broker has to come up with enough cash to close the sale, then wait until the property can be resold to recover the cash (and hopefully, profit). Why not agree to buy the property, on a binding contract so the seller can be sure that it is sold, but not close the sale until a subsequent buyer can be found. In other words, the earnest money agreement can contain a clause allowing the broker several months, if necessary, in order to finalize the purchase. As soon as the subsequent buyer agrees to buy the property, the broker can close the transaction with the seller.

Of course, this is really two transactions. But since both sales involve the same property, and will close at the same time, they can be handled in the same escrow. This is called a **double escrow**, or sometimes a **back-to-back escrow**.

Note that excise taxes must be paid on most real estate transfers, but a broker re-selling a property within nine months is exempt. (See *Real estate excise tax* later.)

A related situation occurs when a seller is selling one property and buying another, but using the proceeds from the sale of the first property to buy the second. In this case we could use a double escrow as well. But many times the properties are listed by different companies and it becomes difficult to arrange for the same escrow to close both transactions. Of course, it is certainly possible to use two separate escrows. When we set up two escrows, with the second contingent on the closing of the first, it is frequently called a **chained escrow**, or sometimes a **split escrow.** Chained escrows can involve more that just two properties and two escrows. In fact, in exchange transactions it is not unheard of to have five or ten properties involved. Such transactions can become very complex.

Foreign Investment in Real Property Tax Act

Investment in U.S. real estate is popular with many foreigners. The U.S. is seen as a safe haven where their assets are not likely to be seized or expropriated. Being a coastal state, Washington receives more foreign investment in real estate than most states.

In the past it was common practice for foreigners to ignore U.S. income tax laws when selling their properties. Under the Internal Revenue Code, capital gains tax is frequently due on the sale of a property. As a result, in 1980 Congress passed the **Foreign Investment in Real Property Tax Act** (FIRPTA). To comply with FIRPTA the closing agent must obtain a certification from the seller that the seller is not a foreign person as defined in the Act. If the seller cannot give the certification and the transaction is not otherwise exempt, the closing agent must withhold 10% of the sales proceeds for the capital gains tax and remit the tax withheld to the IRS. If the closing agent fails to withhold, the IRS can hold the closing agent and any of the real estate agents in the transaction liable for the tax.

The Foreign Investment in Real Property Tax Act is a complicated law with many exemptions. Closing agents are generally aware of the major provisions, but sometimes outside tax counsel is required before the transaction can close.

IRS reporting requirements

While most transactions are exempt from withholding requirements under the Foreign Investment in Real Property Tax Act, the closing agent must still make a report to the IRS on virtually all sales. The report is on a form 1099-S, which is under the seller's social security number. Form 1099 is used for reporting miscellaneous income. The report must include the sales price so the IRS can check the seller's next tax return to see if the seller reported the capital gain. The closing agent is not allowed to charge a fee for preparing and filing the 1099-S.

If the closing agent fails to file the 1099-S the responsibility falls to the lender, and if there is no lender or the lender fails to file the report, then to the real estate broker(s) in the transaction. Because of this reporting requirement escrow agents always insist on the seller's social security number before closing.

Real estate excise tax

Washington law requires an **excise tax** on transfers of real estate. The tax is collected by the county treasurer and remitted to the Department of Revenue. Deeds and contracts cannot be accepted for recording until the treasurer has certified that the tax has been paid or that the transaction is exempt. The tax is calculated on the gross selling price, including the amounts of loans. Normally it is the seller's obligation to pay the tax. However, the tax is a lien on the property until paid, so if the seller doesn't pay it the buyer will become obligated to do so.

Since deeds and contracts cannot be accepted for recording without paying the tax, the normal practice is for the closing agent to pay the tax and obtain the certification from the county treasurer. (Real estate excise tax is covered in more detail in Chapter 8.)

Homeowner's insurance

When a buyer purchases a home the issue of fire insurance must be addressed. In years past this was a simple matter. The buyer just called local insurance agents for price quotes and took the policy with the lowest premium. Frequently this would be the company that already carried the buyer's automobile insurance, since many insurance companies offer attractive package prices. The insurance agent would send a binder to the closing agent as proof of coverage and most lenders would be satisfied and agree to fund the loan on the binder. Occasionally a lender would insist on the issuance of a full policy, but this was unusual.

Today, however, matters have changed. It is no longer a simple matter of ordering the policy. Insurance premiums have been soaring for various reasons, mostly because of increasing claims and the cost of the claims. To help counter this trend most insurers today use a report from the **Comprehensive Loss Underwriting Exchange** (CLUE). The CLUE report tracks both the homeowner (by social security number) and the property. If the property has had a history of claims, the buyer may discover that premiums are very high or that insurance is not available at all. Real estate agents should advise buyers to make application for their homeowner's policy as soon as possible. If the buyer encounters difficulty the best source for assistance is the Washington State Office of the Insurance Commissioner.

There are many different kinds of homeowner insurance policies. In order to give good service to their clients and customers, real estate agents should be aware of some basics.

Homeowner's policies generally offer coverage on the structure, the contents, and liability. Coverage on the structure is what it would cost to rebuild it if damaged or destroyed. However, on older homes this can be an enormous amount, far in excess of the market value. Therefore, buyers of older homes may elect to obtain a replacement cost policy. A replacement cost policy covers the market value of the home rather than what it would cost to rebuild.

Homeowner's policies always exclude earthquake and flood coverage. Earthquake loss can be obtained in a separate policy. Flood insurance is available through the federal government (see below).

Federal flood insurance

The **National Flood Insurance Program** provides federal flood insurance. Policies are written by private insurance companies, with premiums set by the government. Since the insurance companies cannot compete on premiums, they compete on service. Policies are issued in addition to regular homeowner's policies.

The cost ranges from $110 per year for a minimum coverage in a preferred area, to thousands of dollars for coverage of a commercial property in a standard area. Most insurers participate in the program, so the property owner frequently obtains the flood insurance from the same company as their regular policy.

The **National Flood Insurance Reform Act of 1994** requires lenders to notify existing borrowers borrower any time the lender discovers that the property is located in a flood-prone area. The borrower has 45 days in which to obtain flood insurance. If the borrower fails to do so the lender must purchase flood insurance for the borrower, although the lender may charge the borrower for the amount of the premium. In areas identified as prone to flooding lenders must also require flood insurance in addition to a regular insurance policy on all new loans. Whenever a loan requires flood insurance the lender must set up a reserve (escrow) account for the insurance premiums, the same as they currently do for fire insurance and property taxes.

As of the end of 2003 over $4 billion in flood insurance was in force in Washington, representing over 27,000 policies. Without the National Flood Insurance Program most of these properties could not have been financed.

Prorating

Some of the expenses attributable to a property, such as fire insurance premiums, are paid in advance. Yet other expenses, such as interest on a mortgage loan, are commonly paid in arrears. When the title changes hands, these expenses must be apportioned fairly between the principals. This process is called prorating, and the amount of a given expense which is apportioned to one of the principals is called a prorate.

There is no legal requirement that a buyer and a seller prorate these expenses, but it is a rare transaction where prorating is waived. All standard earnest money forms provide that the parties will prorate expenses attributable to the property.

When prorating the question of what to do with the closing date arises. Should we consider that the seller owns the property on the closing date, or the buyer? In some states there are laws stipulating who owns the property on the closing date. In other states there is just a custom. In Washington it is customary to assume that the buyer owns the property on the closing date, although the parties can stipulate otherwise in the purchase agreement. If the agreement is silent, then we presume that the buyer owns the property on the closing date. This means that the buyer will be charged all expenses for the closing date, but will also get any income (i.e., rent on investment property) for the closing date. Most prorates are expense items, not income. The theory behind the custom of saying the buyer owns the property on the closing date is that the buyer will then end up paying the expenses for that day. All buyers will some day be sellers, so then they will get it back. But not all sellers will some day be buyers.

When calculating prorates it is important to distinguish between calendar years and banker's years. A **calendar year** has 365 days, or 366 if a leap year. A **banker's year** is 360 days. In the real world we always assume a calendar year unless the parties have agreed otherwise in the purchase agreement. On exams, however, prorates use a 360-day year. Similarly, in prorating monthly items (e.g., rent), in the real world we use however many days the month in question has, but on exams they assume a 30-day month.

There are four expenses which can be prorated – property taxes, fire insurance premiums, interest on loans being assumed, and rents on investment property. Not all expenses occur in any given transaction, although some occur in almost every sale.

Closing (escrow) fee – Some people would argue that splitting the escrow fee between the parties (a customary practice, although not legally required and sometimes not permitted), should be considered a prorate. However, a true prorate involves a time factor, which simply splitting an expense does not.

Fuel in storage tank – Some might think apportioning the expense for fuel oil in the tank is a prorate, but most people do not consider it a true prorate. It does have to be handled, typically as an expense to the buyer and a credit to the seller.

Prorating taxes – The most common (and most confusing) expense which is pro-rated is the real property tax bill. In fact, it is an unusual transaction where the property taxes do not need to be prorated. The confusion stems from the fact that the property tax year in Washington runs from January 1 through December 31, yet the bill is due in halves on April 30 and October 31. So if you have paid the property taxes in full on April 30 you have paid the taxes four months in arrears (from the preceding January 1) and eight months in advance (through December 31).

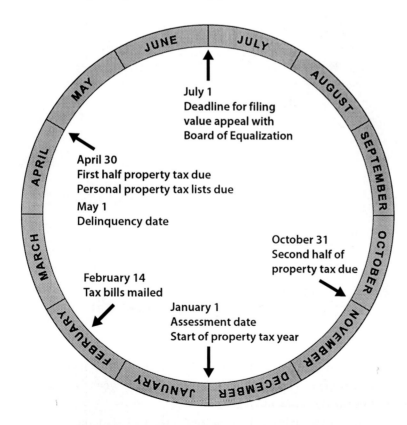

This means that if an owner sells the property between the time the full year taxes were paid and the following December 31, the buyer receives a property with the taxes paid in advance for a time. Logically then, the buyer should reimburse the seller for the amount of the prepaid taxes.

This is easier to understand with some examples. Let us suppose that a sale occurs and the prorate date is to be February 16. If the seller paid the taxes in full the preceding October 31, that paid the taxes only to the end of the year (December 31). The first half of the tax bill is not due until April 30, and cannot be paid before February 15, so it is highly likely the seller has not yet paid the taxes for the first half of the tax year. Yet, the taxes for the first half of the tax year have been a lien on the property since January 1. Therefore, either the buyer can take the title subject to the lien for the unpaid taxes, or the closing agent can pay the taxes and prorate the amount between the parties. However, in almost all cases the earnest money agreement between the buyer and the seller calls for the seller to deed the property to the buyer free and clear. Therefore, as a practical matter, in almost all cases the closing agent must pay the taxes for the first half of the year.

The closing agent can do this one of two ways. One way would be to charge the seller for the full amount of the first half of the tax bill. This will pay the taxes through June 30. But now the buyer will be getting a property with the taxes paid in advance. Therefore, we will make the buyer reimburse the seller for part of the taxes which the seller paid in advance. In accounting terminology, we will debit the buyer and credit the seller the same amount. In the drawing below, the dark part of the band is the time span that the buyer must reimburse the seller for (February 16 through June 30).

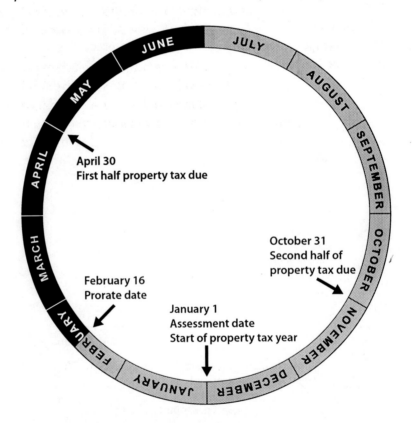

Now that we know what to calculate, we can turn our attention to the actual calculation. The first step is to count the number of days between February 16 and June 30 (the dark band in the drawing above).

Since the buyer is getting a debit in this case, we will debit the buyer for February 16, and for each day thereafter through June 30. Since there are normally 28 days in February, the buyer will be charged for the last 13 of them. And we will charge the buyer for all 31 days in March, all 30 days in April, all 31 days in May and for all 30 days in June. This comes to a total of 135 days.

Now we must calculate a daily factor. Suppose the annual tax bill for this property is $4,264. To calculate a daily factor for the first half of the year, just take half of the tax bill ($2,132) and divide it by 181. (There are 181 days in the first half of the year, but if the tax year is a leap year, divide the half of the bill by 182.)

Assuming we are not in a leap year, our factor should be $11.78 per day ($2,132 ÷ 181 = $11.78). Now we are ready to find the amount of the prorate. Just multiply the daily factor ($11.78) by the number of days (135), which gives us $1,590.30. The correct prorate is therefore to debit the buyer $1,590.30 and credit the seller $1,590.30. However, note that the seller also has a debit for half the year's taxes in the amount of $2,132.

But what would happen if we reversed the above and had the buyer pay the full bill? In this case, the closing statement for the buyer would show a debit for the amount of the taxes for the first half of the year, and then there would be a prorate between the buyer and seller, as before. However, this time the buyer paid the taxes, so the seller should reimburse the buyer for the seller's share of the bill, in other words, the period when the seller owned the property, January 1 to February 16. The drawing below shows the amount of time to prorate for –

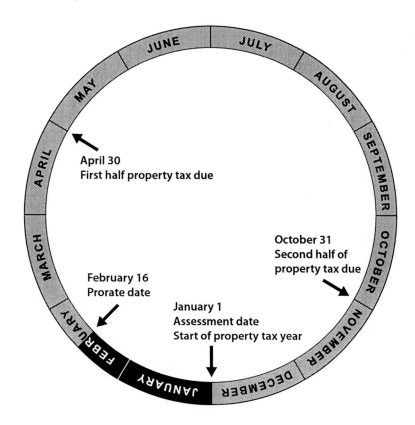

As before, the first step is to count the number of days. We will give the buyer credit for all of January (31 days) and for the first 15 days of February. This comes to a total of 46 days.

To calculate the prorate, we simply multiply our daily factor ($11.78) by 46. The answer is $541.88. Therefore the escrow agent will debit the seller $541.88 and credit the buyer $541.88 on their respective closing statements. Of course, in this case the buyer paid the full bill ($2,132.00), so the buyer is out a net amount of $1,590.12.

Note that we calculated the tax situation two different ways, but each one gave us the same results. In the first way we debited the seller $2,132 and the buyer gave the seller

$1,590.30 of it back, so the seller was out a net amount of $541.70 and the buyer was out $1,590.30. In the second example, we debited the buyer $2,132.00, but had the seller give the buyer back $541.88, so the seller was out $541.88 and the buyer was out a net amount of $1,590.12. In both cases the buyer received the property with the taxes paid through the coming June 30. –

	Seller paid net	Buyer paid net	Total
First way	541.70	1,590.30	2,132.00
Second way	541.88	1,590.12	2,132.00

(The few pennies difference is due to rounding of the daily factor.)

But what would happen if the transaction closed during the second half of the year? Suppose the prorate date was, say, August 16. (Note that we used February 16 in our first problems and August 16 is exactly six months later.) The answer is very simple. Just take the previous two drawings, and mentally slide the black areas 180 degrees around the circle. The way to do the prorate is exactly the same. The only thing to remember is to divide the last half year's taxes by 184 instead of 181, because there are always 184 days in the last half of the year. Note that in Washington we almost always think of tax prorating in terms of half-years.

Now we have seen what to do when the tax bill has not been paid. But what would we do if the tax bill has already been paid by closing date? For example, let's suppose the seller paid the first half of the tax bill on April 30 and the prorate date is to be June 5. The payment on April 30 paid the bill through June 30, so the buyer is getting a property with 25 days taxes already paid on it. The solution is simple. Using the same techniques as above, calculate a daily rate and multiply it by 25. That is the amount of the prorate. Since the buyer is getting the property with the taxes paid in advance, the buyer should reimburse the seller for this amount. Therefore, we should debit the buyer and credit the seller for the 25 days worth of taxes.

Loan reserves – In the real world of selling real estate an agent does not have to do exact prorating to the penny as in the above examples. After all, when selling the property we don't necessarily know exactly what date it is going to close anyway. However, we do need to give the parties at least an estimate.

When estimating the total move-in cost for a buyer we must make an allowance for the tax prorate and for the reserve account the lender will require as well. (The vast majority of lenders require a reserve account.) Of course, lenders figure tax reserves on a monthly basis, not as a daily amount. So the amount the lender will require to be placed into the reserve account at closing will be one-twelfth the annual bill for as many months as are necessary in order for the reserve account to have enough to pay the next tax bill when it comes due.

Looking at our previous example, the annual tax amount is $4,264, so the monthly amount would be $355.33, which the lender will typically round up to the nearest dollar, or $356. After closing, the next tax bill will be due on October 31, and will be for six months worth of taxes. However, lenders also usually demand a two-month cushion (the maximum cushion allowed by the Real Estate Settlement Procedures Act). So by October 31 the lender wants to see eight months worth of taxes in the reserve account.

If the transaction closes on February 16 the buyer's first payment will be due April 1. Adding up all the payments that will come due through October 1 comes to seven months worth of payments (April, May, June, July, August, September and October). In other words, the lender will be short one month's taxes for the reserve account.

Therefore, the lender will require the buyer to set up one month's taxes in the reserve account at closing.

As an exercise, consider different closing dates throughout the year, bearing in mind that sometimes the due date would have to be April 30 instead of October 31. Assuming a closing sometime in the middle of the month, here are how many months remaining for each closing date –

Closing date	Tax due date	Number of payments	Reserve requirement	**Total months**
1/15	10/31	8	0	**8**
2/15	10/31	7	1	**8**
3/15	10/31	6	2	**8**
4/15	10/31	5	3	**8**
5/15	10/31	4	4	**8**
6/15	10/31	3	5	**8**
7/15	4/30	8	0	**8**
8/15	4/30	7	1	**8**
9/15	4/30	6	2	**8**
10/15	4/30	5	3	**8**
11/15	4/30	4	4	**8**
12/15	4/30	3	5	**8**

Now consider the prorates discussed earlier. When the closing date was February 16, the buyer had to pay a total of $1,590, or nearly four and a half months worth of tax. The lender also required another month's worth of tax, so the buyer had to pay at closing approximately five and a half months worth of tax prorates and reserve requirements.

What would happen to the prorate figure if the closing date were the middle of March instead of the middle of February? The buyer's prorate would be one month less, because the seller owned the property for one more month during the first half of the year. So the buyer's prorate requirement would be only three and a half months worth of taxes. But the lender (see chart above) would require two months taxes for the reserve account. Once again, the buyer has to come up with five and a half months worth of taxes at closing.

No matter what time of the year the transaction closes, if the sale is being financed by a loan where the lender will require a reserve account, the buyer's total out of pocket for tax prorate and reserve requirement will be about five and a half months worth of taxes. Therefore, when estimating out of pocket closing costs for a buyer, the selling agent can just take five and a half months worth of taxes as a quick calculation. However, most agents prefer to use six months, just to estimate a bit on the long side.

Prorating insurance: – It is not common today to prorate insurance on residential sales, although it is still sometimes done in sales of improved commercial and industrial property. In residential sales today, the seller simply cancels his or her old policy and receives a refund check directly from the insurance company. The buyer, in turn, just obtains a new policy from the buyer's insurance agent. As a result, there is nothing to prorate between the parties.

If the sale agreement between the parties calls for the buyer to take over the seller's old policy, then the buyer should reimburse the seller for the unexpired term.

Insurance prorates always involve a situation where the seller has paid the premium in advance, so the buyer should reimburse the seller for the amount of time that the policy has remaining. As a result, the closing agent will debit the buyer for the prorate, and credit the seller for the same amount.

However, there is one difference between prorating for taxes paid in advance and prorating for insurance paid in advance. The taxes are almost always paid through June 30 or December 31. Insurance policies, on the other hand, are generally written for a year from the time they are taken out, so the expiration date could be any date during the year. Naturally, if you need to prorate insurance, you will have to know the expiration date of the policy.

For a discussion problem, let us use April 12 for a prorate date. Let us also stipulate an annual premium of $1,100 on a commercial property, which the seller paid for one year on the preceding December 15.

To solve the prorate, we start by calculating the number of days the policy has remaining. Looking at the following drawing of a year, the dark shaded area is the time period for which the buyer should reimburse the seller.

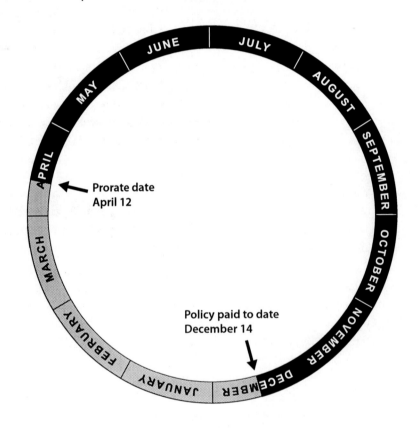

To count the days, remember that the policy was taken out on December 15 for a year, which means that it was paid through the following December 14. To start, we will count all the rest of the days in April (18 days remaining). And we will give the seller credit for all of May (31 days), June (30 days), July (31 days), August (31 days), September (30 days), October (31 days), November (30 days) and the first 14 days of December. This comes to a total of 246 days.

Now we must calculate a daily factor. Assuming it is not a leap year, just divide the annual premium ($1,100) by 365. The result is $3.01 per day. Now we can find the prorate by multiplying the daily factor ($3.01) by the number of days (246). The result is a prorate of $740.46. The buyer will be debited $740.46 and the seller will be credited the same amount.

Prorating interest – While there may be many interest calculations in a real estate transaction, a prorate of interest occurs only when the buyer is taking over the seller's old loan. Real estate loan payments are normally due on the first of the month, yet the sale typically closes with a prorate date somewhere in the middle of the month. Therefore, the interest for the month in question must be apportioned between the buyer and the seller.

For discussion purposes, let us use the same prorate date as in our previous insurance prorate problem (April 12). And let us say that the buyer is assuming the seller's old loan. The seller's old loan has a balance after the April 1st payment was made of $145,068. The interest rate is 8%. The monthly payment is $1,386 which includes just principal and interest, not taxes and insurance.

The important thing to remember about prorating interest is that the interest is paid at the end of the period. So when the seller made the payment on April 1, that payment included the interest for March. Of course, the buyer will make the payment on May 1, since the buyer will be the new owner at that time. Therefore, when the buyer makes the payment on May 1, the buyer will be paying interest for all of April. But the seller owned the property for the first 12 days of April. And therefore we must charge (debit) the seller for 12 days worth of interest, and credit the same amount to the buyer. Then, when the buyer makes the payment on May 1, the buyer will already have been reimbursed by the seller for the seller's share of the interest in that payment.

Notice that we do not prorate the principal. If the principal balance were slightly more or slightly less, the buyer would have to bring in slightly more or slightly less cash to close, but would owe correspondingly less or more on the property, so the net result is no change in the buyer's position. Similarly, if the loan balance is slightly higher or lower, the seller will receive slightly less or more net proceeds, so there is no change to the seller's position either. *Caution:* Do not use the monthly payment in prorating, as it includes principal as well. When prorating interest on loans assumed, the monthly payment is irrelevant and must be ignored.

Therefore, we calculate only a prorate of the interest. As with all prorate problems, we must calculate a daily factor. In this case, we need to know how much interest is accruing on the loan each day. The calculation is very simple.

First calculate an entire year's worth of interest on the remaining principal balance. To get this figure, just multiply the balance ($145,068) by the interest rate (8%). The result is $11,605.44. Now just divide this by 365 (366 if working in a leap year), to get one day's worth of interest. The result will be $31.80 per day.

Now we need to find out how many days to charge for. Remember that the buyer will pay the interest for all of April on May 1, so the seller will be debited and the buyer will be credited. We will debit the seller for the first 12 days of April. Therefore, to find the prorate, just multiply the daily factor ($31.80) by 12 days. The answer is $381.60. On the closing statements, the seller will be debited $381.60 and the buyer will be credited the same amount.

Prorating rent – When investment property changes hands there is usually a prorate of the rent between the parties. In the case of large investment properties, the calculation can become quite complicated, but the principle is very easy. The tenants pay the rent to the seller, generally on the first of the month, which pays their rent for the coming month. When the seller conveys the property to the buyer with a prorate date anywhere in the middle of the month, the buyer becomes entitled to a portion of the rent for the period from the prorate date to the end of the month.

For example, let us use our prorate date of April 12, and let us make the buyer responsible for the prorate date this time. Let us also assume the buyer is an investor buying a rental house which is rented for $1,200 per month, the rent is due on the first of the month and the seller has collected it already.

Since the seller will have to turn over to the buyer the rent for the last part of the month, the seller will receive the debit and the buyer will get the credit. We will give the buyer credit for the final 19 days of April, because the buyer owns the property on the closing date.

Now we must calculate a daily factor. On exams the usual procedure when dealing with rent is to assume a 30-day month. In other words, just divide the monthly rent income by 30 to get the daily factor. (In the real world the customary practice is to use the actual number of days in the month.) In this case, April has 30 days, so the daily factor comes to $40.00 per day ($1,200 ÷ =$40.00). To find the prorate, just multiply this daily factor by the number of days (19), and the prorate turns out to be $760.00. Therefore, the seller will be debited $760.00 and the buyer will receive a credit for the same amount.

Now we must consider the complications. The preceding example was a simple rental house. Let us take a more complicated transaction this time. Let us use the same prorate date (April 12), but this time, let us make the property a four-unit apartment complex. Let us assume that Unit 1 is rented for $900 per month, the rent is due on the first, and the seller has collected it. Let us set the rent for Unit 2 at $1,000 per month, make it due on the third, and presume that the seller has collected it. And let us make Unit 3 rent for $1,200 per month also, but make it due on the fifth, and assume the seller has not collected it. And finally, let us assume that Unit 4 is completely vacant.

While this example may be more realistic, it is also considerably more complex. In fact, it is really four separate problems. Since the due dates are not all the same, the buyer is entitled to prorates for different periods of time. And as for Unit 4, if the seller has not collected the rent, then the buyer is not entitled to any prorate for this unit at all.

To prorate for Unit 1, note that the rent is paid through the end of the month, so we calculate that the buyer is entitled to 18 days of rent, which is at $900 per month. Rent of $900 per month accrues at $30.00 per day ($900 ÷ 30 = $30), so the prorate is to credit the buyer and debit the seller for 18 days, times $30.00, or $540.

To prorate for Unit 2, remember that the rent is due on the third, so the rent collected by the seller paid the tenant's rent through the second of the following month. If we prorate as of the 12th, then the buyer is entitled to 20 days prorate for Unit 2. Remember also that the rate is $1,000 per month, so the daily factor is $33.33 per day. The prorate is therefore 20 days times $33.33, or $666.67. We will credit the buyer and debit the seller $666.67 for Unit 2.

Unit 3 is rented at $1,200, but the seller has not collected it. Eventually, the buyer will collect it. However, part of the money the buyer collects in the future belongs to the seller for the period of time when the seller owned the property. If the rent is due on the fifth, then the tenant's monthly rent check pays the rent through the fourth. Therefore the seller is entitled to rent from the fifth through the twelfth of the month, or eight days. At a monthly rate of $1,200, the daily factor is $40.00. Eight days rent at this rate comes to $320.00. Therefore, we debit the buyer and credit the seller for $320.00 for Unit 3.

Since the buyer receives no prorate for Unit 4, the total prorate is a credit to the buyer of $540.00 (Unit 1), $666.67 (Unit 2), less a debit of $320.00 (Unit 3), for a total credit of $886.67. The same amount will be debited to the seller.

Security deposits – When the tenant has given the seller a security or cleaning deposit this must be transferred to the buyer at closing. Under the Residential Landlord-Tenant Act the buyer becomes responsible for refunding it to the buyer, so it is only fair that the seller turn it over to the buyer. Note that this isn't really a prorate, but people sometimes become confused about security deposits when they think of rent prorates, so it is important to make sure the issue is covered in the sale agreement.

Time calculations – Many beginners in real estate become concerned because they always seem to be one day off, usually due to forgetting which party to charge for the prorate date. In the real world of selling real estate, a listing or selling agent only needs to estimate for the buyer and the seller at the time of making the sale. Since you cannot do better than guess at when the transaction will finally close anyway, being a day off is more than close enough for an estimate. Real estate agents should take special care to be sure the clients are aware that the figures the agent gives them are rough estimates and that the exact figures will be calculated by the closing agent later. It is also a good idea to estimate a bit on the high side for buyers and a bit on the low side for sellers.

Closing statements

Fundamental to understanding how to create a closing statement is a firm grasp of the basics of double entry bookkeeping. Even if you have never heard the term before, you have probably run into it anyway, since it is the most commonly used bookkeeping system in the world.

The basic idea of double entry bookkeeping is that every transaction consists of both a debit and a credit, and the debit must equal the credit and vice-versa. If you ever post a debit without its offset (the matching credit), or post a credit without an offset (the matching debit), you will be out of balance. This makes it easy for bookkeepers to keep themselves in balance – they just have to remember one simple little rule – never post anything without posting its offset as well.

Now, sometimes the offset will be several items. For example, in closing a real estate transaction, the closing agent will be credited with the closing (escrow) fee, but since this fee is normally split between the buyer and the seller, the offset to the credit will be two debits – one debit on the seller's statement for half the fee, and the other debit on the buyer's statement for the other half of the fee. Sometimes there may be dozens of items on one side, all offset with just one entry on the other.

The blank closing statement on the following page is a simple form like those commonly sold in stationery stores. However, in closing a real transaction, this form is inadequate because it completely lacks a statement for the closing agent. If you must use a form like this, you must use a piece of scratch paper and make yourself a statement for the closing agent that looks the same as the buyer's and seller's statements on the next page. This is because many of the entries find their offset on the closing agent statement. If you don't make one, you will have no place for some of the offsets and you will become very confused. In addition, it will be impossible to balance the statements at the end, so you will have no way of knowing if your work is correct.

It should also be noted that the HUD-1 closing statement required by the Real Estate Settlement Procedures Act also shows only the buyer and the seller. (There is a sample of the HUD-1 form in Chapter 14.)

Even with a closing agent statement to work with, many people become confused about where to put the different debits and credits. As we will see in the following discussion, this is not really as hard as it sounds. Sometimes you may have difficulty remembering where to place an item, yet you can save the day because of double entry bookkeeping. Since there must always be an offset, and it has to be the opposite, all you really need to be able to remember is one side of the transaction. For example, suppose you were trying to enter the prorate for property taxes. You know the buyer is getting a debit because the seller paid the taxes in advance. If you are sure of this fact, then it doesn't matter if you cannot remember that the seller gets a credit in this situation – if the buyer gets a debit, the entry on the seller's statement absolutely has to be a credit.

SETTLEMENT STATEMENT WORKSHEET

Property _____

Seller_____

Buyer _____

Settlement date _____

	BUYER		SELLER	
	Debit	Credit	Debit	Credit
_____				
_____				
_____				
_____				
_____				
_____				
_____				
_____				
_____				
_____				
_____				
_____				
_____				
_____				
_____				
_____				
_____				
_____				
_____				

Below are listed the major items which appear on a typical closing statement, together with the rules for where they should be entered.

Purchase price – The purchase price is a credit to the seller and a debit to the buyer. In addition, if there is personal property which the buyer is paying an extra amount for, the extra amount is also a debit to the buyer and a credit to the seller.

Sellers old loan(s) – The seller's old loans are debits to the seller. The offset(s) are credits on the closing agent statement, since the closing agent must write a check to the lender to pay off the loan(s), unless they are being assumed by the buyer, in which case they are credits to the buyer.

Buyer's loan(s) – New loans, as well as loans being assumed by the buyer are credits to the buyer. For new hard money financing the offset is a debit on the closing agent statement. For loans being assumed or for loans to be carried by the seller, the offset is a debit on the seller's statement.

Assumption fee – It is customary for the buyer to pay this, although the parties may agree otherwise. If the buyer pays it, it is a debit on the buyer's statement. The offset is a credit to the closing agent statement, since the closing agent will send it to the lender.

Loan origination fees – Loan origination fees are normally the buyer's responsibility, although it is not unheard of for the seller to agree to pay them. If the buyer is to pay, they are a debit to the buyer and the offset is a credit to the closing agent statement.

Other loan expenses – Fees for matters required by the buyer's lender, such as survey, tax service fee, credit report fee, appraisal fee, inspection fees, and so on, are normally debits to the buyer unless the seller has agreed to pay them. The offsets are credits to the closing agent statement, since the closing agent must forward the money to the lender or other provider of the service.

Charges related to the seller's old loan(s) are debits to the seller and offsetting credits on the closing agent's statement. Examples are prepayment penalties and interest from the date of the last payment to closing date. If the seller's loan is being paid off there may be a credit for amounts held in the seller's reserve account. This would be offset by a debit to the closing agent's account.

Discount points are typically paid by the seller, but also frequently by the buyer. Whoever pays them gets the debit, and the offset is a credit to the closing agent's statement.

Earnest money deposit – The buyer receives a credit for the earnest money deposit. The offset is a debit on the closing agent statement, since the closing agent's trust account is where the funds reside.

Title insurance – Depends on the terms of the contract. Normally, the seller pays for the buyer's policy, so this will be a debit to the seller and a credit on the closing agent's account so the closing agent can pay it to the title insurance company. Sometimes the seller will pay for the standard form buyer's policy, but the buyer will want an extended coverage policy and agree to pay the extra cost. In that case each will receive a debit for their share of the cost, but the offset will still be the closing agent's account so the closing agent can pay it to the title insurance company. However, the buyer generally is responsible for the mortgagee's policy required by the buyer's lender. Therefore, the premium for the mortgagee's policy will normally be a debit to the buyer and a credit on the closing agent's statement.

Fire insurance policy – Lenders will generally not allow the transaction to close unless the buyer has the property insured. Therefore, the buyer will be expected to pay for the fire insurance policy through the escrow. As a result, the premium for the fire insurance policy will be a debit to the buyer and the offset will be a credit on the closing agent's statement so the closing agent will have the funds to pay the premium.

Recording fees – Fees for recording documents are generally charged to the party who benefits from the recording, or whose actions make it necessary. For example, recording the deed from the seller to the buyer gives constructive notice and protects the buyer's interest, so this is normally a debit to the buyer. Recording the buyer's loan documents are also posted as debits to the buyer, since it is the buyer's fault that the loan was necessary. On the other hand, recording the satisfaction of the seller's old mortgage (or deed of reconveyance) is the seller's responsibility. The offset to all recording charges is a credit on the closing agent's statement so the closing agent will have the funds to pay the auditor.

Closing agent fee – This fee is customarily split between the buyer and the seller. However, if the property is being financed with a loan guaranteed by the federal Department of Veterans Affairs, federal law does not allow the veteran borrower to be charged any part of an escrow fee, so the fee must be paid in full by the seller. Otherwise, the parties are free to follow standard custom or to contract otherwise.

Excise tax – Washington law provides that the real estate transfer excise tax is normally the seller's responsibility, but if the seller doesn't pay it, then it is a lien on the title so the buyer will end up having to pay it eventually. Documents cannot be recorded until it is paid, so it is customary for the closing agent to debit the seller for it on the closing statement. The offset is a credit to the closing agent's account, so the closing agent will have the funds to send to the county treasurer.

Inspection fee – Most commonly the buyer pays for the inspection fee. However, it is not uncommon for the parties to agree that the seller will pay it. Whoever pays it receives a debit on the closing statement, and the offset is a credit to the closing agent's account.

Attorney's fee – Most transaction close without the need for an attorney. However, commercial transactions are an exception, and sometimes even simple transactions require the services of an attorney. Normally the party for whom the attorney rendered services is charged, with an offsetting credit to the closing agent's account. As with most expenses, the parties can agree to split it or handle it whatever way they wish.

Brokerage fee (commission) – Normally paid by the seller, so it appears as a debit on the seller's statement. The offset is a credit on the closing agent's statement, so the closing agent will have the funds to write the check to the broker.

Completing a closing statement

Using the preceding rules as a guide, study the narrative below and the closing statement on the next page. Notice that the debit column and the credit column are subtotaled straight across the bottom for each of the three accounts (Buyer's Statement, Seller's Statement, and Escrow Statement). In this transaction the closing agent is an escrow company. Note: This fictitious statement is simplified for demonstration purposes and leaves out many entries which would be found in a real closing statement.

Narrative data

The sales price is $280,000. The buyer has paid $10,000 earnest money which the broker has already transferred to the escrow. The buyer will assume the seller's old loan of $120,000 and will pay a 1% assumption fee. The seller will carry a second trust deed for $80,000. The buyer will pay the balance of the purchase price in cash at closing. The buyer will pay $30 in recording fees and the seller will pay $10. The seller will pay a commission of $19,600. The seller will also pay a real estate transfer excise tax of 1.53% of the sales price. Property tax prorates will be $1,035 credit to the seller and debit to the buyer. Interest prorates on the assumed loan will be $207 debit to the seller and credit to the buyer. The parties will split the escrow fee of $300. The seller will pay for the buyer's title insurance, in the amount of $650. The terms of the earnest money agreement call for the seller to provide utility account data for prorating, and the seller did so, but the house has been vacant, all utilities are turned off, and the final bills paid in full.

	Buyer		Seller		Escrow	
	Debit	Credit	Debit	Credit	Debit	Credit
Sales price	280,000			280,000		
Earnest money		10,000			10,000	
Loan assumed		120,000	120,000			
Interest prorate		207	207			
Assumption fee	1,200					1,200
Second trust deed		80,000	80,000			
Recording fees	30		10			40
Tax prorates	1,035			1,035		
Transfer tax			4,284			4,284
Escrow fee	150		150			300
Title insurance			650			650
Commission			19,600			19,600
Subtotals	282,415	210,207	224,901	281,035	10,000	26,074

Note that the subtotals above for the debit and credit columns for the three statements are not in balance. For example, the buyer has $282,415 in debits, but only $210,207 in credits, meaning the buyer's statement is out of balance by $72,208 ($282,415 − $210,207 = $72,208). You may also have noticed that there is no entry for the buyer's down payment. If the purchase price is $280,000 and the loans total $200,000, then should there not be an entry of $80,000 for the buyer's down payment?

In reality, the down payment is not stated as such on a closing statement. Instead, the closing agent just brings the statement to this point, and then tells the buyer to bring in $72,208 to close the transaction. In other words, the buyer is short $72,208 to close, so the buyer must bring in additional funds. The additional funds include the down payment, as well as all the rest of the buyer's expenses, but less the earnest money already deposited.

Now, the interesting thing about the additional funds that the buyer will bring in ($72,208), is that the funds will become an additional credit on the buyer's statement. And since the buyer will give the funds to the escrow agent, the offset to the credit entry on the buyer's statement will be a debit to the escrow statement. These are normally entered right under the subtotals.

In similar fashion, you will note that the seller has an excess of credits over debits. So the seller will receive a check (an additional debit) for the difference between the seller's total credits and total debits. In the statement above, this is a total of $56,134 ($281,035 − $224,901 = $56,134). And when the escrow writes the seller the check for $56,134, it will become an additional debit to the seller, whose offset is a credit on the escrow statement.

NOTES

When you have finished entering the buyer's additional funds and the seller's sales proceeds, and their offsets on the escrow statement, you can total each account. This should result in statements that look like the following –

	Buyer		Seller		Escrow	
	Debit	*Credit*	*Debit*	*Credit*	*Debit*	*Credit*
Sales price	280,000			280,000		
Earnest money		10,000			10,000	
Loan assumed		120,000	120,000			
Interest prorate		207	207			
Assumption fee	1,200					1,200
Second trust deed		80,000	80,000			
Recording fees	30		10			40
Tax prorates	1,035			1,035		
Transfer tax			4,284			4,284
Escrow fee	150		150			300
Title insurance			650			650
Commission			19,600			19,600
Subtotals	282,415	210,207	224,901	281,035	10,000	26,074
Cash in/out		72,208	56.134		72,208	56,134
Totals	282,415	282,415	281,035	281,035	82,208	82,208

Notice that we forced a balance on the buyer's and seller's statements. If we forced a balance, how do we know that we did not make a mistake? We know that all the figures are correct because the escrow statement balanced when we added it up. In other words, balancing the escrow statement is the proof of the closing. Creating an escrow statement not only allows you to create proper offsets for the entries on the buyer's and seller's statements, it also allows you to create a balance so you know the buyer's and seller's statements are correct.

🔑 KEY TERMS

The key to understanding any new field is the vocabulary used in that field. To maximize your comprehension of the material presented in this chapter, be sure you know the meaning and significance of the following terms. Remember that the majority of test questions primarily test knowledge of vocabulary.

Assumption fee

Assumption letter

Back-to-back escrow

Banker's year

Calendar year

Certified escrow agent.

Chained escrow

Closing statement

Closing

Comprehensive Loss Underwriting Exchange

Credit

Debit

Double escrow

Double entry bookkeeping

Dual agency

Escrow instructions

Escrow agent

Estoppel certificate

Excise tax

Fiduciary

Fiduciary duty

Foreign Investment in Real Property Tax Act

Interpleader

Limited practice officer

National Flood Insurance Program

National Flood Insurance Reform Act of 1994

Offset

Open escrow

Payoff letter

Preliminary title report

Prepaid interest

Principal

Prorate

Scrivener

Split escrow.

Settlement

Title report

Chapter | 24

Property management

✳**M**ANY OWNERS FIND IT EXPEDIENT to hire someone to act as their property manager. Increasing urbanization and greater incidence of absentee ownership creates a need for quality property management. In addition, many owners do not have the time to manage their own property, or simply do not have the necessary knowledge of the law or ability to deal with tenants. And finally, even owners who could manage their own property usually find that they are able to negotiate with tenants better if there is a manager for the tenant to deal with.

Successful property management

A property manager becomes successful largely through word of mouth. If you manage a well-run property with satisfied tenants, they will tell other prospective tenants and you will find it easier to fill vacancies. Similarly, owners who are happy with your services will recommend you to other property owners, and your business will multiply.

Property owners expect their managers to maximize the return on their investments. Profits are at their highest when the tenants are satisfied customers because rents can then be maintained at optimum levels and vacancies will be at the lowest. Keeping tenants contented then, is a primary consideration of a successful manager. Of course, maximizing an owner's return on investment also involves complex decisions to maintain the property in good condition while reducing operating costs, as well as countless other factors.

Successful property managers need to understand that lowering costs does not necessarily increase the owner's return on the investment. In business there is a saying, "you have to spend money to make money." Of course, spending the owner's money foolishly is poor management, but at the same time, funds must be budgeted and expended to maintain the property in top condition. Low-paid employees may also seem cost-effective, until you consider the effect on tenant relations and the expense of redoing the work they may do wrong the first time. Demanding top quality for the best price available is a skill owners insist that their managers possess.

In this chapter we will discuss various matters specific to the management of real estate. But property managers should also be familiar with principles of investment, covered more thoroughly in Chapter 16.

Business cycles

The general business cycle is also a matter of concern to a property manager. Every property manager should know that business tends to expand and recede. During a period of expansion, of course, there will be few vacancies and rents can be raised. But management should also prepare for a recession, when vacancies are high. So as to preserve the owner's asset from the negative impact of a recession, a manager must make extra effort to keep expenses low.

The general business cycle goes through four phases – expansion, recession, contraction and revival. During the *expansion* period production increases, employment increases and economic growth occurs. Demand is high and market rents increase. The point where demand levels off is called *recession*.

However, too much demand can cause inflation. To counter inflation the government, through the operation of the Federal Reserve Bank System and other institutions, acts to curtail the availability of money and credit. Interest rates increase, causing demand to slacken. Unemployment rises and the entire economy goes into a downturn.

This is called **contraction**. The period of maximum recession is called **business contraction**. Ultimately, interest rates are lowered, prices have also lowered due to lack of demand, and consumers are lured back into the market. Thus begins the process of **revival**.

Real estate markets are also subject to the same wavelike cycles as the general business economy. Extremes of over- and undersupply apply to real estate the same as to any other commodity. However, real estate markets tend to lag behind the rest of the economy, sometimes so much so that it appears that real estate is running counter to the rest of the economy. Much of this is due to the fact that mortgage commitments, particularly for large commercial projects, tend to be made for several months in advance of when the funds will actually be used.

Property managers need to keep an eye on the overall supply of rental units in the area, and the demand for them. When there are more units available than tenants to fill them, we refer to this as a **technical oversupply**. If units are vacant because tenants cannot afford them, some economists call this an **economic oversupply**. Similarly, if there are more tenants wanting units than available units, this is a **technical undersupply** (technical shortage), and if there are more tenants who have the means to pay, it is an **economic undersupply** (economic shortage).

Property managers need to be aware of fluctuating vacancy levels. There is not a "standard" or "normal" vacancy percentage. Vacancy percentages always vary with economic conditions, and are always local in nature. Your community may be experiencing a boom and a low vacancy rate, but a tow across the state may have the opposite economic conditions. When making forecasts always base your vacancy figures on the real world around you.

Budgeting and management takeover

Property managers must also be able to handle the tasks involved in taking over the management of a property. Of course, a license is required when managing property for another. You will find extensive discussions of the requirements of Washington real estate licensing laws and rules with respect to property management in Chapter 19, and duties under the law of agency in Chapter 18.

When taking on the management of a new property, the manager's first duty is to analyze the regional and neighborhood market in which the property is located.

The regional market includes the entire metropolitan area or general area of the state in which the property is located. Analysis of this market includes demographic and economic information such as population trends, types of employment available in the area and the projections for future growth in the industries that are located in the region.

Analysis of the immediate neighborhood market in which the property is located includes a multitude of factors such as –

- Definition of the boundaries of the neighborhood and the features of the area, such as zoning, recreational areas, traffic counts along arterials, and the like.
- Transportation facilities, including proposed changes, availability of parking.
- Cost, availability and quality of utility services, particularly for industrial properties.
- Economic conditions, types of industries and level of diversification, and the potential for growth
- Supply and demand in the rental market, including occupancy rates and the potential for change.

- Current population, the number and density, willingness to lease or rent and their financial strength.

Although all these factors are important, for residential property probably the most important is the makeup of the population. If the population is increasing in number or density and its financial ability is improving, this augurs well for the market. For commercial property, on the other hand, traffic counts, competition in the area, availability of transportation services and other factors are more important.

Following regional and neighborhood market analysis, the property manager must prepare a *market rent analysis*, also called a *market rent survey*. This is simply a study of the competition – what other properties there are in the neighborhood and what rents they are able to command. Appraisers define a *neighborhood* as an area bordered by natural and man-made barriers in which the land use, economics, transportation and utilities are homogenous. The goal of a neighborhood market rent analysis is to determine the *market rent* (also called *economic rent*) for the property.

Having determined the market rent, the property manager must calculate the projected expenses. Expenses are categorized in two ways. *Fixed expenses* are those expenses which will occur regardless of occupancy rates or rental income (e.g., property taxes). *Variable expenses*, on the other hand, are expenses which increase and decrease as occupancy and income increase and decrease. Many accountants also categorize certain expenses as *mixed expenses*. For example, fire insurance is completely fixed, because the premium is the same whether the property is full or has vacancies. But if you are charging management fees based on the actual income received, then the owner's management expense is variable. On the other hand, the water bill in most communities is calculated on a base amount, whether any water is used or not, plus an additional amount according to the quantity of water used. Such an expense would have both fixed and variable elements, so it would be called a mixed expense.

Expenses are also categorized as recurring and non-recurring. Most expenses are *recurring expenses*, that is they recur monthly or yearly. The annual fire insurance premium or the monthly water bill are examples of recurring expenses. Some expenses, on the other hand, are one-time expenses. For example, it might become necessary to replace a refrigerator in an apartment. This would be considered a *non-recurring expense*. Non-recurring expenses are budgeted as reserves for replacement (see later).

Information on income and expenses is derived both from the marketplace, and from the owner's financial records. Once the manager has determined the market rent and the projected expenses, the manager can prepare a *projected operating statement*, (or *pro-forma*) to discuss with the owner. The projected operating statement should contain the manager's professional approach to optimizing the owner's investment. Problems to discuss might include abatement of accrued deferred maintenance (rehabilitation), increasing rents, and decreasing vacancies and turnover, and so on. A projected operating statement might look something like the example on the next page.

Note above the entry for "reserves for replacements." *Reserves for replacements* are also a type of maintenance, but include only large projects which are undertaken only every several years, such as re-roofing, exterior repainting, new carpeting, and the like. Reserves for replacements are also sometimes referred to as non-recurring expenses. The manager must estimate an annual allowance for reserves for replacement on the projected operating statement.

The bottom line in the projected operating statement is the net operating income. This is the amount that should be available to service the debt (*debt service*) and provide a cash return to the owner. The amount left over after debt service is sometimes called the *net spendable income*.

Crampington Manor Apartments

Projected Operating Statement (Pro-Forma)

Income

Potential Gross Income (PGI)		$ 450,000
Less vacancy and credit loss		− 22,500
Effective Gross Income (EGI)		$ 427,500

Operating Expenses

Fixed:

Property taxes	40,500	
Insurance	10,000	
Total fixed expenses		50,500

Variable:

Management (5%)	22,500	
Resident manager (5%)	22,500	
Utilities	24,000	
Maintenance	25,000	
Reserves for replacements	20,000	
Miscellaneous	10,000	
Total variable expenses		129,000
Total expenses		− 179,500
Net Operating Income (NOI)		$ 248,000

Investors also consider the return on their investment on a ***cash on cash*** basis. Cash on cash means taking the net spendable income and dividing it by the dollars invested (down payment). This gives the owner the expected annual return on the actual amount of the investment. Remember, you may pay $1 million dollars for a property, but if your down payment was 10% ($100,000), then your investment amount is $100,000, not $1 million.

Another important consideration in the operating statement is the ***break-even point***. In fact, the break-even point is the primary method used by investors to calculate the profitability of the investment. For rental property, the break-even point is the percentage of occupancy necessary to produce enough income to cover all fixed and variable expenses at that occupancy rate. The formula to calculate the break-even point is –

$$\frac{\textbf{Total Expense + Debt Service}}{\textbf{Potential Gross Income}} = \textbf{Percent of Occupancy}$$

In addition to the above formula, there are other more sophisticated ways of calculating a break-even point.

An important consideration in analyzing a property is the amount of rentable area and usable area. In an office structure, there are portions which are not usable or rentable. Property managers refer to the ***construction area*** as the total square footage of the structure as measured from outside dimensions. But the ***rentable area*** is the inside of the structure, including spaces not occupied by tenants such as restrooms, janitor's closets, mechanical equipment rooms, and the like. Rentable area, however, does not include intruding portions of the building structure such as pillars and stairwells. The ***usable*** *area* of the structure is that portion which tenants can actually occupy. Usable area does not include lobbies, common hallways and restrooms, although hallways contained within the tenant's area are considered part of the usable space.

Property managers and investors consider the ratio of rentable area to usable area an important factor in calculating the profitability of a structure and in setting rent rates. The ratio of rentable area to usable area is sometimes called a loss factor. The **loss factor** is a measure of the efficiency of space utilization in the building. When there are multiple tenants on the same floor, the loss factor is sometimes called the **load factor**. For example, if a building has 50,000 square feet of rentable space, but the usable space is only 40,000 square feet, then the rentable/usable ratio, or loss factor, is 125% (50,000 ÷ 40,000 = 1.25). Therefore, if a space is leased to a tenant at $20 per square foot of rentable space (for example), the tenant's real cost per square foot of usable space is $25.00 ($20.00 × 1.25 = $25.00). If rent rates are calculated on rentable area instead of usable area, then buildings with a high loss factor frequently rent at lower rates per square foot to reflect the fact that tenants do not gain as much benefit for their rent dollar.

When setting rent schedules, the market, of course will be the ultimate determiner of rental rates. Nevertheless, property managers and owners need to consider the minimum rent that they can charge in order to meet the expenses of the property and also provide a reasonable return on the investment. The minimum rent is calculated with the formula –

$$\frac{Operating\ Expenses + Debt\ Service + Owner's\ Return}{Rentable\ Area} = Minimum\ Rent$$

The results of this calculation will be the minimum rent that the owner can charge. If market rents are lower than the minimum rent, then the owner should not make the investment.

Rehabilitation

Rehabilitation of a property is a common reason an owner hires new management. The term **rehabilitation** generally means restoration of the property, but not usually alteration of its design, purpose, function, or utility. If a property requires rehabilitation, the manager must have a clear understanding with the owner as to how the work is to proceed and the source of funds to pay for it.

Government subsidized housing

The federal government has made a major impact in residential rental property through the **Section 8 Housing Assistance Payments Program** of the Department of Housing and Urban Development (HUD). Under this program, low income tenants receive a rent subsidy. The tenant pays rent in an amount up to 30% of the tenant's adjusted monthly income. Housing and Urban Development then pays the owner the difference between the rent paid by the tenant and the market rent as negotiated between the owner or property manager and HUD.

To rent a property under the HUD Section 8 Program, the owner must agree to the terms as required by the Program. This is accomplished by a **Housing Assistance Payments Contract**. In addition to the Housing Assistance Payments Contract, the owner must agree to a lease of the property for a specified period, usually at least one year. The lease is also a standard form required by HUD, and is called the **HUD Model Lease**.

The Residential Landlord-Tenant Act

For as long as there have been landlords and tenants their relationships have been the subject of legal disputes. Until recently, the legal relationship between a landlord and tenant has been in many ways out of step with the realities of modern life. In the late 1960s the federal government funded a project sponsored by the American Bar Association to create a Model Residential Landlord-Tenant Code, which was finally published in 1969. Subsequently, the National Conference of Commissioners on Uniform State Laws drafted the Uniform Residential Landlord and Tenant Act (URLTA) in 1972. This was adopted by the American Bar Association at its mid-year convention in August, 1972 with a recommendation that it be enacted in all states. In 1973 the Washington Legislature became one of the first states to enact legislation based on the URLTA when it passed the original Washington Residential Landlord-Tenant Act.

Today many states have adopted residential landlord-tenant laws based on the URLTA, but the laws in each state vary slightly from the original, including the Washington Residential Landlord-Tenant Act. Still, the common elements of state residential landlord-tenant laws today makes it easier for tenants moving from one state to the next to understand the law.

In 1974 the American Bar Association adopted amendments to the original URLTA, most of which were incorporated as amendments to the Washington Residential Landlord-Tenant Act. Since its effective date on July 16, 1973, the Washington Residential Landlord-Tenant Act has seen many other amendments, as well as court interpretations.

As could be inferred from its name, the Washington Residential Landlord-Tenant Act applies only to residential property. Even so, the Act excludes certain rental arrangements, such as –

- Institutional residential facilities, such as schools and colleges, medical care facilities, religious institutions, and other institutions where the reason for the tenant's occupancy is not just residence,
- Rental of a property by a purchaser prior to the closing of a sale, such as when the buyer moves in before closing
- Rental of premises in a hotel or motel on a transient basis
- Premises occupied by a resident manager of a landlord or owner, because the arrangement is for employment more than a rental arrangement
- Agricultural property, when it is rented as a business, but rental of a farmhouse separately is within the scope of the Act

It should be noted that the Manufactured/Mobile Home Landlord-Tenant Act (discussed later in this chapter) includes extensive provisions governing rental of spaces in mobile home parks. However, the Residential Landlord-Tenant Act applies to the rental mobile and manufactured homes where the landlord owns the home (in which case the Manufactured/Mobile Home Landlord-Tenant Act does *not* apply).

Rental agreements – The Residential Landlord-Tenant Act does not stipulate the content of rental agreements, except that certain provisions are prohibited. These include –

- Waiver of the tenant's rights under the Residential Landlord-Tenant Act
- Agreement that the landlord has a judgment against the tenant without having to file suit
- Waiver of landlord's liability (called an ***exculpation clause***)
- Agreement to use a particular arbitrator in the event of a dispute

A landlord who includes any of these provisions may be liable to the tenant for actual damages as well as attorney's fees.

The landlord must state the name and address of the landlord, either in the rental agreement or by posting a notice on the premises. If the landlord does not reside in Washington, then the landlord must designate someone who resides in the county as agent for service of legal process.

Unless the rental agreement stipulates otherwise, the tenancy is presumed to be month to month unless the rent is payable on some other periodic basis, e.g., week to week. Of course, this is merely a presumption. If the parties wish, they can stipulate other arrangements. However, a tenancy from year to year is abolished unless there is a specific agreement in writing creating it.

Deposits – Prior to the Residential Landlord and Tenant Act, tenants were frequently frustrated in their attempts to recover deposits, even though they left the premises in good condition. To remedy this situation, the Act stipulates that a *security deposit* is refundable – that is, it is subject to being refunded. This does not mean that a landlord cannot retain a security deposit if the tenant breaches the agreement. But it does mean that the tenant is entitled to receive a refund of the deposit or an accounting of why the landlord is not refunding the deposit, or a partial refund and partial accounting. The landlord must give the refund or accounting to the tenant within 14 days after the end of the tenancy or the landlord is liable to the tenant for twice the amount of the deposit as damages. Security deposits may not be used to make repairs for ordinary wear and tear.

In addition, if a landlord wishes to take a security deposit the landlord must provide the tenant with a written checklist "specifically describing the condition and cleanliness of or existing damages to the premises and furnishings ..." (59.18.260 RCW). The checklist must be dated and signed by the landlord and the tenant and the landlord must give the tenant a copy.

To ensure that the funds will be available for refund to the tenant, when a landlord takes a deposit it must be placed in a trust account. When an account is labeled as a trust account it means the funds are not subject to attachment or garnishment by a creditor of the landlord, because they are not deemed to be the landlord's property.

If a property rented to a tenant is sold, and the previous owner was holding a tenant's security deposit, the new owner automatically becomes liable to the tenant for refund of the deposit. For this reason, the seller must turn all deposits over to the buyer at closing.

The statute allows a "non-refundable" deposit to hold a unit for the tenant. If the tenant does rent the premises, the landlord is required to credit the tenant with the full amount of the deposit. If the tenant does not rent the premises, then the landlord may retain the deposit, provided there was a agreed upon written statement of conditions under which the landlord is entitled to keep the deposit. At the same time, it is illegal to take a deposit from a tenant merely to place them on a waiting list. If the landlord takes a deposit to hold a unit, the unit must be available.

Tenant screening charge – In the past it was common for landlords to increase their profits by charging a credit report fee (*tenant screening charge*) in excess of their actual costs. The landlord is now prohibited from charging more than what a screening service charges. If the landlord does the screening, then the landlord can charge whatever the landlord's costs are, but not more than the amount a screening service in the area would charge. Because the amount could be disputed by tenants, most landlords use an outside service which simply bills the landlord at a flat rate.

The landlord is prohibited from requiring an applicant screening charge unless the landlord discloses to the applicant the name and address of the screening service the landlord will use, or the process by which the landlord will conduct the screening (i.e., what the landlord will check), and tells the applicant of his or her right to contest any incorrect information. The landlord must also comply with the provisions of the federal Fair Credit Reporting Act.

Landlord obligations – Prior to the Residential Landlord and Tenant Act, there were occasions when tenants were unable to make their landlords provide safe, clean and decent housing. While the majority of landlords were reasonably conscientious about the condition of their property, the law now provides mandatory minimum standards. These include –

- Reasonable weatherproofing of the dwelling
- Facilities adequate to provide hot and cold water, and an adequate heating system, except where the building is not equipped for the purpose
- Electrical, plumbing, heating and other appliances furnished by the landlord maintained in good working order
- Providing a reasonable program to control pest infestation at the start of the tenancy and even during the tenancy unless it is a single-family dwelling or the infestation is caused by the tenant
- Appropriate garbage and rubbish receptacles, including removal, unless it is a single-family dwelling
- Roofs, floors, walls, chimneys, fireplaces, foundations and other structural components maintained in good repair
- Working locks with keys provided to the tenant
- Maintaining the premises to comply with any laws relating to matters which could impair the health or safety of the tenant, including keeping the premises in the condition they should be in, except for normal wear and tear.
- A working smoke detector at the start of the tenancy and a notice to the tenant that the dwelling has a smoke detector. If the building is other than a single-family residence, the landlord must also disclose whether it is hard-wired or battery-operated, whether the building has a sprinkler system, a fire alarm system, a smoking policy, or an emergency notification, relocation or evacuation plan. The notice must also advise the tenant that it is the tenant's obligation to maintain the smoke detector and that the tenant is liable for a fine up to $200 for failure to do so. The notice must be signed by both the landlord and the tenant at the start of the tenancy with copies to each party.

While the landlord is normally obligated to maintain the premises to the above standards, if the problem was caused by the tenant or the tenant's family or guests the tenant loses the right to complain. The tenant also loses the right to complain if the tenant refused to allow the landlord access to make repairs. And the tenant must be current in payment of rent and utilities, although the tenant could still raise the defense that defects in the property lowered its rental value, so the amount of rent the tenant paid should be considered adequate.

If the premises do not meet these standards, the landlord and the tenant may enter into an agreement that the tenant is to make repairs. To do so the tenant must receive adequate consideration for the work as a cash payment or rent reduction.

If the landlord fails to maintain the premises as required by the Act the tenant has various remedies, but first the tenant must give the landlord notice. Except for circumstances beyond the landlord's control the landlord must repair the premises within –

- 24 hours for lack of hot or cold water, heat, electricity, or is imminently hazardous to life,
- 72 hours for lack of use of a major plumbing fixture, or a range, refrigerator or oven if supplied by the landlord,
- Ten days in all other cases.

The tenant can give the landlord an estimate of the cost of repair and if the landlord fails to repair as required within the time limits, the tenant can have the premises repaired according to the estimate, provided the cost is not over one month's rent. The tenant can then deduct the cost from the rent. If the cost is under one half of a month's rent the tenant does not have to give the landlord the estimate.

As an alternative the tenant can bring action against the landlord and obtain judgment for the cost of the repair (not over one month's rent), plus a claim for reduction in rental value. If the court or arbitrator agree that the rental value is diminished and as a result the tenant overpaid rent, the judgment will include the amount of the overpayment.

If the tenant cannot reasonably use the remedy of having the repairs made, and the premises substantially endanger the health or safety of the tenant, the tenant can give the notice as usual and, if the landlord fails to correct the problem, the tenant can ask the local government to inspect the premises (or have them inspected). If the inspector agrees that the premises are unsafe, the tenant may pay the rent into an escrow so as to withhold it from the landlord.

In all cases, as an alternative remedy, the tenant can terminate the rental agreement. If the tenant terminates the rental agreement because of the landlord's failure to repair the premises as required, the tenant is entitled to pro-rata refund of rent and any deposits unless the tenant has breached the rental agreement and given the landlord cause to retain the deposit.

A landlord is prohibited from renting a property that has posted as unfit for human habitation by a local government agency. If the landlord rents the property in violation of the law the landlord is liable for treble damages or three times the monthly rent.

Tenant's obligations – A frequent complaint of landlords is that tenants abuse the premises. To remedy this problem, the Residential Landlord-Tenant Act creates specific obligations of the tenant. The tenant must –

- Not do anything on the premises that is imminently hazardous to others, or assault others, or use a firearm or other deadly weapon
- Keep the premises as clean and sanitary as their condition permits
- Dispose of all rubbish, garbage and other waste from the premises in a clean and safe manner and pay for all necessary extermination and fumigation
- Not allow waste or commit a nuisance on the premises
- Properly use the electrical, plumbing, heating and gas, appliances and fixtures supplied by the landlord
- Maintain the smoke detector, including replacement of batteries
- Not deliberately or negligently destroy, deface, damage, impair or remove any part of the premises including personal property furnished by the landlord, or allow anyone else to do so
- Not engage in gang or drug activity, or allow others to do so
- Restore the premises at the end of the tenancy to the same condition as they were at the start of the tenancy, ordinary wear and tear excepted

Rules – Many times a landlord will find it necessary to adopt occupancy rules. Normally, rules are adopted at the start of the tenancy either by including them in the rental agreement or posting them with reference to them in the rental agreement. Changes to rules can go into effect upon giving 30 days notice of them to the tenant. Rent increases also require a 30-day notice.

Right of access – A landlord is entitled to enter the premises to inspect, make repairs or alterations, supply services, or show the premises to prospective purchasers, lenders, tenants or contractors. Normally, the landlord must give the tenant two days notice prior to entering the premises. However, there are exceptions. A landlord can enter the premises without notice –

- In the event of an emergency
- Under order of a court
- With the consent of the tenant
- If the landlord has reason to believe the premises have been abandoned

The landlord can also enter to show the unit to potential buyers or tenants at a specified time, in which case only one days notice is required.

The landlord cannot abuse the right of access or harass the tenant. If the landlord fails to give proper notice, or harasses the tenant, the tenant may give notice to the landlord that the landlord is in violation. Thereafter the landlord is liable to the tenant in the amount of $100 for each further violation.

Mitigation – If the tenant has abandoned the premises, then the landlord must make a reasonable effort to re-rent the premises for a fair rental value. If the previous tenant (who abandoned the premises) had paid rent in advance, upon re-renting the premises the landlord must refund rent for any overlapping period. The concept is that the landlord may not collect rent for the same space for the same period of time from two different tenants.

Tenant's personal property – The Residential Landlord-Tenant Act contains provisions which balance the landlord's right to recover possession and dispose of abandoned property as quickly as possible, with the tenant's right to be sure that property which is not really abandoned is not lost without proper notice.

At common law a landlord has an automatic lien on the tenant's personal property, which gave the landlord the right to hold the personal property to enforce collection of rent. In most states this is referred to as **distraint for rent**, but in Washington code it is called **distress for rent**. Under the Residential Landlord-Tenant Act, distress for rent is abolished. However, it is abolished only for tenancies covered by the Residential Landlord-Tenant Act, not for all tenancies.

If the tenant has abandoned the premises and stopped paying rent the landlord may enter the premises and remove any of the tenant's personal property. The landlord must place the property in storage and send the tenant a notice that it has been removed and that the tenant can reclaim it by paying the costs of removal and storage. If the tenant does not do so within 45 days (seven days if the value is $50 or less), the landlord may proceed to sell the property or dispose of it. The landlord may apply the proceeds of the sale to any unpaid obligations of the tenant to the landlord, and must hold any surplus for the tenant for up to one year. If the tenant does not claim the funds within the year the landlord may keep them.

If the premises are vacant because the landlord has evicted the tenant, the rules for the tenant's personal property are somewhat different. In this case the landlord can enter and remove the property to a secure place, but if the tenant objects to its storage, then the landlord can deposit it "upon the nearest public property" (59.18.312 RCW). In other words, "out in the street."

If the tenant does not object, and the landlord removes the property to storage, the tenant can reclaim the property any time by paying the landlord's cost of removal and storage. The landlord can give the tenant notice of the landlord's intent to sell or dispose of the property and proceed with a sale or disposal 45 days thereafter (seven days if the value is $50 or less). The landlord can apply the proceeds to amounts the tenant owes the landlord, but must retain any surplus for one year. If the tenant does not claim the surplus within the year the landlord must turn the funds over to the state as abandoned property instead of keeping it.

In cases where the value is $50 or less and the landlord sells or disposes of the tenant's property within seven days the landlord cannot sell or dispose of "personal papers, family pictures and keepsakes."

Retaliatory conduct – The Residential Landlord-Tenant Act allows the tenant to exercise certain rights without fear of retaliation by the landlord and it is illegal for the landlord to take action against the tenant for exercising any of these rights. These rights include –

- Complaining to any governmental agency of violation(s) of codes relating to the operation or maintenance of the premises
- Asserting or enforcing any of the tenant's rights under the Residential Landlord-Tenant Act

It is considered *reprisal or retaliatory action* if the landlord, in response to the tenant exercising the above rights, increases the tenant's rent or other obligations, decreases services, or evicts a tenant.

Nevertheless, the landlord has a rebuttable presumption that an eviction was not a reprisal or retaliatory action if the tenant is in default in paying the rent or otherwise in breach of the rental agreement. "Rebuttable presumption" means that a court must assume the landlord is right unless the tenant can prove otherwise. Also, the landlord does not engage in a reprisal or retaliatory action by evicting a tenant when the property is in such condition that it is necessary to evict the tenant before repairs can be made. It is also a rebuttable presumption that a tenant's complaint was not in good faith if it was made within 90 days of a notice of rent increase. And if the tenant files a complaint and the landlord thereafter raises the rent it is not a reprisal or retaliatory action if the landlord can prove that the rent increase is reasonable under market conditions.

Eviction – When a landlord files a suit to evict a tenant, this is called an *actual eviction*. The legal expression in most states is an action for forcible entry and (wrongful) detainer, sometimes abbreviated "F.E.D." In Washington this is usually referred to simply as an *unlawful detainer*. When a landlord attempts to force a tenant out by refusing or deliberately neglecting to supply essential services, this is called a *constructive eviction*. While constructive eviction is not barred in other types of tenancies, the Residential Landlord-Tenant Act does not permit its use for residential tenancies.

When a landlord gives a tenant proper notice and the tenant remains unlawfully in possession, the landlord may file an eviction proceeding. Similarly, the tenant can move out and terminate the tenancy upon proper notice to the landlord. If the tenancy is month to month or for another period, either party may give the other 20 days notice at any time without needing a reason. If the tenancy is for years (lease), then neither party can give the other notice unless the other party has breached the lease. Leases terminate automatically at the specified end date of the lease without needing any special notice.

For month-to-month tenancies, the landlord can give the tenant –

- Three days notice if the tenant has failed to pay the rent, has allowed waste, is conducting an unlawful business on the premises, or is creating a nuisance
- Ten days notice for any other breach of the rental agreement.

The landlord can also give three days notice to a trespasser. A trespass is different from a tenancy by sufferance in that a tenant by sufferance originally had a legal right to possession but has held over wrongfully after the right expired. A trespasser never had a legal right to possession. Trespass is a criminal act as well as a civil wrong.

If the landlord attempts to evict the tenant for non-payment of rent, or sues the tenant for unpaid rent, the tenant may counterclaim for any damages the tenant feels is owed by the landlord. If the tenant's counterclaim is successful, the court must offset the claims of the landlord by the amount of the tenant's counterclaim.

For example, suppose the landlord files an eviction, claiming that a month's rent in the amount of $1,000 is past due. However, the tenant counterclaims that the property did not meet standards required under the Residential Landlord-Tenant Act and the landlord failed to remedy the situation, causing the rental value to be diminished by $300 per month for the past four months – so the tenant's total counterclaim is for $1,200. If the court agrees that the tenant's counterclaim is just, then the landlord actually owes the difference ($200) to the tenant, and the landlord's suit to evict will be dismissed.

However, where a landlord has sued to evict a tenant and the tenant's counterclaims are less than the amount of rent owing, the tenant must pay the remainder of the rent to the court to retain possession.

To evict a tenant the landlord must file a suit in superior court of the county where the property is located. The complaint must be served on the tenant, who must file an answer within six days of service, although in some cases a longer time may be allowed. If the tenant fails to answer the landlord wins by default. If the tenant files an answer the case will be heard by the court. Even after hearing the case the court may find in favor of the landlord. When the landlord wins the court will grant a **writ of restitution**. The writ of restitution is an order from the court that the tenant must make restitution of possession to the landlord. Once the writ is issued it will be served on the tenant. If the tenant fails to move out the landlord can ask the court to order the sheriff to move the tenant out.

As soon as the landlord files the complaint the landlord may apply for a writ of execution, without even waiting for service on the tenant or the hearing. If the landlord posts a bond sufficient to pay any damages in the event the landlord's case was wrongful, the court can issue the writ of restitution right away. If the eviction is for non-payment of rent the tenant can stop the landlord from forcing the tenant to move out by paying what is due into the court. If the tenant claims offsetting damages the tenant can claim the amount as part or all of the amount the tenant must pay into the court to keep from having to move out.

Victims of violence – In recent years the public has become aware of the plight of tenants who are the victims of violence. The legislature has addressed this issue by providing that if a tenant reports that another tenant has threatened the tenant with a firearm or other deadly weapon and the landlord does not file an eviction against the tenant who threatened the tenant within seven days after the tenant was arrested, the tenant who was threatened may terminate his or her tenancy immediately without liability for further rent.

There have also been cases where the tenancy was held by co-tenants and one of them is the victim of domestic violence by the other. In the past many apartment managers have followed the policy of evicting the tenants under a "zero tolerance" policy. In the case of *Alvera v. CBM Group* heard by the Seattle Office of the Department of Housing and Urban Development, it was held that the defendant's policy of evicting both the perpetrator and the victim violated the victim's civil rights under federal law.

Manufactured/Mobile Home Landlord-Tenant Act

The Manufactured/Mobile Home Landlord-Tenant Act applies only to manufactured home and mobile home parks. (Although the term **mobile home** is still commonly used, the term for a dwelling built after 1976 is **manufactured home**, because after 1976 dwellings were built to national standards created by the Department of Housing and Urban Development.) Mobile and manufactured homes on rented spaces in parks have particular problems, partly due to the fact that they may be financed, so consideration must be given to the rights of lenders, and also because having to move them can be costly for the tenant. Therefore, the Manufactured/Mobile Home Landlord-Tenant Act was created with requirements of the parties the same as the Residential Landlord-Tenant Act, but with certain special provisions. These provisions include –

• The landlord cannot terminate the rental agreement except for substantial or repeated violation of the rules (mediation required), non-payment of rent (five days notice required), or upon fifteen days notice for conviction of a crime which endangers the safety of other tenants, engaging in criminal activity, failure of the tenant to comply with laws relating to mobile or manufactured homes, disorderly or substantially annoying conduct, or any other act that materially affects the health, safety or welfare of other tenants.

• A landlord cannot charge extra for guest parking.

• Rules can be adopted only if they are to further the welfare of tenants, preserve the premises from abuse or make a fair distribution of services to the tenants, and are not used to evade the landlord's duties or retaliatory or discriminatory.

• Rental contracts must be in writing and must normally be for periods of at least one year, and must provide reasonable rules, including rules for guest parking, the name and address of the landlord, the name and address of any party with a security interest in the home, and a covenant by the landlord that the landlord will not change the use of the land for three years, the utilities which will be available to the tenant and their cost, the description of the boundaries of the space, and the current zoning on the land.

• Rental contracts may not provide for towing or impounding of a vehicle without notice to the owner, increases in rent more often than annually (although escalator clauses are permitted), an entrance fee, that the landlord may charge the tenant for guests, that the tenant waives their homestead rights, or that a particular arbitrator must be used in the event of a dispute.

• Landlords are entitled to a landlord's lien on the tenant's personal property up to a maximum of four months rent.

• If the home is financed and the lender forecloses its lien the lender is entitled to continue the rental agreement and notice to terminate the agreement can be by thirty days notice.

• Landlords cannot require removal of a home merely because it has reached a certain age.

• Landlords cannot dictate whom the tenant may choose as supplier of goods or services, although the landlord may reserve the right to approve exterior structural improvements.

• Rental agreements and occupancy rules may not contain provisions which limit the tenants reasonable right to assemble peaceably or canvas on the common areas of the facility, nor can the landlord prevent tenants from speaking or inviting speakers to speak on political issues.

• Landlords cannot increase the rent except on renewal of the agreement and must give at least three months advance notice.

• Tenants must give one months notice of an intent not to renew a rental agreement, except that a tenant can terminate a rental agreement with 30 days notice if the tenant has a change in employment requiring the tenant to relocate.

• Landlords may not transfer the duty to maintain permanent structures in the park to the tenants.

• Landlords may not charge a guest fee if a tenant has a live-in care provider.

• Landlords must maintain the common areas, including roads and utilities and extermination of pests.

• Landlords must respect the privacy of tenants and are not permitted entrance into the tenant's dwelling except in case of emergency, and if the landlord needs access to the tenant's space other than the dwelling the landlord must make a reasonable effort to notify the tenant beforehand.

• If an owner of a home wishes to sell the dwelling, the landlord may not require the owner to remove the dwelling from the park for the purpose of selling it or restrict the tenant's right to sell the home, and the landlord must allow the tenant to assign the rental agreement to the buyer, subject to reasonable credit review.

Commercial property management

When people think of property management their minds almost always assume residential properties. While residential property management may account for the majority of property management activity, non-residential management is no less important. It is especially significant for real estate brokers who specialize in commercial investment property. Being able to manage an office building for a buyer goes hand in glove with commercial brokerage. In fact, many investors prefer to buy only from firms who can also manage the property for them after the sale.

There are many differences between managing residential property and managing commercial property. One difference is the manner in which the agent is typically compensated. In residential management it is customary to collect the rent for the owner, so the property manager normally collects the management fee as a percentage of the rent receipts. In addition, a residential property manager would charge an extra fee for re-renting the property, perhaps half of the new tenant's first month's rent or so.

In commercial management properties are typically leased because business tenants need to know they have the right to a location for a period of time. The role of the property manager becomes less a rent collector and more a mere broker of the lease. In the majority of commercial leases the tenant pays the rent directly to the owner. The property manager just brings the parties together, much as a real estate broker brings a buyer and seller together and negotiates the terms of the transaction.

Since the property manager is not collecting the rent, there is nothing from which to collect ongoing management fees. The solution is for the property manager to charge for the negotiation of the lease in more or less the same way that a real estate broker would charge for arranging a sale – a straight percentage of the rent payments over the total term of the lease.

As with any compensation arrangement, the amount is negotiable. But there is a problem with charging a commission for arranging a lease. A sale is a transaction that is over and done with. A lease may last for decades. Should the property manager charge the same percentage of the rent over the entire term?

Most owners would object. After all, what would happen if the tenant's circumstances changed and the parties voluntarily terminated the lease early? Or if the owner ended up having to evict the tenant after a few years of a long term lease? For these reasons it is customary to charge a higher percentage of the rent for the first years, diminishing over the later years of the lease.

Renewals are another matter to consider when calculating leasing commissions. The agent normally expects to be paid an additional commission if the parties renew the lease, although the amount is typically considerably less than the original fee.

In commercial (and once in a while even in residential) transactions, there are special terms that are sometimes incorporated into a lease. Brokers and property managers also have special names for certain types of leases.

A *flat lease* is a lease where the rental payments are equal throughout the term. It is also sometimes called a *straight lease* or *fixed lease*. In contrast, many leases call for changes in the amount of rent. A *graduated lease* (also sometimes called a *step-up lease*) is a lease where the lease provides for pre-agreed increases in the rent. The part of the lease where this is stipulated is called the *escalator* or *escalation clause*. The rent due under a lease can also be tied to an index (called an *index lease*), such as the Consumer Price Index. Many times the lease will just provide that the rent will be adjusted annually according to the increase in the owner's operating costs and property taxes.

There is an implied covenant of quiet enjoyment in all leases and rental agreements. While a lessor of a residential property cannot escape this because of the provisions of the Residential Landlord-Tenant Act, owners of commercial properties frequently limit their liability with an *exculpation clause* in the agreement.

A *percentage lease* is common in retail centers such as shopping malls. The lease payments are usually stipulated as a base, plus a percentage of the tenant's gross sales. The effect of the percentage lease is to make the lessor the "partner" of the lessee so the lessor has an interest in encouraging shoppers to patronize the lessee's business. At the same time, it provides the lessor with funds which can be used to promote the entire shopping center. The more the lessor promotes the shopping center, the greater the number of customers, resulting in greater sales, thereby generating greater rent income to cover the cost of the promotion.

In most cases the percentage portion of the rent is based on the gross sales, rather than the tenant's net income. The reason for this is the difficulty in defining what constitutes expense. Basing the rent on gross sales causes fewer disputes between the landlord and the tenant. Even so, the lease typically has exclusions for certain items. For example, a typical percentage lease would state that income the tenant receives from interest earned on customer accounts is not considered part of gross sales.

When a lease is based on the tenant's gross sales and nothing else, then it is called a *straight percentage lease*. In most cases the landlord would prefer a base rent, in which case it is called a *fixed minimum percentage lease*. In a fixed minimum percentage lease the portion of the rent attributable to the percentage is called the *overage rent*. It is also common to find a ceiling on the gross sales that are subject to the rent percentage calculation.

Percentage leases also frequently contain a *recapture clause*. This clause allows the landlord to terminate the lease if the tenant's gross sales fall below a stated minimum. A landlord desires the recapture clause, not just because it increases the landlord's rent income, but because a tenant who is not performing is hurting all other tenants in the shopping center as well. For this reason a shopping center lease also typically requires each tenant to participate in *cooperative advertising*.

Shopping centers are very dependent on the existence of one or more anchor tenants. An *anchor tenant* is any major tenant such as a large department or food store or similar type of business. Without an anchor tenant, the shopping center is likely to wither and die, for it is the anchor tenant which draws the majority of the customers. Because they have great bargaining power, it is common for the anchor tenant to be able to negotiate an *anchor lease* at very low rental rates.

The owner of the shopping center typically makes the profit on the smaller tenants. While this may seem undemocratic, the reality is that without the anchor tenant there would be no shopping center in the first place. This is easier to grasp when you consider the process a developer must go through to create a shopping center. Ultimately everything depends on financing, so the first step after identifying the site is to obtain financing commitments. Large shopping centers are typically financed by insurance companies and other large funds. These lenders look first for anchor tenants and will not issue a commitment without first seeing a signed anchor lease.

Which expenses each party will be responsible for during the term of a lease will normally be spelled out in the lease. Real estate agents use the relative terms **net** and **gross** to describe leases. The more net the lease, the fewer expenses the lessor will pay, and vice-versa.

Investors use the special term **net, net, net lease** (or **triple net lease**) to describe a lease where the tenant pays all of the expenses, including maintenance, insurance and property taxes. The opposite of a net, net, net lease is a **full-service lease**, where the landlord provides all services, usually including heat, light and janitorial service. Of course, lessors and lessees may negotiate a lease which is anywhere between these two extremes.

When a commercial tenant leases an entire structure, the owner typically desires to lease it on a net, net, net basis, especially if the lease is relatively long term. The usual reason is that the tenant will likely make improvements to the property. The improvements increase the costs, especially the property taxes. Therefore, the owner's inclination is to have the tenant pay such added costs. By the same token, the tenant also prefers a net, net, net lease because the tenant can better control costs such as utilities and janitorial. The result is that both lessor and lessee prefer the net, net, net lease.

On the other hand, if the structure is large and is occupied by various tenants, it is not usually practical to provide individual utility meters and separate janitorial services for each tenant. Apportioning the insurance and property taxes would also be difficult. As a result, such properties are typically leased on a full-service basis.

Many times a lease contains an **expansion option**. An expansion option is a clause which allows the tenant to lease additional space, usually after a period of time. In reality most landlords would never agree to an expansion option if it requires them to leave premises unrented in case the tenant wishes to exercise the expansion option. However, an expansion option is sometimes used where it gives the tenant the right to additional space from neighboring space when the tenant in that space vacates.

A **ground lease** is a lease of the bare land only, usually on a long-term basis and where the tenant typically intends to build a structure on the land. The term of the lease will usually be for a term equal to the projected economic life of the building which the lessee contemplates building. An advantage to the lessee is that the cost of the land can be cheaper this way, and there are potential income tax benefits for both lessor and lessee. If the lessee had purchased the land the only tax write-off would be the cost recovery on the building because you cannot claim cost recovery on land, whereas with the ground lease the lease payments are also deductible as a business expense. At the same time, using a ground lease can sometimes avoid capital gains tax that the lessor would have had to pay if the lessor had sold the land.

If the lessee wishes to finance the building to be built on ground leased land, there are certain problems which must be addressed. The lender will want to make sure the building is secured as collateral for the loan. Normally a lender would take a note (evidence of the debt) from the borrower, and also a mortgage or trust deed to create a lien on the real property and make it the collateral for the note. In this case, the mortgage or trust deed would have to be a mortgage or trust deed on the leasehold interest, since that is all the borrower holds.

However, an eviction has the effect of extinguishing a lease. Therefore, if the lessee fails to pay the rent, the lessor could evict the tenant and take the property back. If the lender holds a mortgage or trust deed on a leasehold and the leasehold is extinguished, then the lender's mortgage or trust deed is extinguished with it. This leaves the lender with nothing more than an unsecured note. To protect the lender, ground leases where the building must be financed are typically created in such a way as to make the mortgage prior in right to the lease. A simple way to do this is to have the lessor sign the mortgage as well as the lessee. By signing the mortgage, the lessor is agreeing that the lessor's interest is subordinate to the mortgage.

Many times a tenant will desire to install items on the leased premises. Normally items permanently affixed will become part of the real property. However, the law holds that items installed by a tenant remain personal property. Therefore, the tenant may remove the items at the termination of the tenancy. The tenant must do so before the end of the tenancy or they are deemed to be abandoned and become part of the real property. The tenant must also restore the premises and repair any damage caused by their installation and removal.

When items are installed on leased commercial premises we call them ***trade fixtures***. Similarly, items installed on residential property are sometimes called ***residential fixtures*** and items installed on agricultural property are frequently called ***agricultural fixtures***.

KEY TERMS

The key to understanding any new field is the vocabulary used in that field. To maximize your comprehension of the material presented in this chapter, be sure you know the meaning and significance of the following terms. Remember that the majority of test questions primarily test knowledge of vocabulary.

Actual eviction	*Exculpation clause*
Agricultural fixture	*Expansion*
Anchor lease	*Expansion option*
Anchor tenant	*Expenses*
Break-even point	*Fixed expense*
Business contraction	*Fixed lease*
Cash on cash	*Fixed minimum percentage lease*
Construction area	*Flat lease*
Constructive eviction	*Full-service lease*
Contraction	*Graduated lease*
Cooperative advertising	*Gross*
Debt service	*Ground lease*
Distraint for rent	*Housing Assistance Payments Contract*
Distress for rent	*HUD Model Lease*
Economic oversupply	*Index lease*
Economic rent	*Load factor*
Economic undersupply	*Loss factor*
Escalation clause	*Manufactured home*
Escalator	*Market rent*
Exculpation clause	*Market rent analysis*

Market rent survey

Mixed expense

Mobile home

Neighborhood

Net

Net spendable income

Net, net, net lease

Non-recurring expense

Overage rent

Percentage lease

Pro-forma

Projected operating statement

Recapture clause

Recession

Recurring expense

Rehabilitation

Rentable area

Reprisal or retaliatory action

Reserves for replacements

Residential fixture

Revival

Section 8 Housing Assistance Payments Program

Security deposit

Step-up lease

Straight lease

Straight percentage lease

Technical oversupply

Technical undersupply

Tenant screening charge

Trade fixture

Triple net lease

Unlawful detainer

Usable area

Variable

Writ of restitution

25

Real estate arithmetic

REAL ESTATE ARITHMETIC is a subject which most people find relatively easy, and which completely baffles others. There seem to be few in the middle. This is probably due to early life experiences, but blaming your parents and teachers is little consolation now that you want to get a real estate license.

Fortunately, there are few questions on the real estate examinations which require any mathematics at all. In fact, it is an unusual exam if it has as many as 10% questions involving any kind of mathematics. So if you fail every calculation question on the state and national examinations, you would still pass comfortably if you were well versed in the rest of your real estate studies.

For most non-mathematically oriented students, the best thing to do is study other aspects of real estate rather than worry about mathematics. Mathematics is a skill subject and cannot be crammed. Like learning a language, it takes a great deal of practice to master mathematical skills. Unless you have months before you are scheduled to take the examinations, you probably do not have time to become very proficient at it. Nevertheless, even students who are good at mathematics can profit from a review of some simple concepts, and (like learning a language), even if you can't take the time to become fluent, at least you can learn some basics.

Although you may be able to pass a real estate examination with only a rudimentary knowledge of arithmetic and business mathematics, when you obtain your license and start selling real estate you will discover that the world of real estate dishes out a lot of real estate mathematics. For this reason, as well as to help prepare for the real estate exams, you will find on the following pages ad discussion of various kinds of real estate arithmetical computations.

Real estate arithmetic questions can be separated into several categories. Although there are a few questions which are unique, most questions belong to the following types –

- Area and volume problems
- Commission problems
- Part-whole and ratio problems
- Profit and loss
- Legal descriptions
- Interest and loan calculations
- Economic life, book value and depreciation
- Property taxes, insurance and prorating
- Capitalization and return on investment

Many of these problems have been covered in previous chapters in this text. Therefore in this chapter we will concentrate on just area and volume, commission, part-whole and ratio, profit and loss. basic percentage and interest problems.

In the following pages you will find formulas, tips and techniques to solve these kinds of problems, particularly the sort you will find on the exams.

Area problems

Area problems can involve any shape object, but in real estate exam questions they almost always involve squares, rectangles, triangles, and occasionally circles. Of these, squares are the easiest. The formula to find the area of a square is –

$$A = s^2$$

Where "*A*" is the area and "*s*" is the length of a side. As you may recall, the superscripted number "2" in the above formula is read "squared" and means that you multiply the "*s*" (side) by itself. So you could state the same formula as –

$$A = s \times s$$

Now, a rectangle is similar to a square, except that it has two pairs of equal sides instead of four equal sides –

Square	Rectangle

Although the rectangle looks different, you use the same formula to calculate its area, that is, you find the area by multiplying one side by the other. For rectangles, we usually write the formula

$$A = l \times w$$

Where "*l*" is the length and "*w*" is the width. But notice that you still multiply one side by the other, so you can solve area problems for squares and rectangles the same way – just multiply one side by the other.

What is the area of a square which is 6 miles on a side?

Answer   A = s × s
            A = 6 × 6
            A = 36 square miles

What is the area of a rectangle which is 12 feet by 6 feet?

Answer   A = l × w
            A = 12 × 6
            A = 72 square feet

Triangles are also really easy. If you look at the triangle (dark area) below, you will notice that it is obviously exactly one-half of the rectangle that it is inside of –

So the formula for finding the area of a triangle is just to find the area of the rectangle it is inside of and divide the result by two –

$$A = \tfrac{1}{2} \times l \times w$$

Where "*l*" is still the length and "*w*" is still the width. However, for most people it seems to make more sense to call the sides of a triangle the "base" and the "height" rather than the length and the width, so the formula is usually written "$A = \tfrac{1}{2} \times b \times h$."

Notice what would happen if you move the topmost point of the triangle along the top line of the rectangle. If you slide the topmost point back and forth across the top, you get an infinite number of differently shaped triangles –

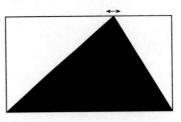

The interesting thing about this is that regardless of where you slide the point to, the area inside the triangle stays the same – as it loses on one side it gains on the other and vice-versa. So you can trust that the formula will work with the base and height of any triangle.

What is the area of a triangle whose base is 18 feet and which is 8 feet high?

Answer   A = ½ × b × h
             A = ½ × 18 × 8
             A = 72 square feet

Occasionally exam questions ask you to calculate the **perimeter** of a square or a rectangle. This is the easiest question of all. Just add up the sides. Officially, the formula for a square is –

$$P = 4 \times s$$

Which means "Perimeter equals 4 times the side." And for a rectangle, the standard formula is

$$P = (2 \times l) + (2 \times w)$$

Which is read "Perimeter equals 2 times the length plus 2 times the width." But rather than remember the formulas, just remember to add up the sides. The rule works equally well for any square, rectangle, or any other figure. Of course, it doesn't work for circles, because circles don't have sides, which means that circles need special treatment.

We'll start with the area of a circle. But before we get started we have to introduce you to π. Practically anything you do with a circle requires that you remember π (π is pronounced "pie" but spelled out in English letters as "pi"). Fortunately, there are hardly any exam questions today which contain circles, although there may be an occasional one. You may remember from grade school that π is 3.14159 (and a lot more decimals without apparent end). Scientists who fire rockets at the moon are interested in taking π to many decimal places, but two places (3.14) is plenty for ordinary real estate work.

You also have to remember that the **diameter** is the distance all the way through the circle, and the **radius** is half way through (one-half the diameter). So if you have the radius, but need the diameter to solve the problem, just multiply the radius by 2 to get the diameter. Similarly, divide the diameter by two to get the radius.

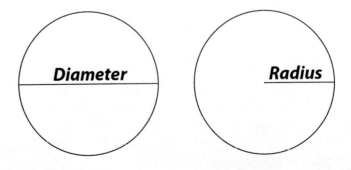

The formula for the area of a circle is –

$$A = \pi \times r^2$$

Which is read "π times the radius squared," or "π r squared." Remember, **squared** means multiplying the figure by itself. So to find the area of a circle, multiply the radius times itself, and then by 3.14.

What would be the area of a circle whose radius is 25 feet?

Answer
$A = \pi \times r^2$
$A = 3.14 \times 25^2$
$A = 3.14 \times 25 \times 25$
$A = 1{,}962.5$ square feet

The distance around straight sided figures such as squares and rectangles is called the perimeter. But the distance around a circle is called the **circumference**. The circumference of a circle is easy to find with the formula

$$C = \pi \times d$$

Which is read "Circumference equals π times the diameter."
How may feet of fence is required to fit around a circular garden with a diameter of 12 feet?

Answer
$C = \pi \times d$
$C = 3.14 \times 12$
$C = 37.68$ feet of fencing

Many times area problems will involve more than one area. Notice the drawings below all contain more than one figure –

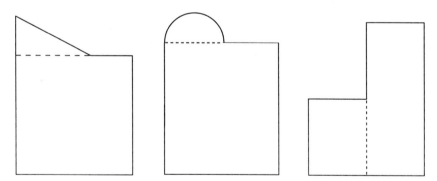

To calculate the area of the whole figure, just calculate each area separately and then add them up.

Volume problems

Questions which involve the volume of squares and rectangles sometimes appear on the exam. Rarely, there is even a question about the volume of a cylinder on the exam. Note that these are solid objects which parallel two-dimensional objects. For example, a square is two-dimensional, but its three-dimensional solid counterpart is the cube. A rectangle is two-dimensional, but when you give it height it becomes three-dimensional and is called a rectangular solid. A circle is two-dimensional, but if you add height it becomes a cylinder and has three dimensions. If you can do the area of a square, rectangle or circle, the volume is simple by comparison.

Whenever volume is involved, you simply calculate the area, and multiply the area by the height. For example, you find the area of a square or rectangle by multiplying one side by the other, then to find the volume, multiply the square area by the height. In some problems, such as problems involving basements, the height will be stated as the depth. Don't worry, just look for the "third dimension" – there has to be a third number to multiply times the square area.

This also works perfectly with circles and cylinders. For example, a storage tank is nothing but a cylinder. To find its volume, just find the area of the circular base, and multiply it times the height of the tank.

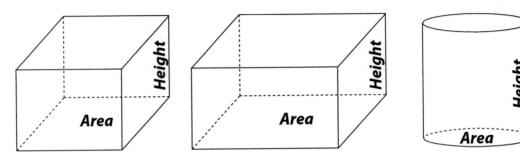

The formula for the volume of a cube or rectangular solid (the first two figures above) is –

$$V = l \times w \times h$$

Which is read "Volume equals length times width times height." To find the volume of a cylinder, use the formula –

$$V = \pi \times r^2 \times h$$

Which means "Volume equals π times the radius squared times the height."

Commission problems

Oddly enough, relatively few students have trouble calculating commissions. The same student who cannot add two and two and get the same answer twice in a row, never seems to have a problem calculating a commission right to the penny. As a result, in order to make commission questions more challenging on the examination, the test makers create questions where they require you to calculate part of the information before you can answer the question.

The basic formula to calculate a commission is

$$C = SP \times R$$

Where "SP" is the selling price and "R" is the commission rate. In other words, just multiple the sales price by the commission rate. But suppose you got a question like the following –

Abraham sold a property for Moses and charged Moses a 7% commission. Abraham's commission came to $13,807.50. What was the selling price?

As you can see, the formula above is set up to solve for the commission. Now we need a commission formula set up to solve for the sales price when we have the commission stated in dollars and cents and the commission rate as a percentage. Recasting the above formula gives us –

$$SP = C \div R$$

Which means "Selling price equals the commission divided by the rate."
Or sometimes the question will ask for the rate, as in –

Job sold a house for one of his sons and charged the son $13,500 commission. The sales price was $150,000. What commission rate did Job charge?

This time we need a formula which will give us the commission rate when the selling price and dollar amount of commission is known. Rewriting the above formula again gives us –

$$R = C \div SP$$

Which means "The rate equals the commission divided by the selling price."

Note that all commission problems contain the three elements, selling price, dollars of commission, and the commission rate. In every problem you will be given, or will have a means to calculate, at least two of the three. You use one of the three formulas above to find the third element from the first two.

Part-whole and ratio problems

Part-whole and ratio problems can be among the most confusing for students. Although really very simple, the logic escapes many people. For an example of such a problem, consider the following story –

Farmer Jones sold a property for $150,000. One-half of the property was in butter beans and was worth twice as much per acre as the other half. How much was the part in butter beans worth?

These questions ask many variations on the theme, but they all seemingly fail to give enough information to answer the question. Nevertheless, there is always enough data, you just have to approach the question using all the logic at your command.

For example, in the above problem, you could realize that if one part of the property is worth twice as much as the other, then you could just imagine dividing the value into three equal parts so you could give one part of the value to one-half of the acreage, and the other two parts to the other half of the acreage (the part in butter beans). You could even write this down as a formula where you define one side in terms of the other. That is, if the side in butter beans has twice the value of the other side, then define the other side as "½BB" for "one-half as much as the butter bean side." The formula might look like this –

$$BB + \tfrac{1}{2}BB = \$150{,}000$$

Now you can do some elementary manipulation of the formula. "BB + ½BB" is the same as saying "1.5 × BB," and substituting the new term makes it clearer –

$$1.5 \times BB = \$150{,}000$$

And now divide both sides by 1.5 –

$$BB = \$100{,}000$$

Notice that you had to create your own formula. That is the difficult part about part-whole and ratio problems. You have to be able to perceive the relationships among the different parts of the whole and then express them in a formula. The formula for each problem will be unique. But once you have a correct formula for the problem, the solution is easy.

Many times part-whole problems involve percentages. These can require great use of logic. Consider the popular "net listing" problem.

An owner wished to sell some property and called a real estate broker. The owner told the broker that the property was to be sold for enough to net the owner $312,000 after the broker's commission. The broker wanted a 7% commission. At what price did the broker have to list the property?

Your immediate reaction is likely to be to add 7% of $312,000 onto $312,000. But try it to see if it will work. Seven percent of $312,000 is $21,840. Adding $21,840 to $312,000 gives us a listed price of $333,840. Now suppose the property sells for the full $333,840. When you calculate a 7% commission on $333,840, you will find that it comes to $23,368.80. And if you subtract $23,368.80 from $333,840, it leaves only $310,471.20. In other words, you just shorted the seller by a little over $1,500.

In order to solve this problem properly, you have to think what the $312,000 is. State it as a formula. Is it not true that the $312,000 is only 93% of what the property must be listed for? So this is the formula we must create –

$$\$312{,}000 = .93 \times LP$$

Where "*LP*" is the listing price we are trying to find. Now we can solve the problem by dividing both sides of the formula by .93 –

$$\$335{,}483.87 = LP$$

So the correct answer is $335,483.87. You can prove this by multiplying $335,483.87 by 7% and subtracting the result from $335,483.87. It will leave you with exactly $312,000.

Now try one more problem, more difficult this time –

Buck Wacker is a developer who owned some property. Two-tenths of the property was zoned residential and this comprised 130 acres. How large was the whole?

You know that the residential is two-tenths (0.2), and this was 130 acres. So you set up a formula to express that fact, using "W" for the whole –

$$.2 \times W = 130$$

Now you solve the problem by dividing both sides by .2 –

$$W = 650$$

So the answer is 650 acres.

Many students find they just can't comprehend these problems. If that is the case, consider an alternative method to get the right answer. If the above question were in exam format, it would look like this:

Buck Wacker is a developer who owned some property. Two-tenths of the property was zoned residential and this comprised 130 acres. How large was the whole?

(A) 100 acres   (C) 350 acres

(B) 130 acres   (D) 650 acres

First, it doesn't take a genius to figure that if part of it is 130 acres, then the whole has to be more than 130 acres. Therefore the first two answers are impossible. Next, just take two-tenths (.2) times answers (C) and (D) in turn to see which leaves you with 130 acres. That must be the right answer. Part-whole and ratio problems on exams lend themselves especially well to this technique.

Of course, in the real world, you won't have four convenient answers to choose from. But then, in the real world, you would just ask Buck Wacker for a map of his property so you could see how many acres the whole property is.

Profit and loss problems

A problem involving profit and loss is very similar to a commission problem. Yet there are some special things to consider in profit and loss problems. Consider the following question –

A speculator bought a property for $296,000 and sold it at a 48% profit. How much was the speculator's dollar amount of profit?

The basic profit and loss formula is –

$$P = R \times I$$

Where "P" is the profit in dollars, "R" is the rate of return as a percentage, and "I" is the original investment in dollars. Applying this formula to the above problem, we get –

$$P = 0.48 \times \$296,000$$
$$P = \$142,080$$

So far, the above problem is relatively easy. But on the exam and in the real world, profit and loss questions frequently require that you calculate something other than the dollar amount of profit. For example, take the speculator problem above and rewrite it –

A speculator bought a property for $296,000 and sold it for a profit of $80,000. What rate of return did the speculator get?

You can solve this problem easily by rewriting the formula as –

$$R = P \div I$$

Which is read as "Rate of return equals profit divided by investment." Applying this formula to the problem gives you "R = $40,000 ÷ $148,000" which results in 27.02%.

Now consider another twist to profit and loss problems –

A speculator made a profit of $56,000 on a sale of property, which represented a 16% profit. How much was the original investment?

Notice that this time the problem asks for the amount of the original investment (*I*), rather than the percentage of return or the dollar amount of profit. Find the answer with the formula –

$$I = P \div R$$

Which is read as "Original investment equals profit divided by the rate of return." Applying the formula to the problem gives you "I = $56,000 ÷ .16," which calculates as $350,000.

In short, profit and loss problems can be solved with one of three related formulas –

$$P = R \times I$$
$$R = P \div I$$
$$I = P \div R$$

However, there is a special issue you must keep in mind when using these formulas. You have to remember that the "*I*" means the *original* investment, not the amount the speculator sold the property for. Consider the following tricky question –

A speculator sold a property for $450,000, which was $99,000 more than the speculator paid for the property. What was the speculator's rate of return?

Your immediate reaction might be to take the formula for the Rate (R = P ÷ I) and plug in the following numbers –

$$R = \$99,000 \div \$450,000$$
$$R = 0.22$$

So you figure the rate is 0.22 (22%). But the original investment was $351,000 ($450,000 − $99,000), so the formula should have been used in this way –

$$R = \$99,000 \div \$351,000$$
$$R = 0.2821$$

So the profit of $99,000 on an investment of $351,000 was 28.21%, not 22%. Always be sure the figures you take from the problem really match the meaning of the letter in the formula.

Return on investment problems are the same as profit and loss problems. The "profit" is the income the property generates. However, when dealing with income properties, the return on investment can get more complicated. The formulas above still work, but sometimes you have to subtract expenses from gross income to find the net income. We calculate percentage of profit on how much the investor takes home (net income), not gross income. Sometimes you are given the income on a monthly basis, which means you have to calculate the annual income before you can solve the problem.

Depreciation problems

Depreciation problems require you to understand the concept of economic life. Every property has a useful life over which the owner will receive benefits of ownership. At any given point in time the property has a number of years of remaining life. The value goes down over the economic life according to the depreciation rate. The value at any given time is called the **book value**.

The usual way to calculate depreciation is straight line. Straight line depreciation means the property depreciates the same amount every year. This is usually expressed as a percentage. For example, if a structure has an economic life of 50 years, then it is depreciating 2% per year. At the end of the tenth year, it will have depreciated a total of 20% or, to put it another way, it has a remaining life of 80%. The percentage is applied against the original cost. For example –

An investor paid $400,000 for a property which had a useful life of 40 years. What was its book value at the end of ten years?

The answer is easily calculated. If the life is 40 years, then the depreciation rate is 2.5% per annum (100% ÷ 40 = .025). This means it will be 25% depreciated at the end of ten years, or to look at it from the aspect of remaining life, it has 75% life remaining. Therefore, the book value can be calculated by multiplying the percentage of remaining life times the original cost. In this case it would be $300,000 ($400,000 × .75 = $300,000).

When calculating depreciation you must always remember that only the structure depreciates. Land is perpetual and indestructible, so it does not have an economic life.

Financial arithmetic

Being a successful real estate agent requires a certain amount of skill with financial and other arithmetic subjects. While every real estate transaction involves non-financial mathematical skills, such as estimating buyers' and sellers' costs, square footage of a structure, and many other things, the financial arithmetic is the most critical. If you can't tell a buyer how much the monthly payments will be, it will be hard to get them to sign the earnest money agreement.

Basic decimal, fraction and percentage problems

Decimals and percentages are used constantly in real estate arithmetic, so we should start with fundamental decimal and percentage concepts. A **decimal** is any number which is less than 1, usually expressed with the **decimal point** in front of it – e.g., ".1," ".23," "0.456," and so on. Note that sometimes the "0" is written in front of the decimal point, although it is not necessary. Zeros are also sometimes used at the end, e.g., ."10," ."230," "0.4560," but zeros at the end are also unnecessary and need not be used. The examples used above could be read aloud as "point one," "point two three," and "zero point four five six." They could also be read as "one tenth," "twenty-three hundredths," and "four hundred fifty-six thousandths."

A **percentage** is really nothing more than another way of writing a decimal. For example saying "50%" is exactly the same as saying "0.5" (or "0.50," "0.500," and so on). If you note that "50%" is the same as ".50," then you can see that a percentage is just a decimal in which the decimal point has been moved over two spaces to the right, and a percentage sign added. Thus

        0.10 = 10%
        0.23 = 23%
        0.456 = 45.6%

And so forth. *Important note:* On most calculators the "percent key" has the function of automatically moving the decimal point two places to the right for you. Experiment with your calculator to see if this is how it works.

As you can see, percentages and decimals are really just different ways of writing the same thing. Similarly, fractions are another way. For example, "50%" is the same as "0.5," and is also the same as "½." Note the following examples –

        .1   = 10%   = $\frac{1}{10}$
        .23 = 23%   = $\frac{23}{100}$
        0.456 = 45.6% = $\frac{456}{1000}$

Some people prefer to do their calculations with fractions, and if you are comfortable with fractions, there is nothing wrong with using them. But most people are more familiar with decimals, especially since decimals are easier to use with calculators.

If you wish to convert a fraction to a decimal, just divide the **denominator** (bottom number) into the **numerator** (top number). For example, to convert $\frac{49}{86}$ into a decimal, just divide 49 by 86, which gives you the decimal equivalent as 0.5697674.

Now, observe that it does not make any difference whether you calculate with a decimal, a percentage or a fraction. Suppose you had a farm which was 1,200 acres and you wanted to know how much $\frac{49}{86}$ of it was. You could calculate it as a –

Decimal:	$0.5697674 \times 1{,}200$ acres $= 683.72088$ acres
Percentage:	56.97674% (push % key) $\times 1{,}200$ acres $= 683.72088$ acres
Fraction:	$49 \times 1{,}200$ acres $\div 86 = 683.72093$ acres

Although using the fraction gives a slightly more accurate result, the decimal or percentage is more than close enough, and most people find it easier to deal with tenths, hundredths, thousands, and other decimals.

One of the things real estate agents need to calculate all the time is the dollar amount of a loan discount. Discounts are measured in terms of points. A ***point*** is nothing more than one percent of the loan balance. For example, on a loan of $100,000, a discount of five points would be 5% of the loan amount, or $5,000. The formula is *Discount = Principal × Points ÷ 100*. We have to divide by 100 in order to convert the number of points (expressed as a whole number) to a percentage.

Interest calculations

Calculating interest is basic to understanding other financial arithmetic. The main formula to calculate interest due is I = PRT, where *I* is the interest in dollars and cents, *P* is the principal balance of the loan, *R* is the interest rate (percentage rate), and *T* is the time over which the interest accrues –

$$I = PRT$$

For example, suppose you had to calculate the interest which would be due at the end of a year on a loan of $12,000 at 11%. The calculation would be "I = $12,000 × 11% (or .11) × 1 year," which comes to $1,320.00 ($12,000 × .11 × 1 = $1,320).

This was a very simple problem. But interest problems are not ordinarily so easy. We usually have to calculate interest over a period of time which is not an even period. In other words, calculating the interest over one year means that the *T* will be 1. What if the interest were accrued over 188 days instead of one year? Then the *T* will be $^{188}\!/_{365}$ (0.5150684 as a decimal). To calculate the interest which will accrue over 188 days, we calculate "I = $12,000 × 11% (or .11) × 0.5150684," or you could substitute "188 ÷ 365" as a fraction for the decimal "0.5150684." The answer will come to $679.89 ($12,000 × .11 × .5150684 = $679.89028).

Note that the *T* in our calculations above is in terms of "years." For example, if the time is six months, this is one-half of a year, so the *T* will be 0.5; if the time is nine months, this is three-fourths of a year, so the *T* will be 0.75, and if the *T* is 3½ years, the *T* will be 3.5. The reason the *T* is in terms of years is because the interest rate (11% in the above examples) is expressed as an annual interest rate.

But what would happen if the interest rate were expressed as a monthly or daily rate instead? The important thing to understand about interest calculations is that the *T* must be expressed in the same terms as the rate. In other words, if the rate is an annual rate (e.g., 11% per annum), then the *T* must be the expression of the number of years or fractions of a year. If the interest is expressed as a monthly rate, then the *T* must be the number of months or fractions of a month. And if the rate is a daily rate, then the *T* must be the number of days.

This can be very confusing because the rate may be stipulated as an annual rate, but the *T* is expressed in months. For example, a problem may state "What is the amount of interest that would accrue on a loan of $12,000 at 11% interest over a nine month period?" This would lead you to believe that the *T* must be nine. In fact, since the rate was stipulated as an annual rate, the *T* must be stated in terms of years, so the proper value for

T is 0.75 (⁹⁄₁₂ of a year). In interest calculations you must always be sure that if the rate is an annual rate, that the T is expressed in years; if the rate is a monthly rate, that the T is stated in months; or if the interest is a daily rate that the T is expressed in the number of days.

So far this discussion has be directed toward calculating interest due. Interest calculations also frequently involve other questions. For example, consider this question –

How big a loan could a borrower afford if the borrower could make annual interest payments of $6,000 and the interest rate will be 9%?

To solve this problem, you need a different formula. You need a formula to calculate the principal balance (P). This formula is actually just a variation of the original interest formula (I = PRT) –

$$P = I \div RT$$

Applying this formula to the above problem, we find the answer is $66,666.67 ($6,000 ÷ 0.09 × 1 = $66,666.666). Again, however, this is a simple problem. In the real world the problem is usually much more complex. Suppose the question were –

A couple can afford interest payments of $10,000 per year and the interest on their loan will be ⅞ of 1% per month. What size loan can they afford?

In this case, the solution is simple, once you realize that the dollar amount in interest (I) is based on a year, but the interest rate (R) is expressed in monthly terms. All that is necessary is to convert the interest to an annual rate before solving the problem. A monthly rate of ⅞ of 1% is the same as 10½% per annum (⅞ × 12 = 10½). Using the annual rate of 10½% gives us the answer to the problem, which is $95,238.10 ($10,000 ÷ .105 = $95,238.095).

Another type of problem is the question of what rate is being charged. A problem of this type might be –

Over a year's time, a lender earned $1,350 in interest on a loan of $12,000. What was the rate of return on the loan?

Again, we must recast the original interest formula to solve this type of problem. The formula to find the interest rate is –

$$R = I \div PT$$

Using this formula, it is easy to find that the answer to the problem is 11¼% ($1,350 ÷ $12,000 × 1 = .1125). And, as with preceding formulas, the problems are made more complex if the T is more or less than one year. For example, consider the following problem –

A borrower paid $1,100 interest in three months on a loan of $40,000. What was the interest rate?

Since three months is one-fourth of a year, the easiest way to solve this problem is to convert the dollar amount of interest to a full year's worth of interest; that is, multiply it by 4 ($1,100 × 4 = $4,400). Now we can calculate the rate using the formula, which gives us the answer 11% ($4,400 ÷ $40,000 = 0.11).

Sometimes we must find out how long it would take for a certain dollar amount of interest to accrue. For example, consider the following problem –

An investor has lent $190,000 at 11% interest. How long will it take to accrue $2,000 interest?

This means that we must solve for the T, so we must rewrite the formula again –

$$T = I \div PR$$

Using this formula we find that the answer to the above problem is about 35 days. To calculate, first multiply the principal by the rate, which results in $20,900 ($190,000 × 0.11 = $20,900). Now divide the interest ($2,000) by $20,900, which gives the result of 0.0956937. Since the rate (11%) is a yearly rate, this represents the portion of a year that it would take. To convert this to the number of days, just multiply by 365. The final result is 34.9282 days (0.0956937 × 365 = 34.9282).

Compounding

It is a common practice to accrue interest on interest that has already accrued. This is called **compound interest**. For example, consider the following example of a loan where the interest (at a 10% rate) has been compounded –

	Compounded	Balance	Simple	Balance
Beginning balance		$180,000.00		$180,000.00
Interest for January	$1,500.00	$181,500.00	$1,500.00	$181,500.00
Interest for February	1,512.50	183,012.50	1,500.00	183,000.00
Interest for March	1,525.10	184,537.60	1,500.00	184,500.00
Interest for April	1,537.82	186,075.42	1,500.00	186,000.00
Total interest earned	**$6,075.12**		**$6,000.00**	

When interest is compounded the interest that is computed each month it is added to the principal balance, and then the interest for the following month is computed on the new balance – which means that the borrower is paying interest on the interest. In the above chart the two columns on the left are compounded and the two on the right are simple interest. The total interest earned by compounding over the four months is greater because the interest is computed each month on the increasing balance. In the simple interest columns on the right the interest is always computed on the original balance. When interest is not compounded, it is called **simple interest**.

Discount interest

Another way of calculating interest is to discount it from the principal balance. This is called **discount interest**. Interest on certain federal treasury obligations, for example, is calculated this way.

If you buy a ten-year treasury bond for $10,000 at, say, 8% interest compounding annually, the total interest income for the ten years will be $5,368.07. Since the interest will be $5,368.07, you would buy the treasury bond today for $4,631.93. In other words, you lend the government the discounted amount, and the loan matures to the face amount at the end of its term. Calculating discount interest requires a financial calculator or present value table.

Amortizing

Non-amortized loans are sometimes called **straight loans**, or more commonly, **interest-only** loans. In an interest-only loan the borrower pays just interest; the principal is all due at the end of the term. Sometimes the interest is paid monthly, or sometimes both the principal and all accrued interest will be due at the end.

However, most real estate loans are made so they are paid off with regular payments and each payment includes a small amount toward the principal. When a debt is retired in regular installments this way, it is called loan **amortization**. The following is a typical loan statement for a bank loan of $180,000 repayable in equal monthly install-ments of $1,570, including interest at 10% –

Payment	Interest	Principal	Balance
Beginning balance			$180,000.00
1,570.00	1,500.00	70.00	179,930.00
1,570.00	1,499.42	70.58	179,859.42
1,570.00	1,498.82	71.18	179,788.24
1,570.00	1,498.24	71.76	179,716.48
1,570.00	1,497.64	72.36	179,644.12

In the above example the loan was set up with level payments of $1,570 per month. Notice in the chart that the $1,570 payment is applied mostly to interest at the beginning of the loan, but as the loan progresses, the portion of the payment which is applied to inter-est declines and the portion applied to principal increases. Setting up an amortizing loan requires the lender to determine the monthly payment necessary to amortize the loan over an even period of time, typically 30 years for a real estate loan. The calculation is done to-day with a financial calculator, although in the past lenders used an **amortization chart**. (For an example of a simple amortization chart, see Chapter 16.)

Some loan amortization schedules take into account that the lender usually re-quires the borrower to include one-twelfth the annual taxes and one-twelfth the annual fire insurance premium with the principal and interest payment. We say such loans are paid "PITI," which stands for "principal, interest, taxes and insurance." If the taxes are included in the payment, but the borrower pays the fire insurance premium directly, we say it is "PIT." When the taxes and insurance are not included, then we say the loan is just "PI."

When the payments include taxes and insurance the lender normally sets these sums aside in a **reserve account**, also sometimes called an **escrow account** or an **im-pound account**. In a few cases, Washington law requires a lender to pay interest on the reserve account, although almost all loans are exempt. If the $180,000 loan in the above example included a reserve account for a $3,000 tax bill and a $350 insurance bill, its amortization schedule might look like this –

Payment	Taxes	Insurance	Interest	Principal	Balance
Beginning balance					$180.000.00
1849.17	$250.00	$29.17	$1,500.00	$70.00	179,930.00
1849.17	250.00	29.17	1,499.42	70.58	179,859.42
1849.17	250.00	29.17	1,498.82	71.18	179,788.24
1,849.17	250.00	29.17	1,498.24	71.76	179,716.48
1849.17	250.00	29.17	1,497.64	72.36	179,644.12

The above example shows the first five months payments on the loan. Note that the principal and interest figures are the same as in the previous statement. However, this statement shows that at the end of the five months the bank will be holding $1,250 in the borrower's reserve account for property taxes and $145.85 for the fire insurance policy.

In the preceding two examples of loan amortization, the payments would be calcu-lated so that each month the amounts applied to interest and to principal would change, yet the amount of the payment itself would remain constant.

Although not common today, it is also possible to amortize a loan with equal installments of principal, but variable amounts of interest. In this case, the amount of the payment would change each month. For example, suppose you made a loan of $180,000 to be amortized in 360 principal payments of $500, *plus* interest at 10%. The chart might look something like this –

Payment	Interest	Principal	Balance
Beginning balance			$180,000.00
2,000.00	$1,500.00	$500.00	179,500.00
1,995.84	1,495.84	500.00	179,000.00
1,991.66	1,491.66	500.00	178,500.00
1,985.50	1,485.50	500.00	178,000.00
1,983,34	1,483.34	500.00	177,500.00

... Continuing, until the last few payments look like this –

Balance after payment #355			2,500.00
520.84	20.84	500.00	2,000.00
516.66	16.66	500.00	1,500.00
512.50	12.50	500.00	1,000.00
508.34	8.34	500.00	500.00
504.16	4.16	500.00	0.00

Notice that the total payment starts out high, and declines over the life of the loan. The reason this method of amortizing loans is not popular today is that it is difficult for young people starting out to make high payments at the beginning of the loan. In fact, some modern loan programs actually make the payments artificially smaller at the beginning, perhaps not enough even to cover the interest expense, and compensating with larger payments at the end of the loan. A "plus-interest" amortization schedule is the opposite of what today's typical borrower needs.

Present value and loan discounting

What if you had the legal right to receive $10,000 one year from today. Suppose further that you wished to sell this right in order to derive cash today. Since money has a time value, your buyer would not likely pay $10,000 today for the right to receive $10,000 in one year – this would mean that the buyer's rate of return would be 0%.

The amount a buyer would pay would be less than the face amount of the obligation. In fact, the less your buyer pays for the right to receive $10,000 in one year, the greater your buyer's return on the investment.

For example, if your buyer paid $8,000 for the right to receive $10,000 in one year, your buyer would stand to make a $2,000 profit on an investment of $8,000. This would be a return of 25% ($2,000 ÷ $8,000 = 0.25). But if your buyer paid $9,000 for the right to receive $10,000 in one year, the profit would be only $1,000, so the rate of return would be 11.1% ($1,000 ÷ $9,000 × 1 = 0.1111111).

Figuring the **present value** of a potential future income requires that you begin with an assumption as to the rate the investor or lender will require. Since rates of return in the marketplace can be readily ascertained, appraisers sometimes use the present value concept when appraising income properties. By calculating the present values of future anticipated incomes, an appraiser can determine what an informed investor ought to be willing to pay for an income property.

Present value calculations sometimes involve a lump sum future income, as in the above example, but more commonly there is a stream of regular payments to be received. A stream of regular payments to be received in the future is called an **annuity**. Calculating the present value of a lump sum payment or of a series of regular payments can be accomplished with a table, but modern investors use a financial calculator.

Now, if you think about it, from a lender's viewpoint, a loan is really an annuity. In fact, "present value" is just a loan calculation in reverse. Instead of starting with a loan amount and calculating the payments needed to amortize it at a certain interest rate, the investor starts with the proposed payments and interest rate, and calculates the principal balance that can be lent. This concept is constantly used in real estate transactions where the seller will carry a contract or trust deed, but then sell the paper to an investor. The investor determines what he or she will pay for the paper according to the yield (rate of return) the investor demands.

Formulas to Master

$A = s^2$	Area equals side squared. Used to find the area of a square.
$A = l \times w$	Area equals length times width. Used to find the area of a rectangle.
$A = \frac{1}{2} \times b \times h$	Area equals one-half the base times the height. Used to find the area of a triangle.
$P = 4 \times s$	Perimeter equals four times the side. Used to find the distance around a square.
$P = (2 \times l) + (2 \times w)$	Perimeter equals two times the length plus two times the width. Used to find the distance around a rectangle.
$A = \pi \times r^2$	Area equals π times the radius squared. Used to find the area of a circle.
$C = \pi \times d$	Circumference equals π times the diameter. Used to find the distance around a circle.
$V = l \times w \times h$	Volume equals the length times the width times the height. Used to find the volume of a cube or rectangular solid.
$V = \pi \times r^2 \times h$	Volume equals π times the radius squared times the height. Used to find the volume of a cylinder.
$C = SP \times R$	Commission equals sales price times commission rate. Used to find the dollar amount of commission.
$SP = C \div R$	Sales price equals commission divided by rate. Used to find the sales price when the commission and the rate are known.
$R = C \div SP$	Rate equals commission divided by sales price. Used to find the commission rate when the dollar amount of the commission and sales price are known.
$P = R \times I$	Profit equals rate of return times original investment. Used to find the dollar amount of profit when the rate of return and original investment are known.
$R = P \div I$	Rate of return equals profit divided by original investment. Used to find the investor's rate of return when the dollar amount of profit and original investment are known.
$I = P \div R$	Original investment equals profit divided by rate of return. Used to find the amount of the original investment when the dollar amount of profit and investor's rate of return are known.
$I = PRT$	Interest equals principal times rate times time. The time and the rate must be in the same period, i.e., if the rate is monthly, the time must be in the number of months, and so on.
$P = I \div RT$	Principal equals interest divided by the rate times the time. Rate and time must be for the same type of period; for an annual rate the time must be in years.
$T = I \div PR$	Time equals interest divided by the principal times the rate. Use this formula to find how long it takes to accrue a certain dollar amount of interest.
$R = I \div PT$	The interest rate equals interest divided by the principal times the time. Use this formula to find the rate being charged when you know the principal amount, amount of interest, and the time over which it accrued

⛐ KEY TERMS

The key to understanding any new field is the vocabulary used in that field. To maximize your comprehension of the material presented in this chapter, be sure you know the meaning and significance of the following terms. Remember that the majority of test questions primarily test knowledge of vocabulary.

Amortization	Impound account
Amortization chart	Interest-only loan
Annuity	Numerator
Book value	Percentage
Circumference	Perimeter
Compound interest	Point
Decimal	Present value
Decimal point	Radius
Denominator	Reserve account
Diameter	Simple interest
Discount interest	Squared
Escrow account	Straight loan

Index